FACING THE OCEAN

BARRY CUNLIFFE

FACING THE OCEAN

The Atlantic and its Peoples

8000 BC–AD 1500

OXFORD
UNIVERSITY PRESS

OXFORD
UNIVERSITY PRESS

Great Clarendon Street, Oxford OX2 6DP

Oxford University Press is a department of the University of Oxford.
It furthers the University's objective of excellence in research, scholarship, and education by publishing worldwide in

Oxford New York
Athens Auckland Bangkok Bogotá Buenos Aires Calcutta
Cape Town Chennai Dar es Salaam Delhi Florence Hong Kong Istanbul
Karachi Kuala Lumpur Madrid Melbourne Mexico City Mumbai
Nairobi Paris São Paulo Singapore Taipei Tokyo Toronto Warsaw

with associated companies in Berlin Ibadan

Oxford is a registered trade mark of Oxford University Press in the UK and in certain other countries

Published in the United States
by Oxford University Press Inc., New York

First published 2001

British Library Cataloguing in Publication Data
Data available

Library of Congress Cataloguing in Publication Data
Data applied for
ISBN 0-19-924019-1

1 3 5 7 9 10 8 6 4 2

Typeset in Dante MT
by Best-set Typesetter Ltd., Hong Kong
Printed in Great Britain
on acid-free paper by
Bath Press Colour Books, Glasgow

Contents

Homme libre, toujours tu chériras la mer!
La mer est ton miroir: tu contemples ton âme
Dans la déroulement infini de sa lame,
Et ton esprit n'est pas un gouffre moins amer . . .

(Charles Baudelaire,
'L'Homme Libre et la Mer', 1852)

Preface

This is a book that I have wanted to write for a lifetime without realizing it. Spending much of my working life in a Midlands river valley, having been brought up on the south coast of Britain and used to the smell of the sea, has made me increasingly conscious of the lure of that fiercely energetic interface between land and ocean. Travelling south from Oxford up over the chalk downs the air perceptably changes as the coast approaches, and always there is that growing excitement of being with the sea again. Imaginative nonsense perhaps but no less real for one who believes it.

It is, I suspect, no accident that many of the archaeological excavations I have directed over the years have been on coastal sites, at the late Roman Shore Forts of Portchester Castle near Portsmouth and Stutfall Castle at Lympne in Kent, at the Iron Age trading ports of Hengistbury Head on Christchurch Harbour and Mount Batten in Plymouth Sound, at various prehistoric and Roman sites on the Channel Islands of Jersey, Guernsey, and Herm, and currently at the coastal promontory fort of Le Yaudet on the north coast of Brittany. But choice of site has been more than the pure indulgence of being near the sea, it was governed by the underlying desire of trying to better understand the social and economic relationships of coastal communities living along the Atlantic seaways in the first millennium BC and first millennium AD. This work, still very much in progress, has encouraged me to read widely, back into the more distant prehistoric period and forward into the Middle Ages, in an attempt to understand what Fernand Braudel has referred to as the *longue durée*—the underlying consistencies that bind communities together and the rhythms that moderate their development over long periods of time.

As the result of all this I have become convinced that the peoples of the long Atlantic façade of Europe have shared common beliefs and values over thousands of years, conditioned largely by their unique habitat on the edge of the continent facing the ocean. They lived in a resource-rich zone, in many ways remote from neighbours by land yet easily linked to others by the sea. Perhaps, even more important, they were constantly aware of the power and the rhythms of the natural forces around them and these were their stimulus. There were times of long, uneventful existence and other times of remarkable inventiveness and energy when the Atlantic communities far outshone those of the more lethargic Mediterranean. This is the story that I hope to tease out.

A book of this scope, covering nearly 8,000 years of human endeavour, must be highly selective yet, at the same time, must try to present the regional scene against its more general European background. It relies heavily on the detailed research of hundreds of scholars only a small number of whom could be specifically referred to in the selective bibliographical guide at the end of this book. Yet all those who have been a particular inspiration are somewhere mentioned. Many friends and colleagues from Ireland, the United Kingdom, Denmark, the Netherlands, France, Spain, and Portugal have contributed in a variety of ways, through sending offprints, by discussion and correspondence, and through their generous hospitality—in the course of this work I have enjoyed excessive amounts of excellent Atlantic food in their company. I owe much to them all but a special debt of gratitude to Sean McGrail who, over the years, has patiently helped me to understand the boatbuilding and navigational skills of our north-west Atlantic ancestors and to Wendy Childs who guided me into The Middle Ages.

This book was written during two terms of sabbatical leave, granted by the University of Oxford, which allowed time for two essential indulgences: access to its incomparable libraries to stock up with facts and ideas, and the leisure to escape from the Midlands valley from time to time to the invigorating coast of northern Brittany there to think about it all. In preparing the book I have enjoyed the help of two colleagues, Alison Wilkins who drew most of the line-drawings and Lynda Smithson who translated my scribble into a correctly spelt and legible typescript. Without the knowledge that I could rely on their tolerance and support I suspect I would not have had the courage to begin. Finally, I have had the good fortune of working with Oxford University Press, who have not only encouraged me to write the book I have wanted to write but have provided a level of care, guidance, and support customary to them, but all too rare in the world of publishing today.

Oxford and Pont Roux
April 2000

Barry Cunliffe

1. Perceptions of the Ocean

To stand on a sea-washed promontory looking westwards at sunset over the Atlantic is to share a timeless human experience. We are in awe of the unchanging and unchangeable as all have been before us and all will be. Wonder is tempered with reassurance: it is an end, but we are content in the knowledge that the cycle will reproduce itself—the sun will reappear. The sea below creates different, more conflicting, emotions. True, there is the comforting inevitability of the tides, but there is also an unpredictability of mood, the sea constantly changing, sometimes erupting in crescendos of brute force destroying and remoulding the land and claiming human life. The sea is a balance of opposites. It gives and takes. It can destroy land and quickly build new; it sustains life and it can kill. Small wonder that through time communities have sought to explain these forces in terms of myth and have attempted to gain some puny influence over them through propitiation.

Nowhere is this relationship more apparent than in the legends and folk traditions of Brittany. In the howl of the wind can be heard the screams and laments of those drowned at sea, and much of human life—birth and the gender of the newborn and death—was believed to be conditioned by the tides. Below a thin veneer of Christianity lie beliefs deeply rooted in time. A century ago, in the parish of Ploulec'h on the north Breton coast, the first Sunday in May saw the people in procession climb to La Croix du Salut—an isolated landmark that could be seen from far out to sea offering assurance of the approach to a safe haven. Here the sailing community gave thanks for their safe returns before descending to the chapel of Notre-Dame across the bay on the headland of Le Yaudet. In the church today, fine model sailing ships hanging from the roof beams are among the more evocative of the offerings made to the Virgin by grateful mariners. The deep underlying awe of the ocean is poignantly expressed in the Breton poem

War vor peb ankenn
War vor peb péden

Sur la mer toute angoisse, sur mer toute prière.
At sea all is anguish, all is prayer.

The first visions of the Atlantic to survive in recorded history are those of the Mediterranean communities aware that their own sea opened into something much vaster—limitless ocean. Between the two was a narrow strait dominated by the Pillars of Hercules erected by the mythical hero at Calpe and Abyla to define the portal to the Atlantic. In the stories of Hercules' labours we glimpse the earliest Mediterranean perception of the Ocean. For his tenth labour Hercules was ordered to fetch the red cattle of Geryon who lived on the island of Erythia in the far west under the rays of the setting sun. It was en route that he set up the Pillars. Soon after, maddened by the intensity of the sun he shot an arrow at it. In response the sun, Helios, lent him a golden cup (which the god used at night to travel from west to east to rise again), and in this Hercules sailed to Erythia to complete his task successfully. When he arrived back at Tartessos he returned the cup to Helios. The geography embedded in this myth implies that the island lay in the Atlantic, and the dominant solar symbolism adds support.

For his eleventh labour Hercules is sent to fetch the golden apples of the Hesperides—apples which Hera had been given by the earth, Ge, as a wedding present and had entrusted to the Hesperides for safe keeping. According to some traditions the Hesperides were the daughters of Atlas and Hesperis, and the earliest version of the legend had them living on an island in the ocean in the extreme west. Here Atlas held the sky and the heavens on his shoulders, keeping them apart from the earth. Hercules enlisted Atlas' help, taking the burden of the sky on his own shoulders but tricking Atlas into reassuming his task after he had returned with the golden apples. Although in later versions of the story the details and the geography change, the Atlantic symbolism of the earlier threads is clear. The Hercules myth has embedded within it a simple, comforting image—our world and our sea separated from the outer ocean by the Pillars of Hercules, and out there, where the sun sets, is the preserve of the gods.

Views From the Inner Sea

One of the earliest versions of the Greek theogony presents the god Ocean—Okeanos—together with his consort Tethys, as the primal parents of the gods. As Homer puts it in the *Iliad*, 'Okeanos, whence is risen the seed of all the immortals'. In this satisfying creation myth everything arises from the mingling of saltwater sea Okeanos and the freshwater stream of Tethys.

Some flavour of the beliefs prevalent in the eighth century BC is captured in the works of the early Greek poet Hesiod in his two extant poems, *Theogony* and *Works and Days*. He writes of the Gorgons, 'who dwell beyond renowned Ocean in the farthest parts towards the night, where are the shrill-voiced Hesperides'. Elsewhere he talks of the glorious dead who, 'untroubled in spirit dwell in islands of the blest by deep-eddying Ocean, happy heroes for whom the grain-giving fields bear rich honey-sweet fruit three times a year', and we learn of Atlas, who 'from strong necessity on his head and tireless arms carries the broad heavens standing at the limits of the earth before the shrill-voiced Hesperides'. The image of the Islands of the Blessed was to remain powerfully attractive well into the Middle Ages.

Whether or not the sources on which Homer based his great works knew of the Atlantic has been a matter of debate for some time. Strabo, writing in the early first century AD, raised the issue, suggesting somewhat obscurely that 'no one could be surprised if . . . the poet had written his mythical account of the wanderings of Odysseus in such a way as to set most of his stories of Odysseus in the Atlantic Sea beyond the Pillars of Hercules' (*Geog.* 3. 4. 4). This said, there is little in Homer that gives any direct link with the Atlantic, though there may be some merit in the suggestion that the monster Charybdis, who was able to suck down the sea to entrap sailors, was a reference to the massive tidal range experienced on the Atlantic shores.

Early Ionian writers, like the geographer Hecataeus, *c.*500 BC, visualized the earth as a flat circle with a wide river, Oceanus, flowing around (1.1). Beyond this was the continent where the dead resided. But later, more sober writers like Herodotus, while accepting the basic concept of a central, inhabited earth with ocean beyond, regarded the whole as more irregular and preferred to leave the question of there being a northern ocean unresolved (1.2). That part of the ocean which lay to the west became known as the Atlantic (after Atlas), but many writers regarded 'Ocean' and 'Atlantic' as synonymous.

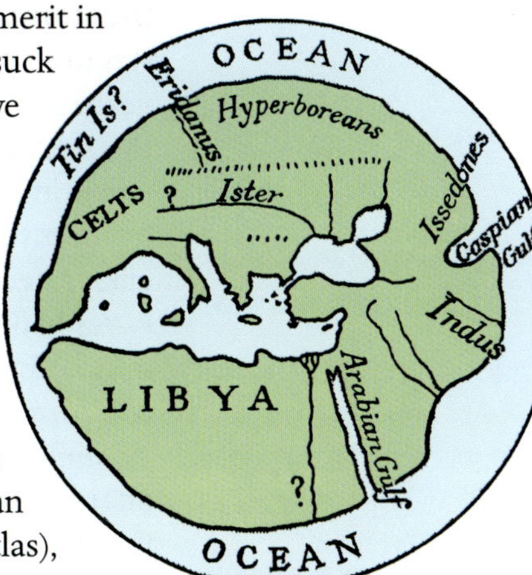

1.1 The world according to Hecataeus of Miletus, about 500 BC.

To this early substratum of beliefs and fables a vivid new theme was added by Plato early in the fourth century with the now-famous legend of the lost continent of Atlantis. He claimed that the story was first heard in Egypt by Solon, who brought it back to Greece round 600 BC. According to Plato, Atlantis was a massive island in the ocean beyond the Pillars of Hercules, larger than Asia and Libya together. It became the preserve of

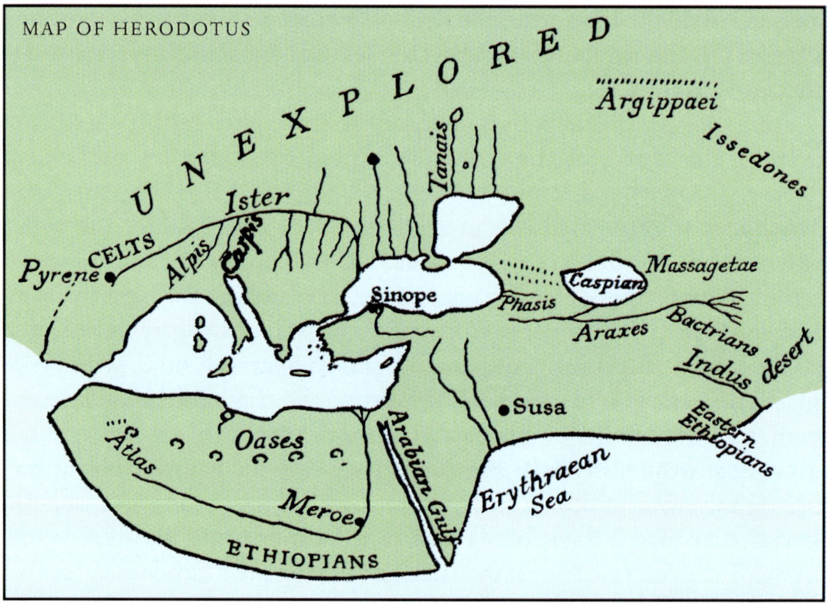

1.2 The world according to Herodotus of Halicarnassus, about 450 BC.

the god Poseidon, whose progeny proceeded to people it. The island was wealthy and peaceful but the people eventually became corrupt and began to conquer Africa and Europe, seeking world domination. They were, however, resisted by the valiant Athenians and, having fallen foul of Zeus, the whole island was swallowed up by the sea in a single night, victim to an earthquake. These events took place, says Plato, nine thousand years before his time. Few of Plato's successors paid much attention to the story, yet it has captured the lively imagination of writers in more recent times, though to little significant effect. It may be that Plato had heard myths like those encapsulated in the poems of Hesiod and simply elaborated his own allegory around them for debating purposes. On the other hand, the whole legend need be little more than a Platonic invention. Whatever the truth, there can be no doubt that he has added a colourful thread to the rich skein of Atlantic myths.

The development of the Phoenician trading port at Gadir (Cadiz), after the early eighth century BC, brought Mediterranean boats through the Pillars of Hercules to the edge of the ocean, and as we shall see later journeys of exploration along the Atlantic coasts were soon undertaken. But as far as one can judge these ships stayed close to land, following the long-established shipping routes of local vessels. The ocean remained a mystery, and a dangerous one at that. The Greek poet Pindar, writing in the early fifth century BC, mentions the Pillars of Hercules, 'situated far from home. What lies beyond cannot be trodden by the wise or the unwise . . . One cannot cross from Gadir towards the dark west. Turn again the sails towards the dry land of Europe.' A journey made by a Phoenician, Himilco, at about this time gives a frightening picture of seas that can scarcely be traversed in four months.

> No breezes propel a craft, the sluggish liquid of the lazy sea is so at a standstill . . . a lot of seaweed floats in the water and often in the manner of a thicket holds the prow back . . . nonetheless the depth of water does not extend much and the bottom is barely covered over with a little water. Here and there they always meet monsters of the deep and beasts swim amid the slow and sluggish crawling ships.

It is a picture designed to deter. Yet a more encouraging view comes from a text, once thought to have been by Aristotle, in which the writer says that after sailing west for four days from the Pillars of Hercules one comes 'to a lonely region full of tangle and seaweed which floats on the ebb tide and sinks on the flood and on it is found a huge multitude of tunnies of incredible size and obesity'. The mention of the seaweed-tangled sea raises the fascinating, but untestable, possibility that some brave spirits had travelled far west to the Sargasso Sea. These travellers' tales, and no doubt many more that circulated in ports like Gadir, painted the open Atlantic as an empty, dangerous place where ships might be becalmed in waters teeming with monsters. Most would have heeded Pindar's advice to trim their sails towards the dry and familiar shores of Europe.

As time progressed so the vision of the world changed. As early as the sixth century BC Pythagoras was putting forward the suggestion that the earth was a sphere, and by the fourth century Aristotle was offering as proof the curved shape of the earth's shadow on the face of the moon. That the earth was spherical was widely accepted. According to Strabo, quoting the third-century geographer Eratosthenes, 'if the Atlantic Ocean were not an obstacle we might easily pass by sea from Iberia to India, still keeping in the same parallel'. He goes on to say that: 'Those who have tried to circumnavigate [the Atlantic] and then turned back say that their voyaging beyond the limit reached was checked not through opposition or prevention by any continent, but through destitution and loneliness, the sea nonetheless permitting further passage.' The text is fascinating in showing not only a sophisticated understanding of geography but also in indicating that attempts, though unsuccessful and tentative, had been made to cross the Atlantic.

Of considerable interest to the Mediterranean writers were the tides experienced along the Atlantic coast. Pytheas, writing at the end of the fourth century, was the first to offer a sensible observation, maintaining, not altogether correctly, that flood tides occur when the moon waxes, ebb tides when the moon wanes. By the end of the first century BC many Greeks and Romans had had first hand experience of Atlantic tides.

Though various explanations were then current for the phenomenon, it was now widely accepted that in some way the tides were directly related to the phases of the moon. Even so, this did not prevent Caesar from misjudging the conjunction of the tides and winds when mounting his expedition on Britain.

Facing the Ocean

One night in the early decades of the nineteenth century a young man, Émile Souvestre, found himself taking refuge from a storm with a small group of people on the island of St Nicholas in the Bay of Douarnanez on the west coast of Brittany. After a supper of fish soup, as 'the wind . . . carried to us the thousand odours of the shore and the sea murmured at our feet with a remnant anger', an old fisherman began to tell a story of Ker Is, a city swallowed up by the waves in the neighbouring bay at some time distant. Souvestre, who came from a Breton-speaking family in Morlaix, recorded the story and subsequently published it in a collection of folktales in his book *Le Foyer Breton* in 1844. A year later the Breton folklorist Hersart de la Villemarqué included a poetic version of the story in the second edition of his famous *Barzaz-Breiz* (*Songs of Brittany*), claiming to have heard it from an old man from the parish of Trégunk in the south of Finistère. The coincidence is not surprising since the legend was widely recounted and, indeed, was first recorded in 1637 in Albert Le Grand's *Vie des Saincts de la Bretagne Armorique*.

The three versions, as might be expected of oral traditions, differ in their detail, but the storyline is consistent. The city of Is, built upon land reclaimed from the sea, was ruled by King Grallon, whose daughter Dahut was of evil character. One night at the instigation of her lover (in one version it is the Devil) she steals the keys to the dykes and opens the gates, allowing the sea to rush in. All the inhabitants are drowned except the king who, forewarned by a holy man, escapes on his horse. Dahut attempts to cling on to her father but the horse refuses to move, and it is only when the holy man intervenes by striking Dahut that the beast continues carrying the king to safety (1.3). Thereafter, as one version recounts, Dahut was changed into a *mari-morgan* (or mermaid) and is sometimes seen combing her golden hair singing an irresistible song which lures young sailors to their death.

The Breton story finds strong echoes in a twelfth-century Welsh poem which tells of the submerging of Cantre'r Gwaelod in the Bay of Cardigan, and in another Welsh folk-tale based on the disappearance of Llys Helig beneath Lake Bala. There are sufficient similarities between the Breton and Welsh stories to suggest that they were part of the same tra-

1.3 King Grallon fleeing as the rising sea drowns the city of Ker Is. A holy man strikes down the king's evil daughter Dahut who opened the gates of the dyke. Painting by 'Evariste-Vital Luminais (1822–1896).

dition, and it is possible that the Cornish legend of Lyonesse—the lost land between Cornwall and Scilly inundated by the sea—belongs to the same folk theme. How these similarities arose is not easy to explain. While it is clear that Villemarqué knew of the Welsh poem and used it to 'improve' his Breton source, the evidence for there being an independent Breton story is irrefutable. One explanation would be to suggest that, lying behind the tradition, was an actual event which passed into folk memory and spread along the Atlantic seaways in the period of increased mobility in the fifth and sixth centuries AD, but perhaps we are seeing in this particular story a more ancient myth common to the Atlantic coasts which helped to explain the unstable equilibrium between land and sea—land is reclaimed from the sea by man and later taken back by the powers of the ocean—the sea gives, the sea takes, and all the time the sea demands the lives of men mediated by the longings of the powerful presiding female spirit.

Echoes of all this are still to be found in the rich sea lore and the superstitions and beliefs found around the Atlantic coasts (1.4). In many places there is the firm belief that a drowning man belongs to the sea, and that if he is saved the sea will claim a substitute, most likely the rescuer. So strong was the superstition in Orkney in the nineteenth century that peo-

ple are known to have turned away from a drowning friend, not from lack of courage but from a deep fear of the sea's inevitable vengeance. There is also the belief, still prevalent in recent times, that to carry a Christian priest on board ship will anger the gods of the ocean and bring bad luck. Here we are seeing strongly reflected the conflicting oppositions of Christian / pagan, land / sea.

If, then, the domains of land and sea were conceived of as separate systems subject to their own very different supernatural powers, the interface between them was a liminal place, and as such was dangerous. In passing from one world to another the traveller would have been constrained to behave appropriately. Examples abound. In the late nineteenth century the departure of the fishing fleet to Iceland from the harbour town of Paimpol took place on 20 February, and was preceded by a procession of the clergy which descended to the harbour where the boats and their crews were blessed. Ceremonies of this kind were by no means uncommon along the Atlantic seaboard, and were no doubt performed well back in time long before the Christian era. The two Roman temples at Colijnsplaat and Domburg on either side of the wide estuary formed by the Rhine, the Maas, and the Scheldt were evidently places where those about to commit themselves to the North Sea paid homage to the goddess Nehalennia, or did so on their safe arrival in the estuary. How far back into the prehistoric period rituals of departure and arrival were practised it is difficult to say, but such portentous acts are unlikely to have gone unmarked in some way.

The power of the boundary between land and sea must always have been very real in the consciousness of those who inhabited the maritime regions. The issue is made quite explicit in a tenth-century text known as the *Colloquy of the Two Sages* preserved in the *Book of Leinster*. The story tells of a young man, Néde, who, 'one day . . . was on the brink of the sea, for poets deemed that on the brink of water it was always a place of revelation of science. He heard a sound in the wave, to wit, a chant of wailing and sadness . . . so the lad cast a spell upon the wave, that it might reveal to him what the matter was.' As the text makes clear, the liminal region between sea and land was a place of communication and enlightenment.

It is quite possible that the curious episode in AD 40, when the emperor Gaius (Caligula) led his army to the seashore near Boulogne intent on conquering Britain, but returned after collecting seashells, may be explained in terms of the emperor first communicating with the gods in the liminal zone before deciding not to proceed to intrude upon the ocean.

The power of the coastal interface may also be reflected in the many headlands cut off from land approach by artificial barriers. These 'cliff

1.4 (*facing*) A romantic nineteenth century vision of the sea: *Sea Nymphs* by Carl von Marr (1838–1936).

castles' or 'promontory forts', as they are frequently called, are usually considered to be primarily defensive works, but the remote and inhospitable location of many of them strongly suggests that other factors may have been at work, the main imperative being to create a defined enclave at the interface between land and sea. Most of these constructions date to the latter part of the first millennium BC, but at several sites boundaries dating back to the Neolithic period have been identified. The interpretation must remain speculative, but it is given some support by the frequent references in the classical sources to sacred capes and sacred headlands along the southern and western coasts of Iberia.

Islands of Paradise

Hesiod's vision of 'islands of the blest by deep-eddying Ocean' where the spirits of happy heroes dwelt in a rich and fruitful land, and Homer's comparable allegories of the happy land of Elysium in the far west near Ocean, were little more than comforting metaphors to help people come to terms with the inevitability of death, much in the way that many current religions have created their own concepts of 'heaven'. In the early Mediterranean belief system the home of the blessed was placed, not unreasonably, beyond the ocean stream which surrounded the earth of the mortals, in the direction of the setting sun. It was a powerful myth which pervaded Graeco-Roman thought, though historians like Herodotus were careful to have none of it, writing simply that 'of the extreme tracts of Europe towards the west I cannot speak with any certainty' (*Hist.* 3. 115).

Plato's myth of Atlantis embroidered on this theme of a paradise in the western ocean, and although, he claimed, the legendary land had disappeared beneath the depths of the sea there remained the possibility, in the minds of some, that fragments of the continent may have survived as islands. The exploration of the Atlantic coasts, which gained momentum in the latter part of the first millennium BC, began to add some threads of credence to these beliefs. In one instance Diodorus Siculus tells the story of a journey made by Polybius along the African coast when he was blown far out into the ocean by a great storm and, after many days at sea, came to a wonderfully fertile island of great beauty 'irrigated by navigable rivers, from which one can see numerous gardens planted with all kinds of trees and orchards . . . The air is so temperate that the fruit of the trees and other produce grow here in abundance throughout the greater part of the year.' It seems that the landfall may have been made on the Canaries or, more likely, Madeira.

At about this time Strabo was putting forward the view that the Hesperides and the Islands of the Blessed were off Cadiz, while Plutarch, describing the Canary Islands, considered that they were generally believed to be the Elysian Fields 'of which Homer sings'. When, in the second century AD, Ptolemy produced his geographical compilation, the Canary Islands were positively identified as *Insulae Fortunatae*.

It was from the fragments of the classical tradition, then available, in combination with biblical writings, that the early Christians began to construct a vision of the far west. Among the more influential texts were two works by the seventh-century writer Isidore, bishop of Seville—*Etymologiae* and *De Natura Rerum*. Isidore's vision of the world was much like that of Hecataeus' twelve hundred years before and was expressed symbolically in the T–O map (1.5) showing the known world surrounded by the ocean stream. The ocean absorbs the waters of the inner seas and sends them out again in the tidal swell. He debates the nature of the tides—was the ocean like a breathing animal or were the tides caused by winds or the heavenly bodies?—in the end it is all too complicated and only God can know.

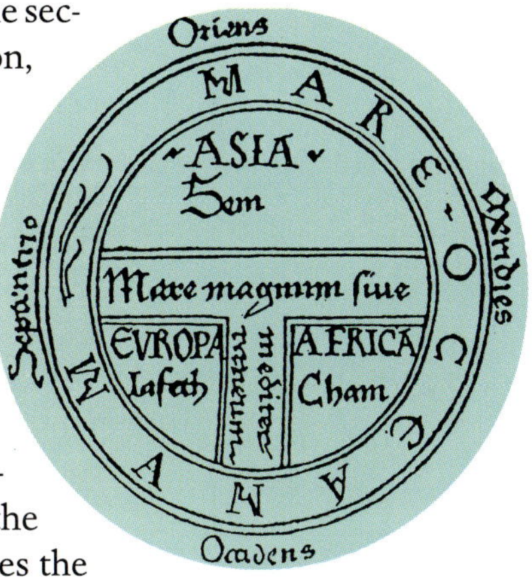

1.5 A fifteenth-century map of the world known as a 'T–O map' which shows the land mass of Europe, Asia, and Africa surrounded by Ocean.

Isidore's cognitive geography envisaged a continental edge fringed with fragments of land—Ireland, Britain, the Orkneys—beyond which the ocean stretched limitless and impassable but not unknown, for the rich biblical traditions told much of its nature. It was the abyss, a place of darkness and of power, and therein were monsters like Leviathan, many demons, and Satan himself and from the ocean would come the apocalyptic beast, the destroyer of humankind heralding the end of the world—yet it was part of God's domain (1.6, 1.8). For Christian commu-

1.6 Ocean beasts inhabiting the sea around Iceland, from a map of 1585 by Abraham Ortel Ortelis (1527–98).

nities living on the fringes of the ocean these were powerful myths—the ocean was a place of constant struggle between good and evil, and as such it was an appropriate place for a Christian monk to join battle on the side of God.

It was in this context that the Irish monks took to the sea, journeying into the 'desert' to find places of solitude for contemplation on the front line in the constant battle against evil: some, as we shall see, reached remote places as far afield as Iceland and settled there, others returned to tell stories of their adventures which soon became enmeshed in a web of fantasy to emerge into literature as the *immrama* (tales of voyages).

The *immrama* are allegories telling of man's journey to the Other World. The journey is made by sea, the pilgrim sailors facing many dangers, including fearsome monsters, before they reach the 'promised land' of fabulous islands far out in the western ocean. One of the earliest stories, 'The Voyage of Mael Dúin's Boat', gives some flavour of the genre. It was probably written in the eighth century and survives in a tenth-century manuscript. In his long voyage over the limitless ocean Mael Dúin and his followers visit thirty-one islands, each as miraculous as the last. On one they encounter ants the size of foals who try to eat them, on another demons enjoying a horse race, while a third, surrounded by a stone wall, was the home of a fabulous beast that ran faster than the wind and had the engaging habit of turning its body but leaving its skin unmoved. A branch plucked from one island produced three apples which satisfied the entire crew for forty days. From another island they collect golden apples, but the earth there is unbearably hot, made so by blazing red swine who by day feast on the apples. And so it goes on—they meet an ancient, hairy pilgrim who tells them that he arrived sailing on a sod of earth which grew to become the island. On another island they are entreated to stay by seventeen attractive young women who provide for all their needs. Finally an Irish falcon, flying to the south-east, guides them back home where they make offerings in the church of Armagh and recount to all the story of their adventures in the western ocean.

If the voyage of Mael Dúin is the earliest of the *immrama*, the best-known is the *Navigatio Brendani*—the voyage of Brendan—composed in the ninth century and relying heavily upon the voyage of Mael Dúin as a model. Brendan and fourteen monks sail west in their currach in search of the Land of Promise of the Saints which, after many adventures, they eventually reach (3.22). The *Navigatio Brendani* was well known throughout the Middle Ages. Its simple, direct language and compulsive story commanded attention, while its allegorical content, rich in metaphor and symbolic meaning, touched the souls of its Christian readers. Many believed in the existence of the Isle of St Brendan and the story remained an inspiration to explorers until as late as the eighteenth century. When maps began to be drawn in the fourteenth and fifteenth centuries it was customary for the Fortunate Isles to be shown varying in number and location. One of the earliest maps, compiled by Marino Sanuto in 1306, indicates some 350 scattered through the western Atlantic.

The Irish were not the only Christians to commit themselves to the ocean. Among the many Breton legends there is the story of a hundred monks setting out 'to contemplate the innumerable wonders of the ocean'. After three years at sea they were guided by statues of the Virgin and of Moses to an island with a golden mountain and a golden town, where they were treated to the food of angels before returning to Brittany. Another tradition records how an archbishop, six bishops, and their Christian followers fled from the Moorish advance through Iberia in the early eighth century. They took ship in Portugal and sailed westwards under divine guidance, eventually arriving at a large island way out in the Atlantic, called Antillia. Here they settled in peace, founding seven cities. The mythical islands first appeared on a chart of 1424 and thereafter constantly featured among the plethora of imagined islands the quest for which encouraged generations of navigators to venture further and further into the unknown Atlantic (1.7).

The Arabs, too, had stories of Atlantic exploration. One tale, reported in the twelfth century by the famous Arab geographer Al Idrisi, records the adventures of eight Muslim sailors who sailed out into the Atlantic—the 'Sea of Perpetual Gloom' as it was called—wherein there were thirty thousand fabulous islands and unforeseen horrors, including man-eating monsters. After facing massive seas and treacherous shallows made the more dangerous by heavily overcast skies, they eventually landed on the Island of Sheep, most likely to be identified with Madeira, before reaching the Canaries and finally making for the safety of the Moroccan coast, which they reached having been thirty-seven days at sea. This particular journey, unlike the legendary travels of the Christian clerics, has all the appearance of being a sober account of an actual adventure.

Of all the legendary islands of the Atlantic the most intriguing is Hy-Brazil, said to lie not far off the west coast of Ireland, so named and placed on charts from the fourteenth century onwards. The legend goes back much further, probably into pre-Christian times, appearing first in the seventh century in the Irish text known as 'The Adventure of Bran Son of Febal', which tells of Bran's visit to this Other World island supported on pillars of gold where games are played, people are always happy, there is no sorrow or sickness, and music is always to be heard—truly a land of the blessed. It emerges from oral and written tradition to pictorial form in a map of 1325 compiled by Angelino de Dalorto, gathering a rich

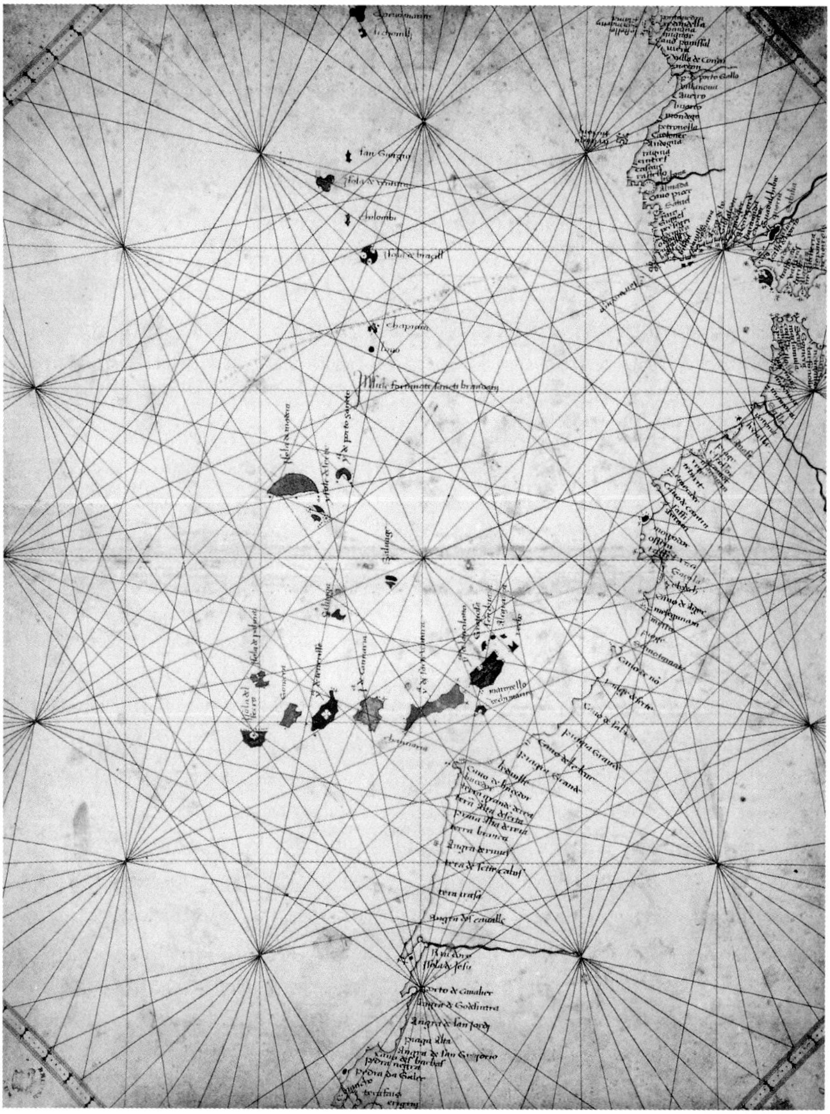

1.7 Chart of the Atlantic by Grazioso Benincasa, 1470, indicating islands both real and imaginary.

mythology around itself. It was seldom seen, being constantly enshrouded in mist and fog, but once every seven years the island would rise from the sea and the mists would part. Many claimed to have seen it. What is remarkable is that so strong was the tradition that 'Brazil Rock' was still marked on charts of 1830, and was not finally removed until 1865. In an article published in the learned journal the *Proceedings of the Royal Irish Academy* for 1912, the antiquary T. J. Westropp claimed to have seen the island three times. Of the last sighting in 1872 he wrote that, on 'a clear evening, with a fine golden sunset . . . just as the sun went down, a dark island suddenly appeared far out to sea, but not on the horizon. It had two hills, one wooded; between them, from a low plain, rose towers and curls of smoke.' Others with him confirmed the story.

Legendary islands in the far west—Elysium, the Hesperides, the Island of the Blessed—provided a powerful and sustaining allegory, made all the more real for those living along the Atlantic shore by the ever-present ocean in all its moods. When monks sang Psalm 106, to the sound of the breakers crashing on the rocks—'Those who go down to the sea in ships and have business in its many waters see the works of the Lord and his great deeds in the deep'—they were expressing a profound belief that all those before them could have shared. The ocean was a place of turbulence and danger to be challenged. Yet beyond it, for those who persevered, lay the islands of peace, calm, and plenty. For many, over the past three thousand years or more, the metaphor and the reality merged one into the other.

The Land Beyond the Ocean

By the second century BC the rational thinkers of the Graeco-Roman world were aware that the earth was a sphere. As we have seen, Strabo, writing at the beginning of the first century AD, clearly stated his belief that the land mass of Europe and Asia stretched partly round the sphere, the extremities being separated by the ocean too vast to navigate. In attempting to establish distances the second-century geographer Ptolemy, dividing the world into 360 degrees of longitude, estimated that the land mass from Cape St Vincent to the coast of China was 177 degrees at the equator. In fact the actual distance is only 131 degrees, but Ptolemy's erroneous estimate, which reduced the perceived ocean journey between Europe and China westwards across the ocean, was an encouragement to early navigators like Columbus. In 1474 Columbus was in correspondence with the famous Florentine humanist Paolo Toscanelli, who wrote encouragingly of the trans-Atlantic journey and the riches to be found in China and Japan. This said, his estimate of the length of the journey between Spain and Japan—some 4,500 miles—was frightening. Columbus was not prepared to accept it, and instead preferred to base his own estimate on the work of a ninth-century Arab scientist, Alfraganus, and arrived at a figure of 3,000 miles—a distance which would have given his financial backers, and his fellow sailors, some reassurance of success. As we now know, the distances discussed in the fifteenth century were serious underestimates, the actual distance between the Canaries and Japan being in the order of 10,000 miles. Given his beliefs, it is easy to see why Columbus was ready to accept the completely unsuspected conti-

1.8 The dangers of sea travel, from an engraving by Olaus Magnus, 1598.

nent of America that so inconveniently intervened as being the east coast of Asia—a view he appears to have held until his death. It took another thirty years for the shape of the Americas to be defined and the true size of the world to be appreciated. Those who lived on the Atlantic fringe of Europe had now to readjust to the understanding that they no longer occupied the edge of the Old World but were on the interface with the New: it demanded a dramatic and unsettling shift in cognitive geography.

Enter Geographers and Archaeologists

In 1902 the Oxford geographer H. J. Mackinder published a book, *Britain and the British Seas*, which can fairly be regarded as the first scientific treatment of the island's geography. In it Mackinder distinguished the two maritime faces of Britain, those lying east and south between Britain and the Continent and those lying to the west and north—essentially the ocean margin. In considering this latter zone he recognized three subzones—the 'marine antechamber' from Brittany to south-west Ireland; the British 'Mediterranean', that is, the Irish Sea; and 'seas of the oceanic border', comprising the north and west coasts from south-west Ireland to the Orkneys. But for Mackinder the seas were seen more as a barrier than as a corridor. The seas divided Britain from the Continent and Ireland from Britain. His was essentially the land-centred view prevalent among historians and geographers at the time.

The first clear statement of the importance of the western seaways as an axis of communication came ten years later from the pen of another Oxford geographer, O. G. S. Crawford, whose early interest in the past ensured that he was to become one of the country's foremost archaeologists. In 1912 Crawford published a paper entitled 'The Distribution of Early Bronze Age Settlements in Britain' in the *Geographical Journal*, showing, for the first time, how the distribution pattern of artefacts in the west of Britain and the Continent was the result of transport by sea. He later went on to develop the theme far more fully in a paper entitled 'The Western Seaways' published in 1936. By this time, however, other archaeologists in Britain had become aware of the importance of the sea. The Welsh geographer H. J. Fleure was writing on the western coasts of Britain and the importance of the seaways in 1915, and these views were further expanded in his book (co-authored with H. Peake) *The Way of the Sea*, published in 1929.

As the distribution of archaeological artefacts came more fully to be known, so the importance of the Atlantic seaways began to be appreciated. One of the earliest accounts of Atlantic trade was published by E. T. Leeds in 1927 as an adjunct to a report on the excavation of Chun Castle, an Iron Age fortified site in Cornwall. Leeds drew extensively on the archaeological record and classical sources to build up a picture of the movements of people along the Atlantic seaways between Iberia and Britain in the later prehistoric period. A few years later, with the publication of his influential book *The Personality of Britain* in 1932, Sir Cyril Fox established once and for all the special character of Atlantic Britain and the intricate pattern of maritime and trans-peninsular routes which bound the maritime communities of western Europe. Archaeologists like Gordon Childe could say, in 1946, when writing of the north-west coasts of Scotland: 'We may picture these grey seas as bright with Neolithic Argonauts as the western Pacific is today.' In a later book dealing with European prehistory Childe went on to develop the idea of seaborne 'megalithic missionaries' sailing along the Atlantic coasts, much as the Christian saints were to do several millennia later, taking with them the belief systems which required communities to build great megalithic tombs. Glyn Daniel, in his book *The Megalithic Builders of Western Europe* (1958), though less sanguine about the concept of missionaries, nonetheless saw the sea as the corridor of communication:

> . . . it is possible to forget that behind these movements there were not only people, but human beings who were intrepid navigators, who survived the first navigational shocks of leaving the tideless Mediterranean and cabotage, for the rigours of the four hundred miles of storm and sea between Finisterre in north-west Spain and Finistère in western Brittany; these people must indeed have thought at times that they were journeying to the ends of the earth.

The importance of the western seaways in the early Christian period has long been recognized through the lives of the many saints who faced the fringe of the Atlantic. The evidence was convincingly brought together by the Welsh historical geographer E. G. Bowen in 1969 in his book *Saints, Seaways and Settlement in the Celtic Lands*, and it was the same author who,

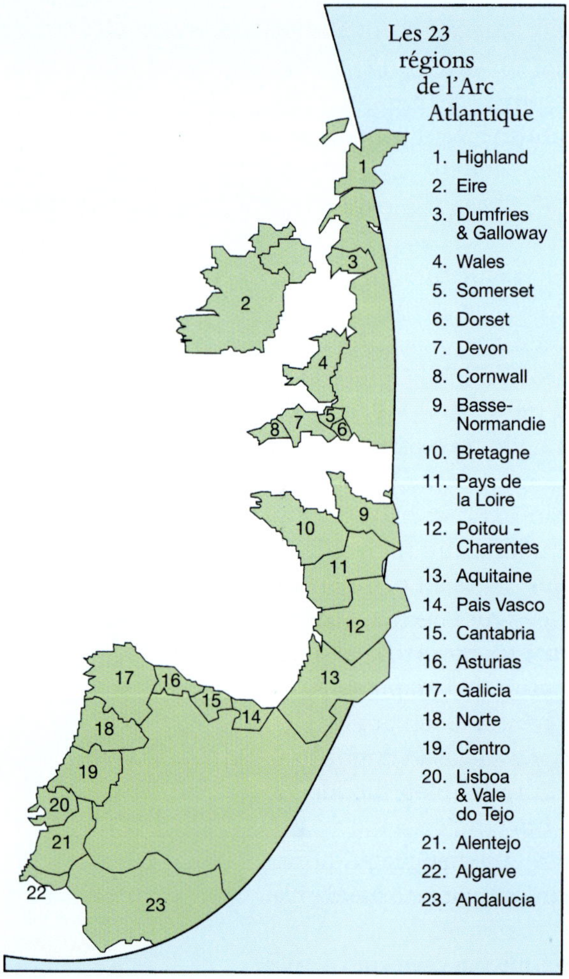

1.9 The 'Atlantic Arc'—a visual representation of a European Union socio-political construct as presented by J. Martray, *Nous qui sommes d'Atlantique* (Rennes, 1991).

in 1972, produced the first overview of the Atlantic seaways through time in his *Britain and the Western Seaways*. With the broadly based scholarly works of Bowen it may fairly be said that the awareness of the vital importance of the Atlantic seaways to the development of Europe in the prehistoric and historic period finally became established.

New Europe—New Myths

The Atlantic is a strong binding force, and inevitably in nineteenth- and twentieth-century politics it has been called into use from time to time to bolster beliefs and underpin aspirations. In 1867 the Breton folklorist and nationalist La Villemarqué called the first Inter-Celtic Congress in Brittany, inviting his 'compatriots' from Wales, 'brothers' from Cornwall, and 'cousins' from Ireland and Scotland, in an attempt to develop a political alliance between the 'Celtic' countries of Atlantic Europe to counter the power of England and France. Just over 120 years later, in October 1989, the general assembly of the Conférence des Régions Périphériques Maritimes was held at Faro. As a result it was decided to create a commission called 'Arc Atlantique' to bring together all the regions that 'constitute the Atlantic façade of Europe' from Scotland to Andalucía to prepare a 'series of actions destined to create, in that part of Europe, a real core of attraction' (*un véritable noyau attractif*) (1.9). The brief is economic, cultural, and environmental, but above all it is intended to provide a political-economic force to counter the power of the industrial regions stretching in an arc from Birmingham to Milan—the so-called 'hot banana'. Are we witnessing the restatement of a timeless geopolitical reality, or is the Ocean creating for us yet another Atlantic myth?

2. Between Land and Sea

From perception of the landscape—the kaleidoscope of cognitive geographies—we turn to the reality of the land itself and of the ocean that gives the Atlantic façade its peculiar definition. Fernand Braudel has warned that 'history is not made by geographical features, but by the men who control or discover them'. So it is, and it is well to carry this reminder with us, yet environment constrains behaviour as well as offering opportunities, and without a congenial environment there can be no men. History, then, is human behaviour controlled and empowered by environment. More starkly reduced, it can be characterized as the dynamic relationship between the organism and its ecological niche. That niche is the landscape: the capes and bays, the prominent landmarks and valleys, the tides and currents, and the very rock itself and the weather that sculpts it. In different combinations, these provide the microenvironments within which the human community creates its history.

The north-western fringe of the Atlantic extends across 40 degrees of latitude from 25°N to 65°N, from the Canary Islands to Iceland, a direct sailing distance along longitude 15°W of some 4,000 kilometres (2.1). In the Canaries the winter temperature seldom falls below 18°C; on the southern coast of Iceland it usually remains at about freezing point in spite of the warming effect of the Gulf Stream. The two extremities of our region were, in the period that concerns us, worlds apart, yet by as early as the 1420s they were being drawn in ever more tightly to the centre. In 1424 merchants from Bristol were visiting the profitable shores of Iceland to bring back the abundant cod; just a year later a Portuguese force, dispatched by Prince Henry, was *en route* to Grand Canary, to initiate the European occupation. In the busy ports of Lisbon and Oporto sailors from both expeditions could have met and exchanged stories. The world was fast contracting.

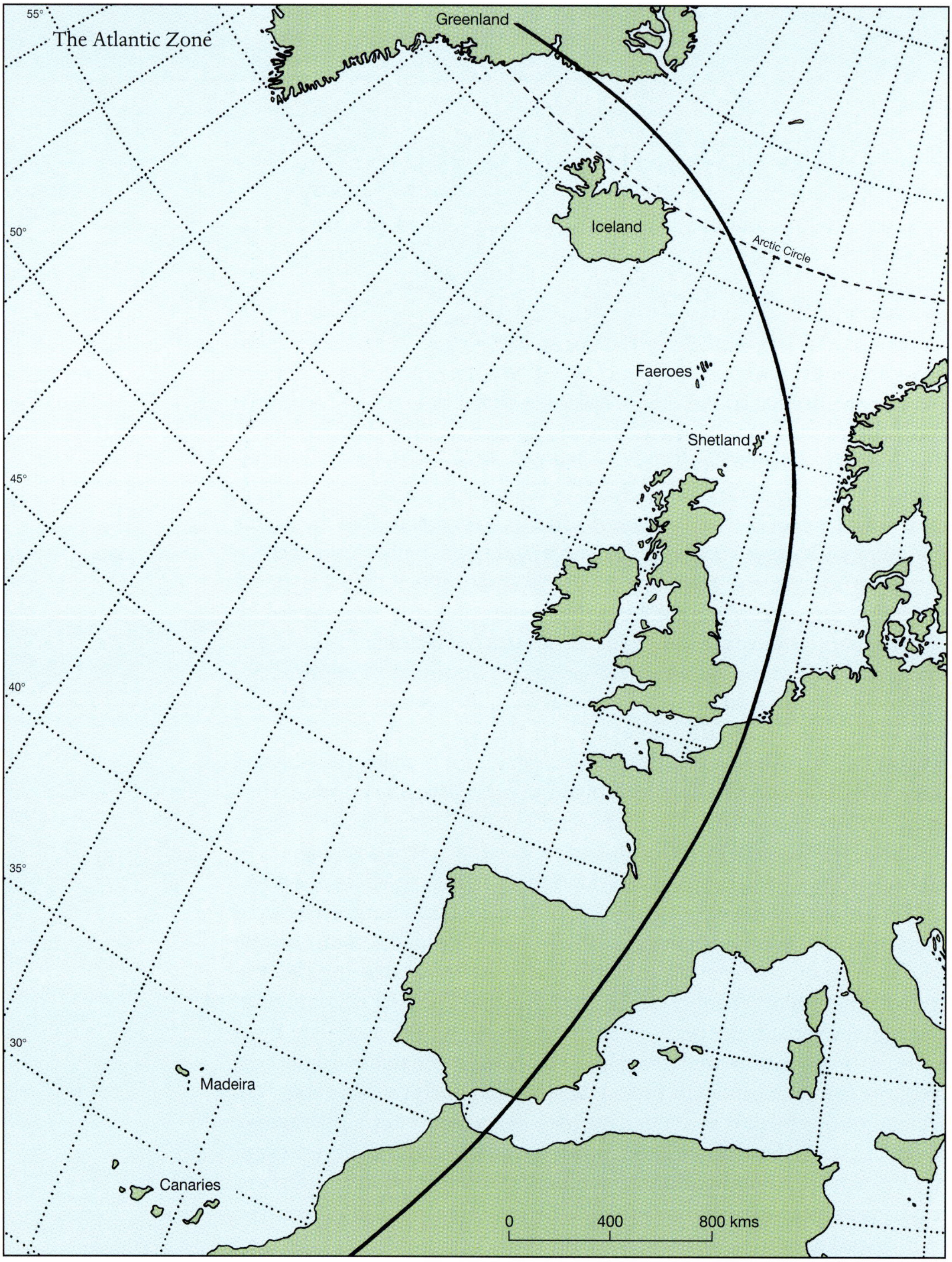
The Atlantic Zone
55°
50°
45°
40°
35°
30°
Greenland
Iceland
Arctic Circle
Faeroes
Shetland
Madeira
Canaries
0
400
800 kms

The Battle Between Land and Sea

Along such a vast interface the land facing the sea varies much in texture and in aspect. The sea and land are constantly at battle as the winds from the west hurl often-mountainous waves at a varied geology. Old hard rocks stand out in craggy headlands (2.2, 2.3), while younger, softer rocks succumb to the sea's pounding and are quickly eroded away. On the European coast the dominant peninsulas of Brittany, Devon and Cornwall, south-west Wales, and south-west Ireland are composed of resilient Palaeozoic rocks, metamorphosized shales, and old red sandstone permeated by granites and other intruded igneous masses, all compacted together and folded with a persistent east–west grain. These four great bastions stand out against the sea, each with its most westerly extremities creating the headlands familiar to sailors for hundreds of generations—Pointe du Raz and Île d'Oussant in Brittany, Land's End in Cornwall, St David's Head in Wales, and the many daunting crags of Co. Cork and Co. Kerry, from Cape Clear to Slea Head.

Further south the Palaeozoic and igneous rocks of the Iberian Peninsula strengthen the two westerly corners of the land mass. In the north-west they form the great bulwark of Galicia with its famous capes of Finisterre and Ortegal, while at the south-west the Serra de Monchique of the Algarve and Lower Alentejo thrusts into the ocean as Cape St Vincent—the sacred cape known to classical writers as the westernmost limit of Europe. Between these resilient extremities the softer rocks of Tertiary and Quaternary date provide a more gentle yielding face to the sea, except on either side of the Tagus where the tough calcareous rocks of the Serra de Sintra and the Serra de Arrábida, ending in the Cabo de Roca and Cabo Espichel, flank the estuary signalling its approach from far out to sea.

South again, past the Straits of Gibraltar and down the African coast of Morocco, the Atlantic coast lacks monumentality until the island of Mogador is reached, beyond which, to the valley of Oued Souss, the ridge of the High Atlas reaches the sea, creating a formidable coastline of towering cliffs more than 300 metres high dominated by Cape Rhir. South of the Souss the Ante Atlas, a lower mountain range parallel to the High Atlas, loses altitude before meeting the sea, providing the last significant heights before the Sahara is reached in the latitude of the Canaries.

The simple process of coastal erosion, with the sea etching out the softer rocks and leaving the more resilient of peninsulas and promontories, is one of the most obvious formative processes at work. Another, less immediately apparent, is the eustatic readjustment of the sea in relation to the land. Relative sea-levels have changed quite considerably over

2.1 (*facing*)
The Atlantic zone.

the last ten thousand years or so, largely in response to the melting of the ice caps which allowed the land to rise once the weight of the ice had been removed. The balance between rising sea-level, caused by the melted ice, and rising land has rarely kept in equilibrium. A further complication has been introduced by uneven warping in the earth's crust. Together, these factors have ensured that every length of coastline has its own particular history.

In general, much of the Atlantic façade has suffered a gradual sinking of the land in relation to the sea. One of the most dramatic results of this has been the progressive flooding of river valleys by the sea. The phenomenon is particularly well demonstrated by the Atlantic coast of Galicia, now deeply indented by wide inlets known as *rias*—a Spanish word universally used by geographers to describe the phenomenon wherever it occurs (2.4, 2.5). The regularity evident in the *rias bajas* of Galicia is due to the corrugated nature of the folded rocks controlling the course of the west-flowing rivers. Here the rise in sea-level has created wide, well-pro-

2.2 (*facing*) Cliffs of old hard rocks standing out against constant battering from the sea. Kynance Cove, Cornwall.

2.3 The sea differentially eroding cliffs. Elegug Stacks, St Govan's Head, Pembrokeshire.

2.4 The ria coastline of Galicia (north-western Iberia). The deep, well-protected inlets are river valleys flooded by a rising sea-level in later prehistoric times.

tected, deep-water inlets penetrating 20–30 kilometres inland, providing safe anchorages for shipping through the ages. The generations of pilgrims arriving by sea to visit the shrine of St James at Santiago de Compostella will have breathed a sigh of relief as their ships entered the long, safe haven of Ria de Arosa after facing the ferocity of the Atlantic smashing against the Galician headlands.

Much the same kind of landscape can be found elsewhere on the

Atlantic façade. The coasts of Brittany are deeply penetrated by drowned valleys, the most famous of which—the Rade du Brest—is a huge expanse of protected water formed by the flooding of the confluence of two river valleys, the Elorn and Châteaulin. On the opposite side of the Channel, the same eustatic processes have turned the lower Tamar into another great naval roadstead—Plymouth Sound—one of a number of rias stretching along the southern shores of Devon and Cornwall between Exeter and Falmouth. In south Wales its equivalent is Milford Haven, while in southern Ireland the Cobh gives life to Cork. But nowhere is the deeply penetrated ria coastline better seen than in the extreme south-west of Ireland where, between the peninsulas of Dingle and Mizen, long fingers of sea and land clench each other in an inseparable hold.

Only where the rocks are resilient has the rise in sea-level created rias, giving rise to a coastline of stark contrasts, both dangerous and welcom-

2.5 The ria coast of Galicia. The drowned valley of the Ria de Muros y Noia looking west to the Atlantic.

2.6 (*facing*) The coastal barrier flanking Les Landes in western France. The great beach runs from just north of Biarritz to the mouth of the Gironde. This view is taken near Lit-et-Mixe, Landes.

ing to sailors. Where the rocks are softer and more easily worn away the situation is quite different. Instead of pounding and penetrating, the sea smooths and builds. This is vividly demonstrated by the Atlantic coast of France from the mouth of the Loire to the Pyrenees, where, on the shelving shores, the sea has built long sinuous bars of sand and shingle, in places discontinuous or linking island to promontory, elsewhere forming immense continuous swaths smoothed and straightened by longshore drift. Behind these barriers, with the land still falling, marshes have developed, fed by silts brought down by rivers trying to find their way to the ocean. The Marais Breton and Marais Poitevin are two of the largest of the many which grew up behind coastal barriers between the estuaries of the Loire and Gironde. Even more impressive is the monotonous coastline stretching from the mouth of the Gironde southwards to Bayonne. Here the great swath of coastal sand dunes up to 7 kilometres wide runs in a straight, almost unbroken, line for some 230 kilometres (2.6). Once constantly on the move, blown landwards by onshore winds, the dunes are now anchored by the roots of deliberately planted pine and willow, a method of stabilization introduced by the engineer Brémontier in 1783. Behind them lies a string of ponded-up lakes and marshes separating the dunes from the sandy heaths of the equally monotonous Landes.

Coastal barriers formed by longshore currents building sediment into protective ridges are found along much of the Atlantic coast, though seldom to the extent of the Landes. In southern Iberia a sandbar, the Playa de Castilla, stretching from Huelva eastwards towards Cadiz blocked the old estuary of the Guadalquivir, creating behind it a great expanse of marshland that is now one of the most important ornithological reserves in Europe (2.7). In the late fifteenth and early sixteenth centuries the growth of the sandbar across the mouth of the river at Sanlúcar de Barrameda posed a serious obstacle to the fleets from the Americas attempting to sail upriver to the home port of Seville. Longshore drift is again at work along the coast of Morocco between Larache and Rabat, the Phoenician ports of Lixus and Sala, building beaches ever southwards, deflecting the mouth of the Oued Sebou, and creating behind the coastal barrier long, narrow, brackish lakes and marshes like the Merja Ras ed Daoura, which today runs parallel to the sea for more than 40 kilometres and is only one of a string of such lakes together extending over twice the distance.

These examples chosen from along the Atlantic façade will suffice to show the sea as a builder of coastal lands, but what was created was seldom to the benefit of human communities. Sand-dunes and marshes may be congenial to wildlife but they tend to isolate communities, separating them from the sea and thus hindering them from using the ocean

for communication. To a traveller sailing along the Atlantic seaways these are coasts to be avoided, inhospitable and of little interest. Being difficult to see from the sea, such dangerous shores are best given a wide berth.

2.7 (*facing*) Satellite photograph of the Golfo de Cádiz from Cape Trafalgar near the bottom to Huelva at the confluence of the rivers Odiel and Tinto, near the top. Cadiz (Gadir) lies at the tip of the narrow strip of land offshore. The marshy estuary of the Guadalquivir is to the north of it. Compare with 2.21.

The land–sea relationship took another form ever present in the minds of those who faced the Atlantic—the power of the sea to engulf land, swallowing up whole communities at will. We have already considered the myth of the lost land of Atlantis, presented in its most familiar form by Plato, and the various, more local legends—the submerged land of Lyonnesse west of Land's End and the legendary site of Ker Is, once part of Brittany, inundated in a single night by the wrathful gods. These stories embody an understanding of the unstable equilibrium between land and sea. Their origins will always remain obscure, but in part the tales may have come about from the need to explain observed phenomena. The remnants of submerged forests, visible at very low tides around various coasts, provided vivid evidence of drowned landscapes. Stories were naturally created to explain them. Viewing the blackened roots of old oaks thrusting through the sand in Mounts Bay, close to Penzance, the monks can be forgiven for conjuring up visions of villages, complete with parish churches, suddenly being overwhelmed when really what they were observing was the forested littoral of the Early Bronze Age submerged over a span of centuries by a gradually rising sea-level. Even more dramatic and worrying to a superstitious medieval mind would have been the sight of megalithic monuments like the stone hemicycle, now on the tiny islet of Er Lannic, its upright stone rows marching down the shore into the Bay of Morbihan (2.8), or the stone core of a megalithic tomb at Kernic near Plouescat, on the north coast of Finistère, now visible only at low tide (2.9).

2.8 The island of Er Lannic in the Bay of Morbihan. The island was once a slight hill in the low-lying coastal region but a rise in sea-level after the Neolithic period flooded much of the area. The hemicycle of standing stones on the hill was partially inundated, an adjacent hemicycle is now wholly below high-tide level.

Examples such as these provide tangible evidence of the sea-level changes which, over the last ten thousand years or so, have created the present configuration of the coasts. In the Mesolithic period, about 8000 BC, much would have been different: Britain would then have been part of the European mainland, the chalk ridge between Dover and Calais cut only by a wide river valley flanked by marshes, while the island of Jersey was a promontory of what is now the Cotentin peninsula.

To anyone familiar with the Atlantic shores one of the abiding memories is of the myriads of islands scattered throughout the coastal

2.9 The allée couverte (a megalithic chambered tomb) at Kernic, Plouescat on the north coast of Brittany. The rise in sea-level after the Neolithic period means that the monument, once on dry land, is now in the intertidal zone.

waters—pieces of land severed from the mainland by rise in sea-level or erosion and now the preserve of the ocean. Islands were special locations. They could provide safe places, extraterritorial, where by agreement foreigners could stop over to create ports-of-trade. Cadiz, once an island settled by the Phoenicians, is a prime example of such a place. From here the Phoenician merchants could trade in peace with the Tartessians of the mainland.

Islands could also be havens of calm, isolated from the world, where men or women could be at peace to communicate with their gods. In the Christian era the Skellig rocks off the coast of Kerry (2.10), the Île Lavret close to the north Breton shore, and Iona, a fragment of land split from the island of Mull, were among the many chosen by small religious communities as places of solitude for contemplation. The attraction of islands for religious observance was not restricted to the Christians. When St. Budoc chose to set up his monastic school on Lavret he may well have been attracted by the Gallo-Roman building already there (2.11). The structure is now ruinous, but it has many of the characteristics of a temple, suggesting a long continuity of religious observance going back to at least the third century ad or even earlier. Nor should we forget the island mentioned by Poseidonius (quoted by Strabo, Geog. 4. 4. 6) somewhere off the mouth of the Loire, inhabited only by women dedicated to a fertility deity whose ritual regime required them once a year to reroof their temple and to complete the day's festivities by eating one of their number. Strabo goes on to tell us of another island 'near Britain' where rites are performed which he likens to the worship of Demeter and Core on Samothrace, implying perhaps a local fertility cult celebrating the chthonic deities.

Islands then, particularly small remote islands, had a special quality. No doubt their isolation and comparative safety provided the conditions desirable for religious and trading communities, but there was surely more to it than that. Perhaps it was the idea of boundedness—the sea serving as the protecting perimeter—that was the attraction. That islands were liminal places, neither entirely of the land nor of the sea, would have endowed them with unusual power in the minds of those who lived at the interface between land and ocean.

While the islands, capes, and promontories were a feature of the isola-

2.10 Skellig Michael, Co. Kerry, off the south-west tip of Ireland, chosen by Christian monks to provide them with seclusion. One of the most daunting of the remote Irish monasteries.

tion of the Atlantic façade, the rivers which flowed into the ocean provided the corridors giving access to Continental Europe. The interface between the two—the river estuaries—were the route nodes where the systems interlocked. If the flow of fresh water was sufficient to flush out sediment and frustrate the efforts of the tide to create coastal barriers, the estuaries were places of potential economic importance. Here, on the shores, cargoes could be transferred from seagoing ships to riverboats and barges and permanent port settlements would grow up. Lisbon and Oporto, Bordeaux and Nantes, Bristol and Hull are all examples of settlements which developed far up estuaries, away from the river mouths,

2.11 The island of Bréhat off the north coast of Brittany and the smaller islets around provided ideal 'remote places' for early Christian monks to settle. One group established themselves in a ruined Roman building on Île Lavret.

usually at the confluence with a tributary where conditions were optimum for providing a safe anchorage of sufficient depth, or easy beaching, together with good access to inland communication.

But what constituted a preferred location for a port in the Middle Ages may not have attracted people in earlier times. There were many interwoven factors at work. Contrast, for example, Christchurch Harbour and Southampton Water. In the Iron Age, Christchurch Harbour, dominated by the headland of Hengistbury, was a favoured port-of-trade playing a pivotal role in cross-Channel exchanges in the first century BC, yet in the early Roman period it was all but abandoned. Southampton Water came into its own in the early Roman period, further developed in late Saxon and medieval times, and became one of the major ocean-going terminals in the nineteenth and early twentieth centuries.

There were many reasons why this shift between the two Solent ports took place, but principal among them were socio-economic imperative and technological demand. In the Late Iron Age a major focus of population lay on the chalklands of Wessex, an area conveniently reached by the two major rivers, the Stour and Avon, both flowing into Christchurch Harbour. The harbour was well protected and easily accessible to seagoing ships small enough to negotiate the narrow harbour mouth and the sandbars which shielded the opening. Thus the attractions of Christchurch Harbour in the prehistoric period were many. But from the beginning of the Roman period onwards the geopoliticical centre of Britain changed, moving towards the Thames and Essex, a process which continued in early medieval times with London eventually emerging as the capital. Given the new focus of power, Southampton Water became the preferred port of entry on the south coast, benefiting initially from an excellent road network created by the Romans, its importance growing as ships of deeper draught came into common use. The lesson is clear—an estuary may develop as a port, but always in response to the changing needs of the community, echoing Braudel's stricture that 'history is not made by physical features, but by the men who control or discover them'.

The Many Different Seas

Chaucer's ship's captain might know 'all the havens that there were from Gottland to the Cape of Finisterre, and every creek in Brittany and Spain', but many of those sailing in Atlantic coastal waters would seldom have had much cause to venture beyond their own seas—the waters they had learned from their elders and their own experience: each seafarer carried with him his own limited cognitive geography. Thus defined, there were many seas along the Atlantic face of Europe. To attempt to characterize them all would be an impossible task, yet some flavour of the great variety must be given.

Within the great swath of the Atlantic façade two zones of prime importance stand out as the twin centres of the maritime system—a *southern core* extending from the Tagus in Portugal to the Souss in Morocco, including the Straits of Gibraltar, and a *northern core* from the Shannon to the Loire, including the English Channel (2.12). What both have in common is that they control the approaches to other maritime worlds—the Mediterranean and the North Sea / Baltic region. Thus they are themselves gateways for maritime exchange. The significance of the *northern core* was recognized a century ago by the Oxford geographer H. J. Mackinder, when he described it as 'the marine antechamber of Britain'. The *southern core* zone could well be called the marine antechamber of the Mediterranean.

The two 'antechambers' are linked by a network of maritime routes which inevitably acknowledge and incorporate the north-western corner of the Iberian Peninsula, where the ria coastlines of Galicia provide an abundance of fine anchorages. Unlike the core zones, with their ease of access to other worlds, Galicia has its back to the mountains—it looks only to the sea. Thus it served essentially as a stepping-stone—a vital one and with valuable reserves of metals to offer—but a stepping-stone nonetheless.

Beyond the core zones the world extended without limits. To the north lay what Mackinder referred to as 'the seas of the ocean border'. He included the west-facing shores of Ireland and Scotland and the Orkneys. To these we must add the Shetlands, the Faroes, Iceland, and Greenland, taking us to the Arctic Circle where the seas freeze. To the south lay a very different ocean border, also scattered with islands, extending down the coast of Africa to where the desert meets the sea. It was along these corridors leading from familiar waters to the unknown that European seafarers—the Norsemen of the north and the Portuguese in the south—first began to explore other worlds.

2.12 (*facing*) An interpretation of the Atlantic region. The shaded areas are the two core zones each experiencing a degree of internal integration and each offering access to other seas beyond. The smaller areas circled indicate important route nodes around the peripheries of the core zones.

There is a certain satisfying symmetry in the simple model sketched out here: it effectively contains the essential elements of the Atlantic seaboard and helps us to understand the broader issues, but it should not be allowed to obscure the underlying complexity of it all or to downplay the areas omitted. The southern part of the Bay of Biscay was the home of the Basque sailors who were to play such a significant role in the history of the sea, while the Irish (or Celtic) Sea—called by Mackinder 'the British Mediterranean'—teemed with maritime traffic throughout the millennia and was a major factor in creating the web of cultural sharings evident around its shores. Sailors from both regions cannot have failed to

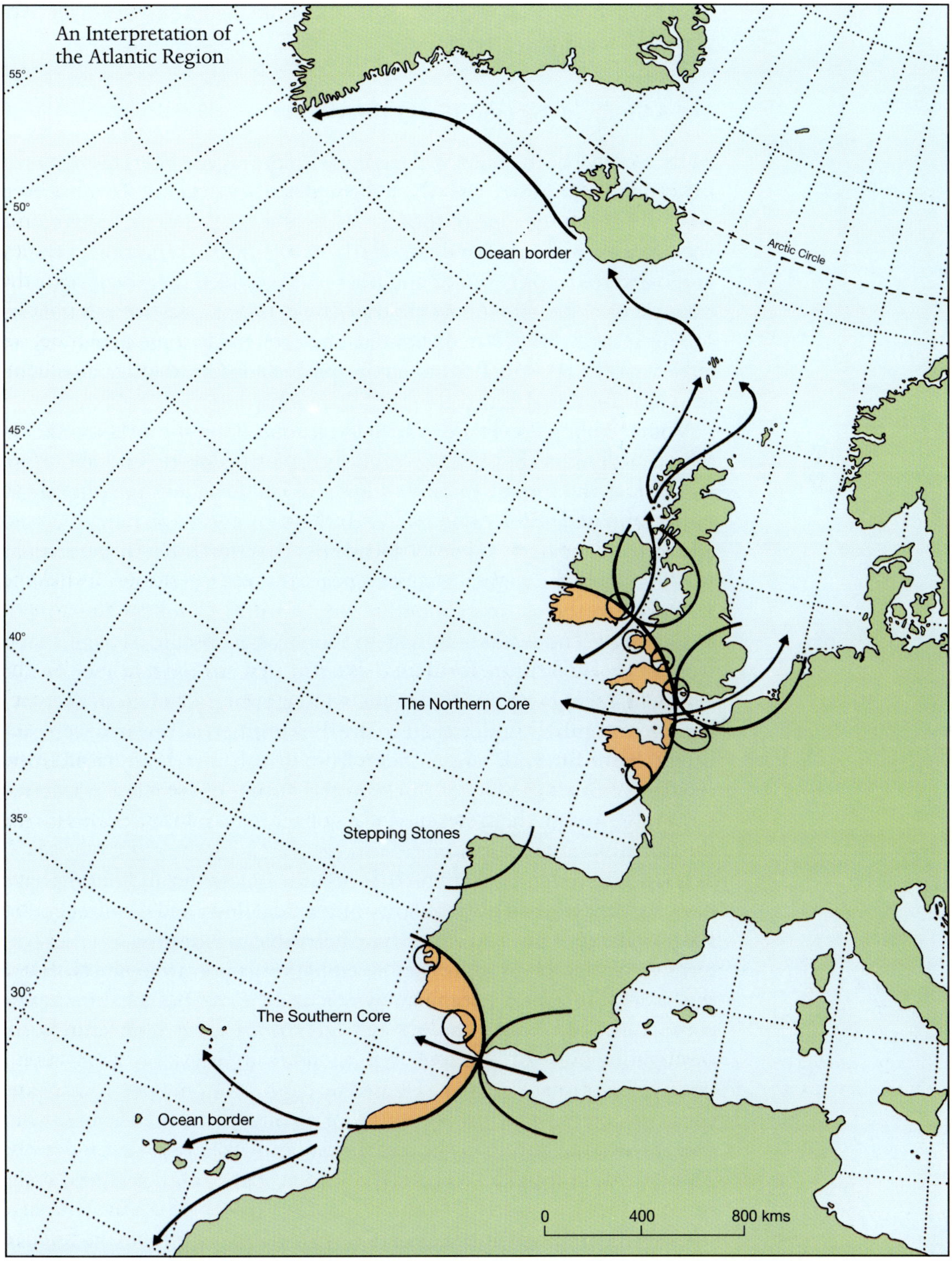
An Interpretation of the Atlantic Region
55°
50°
45°
40°
35°
30°
Arctic Circle
Ocean border
The Northern Core
Stepping Stones
The Southern Core
Ocean border
0
400
800 kms

have been drawn into the wider systems, while their home seas will have played host to many strangers.

The Motion of the Winds and Tides

So far we have been concerned largely with the jagged interface between land and sea, the processes which formed it and its variety. The interface was ever-changing. One of the factors involved in this complex dynamic was the action of wind and tide working together in temporal cycles to erode and to deposit. Winds and tides also provided their own rigorous constraints and opportunities to travel by sea. In the days of sail the season for sea travel was strictly limited, and even today some of the largest ferries may be prevented from making port in adverse weather, as anyone who has attempted to travel to St Malo in midwinter will well know.

Winter sailing is certainly more hazardous along the Atlantic shores than travelling in the summer months. Gales of force 7 and above are eight times more frequent and rough seas occur on average one day in four, compared with one in twelve in the summer. Fogs, rain, and cold add to the dangers. It is hardly surprising, therefore, that in the ancient world, even in the calmer Mediterranean, the sailing season was usually restricted to the summer months from April to October. The Anglo-Saxon elegy 'The Seafarer' tells us, in a somewhat obscure passage, that it was not wise to venture forth until after the first cuckoo had been heard. This said, sailing was possible in the winter, even if ill-advised, and voyages were regularly undertaken where the commercial rewards were sufficient. In the fifteenth century fleets from British ports bound for Lisbon regularly crossed the Bay of Biscay in the summer, returning in December, bringing with them sweet wine and fruit to be sold at a premium for the Christmas market at home.

It is a reasonable assumption that Atlantic sailors throughout the ages have well understood the regularity of the tidal flows and the direction of the prevailing winds, and would have been able to judge the weather patterns with tolerable accuracy before embarking upon a journey. North of the Bay of Cadiz the predominant winds, and the swell which they create, come from the west, varying between north-west and south-west throughout most of the year, but winds from anywhere from south through west to north can be created by depressions moving north-east. Close to land the daily heating and cooling of the land mass causes local breezes onshore during the heat of the day and offshore as the land cools. All of these factors had to be taken into account when a journey was planned.

The wind imposed upon the sea a surface current which, in the English

Channel, could average 6 nautical miles a day in a north-easterly direction. In the Bay of Biscay the current runs inshore in a south-easterly direction. These localized currents are modified by the natural ebbs and flows of the tidal stream, which in turn are affected by the shape of the adjacent coast. Topography can also create massive differences in the tides from one place to the next. In the Severn estuary spring tides can be as much as 14 metres, while on the Solent coast they are about 2 metres, but the Solent has an unusual tidal pattern with a double high water. The effect of this in Poole Harbour is for the tide to be high for fourteen out of every twenty-four hours—a distinct advantage when berthing vessels of deep draught.

A knowledge of all these factors would have allowed the sailor to work the winds and tides so that headway could be made. In open sea the difficulties were not great, and well out from land there was less danger of grounding on rocks or shoals. But inshore sailing presented constant hazards. In rounding capes, so long as the seaman knew his tides he would know when the tide would turn and take him around the cape. A more serious problem would be whether a wind favourable for approaching the cape would also be favourable for taking him on from the cape without having to give the cape a wide berth. The other danger which all sailors feared was to be driven onto a lee shore by onshore winds (2.13, 2.14).

Once south of Cadiz one moved out of the influence of the westerlies into the realm of the North East Trades, which blow persistently southwards down the coast of Africa. Thus while the passage outwards from the Bay of Cadiz was speedy the return was far more difficult. As the Spanish and Portuguese were to find, the return was best accomplished by sailing in an arc westwards to north through the variable winds of Cancer and hoping to pick up a westerly for the passage back to Iberia. It was in this way that the Azores were encountered in the early fifteenth century, first appearing on a chart of 1435. The difficulties of the return journey may well have dis-

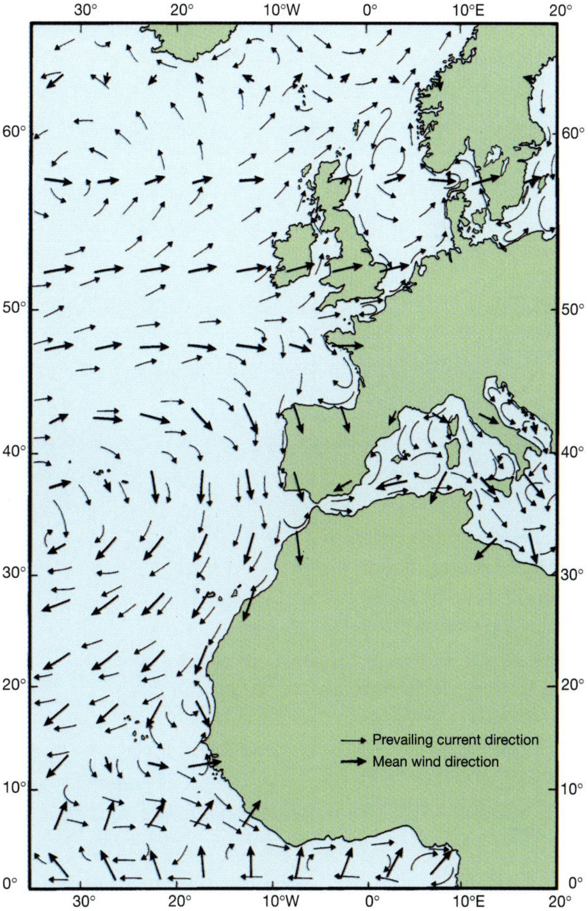

2.13 Pilot chart of the north-western Atlantic for August showing the prevailing current direction and the main wind direction.

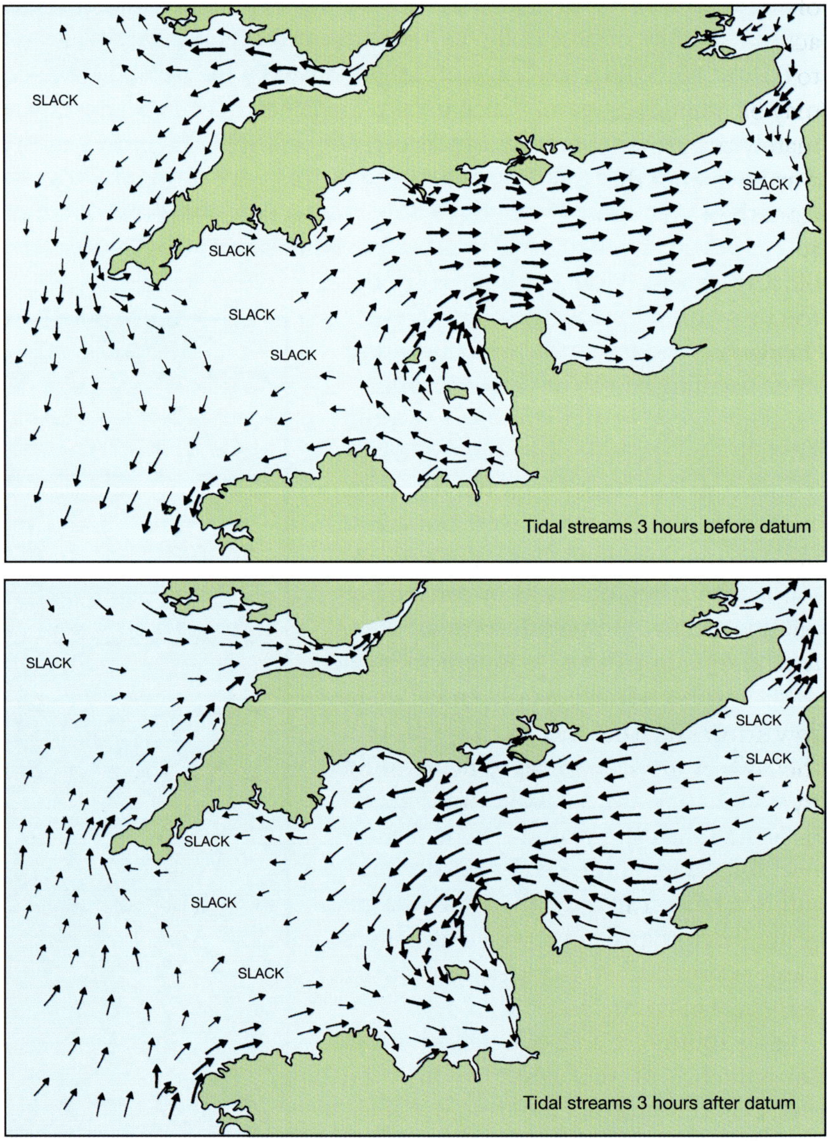

2.14 Chart of tidal streams in the Channel at 3 hours before and 3 hours after datum (high tide at Dover). The arrows indicate flow—the thicker the arrow the stronger the stream. Based on information from the Hydrographic Department, Taunton.

couraged earlier travellers from venturing far down the coast beyond Mogador. It was only the persistence of the Portuguese navigators in their highly manoeuvrable caravels, spurred on by the great wealth to be had, that drew men further south. Diego Cão reached Namibia in 1482 and a few years later Bartholomew Diaz rounded the Cape of Good Hope, returning home safely in December 1488.

One final aspect of the sea needs to be mentioned for the effect which it had on the Atlantic seaboard of Europe—the Gulf Stream—a current of warm water which originates in the Caribbean and flows in an arc across the North Atlantic, warming the European coasts from Scotland to Galicia. The difference in temperature which the stream helps to cause may be appreciated by remembering that Newfoundland is on approximately the same latitude as Brittany and Cornwall. The mixing of the warm water of the Gulf Stream and the nutrient-rich cold water flowing from the polar regions encourages the growth of phytoplankton which sustains huge shoals of fish. The greatest concentration of this plankton biomass extends in an arc up the Atlantic coast of Europe northwards to Iceland, creating in these waters some of the richest fishing grounds in the world.

Corridors from Land to Sea

The communities of the Atlantic seaboard were bound to the hinterland of peninsular Europe by innumerable routes—corridors of communication—which allowed people, goods, and, no less important, knowledge to flow (2.15). These corridors are, in large part, the construct of geography. At a very simple level Europe may be divided into three broad east–west zones separated by mountain ridges.

The Mediterranean, with many islands and peninsulas, has a very narrow littoral strip before the first mountain barrier is reached, comprising the Balkan massif and the Alps, with the Cévennes giving way to the Pyrenees. Beyond, to the south, the Iberian Peninsula presents an unfriendly range of sierras to shut out approaches from the sea. Natural routes leading through this barrier are comparatively few. Around the Julian Alps the valleys of the Drava and Sava can be reached, a few passes penetrate the Alps, but it is the Rhône valley which provides the most convenient way to the north, while the Aude and Garonne lead westwards to the Atlantic.

Beyond the southern mountain barrier lies middle Europe, dominated by the great river valley of the Danube and its tributaries, in its upper course reaching far west to come close to the headwaters of the Rhine, Moselle, Seine, and Saône. Together these rivers give coherence to a swath of highly productive land extending from the Atlantic coast of France to the Black Sea shores of Bulgaria and Romania. The potential of this land can be judged from the power of the empires that emerged there, from the Carolingian to the Austro-Hungarian.

Providing a northern protective barrier to middle Europe is another series of mountain ranges—the Carpathians, Sudeten Mountains, and Erzgebirge in the east, extending westwards in the lesser ranges of the Thüringer Wald, Eifel, and Ardennes. Beyond to the north lies the huge

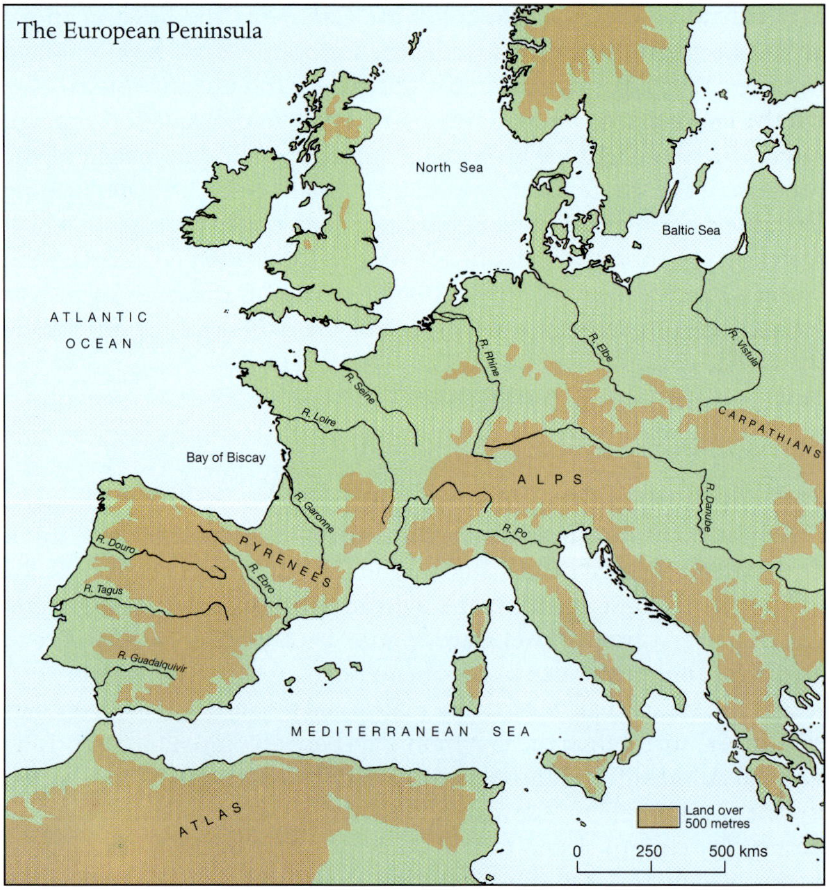

2.15 The European Peninsula indicating the major river routes providing corridors between the seas and the Ocean.

expanse of the North European Plain, stretching, in its extremes, from East Anglia to the Urals. Ways through the mountains linking middle and north Europe are comparatively few. The Morava and Oder, Vltava/Elbe, and the Rhine provide the major corridors, together with the sea routes along the English Channel and North Sea.

A glance at the simplified map is sufficient to make these generalizations clear—peninsular Europe is like a grid of north–south and east–west routes, allowing its disparate territories the more easily to communicate by means of the differing systems of trade, migration, and invasion that together punctuate history. The map also puts into perspective the nature of the Atlantic corridor, entirely transcending the physical divides of peninsular Europe. Before the fifteenth century AD the Atlantic zone provided the means by which the polities of western Europe could interact: bulk products and people could move quickly and in comparative safety. After the beginning of the fifteenth century the zone took on an entirely new role as the broad interface with the rest of the world.

Those states which occupied the ocean façade were optimally located to become the ocean's masters.

So much for the broad sketch. The question which now arises is how did the two systems, the Atlantic and the Continental, intercommunicate? There were a number of locations where major routes came together. Of these the most notable were the two Straits—Gibraltar and Dover—choke-points through which the ships had to pass to get from one system to another.

The Straits of Gibraltar (2.16) are wide—some 9 nautical miles of clear water—and, approaching from the Mediterranean, are well signed by the twin pillars of Hercules, *Mons Calpe*, Gibraltar, rising sheer some 425 metres from the sea to the north, and the lesser *Mons Abyla*, Apes Hill, on the Moroccan coast to the south. If approaching from the opposite direction, from the ocean, the navigator would have been able to judge his position when Punta Marroqui at the southernmost tip of Spain or Cape Spartel on the north-westerly extremity of Africa west of Tangier came into view. Clear signing by unambiguous landmarks provided comfort to the approaching ship's master and allowed him to concentrate on the two variables—the tides and the winds—over which he had no control. In the Straits there is a persistent surface current of cool Atlantic water flowing from west to east at a speed that can reach 5 or 6 knots. A hundred metres or so below a reverse current of warm salty water pours out into the Atlantic, but is of no consequence to shipping. For ships wishing to sail eastwards from the Mediterranean the surface current can be extremely difficult, though it may slacken with a stiff easterly wind. Those seeking the quieter waters nearer the shores could more easily find a way through to the ocean, taking advantage of counter-tidal flows. In coming from the Atlantic the current was always favourable.

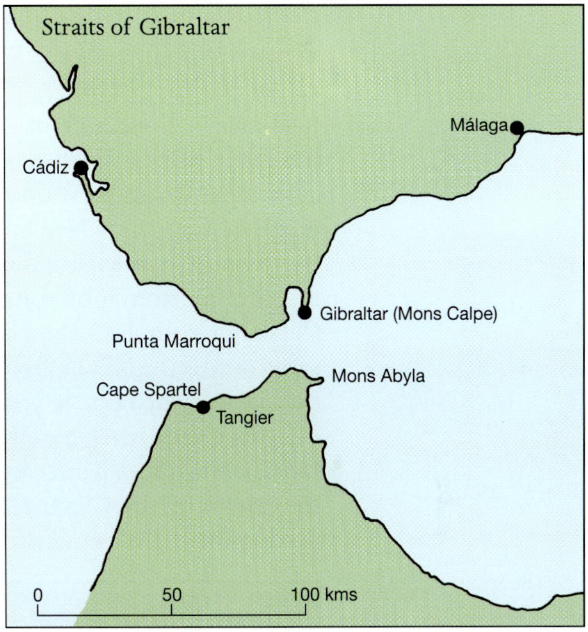

2.16 The Straits of Gibraltar. The 'Pillars of Hercules' were the two prominent landmarks of Mons Calpe and Mons Abyla marking, for a Mediterranean sailor, the portals to the Ocean beyond. For ships approaching from the Atlantic the headlands of Punta Marroqui and Cape Spatel were the guiding marks.

To the sailing ship the winds were all important. In the Straits there were only easterlies or westerlies. The easterlies were generally predominant in March, July–September, and December, with the westerlies filling the months between. The changing wind patterns meant that in the sailing season from April to September vessels would normally have planned to travel into the Mediterranean in the early part of the season and out again after the summer solstice, but weather patterns could be unpredictable and in some years one of the prevailing winds would dominate, negating well-laid plans. In the case of a ship coming from the Mediterranean it might have been necessary to wait for days or even months in the shelter of the coast of Malaga until the winds changed. In extreme cases, the author of the *Ora Maritima* advises, it might be necessary to disembark and offer sacrifice to the gods or even to take an overland route from Malaga to Tartessos, needing nine days for the round trip. Unpredictable delays waiting for the winds to change could well jeopardize safe return to the home port.

The Straits of Dover offer a different set of constraints (2.17). Today the narrowest point between South Foreland and Cape Gris Nez is 18 nautical miles, though Diodorus' estimate of 100 stadia (equivalent to 10 nautical miles), if accurate, might suggest that considerable coastal erosion has taken place over the last two millennia. To any navigator, the chalk cliffs from Dover to Walmer and the corresponding chalk outcropping north of Cape Gris Nez are easily identifiable and give warning of the narrowing Channel. But the behaviour of the sea in the Channel—taking it to be the stretch of water between Land's End/Ushant and Dover/Calais—is complex. The current created by the predominant SW wind sets towards the NE, but is of only marginal significance compared to the tidal flows which can be up to 3 knots on a NE/SW heading in mid-Channel. Since they reverse every 6¼ hours, for any ship attempting to cross the Channel they all but cancel out over a 12½-hour period. When sailing the length of the Channel the main difficulty encountered is with the predominant SW wind. In strong SW winds ships heading westwards

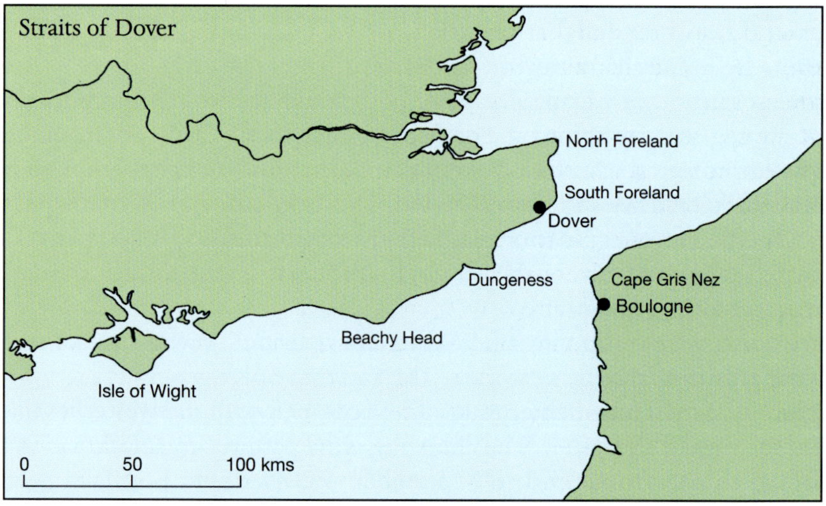

2.17 The Straits of Dover. The approach to the choke point between the Ocean and the seas beyond, the North Sea and the Baltic, was signalled by the two chalk headlands, South Foreland and Cape Gris Nez.

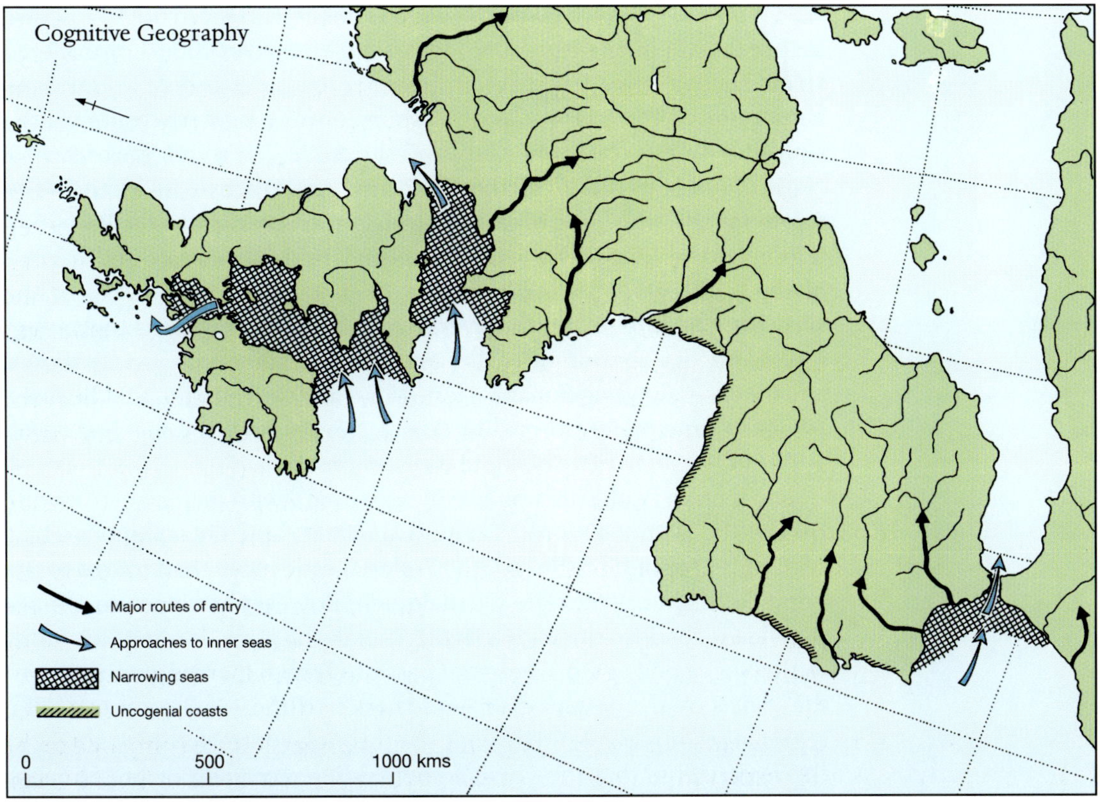

2.18 A cognitive geography of the Atlantic zone as it might have been viewed by an Atlantic mariner.

down Channel may have to wait for a wind-shift, but in lighter winds it may be possible to 'work the tides', that is to sail with the favourable tidal flow for six hours, then to anchor or heave-to for six hours, and so on. Sailing through the Strait is a matter of pilotage, making use of fair winds and tidal flows and observing the landmarks. In crossing the Strait, however, the master has also to allow for the tidal flow by 'aiming off'. In an ideal situation this would mean leaving one side on the ebb and arriving at the other at about the time of the flood. At about 3 knots this could be done, since 18 nautical miles at 3 knots takes about 6¼ hours—the duration of a single tide!

These, then, are the two prime routes by which the sailing communities of the Atlantic were able to reach other seas and other markets. But many, more geographically restricted, corridors were provided by the west-flowing rivers giving access from the Atlantic shores deep into continental Europe (2.18). Strabo, a Greek geographer writing in the early years of the first century AD, lists four major routes, the Rhine, Seine, Loire, and Garonne (*Geog.* 4. 5. 2). Along three of them the Atlantic could be linked to the Mediterranean. The Seine provided access far into northern Gaul, and by overland portage it was possible to reach the Rhône and thence the Mediterranean port of Massilia (Marseilles). The Loire offered an alternative route, and from its upper reaches it was only a short land haul to the Rhône below Lyons. A shorter, more westerly route via the Garonne, the Carcassonne Gap, and the Aude, led to the port town of Narbo (later Narbonne). All these systems were in active use when Strabo wrote for the transport of raw materials and slaves from the barbarian regions to the consuming Mediterranean world. The nature and volume of the traffic would, of course, have been a reflection of needs of the early Roman empire, but the river routes themselves were of high antiquity, as the distribution of earlier prehistoric trade goods vividly shows, and they remained significant arteries for trade well into the Middle Ages, by which time major ports—Bordeaux, Nantes, and Rouen—had developed in the estuaries to facilitate trans-shipment.

The Iberian Peninsula was also well provided with major west-flowing rivers—the Mino, Douro, Tagus, Guadiana, and Guadalquivir—but, with the exception of the last, they offered little more than routes to the immediate hinterland. The Guadalquivir, however, gave rise to a more significant corridor through a fertile, metal-rich zone, leading eastwards to the Sierra de Segura where the pass of Despeñaperros gave access to the valley of the Segura river and thence to the Mediterranean. The regional resources, together with the through route, and easy access to the sea ensured that the Guadalquivir valley remained of pre-eminent importance, as the famous Tartessos in the early first millennium BC, the cradle of Iberian Iron Age culture for the next 400 years, the heart of the fabulously productive Roman province of Baetica, and later the centre of the Arab Caliphate. In the fifteenth and sixteenth centuries the Lower Guadalquivir provided the power driving the colonization of the Americas, in doing so benefiting enormously from trade with the New World.

Further south along the coast of northern Morocco one of the few safe havens for shipping was the navigable River Loukos, at the mouth of which the Phoenicians established the port of Lixus, later to develop as an important Hellenistic and Roman city. The river gave access to a hinterland rich in gold, copper, iron, and ivory which found their way, mostly via the river route, into the all-consuming Mediterranean over the thousand years or so during which the port flourished.

Sailing southwards along the coast for a further 500 kilometres one came to the estuary of the Souss, the last major river of the Atlantic façade, where the roadstead—the Rade d'Agadir—provided shelter from the NE and E winds. The River Souss flowed from the High Atlas, but before the Portuguese established a port at Agadir in the fifteenth century the route was remote from the mainstream of Atlantic communications.

The rivers flowing to the Atlantic seaboard were, then, the routes along which a varied array of stimuli passed between the Atlantic, Continental Europe, and North Africa. The systems were interdependent and interactive: each owed its development, in some part at least, to the information exchanged between them. In this way the natural routes, created in the distant geological past, were to play a crucial role in shaping the development of western Europe.

Preferred Locations: Some Major Route Nodes

Implicit in what has been already said is that some locations were, by virtue of their special geomorphological characteristics, places of particular attraction for human settlement. For communities who constantly faced the sea, sheltered harbours, easy beaching, prominent landmarks, and routes to the interior featured large in their list of desiderata. Some locations were so well endowed that settlement, once established, lasted for thousands of years. Huelva, for example, on the promontory at the confluence of the rivers Tinto and Odiel, has been in constant use as a port from about 1000 BC until the present day. But such an intensive use of a restricted piece of land is rare. More often there has been a shift of focus within a closely defined territory (2.19). In Southampton Water the earliest port, known as *Clausentum*, was established by the Romans on a promontory at the mouth of the Itchen in the first century AD and remained in use at least to the end of the fourth century. Its successor, Hamwic, developed in the eighth and ninth centuries on a new site further downriver, but by the tenth century settlement had migrated again, this time to the tip of the promontory between the Test and Itchen where later the medieval walled town of Southampton emerged to become one of the foremost ports of England. In greatly expanded form Southampton still functions, as a major international container port, today. Among the varied factors which caused the moves, the need for increasingly deep-water anchorages is likely to have been decisive.

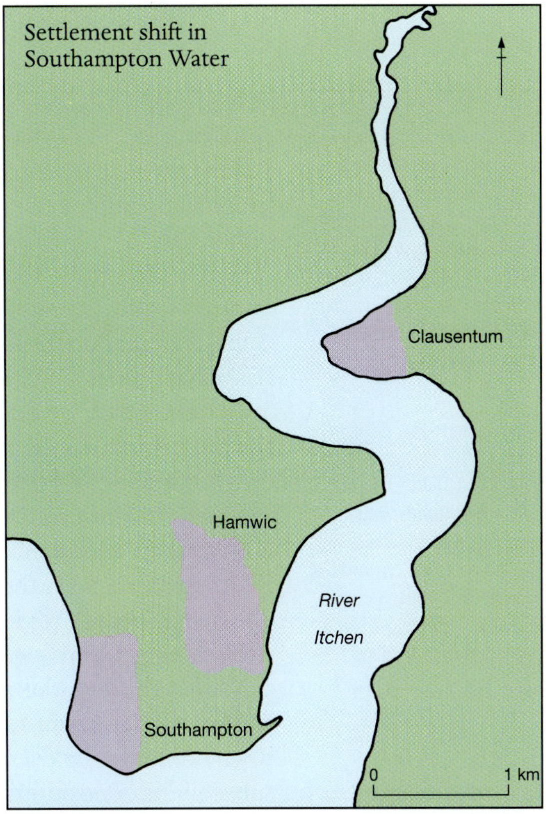

2.19 The shift of settlement focus in Southampton Water between Roman Clausentum, Saxon Hamwic, and medieval Southampton reflects a move towards deeper anchorages.

A comparable example is provided by St Malo in Brittany (2.20). Here settlement began

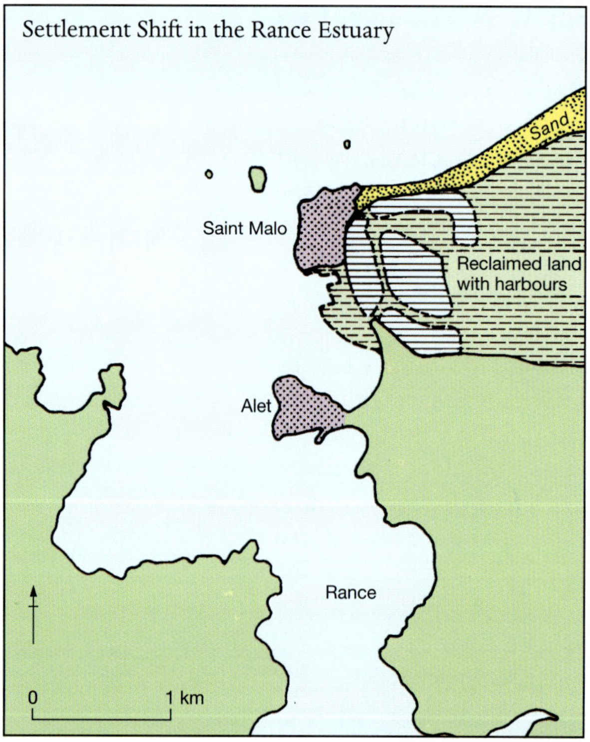

2.20 Settlement shift in the Rance estuary. Alet served as the focus from the first century BC to the tenth century AD. Thereafter St Malo—originally an isolated rock joined by a sand spit to the mainland—took over.

2.21 (*facing*) The Gulf of Cadiz. The coastline, of long sandy beaches and rocky headlands, was uncongenial to sailors but the island of Cadiz and the promontory between the Rio Odiel and Rio Tinto provided favoured anchorages. In the Middle Ages ships sailed up the Guadalquivir to dock at Seville, which became the main commercial centre.

in the Late Iron Age on the promontory of Saint Servin at the mouth of the Rance estuary. The promontory continued in use throughout much of the Roman period and was walled in the late third century. The same enclosure was used in the early medieval period, when a substantial cathedral church was built in the ninth century and rebuilt on an even grander scale a hundred years later. By the twelfth century, however, Saint Servin had been largely abandoned for a new site on a nearby granite island linked to the mainland by a sandbar. Here the medieval walled city of St Malo was built. Its harbours, which welcomed corsairs and north Atlantic explorers in the seventeenth and eighteenth centuries, are now the preserve of pleasure boats, local fishermen, and a flourishing cross-Channel ferry trade.

Huelva, *Clausentum* / Hamwic / Southampton, and Saint Servin / St Malo are all restricted locations that have served as ports over two millennia or more. But to take an even longer perspective it is necessary to broaden our geographical compass to consider maritime contact zones rather than individual sites.

One of the most significant contact zones in European history is the Gulf of Cadiz, stretching from the Cape of Santa Maria, near Faro, to Cape Trafalgar on the approach to the Straits of Gibraltar (2.21). The Gulf has always been a crucial interface. Not only is it central to the *southern core* zone, which we defined above, where the Atlantic system links with the Mediterranean, but it provides the point of contact with the Guadalquivir corridor and the exceptional natural resources of the hinterland, the fertile plains producing the three Mediterranean staples of corn, oil, and wine in abundance, and the metal-rich hills of Rio Tinto and the Sierra Morena with their ample supplies of silver and copper. It is and always has been a region of great vitality, and one whose spectacularly rich resources were legendary throughout the ancient world.

Within this broader region two locations stand out—the promontory at the confluence of the rivers Odiel and Tinto, now occupied by the port town of Huelva, and a small island at the mouth of the Guadalete (which subsequent depositions at the river mouth have turned into a promontory) upon which the city of Cadiz has developed. Between the two, a distance of 100 kilometres, lies the estuary of the Guadalquivir, once a wide, open bay extending inland towards the site of Sevilla. Longshore drift has closed off the estuary with a sandbar, the Playa de Castilla, narrowing the river mouth to a single opening, overlooked by the fishing port Sanlúcar de Barrameda, and allowing an extensive marsh—the Parque Nacional de Doñana (Las Marísmas)—to form behind it.

Huelva occupies a favoured location, not only in relation to the sea and riverine routes to the interior, but also by virtue of the fact that it is the natural gateway to the rich metal resources of the Rio Tinto region on the southern slopes of the Sierra de Aracena. Copper and silver are readily accessible and have been exploited for at least the last three thousand years. A large collection of Late Bronze Age metalwork dredged from the estuary in 1923, and once thought to be from a shipwreck, is now believed to be a ritual deposit dedicated perhaps to the deities who controlled shipping and trade about 1000 BC. Huelva developed rapidly in the seventh and sixth centuries BC, by which time it was linked intimately with the trading networks of the east Mediterranean. It may well be that the extensive town which grew up at this time was the legendary Tartessos.

As Huelva developed on the mainland, so the island of Cadiz—ancient Gadir—emerged as the prime Phoenician station in the west. It was a classic port-of-trade—an island settled by foreign merchants, lying at a safe distance from the native shore. It offered neutral ground for all comers guaranteed by the power of the presiding deity Melqart. The Phoenician settlement was well under way by the eighth century, and controlled the network of exchanges between the Tartessians and Phoenicians throughout the seventh and sixth centuries BC. That the Carthaginian leader Hamilcar Barca chose to land here in 237 BC to begin the Carthaginian domination of southern Iberia, and that its surrender to the Romans in 206 BC signalled the end of the Second Punic War, is some measure of the city's continuing importance. The two towns present an interesting contrast. Huelva (Tartessos?) was essentially a native port town providing a gateway to the hinterland, while Cadiz (Gadir) was an international focus linking the Atlantic system to the Mediterranean.

Although silting and consequential changes to the coastline affected accessibility over the following centuries, both ports maintained, and indeed still maintain, their maritime importance. It is no coincidence that it was from the port of Palos de la Frontera, near Huelva, that Columbus set sail on 3 August 1492, returning there from his first voyage to America the following March. He used the same port again for his second voyage in September 1493, and it was here that Cortés landed in 1528, triumphant from his conquest of Mexico. Similar honours can be claimed by Sanlúcar de Barrameda on the Guadalquivir. It was the point of embarkation chosen by Columbus for his third voyage in 1498, and in 1519 the expedition initiated by the Portuguese explorer Magellan landed here after circumnavigating the world. These staggering events, happening in quick succession over a brief span of thirty-six years, are, in part at least, a reflection of the deeply ingrained maritime traditions of the Gulf of Cadiz. When the moment to conquer the oceans came, shipbuilding

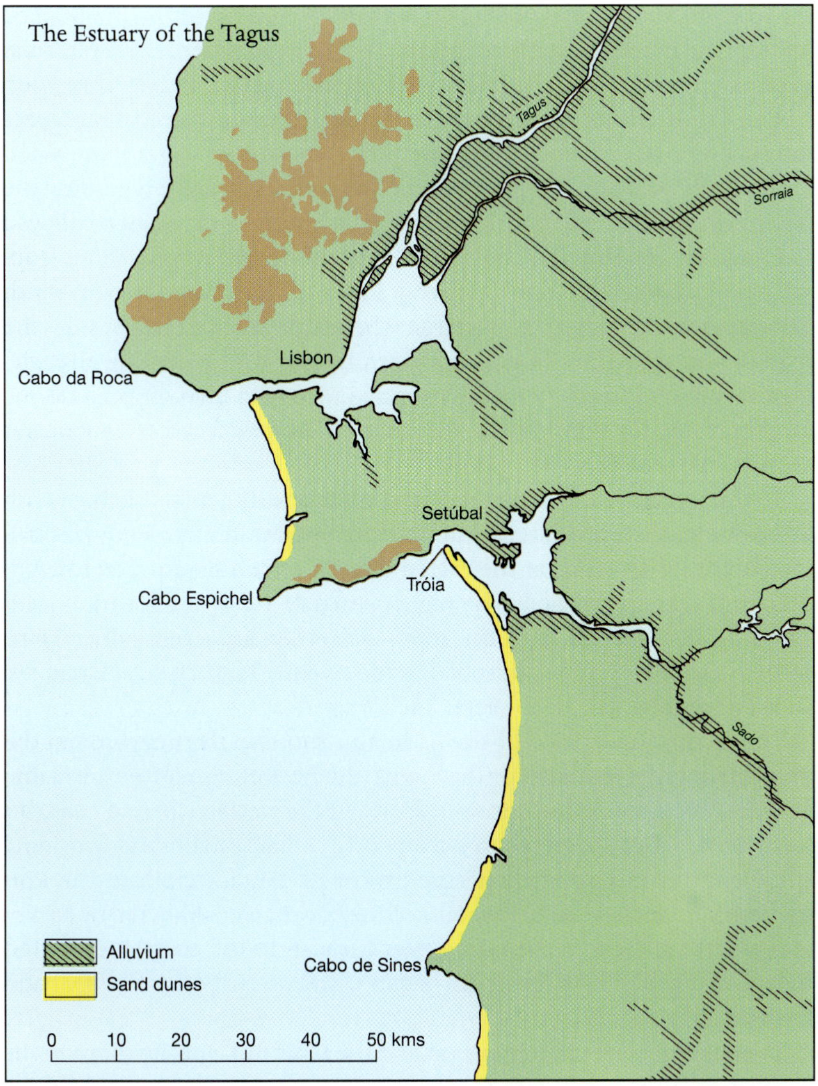

2.22 The estuary of the Tagus. The site of Lisbon remained a favoured port from before the Roman period. In the estuary of the Sado the port of Tróia, in use in the Roman period, was replaced by Setúbal.

technology and experienced sailors were ready to hand to provide the means to fuel the political and entrepreneurial will.

The estuaries of the Tagus and Sado present an interesting contrast to the Gulf of Cadiz, though there are many similarities (2.22). A number of factors combined to make the region highly attractive: the richness of the soil and mildness of the Atlantic climate, as well as the fine harbour and convenient routes to the interior. Throughout prehistory the area was densely settled. It supported substantial and culturally sophisticated Mesolithic communities and was one of the first areas of Atlantic Europe to adopt a Neolithic, food-producing, economy. Later, in the third and second millennia, the local elite built fortified enclosures and maintained widespread maritime contacts, and in the first millennium the region was in regular contact with the Phoenician enclaves at Gadir.

The Tagus, one of the major west-flowing rivers of Iberia, is navigable for 190 kilometres from the sea, and such is its flow of water that its narrow mouth—a deep channel 2 kilometres wide and 13 kilometres long—is kept clear of the clogging sediment which the sea manages to deposit as a sandbar fringing the coast further to the south. Approaching from the sea, the narrow channel opens out into a great expanse of calm water extending upriver for 20 kilometres. The southern and eastern sides are marshy and uninviting, but the northern and western approaches, receiving the full scouring force of the river, are deep with high shores, offering ideal berthing for ships. It was here that the Roman town of *Olisipo* was founded, later to become Lisbon.

To the south the Rio Sado meets the sea in a wide estuary flanked with extensive marshes and largely cut off from open water by a long sandbar, the Peninsula de Tróia, at the extreme tip of which the Roman town of *Celtobriga* was established. The physical instability of the location mitigated against success, and the focus of settlement eventually moved across stream to Setúbal, founded in the twelfth century, which had the added advantage of a deep-water anchorage.

The lesser importance of the Sado as a route to the interior and the overwhelming advantages of the Tagus estuary for shipping ensured that Lisbon soon became the maritime centre of the western Iberian coast. As early as 1378 British merchants from Bristol had established a trading enclave in the city to facilitate the export of English cloth to the Portuguese, and such were the benefits of the haven that in the Age of Exploration Lisbon became the home port for a series of navigators whose spectacular exploits on the ocean began with Vasco da Gama's departure for India in 1497.

The differences between Lisbon and the Gulf of Cadiz lie more in the prehistoric period, when the two regions were developing on different trajectories. Then the catalyst to innovation and exchange was provided largely by interaction with the Mediterranean world, from which Cadiz could best profit. By the fifteenth century AD the geopolitics of Europe had changed dramatically and the Mediterranean was fast becoming a backwater. Now it was access to the Atlantic that provided the stimulus, and both the Tagus and the Guadalquivir could benefit in equal measure.

The River Garonne was identified by Strabo as one of the principal routes between the Atlantic and the Mediterranean in the first century AD, by which time the town of *Burdigala*, precursor of modern Bordeaux, had grown up at the lowest point at which the river could easily be bridged (2.23). Downstream from the town, after its confluence with the Dordogne, the river becomes a broad estuary—the Gironde—here flanked on both sides by inconvenient marshland developing in the protection of the coastal sandbar. Although the configuration of the estuary has changed considerably over the millennia, we may be sure that the combination of longshore drift and the heavy silt load of the river together conspired to keep the estuary mouth fluid and unstable and thus unsuitable for permanent settlement (2.28). *Burdigala* represents the best available location well sited to allow seagoing ships to dock while providing an ideal trans-shipment point for transfer to river transport. The city's favourable position, on the interface of sea and river, is specifically commented upon by Ausonius, a teacher and poet living there in the fourth century AD.

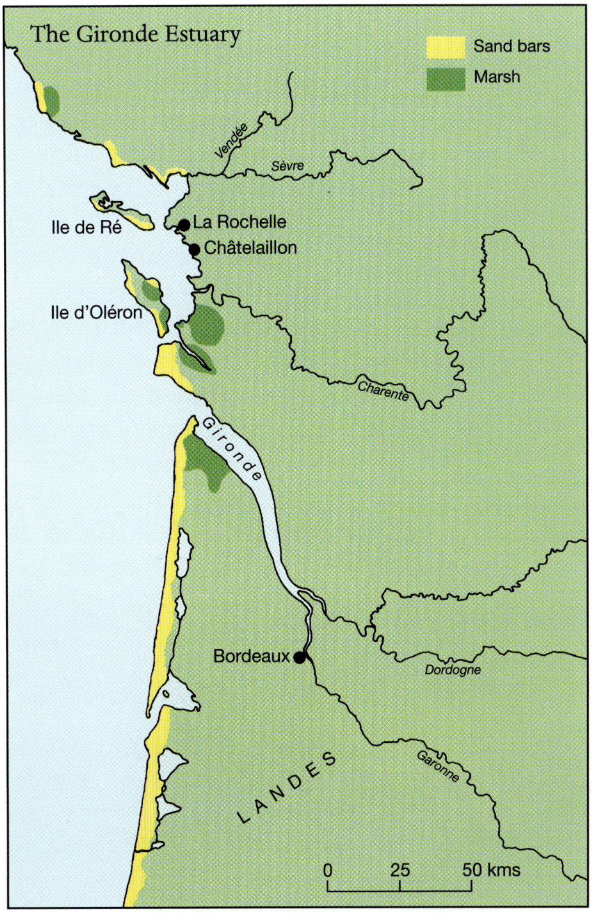

2.23 The Garonne–Gironde provided a major route between the Atlantic and the Mediterranean. To the north the coast was difficult for sailors but La Rochelle rose to prominence in the Middle Ages after the demise of Châtelaillon.

Burdigala was able to control the trade route along the river; it also lay at the centre of a productive hinterland famed for the quality of its wine, which was exported as far afield as Britain in the second and third centuries AD. Wine exportation continued, and in the period 1305–36, when the city was prosperous under English occupation, it is estimated that wine exports from Gascony to England and Flanders reached 750,000 hectolitres a year. This represents the greatest volume of any single product traded internationally in western Europe during the medieval period. Much of the export trade would have passed through Bordeaux. The city continued to flourish, later bolstered by transatlantic trade, and by the end of the eighteenth century was the third largest city in France after Paris and Lyons.

North of the Gironde the coastline is more difficult of access from the sea because of extensive marshlands, rendering the region remote except for one stretch where the Jurassic outcrops near the coast. Here two ports, Châtelaillon and La Rochelle, had developed by the tenth century AD. The destruction of Châtelaillon by the Duke of Aquitaine in 1127 and its subsequent disappearance beneath the invading sea meant that the way was clear for La Rochelle to assume control of maritime trade in the region. By the fifteenth century it had become one of the most important maritime cities in France, growing rich through trade with newly discovered America. La Rochelle can hardly be called a great natural port, nor did it have good communications with its hinterland. Its growth was dictated by economic and political needs rather than being a response to the gifts of nature.

The Loire, like the Garonne, was considered by Strabo to be one of the main arteries linking the Atlantic to the Mediterranean (2.24). He noted in passing that 'formerly there was an emporium on this river called Corbilo' (*Geog.* 4. 2. 1), a statement usually taken to mean that a native port-of-trade once existed somewhere on the estuary. No site has yet been identified that could be such a port, but it may well have lain at Nantes on the north bank of the Loire, where the Romans later established the town of *Condevicnum*. The location was carefully chosen to be where the river was still easily navigable by vessels of quite deep draught and where a

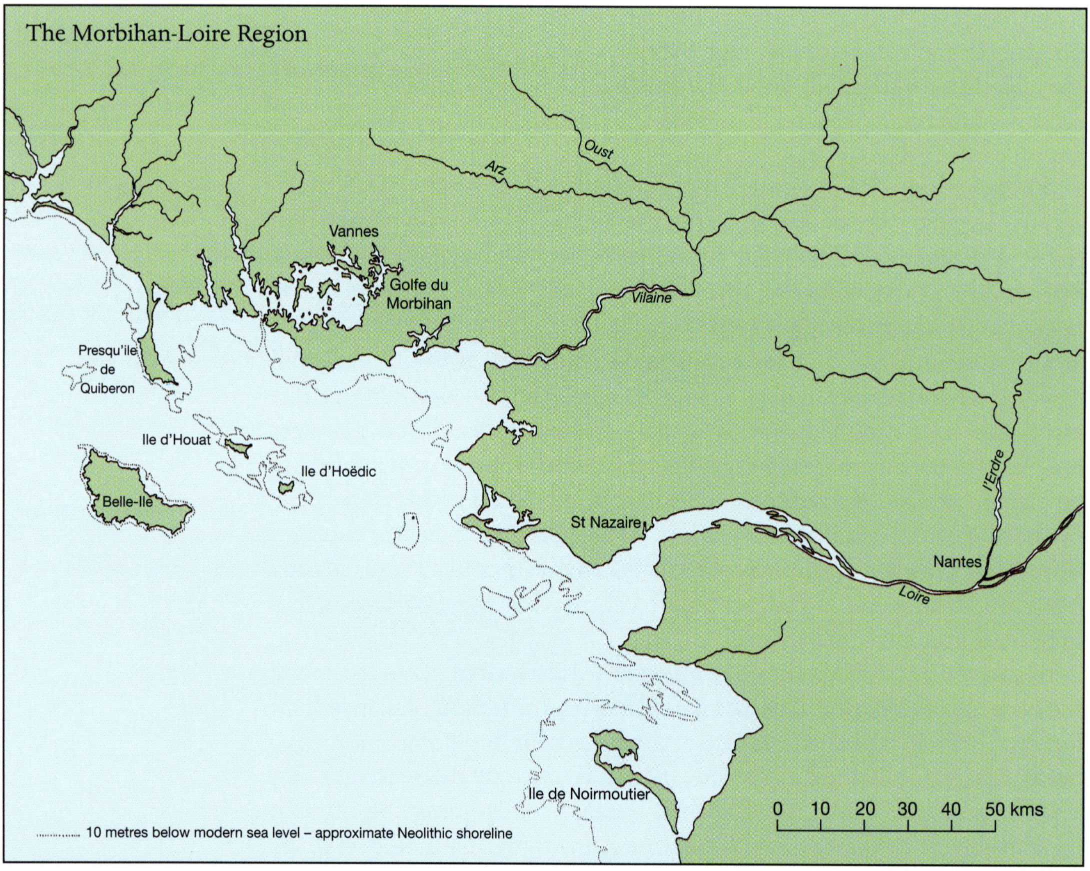

2.24 The Bay of Quiberon protected by a string of islands provided a safe anchorage for ships and allowed easy access to the river routes of the Vilaine and Loire. It was an important zone of contact throughout the prehistoric period. The rise in sea-level after the end of the Neolithic period changed the coastal configuration considerably.

2.25 The Pointe du Raz, one of the most westerly promontories of Finistère, Brittany. For ships passing from the Bay of Biscay to the English Channel it was a welcome landmark and a considerable danger.

bridge could be constructed. Thus *Condevicnum*/Nantes commanded a significant node on the Loire route. Below Nantes, towards the sea, the marshy flanks to the estuary made settlement more difficult until, at the river mouth, a band of igneous rock provides firm ground once more. Here the small harbour of St-Nazaire was developed in the Middle Ages, later, after the mid-nineteenth century, becoming a major deep-water port totally eclipsing Nantes.

To the north of the Loire mouth lies the wide Bay of Quiberon into which flows the Vilaine, one of the major rivers of Brittany. It is a region which has undergone major changes over the last few millennia as the result of rising sea-level—a point vividly made by the partially submerged megalithic monument on what is now the island of Er Lannic in the Bay of Morbihan. Attempts to reconstruct the Neolithic coastline of about 4000 BC suggest that the Bay of Morbihan was largely dry land crossed by water courses, and that the sea would have been 5 kilometres or more further out than the present coast. This would have created a wide bay well protected from the westerly winds and surges by the peninsula of Quiberon and the string of islands springing from it. This bay was, in effect, an antechamber, welcoming maritime traffic from the Loire and beyond and providing a wide interface with the communities of the Breton peninsula, both along the Vilaine corridor and directly overland. In this way social interactions involving trade and exchange were facilitated. The rich archaeological evidence gives ample examples of these processes in action, as we will see below. It is no coincidence that the ships of the Veneti were assembled here in 56 BC to face the fleet that Julius Caesar had had constructed on the Loire the previous winter—a confrontation which proved disastrous for the Veneti. The abortive British landing at Quiberon in 1795 in support of the Royalist cause is a further reflection of the bay's perceived potential as a natural landfall.

It is worth standing back for a moment to view the Atlantic façade of

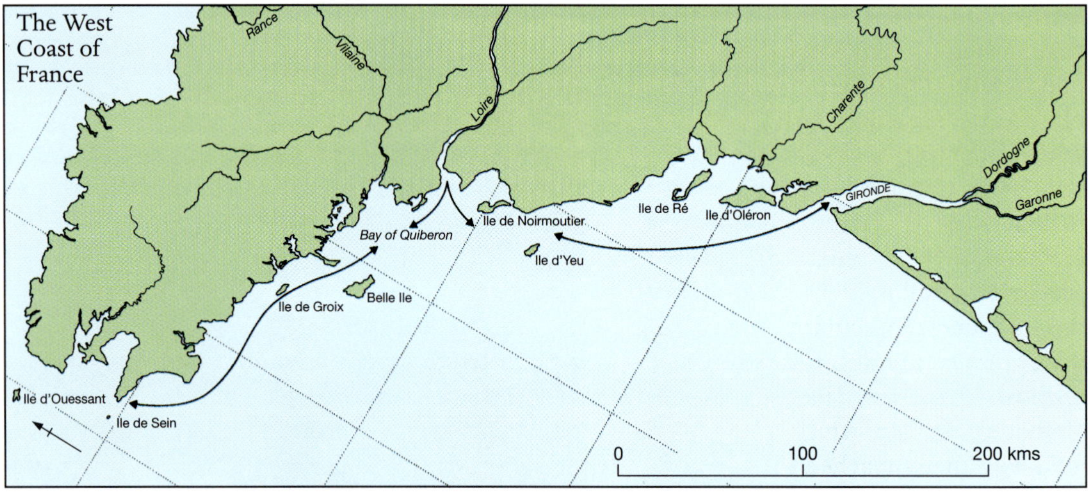

2.26 The Atlantic coast of France, between the Bay of Quiberon and the estuary of the Gironde, was a route node of importance where the river systems of the Loire and Garonne joined the Atlantic maritime zone.

western France as a whole (2.26). The significance of the Bay of Quiberon stands out with great clarity as the nodal point between the river corridors of the Loire and Garonne to the south and the Armorican peninsula and the seas beyond. In terms of the generalized model offered above, it can be seen to be a major contact zone on the southern extremity of the *northern core* region. After the beginning of the second millennium AD the dynamics of the model changed. There were many factors causing this: rising sea-levels rendered the bay less accessible, while larger ships needed deeper anchorages. Thus ports further west along the south coast of Armorica, like Lorient and Concarneau, begin to take on a new importance. But even greater disruption was caused by changing demands for commodities and the increased capability of vessels to sail longer on the open seas. Havens widely embraced in one era could be largely forgotten in the next (2.25).

In the English Channel the greatest concentration of ports of entry lay on the coast of central southern Britain washed by the currents of the Solent (2.27). It is a fragile, fugitive coast carved from the soft Tertiary sands and clays of the Hampshire Basin. Things constantly change—sandbars form across harbours and spits of gravel are built out into the sea, while elsewhere low, soft cliffs crumble. To add to the flux sea-level changes over the last ten thousand years have seen much of what was once the coastal plain disappear beneath the sea. The Solent began its life as a river with the present rivers Frome, Stour, Avon, Test, and Itchen as its tributaries, but for the last two thousand years at least it has been a wide seaway vital to the economy of England.

The combination of river erosion, overall rise in sea-level, and coastal deposition has created a series of havens of which Poole Harbour,

Christchurch Harbour, Southampton Water, and Portsmouth Harbour have all played a significant part in Atlantic communications. Of these only Portsmouth is not served by a major river offering easy access to the hinterland. This lack may explain why its magnificent harbour was not exploited until the Middle Ages, and then for predominantly naval rather than commercial reasons. The other potential havens, on the Hamble, Beaulieu, and Lymington rivers, remained undeveloped largely because as routes to the interior they were insignificant, petering out in forests and heathland.

The evidence provided by archaeological distribution maps shows with great clarity that coastal areas of the Solent, particularly between Durlston Head and The Needles, constituted a contact zone with the Continent through which a range of artefacts, and the concepts associated with them, reached the island in the prehistoric period. Central to this distribution was Christchurch Harbour, dominated by the mass of Hengistbury Head. By the Late Iron Age a major port-of-trade had been established on the protected northern shore of the headland, providing a contact between the resource-rich areas of south-western Britain and the Armorican peninsula. At this stage Poole Harbour seems to have been

2.27 The Solent shore. The medieval ports of Poole, Christchurch, and Southampton were sited on good harbours with river routes to the interior. Portsmouth, commanding a large and well-protected harbour, became the foremost naval base in the region in the Middle Ages. It was linked by a major road route to the centre of government in London.

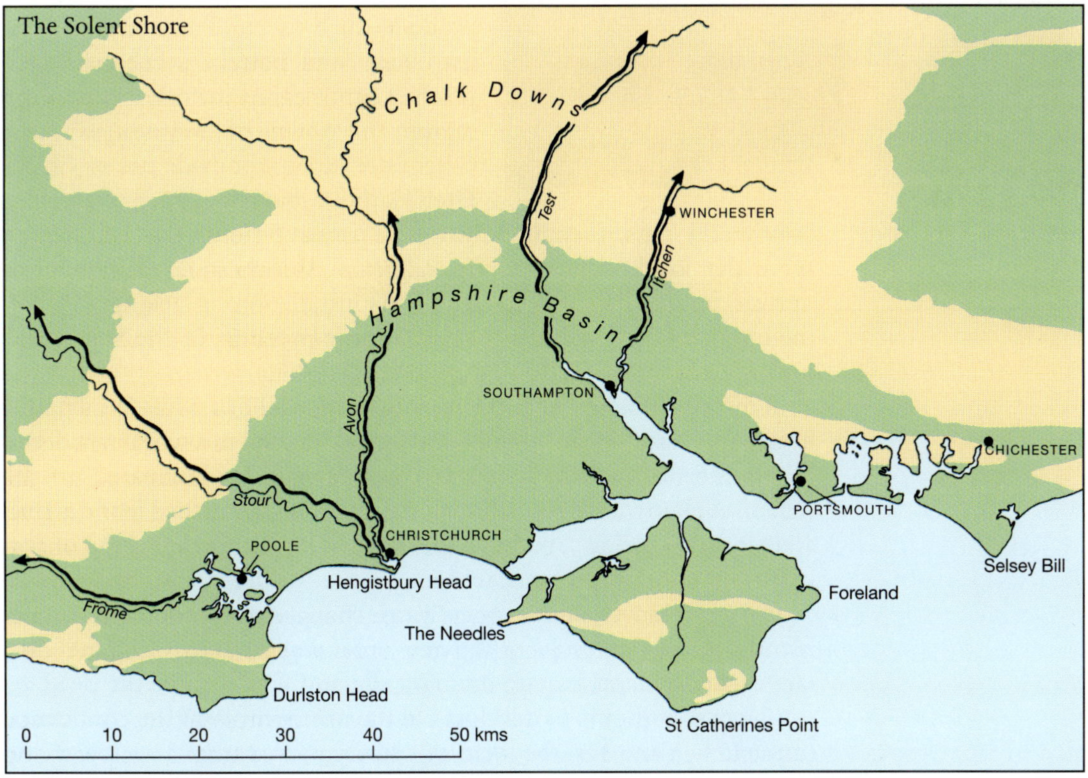

2.28 Sand shoals building out into Archon Bay near the estuary of the Gironde.

linked into the exchange network, but was of subsidiary importance. The Roman invasion of AD 43 introduced a series of new imperatives. At the beginning there was a need for coastal bases to supply the campaigning troops. One lay at Fishbourne, near Chichester, linked by a road direct to London. Another has been identified at Hamworthy in Poole Harbour, served by roads built by the military to hold down the hostile tribes of the south-west. There is also some evidence to suggest an early establishment at Bitterne near the mouth of the Itchen, on Southampton Water.

The military need soon passed, leaving a legacy of port installations and network of roads, but in no case is there evidence of significant commercial development, though Poole Harbour seems to have served as a point of distribution for local products such as building-stone, decorative shale, and pottery, some of which reached Amorica. At the other end of the region the town of *Noviomagus* (now Chichester) no doubt made use of Chichester Harbour, but the nature of the harbour works is at present unknown. The port at Bitterne was well sited to serve the local town of *Venta Belgarum* (Winchester) 20 kilometres upriver, but here again evidence of the installations is lacking. Overall, the impression gained is that the maritime potential of the Solent was underdeveloped in the Roman period.

In the early Middle Ages the picture changed. For a while Winchester became the capital of the kingdom of Wessex, and in a world fast developing international trading contacts a new port was created on the Itchen, at Hamwic, to serve the capital. Hamwic flourished in the eighth and ninth centuries AD, but with the move of England's capital to London its international importance waned.

The Norman Conquest once more changed the geopolitics of the island. One of the results of the new order was that cross-Channel contact began to increase quite dramatically, and with it came the need for south-coast harbours to develop. On the promontory at the confluence of the Itchen and Test the focus of activity moved from Hamwic facing the Itchen to the new site of Hampton on the Test, where the thriving port town of Southampton was soon to develop (2.19). Meanwhile in Poole Harbour the port of Poole emerged, making use of the deeper water on the northern side of the estuary. Both Southampton and Poole were essentially continuing a long tradition of maritime use going back at least a millennium. This was not so with Portsmouth, the third of the Solent ports to be created in the medieval period. Portsmouth lay just inside the narrow entrance to a vast expanse of tidal water, the daily flow of which scoured the channel keeping it clear of clogging sediment. The narrowness of the entrance meant that the inland sea, providing ample safe anchorage, could easily be defended. The site had much to offer, its only real disadvantage being a lack of natural routes to the interior, but this was eventually made good by a road direct to London. Portsmouth Harbour, then, provided a fine roadstead for the rendezvous of naval expeditions to Normandy, and it is as a naval base, rather than a commercial port, that Portsmouth has continued to develop.

If, then, the Solent shore provides the north portal of the Channel corridor, we need briefly to see what equivalence can be found on the south (2.29). Here the broad sweep of the Norman coast from Cap de la Hague to Cap de la Hève presents a contrasting aspect. It is, for the most part,

2.29 The coast of Normandy between the Cherbourg peninsula and the estuary of the Seine offered many havens extensively used in the medieval period. Rouen, up river from the mouth of the Seine, was the principal trans-shipment point from sea to river traffic.

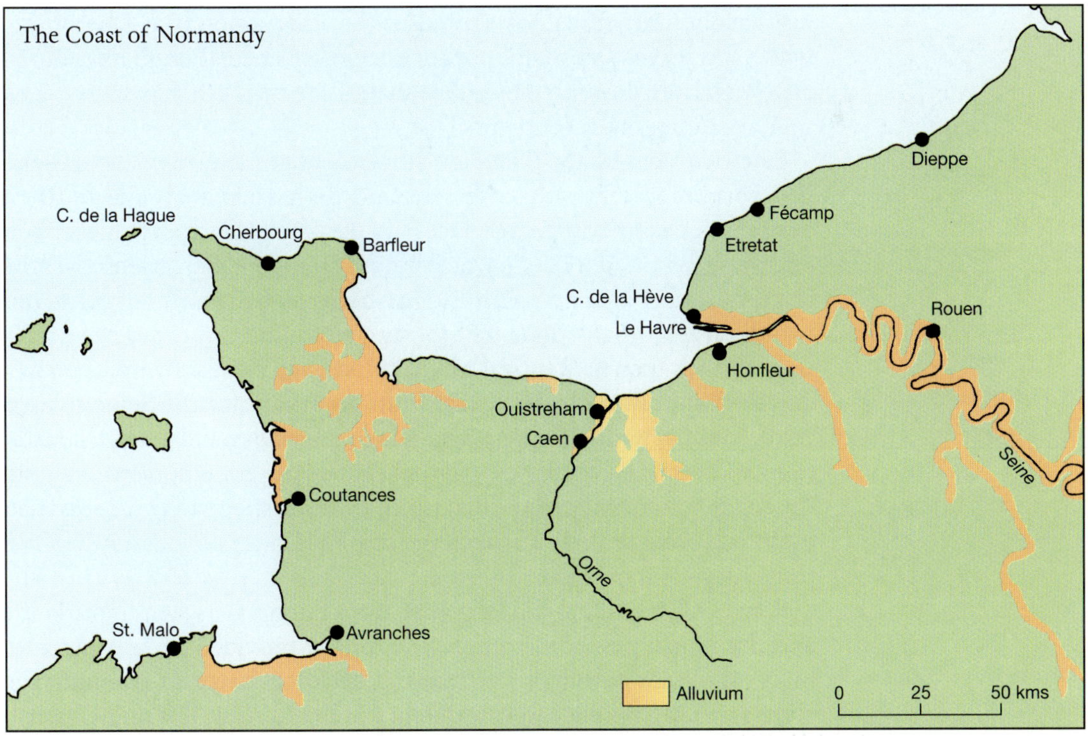

comparatively uncongenial to mariners, offering a face of high cliffs or low-water sands to those approaching from the sea. Only the Seine provides a significant entry with good routes to the interior. It has served as a major corridor of communication for millennia. At the mouth where the sea cliffs end, and before the estuarine sandbars make approach to the shores difficult, two ports developed, Le Havre to the north and Honfleur to the south. Honfleur was a major port of embarkation throughout the Middle Ages, but Le Havre was a comparative newcomer, founded by François I in 1516. More important, however, was Rouen, 80 kilometres from the sea, which began life as the Roman town of *Rotomagus*. Like Nantes and Bordeaux it lies in an optimal position where deep-water ships can penetrate and where the river can easily be bridged. Of the other points of entry on the coast of Lower Normandy, Ouistreham at the mouth of the Orne and Barfleur at the north-eastern tip of the Cotentin developed as much-used ports in the lively cross-Channel political and military interchange of the later Middle Ages.

Of all the Norman locations, Cherbourg and its immediate region can claim the greatest antiquity as a port in the Atlantic system. Just to the west, at Nacqueville, a now partially submerged site of the Late Iron Age seems to have been in trading contact with the Solent ports. It was probably as a result of sea-level changes in the first century BC and first century AD that the port functions shifted to the valley mouth at Cherbourg, which has served as a major port of entry ever since, though its comparatively isolated position, not unlike that of Portsmouth, has encouraged military rather than commercial use.

The two sides of the Channel—the Solent and Norman shores—are geomorphologically rather different, and this has inevitably affected their development as maritime interfaces. Yet they are given a particular coherence by cross-Channel trade which bound them together, at least over the last three millennia or so. The distance between them was not great, nor was the crossing hazardous. The journey from Cherbourg to Poole, a distance of less than 60 nautical miles, could have been accomplished in a day even at only 2½ knots, while from the mouth of the Seine to Spithead, some 85 nautical miles, would take only a day and a half. At faster rates and with fair winds the journeys could have been done well within the daylight hours of a single day. Indeed, Strabo specifically records that, in the early first century AD, from the coast of Lower Normandy 'it is less than a day's run to Britain' (*Geog.* 4. 1. 14).

For travellers sailing the length of the Channel between the Atlantic and the North Sea both shores would have provided reassuring landmarks and safe havens if needed; the deciding factor in planning the course would have been the prevailing winds and tides. The mid-Channel zone, with its facing shores, was a major route node not only between Britain and the Continent but also between the Atlantic system and the North Sea with the Baltic beyond. As such it may be compared with the Gulf of Cadiz: both were antechambers to the narrows leading to different worlds.

St George's Channel, which separates Wales from Ireland, can be regarded as another route node leading from the Atlantic to the inner sea between Britain and Ireland and to the archipelagos of smaller islands to the west and north of Scotland (2.30). At its southern end, between Carnsore Point and St David's Head, it is 100 kilometres wide widening a little at the northern end between Dublin and Holyhead. Of the many fine harbours that line the coasts, like Waterford and Wexford at the south-east corner of Ireland and Pembroke and Fishguard on the opposite shore of south-west Wales, the one that stands out for special comment is Dublin Bay, lying at the mouth of the River Liffey, protected by the headland of Howth from the northerly winds and tides. The potential of the site was appreciated by the Vikings, who established a winter settlement on the south bank of the river about AD 840. By the next century it had grown into an extensive urban agglomeration enjoying far-flung maritime contacts. Thereafter Dublin has continued to develop as an international port.

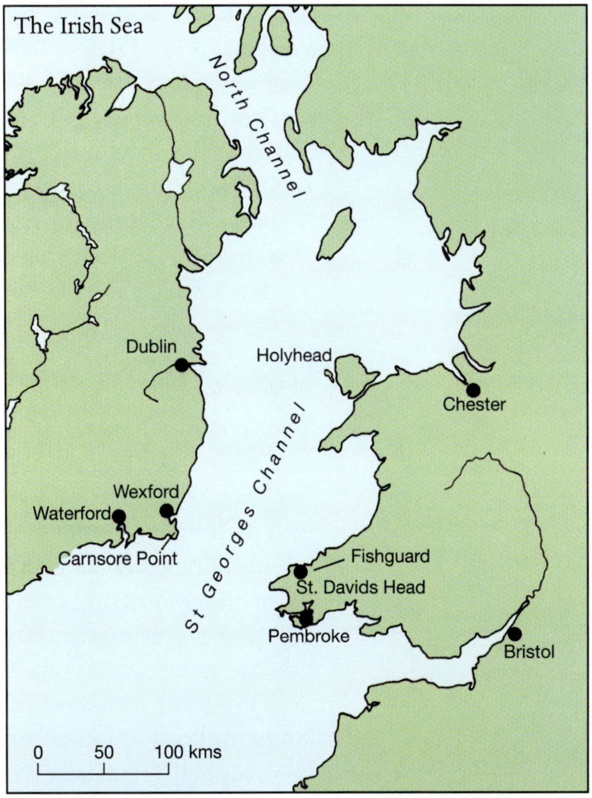

2.30 The Irish Sea—'The British Mediterranean'—was a major zone of entry for long-distance maritime commerce. It also provided a protected route to the North Atlantic.

The bay, with river that serves it, forms a natural entry point to the rich Midlands of Ireland and, at the same time, commands the sea routes throughout the Irish Sea and its approaches. No doubt it was one of the many harbours which, the second-century geographer Ptolemy says, were visited by traders from Roman Britain. Indeed, the distribution of Roman material in Ireland shows a distinct clustering in the country between the Liffey and the Boyne which must reflect, at least in part, the ready accessibility of Roman goods brought from Britain to the Irish coast and traded through local coastal markets. How far back in time Dublin Bay provided an interface for exchanges from overseas it is not easy to say. The distribution maps of earlier material give no hint that the area was of exceptional significance, and indeed it may be that different systems of interaction were then in operation, but these are matters for later consideration.

This brief survey of some of the major maritime route nodes is by no means exhaustive, but it gives some idea of the factors which, at various times in the past, conspired to bring a particular area to prominence. What we have hinted at here, and what will later emerge more clearly, is that time and again it was the same places that were the centres of innovation and exceptional activity. Clearly, geography played a crucial role.

Land and Sea: An Unstable Equilibrium

The 4,000 kilometres of Atlantic coast which we have attempted to characterize in this brief overview constitutes one of the major thoroughfares of Europe. It is like a broad corridor with many doors opening into it along which people, carrying with them beliefs, knowledge, and commodities, have constantly scurried over the last ten thousand years. Over time many things have changed: the traffic has ebbed and flowed, the means of transport have become more sophisticated, and from outside the system have come impulses causing ripples and eddies in the natural flow. All this movement and flux has been played out against a landscape and seascape which, in contrast, appear to be timeless and unchanging. Yet, as we have seen, a fluctuating sea-level and erosion and deposition caused by rivers and the sea modify, often imperceptibly, the delicate interface between ocean and land, while changes in global weather patterns have had long-term effects on prevailing air streams and tidal flows.

This said, there is a degree of consistency about the environment which, when viewed from above as we have attempted to do in this chapter, allows its controlling structure to be more easily defined. What stands out with startling clarity are the two core zones, the *northern core* embracing the wide arc of peninsulas from the Shannon to the Loire, and the *southern core* from the Tagus to the Souss. Each commands the approach to another, contrasting, maritime world—the North Sea and the Baltic beyond, and the Mediterranean—and each provides the way to distant outer peripheries, the one leading to the Canaries and the other to Iceland. The intricate lacing of seaways linking these two cores flows around the isolated yet reassuring stepping-stone of Galicia (2.31).

This is one level of generalizations, but focus down and other patterns come into view. Each core zone is made up of a number of route nodes determined by the opportunities offered by geography. Around the *southern core* the two that stand out are the estuary of the Tagus and the Bay of

Cadiz. At one level these locations provide the points of contact with the seas beyond the core—the Tagus estuary is a stepping-stone to the north while the Bay of Cadiz is the prelude to the Mediterranean—but at another level they are micro-systems, each in its different way binding the sea routes to the interiors. One might reasonably ask if a similar node is to be found at the southern limit of the *southern core* providing an interface with the routes down the west coast of Africa. No such place stands out either geographically or archaeologically, and it may well be that the volume of traffic was never very great. In the middle of the first millennium BC the little island of Mogador served the needs of the Phoenicians. In the Middle Ages the focus had moved to Agadir at the mouth of the Souss, but the establishments were modest, implying a low level of activity.

2.31 Satellite map of north-western Iberia. The congenial ria coastline of Galicia, at the north-west corner, is clearly distinguishable. The west coast is dominated by coastal sand bars while along the north coast the mountain ridge comes close to the sea.

The fringes of the *northern core* were also ringed with route nodes. The Loire / Quiberon region, with its close contacts with the Gironde estuary, was a major crossroads throughout much of the period that concerns us.

So too were the facing shores of the Solent and Lower Normandy, commanding the approaches to the Straits of Dover and the North Sea beyond. Further round, Dublin Bay emerged as dominant over the passage through to the Irish Sea and beyond. At all of these major nodes routes to the productive interior were provided by rivers—the Vilaine, the Seine, the rivers of Wessex, and the Liffey. Between them were clusters of lesser nodes, fine havens where ports like Quimper, Brest, St Malo, Plymouth, Bristol, Pembroke, Waterford, and Cork were to develop, serving their hinterlands and offering comfort to sailors engaged in long-haul ventures. The large number of ports which grew up around the sinuous interface of the *northern core* are a reflection of the intensity of maritime activity in these waters as it was to develop in the medieval period. How far back into prehistory this phenomenon can be traced is the concern of later chapters.

We could increase the focus still more to examine the local sea lanes in even finer detail—the intensive silver trade between Tartessos (perhaps Huelva) and Gadir (Cadiz) in the sixth century BC, the ships carrying Roman wine from Armorica, via Guernsey, to Hengistbury in the first century BC; or the diplomatic and military toings and froings between Portsmouth and Normandy in the thirteenth century AD. In all of these cases and many, many others the ships would have been local and their sailors expert in navigating within their strictly limited worlds.

Throughout the last ten thousand years the Atlantic coasts have teemed with short-haul traffic of this kind. Long voyages, before the first millennium AD, would have been rare, though there were exceptions. Hannos' exploration of the west African coast and Himilco's voyage northwards from the Pillars of Hercules in the fifth century BC were brave expeditions into the unknown, only to be challenged by the remarkable travels of Pytheas who, at the end of the fourth century BC appears to have circumnavigated Britain. These are the voyages we know of—no doubt there were others.

It was with the developing Roman interests in the commercial transport of bulk commodities that longer inter-regional journeys began to get under way on an increasing scale. L. Solimarius Secundinus, who styled himself *negotiator Britannicianus* on an inscription found in Bordeaux, may well have been principally involved in importing Gaulish wine to Britain, while the blocks of pitch found in a Roman wreck in St Peter Port Harbour in Guernsey probably came from the pine trees of the west coast of Gaul. These are tangible traces of the Roman merchant fleets that plied the seas—precursors to the high-volume bulk trade of the medieval merchant venturers.

For the most part these voyages were made by peoples of the Atlantic coasts with an intimate knowledge of the capes and havens and the winds and tides borne of a deeply rooted communal experience, but occasionally peoples from the other seas broke in. The Vikings from Norway and Denmark, in the ninth and tenth centuries AD, spread through the Irish Sea and the English Channel, eventually to sail through the Straits of Gibraltar to reach the Mediterranean. Three centuries later Genoese and Venetian trading vessels were frequenting the Atlantic ports. Whether local or foreign, the men facing the rigours of the ocean fringe were at the mercy of the winds and tides that propelled them and of immutable geology.

Early in November 1836 George Borrow was on a ship approaching Cape Finisterre in north-western Spain when a storm broke. He describes what happened:

> About nightfall Cape Finisterre was not far ahead—a bluff, brown, granite mountain, whose frowning head may be seen far away by those who traverse the ocean. The stream which poured around its breast was terrific . . . By about eight o'clock at night the wind had increased to a hurricane, the thunder rolled frightfully, and the only light which we had to guide us on our way was the red forked lightning which burst at times from the bosom of the big black clouds which lowered over our heads. [At this crucial moment the engine gave out and the vessel was thrown hard on the lee shore] to which the howling tempest was impelling us . . . We were now close to the rock, when a horrid convulsion of the elements took place. The lightning enveloped us as with a mantle, the thunders were louder than the roar of a million cannon, the dregs of the ocean seemed to be cast up, and in the midst of all this turmoil, the wind, without the slightest intimation, *veered right about*, and pushed us from the terrible coast faster than it had previously driven us towards it. (*The Bible in Spain*, ch. 15)

Borrow and his fellow passengers lived to tell the tale, but how timeless was his experience, caught up in the constant battle between land and sea.

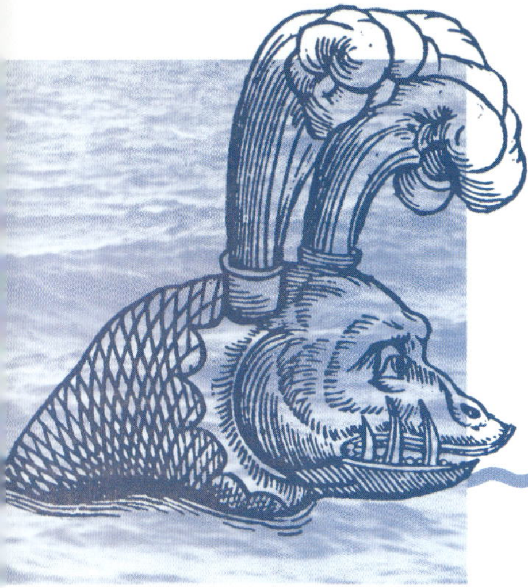

3. Ships and Sailors

In the ancient world seagoing ships and boats were designed primarily for two purposes: to transport cargo and for fishing. Usually cargoes would have been bulk commodities, but in special cases vessels might have been used to transport people—armies of invasion, like Caesar's force of 27,000 men who landed in Britain in 54 BC, settlers like the Scoti who sailed from Ireland to the west coast of Scotland in the fifth century AD, or the constant flow of pilgrims prepared to brave the Atlantic throughout the Middle Ages to visit the shrine of St James at Santiago de Compostella. More rarely vessels were used for exploration or reconnaissance. All who ventured on the sea would have hoped for their ships to be seaworthy and stable, with an adequate capacity for carrying cargo and people and a facility for making passage as quickly as possible. Translated into the science of shipbuilding, the sought-for qualities included buoyancy, strength, durability, manoeuvrability, controllability, and sea-kindliness—the last being the ability of the vessel to respond to the sea with the minimum of stress to its frame or occupants. The skill in designing such a structure lay in the balance of compromise between these often competing qualities.

Seagoing Vessels

Before the Roman period evidence of ships and boats along the Atlantic shores is sparse. A few log boats suitable for river transport have been found, together with five or six fragments of plank boats from river estuaries. To this meagre haul can be added a single boat model made in gold, some sketchy representations on Iron Age coins, and several informative descriptions provided by classical authors. From the Roman period onwards the quality and quantity of the evidence improve. Contemporary texts become more prolific, and several major wrecks have been located and excavated providing a welcome glimpse of reality. By the early Middle Ages, as the textual evidence becomes even richer, contemporary illustrations on coins, town seals, manuscripts, tapestries, and even scratched on walls add immeasurably to the detail.

Techniques of boat-building are conventionally divided into three traditions—log boats, hide boats, and plank boats. The simplest form, and therefore potentially one of the earliest likely to have been developed, is the log boat which, as its name implies, is a craft created by hollowing out a single tree-trunk. A dozen or so have been found along the borders of the Channel in rivers and estuaries dating to the Iron Age or earlier, and many more are known in Denmark. Some sense of the technical competence achieved can be gained from the Hasholme log boat found in 1984 in one of the tributary rivers of the Humber (3.1). It dates to about 300 BC and is 12.78 metres in length and 1.4 metres broad. It was fashioned from a single oak trunk but with a number of refinements, such as a composite bow, an inserted transom stern with tie beams, and with washstrakes fastened to the main hull by wooden pegs. There can be little doubt that the Iron Age boat-builders were working with confidence and skill within a tradition going back for centuries.

3.1 Model of the Iron Age log boat found at Hasholme, Humberside.

The Hasholme boat and the other log boats of this class were well suited to work in rivers, but the inherent instability in the form, with its low freeboard, would have made the basic type unsafe around the more turbulent coasts or in the open sea. If, however, stability was improved by, for example, increasing the freeboard with added planks or attaching lateral stabilizing timbers at the water line or even outriggers, then a vessel capable of sailing in more open water could be achieved. That such developments did occur elsewhere in the world is amply demonstrated by the rich ethnographic record. No such evidence has yet been found along the Atlantic seaboard, but this may be little more than accident of survival.

The log boat tradition is likely to have been very ancient. The earliest so far found in western Europe comes from Pesse in the Netherlands and dates to between 7900 and 6500 BC. Two log boats and their paddles were found at Tybrind Vig on the Danish island of Fyn dating to between 4400 and 3800 BC. Another vessel from the Charente has produced a date of *c.*2600 BC, while a fourth from Locharbriggs in Scotland dates to around 1800 BC. Thereafter examples become more common and the tradition continued in places well into the medieval period. The use of log boats in

Iberia is mentioned by Strabo when writing of Andalucía and in the north-west, but he implies that on the Guadalquivir log boats were by his time antiquated, having been largely replaced by 'built boats'.

Hide boats may have had an equally long ancestry in the west and, judging from the number of times they are mentioned by classical writers, they are likely to have been a common sight in the later part of the first millennium BC. The *Ora Maritima* of Avienus, a poem which is thought to have made use of an early *periplus* of the sixth century BC, refers to the natives of the Oestrymnides (either north-western Iberia or the western tip of Armorica) plying 'the widely troubled sea and swell of monster-filled ocean with skiffs of skin. . . . [They] marvellously fit out boats with joined skins and often run through the vast salt water on leather' (*Ora Maritima* 101–6). Pliny, quoting the historian Timaeus who wrote in the early third century BC, mentions an island, 'six days' sail from Britain', where tin is to be found, 'to which the Britons cross in boats of osier covered with stitched skins' (*Nat. Hist.* 4. 104), and, while writing of the tribes of north-western Iberia, Strabo tells us that into the second century BC the natives 'used boats of tanned leather on account of the flood tides and the shoal-waters' (*Geog.* 3. 3. 7), the implication here being that

3.2 A late seventeenth-century drawing by Captain Thomas Phillips of an Irish currach—'a Portable Vessell of Wicker, ordinarily used by the Wild Irish'.

such vessels were well adapted for local coastal conditions. Some further details are provided by Caesar who, during the Civil War in Spain, ordered boats to be built of the type he had seen a few years earlier in Britain: 'The keels and ribs were made of light wood; the rest of the hulk was made of woven withies covered with hides' (*Bello Civili* I. 54). Particular interest here lies in Caesar's reference to a keel, which is somewhat unusual in hide boats. However, the sixth–seventh-century *Vita St Columbae* describes currachs with keels, and a sketch made by Captain Thomas Philips in 1685 of a currach under construction—described as 'a Portable Vessel of Wicker ordinarily used by the Wild Irish', shows a boat with a prominent keel and stem (3.2).

3.3 A model in gold of a sailing ship of the first century BC. It is possible that the vessel modelled was a currach. Found at Broighter, Co. Derry (National Museum of Ireland, Dublin).

Some indication of the actual appearance of an Iron Age hide boat may be gleaned from a remarkable small gold model, dating to the first century BC, found in Ireland at Broighter, Co. Derry (3.3). It is oval in plan and fitted with nine rowing thwarts, each provided on the quarter with paired oars positioned in grommets. A mast with a yard is stepped, midships, through the central thwart, while the steering oar lies to the rear quarter. The detail of the model even extends to a four-hook grapnel anchor. If the model is an accurate representation of an actual vessel type then we are clearly dealing with a substantial, nine-manned, sea-going sailing currach.

There can be little doubt, therefore, that hide boats were widely used in Atlantic waters, and, like the log boats, may have had a long ancestry quite possibly going back to Mesolithic times. Specific types will have evolved to meet local needs, ranging from the simple, circular one-man currach worked by a paddle for use on the river, to the keeled currachs up to 15 metres long and carrying ten to twelve men, powered by oars and sail, for journeys on the open sea.

The great advantage of the hide boat was the comparative simplicity of its construction, using materials readily available and easily worked. It was also light and could be carried on the shoulders. The disadvantages were that it was easily holed, and even with a keel and steering oar the lightness of the structure meant that the windward performance could be wayward. J. M. Synge in *The Aran Islands*, his brilliantly evocative book of life on the Atlantic fringe, gives a first-hand description of currachs in action at the beginning of the century. On one occasion a vessel that sprang a leak was quickly mended at sea with a piece of flannel cut from a shirt and a splint sliced from an oar. On another voyage a four-man vessel crossing a towering sea was saved from destruction by the lightness of the craft and the skill of the steersman who, as the waves rolled down at right angles, 'whirled us round with a sudden stroke of his oar, the prow reared up and then fell into the next furrow with a crash . . . as it did so, the stern in its turn was thrown up and both the steersman, who let go of his oar and clung with both hands to the gunnel and myself, were lifted high above the sea'. Synge claims to have enjoyed the crossing! 'Down in this shallow trough of canvas that bent and trembled with the motion of the men, I had a far more intimate feeling of the glory and power of the waves than I have ever known in a steamer.' His feeling of closeness to the sea would have been shared by those before him who plied these frail craft back through the millennia.

The tradition of building boats of separate planks can be traced back, around the shores of Britain, to the second millennium BC. The earliest yet known is a single plank of about 1600 BC from Caldicot, on the River Nedern, a tributary of the Severn. Parts of three or four vessels found at North Ferriby on the Humber estuary and much of another found in the River Dour at Dover are from about 300 years later, while the base of a similar vessel—the so-called Brigg 'raft'—dating to about 800 BC—came from the River Ancholme, a tributary of the Humber. All were built of oak planks, fastened with lashings of yew in the case of Ferriby, Dover, and Caldicot or with continuous stitching of willow in the Brigg vessel. They were all flat-bottomed, relatively long, and without stems or significant keels, though the Ferriby 1 boat had a vestigial keel in that the central plank in the bottom was of greater thickness than the rest (3.4). The absence of positive evidence for masts or even oars suggests that these boats were probably without sails and may indeed have been propelled by

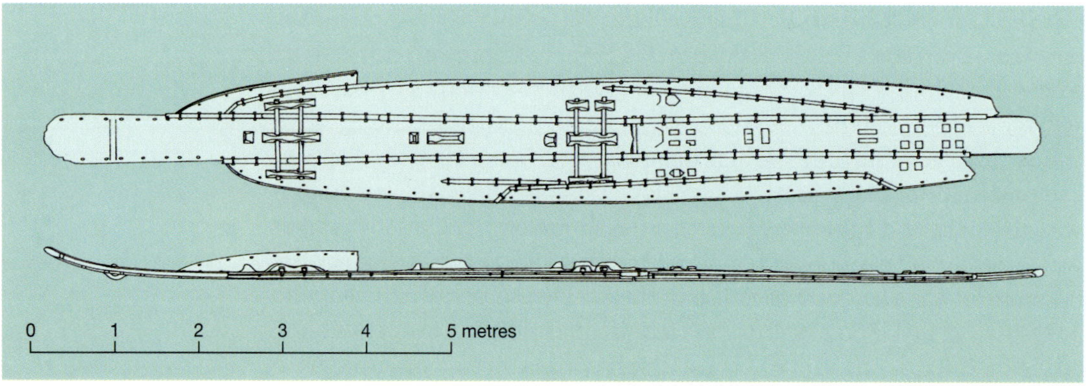

3.4 The Late Bronze Age vessel from North Ferriby, Humberside, as found and reconstructed.

poles or paddles. Vessels of this kind, while well suited to working the rivers and estuaries, would have been difficult to handle at sea. This does not, however, rule out the likelihood of there being plank-built seagoing ships in the second and early first millennia. It is clear from the examples which survive in the rivers and estuaries that the technical skills of the boat-builders were of a high order: they were quite capable of building robust, seaworthy craft.

Caesar's famous description of the ships of the Veneti, a tribe who commanded the trade routes around the Armorican coast from Morbihan to the Loire, is sufficient reassurance that the tradition of plank-built seagoing ships was already well established along the Atlantic coasts by the mid-first century BC. Caesar gives us to understand that the Veneti were the middlemen in a network of long-distance trade stretching from the Gironde to Britain, sometimes acting as carriers, at other times being content to charge dues. His description of their vessels is closely observed and worth quoting in full, though it should be remembered that he was concerned to emphasize the differences in comparison with Roman galleys:

> The . . . ships were built and rigged in a different way from ours. Their keels were somewhat flatter, so they could cope more easily with the shoals and shallows when the tide was ebbing. Their prows were unusually high and so were their sterns, designed to stand up to great waves and violent storms. The hulls were made entirely of oak to endure any violent shock or impact. The frames, of timber a foot thick, were fastened with iron nails as thick as a man's thumb; and the anchors were held firm with iron chains instead of ropes. They used sails made of hides or soft leather, either because flax was scarce and they did not know how to use it, or, more probably, because they thought that with cloth sails they would not be able to withstand the force of the violent Atlantic gales, or steer such heavy ships.

He goes on to describe how in heavy gales the Venetic vessels could run before the wind and weather the storm more easily, 'and heave to more safely in shallow water, and if left aground by the tide, they had nothing to fear from rocks and reefs' (*Bello Gallico* 3. 13).

In short, Caesar was impressed by how well adapted the Venetic vessels were for the fierce seas in which they had to work. Strabo also offers a description of the Venetic ships, adding the detail that they caulked the joints between the planks with 'seaweed' (*Geog.* 4. 4. 1), presumably meaning moss or reeds.

No trace has yet been found of an Iron Age vessel of this type, but an iron anchor, with 6.5 metres of iron chain attached to it, was found in a Late Iron Age context in the hill-fort of Bulbury, not far from Poole Harbour. It could well have come from a vessel working the cross-Channel route (3.5). Of equal interest are schematic depictions of ships on the

3.5 Iron anchor and anchor chain from a hoard of Late Iron Age date found at Bulbury, Dorset

3.6 Coin of the British king Cunobelinus showing a sailing vessel of the early first century AD.

reverses of two coins issued by the British king Cunobelin in the second quarter of the first century AD (3.6). Allowing for the stylized nature of the representations, the ship seems to have been deep-hulled with a square sail set amidships. The mast was supported by a forestay and backstay and the yard was also braced. The fore-stem appears to have supported a transverse spar which may have been to lead the anchor cable. The keel meets the fore-stem in a projecting foot and a side rudder is shown on the starboard quarter. With all their limitations these little images provide a welcome sketch of the kind of native vessel which so impressed Caesar.

The massive sails of hide used by the Veneti in their plank-built vessels and the large square sail indicated by the mast and yard on the Broighter model currach are a clear indication that sails were in regular use along the Atlantic coasts by the first century BC, but when the sail was first introduced into these waters is a matter of debate. Sailing ships of Phoenician origin were regularly working the Atlantic coast from Mogador to the Tagus from the eighth century BC, and no doubt occasionally ventured further. The advantage of the sail in speed and manoeuvrability would not have been lost on other sailors in the region, but there is no need to suppose the introduction was so late. The sail was widely used in the Mediterranean by the beginning of the second millennium BC, and the technology could easily have been picked up by Atlantic sailors in or around the Gulf of Cadiz towards the end of the millennium. The archaeological evidence suggests an upsurge in the volume of Atlantic trade at this time which would be entirely consistent with added capability consequent upon the adoption of the sail. But all this is speculation. The issue can only be resolved by new archaeological discoveries.

The tradition of substantially constructed plank-built ships, so carefully described by Caesar, seems to have continued in the Atlantic and North Sea throughout the Roman period, and is represented by a dozen or so wrecks, scattered between the Thames, Rhine, and Severn estuaries and the Channel Islands, dating to the second and third centuries AD. Vessels of this kind are generally referred to as Romano-Celtic and are characterized by massive floor timbers, very large iron nails, and caulking. Most of those known are river barges but two, the vessel from the harbour of St Peter Port on Guernsey and wreck I from Blackfriars in the Thames at London, had seagoing capabilities (3.7, 3.8). The Guernsey ship was originally some 25 metres long with a maximum beam of 6 metres and a height to the gunwale of 3 metres or more. It was carvel-built in oak with strakes nailed onto forty frames. The strakes were butted and the seams were caulked. The mast was stepped into a large floor timber about a third of the ship's length from the bow. The position is not ideal for a square sail and might have been for a spritsail or lugsail, but the problem is not easy to resolve. Internal dating evidence suggests that the vessel sank towards the end of the third century AD, and it seems to have been engaged in trade with western France when it met its end.

The native tradition of shipbuilding developed against a background of increasing Mediterranean influence. To understand this we must go back a little in time to the expansion of Phoenician influence into the Bay of Cadiz. The Phoenician port on the island of Gadir was well established by the eighth century BC and, as we have said, vessels regularly sailed south as far as Mogador and north to the Tagus and probably beyond. The presence of the high-prowed Phoenician merchant ship introduced an entirely new range of shipbuilding techniques into the Atlantic seaways. One of the results of this seems to have been the development of *hippos*—vessels with high prows decorated with a horse-head and an equally high stern, suitable for fishing and cargo-carrying along the west African coast.

The spread of the Roman army to western Iberia and later to France in the last two centuries BC introduced to the west new concepts of shipbuilding technology. To give some idea of the potential impact a few examples will suffice. In the winter of 56 BC the rebellion of the Armorican tribes posed a serious threat to Caesar's plans for Gaul. To prepare to tackle the problem he ordered warships to be constructed in the Loire, and to man them gave instructions 'that oarsmen should be recruited from the Province and crews and pilots procured' (*Bello Gallico* 3. 9). This force, together with requisitioned native ships from two local tribes, destroyed the Venetic navy of 220 vessels. A large contingent of Mediterranean-style warships suddenly emerging from the Loire must have

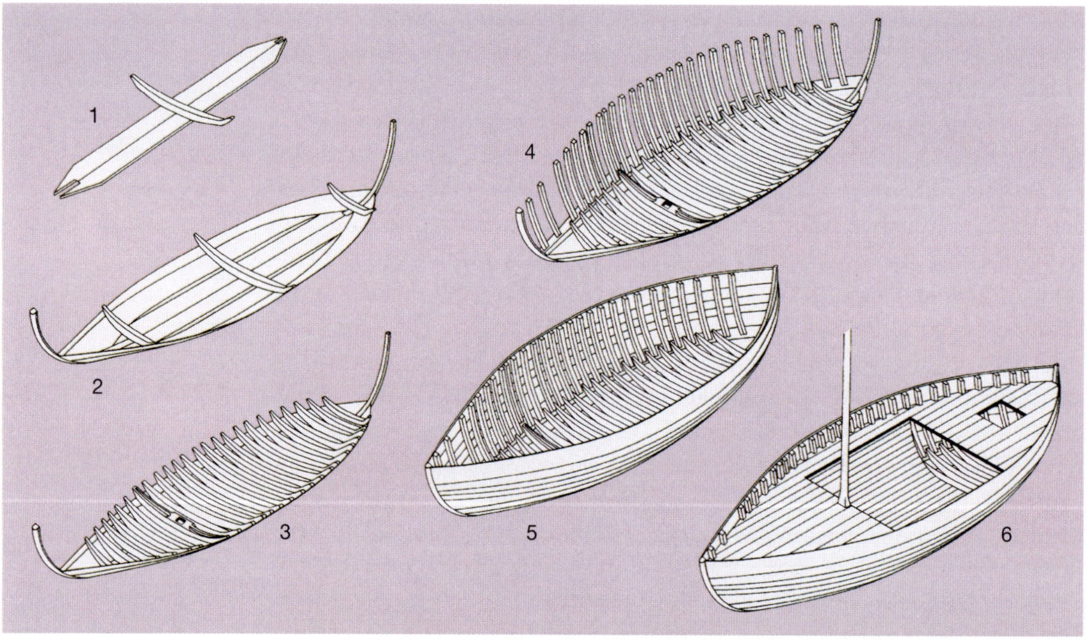

3.7 Stages in building the Blackfriars ship, a Roman–Celtic vessel of the late first century AD found on the north shore of the Thames near Blackfriars Bridge, London.

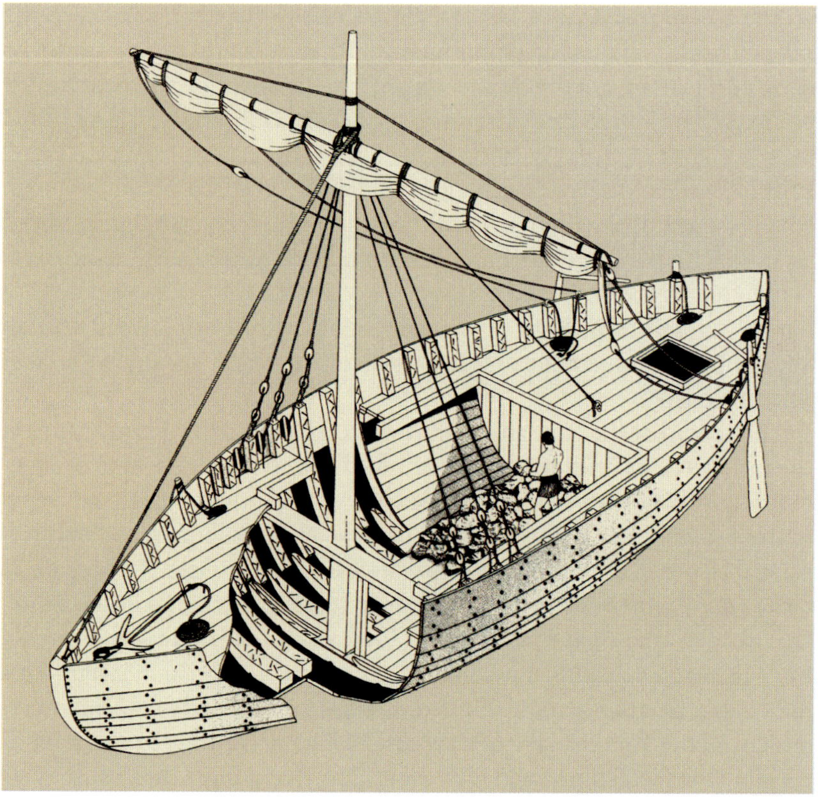

3.8 The Blackfriars ship reconstructed.

made a lasting impression on the maritime tribes of the region. Two years later, in the summer of 54 BC, Caesar assembled an armada of 800 vessels for his second expedition to Britain. While many may have been requisitioned native craft, a high percentage were probably constructed by Mediterranean shipwrights drafted in to work with local labour to build new vessels especially for the occasion.

With the conquest of Gaul all but completed in 50 BC and most of Britain firmly under Roman control by AD 85, the Atlantic seaways were rapidly opened up to Roman shipping. Vessels of Mediterranean and Atlantic type will have docked alongside each other in the ports, and so the long process of assimilation will have begun. One of the Mediterranean techniques that seems to have been quite widely adopted was the morticing of the strakes together. Ships constructed in this way have been found along the Rhine and Thames. The County Hall ship from the Thames, though adopting this Mediterranean style of building, was constructed of local oak. However, that there were Mediterranean-built vessels in British waters is demonstrated by a Roman lead anchor stock dredged up off the coast of North Wales. With Roman power consolidated along much of the Atlantic seaboard, the gene pool of shipbuilding ideas was greatly enriched.

From the fourth until the eleventh century the North Sea became a centre of innovation. It is here that a number of distinct traditions can be discerned, of which the longest lasting was the refinement of the clinker-built, or Nordic, tradition in which the strakes were edge jointed and the joints between them caulked to make good any gaps. The earliest known examples are Danish and can be traced back to the Hjortspring boat ritually deposited in a bog on the island of Als in the late fourth century BC (3.9). In this vessel the planks were overlapped and sewn together. A more sophisticated version of the same technique is apparent in the Björke boat from Sweden, thought to date to about AD 100. Strictly, this vessel can be regarded as a log boat to which two planks have been attached to each side creating a much

3.9 The Hjortspring vessel dating to the late fourth century BC was found in a bog on the Danish island of Als. The reconstruction shows the stern, with quarterdeck. The sketch below gives the vessel in elevation.

3.10 Stages in the building of the Viking Age cargo ship Skuldelev 3 from Roskilde, Denmark. The shell was built first and the strengthening ribs added later in the manner typical of the Nordic tradition.

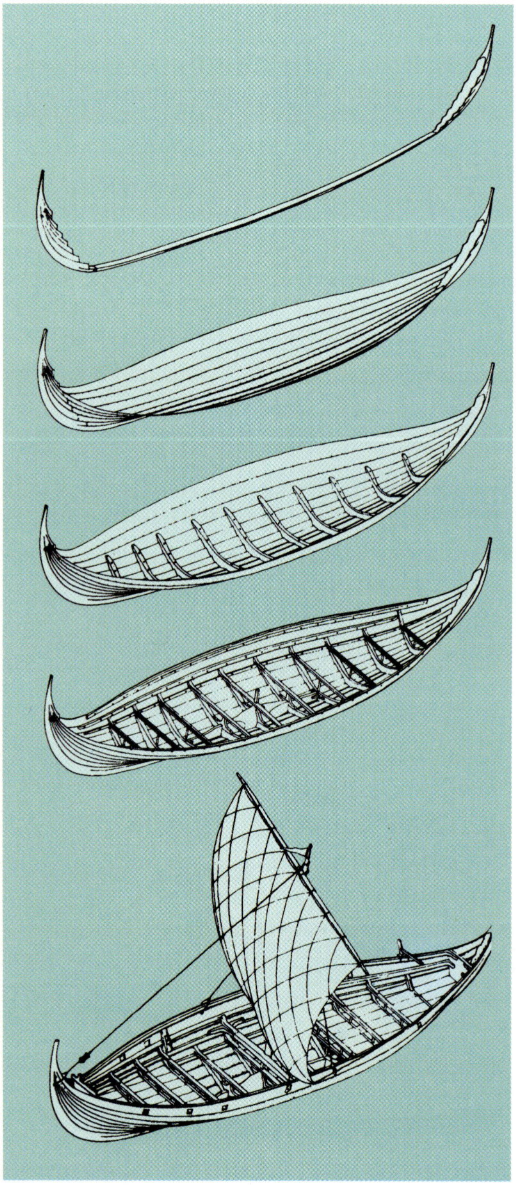

higher freeboard. Björke was a small vessel, just over 7 metres long. A larger and more developed form was found at Nydam in southern Jutland dating to the fourth century AD. The surviving boat of the three originally discovered was entirely plank-built of oak, with five planks on each side creating a vessel of just over 15 metres in length. The particular interest of the Nydam boat is that it represents a fast, seagoing rowing vessel of the type which would have been used in the migration of north European communities to the shores of Britain in the fifth and sixth centuries.

The famous vessel preserved as a soil-mark beneath a burial mound at Sutton Hoo in Suffolk, and built some time around AD 600, though much longer than Nydam (27 metres) and with its planks held together with iron rivets, is in the same tradition. It represents a further degree of boat-building sophistication emerging from the rich, and no doubt complex, traditions to be found all around the North Sea. Yet even by about AD 700 there is still no evidence of the use of the sail. The vessels were rowing boats, so designed that they would be effective in coastal shallows and deep water alike. They were, therefore, ideally suited for North Sea traffic and for working the rivers and estuaries that are so much a feature of the fringes of this sea.

In the Low Countries, and particularly in the various channels of the Lower Rhine, the Nordic tradition continued to evolve to give rise to the small vessels powered by single rectangular sails known to have been used by the Frisians and Franks in their trading expeditions from the English Channel to the Baltic. Although the hull construction belonged to the Nordic boat-building tradition, the sail was in all probability a legacy from the Romano-Celtic vessels which worked the southern North Sea and the Rhine. There can be little doubt that the sail was one of the most important of the technological innovations that made possible the remarkable maritime expansion of the Danes and Norsemen in the period AD 800–1100, allowing them to sail with ease not only around the seas of Britain, down the Atlantic coast, and into the Mediterranean but also across the north Atlantic to Iceland, Greenland, and North America (3.10). It was in this way that the Romano-Celtic and Nordic shipbuilding traditions came together to create vessels familiar along the entire Atlantic seaboard of Europe.

3.11 Cog depicted on the second Seal of Winchelsea c.AD 1300. The vessel is clinker-built with a double-ended hull and castles fore and aft.

Meanwhile, in the seas around Iberia a great variety of shipping was to be seen. The local traditions continued much as before. The Galicians, for example, remained content with their light cargo ships (*sarcinaria*), which worked coastal waters. But after the middle of the ninth century Viking vessels began to make their appearance. The walls of Seville were destroyed in 844 by Northmen and Algeciras was looted in 859. At this time southern and eastern Iberia was under Moorish control. The Muslim kingdom and Taifs of the Peninsula were equipped with technically advanced warships and galleys of Mediterranean type and these were used with increasing effectiveness to raid the north-western, Christian, coasts of the Peninsula. The scourge of these 'Saracens' reached such proportions that in 1115 the Galicians sent messages to Pisa and Genoa, 'where most expert shipbuilders and sailors could be found', calling for assistance. In response war galleys were built and sent to the aid of Galicia. Thus during the period from *c*.800–1200 the Atlantic coastal communities of Iberia became all too familiar with both Mediterranean and the North Sea shipbuilding traditions.

From AD 1100 to 1400 three broad developments can be seen in north-western European shipping. First, the round-hulled, clinker-built vessels underwent a range of improvements, becoming broader and deeper, a form very clearly shown on civic seals of the twelfth and thirteenth centuries. In parallel with this the flat-bottomed tradition of the Frisians evolved into a distinctive and highly functional type known as the *cog*, characterized by high sides with a straight stem and stem post and a stern rudder (3.11). Her deep draught also meant that she was able to carry increased volumes of cargo, while her flat bottom allowed her to be beached and still remain upright. At the beginning of the fourteenth century a Florentine observer noted cogs of Bayonne sailing through the Straits of Gibraltar on buccaneering expeditions. The Genoese, Venetians, and Catalonians were so impressed by the seaworthiness and low

3.12 Hulk depicted on the Tournai marble font from Winchester Cathedral. Made in Belgium *c.*AD 1180.

3.14 Hulk on a coin of 1473.

3.13 Hulk bringing Henry I back to England, from the *Chronicle of John of Worcester*, *c.*1118–1140.

cost of these vessels that they abandoned their own larger ships and began to build cogs instead. The third type to develop in the North Sea was the *hulk*. The principal characteristic of the type was that the hull was so constructed that the plank ends rose high out of the water. The type is known only from contemporary illustrations, like the Tournai marble font in Winchester Cathedral and a few civic seals and coins (3.12, 3.13, 3.14). It would seem, from the port records and seal representations, that the hulk was more common than the cog in the Channel and southern North Sea from the fourteenth century and by the fifteenth century had replaced the cog in the Hanseatic fleet. The cog, however, continued in use.

In the Mediterranean there was also a rapid advance in shipbuilding technology, most notably the development of great galleys with high freeboard and a length-to-beam ratio of no more than 6 to 1 (3.15). By the fifteenth century these vessels came to be widely used for commerce. While designed for the Mediterranean they could sail in the Atlantic, at least in summer, and merchant fleets from the north Italian ports were not infrequently seen in Lisbon, Southampton, and Bruges. Galleys could be rowed if the wind was foul or too light for sail, but their great disadvantage was the large crew size needed to power the oars and the quantity of food and water consumed over long journeys: both took up much of the ship's valuable capacity. For this reason they began to be replaced by distinctive sailing vessels differing from the traditional Atlantic cogs in that their rudders were hung on the quarter and they were powered by lateen sails favoured by Arab shipbuilders. The lateen was a triangular sail laced to a yard hoisted obliquely on a mast which was usually raked forward. The great advantage of this type of sail was that considerable speed could be achieved when the wind was on the beam. The disadvantages lay in the fact that the vessel could not easily put about, and that the length of the yard limited the area of canvas carried. Another problem was the inefficiency caused by the fact that the sail could not be reefed or furled aloft. This meant that the yards had to be lowered when the wind increased so that a smaller sail could be set.

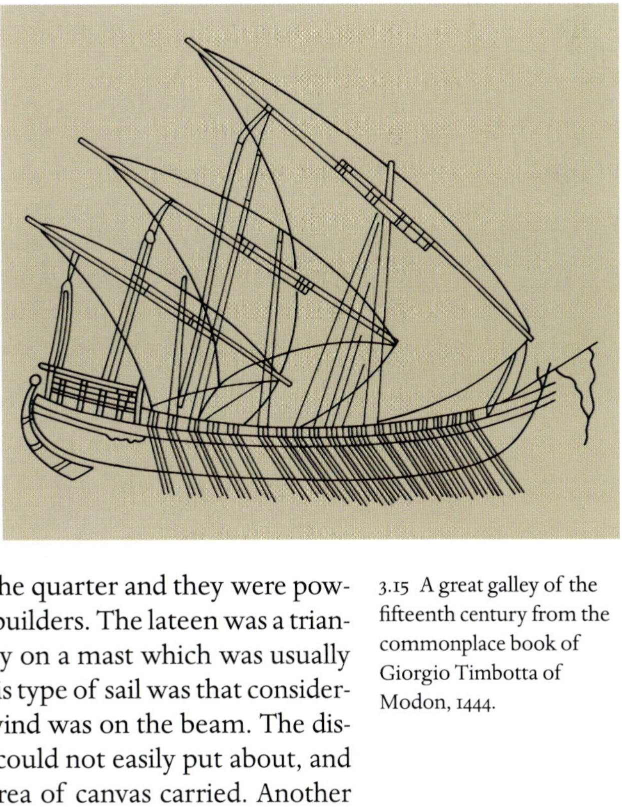

3.15 A great galley of the fifteenth century from the commonplace book of Giorgio Timbotta of Modon, 1444.

Ships built in the Mediterranean and north-west Atlantic traditions came together in the seas around south-west Iberia and hybrid vessels began to appear. By the beginning of the fifteenth century the Portuguese had adopted the lateen sail for their *caravels*, small, fast vessels that performed well along the west coasts of Africa, which at this stage were being intensively explored at the instigation of Prince Henry. The caravels, while rigged in Mediterranean style, were built frame first, which seems to have been a feature that the north Europeans copied from them.

As the mood for exploration intensified during the fifteenth century so ship design became increasingly innovative, the best of the Mediterranean and north-western European traditions being brought together to suit the growing demand for better performance in the open sea. What emerged was a hybrid vessel—the *caravela redonda*—a three-masted, clinker-built, caravel designed so that both lateen and square-rigged sails could be raised in whatever combination they were required. The spirit of innovation and flexibility which prevailed at the end of the century is neatly demonstrated by the ships brought together by Columbus for his first Atlantic voyage in 1492. The *Santa Maria*, which he called a *não* (a ship), was a round-bellied vessel with three masts: the fore and main masts were square-rigged while the mizzen carried a lateen sail. Of his other two ships, the *Pinta* was a *caravela redonda*, while the *Niña* set off as a lateen-rigged caravel but during a temporary stop over in the Canaries, outward bound, was re-rigged to convert it to a *caravela redonda*, a form of sail more suitable for the prevailing winds of the open Atlantic.

Sufficient will have been said, in this brief overview, to show that the development of the seagoing vessel was a complex process. Before the beginning of the first millennium BC our knowledge is sketchy, but already we can discern four broad traditions: the Mediterranean tradition prevalent in the Bay of Cadiz; the hide boats of the north-west Atlantic coasts from Galicia to Ireland; the sturdy, flat-bottomed, plank-built, sailing vessels of the Channel, characterized by the ship of the Veneti; and the clinker-built round hulls of the Nordic region. With the establishment of Roman power in western Europe, Mediterranean ships began to sail regularly into Atlantic waters, parading an array of different structural techniques and solutions, some of which were adopted by local boat-builders. Thereafter, throughout the first millennium AD, intensive indigenous development in the North Sea region and in the Mediterranean gave rise to two robust, but different, traditions. The fourteenth and fifteenth centuries saw elements of these two traditions come together in the seas around south-western Iberia, giving rise to the remarkable ocean-going vessels which set in motion the exploration of the world.

Pilotage and Navigation

Much of the sailing undertaken in prehistoric and early historic times would have been within waters familiar to the ship's master—inshore fishing and short-haul trips within the sight of familiar coasts—but even in prehistoric times longer, and far more adventurous, journeys were made taking vessels into unknown waters and out of sight of land for periods often of several days. For regular trips, of whatever length, the master would have built up a familiarity with the environment through which he travelled, able to assess the movement of his craft in relation to the sea and the winds, to interpret the signs of land still out of sight, and to recognize the shape of land once it came close enough to be visible. What was required was a mental map of the voyage incorporating knowledge gained from all the senses. A Bristol ship's captain bound for Lisbon in the thirteenth century would have been familiar with the Scillies, Ushant, and Cape Finisterre but may have known little of the coasts between—his mental map needed only to identify the landmarks and to know how to progress from one to the other. A local fisherman working around any of those places needed a far more intimate knowledge of the inshore waters to survive.

Whatever the range of the voyage, the ship's master had to be experienced in coastal pilotage, that is, the art of conducting the vessel in close proximity to land usually as a prelude to arrival and departure. When sailing, his mental map of the immediate area and the route to be taken would enable him to choose the moment of departing, taking into account the developing weather conditions and the state of the wind, sea, and tide. Normally vessels would leave on an ebb tide, but oars may have been needed to steer clear of reefs and shoals and to position the vessel in a favourable offshore wind ready to take departure.

When approaching land from the open sea a different range of skills was required. Inshore waters were potentially dangerous, and it was of overriding importance to the master to be able to assess as quickly as possible the approach of land and, when sighted, to judge where the landfall was being made so that his knowledge of the hazards could be brought to bear to ensure a safe landing. Often, from far out to sea land would be signalled by orographic cloud. There were other signs that could be used. Certain birds, such as fulmars, fly landward to roost as night approaches, while the presence of cod in the north Atlantic is indicative of the shallower waters of the continental shelf. Even the smell of the land may sometimes be sensed before it comes into sight.

Another technique widely used to assess position was the sounding lead—a lead weight, hollowed on the underside (3.16). The recess was smeared with tallow to capture sediment from the seabed when the weight was heaved overboard. The kind of sediment accumulating on the sea-floor can be highly specific to location. In the early sixteenth century a Spanish mariner finding fine black sand in his lead judged that the Lizard peninsula was safely abeam of his vessel, but white sand 'and white soft wormes' from shallow waters alerted him that the Lizard was nearby. The value of the lead lay not only in its ability to sample the bottom but also as a measure of the depth of water beneath the vessel. In shoal waters this information was crucial, not least because of the considerable variation caused by tide. In these circumstances the sounding lead, weighing about 7lb, would have been in constant use checking for danger as the vessel moved forward. Further out to sea the deep-sea lead and line would have been of value in giving forewarning of the approach of land. The 100 fathom (*c.*200 metre) contour marked the effective edge of the continental shelf, beyond which the sea bed dived off precipitously. Establishing this position would have told the pilot approaching the Atlantic coast of Iberia that he was 20 miles off land. Further north, around Brittany and south-west Britain, the edge of the continental shelf was about 100 miles from land but, even here, constant soundings taken to build up a picture of seabed contours would have enabled the pilot to judge the vessel's progress against his store of detailed knowledge.

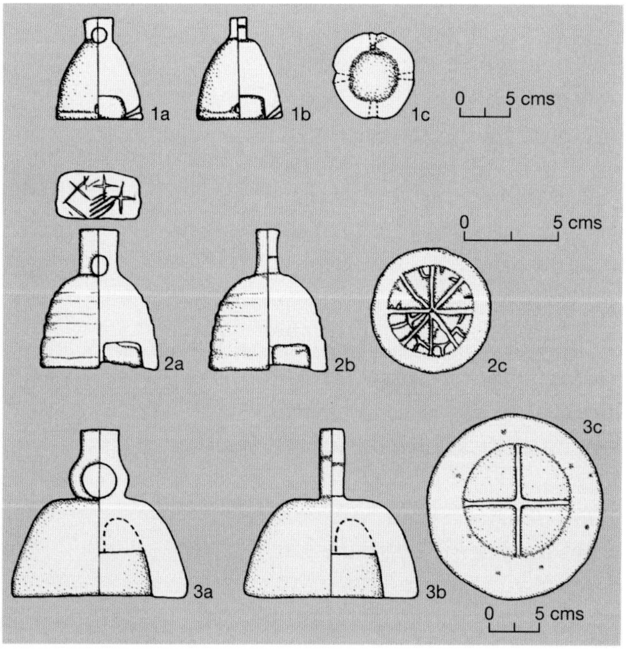

3.16 Sounding leads from the Mediterranean coasts of France dating to the mid first century AD.

The use of the sounding lead is probably as old as sailing. Herodotus was certainly familiar with it in the fifth century BC, while actual examples of leads dating back to the second century BC have been found around the Mediterranean coast of France.

Once land had been sighted it was necessary to identify it. In good visibility land 30 metres high could be seen from a distance of 11 nautical miles, while a headland of 300 metres might be spotted from 35 nautical miles. The profile of the land horizon, the succession of the promontories coming into view, and the colour of the cliffs were all valuable indicators of position. So too were prominent skyline landmarks such as a barrow or standing stone, a clifftop temple, a chapel, or a lighthouse.

Knowledge of such things was essential to a successful mariner. It was committed to memory and passed from one generation to another.

Out of sight of land, skills of navigation were called into use. In essence the navigator had to chart a course between point of departure and destination and to ensure that the vessel remained as close as possible to that course. This required estimates to be made of direction, speed, and distance.

Direction was all important and there were many ways it could be assessed with varying degrees of accuracy. The simplest was the position of the sun, its rising and setting giving east and west, while north and south could be judged by the direction of light and shadow. Another simple indicator widely used in the Mediterranean in early times was wind direction and wind type. Winds coming from different directions had their own distinctive characteristics. Homer noted the west wind as wet, the north as cold, and the south as hot and dry. Even at an early date the eight-point wind-rose was in use and each wind was identified by name. Aristotle added two more, north-north-east and north-north-west, and Timosthenes of Rhodes described the twelve-point rose—a scheme which survived in regular use well into medieval times.

At night-time, with a clear sky, it would be possible to estimate the celestial pole or null point around which all the other stars gave the appearance of moving. Homer was aware of the importance of the circumpolar stars which to him were ever visible. At that time, in the eighth century BC, the star nearest the pole was *Kochab*, rather than *Polaris* as it is now. The third-century BC Greek writer Aratus of Soli, in an astronomical poem, *Phaenomena*, describes the constellation of Ursa Minor (which contains Kochab and Polaris) and goes on to say, 'by her guidance the men of Sidon [the Phoenicians] steer the straight course'. That a knowledge of the importance of the celestial pole was widespread along the Atlantic seaways in early medieval times is shown by references to the pole star in Anglo-Saxon vocabularies and the Icelandic sagas. In all probability this awareness goes back well into the prehistoric period. Indeed, navigation skills were needed even by land-based hunter-gatherer communities following herds in the Mesolithic period and earlier.

It is probable that sailors were reluctant to spend more than one night out of sight of land, but some journeys would certainly have required consecutive nights at sea. The earliest recorded in Atlantic waters was a northern voyage described by the Irish monk Dicuil in the early ninth century, but there is no reason to suppose that it was in any way unusual.

On long journeys, or when the night sky was overcast, other navigation aids would have been used. Of these one of the most valuable would have been the identification of the underlying swell—that is, the movement of the sea set up by the prevailing wind. Swell is not significantly affected by tide or current and persists long after the wind has died down. A practised sailor is able to sense the swell even when it is not visually recognizable and to distinguish this underlying 'mother wave' from more superficial movements caused by the proximity of land. Since the direction of the swell provides a constant over extended periods it can be used as a reliable indicator of direction.

Wind, current, and tidal stream would deflect a vessel from the charted course. The *leeway* caused by wind can be estimated by observing the angle of the wake to the course steered, but drift allowance resulting from the tidal stream is more difficult to judge, though as a very rough approximation it may be thought to be self-cancelling over a 12½-hour period (3.17). An experienced navigator would be aware of all these things and able to make adjustments to maintain the desired track over the seabed.

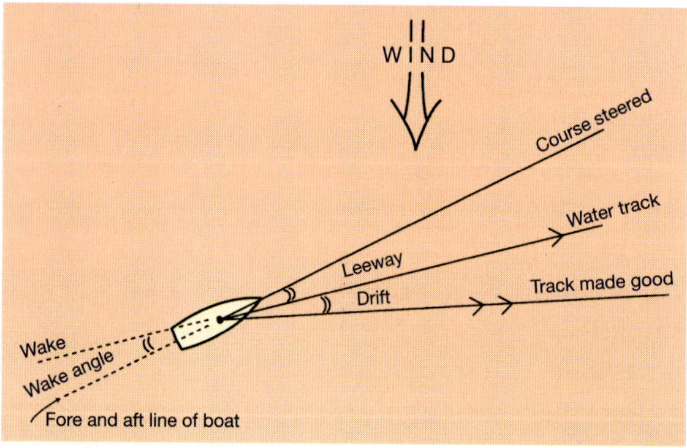

3.17 Diagram to show the relationship of leeway to the course steered and drift due to current and tidal stream activity in the same direction of the wind. The track made good over the sea bed is the result of the combined effect of leeway and drift.

The magnetic compass was to become an important navigational aid, but nothing is known of it before the end of the twelfth century when Alexander Neckham, abbot of Cirencester, describes how a magnetized needle floating in a bowl of water can be used to establish the four cardinal points. A more succinct assessment was made a few years later in 1218 by Jacques de Vitry, a bishop recently back from the Crusades. He describes how 'an iron needle after it had made contact with a magnet stone always turns towards the north star, which stands motionless while the rest revolve being as it were the axis of the firmament. It is therefore necessary for those travelling at sea.' Neckham's description implies that the compass's only use at sea was in foul weather and then only to check wind direction. Even by the end of the fifteenth century, when the compass had become a more sophisticated device, the needle was read in relation to a card, or fly, marked with the eight principal 'winds' with subdivisions giving thirty-two or sixty-four points. Although, therefore, it was possible to establish bearings to five or six degrees, giving compass measurements in degrees was not a common practice until much later.

One method of navigation, which might conceivably have been used by early sailors in Atlantic waters, was latitude sailing, that is, sailing due east or west from a particular location in the certain knowledge of arriving in a specific point on an opposite coast. To accomplish this successfully it was necessary to know the altitude or angular height of the pole star at the ports you were likely to frequent. You would then sail north or south until the pole star was at the required port's altitude and then sail east or west along this latitude, keeping the pole star's altitude constant, until the landfall was made. Establishing the exact altitude of the pole star at the desired destination was of crucial importance. To do this it was essential to make minor corrections, based on the position of the Guards (the stars around the pole star), to allow for the circle which Polaris describes around true north. Without knowledge of the corrections and without instruments to measure the altitude accurately maintaining a latitude could only be done with quite wide margins of error, but the introduction of the mariner's astrolabe and the quadrant in the fifteenth century offered much greater precision. In the age of exploration, when establishing location accurately was of crucial importance in defining and communicating routes, measurement of latitude took on a particular significance. Before that, for the sailor plying the Atlantic coasts, traditional methods of navigation—sighting the pole star and using the lead—were sufficient.

Setting a course was of prime importance in navigation, but it was also necessary to know what point, along that course, the vessel had reached. In other words, the navigator had to 'fix' his position in his mental map of the route. After allowing for leeway and drift the distance travelled could be calculated as a factor of speed and time, but in the ancient world neither could be measured with any degree of accuracy. It was usual, therefore, to estimate distance in terms of a day's travel—the distance a standard boat would travel in fair conditions of wind and sea. Thus, according to Timaeus, the tin-producing island Mictis was six days' sail from Britain. There are difficulties in trying to interpret distances given in this way, for it is necessary to know what a day represents, whether twenty-four hours or only daylight, and speed would vary considerably depending on whether the vessel was being rowed or was travelling under sail. An estimate of Viking and early medieval 'day's sailings' varies from about 30 to 150 nautical miles. In the late Middle Ages, when the use of the hourglass allowed time to be estimated fairly accurately, it became conventional to measure distance at sea in terms of *leagues*—the league being the distance the average vessel would travel in an hour in fair conditions.

To estimate actual speed sailors developed various rule-of-thumb methods to compare speed achieved with standard speeds. The simplest would have been to measure the time taken for a piece of wood to pass the length of the boat or to judge relative speed by the amount of spray turbulence caused. The floating-object method was gradually formalized and by the late fifteenth century became the accepted technique.

The piece of wood—the log—was by then a carefully designed structure with flyers to resist the tow of the ship. It was attached to a line knotted at intervals. When the log was thrown into the stream the time taken for a specified number of knots to run over the stem was carefully timed on a small sand-glass. A record was kept—the log—and the measurement of speed at sea became standardized as the knot, equivalent to a nautical mile per hour.

Knowing the course and wind or swell, corrected for leeway and drift, and the distance sailed calculated in terms of either speed or fraction of a standard day's sail, the navigator could identify his position on his mental chart of the route. Needless to say there were many inbuilt inaccuracies. How significant all this was to the average sailor along the Atlantic seaboard is debatable. A knowledge of the capes and headlands, a clear sight of the stars, and a sounding lead would have been more than sufficient for most journeys. Combined with an intuitive sense of weather and sea, these were all that an experienced sailor needed to ensure a safe return to his home port.

The accumulated wisdom of centuries of sailing experience would have been passed from generation to generation in a rich oral tradition of sea lore, some glimpses of which survive in rare early texts. One of the earliest of these, concerning Atlantic sailing, was the *Massaliote Periplus*, a source thought by some scholars to have been compiled originally in the sixth century BC and eventually used by Rufus Festus Avienus in the fourth century AD in his poem *Ora Maritima*. If such a text once existed Avienus is likely to have had access to it only through quotations found in later writings. The *Ora Maritima* is a confused and frustrating text, difficult to untangle, but this said one of the sections dealing with the Atlantic (lines 172–261) does appear to be based on a *periplus*, or sailing manual, of some antiquity. It gives a reasonably coherent description of the coast from the promontory of Ophiussa (Cape Roca at the mouth of the Tagus) to the Pillars of Hercules (Straits of Gibraltar) in terms which would have been particularly useful to a sailor attempting to make the journey (3.18). Of the Tagus estuary, for example, we are told:

> The bay which spreads widely from there is not all easily navigable by one wind. For you arrive in the middle of the bay with the west wind carrying you, the rest requires the south wind. And again if one should head for the Tartessian shore from there on foot he would complete the journey scarcely on the fourth day. If one prolongs his trip to our sea [the Mediterranean] and the port of Malaca [Malaga] the journey lasts for five days. (lines 174–81)

Thereafter we are given a succession of named features visible from the sea with a brief description of their characteristics. The island of

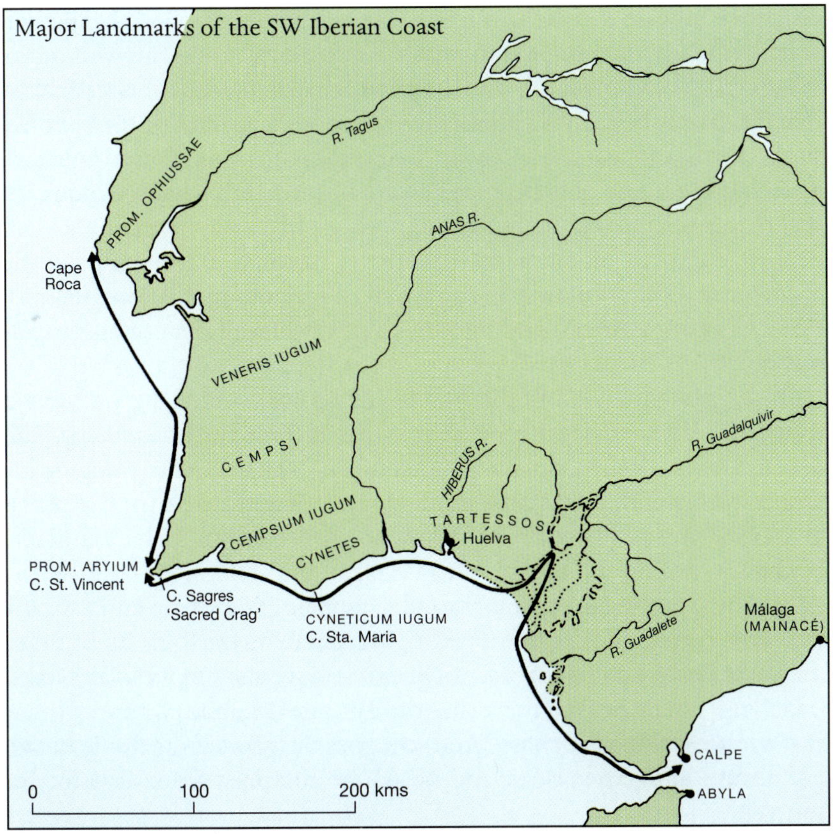

3.18 The major landmarks of the coast of south-western Iberia according to the *Massilliot Periplus* quoted in *Ora Maritima* by the fourth-century AD poet Avienus. The names in capitals are the ancient names used in the text.

Achale, lying beneath the 'Cempsican ridge', for example, is surrounded by a sea which is 'always churned up with dirty mud and the muddy waters are thick with filth' (lines 192–4). The outflow of the River Anas (Rio Guadiana) can also be recognized by the sediment it brings down, and 'here the tops of two islands raise themselves on high' (line 212). A number of capes are also mentioned and identified. One of them, *Cyneticum Jugum* (possibly Cape Sta Maria at Faro), is described as 'rising high where the starlight sets'. There can be little doubt that Avienus was basing this section of his ponderous poem on a very practical sailors' *periplus* compiled to enable ships' masters to navigate the coast of Iberia from the Tagus to Massalia. Even in the garbled form in which it comes down to us it is a remarkable survival.

Information of this kind, first committed to memory and later sometimes in written form, will have been available for every stretch of the Atlantic coast and for the longer sea passages. A good example of the latter are the sailing directions covering the journey from Norway to Greenland recorded in the fourteenth-century manuscript the *Hauksbók*. It describes how, in setting out from Hernar, where the fjord of Bergan reaches the sea, one should sail west to reach Hvarf, Cape Farewell, at the southern tip of Greenland, 'and then you are sailing north of Shetland, so that it can only be seen if visibility is very good; but south of the Faeroes, so that the sea appears half way up their mountain slopes; but so far south of Iceland that one only becomes aware of birds and whales from it.' In reality this would have meant sailing well south of west to about 40 nautical miles north of Shetland, passing 30 nautical miles south of the Faroes and 90 nautical miles or so south of Iceland. In this way the master would have used his land sightings but stayed well clear of all dangerous shores.

By the fifteenth century the Atlantic navigator would have had access to ample written advice if he were able to read. One such document, *Sailing Directions For the Circumnavigation of England and For a Voyage to the Straits of Gibraltar*, as its name implies, was designed to be used at sea. It gives very precise instructions of how to proceed from each identifiable landmark, noting the direction to be taken and offering advice on the tides. Thus (putting the text into modern spelling): 'In Spain and Brittany this is the course and the tide. From St Matthieu [on the Rade du Brest] to the Île de Bas the course is east north east and west south west, and upon [reaching] the Île de Bas [there] lies the Tour de la Lande [where] it flows east and west along the coast.' And so it goes on, providing minute detail, not always altogether clear, and no doubt compiled from a variety of sources.

The fifteenth-century *Sailing Directions For the Circumnavigation of England and For a Voyage to the Straits of Gibraltar* is the earliest of the north European pilot books known as 'routiers' or 'rutters'. In the Mediterranean these *portolani* as they were known—directions for coastwise passage—had been in use for centuries. By the late thirteenth century individual sets of notes had been brought together in a single volume, the *Compasso da Navigare*, which gave sailing instructions from port to port all around the Mediterranean and the Black Sea in a systematic manner, beginning at Cape St Vincent in south-west Portugal and ending at Safi in Morocco. Compared with *Sailing Directions*, the *Compasso* is a sophisticated document giving bearings, distances, and depths of anchorages in considerable detail. Mediterranean sailors had other advantages. By the beginning of the fourteenth century traverse tables, enabling the ship's master to work out his distance along his course for each track sailed, were in common use and drawn charts were available. The earliest survey chart—*The Pisan Chart* of the Mediterranean—dates to about 1290, but the first recorded use of a chart was twenty years earlier.

The sailor in the Atlantic, before the fourteenth century, had no such

3.19 (*facing*) Chart of western Europe by Pietro Vesconte, 1325.

sophistications (3.19). He had to rely on his knowledge of the difficult, dangerous, and often fog-bound coast and his ability to navigate by dead reckoning using only the stars and his lead. He was heir to a long tradition of mariners schooled in the most dangerous and demanding of the European seas. Thus, when the challenge of the oceans was finally taken up in the fifteenth century it was the Atlantic community who provided the men, fitted by tradition and temperament, for the task.

Exploring the Ocean

There is ample evidence, from the few scraps of anecdotal evidence that have come down to us from the ancient world, that long voyages were made to explore the coastal regions of the Atlantic at least as early as the middle of the first millennium BC. The earliest of these tales centre around the entrepreneurial activities of the Phoenicians, whose main home ports of Tyre, Sidon, and Byblos lay on the Levantine coasts of the east Mediterranean. It was the Phoenicians who sailed through the Pillars of Hercules to found their trading colony on the island of Gadir (Cadiz), thus being the first Mediterranean state to establish a base in the Atlantic.

3.20 The journeys of Phoenician explorers in the sixth and fifth centuries BC.

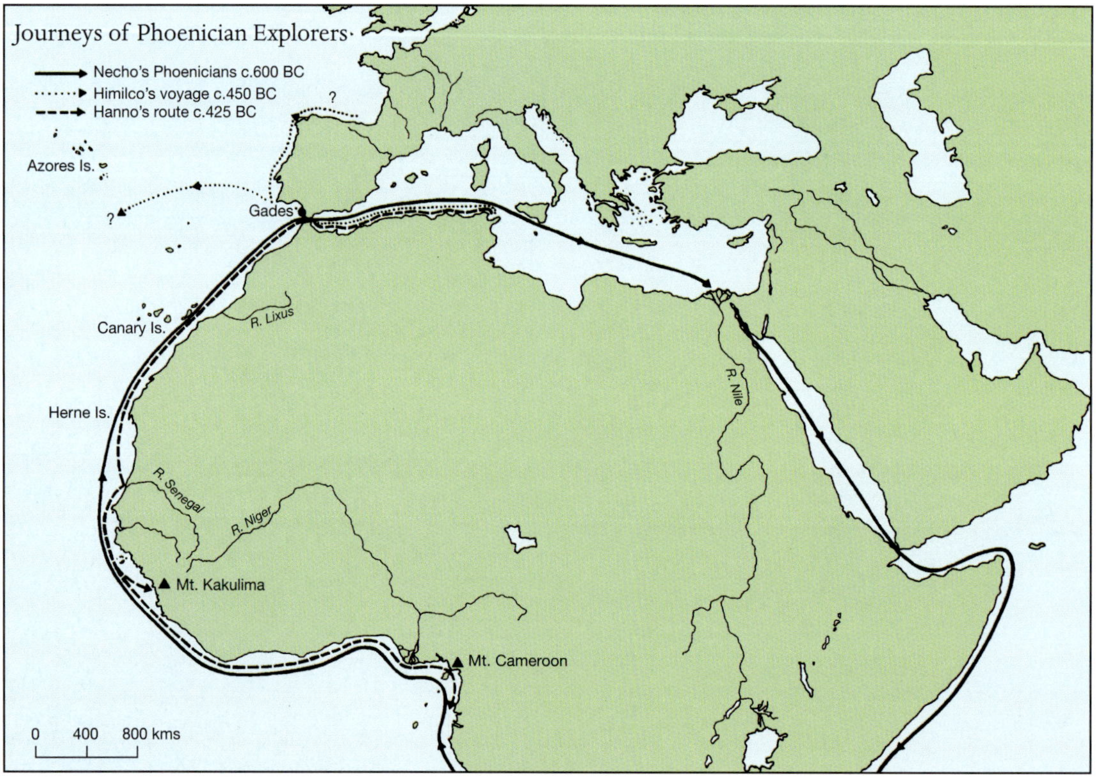

The presently available archaeological evidence shows that Gadir was a going concern in the eighth century, but the traditional date of foundation, widely accepted in the classical world, was *c.*1100 BC. There is no reason to dispute a date as early as this except for the lack of positive archaeological evidence to support it. From the eighth century we can be sure that regular maritime contact was maintained between Gadir and the east Mediterranean home ports. This was no mean feat of seafaring, and establishes the Phoenicians as one of the more adventurous, and presumably technically able, of the Mediterranean states.

Herodotus tells a remarkable story of Phoenician endeavour (3.20). It was widely believed that Africa was almost an island—as Herodotus puts it, 'washed on all sides by the sea except where it is attached to Asia'. To prove this the pharaoh Necho II (609–593 BC) sent out a number of ships manned by Phoenicians from the Red Sea with orders to make for the Pillars of Hercules and return to Egypt. It was a rationally constructed experiment of some daring and, miraculously, it appears to have succeeded. The circumnavigation was said to have been completed in just under three years, the sailors stopping each year to sow crops and setting off again after the harvest was collected. Herodotus was understandably sceptical about the story, and in particular he found it hard to accept the claim that 'in sailing round Libya [Africa] they had the sun on their right hand'. He could not have known that this observation in fact provided the most convincing evidence that the journey actually did take place!

The next recorded Phoenician journeys into the Atlantic took place towards the end of the fifth century, about, or soon after, 425 BC. Two expeditions set out, probably from Gadir. One, led by Hanno, sailed south down the west coast of Africa while another, commanded by Himilco, appears to have sailed northwards. Hanno's voyage is remarkably well recorded, because his own account of his exploits was set up in the temple of Baal at Carthage, and although the inscription no longer survives the text is reported, through a somewhat garbled form, in a manuscript of the tenth century AD. The account suggests that the expedition set off specifically to found colonies along the African coast, claiming that 30,000 men and women were carried in sixty penteconters—long, narrow ships usually used in war. At various points down the coast settlements were established as far as the River *Lixos*, usually considered to be the Oued Draa, which lies on the south side of the Ante Atlas before the Sahara begins. Here interpreters were taken on and the ships (how many were left by this stage is not recorded) moved on. After three days another settlement was made on the island of *Cerne*, probably at or near the mouth of the Senegal. At this point it seems that the expedition changed from a colonizing venture to one of pure exploration.

In the rest of the journey, southwards, the expedition encountered a number of wonders: a river teeming with crocodiles and hippopotamuses, an immense gulf, an extensive forest where they 'heard the sound of flutes and of beating of cymbals and drums and a great din of voices' and quickly departed, volcanoes pouring lava into the sea, and finally an island full of shaggy 'savages . . . whom our interpreters called Gorillas'. Three females were caught and killed and their skins were eventually carried back to Carthage. At this point supplies ran low and the expedition returned. How far Hanno had penetrated is a matter of speculation. Some commentators believe that he got no further than Sierra Leone, others would allow that the ships reached the Cameroons. At any event the expedition must rank as one of the great voyages of discovery in Atlantic waters.

Himilco's travels are far more obscure since all that survives are a few lines in the *Ora Maritima* of Avienus. The usual interpretation, but one by no means certain, is that he reached as far north as Britain and Ireland, but if taken at face value, in its mention of a voyage lasting for months, of sluggish windless seas, and of masses of seaweed that 'holds the prow back', the text could be hinting at a voyage far out into the Atlantic. This might have been what was in Pliny's mind when he notes that Himilco was sent to explore 'the parts beyond Europe' (*Nat. Hist.* 2. 169)—but sadly we will never know.

The west coast of Africa retained its fascination for explorers in the centuries following Hanno's expedition. Euthymenes from Massalia seems to have got as far as Senegal, for he too saw rivers teeming with crocodiles, and just before the destruction of Carthage in 146 BC the historian Polybius seems to have made a similar journey, also noting crocodiles. A few years later, *c.*120 BC, another entrepreneur, Eudoxus of Cyzicus, tried his luck. He was an experienced sailor who normally worked the Black Sea and had twice voyaged to India. According to a story preserved for us by Strabo, Eudoxus decided to make another trading voyage to India but this time to sail round Africa to avoid having to pay dues to the Egyptians. It was a decision which suggests that he can have had little concept of the size of the continent. At Gadir (Cadiz) he 'rigged out a large sailing vessel and two smaller boats like those that pirates use' and set sail. Whilst en route he was persuaded to put in to shore but in doing so ran his main vessel aground. The ship stuck fast but was not badly damaged so he was able to remove the cargo and dismantle the vessel, building from the salvaged timbers a new craft 'about the size of a penteconter'. The expedition proceeded but was eventually aborted, and after various adventures Eudoxus made his way back to Spain. Undaunted he prepared for a new expedition, choosing as transport 'a round merchantman and a long penteconter, the one for the open sea, the other for exploring the coast.' This time he was better prepared, taking on board agricultural tools, seed corn, and carpenters, intending, if necessary, to overwinter on an island he had previously discovered, 'there to sow the seed and reap the harvest and then complete the expedition as planned'. At this exciting juncture in the narrative Strabo breaks off, leaving us in the air with the throwaway line: 'That is as far as I can go in the story of Eudoxus . . . Perhaps those who live in Gades or in Spain may be able to tell what happened to him after all!' (*Geog.* 2. 3. 4).

The account, frustrating though it is, provides a fascinating insight into coastal exploration at the time and the innovative attitudes of those prepared to face the dangers of the Atlantic south of the Pillars of Hercules.

The northern seas were no less fearful. Anecdotal scraps of information, incorporated in *Ora Maritima* (including all we know of Himilco's voyage) imply that there was some knowledge of the seas north of the Tagus, but how systematic was the exploration of these regions before the end of the fourth century BC it is impossible to say. The breakthrough came with a remarkable northern journey made by Pytheas of Massalia some time before 320 BC. Pytheas must have written an account on his return to the Mediterranean. Of the original treatise *On the Ocean* nothing survives, but his observations are reported by no less than eighteen ancient writers all crediting Pytheas by name, though many of these texts survive only as quotations in later works. Early writers like Timaeus, Eratosthenes, and Hipparkhos were evidently respectful of Pytheas and the copious body of astronomical and other data he recorded, but at the pens of Polybius and Strabo his reputation was savaged. The elder Pliny, who made extensive use of Pytheas' observations in his *Natural History*, was less dismissive. What emerges from the fragments is that Pytheas was a keen and accurate observer who made a number of measurements important to science. He recorded, for example, the lengthening of the day as his journey proceeded northwards, he took the height of the sun from which it was possible for Hipparkhos to calculate latitudes, and he noted that there was no star at the exact pole. These are no mean contributions to science and have suggested to some that the purpose of his expedition was essentially scientific. It is more likely, however, that he was simply a skilled mariner practising the normal procedures of his trade.

His journey can be traced in some detail. It is usually assumed that he boarded a Greek ship in Marseilles and sailed around Iberia to the Bay of Biscay and thence northwards. There is, however, no evidence for this and, as we will argue later (pp. 306–7), it seems more likely that he travelled over-land to the Gironde and joined a local ship, making his whole remarkable exploration in local vessels, changing ship as he progressed. From the Gironde it was three days' sail to *Uxisame*, which is plausibly to be identified with Ushant off the coast of Finistère. There he noted other islands and a prominent cape, *Kabion* (Pointe du Raz?), peopled by the *Ostimii*. From western Armorica, it seems that he crossed to Britain—the *Prettanic Isles*—probably using native vessels. If so it would suggest a direct journey to the tin-producing region of the south-west, the promontory of which he calls *Belerion* (Land's End). He also named two of the other promontories of Britain, which he regarded as triangular, as *Kantion* (Kent) and *Orkas* (Orkney). His circumnavigation of the island enabled him to estimate the lengths of each side, but while his proportions were correct his estimated lengths were almost double the reality, suggesting that in translating a day's sailing into distance the speed of the vessel was overestimated. Perhaps he was using a Mediterranean estimate for the slower local vessel on which he was travelling. In passing he noted Ireland. Much of the detail about Britain and Ireland to be found in the works of later authors is likely to have been gleaned from Pytheas' treatise, not least about the ever-interesting theme of tin from the south-west peninsula. It may well be that one of the objectives of the voyage was to establish direct contacts with the tin-producing peninsulas of Armorica and Britain.

There are clear indications, in the surviving text fragments, that Pytheas' travels took him along the North Sea coast of Europe at least as far as the Elbe estuary where amber, washed up on an offshore island, was to be had. Whether or not he reached the Vistula is debatable. So too is the question of how far north he ventured. Mentions of the land of Thule in the far north, six days' sailing from Britain, of frozen sea, of volcanoes that boil the sea, of a place where it is daylight for six months a year, and many other wonders, have intrigued commentators ever after and still the debate rages. Some argue that he reached Iceland, others that he got no further than Shetland but there collected travellers' tales of more distant places. The sad truth is that we will never know. The surviving texts, full of half-observed and half-remembered hearsay, will, however, remain a rich source for ingenious speculation for decades to come.

But this is not to belittle Pytheas' expedition. His journey, even if only to the Elbe and Shetland using local ships, was an outstanding achievement. It brought to the narrow confines of the Mediterranean world an entirely new awareness of what lay beyond and it introduced a new array of astronomical data for scientists to practise on. But there was also a sound practical result. The voyage brought back to the home port of Massalia a detailed knowledge of the tin-producing areas of the west. The long-established trade route along the Aude and Garonne to the

Gironde could now be linked, by a short coastal sea route, direct to the producers of the Morbihan and beyond. Thereafter the tin trade was to flourish. By the first century BC these same shipping lanes were to carry a considerable bulk of Roman wine in exchange for barbarian products.

In journeying to the northern fringes of the British Isles Pytheas benefited from the expertise of native seafarers whose knowledge of the local waters would have been encyclopaedic. He may well have gleaned his stories of the far north and even of the sources of amber from British sailors without visiting the regions for himself. The archaeological evidence shows, with great clarity, that the sea lanes around the Atlantic coasts from Ireland to Shetland were in active use at least as early as the Neolithic period. Most of the traffic would have been short-haul and coastal, but there is no reason to doubt that occasional adventurers made more daring voyages, bringing back stories to be woven into the local folk tales. The frozen seas and volcanoes that make the sea boil sound much as though Britons had reached Iceland, led northwards perhaps by the migration patterns of birds, long before Pytheas entered British waters to learn of these wonders.

Adventuring continued throughout the first millennium AD and is reflected, albeit often obscurely, in the *immrama* (voyages) recording the wanderings of Irish monks. Perhaps the most famous, but in many ways the least informative, is the *Voyage of St Brendan*—a mixture of fact, fantasy, and allegory reflecting the life of a monk in the sixth century (3.21). Whilst the geographical content of the legendary voyage is unintelligible, the story is, in its very essence, a tale of the sea composed for, and by, those who lived and breathed the ocean. A more realistic picture of the achievements of Irish sailors is offered by the Irish monk Dicuil in his book *Liber de Mensura Orbis Terrae* written in AD 825. His sober account is based on stories brought back by travelling monks—the *peregrini*. In the ocean to the north of Britain, he tells us, there are many islands inhabited by hermits who had sailed from Ireland. They were uninhabited when the Irish arrived about a century before, but at the time he was writing many had been abandoned in the face of incessant raids by Norse pirates, leaving only the sheep. The Faroes were certainly occupied by the Irish as early as AD 700, and when the first Norse settlers arrived in Iceland in 870 the Irish monks had only recently departed, their presence evident from the 'books, bells, and croziers' which they left in their flight. That the Irish sailors were very familiar with the northern ocean is apparent from the story that it was Irish captains who guided the Norsemen to their safe landing on the island.

In the *longue durée* it is tempting to see this exodus of peregrini from Ireland to the islands of the far north in the seventh and eighth centuries

3.21 (*facing*) St Brendan and his followers land their boat on an island that turns out to be a giant sea beast.

as simply a continuation of voyages of exploration which were already under way in the Neolithic period.

In the last decade of the eighth century AD Viking ships began to attack the coasts of Britain and the Continent, intent, in the first instance, on gaining plunder from unprotected Christian monastic communities. The first recorded raid was on the island monastery of Lindisfarne in 793. The next year another Northumberland monastery, probably Jarrow, was attacked. In 795 the raids extended to the west coasts, with communities on Skye, Iona, and Rathlin succumbing. These early raids were the work of the Norsemen (from Norway) who had already established permanent settlements on Shetland and Orkney. At about this time three Norse ships landed on the south coast at Portland and were mistaken for merchants by a royal reeve (for whom the error proved fatal). The first recorded attack on the Continent came in 799, when the monastery of St-Philibert, on the island of Noirmoutier near the estuary of the Loire, succumbed. The English Channel had by then become a danger zone. Pirates who 'infest the Gallic sea' caused Charlemagne to look to the defence of the coast north of the Seine, while in Kent similar preparations were being made.

By the middle of the ninth century the intensity of the Viking activity in the west had increased dramatically. The Norsemen had, by this stage, settled the Hebrides and had established permanent bases at Dublin and Cork. They had also explored the west coasts of Ireland. Raiding continued in the area: between 822 and 829 fifteen monasteries were plundered, and from 830 to 845 fifty attacks were listed. Meanwhile, in the Channel, Danish Vikings were beginning to become involved, their first recorded attack, on the prosperous port of Dorestad, in the Netherlands, taking place in 834. Although divisions between the spheres of influence of the Danish and Norse Vikings became blurred, the archaeological and linguistic evidence shows that the settlements in the Northern Isles, the Hebrides, and Ireland were Norwegian while those in eastern England and northern France were predominantly Danish.

The type of vessels in use at this time can be appreciated from the extremely well-preserved ship found in the burial mound at Oseberg, west of Oslo fjord, dated by dendrochronology to *c.*AD 820. The vessel (3.22) is 21.5 metres long and over 5 metres broad, with its mast just forward of midships. The depth amidships from keel to gunwale was 1.4 metres, but with high upcurving stems as befits a fast sailing vessel. These characteristics, of sail and high stems, are shown on picture-stones in Gothland from the beginning of the seventh century. To give the vessel greater stability at sea an angle was created between the comparatively flat bottom and the sides, and to accommodate this the ribs were made of

Est belua in mari que grece aspido delone dicitur. Aspido ul
Latine u aspido testitudo. Cete etiam dicta. ob cete.
immanitate corporis. est enim sicut ille qui excepit

several pieces, adding to the strength of the hull along the water-line. The Oseberg vessel lies at a period of transition in the development of Viking shipbuilding. The greatly increased activity from the late eighth century, involving exploration, raiding, settlement, and trade, encouraged experiment and innovation on an unprecedented scale.

3.22 (*facing*) Replica of the Oseberg ship.

The settlement of Iceland beginning about AD 860 followed a period of exploration. The earliest Norsemen adventurers found Irish monks already established but, as we have seen, by the time that settlement began in earnest the monks had fled. The *Íslendingabók*, a history of Iceland compiled by Ari the Wise in about 1130, describes the first three voyages, one led by a Swede and two by Norwegians. Thereafter, over the next fifty or sixty years, settlers arrived in some number, more than half of them from the region of Bergen, though some came from the Viking settlements in Britain. By the mid-tenth century the population is thought to have been as great as 60,000 people.

From Iceland, Greenland was no great distance. Travellers' talk of this huge, largely inhospitable land mass circulated among the Icelanders for some time before the first detailed exploration of the west coast was made by Erik the Red in about 980. It was he who named the country Greenland and initiated the first settlements.

Not long after, so tradition records, a Norse ship's crew sailing further west beyond Greenland were the first Europeans to see America. They did not land but returned to Greenland with their story, and it was Erik's son Leif who led the first exploration of the land, calling it Helluland, Makland, and Vinland. Firm archaeological confirmation of the Viking achievement came in 1961 with the discovery of Viking houses, dating to the eleventh century, at L'Anse aux Meadows, near the northernmost tip of Newfoundland. The Atlantic had now been crossed.

The Norse exploration of the north Atlantic in the ninth and tenth centuries was in no small part due to the sheer spirit of adventure which drew men on further into the unknown, but behind it all lay the normal human desire to find good land to settle and desirable commodities to exploit. So it was with the Portuguese in the fifteenth century, though here a complicating motivation (or justification) was the desire to spread Christianity.

If a Norseman in Reykjavik looked westwards towards his unknown a Portuguese at Sagres looked south, along the west coast of Africa. Portugal was admirably located to explore this southern unknown, her shores swept by favourable winds and currents. The impetus behind the early-fifteenth-century voyages is usually ascribed to Prince Henry, son of John I and Philippa (daughter of John of Gaunt). Henry became governor of the Algarve in 1419, and through his patronage encouraged Portuguese captains, still bound up in a code of late-medieval chivalric values, to vie for his approval by engaging in increasingly daring voyages of exploration. Such was his success that largely apocryphal stories grew up about his deep involvement with maritime matters, leading one English historian of the nineteenth century to give him the sobriquet of 'the Navigator'—something of an exaggeration given that Henry had never travelled further than Tangier. This said, the remarkable voyages undertaken between 1419 and his death in 1460 owed much to his inspiration and support.

In about 1419 ships left Sagres to colonize Madeira, and soon after annual expeditions were sent out to explore the western coast of Africa—the first systematic attempt we know of after Eudoxus' voyage *c.*1540 years earlier! The psychological barrier of the treacherous Cape Bogador (on the coast of the western Sahara south of the Canaries) was passed in 1434. The Cape had an infamous reputation and was believed to be the end of the world, beyond which it was unsafe to travel:

> For, said the mariners, this much is clear, that beyond this Cape there is no race of men nor place of inhabitants: nor is the land less sandy than the deserts of Libya, where there is no water, no tree, no green herb—and the sea so shallow that a whole league from land it is only a fathom deep, while the currents are so terrible that no ship having once passed the Cape, will ever be able to return. (Azurara, *The Chronicle of the Discovery and Conquest of Guinea*)

Putting fear aside, Gil Eannes rounded the Cape in 1434 and lived to tell the tale. By this time the Azores were known, having probably been found by accident by returning ships taking a wide loop westwards to catch the north-westerly winds.

In the 1440s Henry's brother Pedro, now regent, became the driving force as a sponsor of exploration. By the time of Henry's death in 1460 the coast at least down as far as Sierra Leone had been explored and charted, and a little later the Cape Verde Islands were discovered. Thereafter the momentum to explore increased, fed now by commercial imperatives, not least the lure of trade with India and the East, and facilitated by improved navigational methods. Diego Cão sailed up the Congo river in 1483, and in 1488 Bartholomew Diaz rounded the Cape of Good Hope. The century culminated with the voyage to India and back led by Vasco da Gama in 1497–9. It is interesting to reflect that much of the same journey, though in reverse, had probably been made by a Phoenician mariner two thousand years before: the two journeys took about the same length of time.

The Norse adventurers in the north Atlantic and the Portuguese in the south Atlantic take us beyond the geographical scope of this book. The crossing of the Atlantic by Columbus in 1492 is the moment when

3.23 Columbus landing at San Salvador with King Ferdinand looking on across the Ocean. From a fifteenth-century woodcut.

the ocean-facing communities of Europe had suddenly to readjust their perspectives—the endless ocean stretching out in front of them was no longer endless (3.23).

Voyages of Commerce

The voyages of exploration were inextricably bound up with the desire to trade, even if other factors such as curiosity and personal prowess were the prime movers. After the shipping lanes became established more organized bulk trade usually followed. The evidence for this is disparate and varies from text-free archaeology to the heavily documented history. Much of the detail will appear in the chapters to follow. Here we will extract a few strands of evidence which allow us to glimpse something of the role of ships in that trade and the way in which the fleets were organized.

Before the Roman period there is very little tangible evidence for trade other than the distribution maps drawn by archaeologists of items which can be shown to have been moved far beyond their centres of production. The distribution of *amphorae* made in Italy, for example, demonstrates the extensive export of wine taking place over considerable distances in the first century BC. Some of that product, taken by river and overland portage to the Gironde, will then have been loaded on ships for onward passage to Armorica and Britain (pp. 390–1)—a deduction supported not only by the finds of amphorae on land but also by wreck sites like the one indicated by amphorae found at sea off Belle-Île in the Morbihan. Strabo, writing in the early first century AD about trade with Britain, before the island became part of the Roman empire, mentions the heavy duties which the natives were prepared to pay on both exports and imports, adding, rather scathingly, 'these latter are ivory chains and necklaces, and amber-gems and glass vessels and other pretty wares of that sort' (*Geog.* 4. 5. 3). Elsewhere, in commenting on exports from the island he lists 'grain, cattle, gold, silver and iron . . . also hides, and slaves and dogs that are by nature suited to the purposes of the chase' (*Geog.* 4. 5. 2). Taken together with the archaeological evidence the implication would seem to be that trade was, by this time, well organized.

More direct evidence for maritime trade is available for the Roman period. Several wreck sites have been sufficiently well studied to be informative. In the Thames estuary off the north coast of Kent a vessel carrying a cargo of pottery from Gaul foundered on the Pudding Pan rock in the late second century. Another vessel was smashed trying to negotiate the notorious Sept-Îles off the north coast of Armorica opposite Ploumanac'h. From its cargo divers have recorded 271 ingots of lead with a total weight of 22 tonnes. Some of the ingots were stamped with the names *Brigantes* and *Icenes*, suggesting that the cargo may have come from mines in the Pennines and was shipped out through an East Anglian port. A third wreck dating to the late third century had evidently caught fire in the harbour of St Peter Port on Guernsey. Its cargo included blocks of pine 'pitch', of which about half a tonne remained, and oak barrels which could have carried wine or fish sauce. It is not clear where the cargo was taken on board, but the west coast of France is a reasonable possibility. The three examples—all by definition unsuccessful enterprises—give a glimpse into the varied cargoes that were carried around the Atlantic coasts in the Roman period, but they do scant justice to the variety and sheer bulk of the trade.

Little is known specifically of the organization of the maritime trade in the Atlantic at this time, except by analogy with the better-recorded Mediterranean. There were, however, a number of *negotiatores* (traders) at work whose names and origins are recorded on inscriptions. One of the most valuable collections comes from two temple sites on the Dutch coast at Colijnsplaat and Domburg which originally flanked the ancient estuary of the River Scheldt. Here traders set up altars to ensure the safety of their ventures. Merchants specializing in the export of pottery, wine, and salt were all present. One of them, Placidus, son of Viducius, originally came from the lower Seine region but styles himself *negotiator Britannicianus*. He seems to have made his home in York, where he erected another dedicatory inscription in AD 221. Presumably he made his living shipping goods across the North Sea between the Rhine and the Humber. Another York resident involved in long-distance trade at about this time was Marcus Aurelius Lunaris, a '*sevir Augustalis* of the colonies of York and Lincoln'. He erected an altar to the goddess Tutela Boudiga at Bordeaux in AD 237, having promised to do so when he set out from York. He may well have known a fellow *negotiator Britannicianus*, L. Solimarius Secundinus, a Treveran by origin, who died in Bordeaux and was buried there. Perhaps these two men were involved in exporting the local claret to Britain along the route that had been used to carry Italian wine to the island three centuries earlier.

Organized merchant shipping continued throughout the immediate post-Roman period, though on a much reduced scale. Some vague reflection of this occurs in the fascinating story of the legendary early life of St Patrick, who made the three-day crossing from Ireland to Gaul on a merchant ship carrying a cargo of dogs. It is tempting to think of them as hunting dogs of the kind that Strabo listed among the exports of Britain four hundred years earlier.

That trade continued on an international level is amply shown by the archaeological record, which we will be considering in some detail in its appropriate place. By the end of the eighth century, as western Europe was beginning to enjoy the new stability created by Charlemagne, more formal organizations were beginning to emerge. International ports-of-trade had developed around the North Sea and the English Channel—places like Hamwic in Southampton Water, Ipswich on the River Orwell, Dorestad at the confluence of the Lek and the Rhine, and Quentovic near Étaples on the coast of northern France. Similar emporia served the Baltic region. The increased volume of commerce called for negotiated trade agreements between states. One such is incorporated in a letter written in 796 by the emperor Charlemagne to Offa, king of the powerful English state of Mercia. After complaining that British traders had passed themselves off as pilgrims to avoid paying tolls 'in the regular places', he goes on, 'we would have them enjoy our protection and defence within our realm as we have ordained, according to the ancient custom in commerce, and if in any place they are distressed by unjust oppression let them appeal to us or our judges, and we will order justice to be done to them. Show like favour to our merchants . . .' The letter is essentially a confirmation of 'ancient custom', but that it was written at this time is an indication of the growing intensity of international trade and the importance which heads of state attached to it.

The trading energies of Muslim Iberia were firmly focused on the Mediterranean, but its merchants were by no means neglectful of the possibilities of the Atlantic (3.24). The famous Arab geographer Al Idrisi, in discussing maritime traffic along the Atlantic coasts of Africa and Iberia, refers to it, with evident dislike, as 'the sea of perpetual gloom' and makes it clear that shipping kept close to the coast and sailed only in the short summer season. Nonetheless the resources of the coastal plain of Africa, most notably its grain, so much in demand in Andalucía, were widely exploited. Coastal towns, like Rabat founded in the ninth century, also served as collection points for gold coming from deeper within the Continent. Another resource which gained wide fame was ambergris, a

3.24 A Muslim ship in a Spanish port being loaded with bales of wool (*Cántigas de Santa Maria, XXV*).

grey, waxy substance secreted by the sperm whale, which was collected from the Atlantic coast of Iberia and taken to Seville and the other markets of al-Andalus. Ambergris was used in medieval times in cooking and making perfumes. Iberian ambergris could be sold for thirty times its local value in the markets of Egypt or Baghdad.

An interesting insight into the working of trade at grass-roots level is provided by the life of a hermit, Godric, who died at Finchale near Durham in 1170. In his early years Godric was a merchant living in Norfolk. He began in a small way, peddling 'small wares around the villages and farmsteads of his own neighbourhood; but in process of time he gradually associated himself by compact with city merchants'. Gradually he built his business and began to travel abroad. When he returned to Britain he and 'other young men eager for merchandise . . . began to launch on bolder courses, and to coast frequently by sea to foreign lands . . . he laboured not only as a merchant but also as a shipman . . . to Denmark and Flanders and Scotland', carrying many goods from port to port. By selling 'dear in one place the wares which he had bought elsewhere at a small price' he grew rich. With the profit he purchased half a merchant ship and later a quarter share in another. 'At length, by his skill in navigation . . . he earned promotion to the post of steersman . . . He knew, from the aspect of the sea and stars, how to foretell fair or foul weather.' After sixteen years at sea he turned to the church and ended his days in fasting and in prayer.

The story of Godric's early life as a merchant is probably typical of that of many energetic young men who, in the early Middle Ages, turned to overseas trade as a means of livelihood combining the skills of simple peddler, investment broker, and sailor. It was entrepreneurs of this kind who were soon to become the merchant venturers who opened up the Atlantic seaways to a volume of trade never before experienced.

With the increase in volume and complexity of trading ventures came more complex systems of control. National laws governing the behaviour and rights of alien merchants were constantly reviewed and toughened to safeguard local monopolies. Thus, by the twelfth century it was forbidden for a foreign merchant to stay in England for longer than forty days, and then he must stay with an Englishman who was responsible for overseeing all commercial transactions. By the thirteenth century many British towns had charters restricting the goods which foreign merchants could deal in, but those who could supply commodities that were in particular demand were given special privileges. The woad merchants of Amiens were welcomed to London and Norwich, where they could dwell within the city as long as they liked and sell woad 'to whomsoever they will, whether foreigners or natives'. The restrictive practices of the markets of medieval Europe were carefully tuned to the benefit of local economies, but all recognized that trade was their life-blood.

The merchants organized themselves for their mutual benefit and safety. Already by the early thirteenth century the English merchants had created a fraternity which became known as the Merchant Adventurers, organized under a 'major, captain, or consul' and holding a regular assembly and court. They were essentially trading capitalists concerned only with foreign trade, to distinguish their sphere of activity from home-based merchants now organized in livery companies. Under the patronage of successive English kings the different groups, scattered around the Continental cities, were protected by charters specifying their rights and privileges. It was in the interests of the authorities, English and foreign alike, that these revenue-generating entrepreneurs were allowed to practise their profession in comparative freedom.

Each country had its own fraternity of merchants. The 'Men of the Emperor of Germany' existed in Britain before the Norman Conquest. Out of this organization grew the Hanseatic League, also known as the Easterlings, who had gained for themselves an impressive array of rights and privileges. The towns of the Hanse included Lübeck, Danzig, and Brunswick. But other trading cities, like Cologne and Hamburg, set up their own 'Hanse' in partner cities such as London.

National politics inevitably played an important part in the activities of merchants. When Bordeaux finally fell to the French in 1453 the highly profitable Gascon wine trade was for a time severely disrupted. Whereas before French and British merchants engaged freely in trade in the city, now they were able to do so only under special licence from both kings. Trade fell away, and many of the Gascon merchants made for British ports. The vacuum was filled by Breton shipowners quick to assume a lucrative role as middlemen in the transport of wine and cloth between Britain and Gascony. However, within a decade the French king Louis XI, mindful of loss of revenues, did much to re-establish direct links between the two ancient trading partners.

Political allegiances played a large part in the development of the massive trade between Portugal and Britain from the middle of the fourteenth century, particularly after the Treaty of Windsor signed in 1386 by Richard II and John I of Portugal. All the privileges which had previously been enjoyed by Pisa and Genoa were now extended to British merchants. In the two principal ports of Oporto and Lisbon the British could feel secure under the protection of law. A proctor was appointed to oversee prompt payment for English cloth, and a special judge was given powers to settle cases of dispute between English and Portuguese, obviating the need for lengthy trials. Under these favourable conditions trade flourished and Portuguese wines and fruit became familiar in English dining-rooms. For their part English merchants found Lisbon and Oporto congenial places to set up resident factories which, by the seventeenth century, had become a powerful political, social and commercial force.

Thus, the regulation of trade by nations and protective practices by alien merchants became the hallmark of medieval mercantile endeavour as the Atlantic shipping lanes settled down to an ever-increasing volume of traffic varied only by fluctuations in the prevailing political climate.

By far the greatest volume of Atlantic trade was articulated by the ships of the Atlantic ports, but direct links with the city states of Italy began to develop, particularly after the *Reconquista* had freed some of the more important Iberian ports from Muslim control. Cartagena passed to the Christians in 1245 and Seville and Cadiz three years later. As the Straits of Gibraltar became a safer passage the Genoese were first to respond to the new political geography. In 1277 a ship of Genoa docked at Sluys in Flanders. The next year ships arrived at Southampton, Sandwich, and London. The way was now set. Others followed, and in 1314 the first Venetian galleys joined in making for Flanders. Vessels from Lucca, Florence, and Pisa were less frequently to be seen. The journey from Italy to England took about three months. En route the Italians, less happy with open-sea sailing, often put in at Lisbon, the Galician ports, La Rochelle, and at some of the more favoured harbours of Brittany.

Every year from 1314 until 1532 a fleet of merchant vessels, known as the 'Flanders Galleys', was sent by the Venetian state to trade with Flanders and England. Their main aim was to acquire wool, cloth, and tin, in return for which they offered a wide variety of Mediterranean commodities ranging from currants, spices from the East, silks, sweet wines, sugar, and other 'extravagant trifles' to more mundane commodities such as alum from Chios for use in treating cloth. The arrival of these large exotic craft was eagerly awaited, but the inevitable tensions arose. At one stage Parliament received a petition claiming that, instead of restricting themselves to trading in Mediterranean products, the Venetians were picking up other commodities along the Atlantic coast and thus competing with English shipowners. On another occasion it was complained that the Italian merchants were buying their cloth, wool, and tin with cash direct from inland markets rather than through the merchants in the ports of London, Southampton, and Sandwich who dealt with their suppliers on a credit basis, and no doubt added a significant percentage to the price for their services. In 1456 and 7 rioting broke out against the Italians in London, with the result that the Venetian Senate prohibited the 'merchants of the Italian nation' from going to the city to trade, but the embargo was short-lived. Tensions of this sort were

3.25 Currachs at work on the shore of the Aran Islands. The vessels are built of a light timber framework covered with tarred canvas.

endemic in trading ventures. The events in London in the 1450s were probably not very dissimilar to those in the newly established port of Londinium fourteen hundred years earlier.

In this all-too-brief chapter we have attempted to review the relationship between man and the ocean over a period of some five thousand years or so, from the earliest log boat to the merchant fleets of the Middle Ages. The sailing vessels were the servants of the community and as such adapted to changing needs, but where a vessel type performed its function adequately a comfortable conservatism prevailed. The spirit of the skin boats of the prehistoric period is still with us in the currachs used in the Aran Islands today (3.25). Dimly represented in the all-too-fragmentary record is the sense that in boat-building we are witnessing the emergence of three largely separate traditions—the Mediterranean, the Nordic, and the Atlantic—which, from time to time, interacted to enliven each other. The antechambers between the seas—the Bay of Cadiz and the English Channel—were zones of overlap and experiment through which the different ideas were transmitted and transmuted. The Mediterranean offered the sail: much later the North Sea contributed clinker building.

With navigation, the most significant force over most of the period before us was the simple ability of the sailor to observe his ever-changing environment, to use his observations to anticipate further change and to plan ahead. Thus the heavens, winds, tides, swell, atmosphere, and the sight and smell of the land all contributed to his sense of place and direction. If observant he survived and his enterprise flourished; if not, in failure lay disaster. The accoutrements of more sophisticated navigation, which developed in the Mediterranean in the thirteenth and fourteenth centuries, gave no particular advantage to the coastal sailor well schooled in his locality, but they came into their own, as life-preserving necessities, when the open ocean began to be faced and it became essential to record journeys out of sight of land so that they could be repeated.

There have probably been voyages of exploration as long as there have been seagoing vessels. Human curiosity is innate and timeless. The staggering achievement of the Phoenician sailors who circumnavigated Africa in about 600 BC is remarkable for the sheer audacity of the venture rather than for the distance covered and the methods used. After all, Phoenician sailors regularly sailed the length of the Mediterranean: the journey round Africa, outside the Pillars of Hercules, was only five times as long. What is perhaps more interesting is that the exploit appears not to have been attempted successfully for another two thousand years.

The various Phoenician ventures, the travels of Pytheas, the Viking odyssey across the north Atlantic, and the activities of the Portuguese explorers in the south Atlantic, are spectacular achievements, but they are probably only the tip of the iceberg—the few incidents to survive in literature of a long tradition of exploration going back into the distant past. After all, someone in the Neolithic period five thousand years ago must have sailed in a small skin boat northwards from Orkney to see what lay beyond so that others, with their livestock and seed corn, could follow to set up their homes on Shetland. The motivation of this anonymous explorer may not have been very different from that of his better-known successors.

The sea provided an ideal means for transporting goods over long distances, and there is ample evidence that it was used for these purposes at least from the Neolithic period. Indeed, it could reasonably be argued that for much of the time most of the shipping along the Atlantic coasts was engaged in trade, whether it was the movement of polished stone axes in cycles of exchange between the Channel Islanders in the fourth millennium BC to help societies maintain their delicate social equilibria, or the transport of wine in bulk from Bordeaux to Southampton by a skipper intent on making a cash profit in the fourteenth century AD. Only the scales of the enterprise and social contexts were different. What was happening is summed up very succinctly by the merchant in the 'Colloquy' of Abbot Ælfric, written in the tenth century

I go on board ship with my merchandise. I sail to regions beyond the sea, and sell my goods, and buy valuable produce, that is not made in this country, and I bring it to you here. I face great dangers in crossing the ocean, and sometimes I suffer shipwreck with the loss of all my goods, hardly escaping with my life.

He adds:

I maintain that I am useful to the king and to the nobles, and to the wealthy and to the whole people.

4. The Emergence of an Atlantic Identity: 8000–4000 BC

The four thousand years or so following the end of the last Ice Age was a time of dramatic reordering in western Europe: the boundary between the land and sea was constantly changing, with the sea gradually encroaching, while across the land spread woodland, open at first but becoming a dense forest over time and bringing with it a fauna suited to the changing conditions. As the climate improved human communities moved in, at first gathering and hunting their food but later adopting strategies of food production requiring them to care for domestic flocks and herds and to adopt a more sedentary way of life, growing cereal crops in fields around their settlements. In the favoured environment of the Atlantic fringe the population grew rapidly, generating an energy over and above that needed simply to ensure a constant and sufficient supply of food. That surplus energy was transformed into fine goods, like polished axes, used in gift exchanges, and into monumental tombs built to house and to commemorate the ancestors. Thus in four millennia the face of western Europe changed dramatically, and it was during this transformation that a distinctive Atlantic culture emerged.

The Earth and Sea Readjust

When exactly the Ice Age came to an end is a matter of debate. The long period of intense cold of the last glaciation ended about 13,000 years ago and the earth began to warm up. It was, however, a false start, for just as human groups began to adapt to the improved conditions and to colonize further and further north there was a sudden, short-lived cold snap lasting for about a thousand years before the warmth returned, this time to stay. By about 8000 BC the Post-Glacial period had finally begun. Broadly coinciding with this was a change in flint implement technology: the larger-blade implements characterizing the Upper Palaeolithic began to give way to the smaller 'microliths' of the Mesolithic. The boundaries between these two technologies and the chronology of the change are blurred, but the long-established terminologies of Upper Palaeolithic and Mesolithic are still useful as a broad generalization, and the date of *c.*8000 BC provides a convenient starting point for the processes of change which are the concern of this chapter.

As the temperature rose and the ice-caps receded two processes were set in motion which greatly affected the land/sea relationship. The first was the isostatic readjustment of the earth's crust as the weight of the ice was removed. The overall effect of this was a comparatively rapid rise in the absolute height of the land mass, the rise being proportional to the weight of ice removed. Some areas like Scotland and Scandinavia rose very rapidly, while other zones, which lay beyond the limits of the ice-cap, readjusted more slowly (4.1). The process is still happening today. In Britain, for example, the west of Scotland is rising at the rate of 2 millimetres per year while East Anglia is falling at about the same rate: the axis across which the island is tilting (the line of zero movement) runs roughly from Anglesey to the River Tees.

The second process is a eustatic rise in sea-level caused by the freeing of water once locked in the massive ice-caps. Unlike isostatic readjustment, which occurs differentially and is comparatively slow, eustatic readjust-

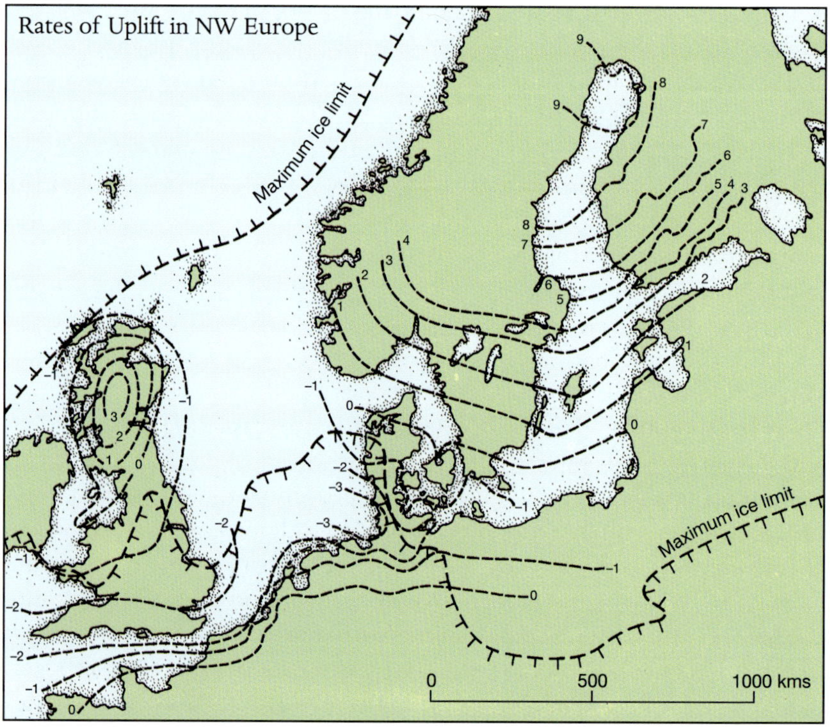

4.1 The rate of uplift and subsidence in north-western Europe in the present day in mm per year as the result of adjustments following the melting of the icecap (the – values representing subsidence).

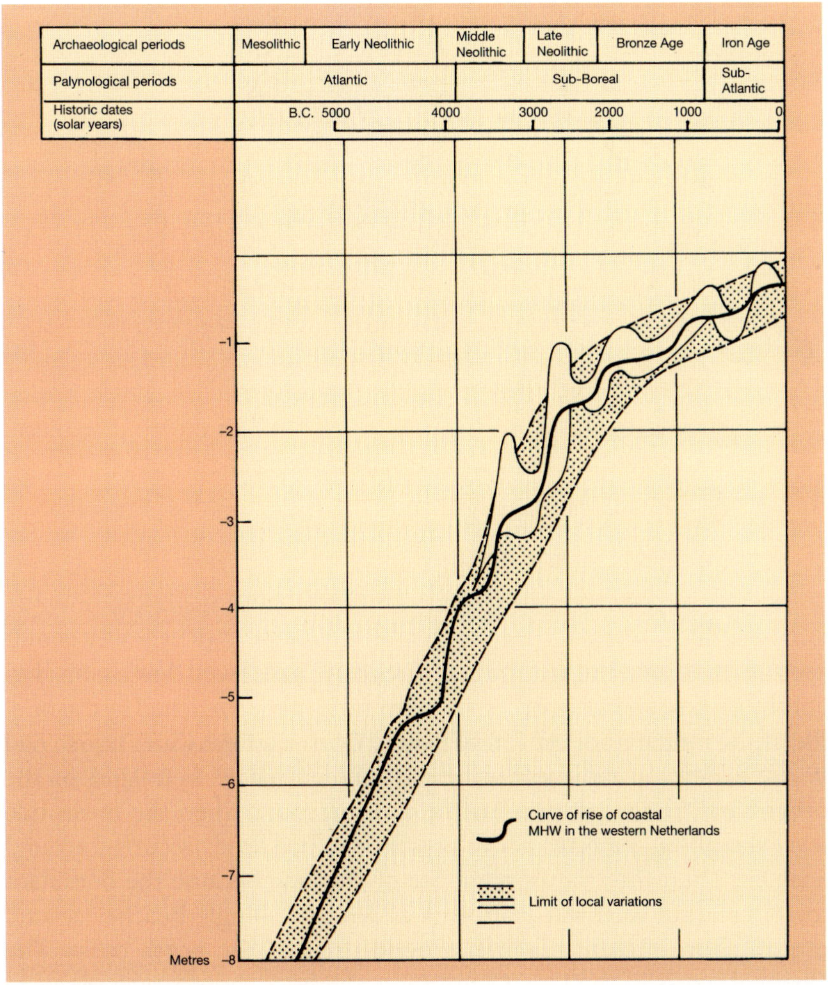

4.2 The rise in mean high-water level in the Netherlands in the 5,000 years BC.

ment affects all areas evenly and is much more rapid. It is the interaction of these two processes working in opposite directions, and distorted by regional variation, that has given rise to the changing coastline of our region.

Although it will be clear from what has been said that each area of the coast has its own dynamic, the overall picture is of a general rise in sea-level, fast at first but slowing down considerably by the end of the first millennium BC (4.2). Using a range of evidence, it is possible to produce general maps of the coastline at different periods (4.3). About 9000 BC Britain and Ireland were firmly part of the continent of Europe, and Denmark and Sweden were joined so that what is now the Baltic was then a large freshwater lake. As the relative sea-level rose Britain became an island around 6500 BC and the Baltic was joined to the North Sea about

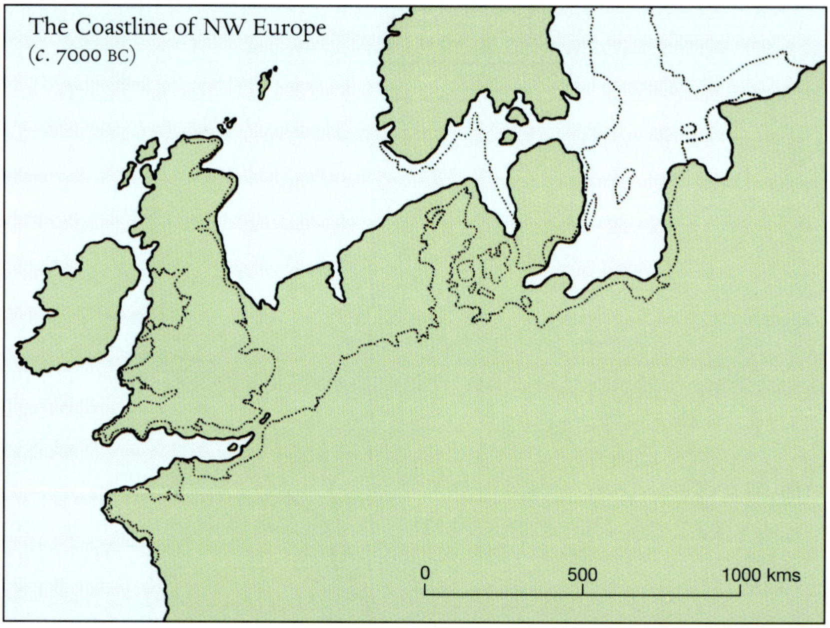

4.3 The coastline of north-western Europe about 7000 BC. The present coastline dotted.

5000 BC. In Britain the marine transgression had slowed down considerably by 5000 BC and a degree of equilibrium had been reached by the middle of the millennium. At Chesil Beach, Dorset, a freshwater marsh had begun to develop above estuarine clays about 4400 BC. In Ireland, on the other hand, the maximum marine transgression, when the mean tide level was about 4 metres above present day tide level, occurred around 4000 BC. Thereafter the isostatic rise of the land became the dominant force, creating wave-cut platforms and raised shingle beaches several metres above present sea-level around parts of the north coast. The Channel coasts of the Low Countries and France show a general rise in sea-level throughout the prehistoric period, but the process was not everywhere entirely even. Around the shores of Armorica, where much detailed work has been done, in the sixth millennium BC the high-tide level was *c.*-12 metres and by the middle of the fifth millennium it was at *c.*-6 metres. Thereafter fluctuations in the rate of transgression are evident about 4000 BC and again about 2000 BC and 600 BC, when there were brief periods of deceleration leading to the formation of peat bogs in estuarine regions.

The climatic change which came about over the period 9000–4000 BC was considerable. In Denmark it is estimated that summer temperatures rose from 9 °C to 18 °C—that is, from a subarctic to a temperate climate—in as little as half a millennium. In southern Europe, well away from the former ice sheets, the increase was less dramatic. Even so changes in vegetation affected all regions. From pollen sequences recovered from peats and lake sediments across Europe, the evolution of the flora has been charted in considerable detail. In north-western Europe the process of vegetational change escalated about 8300 BC as the open park tundra was colonized first by an open birch forest and then by aspen and birch and later by pine. About 7000 BC hazel began to dominate; then followed elm, lime, oak, and alder, and by about 6000 BC the hazel–pine forest had given way to a stable primeval forest dominated by shade-creating trees, particularly lime, oak, and elm. In southern Europe, especially Iberia and southern France, pine spread to the higher altitudes while the rest of the land was covered with oak forests, with a much lower percentage of the other trees found in the primeval forests of the north.

The change of vegetation from a subarctic steppe to mixed oak forest over most of western Europe brought with it a dramatic change in fauna. The herds of large mammals all but disappeared. Several species, such as mammoth, woolly rhino, and giant deer, became extinct, while reindeer and elk migrated to the far north. In their place came smaller mammals such as red and roe deer, aurochs, and wild pig, with a much more diverse fauna of smaller creatures inhabiting the many varied ecological niches provided by the forest. Unlike the large herds of the steppe with their long-distance seasonal migrations, the new, more diverse fauna lived in smaller groups with much more restricted movements. This, inevitably, led to significant changes in behaviour by the human groups who depended on hunting for their livelihood. Other important food sources were provided by the many rivers and lakes and by the coasts and the sea. There was now much diversity in the landscape.

The brief but sharp cold spell at the very end of the Late-Glacial period drove human groups from the northern parts of Europe and created tundra / steppe conditions over huge areas, requiring major adjustments in the lifestyles of those who attempted to live at the fringes, but with the rapid improvement in climate after 8000 BC and the spread of forests over most of Europe human populations moved gradually northwards, adapting their foraging strategies to suit the woodland resources. Given the diversity of the landscape and the paucity of the archaeological data it is impossible to guess the size of the population with any degree of accuracy, but estimates of between one person for every 2 square kilometres and one for every 200 square kilometres are not unreasonable when compared with the population densities of more recent foragers elsewhere in the world.

The activities of Mesolithic hunter-gatherers are known largely from the stone artefacts and stoneworking debris found at their camp sites and studied with loving care by archaeologists in an attempt to characterize chronology, cultures, and activities. The most favoured material, and the most widespread, was flint, though other stones such as quartz and slate were also used. Flint blades struck from cores were usually broken into smaller elements and retouched along one or more edges. These microliths, as they are called, formed the cutting and piercing elements of composite implements such as arrows, spears, cutting tools, and food graters (4.4). Other stone implements included scrapers used for skin preparation and axes for tree cutting and woodworking. Antler, though comparatively rare in the archaeological record because of poor survival, was used for harpoon heads. The organic component of the material culture—wood, bark, wicker, skins, and so on—must have been considerable, but except in rare waterlogged situations very little has survived.

Through the study of flint artefacts it has been possible to construct a broad chronology based on changes in the tool-kit. Over much of north-western Europe the eighth millennium was characterized by use of broad blades to make the microliths, the majority of which were obliquely blunted points. In the seventh millennium narrower blades come into regular use and there is a greater variety in the shape of the small microliths. After about 6000 BC tool-kits become dominated by blades and trapeze-shaped microliths. Details such as these are useful in tracing changes in the settlement pattern through time, whilst a study of even finer typological differences allows cultural patterns to be proposed. What does emerge is that very broad similarities in flint technology occurred over large parts of Europe, reflecting the mobility of hunting

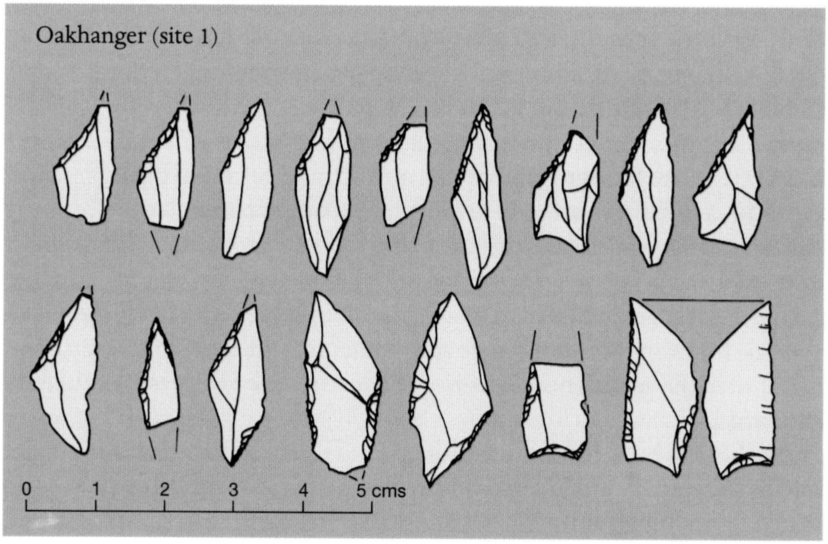

4.4 Microlithic flints of Late Mesolithic date from a camp site in the Weald at Oakhanger in eastern Hampshire.

groups and the degree of intercourse between them. It could, however, also reflect, at least in part, the relative conservatism in tool technology once the tool-kit had reached optimum efficiency for the way of life.

That widespread interaction between groups did lead to broad similarities in culture over large areas is suggested by the fact that British tool-making traditions developed in parallel to those on the Continent until about 6000 BC, by which time sea-level rise had severed Britain from the Continent. Thereafter the flint industries of the island and the mainland began to diverge. Much the same is true of Ireland where, after the middle of the sixth millennium, the insular Late Mesolithic communities abandoned the use of microliths in favour of larger flake tools. In this way the increasing isolation of communities along the Atlantic seaboard began to lead to the emergence of distinct regional styles.

The Riches of the Land and Sea

Western Europe in the Mesolithic period was a mosaic of microenvironments, each the result of the interaction of a number of different factors. Latitude, altitude, geology, drainage, and proximity to the ameliorating effects of the oceanic climate all had their impact. This said, certain broad zones can be defined. The most extensive, in terms of land area covered, was the mixed oak forest which extended from Iberia to southern Scandinavia.

To the south, in the Iberian Peninsula, the forest, where it existed, was dominated by pine, oak, and hazel with tracts of Mediterranean evergreens. By about 5000 BC it is likely that stands of wild cereal grasses, legumes, olives, grapes, and strawberry trees were widely to be seen. Important too were the many bulbous plants such as the onion family (*Allium* spp.), orchids, lilies, and crocuses, and plants with edible roots including *Asphodel*, *Arum*, and *Carum* which were widely distributed and locally abundant in favoured microregions like the damp intermontaine valleys. Plant food was to be had in quantity. One estimate suggests that the biomass offered some 400 edible species, of which most areas would have been able to provide 100–150. Add to this the abundance of animals—the aurochs, horses, deer, sheep, and goats—and the rich fauna of the rivers, marshes, and coasts, and the particular attractions of the varied Iberian landscapes for early foragers can be readily appreciated.

Temperate Europe, north of the Pyrenees and Alps and up to the Baltic, was blanketed in forests dominated by elm, lime, and oak but with significant stands of pine, hazel, beech, and alder. This huge deciduous forest was characterized by annual leaf loss over a period of from three to five months. Each year this leaf fall, together with crashing branches and dead trunks brought down in heavy winter winds, added to the layer of rotting organic matter creating a thick, rich humus to support an intermittent ground cover of fungi, mosses, and liverworts. Above this several 'layers' of forest extended upwards, depending in their variety on local conditions of light and shade. The field layer might contain a number of perennials as well as ferns, bracken, and bulbous plants. Above this came a shrub layer comprising bramble and other berry-producing plants, as well as hazel, while at the highest level was the forest canopy of the tall oak, elm, and ash trees. Each stratum of vegetation was rich in food resources, together offering up to 450 different species including fungi, bracken rhizomes, bulbs and tubers, a wide variety of berries, fruit and nuts, in particular hazel, acorns, and, where they occurred, beech nuts and pine kernels, together with young leaves and shoots. The rich and varied plant ecology was attractive to a great variety of animals, most particularly deer, aurochs, and boar, as well as smaller fur-bearing creatures. Nor should we forget the birds and fish that abounded in and around the rivers and lakes.

For gatherers–hunters–fishermen the temperate forests of western Europe, extending right up to the Atlantic fringes, were rich indeed. Throughout the growing season food could be picked and eaten and animals could be hunted by groups moving around a limited territory. All the local resources would have been well known and the knowledge passed from generation to generation. At the onset of winter a more sedentary existence would have prevailed. At base camps food such as roots, nuts, meat, and fish would have to be prepared for storage and stockpiled to ensure adequate supplies over the five months when the temperate ecosystem was dormant. This was a time when skins could be cleaned and prepared, and tools and weapons manufactured or repaired. The importance of plant food should not be underestimated. The long rhizomes of bracken (*Pteridium aquilinum*) provide an excellent source of stored carbohydrate and its growth is prodigious, yielding annually some 20–50 tonnes per square kilometre. Acorns and hazelnuts, which complement the diet with their high fat and protein content, can be gathered in the tens of thousands of kilograms from favoured stands in temperate forest. There is little doubt that foraging groups deliberately created clearings in the woodland canopy, probably by ring-barking and burning, to allow in light to encourage the growth of hazel. At a Mesolithic camp site at Oakhanger in the Weald the pollen sequence shows a high percentage of hazel against a background of scrub woodland vegetation of alder, lime, oak, and some elm. The site was evidently an extensive and long-lived base camp, and the suggestion that the vegetation was 'managed' to increase the yield of hazelnuts gains some support from the considerable quantity of nut shells found in contemporary archaeological layers.

The temperate deciduous forests and the Mediterranean mixed woodland were highly efficient in converting the available sunlight, through photosynthesis, into carbohydrates and in concentrating minerals and water into their plant cells, to provide a ready, balanced, food resource for herbivores. Estimates suggest that the mixed Mediterranean woodland could produce between 200 and 2,000 dry grammes of edible food per square metre per year, while for the temperate deciduous forests the figures rise to between 600 and 3,000 grammes, the difference being partly the result of the quantity of sunlight and partly the incidence of drought conditions. These edible foods were available for omniverous humans either directly from the plant or, with considerable loss of calorific value, by eating herbivores and other omnivores.

In any single ecological regime the availability of food for human foragers would have been precarious: the range of food sources was restricted, and failures in any one of them would therefore have been potentially disastrous. Thus the favoured areas for occupation would have been those where a variety of ecological zones were close enough together to be exploited by a single community. Within each of the forest zones local differences in geology or altitude or the existence of a river or lake will have offered attractive ecological variations for exploitation. But western Europe was also blessed with a long interface with the ocean. Here there was not only the littoral zone itself, with its marine shallows and continental shelf, but also the estuaries and deltas of the many rivers, and the swamps, marshes, and lagoons created in the deltas and behind the long sandbars laid down by long-shore drift. These aquatic and maritime environments were immensely productive of readily available food. The swamps and marshes could produce grasses like *Glyceria fluitans* (a kind of wild rice) and the club rush (*Scirpus lacustris*) with its highly nutritious seeds, stems, and tubers, as well as a range of other floating water plants such as the cresses, water chestnuts, and water lilies. In the more exposed littoral zone edible plants included sea parsnip, sea fennel, sea rocket, and sea kale as well, of course, as a range of delicious edible seaweeds rich in health-giving minerals. To these plant resources may be added the huge range of birds inhabiting the marshes and the estuaries, the shellfish and crustaceans, and a wide variety of fish, as well as sea mammals, notably seals and stranded whales.

The Atlantic coasts with their high tidal energy system offer a complex range of inter-tidal habitats which, combined with the benefits of the warm Gulf Stream bringing in nutrients from the ocean, create a variety of coastal habitats unsurpassed elsewhere in Europe in the richness of

4.5 The estuary of the River Léguer in the Côtes-d'Armor, Brittany at low tide. The wide sandy bay and rocky shore are rich in shellfish—a resource exploited by people living on the headland of Le Yaudet (from which the photograph is taken) throughout the prehistoric, Roman, and medieval periods.

their food resources. Add to this the many great rivers that flow into the Atlantic bringing down nutrient-rich sediments to feed their deltas, estuaries, and coastal swamps, and the unique quality of the ocean fringe begins to become apparent (4.5).

For communities whose very existence was based on gathering, fishing, and hunting the wide zone where the primeval temperate forests of the Continent met the Atlantic would have been a most congenial place to live. By its very nature the zone was highly diverse in its habitats. This diversity not only added a desirable variety to the diet but it provided an assured supply of alternative food sources should any one of them fail. The multitude of different ecological zones closely juxtaposed in this coastal region also meant that communities had no need to move far when forced by the seasons to vary their foraging regimes.

Any attempt to assess the archaeological record for this crucial four thousand years of human activity is faced with the difficulty that huge areas of the coastal zone, once available to the foragers, have now been lost because of the rise in sea-level. One of the greatest estuaries in Europe, the Thames/Rhine/Meuse/Scheldt, extending over 20,000 square miles, is now the North Sea, while the Somme / Seine / Solent estuary has become the English Channel. Ever since the Late Mesolithic period, by which time the coastline had receded to about the present 10 fathom line, large areas of the coastal zone have been lost, as the map (4.3) will amply demonstrate. Except in the north, where isostatic uplift of the land has outstripped eustatic rise in sea-level, what remains of the present coastal distribution of Mesolithic sites is only a pale reflection of what was once there. Even so, enough remains to give an idea of the character of Atlantic Mesolithic culture.

The Hunter-Gatherers of the Atlantic Fringe: Denmark, Britain, and Ireland

In Denmark a long tradition of archaeological endeavour, combined with conditions conducive to preservation, have produced an unusually full archaeological record—more detailed than for any other part of western Europe. Three broad phases can be recognized. The first, named after the site of Maglemose, lasted for about 1,500 years. The economy was based on collecting a wide variety of vegetable foods, fishing, and the hunting of elk and aurochs, with red deer, roe deer, and wild pig gaining in prominence as the period progressed. Summer camps, representing small groups about the size of single nuclear families, are found close to inland fresh water. The winter camps represented larger groups who chose higher, drier locations. Throughout this period the relative abundance of food and the improving weather conditions led to an increase in population, but after the middle of the seventh millennium several factors combined to create stress. Large game animals became less plentiful as the forest canopy became denser, affecting the availability of browse, while at the same time the rise in sea-level significantly reduced the overall land area. It was quite possibly because of this combination of factors that increasing use began to be made of coastal resources in the sixth and fifth millennia to augment the traditional woodland economy.

The sixth millennium cultural and economic developments are named after the type site of Kongemose. Two types of seasonal settlement have been identified: inland camps, set up by streams or lakes, from which the large game animals continued to be hunted; and coastal settlements, usually in sheltered bays or inshore islands providing easy access to the entire marine environment producing shellfish, fish, sea mammals, and coastal birds as well, no doubt, as the rich array of vegetable resources. Some of these coastal camps were intensively occupied by larger groups than before. How the two types of settlement articulated into a single economic system it is difficult at present to say, but it seems likely that they

4.6 The shell midden at Ertebølle, Jutland (Denmark) during the excavations of 1893–7.

represent the seasonal activities of the same social groups now utilizing a wider range of resource potentials.

By the fifth millennium a new equilibrium had been reached as the use of the coastal resource intensified and a more sedentary life-style developed. This culture is named after the site of Ertebølle. Of the different ecological zones now utilized by far the most resource-rich were the estuaries, productive enough to allow all-year-round settlement. The inland rivers and lakes were also important but on a more seasonal basis in the summer months, while the outer maritime zone of islands and peninsulas was also probably seasonally exploited. The dense inland forests were no longer a significant resource, but they were still visited by small hunting parties in search of deer, pig, and fur-bearing animals.

The change in emphasis from the forest to the coast over a period of two thousand years or so may in part have been the result of the increasing richness and diversity of the coastal environment brought about by climatic amelioration, but it may also have been a change in food-gathering strategy away from the high-risk, high-yield, high-energy-expenditure strategy of game hunting to a low-risk, moderate-yield, low-energy-expenditure strategy of gathering and collecting in the estuaries, valleys, and sheltered coasts.

The type site of Ertebølle, on Limfjord in northern Jutland, provides a fascinating insight into the economy of the period. It was first excavated in 1893–7 and re-examined in 1979–84 using a range of modern scientific methods. The most striking element of the site was a massive 'kitchen midden' composed of millions of shells interspersed with animal bones, artefacts, and hearths, covering an area of 140 by 20 metres along the contemporary shoreline to a depth of up to 2 metres (4.6). This vast mass of food debris represents occupation over a period of 700–800 years by communities who seem to have been present for most of the year. While the huge quantity of shells might at first sight suggest a large population, it is as well to remember that to match the calorific value of a single red deer carcass it would have been necessary to eat 50,000 oysters or 30,000 limpets.

The economy of the Ertebølle community was based on gathering, fishing, and hunting. The nature of the site preservation has left little trace of the vegetable component of the diet, apart from a single charred hazelnut, but the shells show that oysters, mussels, cockles, and periwinkles were a significant food source. Among the hunted food animals the most important were roe deer, red deer, and wild pig with the occasional elk and aurochs. Grey seals, swans, and ducks were also caught and so were fur-bearing animals such as wild cat, lynx, fox, otter, wolf, and pine marten. Fishing, as one might expect, was of particular importance. The sea produced cod, garfish, flounder, and herring, but what is more surprising is that freshwater species from the streams and lakes, including eel, roach, and pike, were of particular importance. Taken together the fauna from the midden shows that, while the community was exploiting a range of resources, most of the species were readily available within a radius of 5–10 kilometres from the site (4.7, 4.8).

Whilst the organic component of the archaeological record is poorly represented in dry-land sites such as Ertebølle, this was more than compensated for by the finds from the submerged site of Tybrind Vig on the western side of the Danish island of Fyn. The settlement occupied dry land, but debris from it was thrown into the nearby reedy fringes of the open water and, because of eustatic rise in sea-level, is now some 3 metres below water. Here, in addition to the food sources evident at Ertebølle, quantities of hazelnuts and acorns were also recovered, but the importance of fishing to the diet was demonstrated by the stable iso-

4.7 Bone fish hooks from the Late Mesolithic site of Tybrind Vig, Denmark.

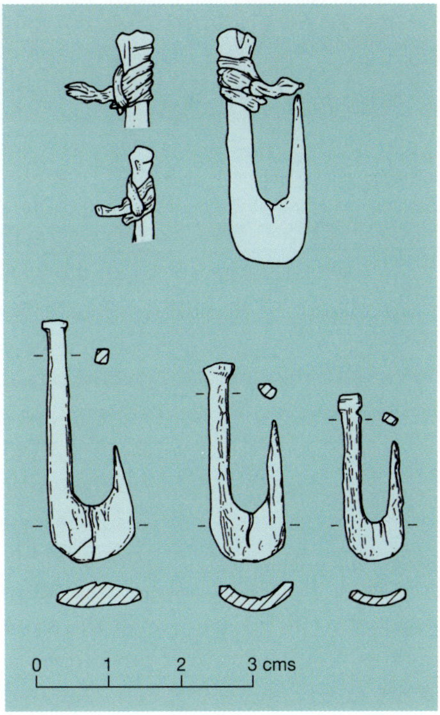

4.8 Part of a wickerwork fish trap of Mesolithic date from Agerod V, Denmark.

tope C^{13} analysis of a human burial which showed that the young female tested had lived mainly on a diet of fish, shellfish, and seal meat.

The waterlogged conditions also preserved bows and arrows suitable for stunning birds, fish-hooks and spears, ropes and woven textiles, together with two log boats—one 10 metres in length—and ten paddles of which two were decorated (4.9). Vessels of this sort were well suited to fishing at sea and in the sheltered waters around the island.

Altogether the Danish Mesolithic sites provide a remarkably full picture of the life of communities living in the maritime environment in the seventh to fifth millennia. By the end of this period population density had increased and there is convincing evidence that life was far more settled, with much of the community spending most of its time at the coastal settlements. Domesticated dogs now accompanied the foragers, while the techniques of pottery manufacture had been adopted, learned from more sedentary food-producing communities of the North European Plain to the south.

Across the rapidly extending North Sea, coastal Scotland offered a similar, though somewhat harsher environment. Mesolithic settlements are known in the valleys of the east-flowing rivers, particularly the Tweed and the Forth, and more extensively round the western coasts and islands where the culture has been named Obanian. Here, because isostatic rise of the land has outstripped the eustatic rise in sea-level, the Mesolithic occupation sites once on the shoreline are now several metres above the sea. Some of the best-studied sites are on the Western Isles of Oronsay and Jura.

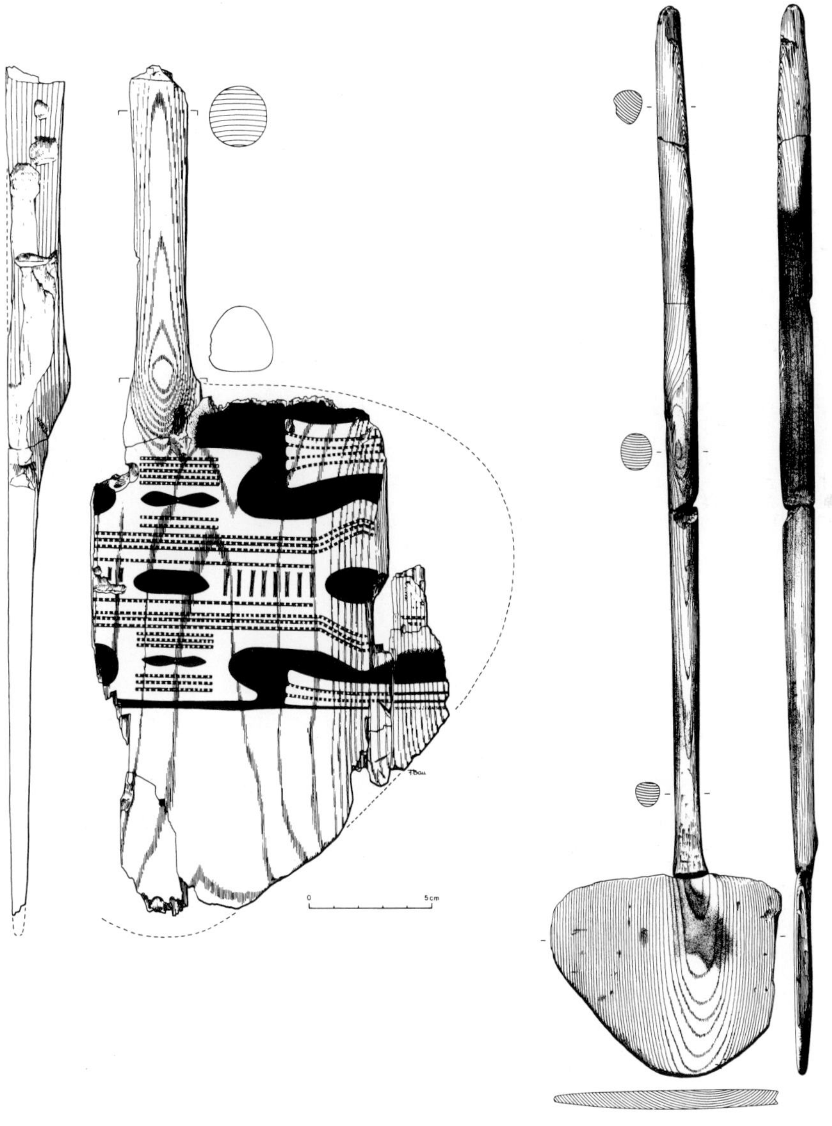

4.9 Wooden paddles from the Late Mesolithic site of Tybrind Vig, Denmark.

Oronsay, even in the Mesolithic period, was a small island of barely 5 square kilometres, yet it has produced five shell midden sites (4.10, 4.11). The middens were composed of huge quantities of mollusc shells including limpet, periwinkle, whelk, oyster, cockle, scallop, and razorshell. Fish, particularly saithe, were abundant and must have formed a major part of the diet, but land mammals and birds were scarce. Following the

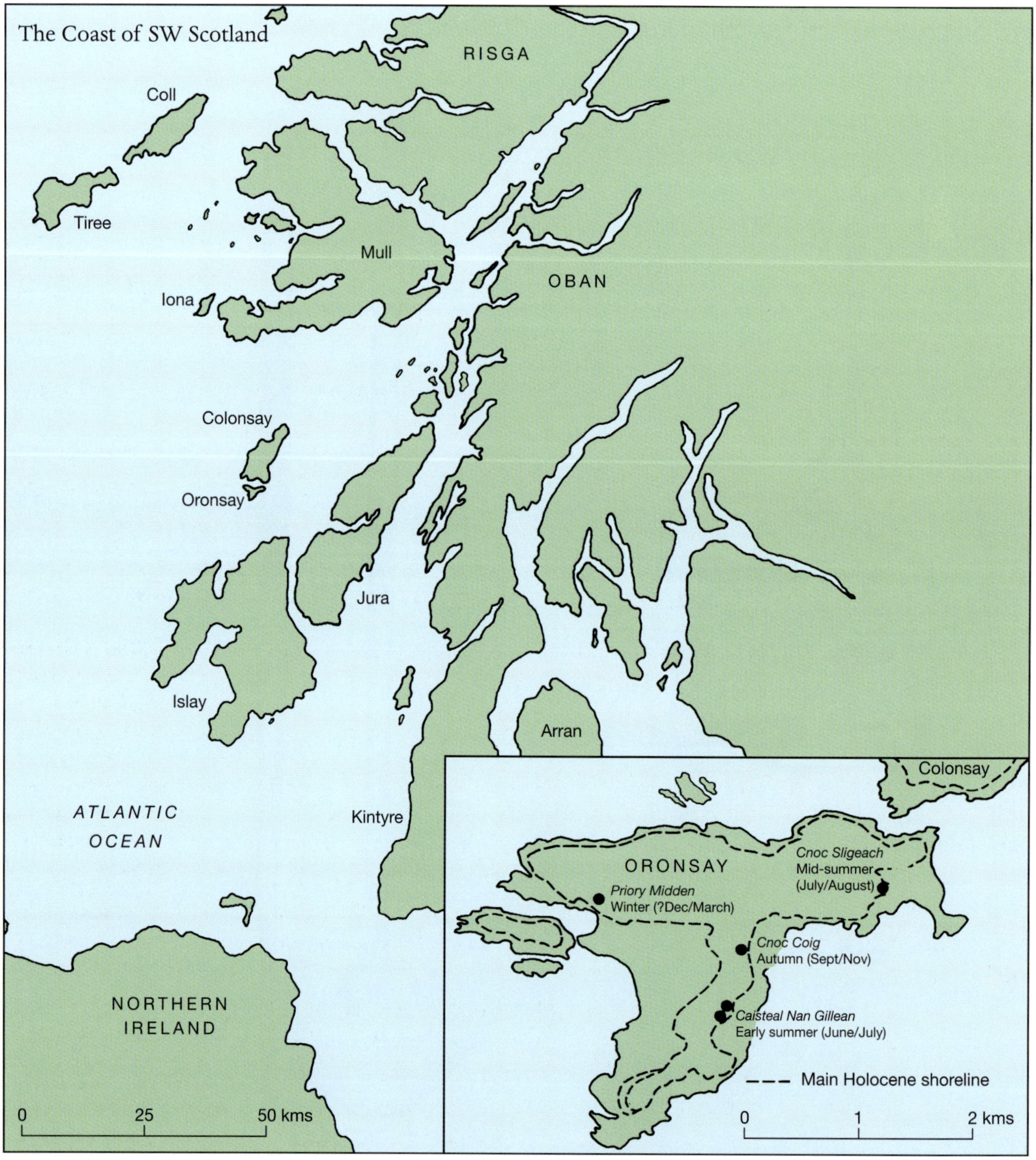

excavation a detailed analysis was carried out of the ear-bones (otoliths) of the saithe. Because the fish grows rapidly in its first two or three years the ear-bone lengthens measurably as the year progresses, and for this reason the season of kill can be estimated with some precision. This rather esoteric study has shown that the middens were all occupied at different times during the year, raising the possibility that the island might have been occupied by a single population moving around the coast as the year progressed. Another possibility is that foragers from the mainland camped at intervals throughout the year on the island for fishing expeditions, their choice of camp being conditioned by prevailing weather conditions.

Something of the richness of these island habitats is shown by the debris from the settlement on the island of Risga in the mouth of Loch Sunart in North Argyllshire. Here, in addition to the usual range of shellfish, common crab and fiddler crab were eaten, while the fish caught included tope, spiny dogfish, angel fish, skate, thornback ray, conger eel,

4.11 The island of Oronsay from the air. The northern part is rocky but the south-eastern parts are covered by deposits of blown sand. The rock outcrops of the intertidal zone provided an ideal habitat for molluscs and crustaceans.

4.10 (*facing*) The coast of south-west Scotland locating the Mesolithic sites of Oronsay, Risga, Oban. *Inset*: the island of Oronsay, showing the four seasonal fishing camps in relation to the contemporary Mesolithic shore line.

4.12 The Early Mesolithic site at Mount Sandel in Northern Ireland. The post-holes and stake-holes of a large timber structure can be clearly seen cut into the natural bedrock.

grey mullet, haddock, and black sea-bream. The birds eaten included great auk, gannet, goose, cormorant, shag, red-breasted merganser, water rail, gull, tern, razorbill, and guillemot. Common seal and grey seal were also caught, and other meat sources included red deer and wild pig. Together with locally available vegetable foods the inhabitants enjoyed a rich and varied diet gleaned from their maritime habitat. Those communities of the littoral, who were able to exploit the sea and the land, need not have travelled far in search of food.

In Ireland the known Early Mesolithic sites are most numerous in the north-west in coastal locations and clustering along the valley of the River Bann. The best-known of these sites is Mount Sandel situated on a bluff overlooking the river. Here at least four huts were identified each about 6 metres in diameter and framed with stakes over which skins or vegetable material would have been draped to provide protection from the weather (4.12). A careful analysis of the copious food remains suggests that the settlement was occupied throughout the year: large quantities of salmon bones point to summer fishing, while the many young pigs found were butchered in the winter. Quantities of hazelnuts, water lily seeds, wild pear, and crab apple reflect autumn gathering and storage. Taken together the faunal and floral assemblage suggests that a foraging band used Mount Sandel as its permanent base camp but ranged wide over a radius of about 10 kilometres (two hours' walking). Within this territory they would have been able to exploit the river valley, the estuary, and the coast.

After the middle of the sixth millennium, by which time Ireland had been severed from Britain, the implement technology began to rely on the use of flint blades rather than microliths. In this later period large numbers of coastal shell middens developed, suggesting perhaps that here, as in Denmark, a greater reliance was now being placed on maritime resources. Some of these middens were massive. One, at Sutton, Co. Dublin, reached as much as 100 metres in length, while at others, like Dalkey Island, Co. Dublin, occupation continued over a long period of time. The majority of the Irish Mesolithic sites were so sited that they could exploit coastal or estuarine environments, but a significant number relied wholly on the resources of rivers or lakes.

Many of the foraging communities of Ireland will have continued their traditional food-gathering activities long after food-production techniques of the Neolithic period had been introduced. In the fourth millennium, at Ferriter's Cove on the Dingle peninsula, a small community managed to eke out a living clinging to the cliff edge (4.13). They hunted pig, caught sea fish by long line or net, and collected molluscs, mainly limpets, but they were in contact, however distant, with farmers who reared cattle and made polished stone axes. Perhaps they were living in some form of symbiotic relationship with these settled agriculturalists, but it is equally possible that the foraging community was now beginning to adopt aspects of the Neolithic food-producing package which was being established at this time along the Atlantic seaways.

Moving now to southern Britain, a far greater density of material makes the situation appear to be more complex, but an analysis of the stone assemblage has allowed two broad 'social territories' to be identified, a South-Western and a South-Eastern. The South-Western covers what is now Cornwall, Devon, and Dorset. Here the distribution of sites is predominantly coastal, occupying the present clifftops along both the Atlantic and English Channel coasts, but there are significant concentrations of finds on the upland granite massifs of Dartmoor, Bodmin Moor, and St Austell. The economy of the coastal sites involved, as might be expected, the exploitation of the maritime environment. At Westward Ho! on the north Devon coast shellfish (oyster, mussel, limpet, whelk, and dog whelk) were common, but red deer, roe deer, aurochs, and wild

4.13 Ferriters Cove on the Dingle peninsula in the south-west of Ireland was the site of a Mesolithic hunters' camp. The resources of the sea were extensively exploited.

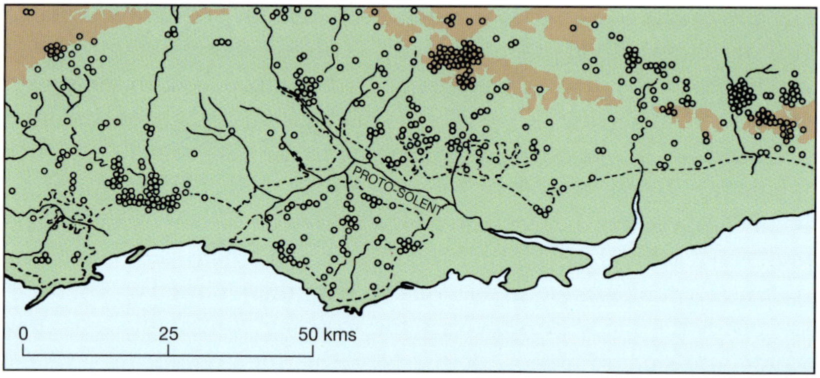

4.14 Mesolithic settlement in the Solent region in relation to the contemporary coastline showing how much of the coastal zone has been lost to the rising sea-level.

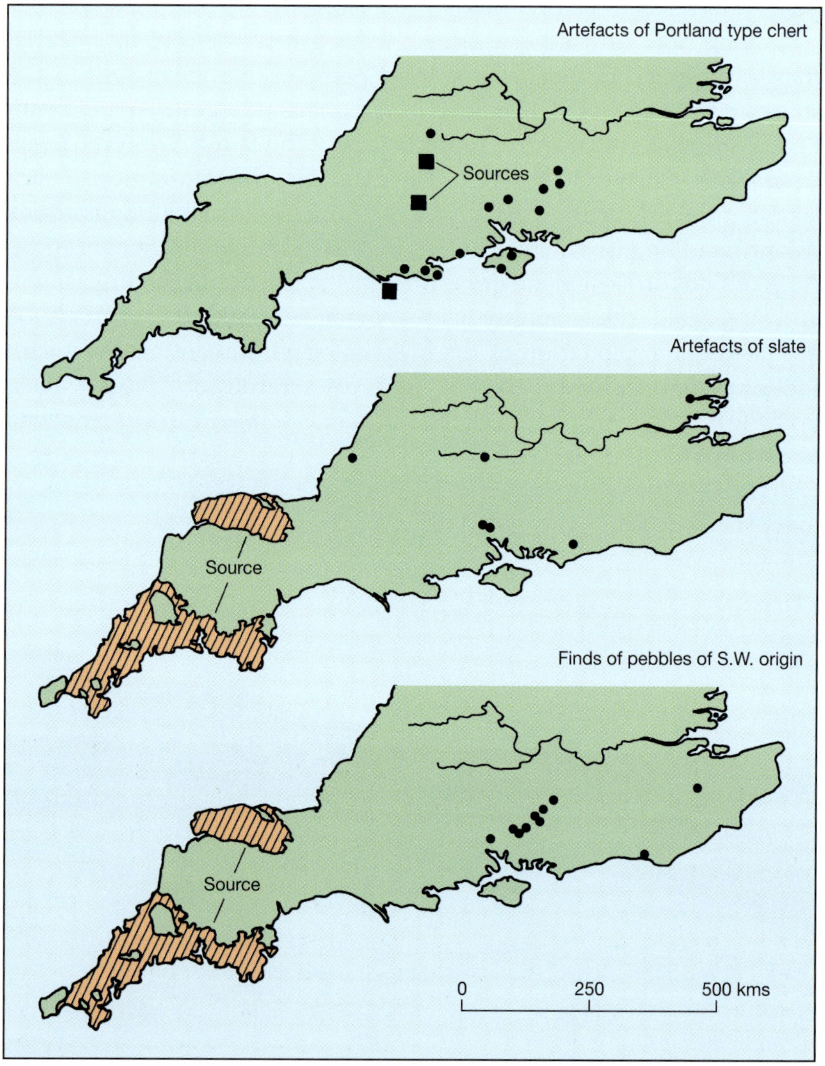

4.15 The distribution of stone artefacts well outside their zones of production provides evidence for the patterns of exchange between Mesolithic communities in southern Britain.

pig indicate the importance of hunting in the hinterland. The large settlement at Culver Well on the Isle of Portland produced thick layers of limpet and winkle, together with hearths and stone floors suggestive of permanent structures. On the granite uplands the acid soil conditions are destructive of animal bones and shells, making any estimate of the economic base of these settlements difficult, but the fact that most of the flint used here derives from beach pebbles and the close typological similarities of both upland and coastal tool assemblages would argue in favour of the two habitats being used at different times during the year by the same foraging communities.

The South-Eastern 'social territory' is more difficult to assess because the rise in sea-level has drowned considerable tracts of Mesolithic coastal plain (4.14) and the wide estuary of the Solent/Arun, once a prime resource, is now completely submerged. Altogether a strip of between 10 and 20 kilometres has been lost, but what does emerge is the very considerable density of settlements on the lighter soils of the sands of the Hampshire basin and the Weald, on the more exposed chalk downs, and along the gravel of the river valleys. Presumably, in these distributions, we are seeing only one element of the foraging system that will once have included the intensive use of the littoral and the estuaries.

The picture which is beginning to emerge, then, for both the South-East and the South-West is of the utilization of a range of resources by foraging bands within a seasonal pattern of movement, some groups from the bands working more distant territories while others enjoyed a more restricted foraging from the base camps. In such a system some bands may have combined with 'foreign' bands at certain times during the year. At such times gifts may have been exchanged. It was probably by this kind of social interaction that exotic materials such as Portland chert, slate, or pebbles from the south-west peninsula were moved over considerable distances across 'social territorial' divides (4.15).

The Hunter-Gatherers of the Atlantic Fringes: Brittany and Iberia

Comparatively few Mesolithic sites have been found in Brittany, and of those that have by far the largest number are coastal, occupying promontories, clifftops, and islands (4.16). Even allowing that the sea-level was lower at the time, these sites can all be regarded as being within the maritime zone. Five of the known Mesolithic settlements were substantial shell middens: La Pointe de la Torche in the bay of Audierne; Hoëdic and Téviec now on islands off the coast of Morbihan; Beg-er-Vil on the Quiberon peninsula; and St Gildas close to the mouth of the Loire. The shell midden at Téviec covered some 200 square metres and is up to 1 metre thick; that at Hoëdic occupied much the same area but was only 30–40 centimetres. The midden at La Pointe de la Torche was about half the area of the others but had accumulated to a depth of 1 metre and contained a number of hearths throughout its thickness. These known sites can only be a pale reflection of the many that must have been inundated or eroded away by rising sea-level.

The middens at Téviec and Hoëdic were extensively explored earlier this century. In addition to the huge quantities of shellfish and fish, meat was supplied by wild pigs and red deer, with smaller quantities of roe deer. Whales and seals are also represented, while birds included duck, guillemot, razorbill, and stork (all from Téviec). Other animals, such as marten, beaver, fox, and wild cat, were probably hunted for their furs. Plant materials are not well represented but included wild pear and hazel-

4.16 Late Mesolithic sites in the Bay of Quiberon, Brittany, in relation to the Mesolithic and Early Neolithic sea-levels.

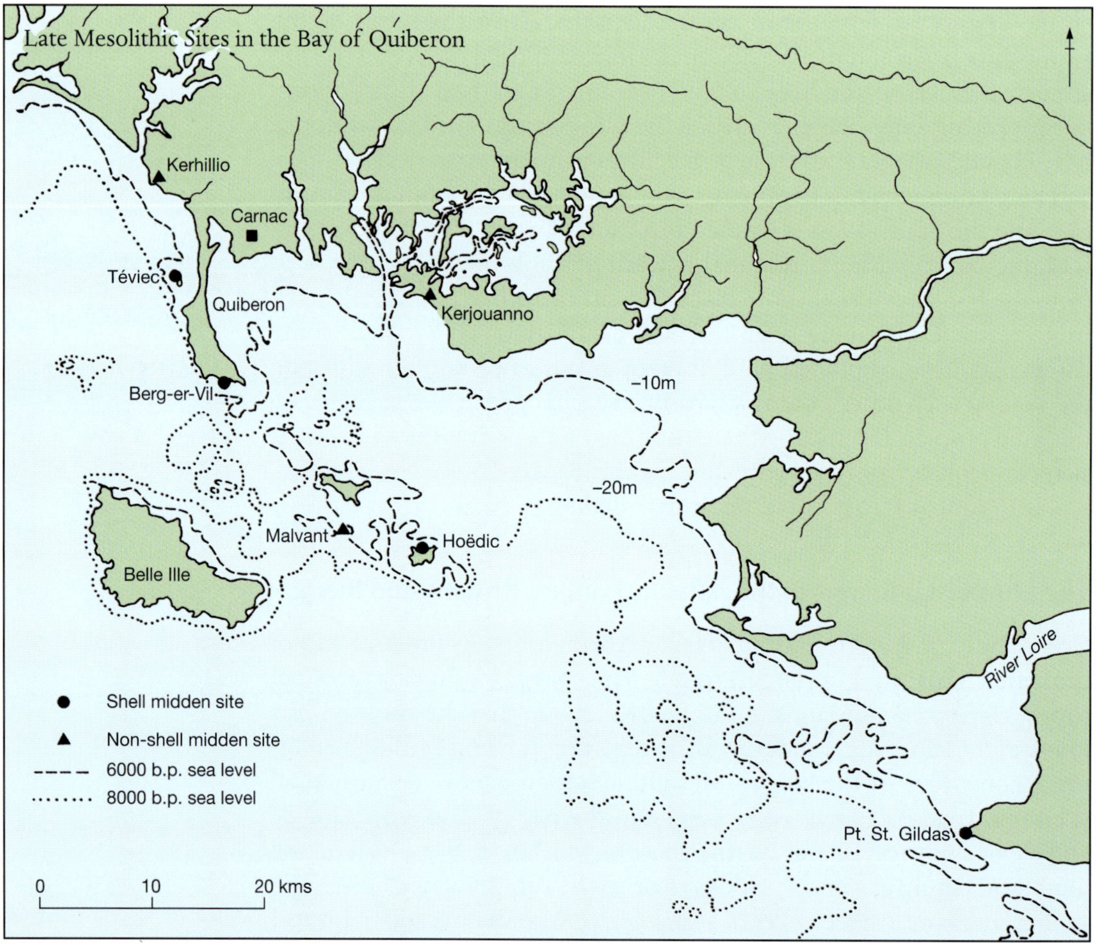

4.17 Painted pebbles from the Mesolithic site of Mas d'Azil in southern France (Musée Nationale, St-Germain-en-Laye, Paris).

nuts. The general range of species represented is very similar to the other sites we have considered in Ireland, Scotland, and Denmark and takes with it the implication that these middens may well have been occupied throughout the year by communities working a territory up to 10 kilometres or so in diameter but with a strong emphasis on the coastal resources. The communities had domesticated dogs, and a single tooth of sheep/goat, claimed to have come from Téviec, may suggest contact with distant farming groups. Both sites produced human burials, but these will be considered in more detail below.

In Iberia two separate cultures with an Atlantic coastal distribution have been identified. The Azilian culture covers much of the northern coast of the Peninsula extending into the Cantabrian Mountains and the Pyrenees, while the Asturian extends along the entire north and west coasts. It is generally agreed that the Azilian culture (4.17) was a late development from the rich Upper Palaeolithic Magdalenian culture of southern France and northern Spain, now best known for its famous painted caves. For this reason the Azilian is often presented, somewhat unfairly, as a pale reflection of former glories, when really it is better considered to be an efficient adaptation to rapidly changing environmental conditions following the end of the Ice Age. Azilian communities spread from the coastal zone to the highlands and made use of a wide variety of game animals, in upland regions concentrating on the ibex.

The far more extensive Asturian culture overlapped in time with the Azilian and appears to have been more restricted in the ecological niche which it occupied, being primarily a lowland estuarine and coastal culture focusing on the hunting of red deer, roe deer, and wild pig. Along the north and west coasts of Iberia settlements occur in some number, quite often taking the form of considerable shell middens. These settlements are particularly prolific along the ocean fringe in northern Portugal between the Lima and Minho. Among the artefacts recovered is a range of simple fishing weights fashioned by notching a flat pebble. Comparison with modern examples used in the region today suggests that one type would have been useful for drag-nets while another was better adapted for line fishing. If used in this way a rich haul of bass, mackerel, sardines, whiting, tuna, and conger eel could have been won to supplement shellfish.

In central and southern Portugal it is possible to distinguish between an Early Mesolithic dating to about 8000–6000 BC and a Later Mesolithic which lasted until about 4500 BC. The earlier sites tended to be small, scattered, and had a predominantly coastal distribution, but by the Later Mesolithic three very distinct clusters can be identified focused on the estuaries of the Tagus, Sado, and Mira (4.18).

The Muge sites of the Tagus are best known for the enormous shell middens which developed as the result of prolonged use and for the large number of human skeletons buried at different times within the middens. Scientific analysis of some of the skeletons, using stable isotope analysis, suggests that the diet was balanced between terrestrial and aquatic resources, and this is borne out by the food debris found in the mounds.

Besides the usual remains of shellfish, crustaceans, and fish, bones of wild boar, red deer, and aurochs were found. The size of the middens varied, but some are up to 100 metres across and several metres high, strongly suggesting prolonged year-round occupation by resident communities well adapted to utilizing the rich estuarine resources. The fact that 300 or more human skeletons have been found at various levels is another indication of social stability and an attitude to the mound itself seen, perhaps, as a symbol of group strength and tradition.

Further south in the inner estuary of the Sado a cluster of similar shell middens has been found which together have produced a hundred burials. The analysis of the faunal remains indicates some element of specialization in the collecting strategies, suggesting that, while some of the sites were the home base camps, others may have been more specialized camps from which specific resources were procured. Much the same system seems to have been in operation in the estuary of the Mira. Here the site of Fiais, 20 kilometres inland from the river mouth, was evidently a permanently occupied settlement to which many other foodstuffs were brought and where the community lived and worked in designated activity areas. One of the subsidiary sites, Vidijal, lay 30 kilometres to the north. The predominance of molluscs and rarity of animal bones suggested to the excavator that it may have been a specialized camp concentrating on exploiting a limited food resource.

These central and southern Portuguese sites, with their three geographically distinct clusterings, each focused on a major estuary, imply that the Late Mesolithic systems were strongly territorial and had developed a high degree of social and economic stability.

In this somewhat lengthy discussion of the different coastal communities

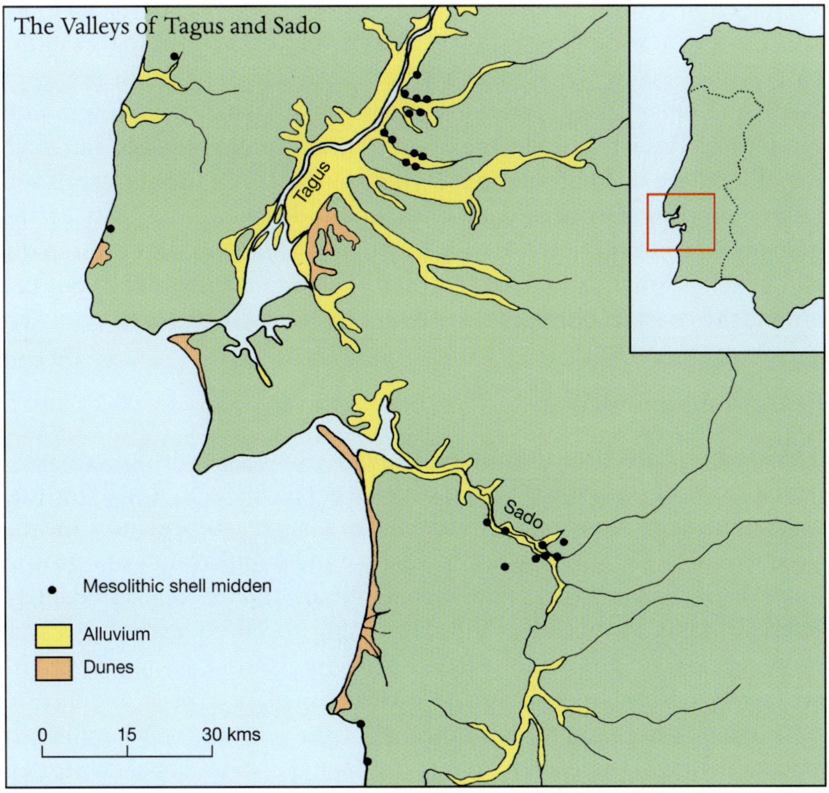

4.18 The valleys of the Tagus and Sado and the adjacent Portuguese coast showing the distribution of the Mesolithic shell midden sites clustering close to the valley edges.

we have emphasized the economic base underpinning the disparate social groups. Although there are recognizable differences in implement typology, what stands out are the considerable similarities in the general way of life of these foragers. They were people of the ocean fringe, and as such they were privileged by what the sea had to provide. The littoral zone, with its many estuaries and marshes, created a myriad of microenvironments offering a broadly-based resource potential. From the coastal base camps the river valleys and forests of the hinterland and the open sea could be accessed and utilized. If any one source of food temporarily failed there were others to rely on. Such was the stability which this rare interface offered that life could take on a more sedentary style and the population could begin to grow. By the fifth millennium a stage had been reached when more formal social behaviour begins to become evident, manifest in the archaeological record by careful burial reflecting the status of the individual.

To what extent similarity in culture over large areas implied long-distance movement of people is debatable, but that there were colonizing movements into territories previously uninhabited is clear. Communities must have moved north, as the forest and its wildlife spread, to colonize what had once been tundra, but these movements were probably gradual, like the inexorable flow of the rising sea-level. Archaeologists in the past, impressed by the similarities between Azilian harpoon points in Iberia and Obanian examples from western Scotland, once toyed with the idea of Azilian 'colonization' along the Atlantic seaways, but such hypotheses are no longer seriously entertained. Given the density of settlement in these favoured coastal regions and the local mobility of the individual communities, it is easy to see how ideas could spread rapidly and beneficial innovations be accepted. The broad similarity of culture among the coastal communities is better explained in this way.

Expressions and Beliefs

The extent to which a community defines its identity, to distinguish itself from others, depends on the need which it perceives to do so. All the time that populations were sparsely scattered in a largely empty landscape the need would be slight, but as sea-levels rose and populations grew groups more often came into contact with neighbours and the need for identity, boundaries, and procedures for articulating social interaction became more necessary. How this social behaviour translates into tangible, archaeologically recognizable data varies from place to place and time to time. Among the Atlantic communities of the seventh to fifth millennia evidence is slight. Artefact typology can hint at distinct social territories.

It allows, for example, a distinction to be made between South-West and South-East Britain. At a much more local scale, in the late Ertebølle culture of eastern Zealand, different styles of flake axe manufacture define three distinct coastal territories, each about 30 kilometres across. The axe forms were quite possibly seen to be symbolic of different social allegiances. Adjacent social groups would, however, need to develop mechanisms of communication, such as gift exchange, to allow a degree of harmony to be maintained. The distribution, in the South-Eastern territory of southern Britain, of the slate artefacts and whetstones derived from the South-West may be the tangible result of such exchanges.

Of the many ways in which social groups may choose to display their identities, style of artefact and decoration are the most frequently used. One has only to look at the enormously rich visual culture of the Nootka and Kwakiutl, sedentary foragers living on the north-west Pacific coast of what is now Canada, to see what a vital part images—painted, woven, and carved—played in publicly defining social identity. It is not unreasonable to suppose that the foragers of the north-west Atlantic coast also had a rich visual culture. Tantalizing glimpses of it survive in a few carved bones, like the decorated antler from Sjöholmen in southern Sweden (4.19), and the more simply decorated bone pin from Beg-er-Vil in Brit-

4.19 An elaborately decorated red deer antler from the Mesolithic site of Sjöholmen in southern Sweden.

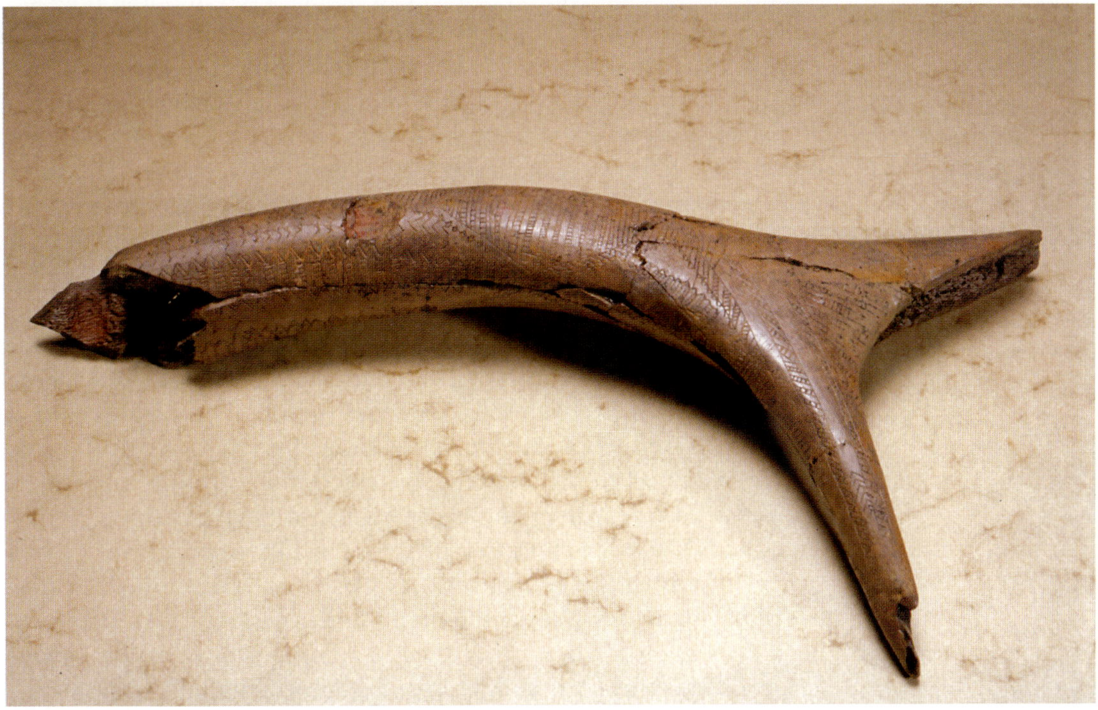

tany. But it is the wooden paddle from Tybrind Vig (4.9), intricately carved and inlaid with a brown substance, that gives an idea of how visually exciting may have been the everyday cultural environment in which the foragers lived. Nor should we forget the use of pigment, reflected now only in the painted pebbles of the Azilian culture of the Pyrenees. These simple artefacts show that standardized combinations of motifs were created in colour. Pigment could also be used in body decoration, widely adopted by human groups in many parts of the world to define group identity and individual status.

It is among the foraging groups of the Atlantic coasts that careful burial in cemeteries first becomes evident in Europe. Cemeteries have been excavated in the Ertebølle culture of Denmark and southern Sweden, the Armorican Mesolithic, and the Concheiros or Mugien culture in the Lisbon region of Portugal. All the major cemeteries known are found in the coastal zone associated with shell middens. The cemeteries vary considerably in size. At Cabeço da Arrunda, near Lisbon at least 175 individuals have been identified; at Skateholm in Denmark there are eighty-six and at Téviec in the Morbihan twenty-three. In other examples only one or two individuals have been found, but it should be remembered that the number of bodies recovered is often a factor of the extent of the archaeological deposit excavated.

The considerable variety which can be observed in burial practices reflects both the varied belief systems and social practices of the different groups and also changes in ritual through time. For the most part (though not invariably) the bodies were buried in single graves which, after filling, were left undisturbed. Occasionally several bodies were interred together. At Skateholm I an elderly male was buried with a young female, while at Tybrind Vig a teenage girl was accompanied by a newborn infant. The Armorican cemeteries of Téviec and Hoëdic were rather different. At Téviec the twenty-three bodies were found in ten individual graves, seven of the ten graves containing more than one individual. At Hoëdic the fourteen bodies occupied nine graves. At both sites the multiple burials were not contemporary interments—the graves were in reality collective tombs used over a period of time, each new interment causing some disturbance to earlier burials. Grave K at Téviec, which contained six individuals, was associated with a hearth which appears to have been lit on successive occasions, quite possibly each time a new body was laid to rest. One of the individuals in the grave, a young man who had been killed by arrows (two of which were embedded in his backbone) was given special treatment in that his body was in a stone-lined depression and was not disturbed when new bodies were added. The collective burial rite and the use of stone-lined tombs at the Morbihan cemeteries in the second half of the sixth millennium is of particular interest when we come to consider the development of the megalithic collective tombs in Armorica in the fifth millennium (below, p. 145 ff).

Many of the burials in the Atlantic coastal cemeteries were provided with grave goods, most usually personal ornaments such as perforated shells, animals' teeth, stone pendants, bone pins, and so on. Variation in the 'richness', that is, the number and variety of the placed objects, may be taken to indicate differences in status (4.20, 4.21, 4.22). At Téviec it was possible to distinguish patterns suggesting that gender and age influenced quantity and type of grave goods, but what was most interesting was the observation that at both Téviec and Hoëdic some of the children were buried with elaborate ritual and 'rich' goods. The implication here is that status could be acquired through birth: in other words, the society had become sufficiently complex to have developed a system of hereditary inequality.

While there were differences in ritual between the coastal cemeteries there are also some remarkable similarities. Red ochre was spread over some of the bodies in Denmark, Morbihan, and Portugal, while at Skateholm, Bogebakken, Téviec, and Hoëdic individuals were accompanied by collections of red deer antlers.

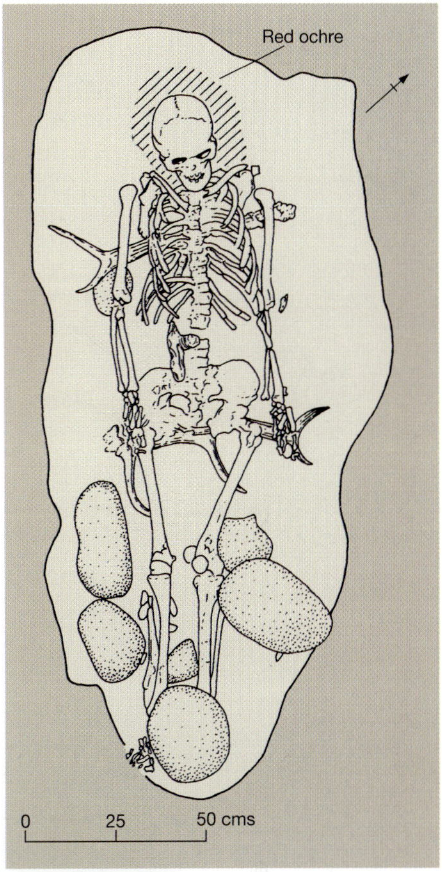

4.21 (*above*) Burial of an adult male from the Mesolithic cemetery at Vedbaek, Zealand (Denmark). The body lies on two red deer antlers and has red ochre pigment around its head.

4.20 (*left*) Reconstruction of a burial from the Mesolithic shell midden on the island of Hoëdic in the Bay of Quiberon in southern Brittany. The burial, a double interment of a female and child, dates to *c*.4600 BC.

Clearly these patterns of behaviour must reflect deeply-held beliefs extending across very considerable areas. What they mean is now beyond recovery, but it is tempting to think that those individuals graced with sets of antlers may have been the shamans who acted as intermediaries between the social group and the spirits.

4.22 Burial of a female and child from the Mesolithic cemetery at Vedbaek, Zealand, Denmark. Beside the skull of the adult are many teeth of red deer and pig, possibly from a necklace. The grave also contains much red ochre pigment.

Standing back from the detail, what is clear is that the Atlantic coastal cemeteries known to us (surely only a very pale reflection of those that once existed) demonstrate that a high degree of social complexity had been reached along the ocean fringe by the fifth millennium. Nothing like it is known in any preceding period anywhere in Europe. Such complexity developed over a long period of time as the population increased and foraging regimes evolved to maximize use of the resource base. Those communities who controlled the littoral with its adjacent sea and forest were privileged. They were able to become increasingly sedentary, and with that came the inevitable progression towards more complex social behaviour.

It is no accident that the earliest organized cemeteries were located in areas where the marine environment was most extensively exploited.

Before leaving this theme we must briefly consider the intriguing question of whether or not the foraging communities created monuments. To some extent the cemeteries themselves are monuments in that they are spaces endowed with the power of ancestors. The creation of mounds over some of the burials at Téviec may be considered to be among the first physical constructions erected to monumentalize a concept. How much else of this kind has been lost to us we will never know, but one example will suffice as a reminder. When the car park at Stonehenge was being extended a row of three large pits, each 1.5–2 metres in diameter and up to 1.3 metres deep, were found. Each had held a large, upright pine-tree trunk three-quarters of a metre in diameter. Dating evidence suggested that the posts were erected in the second half of the eighth millennium BC, and pollen analyses showed that at the time the landscape was covered by a forest dominated by birch and pine. These three timbers (and there may be more) represent the first truly monumental structure of the Mesolithic period known to us. What form they took (carved totem poles perhaps?) and the reason for their erection we will never know, but the Stonehenge timber alignment is unlikely to be unique.

The Arrival of Agri-Pastoralism

The three thousand years from 7000 to 4000 BC saw the gradual introduction over most of Europe of techniques of food production. The two most dramatic aspects of this spread were the establishment of settlements, often villages, occupied over long periods of time, and the gradual opening up of the primeval forest cover as land was brought into cultivation. The origins of the innovations, constituting what is traditionally called a Neolithic economy, lay in the Near East. Geography suggests, and archaeology confirms, that the first part of peninsular Europe to adopt the new subsistence package was Greece and the Balkans, from where the practice of food production spread, in the south via the Mediterranean and in the north by means of the Danube valley and the other great rivers of the North European Plain. By what actual mechanisms knowledge of food-producing techniques spread, whether by migrating populations or the copying of innovations by indigenous populations, has to be debated area by area in the light of the detailed archaeological evidence. It is, however, agreed that the processes were complex and, for much of Europe, are still rather ill-defined.

The 'Neolithic package' involved the growing of cereal crops and the care of domesticated flocks and herds. The most widely used cereals were varieties of wheat and barley which were not native to Europe and had therefore to be brought in from the Near East. The principal domesticated animals were ovicarps (sheep and goats), cattle, and pigs. Wild cattle and pig already roamed the European forests and, as we have seen, featured largely in the diets of the foraging indigenes, but the domesticated varieties were so different that there can be little doubt that they too were introduced from the Near East. Rather more uncertainty attaches to the ovicarps. Although the majority opinion regards them, too, as an eastern import, there is a possibility that colonies of sheep may have survived the last glacial episode in favoured niches in the west Mediterranean and might therefore have been available to communities of hunter-gatherers in Iberia and southern France. Two technological innovations which frequently, though not invariably, accompanied the food-producing economies were the use of pottery and the polishing of stone, usually to make axes.

Before beginning to consider the spread of agri-pastoral regimes to the Atlantic region it is necessary to say a little about the two principal routes by which the new technologies flowed westwards across Europe.

The spread of Neolithic economies throughout the Mediterranean is not particularly well understood, but it is possible that different aspects of the package spread separately and at different rates (4.23). The characteristic earliest pottery, known as 'Cardial Ware' because it is usually decorated with the impressed edge of the *cardium* shell, has been found in Italy, the Mediterranean coast of France, and southern Spain in contexts dating to the early seventh millennium (4.24), but in none of these early sites has any trace of cereal-growing or of domesticated animals, other than sheep, been identified. If the sheep were indeed indigenous, as some scholars argue, then these sites may be the settlements of local hunter-gatherers adopting pottery manufacture, much as the Ertebølle communities did in the north, and beginning to domesticate the flocks of wild sheep with which they would already have been familiar. Gradually, as

4.23 The spread of Neolithic 'farming' economies across Europe from the initial farming zone in the Balkans. The Linear Bandkeramik spread across the löessic soils while the Impressed ware groups appear to have spread largely by sea.

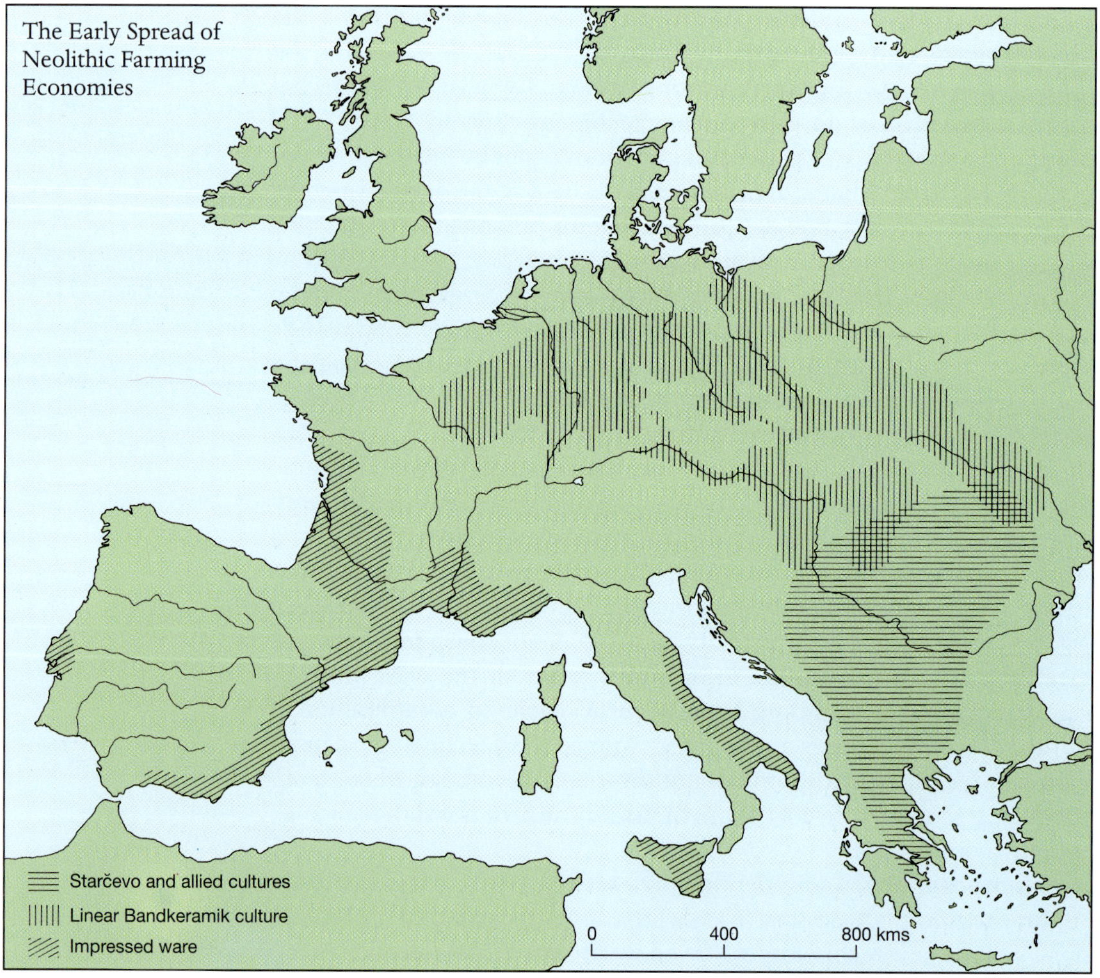

maritime contacts with the central and eastern Mediterranean developed, cereals were introduced and by 5300 BC emmer, einkorn, club wheat, and naked six-row barley were being grown in eastern Iberia. The period from 5500 to 4500 BC saw the spread of Cardial pottery to the Atlantic coasts of Iberia and France. In all probability the technology spread by a variety of routes, by sea through the Straits of Gibraltar and across France by way of the Garonne. The earliest dates in Portugal are 6000–5500 BC and in western France *c.*5500 BC.

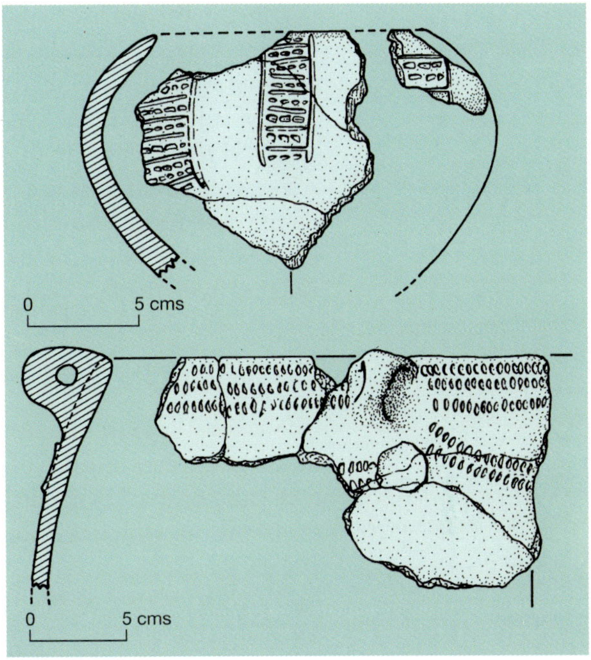

4.24 Cardial ware vessels from Gruta do Caldeirão, Tomar, Portugal. The site is a cave dominating the valley of the Nabão, a tributary of the Tagus.

The progress of the Neolithic economy westwards through temperate Europe has been extensively researched. Neolithic communities were well established in the middle Danube valley and the Hungarian Plain by the middle of the sixth millennium, but expansion beyond this does not appear to have begun until after 5500 BC, significantly later than the initial Cardial ware expansion to the western Mediterranean and west Europe, but once under way movement was rapid, reaching northern France, southern Belgium, the Netherlands, and the North European Plain by 5000 BC. The speed with which these pioneer horticultural groups were able to spread through the forested loess lands of middle Europe was remarkable. It may, in no small part, have been aided by the sparseness of the foraging population. The forests of the loess were dense, and over very large areas supported insufficient biodiversity to attract hunter-gatherers. For horticulturalists ready to ring-bark ancient trees and to burn undergrowth, allowing the ash to fertilize the soil, the old forest was a congenial zone to colonize. By 5000 BC huge tracts of Europe from the Vistula to the Seine had been settled by communities living in well-built timber longhouses, equipped with the general-purpose polished-stone 'shoe-last' adze and using distinctive round-bottomed pottery decorated with incised lines or dots arranged in spirals or meander patterns. It is this pottery which gives the culture its archaeological name—the Linear pottery, or Bandkeramik, culture.

Thus by the end of the sixth millennium BC the hunter-gatherer communities of the Atlantic zone had begun to come into contact with immigrant groups who herded domesticated animals and grew crops. Those occupying the Atlantic coasts from the Straits of Gibraltar to the Loire estuary shared a broadly similar tradition of cardial-impressed pottery which may well have been learnt from the farming communities of the Midi of southern France and the Spanish Levante. To the north, from the Seine to the Baltic the linear pottery groups had expanded to within 100–200 kilometres of the coast. Between the Loire and the Seine the situation was more complex and influences from both groups have been claimed. Across the Channel, Britain and Ireland were still, at this stage, isolated from the fast-changing European scene.

The Western Shores of Iberia

The coastal region of Portugal from Sagres to Cape Modego has produced a number of finds of the Earliest Neolithic cardial-impressed pottery, but comparatively little is yet known of the contexts, cultural and economic, to which the pottery belongs. The general similarity of these vessels to those found in Neolithic contexts in the western Mediterranean has led to the belief that there were seaborne movements of people from the Mediterranean bringing with them domesticated animals and seed corn as well as the technical knowledge to make pots and polish stone: the nature of the distribution would certainly tend to support this. The Latest Mesolithic sites, as we saw, concentrated in the valleys of the Tagus, the Sado, and the Mira. The Earliest Neolithic sites avoid these regions and, as far as one can judge from the limited data so far available, seem to concentrate on the land between the densely settled Mesolithic territories. There is a particular emphasis on the northern Extremadura, between the Tagus and Mondejo rivers, where a cluster of sites producing the earliest Cardial pottery has been located. It is tempting to see this as an enclave of early agri-pastoralists establishing themselves in a distinct niche between the successful hunter-gatherer groups of the Tagus, Sado, and Mira estuaries and the Asturian Mesolithic settlements of Cantabria. Radiocarbon dates for the earliest Cardial pottery suggest that the Neolithic colonists were established between 6000 and 5500 BC.

From the northern Extremadura enclave elements of the Neolithic 'cultural package' seem to have been adopted by the hunter-gatherers to the south some time around 5000 BC. At first much of the traditional Mesolithic culture was retained. At Vale Pincel, in the Alentejo, the lithic industry was still dominated by microliths, but gradually as the food-producing economy took root the artefacts of the Neolithic package became more prolific. The occupants of the later site of Salema, also in the Alentejo, had access to large numbers of polished stone axes as well as quern stones for grinding corn.

For convenience this period can be referred to as Neolithic I. The following period (Neolithic II), dating from about 4800 to 3400 BC, saw the appearance of a range of stone-built 'megalithic' tombs clustering in the coastal region of the Alentejo, particularly around the Tagus estuary, and the Algarve with an inland group in Extremadura. Although a great variety of tomb type is evident there are three basic styles: simple dolmens, passage graves, and rock-cut tombs. On present evidence the passage graves, such as Gorginos and Poço da Gateria in the valley of the Guadiana, are the earliest, with thermoluminescent dates around 4500 BC. Dolmens like Carapito and Seixas are dated later by radiocarbon, to about 3800 BC, but until far more sites have been securely dated too much significance should not be placed on the precise dates or implied sequence. What is important is the fact that megalithic tombs were being constructed in the area as early as the fifth millennium. As we will see, the same phenomenon was happening in Armorica at about the same time.

It was for some time believed that the Portuguese megaliths were introduced from the Mediterranean, but radiocarbon chronology has shown that this is most unlikely to be the case. In all probability the communal burials of the Neolithic period developed locally from the complex funerary traditions of the preceding Mesolithic.

North-Western France

In western France a cluster of sites producing cardial ware and occupying the maritime zone between the Gironde and the Loire has yielded radiocarbon dates within the bracket 5500–4500 BC, that is, broadly similar to the Portuguese sites (4.25). Further inland, in the valleys of the rivers flowing from the edge of the Massif Central to the Garonne, a rather different kind of impressed pottery has been identified and named after the site of Roucadour in the Lot valley. While the radiocarbon dates cover a somewhat wider bracket, from *c.*6800 to 4800 BC, the Roucadian group is probably best regarded as a regional variant of the Atlantic Cardial culture.

Cereal grains, grindstones, pottery, and the bones of domesticated sheep, cattle, and pig found in the western French sites are sufficient to show that elements of the 'Neolithic package' were being absorbed by local communities in the late sixth millennium. The predominance of microlith flintwork made in the traditional manner, however, suggests that the indigenous population remained dominant. In the pre-Neolithic period there is some evidence to show that well-established links existed between the hunter-gatherer groups of southern France and those of west central France by way of the Garonne valley. It may be that social

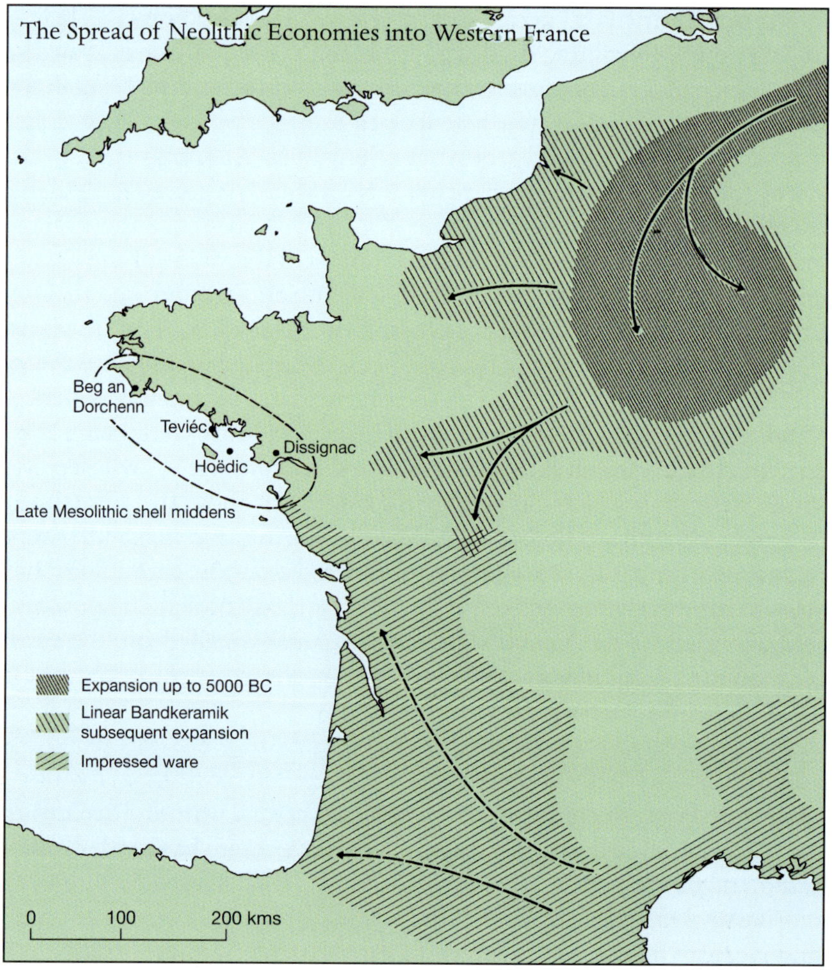

4.25 The spread of the earliest Neolithic economies into western France in the period *c.*5500–4700 BC. The Impressed ware complex may have resulted not from a movement of people but from a spread of the knowledge of pottery-making and the exchange of domestic animals. The Bandkeramik culture is more likely to represent the movement of people.

communication continued throughout the sixth millennium, allowing the novel technological developments of the Mediterranean coastal communities, and the food-producing systems which were taking root there, to be gradually introduced into the hunter-gatherer communities of Atlantic France.

While these processes of acculturation were under way in west-central France, Neolithic horticulturalists of the Bandkeramik cultural complex were establishing themselves in the Netherlands, Belgium, and northern France as far as the Seine valley. The radiocarbon dates at present available suggest that the settlement was well under way by about 5200 BC. Elements of the Neolithic cultural package, in particular pottery and polished stone axes, were soon adopted by communities to the west of the Bandkeramik region as far as the eastern border of Brittany and the Channel Islands. This broad zone of north-western France is divided by archaeologists into two cultural regions, named after the type sites of Villeneuve-St-Germain and Cerny, the division being based largely on subtleties of pottery typology the exact significance of which is still subject to much discussion. These peripheral developments (which can more simply bereferred to as Middle Neolithic I) take us up to about 4500 BC.

It is necessary to pause for a moment to take stock of the fast-changing situation so as better to understand the crucial developments that are about to take place in the Atlantic region of France. About 5000 BC western central France up to the Loire valley was occupied by communities of hunter-gatherer ancestry who had absorbed aspects of the Neolithic way of life from the Mediterranean coastal zone and were characterized by the use of impressed-decorated pottery. In the north, Neolithic settlers of the Bandkeramik group had colonized as far west as the Seine valley and their influence was spreading westwards through Normandy. Meanwhile in Brittany, particularly along the southern coasts, the hunter-gatherer communities, whose shell middens and burials we have already considered, were firmly established in their well-provided environment, having developed a complex and stable social system. A radiocarbon date for the shell midden of Hoëdic indicates occupation within the bracket 5500–5100 BC. The interaction of these various cultural forces led, in the first half of the fifth millennium, to the development of a remarkable cultural phenomenon characterized by the appearance of the large stone- or earth-built burial mounds heralding the beginning of the megalithic tradition of grave architecture.

The origins of this phenomenon in Armorica are difficult to untangle and remain the subject of heated discussion. Since much depends on acquiring accurate dates for the earliest constructions, the debate hinges on the reliability of the growing number of radiocarbon dates for the building and use of the monuments themselves and the dating of distinctive pottery which may be associated with monuments otherwise undated. If we accept that the radiocarbon dates are, by and large, an accurate reflection of true chronology then two classes of burial monument become relevant to the discussion: *long mounds* concentrated in the Carnac region of the Morbihan, and *passage graves*, which at this early date are found mainly in the west of Brittany.

The long mounds (*tertres tumulaires*) were, as the name implies, long, low mounds of earth and stone, usually rectangular or trapezoidal in plan, boarded with upright slabs or drystone walling. Within the body of the mound may be found a variety of structures, from hearths and post settings to small stone-built cists (*coffres*) often containing human

4.26 (*below*) La Table des Marchand, Le Grand Menhir, and a line of pits discovered during excavation which once took an alignment of standing stones. Le Grand Menhir may well have been one of the alignment stones standing in the southernmost of the stone holes.

skeletal material. The monuments are found in a restricted region of the Morbihan overlooking the Baie de Quiberon. Associated pottery is classified as Middle Neolithic I, which belongs to the period approximately 4700–4400 BC and is consistent with radiocarbon dates for the monuments.

The question which has engaged a number of archaeologists is what can be said of the origins of the long mound tradition? One strongly held view is that it was adopted from the Bandkeramik region in the Seine valley along with other elements of the Neolithic package such as pottery, polished stone, and cereal growing and domestication, whether by acculturation—that is, the borrowing of these elements by the indigenous population—or as a result of small immigrant groups moving west to settle. An alternative view would be to see the long mounds emerging as an essentially local phenomenon—a development of the complex burial tradition already apparent in the cemeteries of Téviec and Hoëdic, where stone-lined cists and mounds were in evidence half a millennium or more earlier. The question is not easy to resolve and the two extreme explanations need not be entirely exclusive.

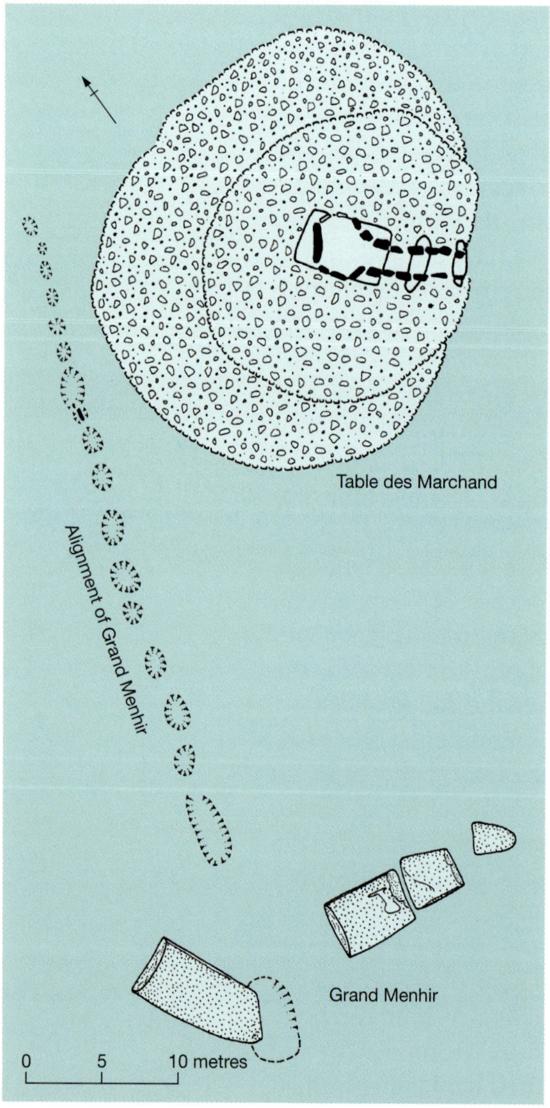

Associated with the long mounds were a series of remarkable large standing stones (menhirs), some of which were elaborately carved. The most impressive of these is Le Grand Menhir Brisé at Locmariaquer (4.26, 4.27, 4.28). As its name implies it now has broken, but had it originally stood it would have been over 20 metres high. It was carved with a curious motif, the uncertain nature of which is inherent in the name 'axe-plough' used by archaeologists to describe it. Excavation has shown that the Grand Menhir was one of a row of menhirs of decreasing size represented now only by the holes in which they were once placed. One of them may well have been the stone known to have been broken into three parts, each used as a capstone in three different passage graves, La Table des

4.27 (*previous page*)
The megalithic tomb of La Table des Marchand after partial reconstruction and Le Grand Menhir Brisé beyond, right. In the foreground (right) is the cairn (long burial mound) of Er Vinglé.

4.28 Some of the large carved menhirs of the Carnac region in southern Brittany showing the way in which the stones were broken and fragments reused in later passage graves.

Marchands, Gavrinis, and Er Grah. It was decorated with an 'axe-plough', an axe, and the heads of two bovines. A third decorated menhir, also broken, was used to provide three of the capstones of the passage grave of Maré-Rutual. Other fragments of similar stones were incorporated in the passage graves of Maré-er-Hroëk and Le Petit Mont, and it is likely that the end slab in La Table des Marchands is a small complete decorated menhir.

The decorated menhirs represent a colossal investment of labour. The Grand Menhir, which weighs 348 tonnes, had to be dragged 4 kilometres from its source to its place of erection, a task which it is estimated would have required the mobilization of more than two thousand people.

What is of particular interest is that many of these decorated menhirs were pulled down some time around 3800 BC and broken up for reuse in passage graves. This deliberate act must surely have been an event of great social and religious importance in the region, marking perhaps the end of one social order and the beginning of another. It is tempting to associate this 'event' with the demise of the long mound tradition and its replacement in the Morbihan by a new belief system characterized by passage graves.

The second burial tradition, reflected by the passage graves, was, in the first half of the fifth millennium, largely restricted to coastal positions in the west of Brittany. Passage graves were stone-built mounds covering one or more burial chambers, each accessible to the outside by means of long passages. The most famous of the Armorican passage graves is Barnenez, lying on the coast some 10 kilometres north of Morlaix (4.29, 4.30). The monument had a complex history. It began as a cairn of stone rubble 35 metres long and up to 20 metres wide revetted by two drystone walls. Within the mound were five burial chambers, each accessible to the outside by long narrow passages. Four of the chambers were corbelled while the central one was built of upright slabs with a massive capstone for a roof. One of the chambers (G) produced a radiocarbon date between *c.*4800 and 4500 BC. At a later date the cairn was extended to the west to accommodate six more burial chambers, some of corbelled structure, others megalithic. A radiocarbon date from chamber A gave a date bracket of *c.*4500–4000 BC, while one from chamber F lay between *c.*4500 and 4200 BC. The dates are therefore consistent and suggest an initial building in the first half of the fifth millennium, with the addition being made early in the second half of the millennium. Another passage grave cemetery, on Île Carn on the north-west coast of Finistère, has also produced a series of three early radiocarbon dates all lying within the period 4500–4000 BC. Four other Armorican passage graves have yielded fifth-millennium dates. To these may be added the tomb of Bougnon, south-west of Poitiers, with three dates in the same range.

Taking this evidence together, it seems that two distinct burial traditions developed in Armorica and the Vendée in the early fifth millennium—a geographically restricted long mound tradition associated with decorated menhirs, and a more extensive passage grave tradition. The

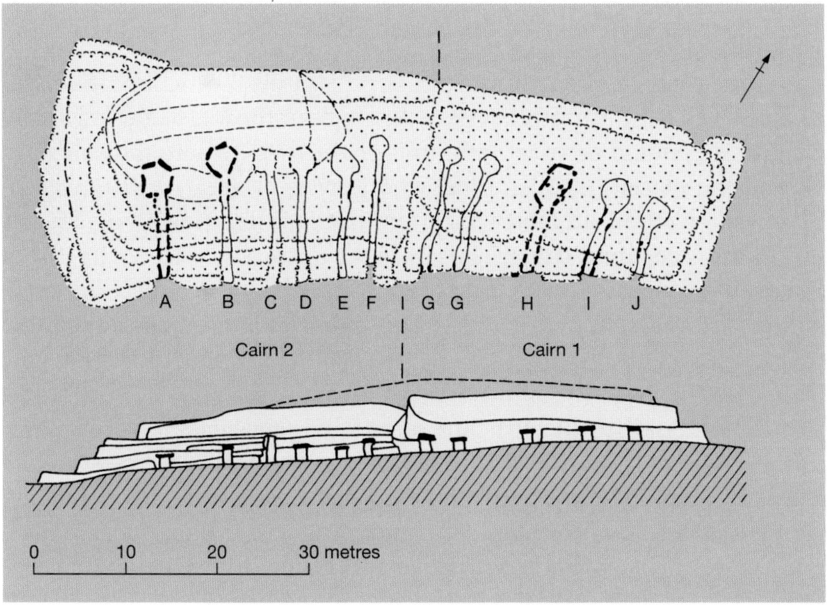

4.30 The burial mound of Barnenez showing the two-phase construction of the monument, the eastern end being the original structure.

long mound tradition seems to have been comparatively short-lived, and was replaced by the passage grave tradition which had spread to the Morbihan by the beginning of the fourth millennium. The sequence is well demonstrated at Le Petit Mont, on the Golfe du Morbihan, where a passage grave was built over a long mound, and by the incorporation of the decorated menhirs into the new passage graves.

Whilst the evidence of the fifth millennium cultural developments in north-western France is now reasonably clear, by what processes the remarkable 'megalithic' phenomenon generated its dynamic energy and from what sources came its inspiration are the unresolved questions of the continuing debate. The simplest approach would be to say that a coming together, in the Atlantic fringes of the region, of a number of factors, most notably the strength and stability of the coastal socio-economic system and the infiltration of elements of Neolithic technology and ideology from the south along the Garonne and from the Seine valley, coalesced in the coastal zone, creating a new social energy and purpose which manifested itself in the mobilization of labour on an unprecedented scale. One of the most evident results was the creation of spectacular architecture, much of it focused on the glorification of ancestors.

Once established the monumental tradition took on a remarkable dynamic, but these are matters to which we shall return in the next chapter.

4.29 (*facing*) The partially restored tumulus of Barnenez on a hill overlooking the bay of Terenez opening to the estuary of Morlaix on the north coast of Brittany. The mound was partially quarried away, before the nature of the site was recognized, exposing some of the chambers of the passage graves.

The Continental Coasts of the North Sea

By about 5000 BC the fast-moving Bandkeramik horticulturalists had established a fully Neolithic system throughout the loess lands of northern Europe, but at the northern limit of the loess, where the land gave way to the glacial outwash sands and gravels of the North European Plain, colonization stopped except for limited infiltration along the valleys of the Oder and Vistula. Thus from the north of France to the east of Poland there remained a zone up to 200 kilometres wide where, for up to a thousand years, hunter-gatherer communities continued to maintain their traditional way of life. This heavily wooded region, through which flowed all the great rivers of northern Europe, from the Somme to the Vistula, with its intricate coastline of estuaries and marshes, promontories and islands, provided rich and varied resources for those who had learned to exploit them to the full. We have already seen how the highly favoured coastal environment, encompassing eastern Jutland and western Sweden, developed a distinctive and stable hunter-gatherer economy—the Ertebølle culture. In the coastal regions of the Netherlands another stable hunter-gatherer group, the Swifterbant, developed. Two phases can be recognized. In the earlier the camp sites were entirely without pottery, but after about the middle of the fifth millennium pottery makes its appearance, representing the selective adoption of 'Neolithic' traits learnt from the inland settlements of the Bandkeramik farmers by the stable Mesolithic communities of the coastal region.

Throughout much of the fifth millennium the two traditions, the hunter-gatherers of the coastal zone and the farmers of the loess, retained their separate identities, although there was, as might be expected, evidence of exchanges. The distribution of Neolithic polished stone axes throughout the North European Plain is a clear indication of what the farmers could offer to their neighbours. These axes were probably passed among the hunter-gatherer communities as desirable gifts in cycles of gift exchange. Other concepts will have filtered northwards. Knowledge of pottery manufacture, which first appears in Ertebølle about 4700 BC, was probably learned from the Neolithic farmers of the south. It is also reasonable to suppose that domesticated animals or cereals may from time to time have been items of exchange.

The equilibrium, which allowed the two economies to coexist in their different regions, finally broke down about 4200 BC, after which those living in the broad coastal zone rapidly adopted the Neolithic life-style, now typified by the widespread use of a suite of pottery of which the funnel-necked beaker is the most characteristic form. The funnel-necked beaker (or TRB) culture, as it is called, extended over Poland, east Germany, and

Denmark while its western equivalent, the Michelsberg culture, covered much of a broad zone from the Alps to the Channel coast. Both 'cultures' are late developers, springing ultimately from the pioneering Bandkeramik but covering a much wider area and merging with the indigenous hunter-gatherer population. Within this broad zone a megalithic burial tradition was to develop in the early centuries of the fourth millennium.

Offshore Islands: Britain and Ireland

For the sake of completeness we may look briefly at Britain and Ireland. Here the Neolithic economy was introduced to most habitable parts of the landscape between 4500 and 3500 BC. The earliest evidence for forest clearance appears in pollen sequences about 4500 BC. These were restricted in extent and of short duration and may have been little more than limited clearances caused by hunter-gatherers intent on encouraging the growth of hazel scrub or improving browse to encourage wild animals to congregate. Thereafter evidence for farming becomes more widespread. A Neolithic economy was being practised at Shippey Hill, Cambridge, by 4300 BC and at Broome Hill, Norfolk, about 4200. By 4100 there is evidence from Cross Mere, Shropshire, and Ballynagilly in Northern Ireland and by 3900 BC Neolithic settlements had been set up in Northumberland, Grampian, and as far north as Shetland. The extent to which the taming of the land had taken hold by the early fourth millennium is shown by the construction of a timber trackway across the Somerset marshes using timbers which the dendrochronological evidence shows were felled in 3807/6 BC. By this time the first burial mounds—long barrows—built of chalk and earth were beginning to appear in Wessex, and the earliest ditched enclosures (causewayed camps) came to dominate the same landscape in the centuries after 3500 BC.

In broad historical terms the spread of the Neolithic way of life to Britain was roughly contemporary with the Neolithicization of the hunter-gatherers of the north European coastal zone and was accompanied by the creation of long mounds to commemorate ancestors. To this extent it can be considered to be part of the same broad process. That the earliest dates so far known for Neolithic activity come from the east of England offers some support for this view.

We should not, however, overlook the potential importance of the western seaways in the spread of Neolithic systems. A group of dates for three Neolithic sites in Cornwall and Devon lie between *c.*4000 and 3700 BC, a site at Landergai in north-west Wales produced a date of *c.*4000, while Ballynagilly and Carrowmore in Ireland both yielded late-fifth-millennium dates. We have already seen that the isolated group of hunter-gatherers living in the extreme south-west, on the end of the Dingle peninsula, was able to acquire polished Neolithic axes and cattle about 4100 BC.

In the wake of the spread of agri-pastoral economies to Ireland and the west of Britain there developed a burial tradition characterized by megalithic monuments, of which the most famous are the great tombs of the Boyne valley. In the fourth millennium simple *portal dolmens* and the more elaborate *passage graves* were to become a common feature of Ireland and the Atlantic coasts of Britain, as we will see in the next chapter (4.31). When the tradition for building large stone monuments for collective burial was first introduced into Ireland and the Atlantic coasts of Britain is still in debate; so too is the nature of the inspiration which led to the rapid acceptance of the concepts which lay behind their construction. It has been claimed, on the basis of radiocarbon dates, that some of the tombs in the cemetery of Carrowmore, Co. Sligo, date back to the early fifth millennium. If so, they would be broadly contemporary with the earliest Breton passage graves and would pre-date by more than 500 years the appearance of the Earliest Neolithic in Ireland. Many archaeologists find the early dates difficult to accept and the question therefore remains unresolved, but there is nothing inherently unlikely in supposing that long-established maritime links between Brittany and Ireland provided one of the routes along which new ideas were transmitted northwards to be rapidly adopted and adapted by the Atlantic communities of Ireland and Britain.

Britain and Ireland, by virtue of their geographical position, were in contact both with western coastal Europe along the Atlantic seaways and northern Continental Europe across the Channel and the southern reaches of the North Sea. From both regions the concepts of the Neolithic way of life reached the islands along with the breeding stock and seed corn which must have been carried across in boats. In the comparatively brief period from 4300 to 3800 BC the practical aspects of food production had penetrated the far west and the far north. So rapid was the spread that there can be little doubt that the already well-developed maritime networks played an important part.

The Emergence of an Atlantic Identity?

Sufficient will have been said to show that in the period from 8000 to 4000 BC the communities fronting the Atlantic developed in a distinctive, sometimes precocious, way that set them apart from their neighbours occupying the more inland regions. The coastal settlers shared two

4.31 The passage grave cemetery of Loughcrew, Co. Meath, Ireland, one of the four large passage grave cemeteries of Ireland.

things: the maritime and estuarine resources which they commanded were rich and varied, giving an assured level of productivity, while their land lay at the edge of the world—it was the last land—there was nowhere else for them to go. It is tempting to believe that these two factors combined to create an Atlantic mind-set. Since movement was circumscribed, hunter-gatherer bands began to develop a more sedentary life-style. This is not to say that foraging or hunting expeditions were necessarily restricted—clearly they were not—but home bases were established, quite often at the interface between land and sea, where the population, or a large sector of it, lived for much of the year, creating substantial middens. It is possible that the midden itself was regarded as a symbol of stability—a monument which proclaimed possession and embodied the history of the band. In such a context it is easy to see why the dead were buried in middens—the midden had become the outward and visible signs of ancestry. The act of returning to the cemetery to inter the newly dead in separate graves, or in communal tombs in the case of the Morbihan, was a social re-enactment that symbolized continuity. The Mesolithic cemeteries of the Tagus, the Morbihan, and southern Scandinavia are remarkable reflections of the level of social complexity that had been reached by the sixth and fifth millennia—a complexity unmatched elsewhere in western and central Europe at the time.

If the rich array of food resources readily to hand was a prime factor *allowing* the emergence of social complexity, the *causes* for such a development are more difficult to discern. Most archaeologists would agree that there was a gradual but significant population increase in these coastal areas. The resource base would have supported this to the point at which the holding capacity of the environment was reached, but there was always the possibility that the population would rise beyond the holding capacity. In such a situation a greater sense of territoriality would have developed, leading to social stress reflected in aggression. This indeed seems to have been the case. The emphasis on the social possession of the midden is a demonstration of territorial claims, while aggression may be reflected in a significant number of deaths through arrow wounds. Another response to population pressure is migration, with a sector of the population moving off to colonize a new ecological niche. Here the nature of the archaeological evidence is very imperfect, not least because so much of the contemporary coastal habitat has been destroyed by sea-level rise, but it might be possible, in some favoured areas, to demonstrate progressive colonization of once-marginal territory. The ocean, however, was always the ultimate boundary.

A third way in which the holding capacity of the territory could be increased was by exploiting new resources, which may have required the development, or acceptance of, new technologies. In the case of the Atlantic communities an obvious resource was the sea. The littoral zone and inshore waters were worked from the beginning but the deeper waters presented more of a challenge, and yet the great wealth of bottom-feeding fish like cod, haddock, ling, and hake offered an unlimited food resource to those with the technology and courage to pursue it in the open sea. In the eighteenth century a six-man boat off the coast of Co. Waterford could expect to take a thousand hake by hook and line in a single night. There is ample evidence of deep-sea fishing in Later Mesolithic times. In southern Sweden, for example, bones of cod, haddock, and ling were comparatively common in midden deposits, with some of the cod reaching 1.5 metres in length and ling up to 1.7 metres. The archaeological record shows ample evidence of sophisticated fish-hooks of the kind suitable for such a catch. By implication, then, we must suppose that adequate vessels, presumably hide boats, were in regular use.

The other resources which became available in the fifth millennium were cultivated cereal and domesticated animals, introduced into the west by the Bandkeramik horticulturalists moving from the loess lands of the north and the Cardial Ware farmers from the Mediterranean. In Portugal it seems likely that actual settlers arrived by sea, coast-hopping from the Mediterranean, but elsewhere in the western coastal zone, from the bay of Gascony to the Baltic, while there may have been limited inward movements of farming groups, it is more likely that the indigenous hunter-gatherer populations gradually adopted aspects of the new agri-technology starting, perhaps, with small flocks of sheep or goats or a few cattle, treating them essentially as supplements to the traditional hunting-gathering regime. There is no need to assume that once cultivates and domesticates became available they were avidly snapped up by the hunter-gatherers. In fact, quite the opposite seems to have been the case. In a broad zone from the Channel to the Baltic the coastal hunter-gatherers maintained their traditional life-styles for a thousand years or so. At the end of the fifth millennium, however, there seems to have been a rapid and wholesale adoption of the Neolithic way of life. Why this should have happened so quickly is an intriguing question. It may be that a threshold of stress had been reached, either as the result of rise in population above a critical level or because of a decline in resources, or both. One possibility is that climatic change, leading to a diminishing of coastal resources, was the catalyst. Thus, to meet the growing nutritional needs of an increasing population the communities of the Atlantic developed two new food resources—on the one hand they embraced the ocean itself, and on the other they adopted the agri-technologies of their inland neighbours.

Both developments had far-reaching effects on social development. Domesticated animals and cereal growing intensified the sedentary nature of society, giving a new imperative to the need to define and identify territory. The emergence of prominent cemeteries—the early megalithic tombs of the Atlantic zone—was little more than an elaboration of trends already apparent in the sixth millennium. The tombs served as territorial markers proclaiming ancestral rights to land. The very concept of the passage grave, a hidden tomb opening to the exterior, linked the world of the ancestors to the living world. At the same time it represented continuity—the burial of the dead was a process without end. One wonders what symbolism lay behind the great tomb dominating the Breton landscape at Barnenez. The original structure was built of local dolerite but the addition was capped with granite that had to be brought from 2 kilometres away. Could this have been a statement of territorial expansion? The burial chamber in the massive passage grave at La Hougue Bie in Jersey was built of orthostats of granite from up to 7 kilometres away. Does this deliberately signal the power of the social group who built it over a defined territory? The hints are tantalizing.

We have left until last the question of the ocean. A prehistoric community that takes to the sea in search of fish acquires a degree of mobility far greater than it is possible to develop on land. In their lightly framed hide-covered boats sailors could cover considerable distances in pursuit of their catch. Some years ago the prehistorian Graham Clark put forward the suggestion that it was the mobility of fishermen, following migratory shoals of fish like hake, cod, haddock, and ling, that first established networks of communication along the Atlantic seaways. In this way disparate areas were brought into contact with each other. The migratory routes of the fish were replicated by seasonal shipping movements, encouraging ideas to spread. It is a compelling argument which provides a simple way of explaining the remarkable cultural similarities seen along the Atlantic façade, from the antler-bedecked Mesolithic burials of Scandinavia and Armorica to the passage graves stretching from Portugal to Orkney.

Thus, as early as the sixth–fifth millennium we can see themes coming into focus which will pervade the rest of the story—the favoured, resource-rich, innovative Atlantic coastal zone, its cultures uniquely fashioned by being at the extremity of the world, bound together over vast distances by maritime networks. With the ocean their limit, communities would be responsive to influences from inland, absorbing and adapting that which was acceptable while retaining a vigorous originality.

5. Ancestors and Ritual Landscapes: 4000–2700 BC

By the beginning of the fourth millennium much of Atlantic Europe—from the valley of the Vistula to the Straits of Gibraltar, including the offshore islands of Britain and Ireland, had adopted a Neolithic lifestyle. Food production, involving the cultivation of cereals and the management of domesticated animals, was now widely practised as an adjunct to hunting and gathering, and simple technologies such as the grinding of stone to make axes and the firing of clay to make pottery had been adopted throughout much of the region. The change to a Neolithic economy was not sudden, nor was it universal. In some areas hunter-gatherer economies survived for some time alongside agri-horticulturalism, and over the broad Atlantic region there was great diversity.

By 4000 BC some communities within the Atlantic zone had already begun to develop a specific form of monumental architecture involving the building of large tombs, designed to display their ancestral legitimacy and their claims to territory. The fourth and early third millennia saw the further development of this remarkable practice and its spread throughout the entire Atlantic zone, giving the region a highly distinctive character and a degree of cultural coherence which served to distinguish it from the rest of Europe. The building of large megalithic monuments was an Atlantic phenomenon without contemporary parallel. But before considering these developments in any detail it is necessary to outline what was happening elsewhere on the Continent, not least because the increasing complexity of these European systems was eventually to have a profound influence on the communities of the Atlantic.

European Perspective

In south-eastern Europe from the shores of the Aegean and Black Sea to the eastern fringes of the Alps certain communities, perhaps motivated first by curiosity, began to turn their technical, and in particular pyrotechnical, skills to the extraction of metals. Copper, in the form of simple, brightly coloured, green and blue compound ores, and gold in its native form recovered from riverine deposits were readily to hand and were easily extracted. In their cast or beaten forms these metals were distributed as items of prestige and could be accumulated by favoured social groups in considerable quantity. At Varna, on the Black Sea coast of Bulgaria, a cemetery dating to about 4000 BC produced no less than 6 kilograms of gold and even larger quantities of copper, all deposited in a display of conspicuous consumption with the elite dead. At this stage both metals were luxury commodities, and although the copper was now cast to form shaft-hole axes and adzes these were symbols of power and prestige rather than practical tools and weapons. So extensive and varied was the production of copper in Romania and Bulgaria that it seems that the south-east European producers had developed a momentum quite separate from that of Anatolia and the Near East some time in the fifth millennium.

The suggestion that copper metallurgy may have developed separately in more than one area is further strengthened by the recent discovery, at Cerro Virtad, Almería in south-east Spain, of evidence of copper smelting as early as the first half of the fifth millennium. However, unlike the metalworkers of Bulgaria and Romania, the Spanish craftsmen did not develop the same range of skilled casting techniques.

A second development of far-reaching importance took place on the southern edge of the North European Plain in a broad zone from western Ukraine to eastern Germany around 3000 BC. This was the homeland of the Corded Ware/Battle Axe 'culture'. As the archaeologically inspired name implies, the type-fossils of this cultural expression include distinctive handleless drinking vessels, with a capacity of about a litre, frequently decorated around the upper register with cord impressions, and stone battleaxes perforated to take a central haft, the two usually found accompanying male burials (5.1). The burials were single and closed—quite different from the collective tombs of the west.

The origin of the Corded Ware / Battle Axe phenomenon is a matter of continuing debate. The use of cord decoration was well known among eastern communities extending to the steppes, while the stone battleaxes were evidently copied from metal forms already well established among the copper-using communities of south-eastern Europe. In the past it was conventional to explain large-scale culture change in terms of invasions. Thus, some archaeologists argued that the Corded Ware / Battle Axe 'culture' reflected a mass migration of warriors moving into northern Europe from the Russian steppes. Explanations of this kind are no longer in favour, and it is now generally accepted that the development is

5.1 Corded ware beakers and their associated stone battleaxes found with burials dating to 3000–2400 BC in Denmark. Burials of this kind were found right across the North European Plain as far east as Moscow.

likely to have been largely indigenous, growing out of contacts between the local farming groups of the TRB (Funnel-necked Beaker) culture, the metal-using communities of the south, and pastoralists on the Pontic steppes where the domestication of the horse had taken place. It is not difficult to imagine how the long-established farming communities of the North European Plain, in developing an increasing complex social structure, came to adopt and adapt symbols of status selected from the systems of their southern and eastern neighbours.

By about 3000 BC the evolving social system had emerged into archaeological visibility with the beaker, the battleaxe, and the rite of individual burial as its defining characteristics. However we choose to interpret these symbols—the communal nature of the drinking vessel, the axe as an icon of aggressive power, and single burial showing reverence for the individual—the 'package', and thus presumably its social meaning, was widely adopted over a huge territory extending from Moscow in the east to Denmark, the Netherlands, and Switzerland in the west. These developments were taking place in the early centuries of the third millennium and were to impact on the Atlantic zone after about 2700 BC.

This brief overview does scant justice to the fascinating and fast-moving cultural development of Europe, but it provides an indication of the energies at work and the pressures building. Meanwhile, throughout the Atlantic zone the social dynamics, already apparent at the end of the fifth millennium, were bringing into being monumentalized landscapes that were both original and highly distinctive. Along this Atlantic zone the archaeological record for the period 4000 to 2700 BC is enormously rich and varied. While in the following discussion we will, necessarily, be selective, focusing on those regions where the most innovative developments were under way, it will be possible to recognize broad similarities throughout the littoral region and, at the same time, to appreciate the distinctive responses of the different communities each contributing to the broad Atlantic continuum that emerged.

Armorica and West-Central France

We saw in the last chapter that by about 4000 BC the coastal communities of Brittany had developed a monumental architecture. In the Morbihan this involved the construction of long burial mounds (*tertres tumulaires*) and the erection of menhirs, some of them in long rows, like that at Locmariaquer, and some, perhaps, arranged in smaller settings or set up singly. At least eight of these menhirs are known to have been decorated with carvings, representing the earliest manifestation of 'megalithic art'. Elsewhere at this time, particularly around the coasts of Finistère, passage-grave tomb building had begun. It is tempting to argue that these two different expressions of monumentality reflect two separate traditions which, in the early fourth millennium, coalesced.

That some significant change of direction occurred in the ritual development of coastal Morbihan is implied by the destruction, some time in the early fourth millennium, of many of the decorated menhirs and the incorporation of their fragments in newly built passage-grave tombs. A round date for this 'event', if such it was, would be about 3800 BC. A major reorganization of this kind, involving the virtual obliteration of an earlier ritual landscape, must signal a significant 'dislocation' in the socio-religious system of the Morbihan, possibly a break in the legitimacy and power of the local elite, but on this we can only speculate.

What emerged was a different, and even more impressive, ritual landscape. It is probably to this period that the *Grand Tumulus* monuments of the Carnac region belong. Only seven are known, and all lie within 20 kilometres of Carnac. Typically these structures comprise a massive circular or elongated mound containing one or more closed megalithic chambers. The largest of these, Le Tumulus-St-Michel, is 125 metres

5.2 The *grand tumulus* of Saint-Michel, one of a small group of such monuments found in the Carnac region of southern Brittany. The photograph shows the excavation in progress about 1900.

long, 60 metres wide, and 10 metres high (5.2). Where a sufficient archaeological record survives, several of the *Grand Tumulus* monuments have proved to be composite, beginning as small circular cairns above a chamber and only later being extended into massive mounds. These later stages are associated with evidence of complex rituals involving the construction of smaller cists, the erection of menhirs, and, in the case of Mané-Lud, the deposition of horse skulls. The primary chambers contained human bone accompanied by grave goods, usually of exceptional value, most commonly finely polished axes fashioned from visually attractive stones such as fibrolite and pyroxenite (5.3); stone beads and oval pendants made from variscite ('callaïs') were also found (5.4). In all, from the four chambers excavated, 169 axes and over 400 beads and pendants have been recovered. The value of these grave goods, in terms of the rarity of the materials and the time lavished on them to create the desired final product, taken together with the huge input of labour

required to build the mounds, demonstrate the exceptional power invested by society through the coercion and co-ordination of surplus labour. Lack of precise dating makes it difficult to place the *Grand Tumulus* monuments exactly in the local sequence, but the fact that two of them incorporated fragments of decorated menhirs (5.5) indicates that they were erected after the iconoclasm of *c*.3800, at about the same time as the early passage graves were being built in the Morbihan.

5.3 (*facing, above*) Axe of fibrolite and a pendant of variscite from the tomb of Mané-er-Hroék in Morbihan (see Fig. 5.5).

5.4 (*facing, below*) Necklace of variscite found in the grave of Tumiac, Arzon in Morbihan.

Of the many passage graves constructed throughout the fourth millennium in the Morbihan the most elaborate is Gavr'inis, set originally on a dominant hillock, now an island in the bay. The chamber, reached by a passage nearly 12 metres in length, was embedded in a cairn 60 metres in diameter, faced with drystone walling, and stepped in tiers (5.6). Of the twenty-nine upright stones which comprise the passage and chamber twenty-three are elaborately carved with a variety of complex patterns (5.7). These will be considered in a broader context below (p. 200–1), but here we might note that on two of the slabs there are clear representations of fine polished axes of the kind found in the *Grand Tumulus* monuments. Given the unusual size and elaboration of Gavr'inis it is tempting to suggest that it may have played a special, perhaps focal, role in the fourth-millennium ritual landscape. It is even possible that the highly decorated interior was not for burial but served some other function, perhaps as a shrine.

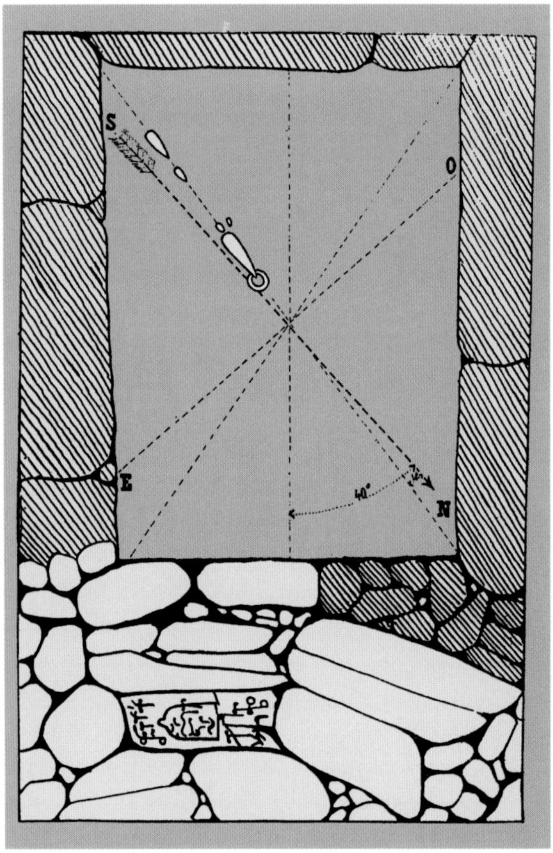

5.5 Plan of the chamber in the tomb of Mané-er-Hroék showing the careful arrangement of the axes and pendants. From the original excavation drawing of 1863.

The other dramatic components of the Carnac ritual landscape are the famous alignments which fall into three groups, Le Menec, Kermario, and Kerlescan, together incorporating some 3,000 stones varying in height from half a metre to 4 metres. Remains of at least three other alignments are known, spread across 8 kilometres of landscape. The most extensive of all is Le Menec, which runs for almost exactly a kilometre in twelve rows laid out between two roughly egg-shaped enclosures (5.8, 5.9). There is one change of alignment part way along the length. The Kermario alignment has three. The association of alignment and stone 'circles' is also repeated at Kerlescan, where the wide end of a diverging series of alignments ends on a roughly square stone-defined enclosure with

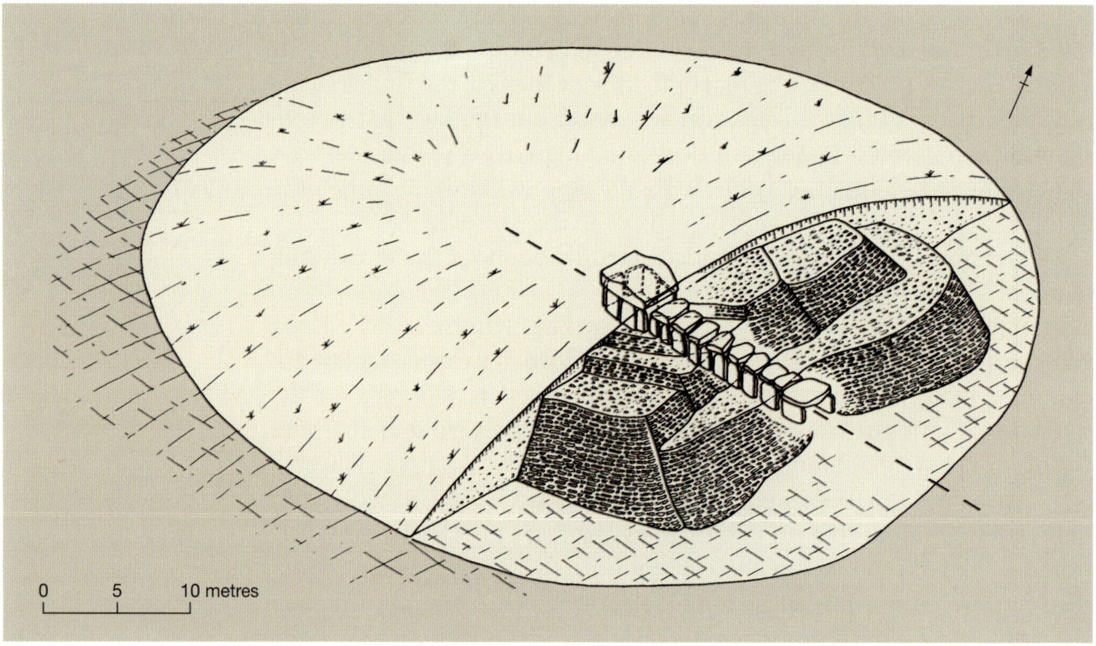

5.6 The tomb of Gavr'inis in the Morbihan: a reconstruction drawing to show the relationship of the megalithic chamber to the stone-built façade.

5.7 (*facing*) Gavr'inis. One of the orthostats of the tomb passage wall carved with eighteen axes.

a large hemicycle of stones nearby. Elsewhere in the region there are a number of isolated 'enclosures', or more usually partial enclosures, like the spectacular pair of conjoined hemicycles now largely submerged in the Golfe du Morbihan, one part of which rises onto dry land on the little island of Er Lannic (2.8).

How these various elements relate to one another and what was their function or meaning it is very difficult to say. Such dating evidence as there is suggests an early-fourth-millennium date, but there is no need to suppose that all the alignments and circles are exactly contemporary. At Le Menec the circles are likely to pre-date the alignment, but not necessarily by very long. However, the way in which the alignments of Kermario march relentlessly over the long mound at Manio leaves little doubt that the long mound had lost its original significance by the time the alignment was erected.

But what to make of it all? There has been, and there will continue to be, much speculation. On the one hand there are those who regard the alignments and circles as having a socio-religious function, being places of assembly or procession or even serving as astronomical markers. An alternative view is that the act of creation was the end in itself—construction being a one-off means of expression. In such a context the result of the act remained but was itself of no further use, except perhaps as a symbol of society's ability to cohere.

Whatever the meaning of this unique ensemble, the fact remains that the energy invested in creating a ritual landscape in the coastal regions of the Morbihan in the fourth millennium was without parallel. It reflects a society living well above subsistence level, with a surplus of energy to devote to its beliefs and sufficient coercive power within itself to ensure that those beliefs were given expression in the form of lasting architecture.

5.8 (*facing*) Part of the stone alignment of Le Menec at Carnac in the Morbihan.

The complex of monuments in southern Morbihan is exceptional. Some elements, such as the carved menhirs, the long mounds, and the *Grand Tumulus* monuments are restricted to this one small area, but the passage graves and alignments of various kinds are more widely spread throughout the peninsula. The combination of alignments and enclosures is less common, but occurs as far afield as St-Just in the valley of the Vilaine and on the Crozon peninsula of western Finistère.

Taken together, the evidence leaves little doubt that during the fourth millennium the Carnac region was one of great energy and inventiveness. But the belief systems which motivated the community were widely held, not only across the Armorican peninsula but also in Lower Normandy, the Channel Islands, and west-central France. To untangle the social and economic implications of all this is not easy, but the long mounds of the late fifth millennium and the *Grand Tumulus* monuments of the fourth millennium may be thought to imply the existence of a powerful elite. The iconoclasm of the early fourth millennium and the incorporation of parts of the old decorated menhirs in new passage graves—often massive constructions—may be read as a conflict of ideologies possibly resulting from some kind of competition within society. What provided the economic force behind these developments, whether the productive capacity within the region or the ability of the elite to control exchange systems, is a matter to be considered in more detail later (pp. 206–11).

The date of *c.*3500 BC is conventionally taken as the divide between the Middle Neolithic and the Late Neolithic periods—phases defined conveniently in terms of changing pottery assemblages. Passage graves contin-

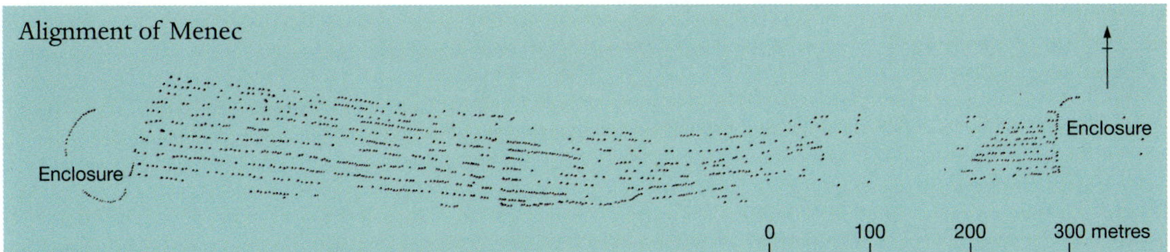

5.9 Plan of the stone alignment at Le Menec, Carnac, in Brittany.

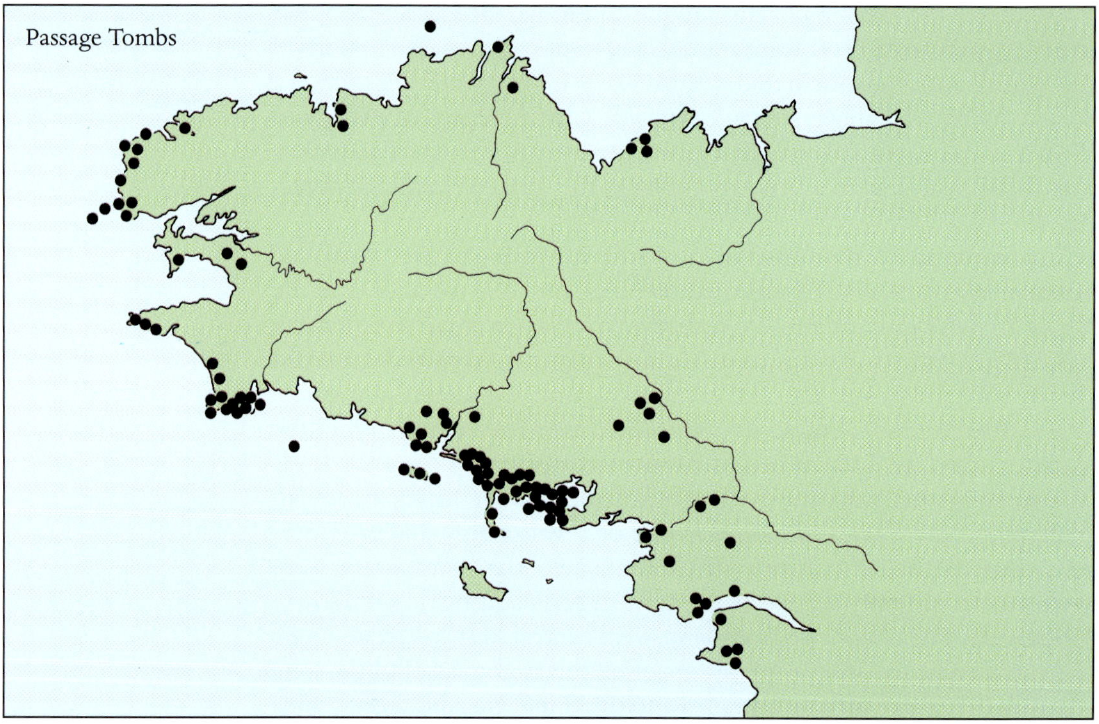
Passage Tombs

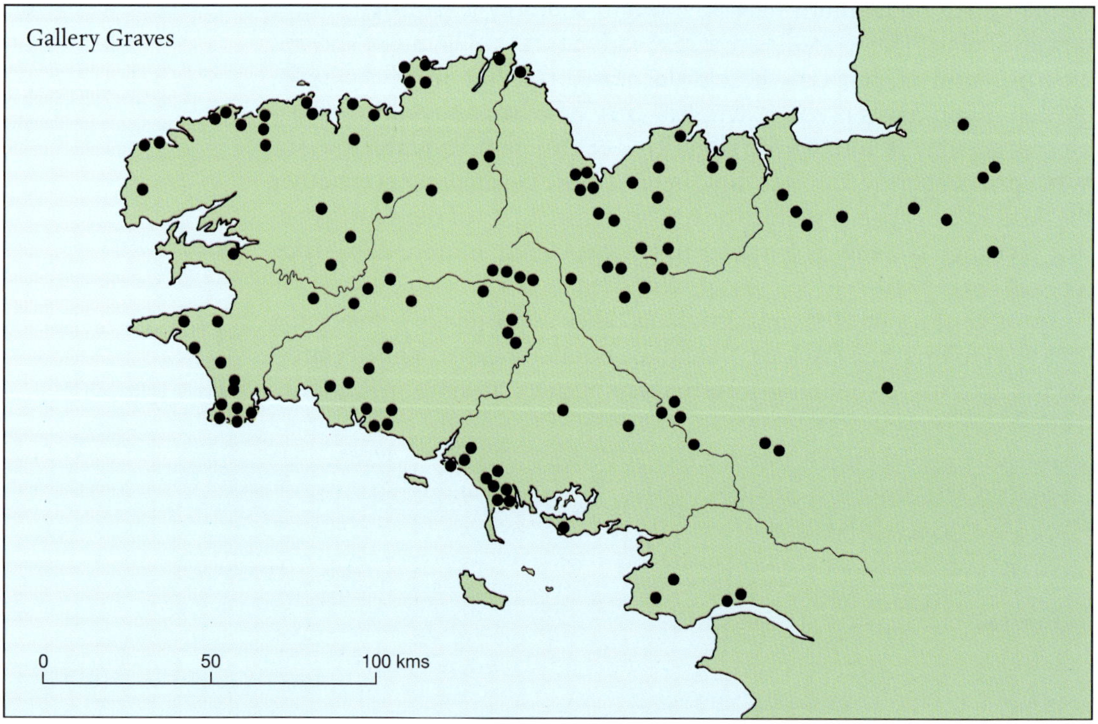
Gallery Graves
0
50
100 kms

ued to be used and built throughout the Middle Neolithic, but after *c*.3500 there is no evidence of new building, though some existing tombs remained in use. Instead, rather different and somewhat simpler types of megalithic tombs, generally known as gallery graves (*allée couverts*), were widely constructed. Mostly they were, as the name implies, simple elongated chambers, but in the southern Morbihan and coastal Loire-Atlantic a variant grave type developed known as an angled gallery grave or, better, *sépulture coudée*. These have the terminal chamber, largely undifferentiated, set at right angles to the entrance passage and are best regarded as a late and highly localized development of the passage grave—the last manifestation of the uniqueness of the Morbihan megalithic tradition—dating to the latter centuries of the fourth millennium.

5.10 (*facing*) The distributions of passage tombs and gallery graves in Brittany emphasizing the essentially coastal distribution of the earlier passage tombs.

Throughout Armorica and large tracts of western France the simple 'gallery grave', in a number of variant forms, became widespread. Gallery graves were essentially elongated chambers composed of parallel uprights roofed with massive capstones, and while some may have been embedded in earthen mounds, since removed, it remains a possibility that many were free-standing or only partially buried. In other words, the gallery graves were far simpler in form than the earlier passage graves and involved far less expenditure in labour. What stands out in particular is that, while the earlier passage graves were largely coastal in their distribution, the gallery graves were distributed throughout Brittany, with a number of notable inland concentrations focusing on the major riverine routes, such as in the valley of the Oust, and in the centre of the country on the major cross-peninsular route created by the rivers Blavet and Trieux (5.10). This would suggest that the hitherto sparsely occupied interior was now, in the Late Neolithic period, beginning to be opened up to settlement.

Elsewhere in western France gallery graves occur in some numbers, suggesting that here, too, new land was being colonized and populations were increasing. In the Charente Basin, for example, major concentrations are found, particularly at the confluences of the main river and its tributaries. Gallery graves also spread to western Normandy and into the Paris Basin. It used to be thought that this particular type of burial chamber originated in the Paris region and the idea was transmitted westwards, but it is more reasonable to see it as evolving from the late passage graves of Armorica and western central France, eventually becoming the principal burial monument both in the long-occupied coastal regions and in the newly settled interiors. The social implications of all this is that the old tradition of collective burial, with its emphasis on the importance of ancestral links with territory, was now becoming widely adopted in the west as settlement spread into hitherto sparsely occupied regions. The

5.12 (*facing*) The distribution of portal dolmens and passage graves in Ireland.

apparent lack of exceptionally grand or richly endowed monuments is a hint that a new, less steeply hierarchical society might now be emerging. Gallery graves continued to be built throughout the late fourth and early third millennia and many remained in use to the beginning of the second millennium, by which time belief systems had undergone a major reorientation and the megalithic tradition was at an end.

Ireland and the Irish Sea

The distribution of all megalithic tombs in Britain and Ireland shows that there are two zones where the tombs concentrate, one looking inwards to the Irish Sea, the other outwards to the Atlantic. Such a pattern allows only broad generalizations since it represents two thousand years or more of activity covering many complex regional developments, yet,

5.11 The portal dolmen from Ballykeel, Co. Armagh, Ireland. The excavation of the chamber produced material of Early Neolithic date.

taken at the simplest level, it offers a clear indication of those regions where the belief systems reflected in the megalithic burial tradition were dominant.

Although very large numbers of monuments are known, and the majority of them have been planned and classified, the chronological development of the various types is still largely obscure. All that can safely be said is that the earliest megalithic tombs seem, on present evidence, to belong to the early part of the fourth millennium, and a reasonable case can be made for arguing that the simplest types—dolmens made of boulders and the slightly more elaborate portal dolmens, comprising a single chamber flanked by a pair of stones reminiscent of a blind entrance (5.11)—may be among the earliest to develop in the region. This does not, of course, imply that all simple dolmens and portal dolmens are early, since the very simplicity of the type may have encouraged its longevity. The distribution of these monuments shows a distinct maritime focus (5.12). They are found around the shores of the Irish Sea and its southern approaches and along the Atlantic coasts of north-west Ireland. There is also an inland band stretching across the island from the Boyne valley to the bays of Sligo and Donegal, hinting perhaps at a route of communication between the two shores. The wide geographical distribution and coastal bias of these simple monuments is another factor suggesting the early spread of the megalithic idea to all parts of the region before distinctive local development began. Few portal dolmens have been dated, but at Poulnabrone in Co. Clare a range of radiocarbon dates from successive burials suggests that the tomb

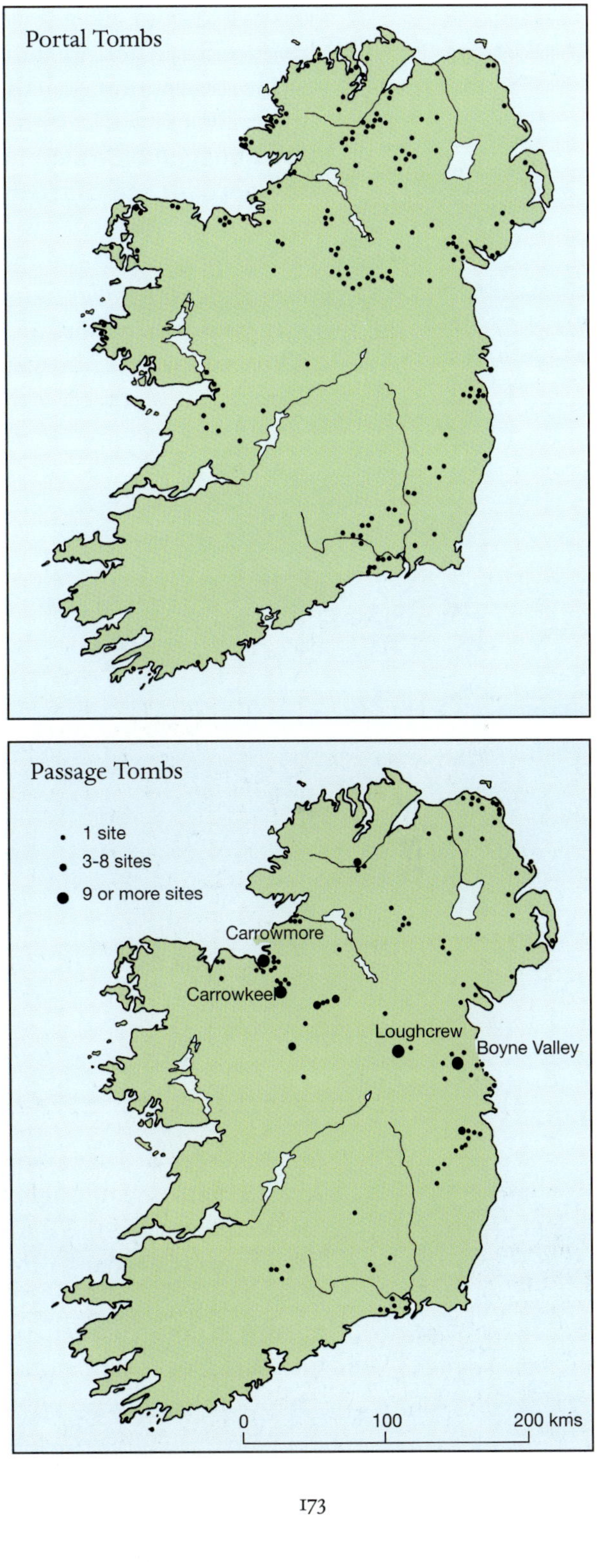

was in use from around 3800 to 3200 BC, while in Wales portal dolmens have produced pottery thought to date from around 3800–3500 BC.

The distribution of the portal dolmens, throughout south-west Britain, Wales, and Ireland, is echoed by that of the more complex *passage graves*, suggesting either that the two types of burial chamber may have developed (or been introduced) together in the early fourth millennium or that their emergence was subject to the same factors. In any event the passage graves became the dominant type, and continued to be built throughout the millennium.

In the northern part of Ireland the concentration of portal dolmens and passage graves is very similar to the distribution of an even more prolific burial monument known as *court tombs* (5.13, 5.14). These are characterized by a large 'courtyard', partly or wholly enclosed by wings extending from the tomb mound, from which the roofed burial chamber is entered. Among the 390 or so examples recorded there is inevitably variation: in some cases two tombs face each other sharing a court in common, in others two may share a mound back to back each with a separate court. The type is distinctly Irish and must be a local innovation, but it shares many features with a group of Scottish tombs known as *Clyde cairns* found along the west coast of Scotland concentrating around the Firth of Clyde. The structural similarities and close geographical proximity of the Irish and Scottish monuments—separated only by the narrow North Channel—is an indication that the two areas may well have been in regular contact with each other. The few radiocarbon dates available suggest that court tombs were being constructed and used throughout the fourth millennium.

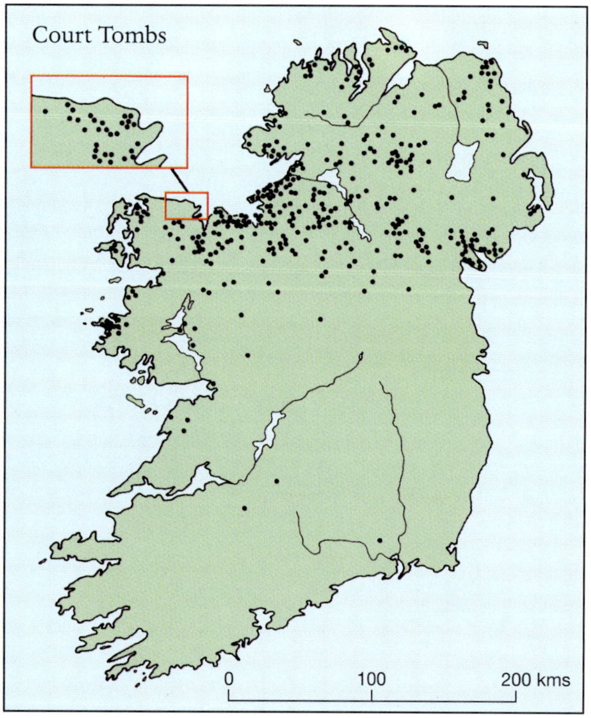

5.13 The distribution of court cairns in Ireland.

The majority of the tombs found in Britain and Ireland are comparatively modest structures. In comparison with contemporary monuments in the Morbihan, they required only a limited investment of communal energy in construction and decoration. However, among the passage graves of Ireland and north-west Wales are to be found examples redolent of the exceptional power of the community.

In Ireland some 230 passage graves have been recorded occurring

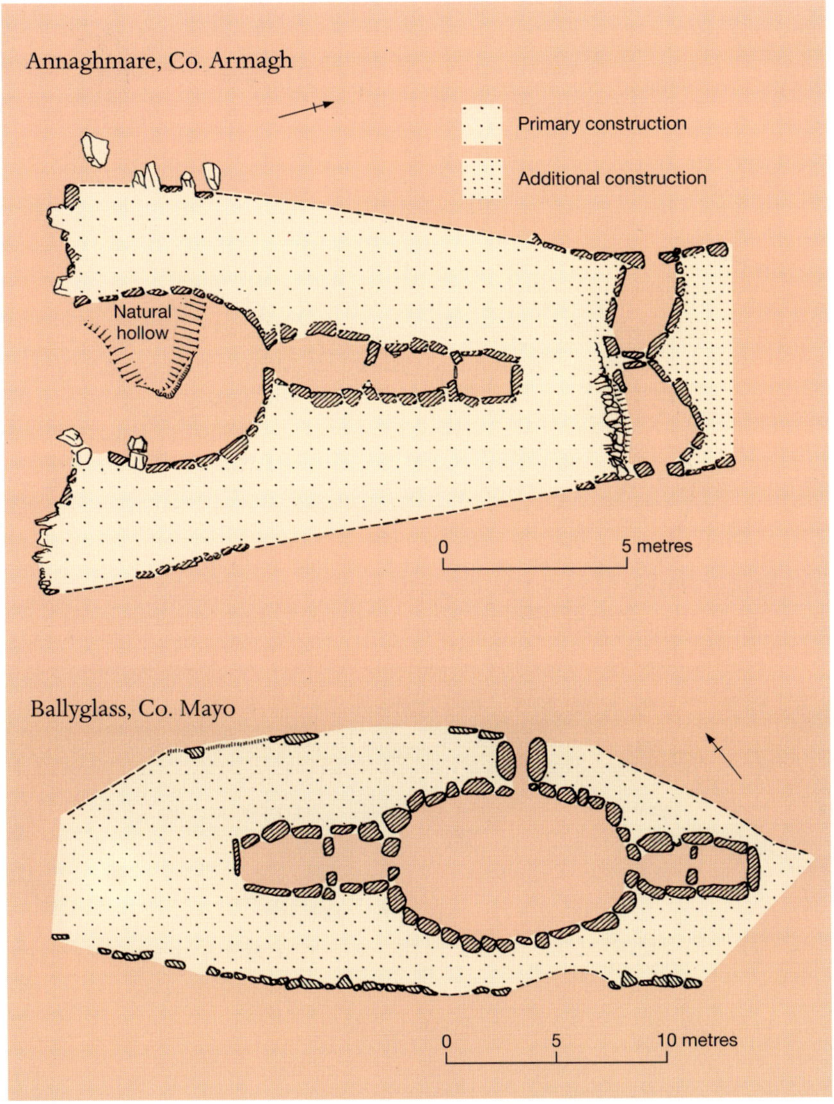

5.14 Court cairns at Annaghmare, Co. Armagh and Ballyglass, Co. Mayo.

singly or, less often, in cemeteries (5.12, 4.31). Four large cemeteries of more than nine tombs survive, at Carrowmore, Carrowkeel, Loughcrew, and the Boyne valley. They vary considerably in size and elaboration, from Carrowmore with sixty or so individual tombs to Carrowkeel with fewer than twenty. By far the most impressive, and justifiably the best known, is the Boyne valley group spread across a territory of over 5 kilometres along the river (5.15) and dominated by the three massive tombs of Knowth, Dowth, and Newgrange, each about 85 metres in diameter and standing to a height of up to 11 metres. It would be tedious to list too

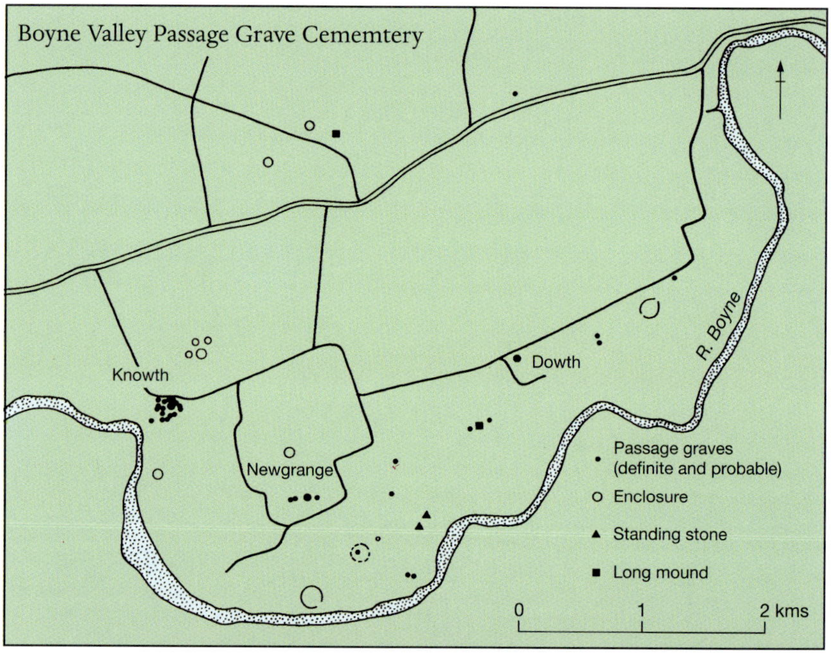

5.15 The passage graves and other monuments in the Boyne valley.

5.16 Newgrange in its restored state. The kerb of stone and the standing stones beyond are original. The revetting wall built on the kerb is an attempt to reproduce how the monument may once have looked.

many statistics, but to give some idea of the enormous labour involved in construction a few facts about Newgrange may be offered (5.16, 5.17). To build the cruciform chamber, the long passage, and the surrounding kerb would have required the quarrying, transport, and erection of at least 450 stone slabs, some weighing more than 5 tonnes, while the mound itself, composed of turf and boulders, comprises some 200,000 tonnes of mate-

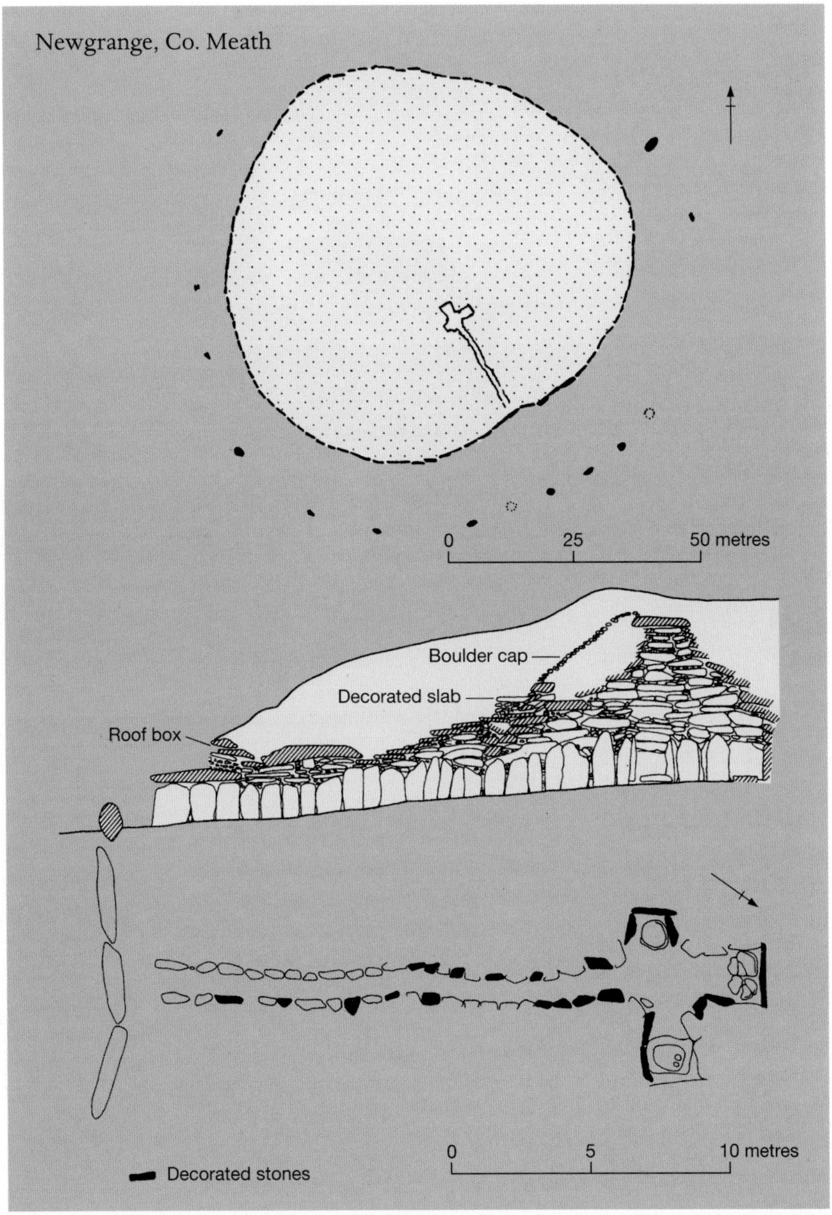

5.17 Plan of the Newgrange passage grave with details of the burial chamber.

rial. Some of the stone for this was deliberately selected and came from many kilometres to the north. The mound was evidently meant to impress not only by its sheer size but by its external appearance. The excavator has suggested that the kerb surrounding the tomb was topped by a sloping drystone wall some 3 metres high, allowing the mound to be flat topped. This arrangement is not at all unlike that seen in several of the larger Breton passage graves. An added refinement was that on the entrance side the wall was enlivened by insetting angular pieces of sparkling white quartz. The spectacular exterior prepared the visitor for the drama of the interior—a long passage leading to a cruciform chamber roofed with a corbelled vault 6 metres high. At the entrance lay a richly carved stone, while many of the kerbstones and the stones of the passage were similarly decorated. To add to the refinements a slot had been created above the capstone at the beginning of the entrance passage so that daylight could enter. Through this slot, beneath a decorated lintel, at dawn on the day of the midwinter solstice the light of the rising sun shines along the passage and into the chamber at the end (5.18). Five thousand years ago, when the tomb was newly built, the sun's rays at that moment would have lit up a triple spiral carved on the back orthostat. We will return to consider this almost unbelievable astronomical sophistication later. Here its relevance is what it tells us about the power and awareness of the society which created the perfection of Newgrange.

5.18 (*facing*) Newgrange. The corbelled chamber inside the tomb. Five thousand years ago the stone with the triple spiral would have been struck by the rays of the sun at the midsummer sunrise.

Just over a kilometre to the north-west another great mound—Knowth—dominates the landscape (5.19). It is about the same size as Newgrange but has two burial chambers, one entered from the east and one from the west. In the eastern burial passage many of the stones are carved, particularly around the northern chamber of the cruciform end. This was evidently a highly significant place, for here lay a large stone basin surrounded by cremation burials accompanied by pins, stone beads, and a perforated mace-head, made from flint, worked in a most elaborate manner.

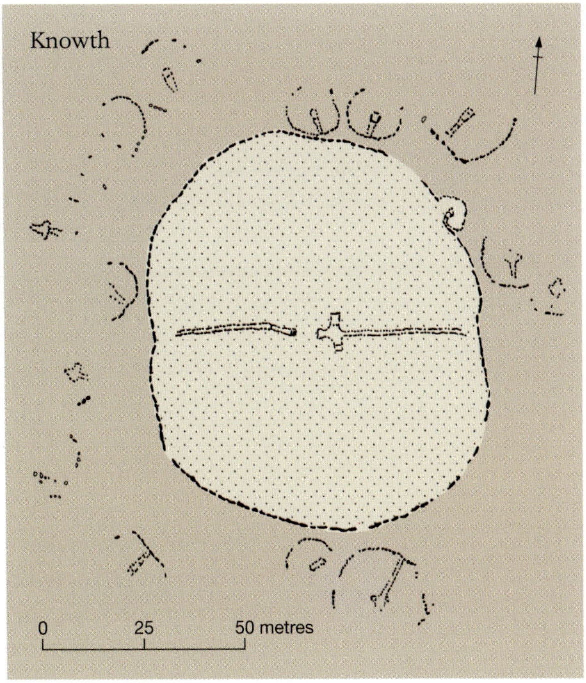

5.19 The great mound at Knowth with its smaller satellite tombs around.

The tomb of Knowth was surrounded by eighteen 'satellite' burial mounds up to 20 metres in diameter. Some at least must pre-date the great mound and may well represent an earlier-phase cemetery when the central burial, or burials, were less grand—before society had decided to lavish so much of its surplus energy in creating its final great monument.

The third of the great tombs, Dowth, comparable in size to Knowth and Newgrange, has not been examined under modern conditions, but extensive and damaging exploration in the nineteenth century established that, like Knowth, it too contained two separate tomb chambers.

The three massive tombs form part of the ritual landscape stretching along the valley of the Boyne. In addition to the groups of passage graves clustering around Knowth and Newgrange, eleven other tombs are known scattered across the landscape, together with several standing stones and a number of large enclosures of unknown date. Many other features may lie undetected beneath the soil. Clearly, a complex of this size developed over a period of time. Radiocarbon dates for the construction of Newgrange and Knowth suggest that the building took place within the period 3300–3000 BC. Other dates from two of the 'satellite' mounds at Knowth fall into the same bracket, while a third is most likely to date to the early centuries of the second millennium.

Where the great mounds fit into the development of the 'megalith' phenomenon in Ireland has been the subject of much debate. Some have argued that they lie at the beginning of the tradition and that, as the passage grave idea spread westwards across the island, tomb building became more impoverished. Others have suggested that the passage grave tradition began with the small tombs of Sligo and spread eastwards, becoming more elaborate with time. In all these debates reliance is placed on tomb typology supported by the few radiocarbon dates at present available, but both are fickle indicators and much ambiguity remains. This said, the most coherent model to be proposed so far suggests that the sequence began with small simple tombs with polygonal or cruciform chambers enclosed by a kerb which may have bordered a covering mound. These tombs have a distinctly coastal distribution. In Ireland they occur around the coasts of Sligo and Mayo in the west and Antrim in the north-east. Similar tombs are found in west Wales, in Pembrokeshire and Anglesey, and along the west and north-west coasts of Scotland as well as in Brittany, where they concentrate in the Morbihan. Dating is imprecise, but a series of assessments from the Carrowmore cemetery suggests that tomb building here may have begun early in the fourth millennium. By the middle of the millennium the passage grave tradition had spread to other parts of Ireland, including the Boyne valley, and by the end of the millennium culminated in the massive constructions of Dowth, Knowth, and Newgrange. Throughout the development there was a progressive increase in size, from an average of 10–20 metres in diameter for the earliest mounds to the 85 metres of the Boyne tombs.

The similarity of the earliest passage graves along great stretches of the Atlantic seaways can most economically be explained, as we have already suggested, in terms of extensive maritime contact some time around 4000 BC. Recurring similarities in tomb architecture, art, and other aspects of material culture throughout the fourth and early third millennia are sufficient to indicate that contacts were maintained. These are questions to which we shall return (p. 197 ff).

Against this background of continuing, if sporadic, maritime exchange must be seen the internal social dynamics of the different communities surrounding the Irish Sea. The growth in size and elaboration of passage graves in Ireland is redolent of social competition made manifest through conspicuous consumption. Reverence for ancestors was used as an outward and visible sign of the community's social prestige. Once established as a means of social display, tomb building developed a dynamic of its own, those communities wishing to compete being forced to build bigger, more elaborate, and more highly decorated structures. At the end of the cycle, about 3000 BC, the elite responsible for the construction of the great Boyne tombs, by the use of highly intricate carving and by relating their structures to major celestial phenomena such as the solstices, were laying claim to a special relationship with the deities.

Whilst the discussion here has focused on the passage graves of Ireland, other areas of the Irish Sea zone should not be overlooked. In Anglesey, for example, the passage graves of Barclodiad-y-Gawres and Bryn Celli Ddu clearly belong to the same general tradition as the Boyne tombs, as the cruciform burial chamber of Barclodiad-y-Gawres and elaborate carving on several of its stones amply demonstrate. Passage graves are also a recurring component of the megalithic tradition of Galloway, though by comparison with the Irish graves they are modest.

The passage graves, as we have already seen, were only one of the characteristic types of megalithic burial chamber in the Irish Sea region. The court graves of northern Ireland and the closely similar Clyde cairns of western Scotland represent regional developments in parallel with the passage graves extending across the same broad territories. To explain this dual development is not easy. It could be that they represent divergent belief systems related to ethnic or status differences, but the archaeological evidence is not yet of sufficient quality to allow subtleties of this kind to be addressed.

The Northern and Western Extremities of Britain

In the extreme north-west of Britain, on the island of Lewis, the largest island of the Outer Hebrides, and on the collection of islands that constitutes Orkney, the fourth and early third millennia was a time of remarkable cultural development recognizable now in some of the most spectacular monuments known in prehistoric Europe.

Orkney, with its generally fertile soils and rich marine resources, was settled by farming communities in the early fourth millennium. The original settlers, most likely coming from mainland Scotland, would have had to brave the uncertainties of the Pentland Firth in flimsy skin boats, carrying their domesticated animals and seed corn with them. By about 3100 BC their descendants were living in permanent settlements, like the well-known example at Skara Brae, in houses built and furnished from the local sandstone—a rock that splits easily into convenient slabs to serve in place of large timbers in which the islands were deficient.

The dead were buried in collective tombs. The simplest, and perhaps the earliest of the tombs, were small cairns with tripartite chambers, the internal divisions created by two pairs of upright slabs. These are at present undated but probably belong to the period 3500–3100 BC and may have been introduced from nearby Caithness, where broadly similar types are known. From this simple version more complex forms seem to have developed. On the island of Rousay *stalled cairns*, with long chambers divided by septal slabs, predominate, while on Mainland there is a different tomb form typified by the monument of Quanterness. These are circular cairns containing an elongated corbel-vaulted chamber entered in the middle of a long side by a passage leading from the exterior. From the main chamber other chambers may open: in the case of Quanterness there were six. The radiocarbon dates from Quanterness and the similar tomb of Quoyness suggest that these types were being built in the first half of the fourth millennium and remained in use for up to a thousand years.

The Orkneys are unusually prolific in chambered tombs. Some fifty-three survive, of which five can be shown to be definitely of the complex Quanterness type. Such a large number in such a comparatively small area (the Orkneys are less than 1,000 square kilometres in extent) implies a reasonably large Neolithic population; it also suggests that society was divided into a number of comparatively small lineage groups of roughly equal status, each demonstrating its identity and laying claim to its territory through its ancestral tombs. Careful estimates of the time taken to build Quanterness arrive at a figure of approximately 10,000 person/hours, which could have been accomplished quite easily by a community comprising no more than twenty individuals.

5.20 (*facing*) Aerial view of the burial mound of Maes Howe, Orkney with the Loch of Harray and Loch of Stenness beyond. The strip of land between the lochs is the site of several stone circles and standing stones (see Fig. 5.21).

Island society, divided into its small, self-contained communities, seems to have remained little changed throughout the fourth millennium. In this the islands were unexceptional. But at the beginning of the

third millennium a sudden change of pace can be detected, the new momentum leading to the creation of a ritual landscape of unusual quality and complexity which could only have been created by the co-operation of a large number of people prepared to pool their energies and expertise.

The landscape chosen occupied a central position on Mainland, a narrow strip of land between two expanses of inland water, the Loch of Harray and the Loch of Stenness, at a point where the island narrows creating easy access between the east and west coasts (5.20, 5.21). In terms of the local geography the location chosen was the natural centre of the island. Here, within a comparatively restricted compass, a number of exceptional monuments were built, including the massive collective tomb of Maes Howe and at least three circular monuments of the type generally classified by archaeologists as 'henges', the Stones of Stenness, the Ring of Brodgar, and the Ring of Bookan. In addition to these spectacular structures, standing stones and several clusters of small burial mounds are to be found scattered across the landscape.

The focal point of the complex, though not centrally sited, is the great grave mound of Maes Howe—a tumulus some 30–40 metres in diameter

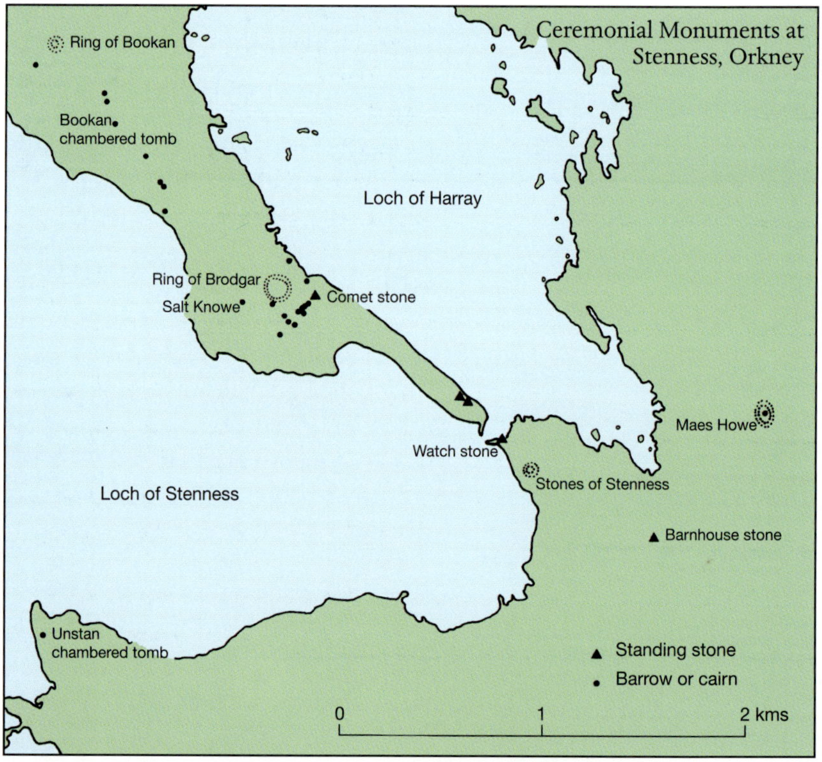

5.21 The complex of ceremonial monuments at Stenness, Orkney.

containing a central rectangular chamber reached by a long passage. From the main chamber four side chambers open, but with entrances well above the main chamber floor. The quality of the building is superb: Maes Howe must rank among the finest architectural achievements of prehistoric Europe (5.22). The main chamber was 4.6 metres square and originally had a corbelled roof which would have been about 5 metres in height. In each corner an elegantly built buttress gave support to the roof. All the stone slabs used were carefully worked and dressed, and where necessary smaller flakes of stone were used to level the courses. Even more impressive was the skill shown in creating the corbelled roof by choosing slabs that had broken obliquely across the ends, and placing them so that the angle reflected the narrowing of the vault.

5.22 Maes Howe.
The interior of the tomb. The central chamber was carefully built of the laminating local stone. The upper part of the structure was corbelled to roof the chamber.

The visual significance of the tomb was further enhanced by a surrounding earthwork consisting of a wide, flat-bottomed ditch with a bank along its outer lip. Earthworks of this kind are typical of circular 'henge monuments'. This combination of burial monument and henge is unusual. Of the other henges in the ritual landscape the Ring of Brodgar is the largest. The massive enclosing ditch, hacked out of the solid rock, would have required a team of a hundred workers labouring for three months to complete. Within this enclosure was erected one of the largest stone circles in the British Isles, with a diameter of nearly 104 metres. The stone circle at Stenness was substantially smaller—some 31 metres in diameter. Originally it consisted of a circle of twelve standing stones, with others inside, surrounded by a ditch with a single entrance. Maes Howe, Brodgar, and Stenness are undoubtedly the most impressive of the Orkney monuments but, as the plan will show (5.21), they are only a part of a far more extensive ritual landscape.

The first question to arise out of this is the date of it all. Here, admittedly, the evidence is limited. Radiocarbon dates from the ditch around Maes Howe suggest that the monument was probably constructed a little before 2800 BC, and the evidence from the Stones of Stenness is consistent with this. It is reasonable, therefore, to argue that the main elements of this focal religious landscape were being created within a comparatively short period soon after 3000 BC. The labour requirements were massive. It is estimated that Maes Howe needed ten times the labour input of a normal tomb, Brodgar eight times, and Stenness at least four times. The implication must be that the entire island population was mobilized in a supreme effort to create a single ritual complex without parallel. It is interesting to note the broad contemporaneity of the events here on Orkney and those 700 kilometres away in the Boyne valley.

The Outer Hebrides, even more remote in their Atlantic isolation, were also well endowed with megalithic monuments. This is particularly true of the southern islands of North and South Uist. The larger island of Lewis and Harris is more rugged with less cultivatable land, a fact reflected in a correspondingly smaller number of tombs. Yet the island can boast an unusual ritual landscape focused on the hill of Callanish at the head of Loch Roag which opens to the Atlantic. Here, dominating the landscape and visible from the ocean, is a stone circle of modest size, about 12 metres in diameter, from which radiate four stone rows, an avenue of standing stones running along the ridge in a northerly direction with single alignments running east, south, and west. Callanish lies at the centre of distribution of a number of other stone settings, all sited to be intervisible. No dating evidence is available, but it is a reasonable supposition that Callanish may be broadly contemporary with the stone circles of Orkney.

The monuments of Orkney and Lewis are remarkable for their complexity and sophistication, but they are only two among many rich ritual landscapes found around the extremities of northern Britain extending down the sheltered and more fertile coasts from Caithness to the Moray Firth. Throughout this zone chambered tombs occur in some number, interspersed with henge monuments and other ritual structures.

One of the most distinctive of the tomb groups are the Clava Cairns which form a tight cluster around the Moray Firth where the Great Glen—a natural thoroughfare through the Highlands—reaches the North Sea. In form the Clava Cairns are simple passage graves, their very simplicity once suggesting to some writers that they represented an early introduction of the passage grave concept by an immigrant population. It has even been mooted that the passage graves of Boyne, Orkney, and Clava were so closely related that they implied the movement of populations between these three disparate regions. All this speculation was possible when the only evidence available for discussion was the actual form of the monuments, but now radiocarbon dates from Clava indicate construction in the period 2200–2000 BC—that is, a full eight centuries after the building of the great monuments of the Boyne and Orkney. The Clava tombs can therefore at last be placed in their correct context as a late, regional development, maintaining the memory of far more ancient structural forms.

The British Isles, East and West

So far the discussion has concentrated on what can loosely be called the passage grave zone of Britain and Ireland—a great swath of sea-linked territory stretching from Cornwall to Orkney and down to the Moray Firth (5.23). Within this Orkney and the Boyne valley stand out, emerging about 3000 BC as centres of enormous focused energy and innovation, having in common, as we shall see later, a ritual art and a highly developed cosmology.

In the rest of the British Isles the east- and south-facing aspects between the Moray Firth and the English Channel—while not sharing in the Atlantic tradition—was at this time undergoing a period of internal development, most dramatically reflected in its ritual monuments. The archaeological record is unusually prolific, not least thanks to the hundreds of excavations undertaken in the last thirty years. As a result, it is now possible to define a broad similarity in the structural response to ritual needs throughout this vast territory and to identify within it innovative regional developments.

The common characteristics found throughout the zone were the use of long mounds for burials, the construction of circular ritual monuments of various kinds (classed together under the all-embracing term 'henge'), and the definition of elongated strips of land, usually by ditches

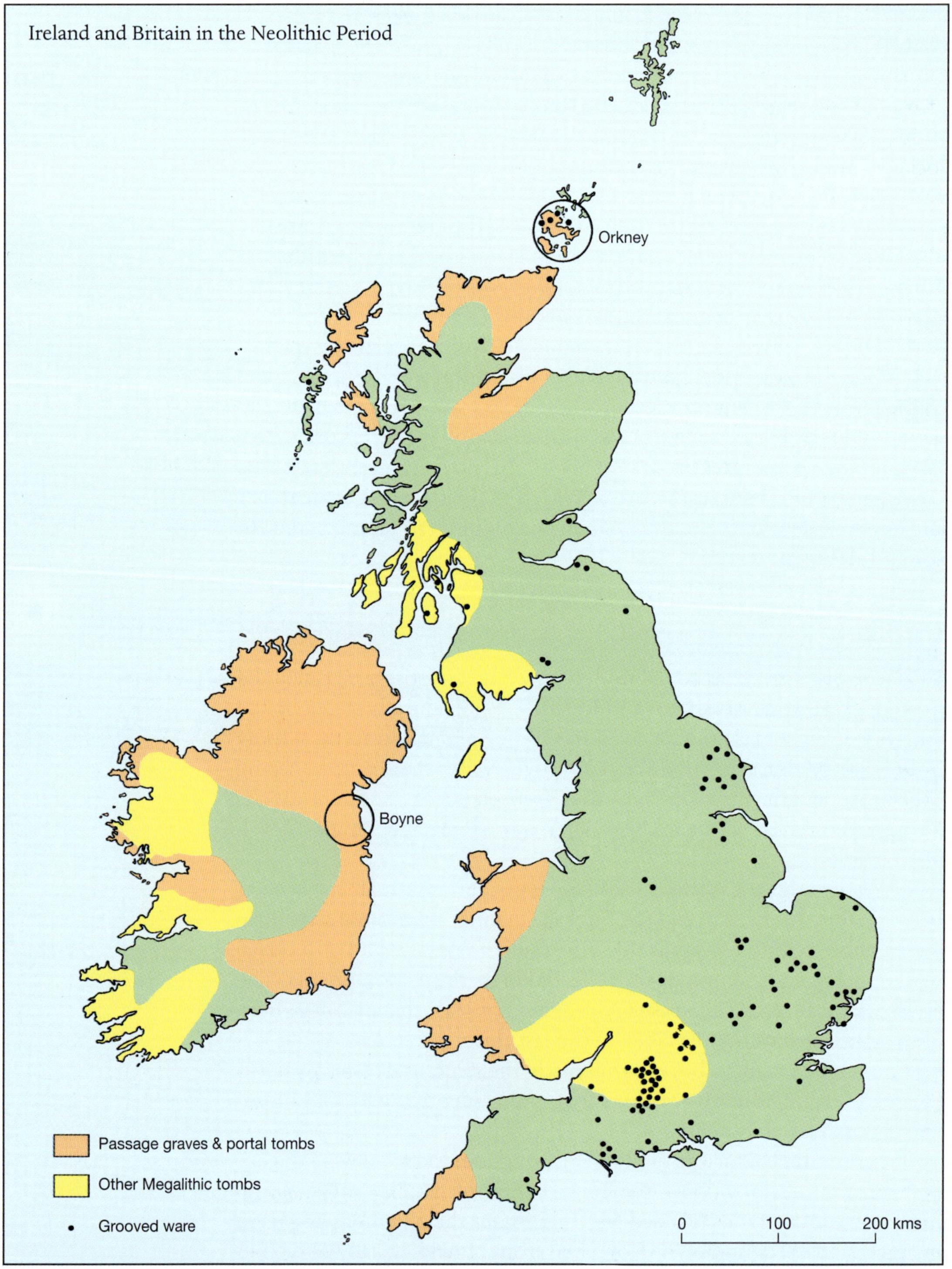
Ireland and Britain in the Neolithic Period
Orkney
Boyne
Passage graves & portal tombs
Other Megalithic tombs
Grooved ware
0
100
200 kms

but occasionally, in Scotland, by lines of pits—structures which are still referred to as 'cursus' monuments following the lead of antiquarians in the eighteenth century. In the south and east of the country another type of monument, the causewayed camp, is comparatively common. These are ditched enclosures which seem to have been used for a variety of social purposes. Many of these elements, the causewayed camps, cursus-style monuments, and long burial mounds, are found in different combinations and styles in continental Europe in a region spreading from west-central France to Poland. Thus eastern and much of southern Britain shared in a broad North Sea cultural continuum. The henge monuments, on the other hand, appear to be a more insular phenomenon and, given their early occurrence on Orkney, it is possible that the religious motivation behind these constructions may first have originated in the northern part of the Atlantic zone.

5.23 (*facing*) Ireland and Britain in the Neolithic period, *c*.3000 BC. Orkney and the Boyne valley were two centres of innovation.

One area where the concept of the henge monument developed to monumental proportions was Wessex. Here, in a broad arc sweeping across the chalk, from the Marlborough Downs almost to Weymouth Bay, five extensive ritual complexes were created, each focused around a massive henge monument—Avebury, Marden, Durrington Walls, Knowlton, and Mount Pleasant (5.24, 5.25, 5.26). Each of the henges consisted of a substantial ditch with a bank on the outside with two or four entrance gaps. Inside, in those cases where excavation has taken place, one or more large, circular timber buildings have been identified. The size of the henges varies from 250 metres across at Knowlton to about 400 metres at Durrington Walls. The henges themselves are only one element in very complicated monument ensembles which include massive barrows (at Knowlton and Durrington), the unique Silbury Hill, and the stone avenues of Avebury, together with smaller henges and hengiform structures such as the complex wooden monuments of the Sanctuary near Avebury and Woodhenge near Stonehenge. Each of the ritual landscapes

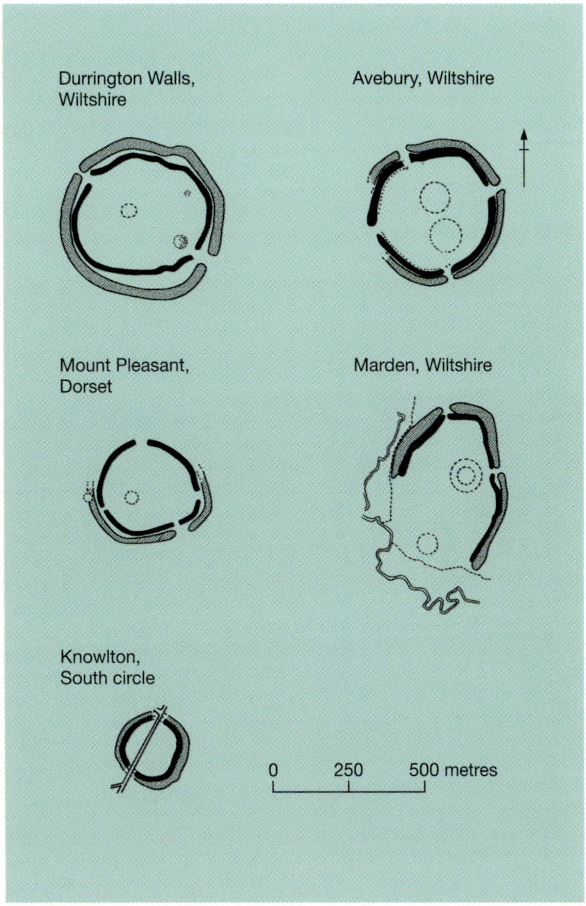

5.24 The great henge monuments of Wessex.

is different and, as new discoveries are constantly reminding us, only a fraction of each complex is at present known.

The great Wessex henges seem to have been built around 2500 BC—a full half a millennium later than the Orkney henges—but they were probably the culmination of a tradition that had already become rooted in the area centuries earlier, that is, they were a highly regional interpretation of an earlier and more widespread concept. The first phase of Stonehenge, dating to *c.*3000 BC, is an example of an early henge. At this stage the monument consisted of a circular ditch, 110 metres in diameter, with an internal bank inside of which was a circle of fifty-six large pits, now thought to have held upright timbers. Stonehenge 1 bears many similarities to the Orkney henges with which it is broadly contemporary.

One further comparison can be made. Many of the ritual monuments extending from Orkney to Wessex are associated with a distinctive type of pottery known to archaeologists as Grooved Ware (5.27). That similar forms and decoration occurred over such considerable areas—across a distance of 1000 kilometres—is quite remarkable (5.23). So too is the fact that in Wessex Grooved Ware was in use throughout the third millennium. This uniformity and persistence, coupled with the fact that Grooved Ware is usually found in ritual contexts and not on domestic sites, has led to the suggestion that it was made specifically for cult purposes. In other words, henge monuments and Grooved Ware were part of a widely adopted 'ritual package' extending the length of the British Isles. The radiocarbon dates from Orkney suggest that Grooved Ware may have developed locally some time about 3200–3100 BC. If so, then this clearly has fascinating implications, for the totality of the evidence would support the view that the ritual package may have emerged in Orkney and from there spread very rapidly to the rest of eastern and southern Britain. The only reasonable context for such a rapid and extensive spread would be in the adoption of the belief system of which the henge and Grooved Ware were the few surviving remnants. That beliefs could spread in this way need occasion no surprise, as we will see later in discussing exchange systems.

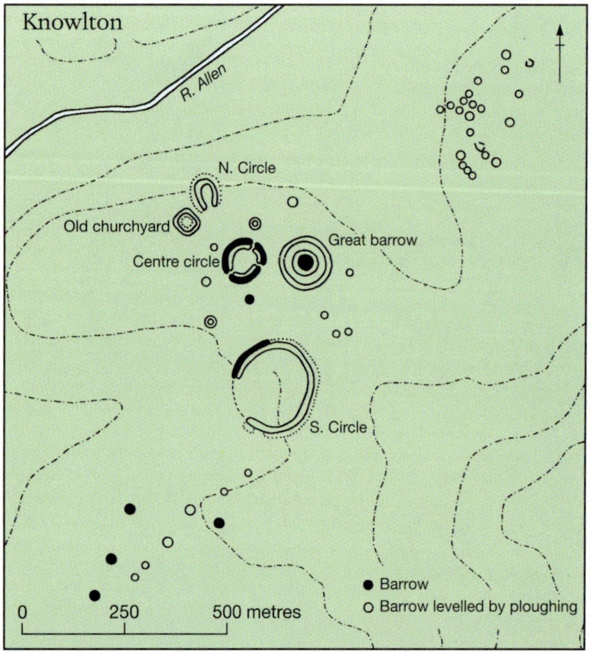

5.25 The Late Neolithic and Early Bronze Age monuments at Knowlton, Dorset. The round barrows, of Early Bronze Age date, were built around the cluster of henge monuments and the Great Barrow of the early–mid third millennium BC.

5.26 Part of the ritual complex at Knowlton, Dorset shown in Fig. 5.25. The ruined church is in the Centre Circle.

5.27 Grooved ware vessels from various sites in eastern Britain.

There remains one part of the British Isles still to consider—the Severn valley, which lies on the interface between the passage grave zone of the Irish Sea and Wessex. Centred on the estuary and the lower valley of the river is a group of distinctive megalithic tombs known as the Severn–Cotswold group. About 175 have been identified, the greatest concentration lying on the Cotswold Hills of Gloucestershire. The principal characteristic shared by all is that the burial chambers lie within a long mound, usually trapezoidal in shape. Three basic subtypes have been identified based on the nature of the burial chamber—simple terminal chambers, transepted terminal chambers, and lateral chambers. Although much has been written about the typology of the Severn–Cotswold tombs and comparisons made with tombs of Armorica, it is difficult to present a convincing development sequence or to place the group within its proper time frame. However, radiocarbon dates from four tombs indicate that in these cases construction took place between 3900 and 3600 BC. Material from grave chambers, however, shows that burials continued to be made in some tombs up to the beginning of the second millennium. It would seem, therefore, that the Severn–Cotswold tombs began, like the other tomb series of the Atlantic zone, some time around 4000 BC or a little earlier, possibly with simple chambers of the portal dolmen type, and over a thousand years or so developed a series of regional variants. It may well be that the long trapezoidal mounds, so common among the tombs of the group, were a feature adopted from the long barrow tradition of the Wessex chalkland, in which case the Severn–Cotswold group could be seen to be combining the traditions of the west and the east.

Within the area of distribution of the Severn–Cotswold tombs, at Stanton Drew, 10 kilometres south of Bristol, lie the remains of one of the most impressive megalithic ritual monuments in England. What now survives above ground are the remains of three circles, two of them with stone avenues attached. The largest of the circles is 113 metres in diameter (second largest in England after Avebury), and has recently been shown by archaeomagnetic survey to contain a number of concentric circles of pits which may have taken standing posts or stones. The complex is clearly a ritual site of some importance comparable to those of Wessex and Orkney, though from which direction its inspiration came—west via the Atlantic or east via Wessex—is a debatable issue.

Western Iberia

In the foregoing discussion we have shown that the northern part of the Atlantic zone from west-central France to the Shetland Isles shared in a common cultural tradition. It is now necessary to look to the south of the Bay of Biscay to see what was happening there in the fourth and early third millennia in Iberia.

A simple distribution map of megalithic tombs shows that the entire Atlantic façade of Iberia was densely scattered with monuments of this general kind. When examined in detail the majority of them can be shown to belong to the passage grave tradition. Within this broad zone the centre of innovation lay in central Portugal around the estuaries of the Tagus and Sado. As we will see in the next chapter, the region, already densely exploited in Mesolithic times, retained its pre-eminent position throughout the second millennium.

The archaeological record, though unusually rich, tends to lack the

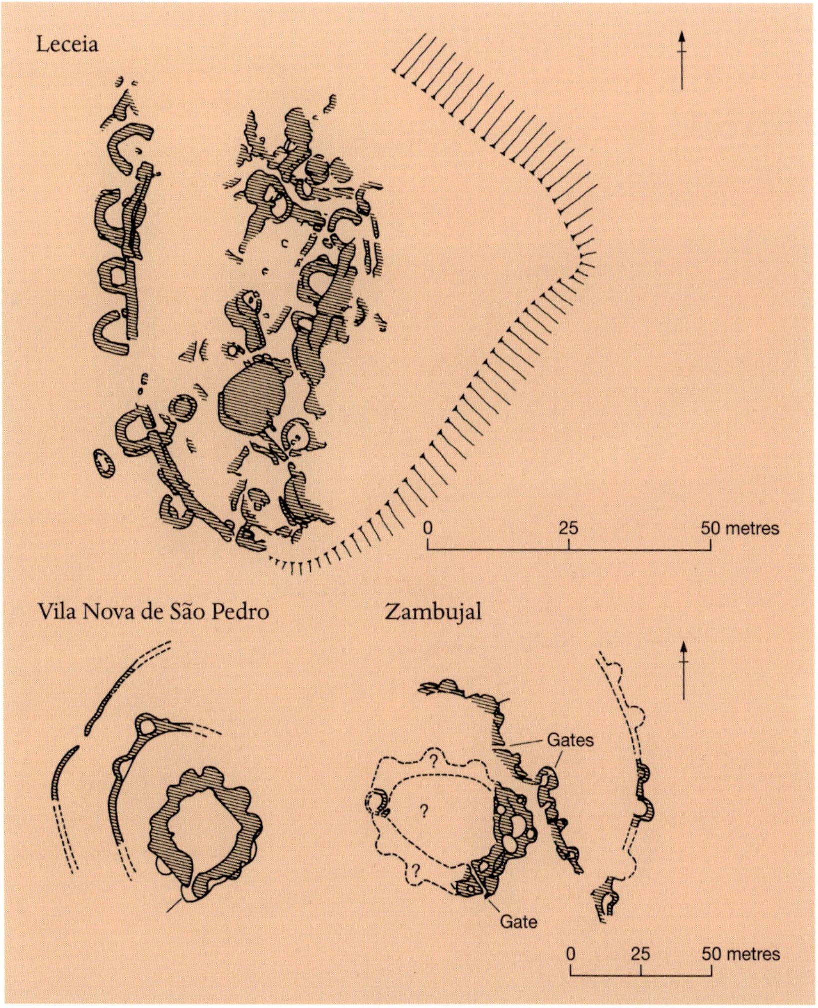

5.28 Plans of fortified settlements of the third millennium from the Tagus region, Portugal.

stratigraphical precision that allows the development of culture to be clearly charted. Recent work, however, is helping to clarify some of the issues. Two types of site dominate the landscape, megalithic tombs and heavily defended villages (5.28), both of which were in use throughout the third millennium although the tombs begin earlier. Archaeologists have named the local 'culture' after one of the fortified settlements, Vila Nova de São Pedro (or VNSP for short), situated some 60 kilometres north of Lisbon. Settlements like Vila Nova de São Pedro and Zambujal, near Torres Vedras, were occupied over a long period of time, during which complex, stone-built defences with forward-projecting bastions were built and extended. At Zambujal (5.29), where the evidence is better-recorded, it was possible to show that the walls were thickened over time

5.29 The fortified settlement of Zambujal under excavation, 1968. The successive walls with their circular bastions can readily be distinguished.

by the addition of successive faces until, in some places, they reached up to 4 metres in thickness. Such massive structures were out of all proportion to defensive needs and suggest that rebuilding may have been undertaken to reassert status on a periodic basis rather than as a response to aggression.

Careful stratigraphical excavations at Leceia near Oeiras in the Portuguese Extremadura, exposed the remains of another long-lived settlement. Here a series of radiocarbon dates were obtained, showing that the limestone promontory had first been occupied by an open settlement in the period 3400–2900 BC, and that after a gap of a century or so three lines of massive stone defences had been built. The defended settlement which remained in use over the period 2800–2600 BC depended for its livelihood on wheat and barley cultivation and the rearing of cattle, sheep, and pigs, but there was also evidence of intensive use of the nearby maritime resources both for fishing and collecting a wide variety of shellfish. The community was evidently well established and able to maintain its complex defences on its productive surplus.

The collective tombs, which tend to cluster around the settlements, have yielded a rich haul of grave goods and a few, excavated according to modern standards, have allowed a clear distinction to be made between the Neolithic assemblage and the later Beaker material. At Praia das Maçãs, in Sintra, a later tomb blocked the entrance of an earlier structure which produced only Neolithic material, including highly characteristic incised schist plaques representing, though at some remove, stylized idols (5.38). The distribution of these plaques is restricted to the southwestern corner of Iberia and can be taken to represent a broad cultural zone sharing the same religious symbolism.

There is much variation among the tomb types, but the passage grave tradition is well in evidence in tombs such as Pai Mogo, near Torres Vedras. Here the circular burial chamber, reached by a long narrow entrance passage, was built of drystone work, partially corbelled but roofed with a single capstone. The internal stratigraphy showed that the tomb was in use for burial over a long period of time and only in the later stages were Beaker and copper items found. Other common tomb types are simple dolmens and rock-cut tombs.

There has been much discussion over the years about the origins, date, and development of the Portuguese tombs, and for some while it was believed that collective burial, together with the technique of building defensive walls with bastions, was introduced by immigrants from the east Mediterranean. With the advent of radiocarbon dating this view was, quite decisively, shown to be wrong—consigning to the backwaters of archaeological historicity a considerable body of literature! Although radiocarbon dates, and dates produced by a different scientific method called thermoluminescence, are still too few to provide finely graded sequences, it is now clear that passage graves were being constructed at least as early as 4500 BC in the Upper Alentejo, while tombs with circular chambers and corbelled roofs were in evidence by 3000. Dates for the simple dolmens lie in the first half of the fourth millennium. At best this shows that in central and southern Portugal the megalithic tomb-building tradition probably began in the early fifth century, at about the same time as the earliest passage graves were being built in Brittany.

In Galicia, in the north-western corner of Iberia, where megalithic tombs are numerous, simple chambered tombs had probably begun to be built by 4500 BC and continued to be constructed for about 1,500 years: on present showing passage graves are not known before about 4000 BC.

Taking the evidence on its face value, it does seem to support the view that the megalithic tradition began in western Iberia with simple chambered tombs found along the entire seaboard, and from this early beginning the more sophisticated types of passage graves were soon to develop. The principal difference between north-west and south-west Iberia lay in the cultural richness of the south-west, and in particular the zone around the Tagus estuary where monumental defensive architecture began to develop to proclaim the exalted status of those who could command its construction.

Southern Scandinavia and Northern Germany

Finally, in this brief review of regional coastal traditions, we return to southern Sweden, Denmark, and the northern coasts of Germany and Poland where, in the fourth and early third millennia, the local Neolithic communities had developed a degree of cultural similarity, known in the archaeological literature as the Funnel-necked Beaker culture (or TRB). Here two broad funerary traditions evolved: burial beneath long earthen mounds, and burial in stone-built chambers embedded in mounds. The earthen long mounds extend across a wide coastal zone from the Vistula to the Elbe and northwards into Jutland, while the megalithic burial chambers seem first to have emerged in a more restricted area, roughly coincident with the old Ertebølle culture covering the mainland coasts and islands between eastern Jutland and south-west Sweden and the north coast of eastern Germany. The earliest of these tombs, found on Zealand, were built about 3700 BC. Thereafter they proliferated: in Denmark alone there were between 5,000 and 6,000.

Such a large dataset has invited classification, and many schemes, usually evolutionary, have been offered, though their value remains in doubt.

The simplest of the dolmens (Danish: *dysser*) consisted of four boulders or slabs of stone placed upright to form a rectangular chamber roofed with a single capstone. More elaborate forms were polygonal or elongated, and some were provided with a short entrance passage allowing access. Those without such a refinement could be entered only by removing the capstone, which may well have been possible since the mounds surrounding the chambers were low enough to leave the capstones exposed. More elaborate tombs, or passage graves, were fully buried within the mound, but their oval-shaped or elongated chambers were accessible through long entrance passages opening from the perimeter of the mounds.

The typological similarity of these northern dolmens and passage graves to those of Britain, France, and Iberia has naturally long excited comment, and although the northern developments are significantly later than those of the more westerly Atlantic tradition, there is no denying that seaborne contact may have inspired the nascent Nordic megalithic tradition. This said, there is little else to indicate maritime intercourse with the Atlantic zone. The concept of erecting a dolmen to contain burials is not exceptional. There is growing evidence to show that the Funnel-necked Beaker burial rite was complex and varied. Many of the long earthen mounds were used for collective burial instead of the more common single burial. Bodies seem to have been exposed before bones were collected for deposition in structures beneath the mound. The dolmens also functioned as receptacles for gathered human remains, and it would have been a simple step to provide an entrance so that more bodies could be added. In other words, it would be entirely reasonable to explain the northern burial tradition in terms of local development—no outside inspiration need have been required.

Yet the coincidence remains that it was in the disparate coastal regions with stable, high-density Mesolithic populations that traditions of burial in stone-built tombs first emerged. Perhaps the dominant linking factor is *collective burial*, the stone-built tombs emerging as a response to this rite. Collective burial implies complex belief patterns about the importance of co-locating past members of the lineage at a particular place—the ancestors being interred in the ancestral territory. It is this concept that distinguished the coastal communities of Neolithic Europe, ever conscious that they lived at the end of the world.

Shared Beliefs

This rapid regional survey of the ritual monuments of western Europe has given some idea of the diversities and similarities between the different regions. The similarities have long impressed archaeologists, who in the past have been led to write of 'megalithic colonization' or the movements of 'megalithic missionaries', but such concepts are too simplistic to account for the full richness of the archaeological record as we have now come to understand it. The advent of radiocarbon dating, which allows tolerably accurate assessments of absolute age to be made, has changed our perceptions by extending the time-span covered by these developments back for more than two thousand years, thus removing the need to see everything as the consequence of influences emanating from the East via the Mediterranean. The 'megalithic culture' of the Atlantic coasts emerges as an entirely indigenous phenomenon originating in the fifth millennium, flourishing in the fourth, and continuing into the third: it is a manifestation of local Atlantic genius.

Once freed from the constraints of having to explain everything by reference to the Mediterranean, and armed with a growing battery of radiocarbon dates, the inevitable quest for origins began: where along the Atlantic seaboard did the 'megalithic package' first emerge? Some have argued for Portugal, others for Brittany. Both regions have monuments dating to the fifth millennium and either could, on present showing, have been the primary focus of innovation. Yet need there have been a single focus? Could not the cultural developments we have outlined have evolved across a broad front among communities intricately linked by the sea? Before facing this question we must consider a further range of evidence.

Much has been made of tomb architecture, not least because there are a bewildering array of tomb types to make sense of. Yet the general pattern of development is really quite straightforward. In most areas one of the simplest of the earliest tomb types is the 'dolmen', a rectangular chamber usually built of large stone blocks. It is the kind of response to the need to dispose of the dead that could emerge anywhere in the world at any time, so long as there were large stone blocks readily to hand, and once established such a basic form is likely to have continued long in use. Simple dolmens are found throughout the entire Atlantic zone, and in Portugal, Brittany, Britain, and Ireland are demonstrably early. In Brittany antecedents may be seen in the Mesolithic stone-lined graves of Téviec. The more sophisticated grave type, with an entrance corridor leading to a central chamber—the passage grave—was soon to appear in Portugal and Brittany, reaching Ireland and northern and western Britain probably by the beginning of the fourth millennium. Thereafter throughout the megalithic zone a wide variety of tombs were built showing much regional variation. In some areas—the Morbihan, the Boyne valley, and Orkney—huge structures were constructed requiring massive input of labour. After the end of the fourth millennium, although new tombs continued to be built in many areas, they were more modest in scale.

The broad parallelism in the development of tomb architecture throughout the entire Atlantic region should be seen against widespread occurrences of other forms of architecture, in particular circular ritual monuments built of standing stones or timbers, or defined by banks and ditches, and the long rows of standing stones in single or multiple alignments. The similarities are such that the only reasonable explanation is to suppose that the maritime communities maintained contact with each other throughout this period.

These various structures are specific enough to imply a shared system of beliefs. Even more compelling evidence for this is the widespread adoption of a restricted set of symbols and a sophisticated cosmology.

The carving of symbols on free-standing menhirs and on the orthostats, lintels, and kerbstones of tombs is a phenomenon found throughout the Atlantic zone from southern Portugal to Orkney. Painting is more restricted, and is at present known only in Iberia, but this may, in part at least, be an accident of survival. Decoration of these kinds, though geographically extensive, is not frequent, being restricted to forty-two sites in Iberia, forty-six in north-west France, thirty-nine in Ireland, and six in Britain.

In Brittany four chronologically and stylistically distinct sets of designs can be distinguished. One of the earliest groups adorned the free-standing menhirs, the broken fragments of which were later reused in passage graves. The range of motifs were fairly restricted (5.30), being confined to isolated symbols such as bovines, complex axe-like structures, axes hafted in crooks, simple crooks, and an anthropomorphic rendering inappropriately called a 'buckler' or an 'écusson'. Some of the same motifs are also found on the walls of early passage graves together with 'waves', 'yokes', U-motifs, crosses, triangular axes, and so on. It may well be

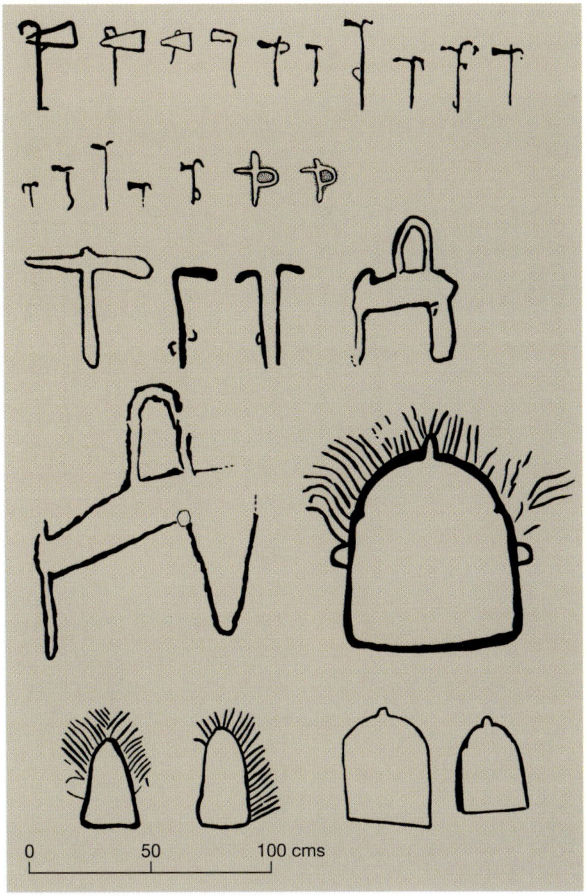

5.30 Selection of motifs carved on menhirs and passage grave tombs in Brittany.

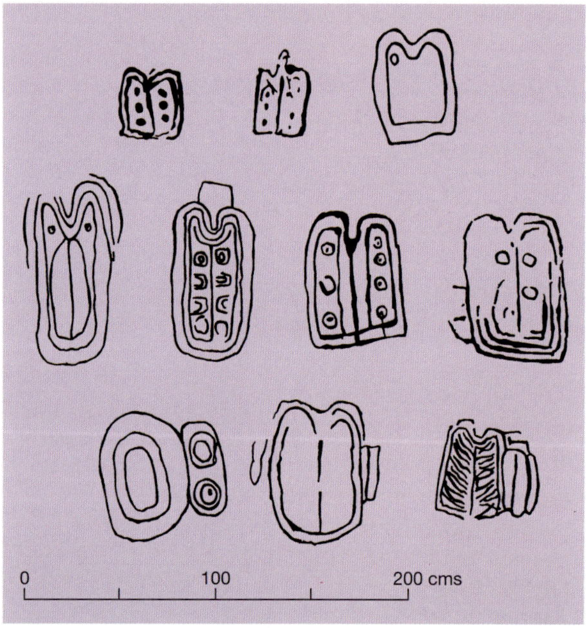

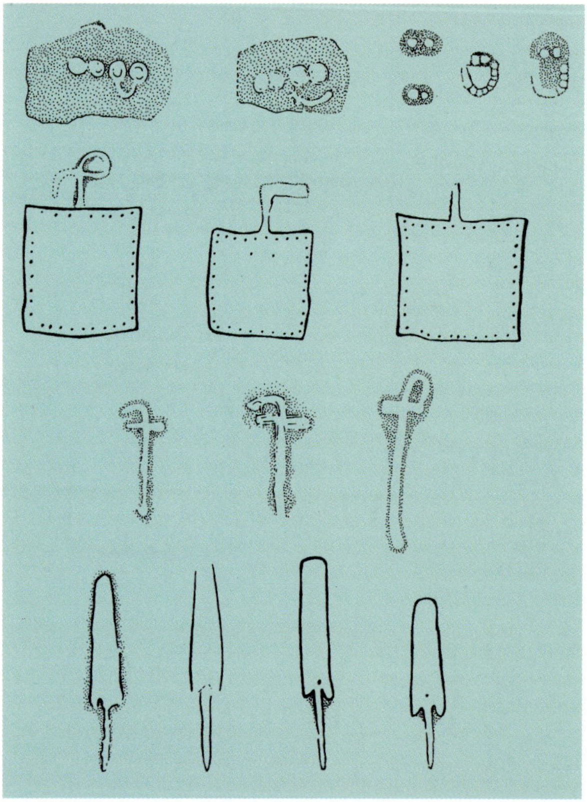

that the early passage grave and the menhir traditions began separately and were later combined by using parts of menhirs in the later passage graves and by adopting some of the motifs for transfer to the orthostats of tombs.

The menhir/passage grave repertoire is quite distinct from the motifs carved on the angled passage graves of the Morbihan. The restricted range of forms, easier to illustrate than to describe (5.31), appear to be anthropomorphic and for the most part have a strict bilateral symmetry. A different repertoire again is represented in the gallery graves and is probably the latest of the Breton styles (5.32). The motifs include hafted axes, tanged daggers, pairs of breasts, sometimes with attached necklaces, and enigmatic square motifs with a projection.

The one monument that stands apart from all the others is the passage grave of Gavr'inis. Almost all of the orthostats which line the passage and chamber are covered in carvings involving complex juxtapositions of whorls, multiple waves, and zigzags giving the impression of manic energy (5.36). Amid it all other shapes and structures are dimly recognizable, the clearest being long, triangular-shaped axes, often occurring in pairs. One quite plausible suggestion is that these are entopic images, that is, images generated under conditions of altered consciousness. Such conditions can occur during hallucinations brought on by drugs or trances caused by exposure to rhythmic beating or other kinds of sensory deprivation. In neurophysiological experiments carried out to study this phenomenon the participants might identify recognizable objects among the entopic images. Such could be the explanation for the axes at Gavr'inis. In any event the unique decoration of the monument sets it apart and supports the suggestion that Gavr'inis may have served more as a shrine than a tomb.

To read meaning into the symbols displayed on the Breton megaliths is an impossible task, but the one recognizable item, recurring on many monuments, is the axe, shown either hafted or as a separate blade. These may well be representations of the finely polished stone axes found as grave goods in several of the tombs. Clearly the axe, whether real or depicted, was a potent symbol in Brittany.

5.33 Selection of motifs engraved on stones from Irish passage graves.

In Ireland and adjacent parts of Britain a distinct passage grave art developed in the late fourth and early third millennia. Nineteen site occurrences have been noted in Ireland, two of them, the cemeteries in the Boyne valley and at Loughcrew, together producing more than four hundred decorated stones. In Britain similar art is represented at three sites in Orkney, two in Wales, and one in England. The range of motifs employed is varied, but most compositions employ zigzags, lozenges, concentric circles, spirals, U-motifs, and radial motifs usually combined in elaborate overall patterns (5.33, 5.34). A distinction has been made between two dominant styles, the Fourknocks style and the Loughcrew style: in the former the overall effect is of careful planning and order; in the latter, to the modern observer, there is no evident attempt to control the spacing of the individual elements. The most elaborate example of the Fourknocks style is the entrance stone from Newgrange in the Boyne valley, with its surprising balance and harmony (5.34). The close similarities between the passage grave art of Ireland, Orkney, Anglesey, and the Calderstones, near Liverpool, leave little doubt that the British and Irish sites can be considered as sharing in a single artistic continuum.

The megalithic art of Iberia may be divided into two groups on stylistic and distributional grounds. In the Viseu region of Portugal a limited range of painted motifs are found on the orthostats of passage graves. They include human figures, a 'skin skeuomorph', so named because it looks like the flattened skin of an animal, rows of triangles or Vs, sawtooth motifs, and serpentiform lines (5.35). Monuments decorated in this

5.31 (*facing, above*) Selection of motifs carved on the walls of angled passage graves in Brittany.

5.32 (*facing, below*) Selection of motifs carved on the walls of gallery graves in Brittany.

way form a distinct group between the Douro and the Mondego. Elsewhere, in the north-west and south-west corners of the peninsula carving prevails, the most common motifs being sawteeth, serpentiforms, radials, circles, and U-motifs.

5.34 (*facing*) The highly decorated entrance stone at the tomb of Newgrange (*above*) with one of the decorated kerbstones (*below*).

Comparison between the three broad geographical groups into which megalithic carving and painting can be divided—Iberia, Brittany, and Ireland–Britain—shows that the most basic of the motifs, serpentiform and zigzag lines, radials, U-motifs, cup mark, and concentric circles, were common to all, but so universal are such basic symbols that too much significance should not be placed on this. When the more complex motifs are considered each of the three regions stands out as distinct, Iberia with its opposed sawteeth, Brittany with its axes, and Britain and Ireland with its spirals and chevrons. But the individual motifs aside, what is significant is that throughout the entire length of the Atlantic zone the belief systems which lay behind the construction of the megalithic tombs also involved using the stones themselves, through the symbols carved or painted on them, as a means of communication. While we may not be able to understand the messages which they conveyed we can be tolerably certain that the images served to link the real, everyday world with the other world of the spirits and the gods. Behind what may now appear to be incomprehensible disorder would have been structure and meaning.

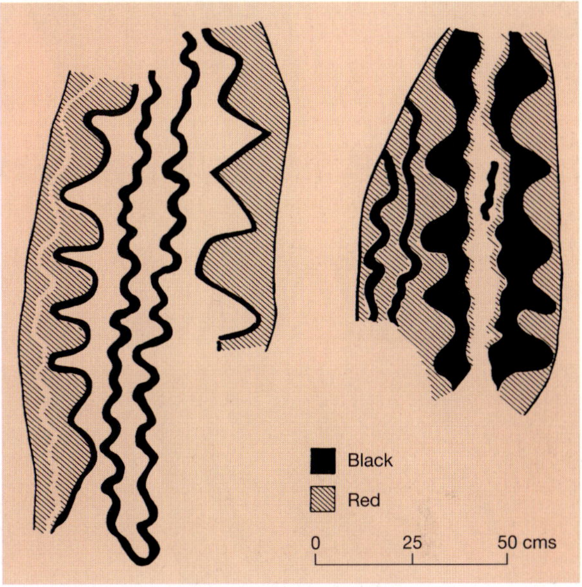

5.35 Painted decoration from the megalithic tombs of Portugal.

Where we can begin to approach the minds and motivations of the fourth-millennium Atlantic communities is through our shared knowledge of astronomy. It has long been believed that megalithic monuments were in some way related to the celestial cycle, and that the midsummer sun rose on the axis of Stonehenge was well known by the eighteenth century. Thereafter there have been many attempts to read astronomical significance into megalithic monuments and to endow them with remarkable mathematical sophistication. Some of what has been written is completely spurious and some is unproven. Yet there remains the unshakeable fact that a number of our most impressive megalithic tombs were designed with immense skill to relate precisely to significant solar or lunar events. A few examples will demonstrate the point.

5.36 (*facing*) Decorated orthostats from the tomb of Gavr'inis, Morbihan.

At Newgrange in the Boyne valley the passage of the tomb was carefully aligned on the midwinter sunrise. It was so designed that the 'roof box'—a narrow window built above the capstone at the beginning of the passage, allowed the rising sun, at dawn on the midwinter solstice, to flood the chamber with light for a brief period of fifteen minutes or so. This happens for a week before and after the solstice, but it is only on the day itself that the beam enters the end chamber. Since the monument was built, five thousand years ago, there have been slight changes in the earth's relation to the sun, but it has been calculated that in about 3000 BC the beam would have exactly bisected the chamber, lighting up the unique triple spiral carved on the orthostat forming the back wall.

The nearby monument at Knowth was also laid out with great deliberation. Its two separate passages are aligned exactly east to west, so that while the west-facing passage exactly catches the setting sun on the spring and summer equinoxes (21 March and 21 September), the east-facing passage is oriented on the rising sun. Of the third great Boyne mound, Dowth, it has been claimed that the shorter passage is aligned on sunset on the midwinter solstice and that the three decorated stones in the chamber were carefully placed to receive direct or reflected sunlight during the solstice period. The longer passage at Dowth has not yet been tested, but its general west-south-west orientation could suggest an alignment on the setting sun on the winter cross-quarter days in November and February, which lie exactly halfway between equinox and solstice. There also remains the possibility of another, yet undiscovered passage in Dowth, perhaps with another significant orientation. Leaving aside these more speculative matters, the established facts are sufficient to show that the three great Boyne tombs were designed to acknowledge significant times in the winter celestial cycle.

Such sophistication is not restricted to Ireland. Maes Howe in Orkney is aligned on the midwinter sunset. A slab which partially blocked the entrance was deliberately set low to create a window, rather like the 'roof box' at Newgrange. At sunset on the solstice the sun's rays shine right down the passage and into the chamber at the end. Claims have also been made that the Ring of Brodgar was designed to allow lunar observations to be made, but these are more difficult to demonstrate.

Finally, let us return to Gavr'inis in the Morbihan, a monument which, by virtue of its size and elaborate decoration, stands out as one of central importance in the region (5.36). Its alignment has been argued to be significant, for the central axis, at 134 degrees, is close to that of the major southern moonrise, while a second axis at 128 degrees (running from the right-hand outer corner of the passage to the left-hand inner corner) aligns with the midwinter sunrise. That the two axes cross at a point where a large quartz slab has been set up in the wall may be nothing more than an intriguing coincidence. While the evidence from Gavr'inis lacks the full conviction of that from the Boyne tombs and Maes Howe, it may fairly be included in the list of monuments with significant celestial alignments.

Similarities in tomb form, collective burial, the adoption of carved and painted symbols, and attention to celestial events combine to provide convincing support for the case for there having been significant social interaction between the many communities living along the Atlantic façade in the fourth and early third millennia. As one might expect, regions close together show the greatest similarities, but even so the Irish Sea zone, Armorica, and western Iberia were sufficiently alike all to be regarded as being part of a single Atlantic cultural province loosely threaded together by a web of maritime movements.

Systems of Exchange

To approach the question of how societies may have articulated themselves at this time we have to rely largely on interpreting distributions of artefacts preserved in the archaeological record. One of the most informative of these is the polished stone axe, of which tens of thousands of examples have been found in the Atlantic region. The advantages of using items of this kind are that stone, by its very nature, tends to survive well, but more important is the fact that the type of stone from which each axe was made can be identified, and quite often the outcrop of rock it came from can be reasonably closely located. In some cases it is even possible to find the actual quarry. Another advantage is that there is an extensive anthropological literature concerning the use of axes in patterns of gift exchange throughout the world. While it is unsound to argue directly from ethnographic analogy, understanding how exchange systems operate elsewhere helps to open the mind when addressing dead archaeological objects. Studies in New Guinea and the Solomon Islands, for example, show that polished axes were given, often in some number, as bride wealth, payments for funerals, and on other ceremonial occasions. For certain types of transaction only axes of a particular stone were acceptable, and some individual axes, by virtue of their quality or historical associations, were accorded exceptional value. It was no doubt in intricate exchanges of this kind, bedded deep in the social systems through which communities articulated, that the Neolithic axes of the Atlantic zone were moved from source to final resting place.

One clear example, demonstrating the intricacies of the exchange system in operation, is provided by the distribution of axes in the Channel

Islands, where good hard stone suitable for axe manufacture is readily available. On the island of Jersey, at a site called the Pinacle, a major production centre has been identified where a dolerite (known as dolerite Type P) was quarried for axe manufacture. Large numbers of these axes were exchanged with the neighbouring island of Guernsey, where 31 per cent of all the axes known are of this type, and it was probably from Guernsey that the much smaller island of Sark received its dolerite Type P axes, amounting there to 21 per cent of the island's axes. What is interesting is that on Jersey only 16 per cent of the total of all known axes were from the local dolerite source. This seems to suggest that the greater part of the Jersey production was used for exchanges with other islands rather than for local use, while Jersey itself received 28 per cent of its axes from Brittany and 16 per cent from Normandy. Exactly what this meant in contemporary social terms it is impossible to know, but the figures reflect quite complex patterns of exchange in which 'foreign' axes were evidently endowed with a value above that of local products. Since the only way in which the axes could have been transported was by sea, it may be that periodic seaborne expeditions organized by the elite bound the islands and mainland together in complex cycles of gift exchange, rather like the kula exchange cycle of the Melanesian islands made famous by the anthropologist Malinowski. In such a system those able to command the seagoing vessels and the navigational skills were the important people.

In Brittany the production and distribution of stone axes is very well attested in the archaeological record. Five major sources have been identified. The most prolific of these was at Sélédin, Plussulien, in the Côtes-d'Armor, where an extensive quarry for dolerite (dolerite Type A) has been examined. Sélédin produced about 50 per cent of all the axes found in Brittany. Other sources include fibrolite found near Brest and in the Morbihan, hornblendite from Pleuven near Quimper, and eclogite from near Nantes. Eclogite is very similar to jadeite, from which the spectacular ceremonial axes found in the Carnac region were made. No certain local source has been found, and it may well be that the jadeite axes were imported from the Alps, but the possibility remains that the Breton axes may have been made from rock obtained near Île Groix from an exposure no longer accessible because of changes in sea-level.

The axe-production factories at Sélédin have been studied in detail and present a fascinating insight into the scale of production. The workings were massive, extending over an area of a square kilometre, and are estimated to have produced about 6 million tools over the twelve hundred years that the quarries were in use—that is an average of about five thousand axes a year! It is thought that to make a single finished axe would have taken one person/day. Thus, if one person worked for 250 days a year, twenty people would have been needed to maintain output. Figures of this sort give some idea of the complexity of the social organization involved.

Production on this scale was hardly necessary to satisfy the practical needs of the Breton community, but if the axes were essential to maintain systems of gift exchange then the scale of the operation can be understood. The distribution of the axes from Sélédin offers a particularly clear picture of the contemporary exchange networks (5.37). In Brittany itself they account for nearly half of all axes found. Beyond this the density decreases, but what the map shows clearly is the importance of the Loire as an axis of communication. There can be little doubt of the strength of the social bonds which linked the Breton communities to those commanding the valley route. It is also interesting to see how far beyond north-western France the axes were exchanged. The four finds from Britain, two close to the Solent shore and two on the Severn estuary, probably reflect the maritime contacts that must have been in operation at this time.

Another of the Breton quarries, that at Pleuven near Quimper, which produced elegant battleaxes some time around 3000 BC, seems to have been serving much the same distribution network (5.37), even though its output was on a more restricted scale. What stands out here is the significance of coastal traffic down the west coast of France to the Garonne as well as the dominance of the Loire route.

5.37 The distribution of dolerite axes made at Plussulien in central Brittany and the distribution of shaft-hole axes of hornblendite from south-western Brittany.

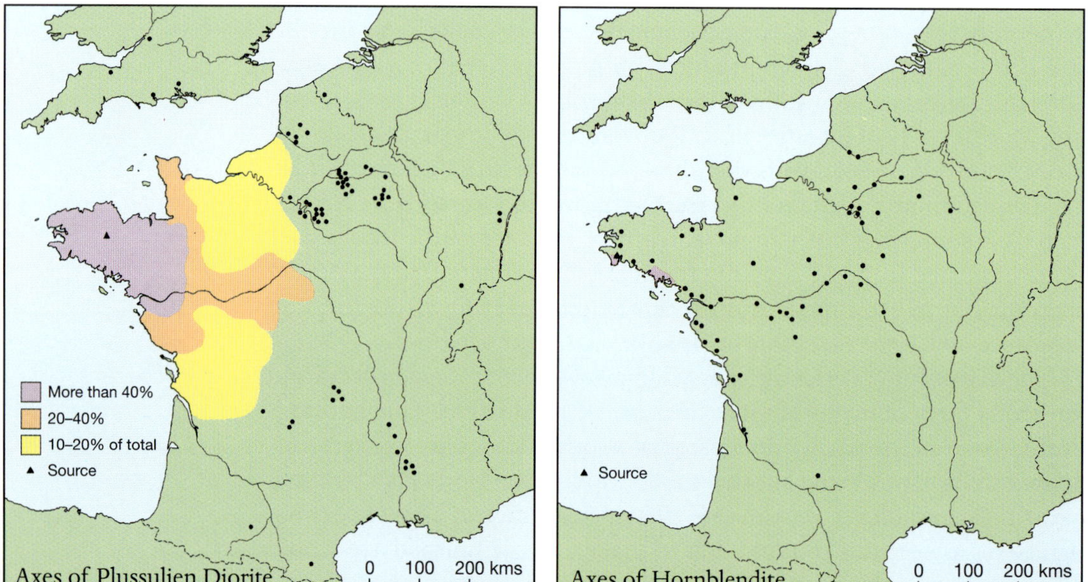

The processes involved in the transport of axes from the quarry to the places where they are found will never be known with any degree of certainty, but that the movement was bound up in patterns of complex social behaviour we can be tolerably certain. One tantalizing hint is provided by the ritual site of Er Lannic—two conjoined hemicycles of standing stones now partially submerged in the bay of Morbihan. Here excavation has revealed a number of hearths associated with unusually large quantities of pottery, together with ample evidence that axes were being gathered for final polishing. The collection contained twenty-seven fibrolite axes and eleven others (some of dolerite Type A), as well as hundreds of fragments and a number of polishing stones. The nearest source of fibrolite is at Pont-Navalo 2 kilometres away. It seems reasonable, therefore, to suppose that Er Lannic may have played a significant role in the systems of distribution. The fires and broken pottery suggest some kind of structured behaviour, possibly feasting, the whole process being governed by ritual. That two of the standing stones of Er Lannic bear carvings of axes may also be relevant to the function of the site.

As we have seen, Er Lannic is not alone in bearing carvings of axes. They are a recurring motif in Breton megalithic art, the most elaborate depictions coming from the chamber of Gavr'inis. Axes of exquisite quality made from rare stone are also found as grave goods, most notably in the *Grand Tumulus* monuments of the Morbihan. Taken together the evidence leaves little doubt that the polished axe played a highly significant role in social interactions in Armorica and in articulating relationships between the communities of the Morbihan and adjacent areas of Europe.

The importance of the axe in social intercourse is also amply demonstrated by the number of 'axe factories' in production in Britain and Ireland during the fourth and third millennia, and by the extent of their distribution well beyond the place of origin. One good example of this are the axes made from a blue-grey porcellanite found to outcrop at Tievebulliagh, Co. Antrim, in Northern Ireland. This single source provided more than half the total number of axes found in Ireland, the majority of them being found within 150 kilometres from the source. A significant number were, however, distributed across the sea to Britain, occurring in greatest number in Scotland and the Isle of Man. What is particularly interesting is the persistent scatter found through the Western Isles to Orkney and Shetland. Whatever social mechanism caused these prizes to be dispersed, they must have been physically carried in boats, their distribution closely reflecting the northward extent of the passage grave tradition. The virtual absence of Tievebulliagh axes in Wales and south-western Britain is, at first sight, surprising, but since both regions have prolific axe-production centres of their own it may be

5.38 Schist plaque from the tholos tomb of Escoural and a schist crozier from Anta da Herdade das Antas, both from Montemor-o-Novo, Portugal .

that cultural preferences were being expressed. Axes of Cornish gabbro were, however, finding their way into Ireland.

While the distribution of polished stone axes provides a striking reflection of social links between communities, it is as well to remember that a wide range of other products, archaeologically invisible, were exchanged as well, and some may have been of equal or greater significance. Woven fabrics are one possibility. Some of the Irish/British passage grave art could have been meant to represent elaborate fabrics, as indeed could the tomb painting in central Portugal. Similar patterns, possibly representing clothing, are also inscribed on the anthropomorphic schist plaques found in the region (5.38). There are many examples in the ethnographic record in which finely finished fabrics featured in cycles of gift exchange. The nature of archaeological evidence is, however, such that it is unlikely ever to throw much light on the question. This said, the recurrence of decorated pins in Irish and Iberian passage graves is a reminder that fabrics were worn by the dead.

Other rare commodities, indicative of early exchange networks, include ivory from the Maghreb which was found in a number of Portuguese tombs. The anthropomorphic schist plaques so characteristic of the tomb furniture of central southern Portugal are also likely to have been a specialized product distributed through networks of social exchange.

5.39 The main centres of innovation along the Atlantic zone in the early third millennium BC and their broader zones of influence.

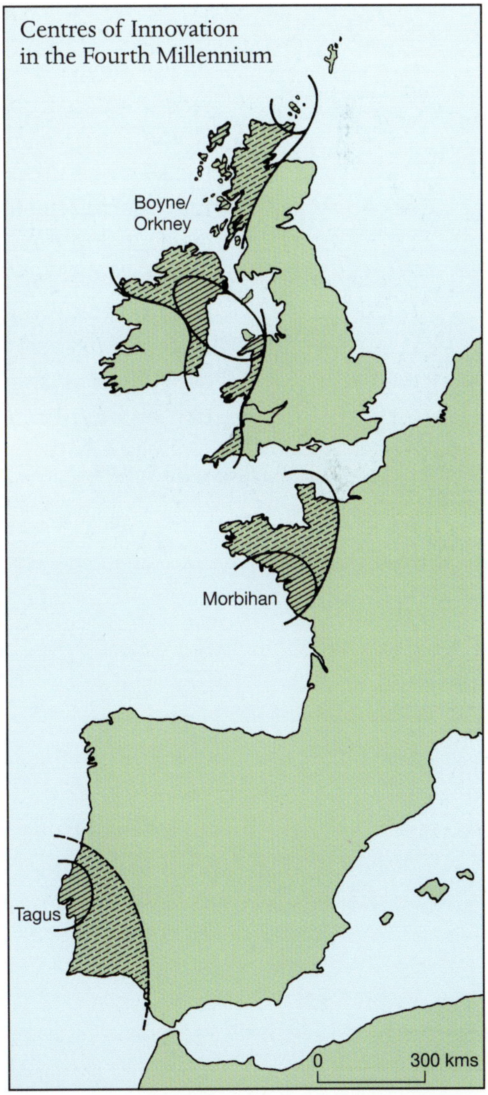

Atlantic Society in the Fourth–Early Third Millennium

In the comparatively brief period from about 4000 to 2700 BC the cultural landscape of the Atlantic zone had changed out of all recognition. At the beginning of the period food-producing strategies had barely had time to make a mark; by the end the tombs of ancestors were everywhere to be seen, proclaiming the power of lineages and signalling to all their claims to the land. There was much cultural diversity, but there was also a remarkable thread of cultural similarity running throughout the whole of the Atlantic zone, expressed most clearly in the ritual monuments.

Against this background three regions stand out as centres of power and innovation—the Tagus region, the Morbihan, and the more diffuse Boyne–Orkney axis (5.39). In each there is ample evidence of the emergence of powerful elites able to mobilize labour to create great monuments. Such power speaks of growing social complexity, and of the individual lineages being brought together in allegiance, perhaps under a unified authority. In the south-west the most obvious manifestation was the fortified settlements; in the north-west it was the great tombs, created to be in harmony with the celestial cycle.

That maritime contact played a crucial role in maintaining a stream of shared ideas along the Atlantic façade is abundantly clear. The Irish Sea was closely bound to the ocean shores of Armorica, while south-western Iberia was linked to Galicia and the Cantabrian littoral. But between the south and the north the deep bight of the Bay of Biscay intervened offering something of a separation, though coastal traffic, and more adventurous open-sea crossings between Finistère and Finisterre, may have been unexceptional, and after all these open waters would have been attractive to fishermen following the shoals.

By stressing the maritime routes we must not underestimate the cultural exchanges which linked the Atlantic communities to those deep within the Continent. The east of Britain looked to northern France, Armorican roots penetrated far along the Loire and Garonne, while south-west Portugal shared much with southern and eastern Iberia. That ideas flowed between the coasts and the Continental hinterland is abundantly reflected in artefact distributions. Beautiful and highly finished jadeite axes, probably from the fringes of the Alps, reached Armorica, Britain, and Ireland, while the idea of the hafted battleaxe, dominant in the east of Europe, was taken up in western Armorica by communities reproducing the novel form in their own hornblendite. In both cases the artefacts are symbols reflecting shared values binding the ocean-fringe communities to the heart of Europe. If, in the fourth millennium, the Atlantic community had established its unique and sophisticated ritual system reinforcing its maritime identity, the third millennium was to see the Atlantic system brought into the European ambit and bound closely to it by vigorous networks of exchange.

6. Expanding Networks and the Rise of the Individual: 2700–1200 BC

Until the beginning of the third millennium Europe was a patchwork of different cultures developing along their own largely separate trajectories, but with the growth of Minoan–Mycenaean power in the Aegean the pattern began to change—the world was becoming more complex and the disparate communities more interdependent. Population increase and the development of social systems demanding larger quantities of raw materials to fuel their cycles of conspicuous consumption added to the intensity of life. Gradually, even distant parts of Europe were drawn more and more tightly into networks which ultimately led back to the Aegean power centres. When, in the twelfth century BC, the Mycenaean world fell apart the shock waves reverberated throughout Europe.

With the Aegean world becoming an innovating and consuming core in the third and second millennia, and the rest of Europe readjusting to become its periphery, a simple 'world system' emerged. The demand for raw materials grew and, inevitably, the natural routes threading the Continent began to be more and more actively used: along them flowed not only goods but also ideas, and no doubt, in small measure, people. Those communities, favoured by nature with sources of desirable raw materials and those able to control the flow of goods by virtue of their command of the routes benefited. They had access to new ideas and, potentially, to wealth; they were also able to learn quickly of other elite systems and adopt for themselves those aspects which suited their own aspirations. The result of all this was a quickening and a convergence.

Until about 3000 BC the communities of Atlantic Europe had developed along their own trajectory little influenced by what was happening elsewhere in the more inland parts of the Continent. But some routes had begun to come into regular use. We have already seen that the Loire provided a major axis of contact along which stone axes manufactured in

Brittany were exchanged, reaching as far inland as the Seine valley. The Garonne, too, was developing as a significant route between the Atlantic and the Mediterranean. Further south the maritime route linking the Mediterranean and the Atlantic coast of Iberia was also in active use. These were the natural axes of communication which had been used for hundreds, possibly thousands, of years; the third millennium was to see the exchange networks intensify dramatically as the mineral wealth of the Atlantic zone came to be recognized and exploited.

6.1 (*facing, above*) The assemblages from three Bell Beaker graves from Oxfordshire. Left Radley, middle Dorchester, and right Stanton Harcourt.

6.2 (*facing, below*) An early Bell Beaker grave from Gaderen, Veluwe, Holland. The beaker is an All-Over Cord Bell Beaker. It was accompanied by amber beads, a battleaxe, a flat axe, and a dagger of Grand Pressigny flint.

The greatest change to come about within the Atlantic zone was the gradual abandonment of the long-established tradition of collective burial in megalithic monuments and its replacement by a new rite of single burial. The body was now treated as that of an individual by separate burial and by the provision of a set of equipment appropriate to the status of the deceased. This single burial tradition seems to have originated in the Corded Ware zone of northern Europe some time about 3000 BC, and to have spread rapidly until, by about 2300 BC, the rite had been adopted over much of western and central Europe, from Morocco to Scotland and from Ireland to Hungary. The new burial style usually involved interring the dead person with a pottery beaker. In many areas a standardized grave set was provided, including barbed and tanged arrowheads, a perforated stone wrist-guard, and a tanged copper alloy dagger (6.1). In other regions stone battleaxes were the normal accompaniment (6.2). So alike were the pottery beakers and so similar and novel was the burial rite found over extensive tracts of Europe (6.3) that archaeologists came to write of 'Beaker Folk' and to debate where these energetic migrants originated and by what routes they spread. The frequent occurrence of copper alloy objects in Beaker assemblages led some to assume that the earliest bands of 'Beaker Folk' were explorers searching for metals.

As new data became available and the different regional manifestations of the Beaker phenomenon were studied in detail the old model was found to be untenable: it was too simplistic to explain the complexities of the evidence, and the long-held belief, that major cultural changes in prehistory could only be brought about by movements of population, was beginning to be recognized as too naive. It is now widely believed that the 'Beaker package', as it is most conveniently called—that is, the belief system that celebrates the individual, and defines his status by the technosymbols required to be buried with him—was adopted in a short space of time by indigenous communities throughout western Europe. Such a rapid spread could only have come about if the territories involved were already bound together by networks of exchange, and if they had reached a state of social development in which their emerging elites were

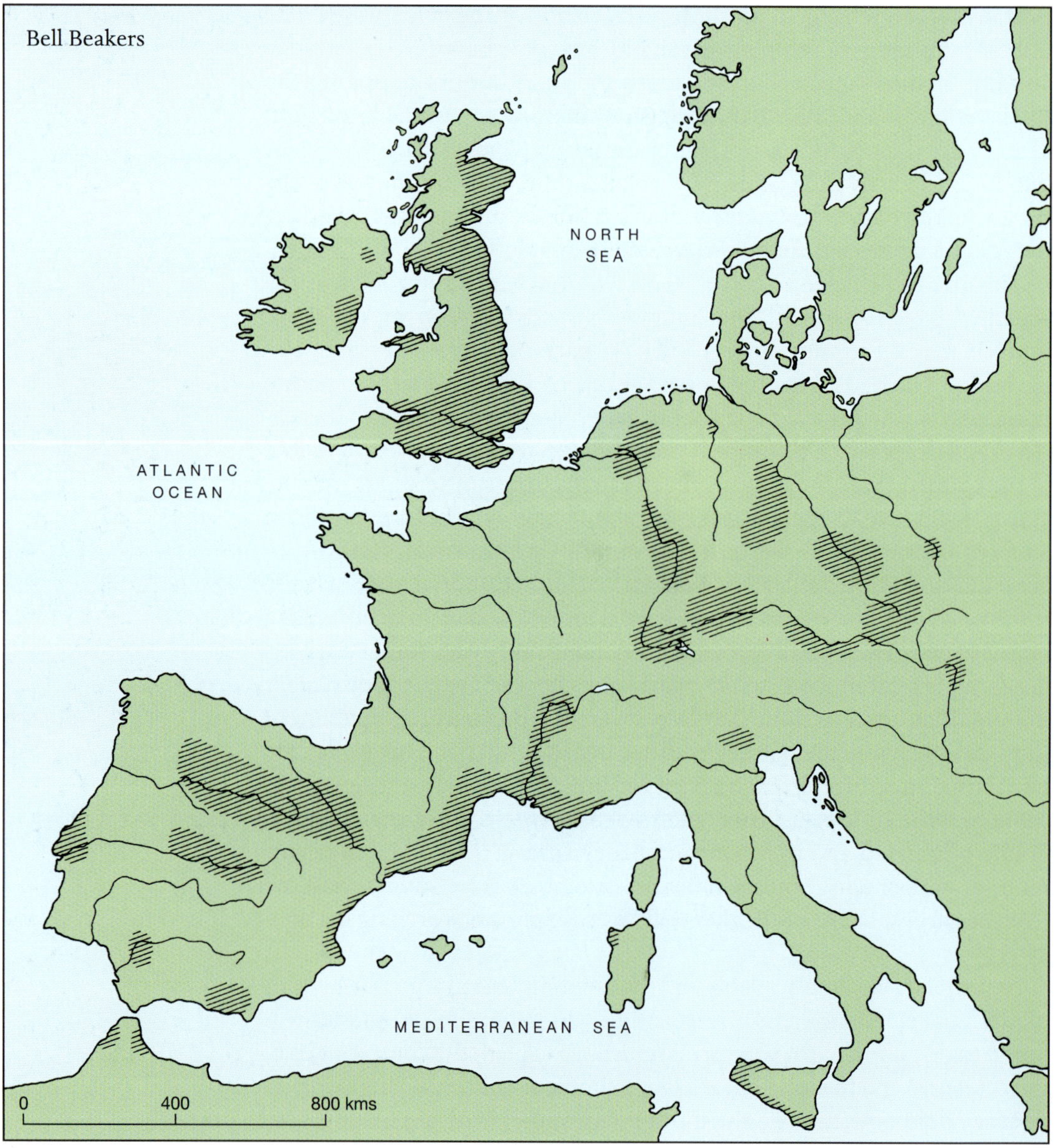

6.3 The distribution of the principal concentrations of Bell Beakers in Europe.

seeking new ways to distinguish themselves. It is often the case in prehistory that the burial customs of neighbouring societies, perceived to be desirable because of their exotic nature, may be adopted by other elites in order to distinguish themselves from those of lower status in their own society.

All this may sound a little over-elaborate, but it does better contain the evidence as we know it. Disposing of the 'Beaker Folk' as an explanation does not, however, make the dramatic changes of the third millennium any the less remarkable.

Prelude, c.3000–2500 BC

The origin of the Beaker phenomenon has been widely debated, and although views have changed quite radically over the years, most archaeologists would agree that while the single-burial tradition emerged on the Middle Rhine there were many contributory threads, of which some of the more important most likely came from the Tagus region of Portugal. Before we can begin to look at the communities of the Atlantic zone and explore their role, it is necessary to say something of the formative processes in northern Europe.

We saw, in the last chapter, how there emerged in a broad swath of the North European Plain, from eastern Germany to west Ukraine, a distinctive cultural grouping known as the Corded Ware, or Corded Ware–Battle Axe, culture. This helpfully explicit archaeological nomenclature makes clear that the type-fossils of the culture were cord-decorated vessels in the form of handleless beakers and stone battleaxes which accompanied the dead individual, invariably a man, in his grave. The Corded Ware culture emerged about 3000 BC and continued until about 2400 BC, during this time spreading into neighbouring territories—into Denmark, the Netherlands, and Switzerland in the west as well as deep into Russia, towards Moscow, in the east. While some archaeologists still believe that the expansion was the result of at least some element of folk movement, most would agree that the cultural package—single burial and the accompanying burial set—spread mainly by emulation. In other words, neighbouring societies simply adopted the rite and symbols of elite burial.

Significant transformation took place in the Lower Rhine valley, where archaeologists have studied the burial pottery in detail, defining a sequence which shows the evolution of forms beginning with Corded Ware Beakers and developing to an All-Over Ornamented Beaker (AOO) and then to the classic Bell Beaker—the general form that is found widely throughout Europe (6.4). One of the AOO types, decorated overall with cord impressions, is found commonly in the Rhine valley, the Netherlands, and Britain with a scattering in Atlantic France. Another type, which it has been claimed developed from form AOO, is the Maritime Bell Beaker. This type has distinctive ornamentation consisting of thin, evenly spaced horizontal bands of decoration. One of the commonest varieties of this type has its patterns formed of comb impressions with alternate bands infilled in opposite directions to create a herringbone pattern. The distribution of these vessels is entirely different from the All-Over Cord Beakers. They concentrate in Iberia and southern and western France, with particularly large numbers coming from the Lisbon area and from Brittany. Although it has hitherto been accepted by many scholars that the Maritime Bell Beaker type arose in the Mid-Rhine, the view is now developing that, while the type was certainly present in the Rhenish sequence, the inspiration may have come from outside, probably from somewhere along the Atlantic seaboard. This is a question of some importance to our theme, and we will return to the implications later. The AOO Beakers developed in the period 2700–2500 BC and the earliest dates for the Maritime type in the Netherlands are around 2500 BC.

The grave goods found with the beakers in the Rhine valley differ according to the type of beaker. AOO Beakers are often found with battleaxes, flint daggers made from Grand Pressigny flint from western France, and with amber beads. The battleaxes look back to the early

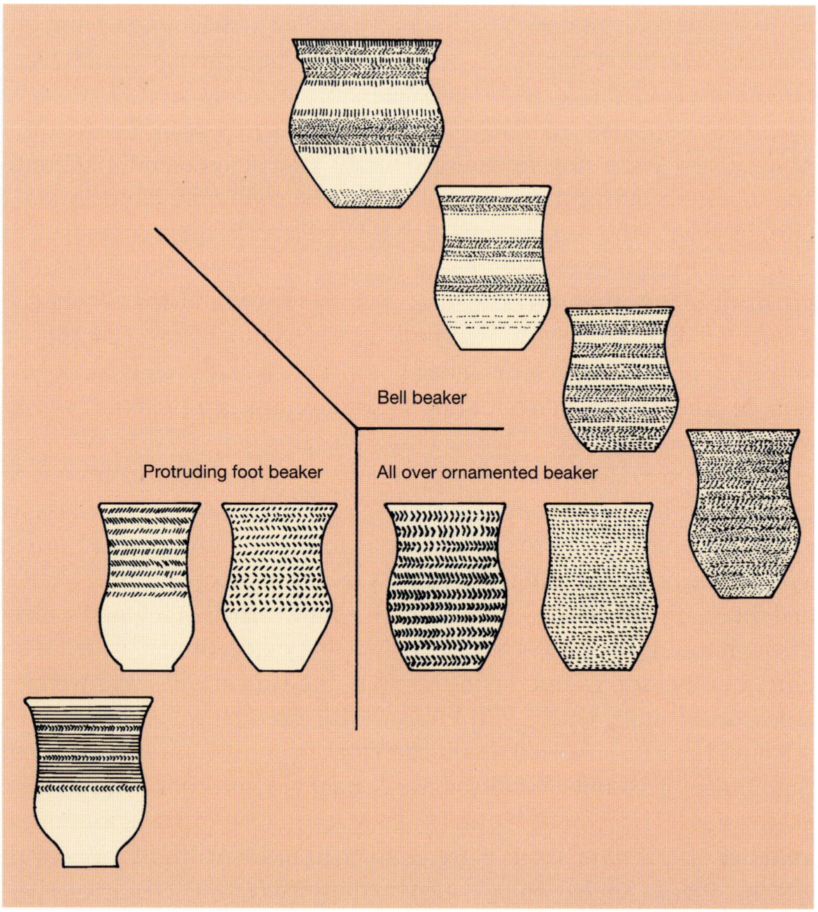

6.4 A typological scheme showing the development of Bell Beakers in the Netherlands. The earliest vessels are at the lower left corner.

Corded Ware heritage, but the presence of Grand Pressigny flint, which could only be acquired through long-distance exchanges, reflects the opening up of northern Europe to west European influences, further reflected in the pan-European nature of the Beaker phenomenon. At a slightly later date, after the initial spread of AOO and Maritime Beakers, a number of provincial styles of Bell Beakers develop and with them we find the classic sets of Beaker grave finds, including archers' equipment in the form of barbed and tanged flint arrowheads, stone wrist-guards, and sometimes arrow shaft straighteners of stone, together with items of copper and bronze such as awls and knives. The earliest archers' equipment occurs in the Iberian Peninsula around 2800–2700 BC. Archers' equipment is found all along the Atlantic seaboard, with concentrations in southern Portugal and Brittany and Mediterranean France, but is distinguished from the central and north European assemblage in that the western communities showed a distinct preference for a narrow wrist-guard rather than the wide version prevalent in central and northern Europe.

It has been necessary to lay out these rather esoteric archaeological niceties to provide a background for our discussion of the social changes which came about along the Atlantic façade in the third and second millennia. What is startlingly clear is that the Atlantic zone was now closely bound up with the changes gripping the whole of central and western Europe.

To attempt to understand the nature of the contacts between the Atlantic and the more inland regions of Europe we turn, yet again, to the distribution of artefacts. We have already seen how, during the fourth millennium, the Breton axe factories working the dolerite at Plussulien were contributing to an interregional exchange network, with the Breton axes being transported in very large numbers along the Loire as far west as Orleans (5.37). The map also shows notable concentrations of axes in the Paris Basin, along the Seine, the Oise, and the Aisne, and it was to exactly these areas that the megalithic burial rite, adopting gallery graves, was to spread in the late fourth and early third millennia. Taken together, the evidence suggests that the Loire–Paris Basin axis was a major corridor of communication along which ideas as well as objects passed in complex processes of social interaction binding neighbouring communities together.

Overlapping chronologically with the production of the dolerite axes were the more sophisticated battleaxes made from hornblendite from near Quimper. Their distribution is particularly interesting (5.37). There are dense concentrations in the vicinity of the quarry and in the Morbihan, but elsewhere in Brittany they are comparatively rare, suggesting that, unlike the simple dolerite axes, they were not made for local consumption but specifically for external exchanges. Outside Brittany the pattern of finds replicates that of the dolerite axes, with its focus on a broad arc stretching along the Loire and then northwards to the Paris Basin and northern France right up to the Somme. There is also a significant distribution down the Atlantic coast of western France to the Gironde. The importance of the hornblendite battleaxe is that the type was totally alien to the Breton tradition and was clearly made in imitation of the battleaxes of northern Europe, presumably copying imported types like the copper alloy examples found at Kersoufflet in Morbihan and Bon Amour in Côtes-d'Armor. The motivation behind the copying is beyond recovery, but it may be that the battleaxes were made specifically to articulate exchanges between the Atlantic coast and the Paris Basin and beyond.

Another product which adds to our understanding of these routes is Grand Pressigny flint, an iron-rich, honey-coloured flint from the valleys of the Claise and Creuse not far from Poitiers. The flint was exported widely in the third millennium as a prestige product, occurring in grave assemblages as long, narrow blades, long daggers or lance-heads, and large cores, the shape and colour of which give rise to their archaeological name—*livres de beurre*. The volume of production was prodigious and the distribution wide, extending from Brittany in the west to the Paris Basin, where the flint occurs in quantity, and north into the Netherlands where, as we have seen, the finely flaked daggers are found accompanying single burials provided with AOO Beakers and sometimes battleaxes. Thus the distribution of Grand Pressigny flint replicates part of the Armorican axe network but extends far deeper into northern Europe. What emerges from all this is that there was an extensive and well-developed exchange network stretching from the mouth of the Loire to the Paris Basin and thence to the Moselle and Rhine throughout the third millennium (6.5). It is easy to see how new belief systems and modes of elite display developing in the Rhine valley could quickly be transmitted to the Atlantic coasts. Such a network, working in reverse, would also explain how styles of beakers, like the Maritime Bell Beaker, which may have developed somewhere in the Atlantic zone could have been introduced into the Mid-Rhine region.

To complete the picture it is necessary to say something about the links between the Atlantic and the Mediterranean. That there was a corridor of contact going back in time is evident from the spread of Cardial ware and the knowledge of the techniques of food production in the fifth millennium. No doubt the valley of the Garonne provided the major axis, and one may suppose that a network of social interactions was maintained

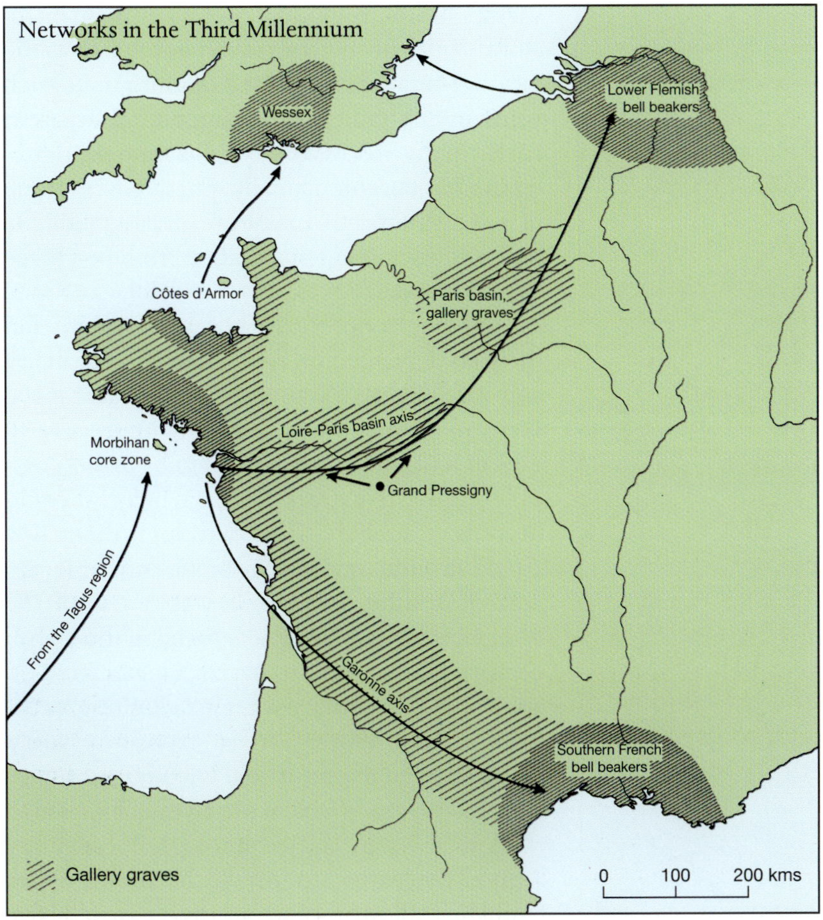

6.5 The major exchange networks of France and adjacent regions in the third millennium BC.

along its route throughout the fourth and third millennia. There is little direct artefactual evidence to support this, but the spread of the Atlantic megalithic gallery grave tradition along the Garonne and its tributaries, deep into western France, is sufficient to demonstrate the importance of the Garonne axis.

The Loire and the Garonne, for long the natural routes by which the communities of Atlantic France and western Brittany maintained social contact with inland Europe, now, in the third millennium, became the arteries along which vital supplies of metal flowed from the metal-rich west to the consuming centres of central and Mediterranean Europe.

The Metal-Rich West

Much of the Atlantic façade of Europe is composed of old hard rocks which, on several occasions, were penetrated by once-molten igneous

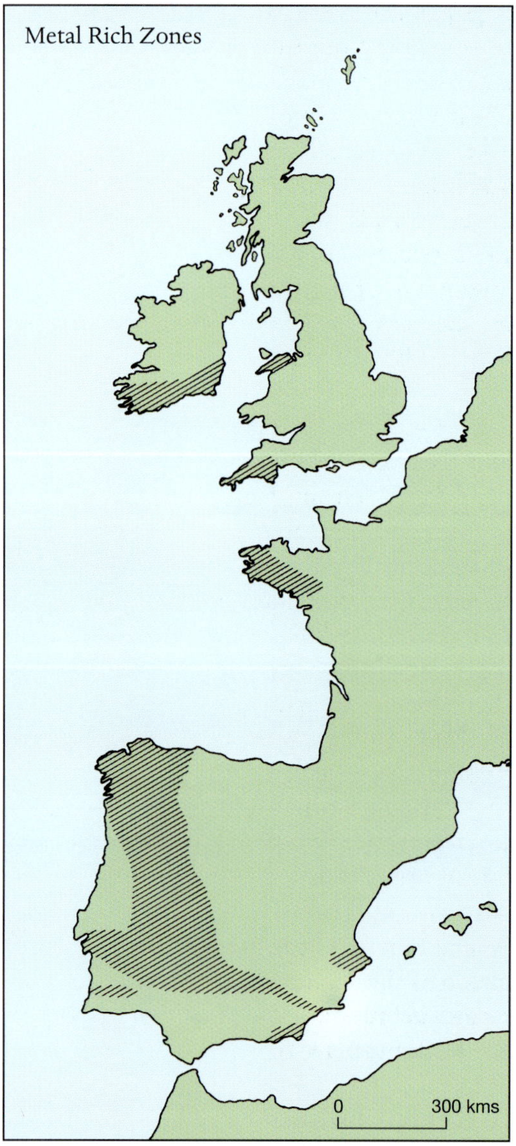

6.6 The main metal-rich zones of Atlantic Europe.

masses. With the gradual cooling of these intrusions, zones of mineralization developed as the gases generated crystallized out into metal-rich veins in the faults and fissures of the parent rocks. In the process of crystallization the different metals became spatially separated, resulting in a distribution of metal ores throughout the region showing much variation from one place to another (6.6).

Whether or not the metals were exploited in the past depended on two factors—desirability and accessibility. Only when there was a social demand for metal was there any imperative to exploit it (it follows that it had to be technologically feasible to extract the metal before it could become desirable). Thus, although there was ample silver in the Sierra Morena and Rio Tinto area of southern Iberia, it was not until the Phoenicians established a demand in the eighth century that it seems to have been extracted on any scale. Accessibility was also a limiting factor in prehistoric times. Surface exposures would have attracted attention and encouraged superficial quarrying, which in turn would have led to shallow mining, but technological capability limited the extent to which the deeper lodes could be exploited. More accessible would have been alluvial deposits of tin and gold eroded from the parent rock and concentrated, because of their weight, in river gravels. Cassiterite (tin oxide) and native gold could have been extracted by simple panning with comparative ease.

One of the greatest of the metal-rich regions in the west was the pyrite zone of Iberia, a broad arc of mineralization sweeping through the Peninsula from the north shores of Galicia to the Mediterranean Levante. Throughout this broad band, though with varying degrees of accessibility, an array of metals was available, from the rich sources of copper and silver in the south-west to tin and gold occurring in a wide zone along the west side of the Peninsula to Galicia and Asturia, where the concentrations were especially rich.

Surprisingly little is known of the exploitation of these resources in the third and second millennia, but the comparatively large quantities of copper alloy in use in the Tagus region, and in a zone stretching from the Algarve to Huelva in the third millennium, argue that local resources were being exploited well before the appearance of Beaker pottery some time about 2700 BC. Analysis of pre-Beaker and Beaker-period artefacts shows no significant difference in the alloys used. In both periods there was a preference for copper alloyed with about 2 per cent arsenic, which provided a metal stronger than pure copper. Some artefacts are also known in a tin/copper alloy heralding the later development of regular bronze. The closest sources of copper to the Tagus are the carbonate ores from Obidos and mines near Grândola, where copper, readily recognizable in its native state, has also been found.

Gold was rarely used in the Tagus region before the development of Beaker pottery, but thereafter becomes more frequent in grave deposits. Alluvial gold is known in the gravels of the River Guadiana, but more extensive deposits lay further north in the river systems of the Duero and Minho.

The major source of tin in Iberia was cassiterite, found in the gravels of the Galician rivers. With the development of regular bronze, containing 10–11 per cent tin, in the first half of the second millennium Galician tin will have become much in demand and must have been extracted on an industrial scale. So important was the metal in the first millennium that the *Cassiterides*—the tin-bearing islands—entered classical mythology.

The Armorican peninsula was also a metal-rich area of some importance in the prehistoric world. Like Galicia, its prime significance would have been as a source of tin which occurred in alluvial deposits found extensively along the southern side of the peninsula, in the hinterland of the coast of Morbihan, around Quimperlé and to the south of Quimper, as well as in Léon in the extreme north-west. Armorica was also a source of alluvial gold found in the centre of the peninsula around Mur-de-Bretagne and in the Montagne Noire of the south-west. Both metals were presumably exploited in the third and second millennia. More doubt attaches to copper. Although there are deposits in various parts of Brittany, the ores are not prolific and were probably only sufficient to make a limited contribution to the total amount of copper consumed locally.

The south-western peninsula of Britain is similar to Brittany. Cornish tin, available in alluvial deposits, was the most important resource, but while there can be little doubt that it was worked on a large scale in the prehistoric period, little direct evidence has survived later workings. Tin would also have been present in the gravel beds of the rivers flowing southwards from Dartmoor. Small quantities of gold have also been recorded around the fringes of Dartmoor, but it is unlikely that it

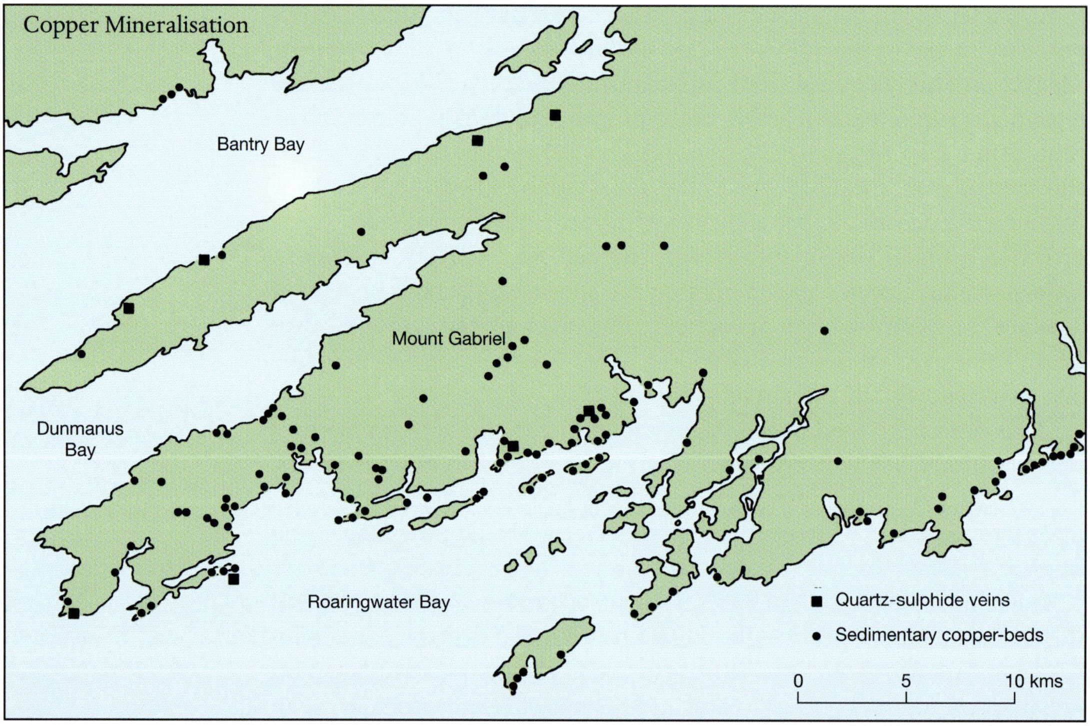
Copper Mineralisation
Bantry Bay
Mount Gabriel
Dunmanus Bay
Roaringwater Bay
Quartz-sulphide veins
Sedimentary copper-beds
0
5
10 kms

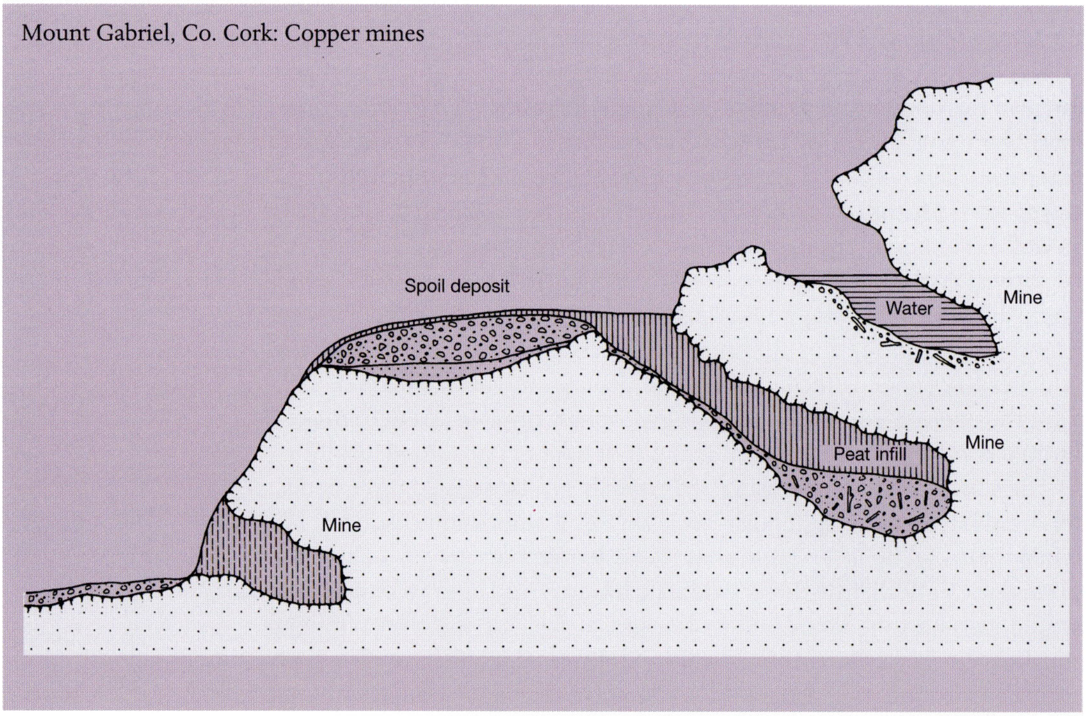
Mount Gabriel, Co. Cork: Copper mines
Spoil deposit
Water
Mine
Mine
Peat infill
Mine

occurred in sufficient quantity to have attracted much attention. Copper occurs in the south-west, but only in limited amounts. There is no direct evidence that it was worked before the first millennium, but it is unlikely to have been overlooked even if the quantities extracted were comparatively limited.

The main source of copper in the northern part of the Atlantic zone in the third and second millennia was Ireland, where the earliest evidence of mining activity in Atlantic Europe has been identified. Two major mining complexes have been located in the south of the country, together spanning the period from *c.*2400 to 1500 BC. The earliest so far known is at Ross Island on the eastern shore of Lough Leane in Co. Kerry. Here cave-like mines were opened up in the limestone to follow mineralized fissures. The rock was first weakened and cracked by fire-setting, then the fractured rock was prised away and the ore extracted and broken up with stone hammers. The later stages of working took place at a nearby campsite where the ore was crushed still finer and smelted in small bowl furnaces to produce an arsenic-rich metal. The available dating evidence suggests that the mines were in operation from 2400 to 2000 BC, during which time Beaker pottery was in use.

A later, more extensive series of mines was opened at Mount Gabriel on the Mizen peninsula of west Cork (6.7–6.9). Here, just below the summit of the hill the bands of copper ore were exposed naturally in the vertical rock outcrops: these were followed by the miners, creating shafts up

6.7 (*facing above*) Copper deposits of the Mizen peninsula, Co. Cork, Ireland.

6.8 (*facing below*) Diagrammatic section through the Bronze Age copper mines at Mount Gabriel, Co. Cork.

6.9 Mount Gabriel, Co. Cork. One of the Bronze Age copper mines, now partially silted up, cut into the limestone hillside.

to 10 metres long. Fire-setting was used to loosen the rock, which was broken and crushed with hammerstones to extract the mineral-rich deposit before removal for smelting. The Mount Gabriel mines were in use over about two centuries from 1700 to 1500 BC, during which time estimates suggest that anything from 1.5 to 26.5 tons of copper might have been produced. The annual yield was probably quite low, no more than about 20 kilograms a year—enough to make forty or fifty axes.

The copper deposits of Ireland were concentrated in the extreme south-west of the country and constituted a major source of supply. Less certainty attaches to tin and gold. The most likely source of alluvial tin in Ireland was the Wicklow Mountains in the south-east, where cassiterite is found together with stream gold. Since these deposits probably provided much of the gold circulating in Ireland in the prehistoric period it is highly likely that they were made to yield tin as well, although whether in sufficient quantity to service the entire bronze industry is unclear.

Finally we must turn to Wales, where some thirty mining sites are now known, mainly in the north and centre-west of the Principality. Of these four have produced radiocarbon dates showing that they were in operation in the first half of the second millennium. The most spectacular workings are those at Great Orme's Head on the north Welsh coast, where an intricate series of tunnels and shafts followed the mineralized zones in the limestone to a depth exceeding 30 metres. As in Ireland, fire-setting was used to fracture the rock and massive stone hammers, some weighing 30 kilograms, were employed to break it up for removal and to crush the ore.

Our knowledge of early metal extraction in the Atlantic zone is limited, partly by lack of adequate fieldwork in many areas and also by the fact that later mining activity has frequently obscured or destroyed all trace of prehistoric workings. The picture will always be incomplete, but on present evidence the earliest copper mining identified in the region is in the south-west of Iberia, where copper was being extracted for local use by as early as 3000 BC, well before the development of Beaker pottery. It was not until *c.*2400 that the Irish sources at Ross Island began to be exploited. Thereafter, in the early second millennium, mines in south-west Ireland and north Wales came into active production.

The tin needed to produce bronze probably came from a number of sources, the most important being Galicia, Armorica, and Cornwall, with the possibility of Irish production centring on the Wicklow Mountains. All of these areas could also have produced gold, but the most prolific source at this time is likely to have been the Wicklow Mountains.

The movement of copper, tin, and gold through the systems of exchange which bound the Atlantic communities together and linked them to the rest of Europe intensified throughout the period, as elites came to require increasing quantities of exotic materials to incorporate in their burial rituals in displays of conspicuous consumption. Thus there was a new imperative to win the raw materials from the rock, to fashion them into desirable items, and to feed these into the ever-demanding exchange cycles. In this way the Atlantic communities were drawn into the new pan-European value system symbolized by the almost universal use of the beaker.

Portugal and the Rest of the Iberian Peninsula

By the beginning of the third millennium a vibrant food-producing society had developed in the coastal region of central Portugal, with its focus around the estuary of the River Tagus. Here, between the Lower Tagus and the sea and between the estuaries of the Tagus and the Sado to the south, the soil is unusually fertile. For the most part the underlying rock is limestone, giving rise to a rich *terra rossa* soil which is further enriched, in the hills above Lisbon, by a mineral contribution from the many basalt dykes which intrude through the calcareous rocks. Add to this the mild dampness of the Atlantic climate and the attractions of the area for prehistoric settlement become apparent.

The rich Neolithic and Chalcolithic culture which developed here is named after the fortified settlement of Vila Nova de São Pedro (abbreviated VNSP). Although a firm chronology based on reliable stratigraphical evidence is somewhat lacking in the region, recent excavations have allowed a broad sequence to be proposed in which two successive early phases (VNSP I and II) are followed by a third phase characterized by the appearance of Maritime Beakers (VNSP III). This, in turn, is followed by a phase named after the site of Palmela, distinguished by a type of tanged bronze point and by pottery decorated by incisions. What is of particular relevance to the present discussion is whether the sequence displays continuity or discontinuity—in other words, are we looking at an entirely uninterrupted local development or does the Portuguese sequence suggest extensive foreign influence?

It will be no surprise to learn that there has been much debate about these issues, and while, inevitably, there are still uncertainties in interpretation, continuity is now stressed. It can be shown, for example, that the major settlements like Vila Nova de São Pedro and Zambujal remained in use throughout this period, developing increasingly massive defences but exhibiting no cultural dislocation. At Leceia it was also possible to demonstrate that the massively defended settlement of the Early Chalcolithic period (above, p. 195), dating to *c*.2800–2600, continued in use into the Middle Chalcolithic period (*c*.2600–2200), during which time Beaker pottery appeared, but by this stage the walls were in disrepair. The same story is told by the collective tombs. Many of those, built in the early period, continued in use unchanged after beakers had made their appearance.

Even more impressive is the continuity in metallurgy. There is clear evidence to show that copper extraction was under way in three regions of southern Iberia, the Tagus, in a coastal zone stretching from the Algarve to Huelva, and in Almería, before the appearance of Beaker pottery. In the Tagus region a rich and productive industry developed in the second half of the fourth millennium producing flat axes, saws, knives, daggers, awls, chisels, and arrowheads. Most of these types continued to be made after Beaker pottery had appeared, and scientific analysis of the metal used shows that there was no significant change in technology corresponding with the first occurrence of beakers. It is clear, therefore, that the development of copper-using technology in the region was unrelated to the Beaker phenomenon and indeed preceded the appearance of beakers by many centuries. This is in contrast to many other areas of western Europe, like Ireland, where the first metallurgy is associated with beakers.

The question which then arises is, could the Maritime Beaker have evolved locally in the VNSP culture? A careful consideration of ceramic styles and technology in the pre-Beaker phase shows that all the major traits—form, colour, fabric, decorative motifs, and use of combs for decoration—were already present in the region. It is, therefore, a perfectly reasonable hypothesis to suggest that the Tagus Maritime Beakers had a local origin. That this was so gains further support from the fact that beakers occur alongside traditional indigenous forms in VNSP III contexts. In other words, the beaker appears to be simply a specialized type of fine pottery evolving within an essentially local tradition.

The exact chronology of these archaeological subtleties has still to be worked out, but the radiocarbon dates now available from Zambujal and Leceia show that the climax and end of the Beaker phase lies in the period 2600–2300 BC, when both Maritime and All-Over Ornamented (AOO) Beakers were in use. This would indicate that the first appearance of Maritime Beakers in the region should probably be placed about 2800 BC, that is, earlier than this type is known anywhere else in Europe. Taken together, then, the evidence does seem to support the long-held hypothesis that Maritime Beakers emerged first in the Tagus area, where a copper-producing technology was already well established, and that these early developments owed nothing to the cultural processes at work in the Mid-Rhine.

The final stage in the cultural sequence of the Tagus region, before the fully developed Bronze Age, is characterized by the Palmela complex. The most obvious distinguishing features are the pottery bowls enlivened with impressed decoration. Associated with this complex are new customs, including the fashion for single burial and the appearance of a new set of equipment, often buried with the dead, including archers' wrist-guards, tanged daggers, and V-perforated buttons. The Palmela complex is best seen as an indigenous development adopting ideas and concepts from the Ciempozuelos culture of central Iberia dating to as early as 2400–2300 BC. The rite of single burial and the accompanying grave goods probably result from central European influences. While these elements were never particularly important on the Atlantic coast of Iberia, they do imply the acceptance of the value systems which were now spreading throughout much of western Europe.

The cultural developments in the Tagus region in the third millennium reflect a vibrant, innovative society. The most dramatic manifestations of this are the fortified settlements, of which Vila Nova de São Pedro and Zambujal are the most famous (5.28). At Zambujal the nucleus of the settlement was immensely strongly defended, with an enclosing wall bristling with circular towers provided with arrow slits and with a massive rock-cut ditch 4 metres wide (5.29). Beyond this were two outer lines of defence, both with towers. The structure of the defensive circuits showed that the settlement evolved gradually, with new strengthenings being added from time to time until some of the walls achieved a thickness of 4 metres. In one phase a copper-working site in the main ditch, associated with Beaker pottery, was buried when a new circular tower containing some beaker sherds was added to the inner wall. The observation is important in showing that the fortifications were still evolving during the Beaker period. The site of Vila Nova de São Pedro was broadly similar, but the inner enclosure was a little smaller, barely 25 metres across, and the structural sequence has been less clearly researched.

It is difficult to assess the social function of sites of this kind and the messages which those responsible for them were trying to convey. The space within the inner fortifications could hardly have been sufficient to provide for a group larger than an extended family, while the size of the fortifications seems excessive to meet the needs of defence. The most likely explanation is that these sites were the residences of the elite who were able to call upon the services of others to aggrandize their enclosing walls, successive acts of rebuilding proclaiming their continued control of power.

The continuity of the social order is also reflected in the continued use of the collective tombs, and it is notable that tombs with rich burial assemblages in the early period frequently continued as rich tombs into the later Beaker period. No doubt the lineages who had built and continued to use these structures were those responsible for maintaining the fortified settlements.

The increasing desire to display elite status, evident throughout the third millennium in settlement architecture, is reflected in the demand for greater quantities of prestige goods for manipulation in burial ritual. Copper, ivory, callaïs (a decorative stone), and, to a lesser extent, gold, were all used in funerary contexts in the pre-Beaker period and continued to be acquired, though in greater quantities, for burial alongside beakers, which themselves may have embodied a statement of status. None of these commodities could be procured from the locality: even the copper probably came from the Algarve–Rio Tinto area. Copper was almost invariably used to make tools, only rarely weapons, and never personal ornaments. As such, therefore, it occupied a different position in the social symbolism of acquired goods from the more esoteric materials which were used primarily for ornaments.

In the pre-Beaker period ivory, brought in from the Maghreb, was used to make a variety of smaller objects such as idols, combs, and wands. Importation continued in the Beaker period, when it was also used to make V-perforated buttons, and similar buttons have been found in later Palmela complex assemblages. That reciprocal exchanges were entered into is shown by the discovery of Maritime Bell Beakers of Portuguese type in Morocco at Cat-Taht-el-Gar and Gar Cahal. Other Moroccan sites have produced pottery and bronzes of the Palmela complex, including two of the characteristic Palmela points. Although the evidence is not prolific, it indicates maritime contact linking the Tagus estuary to the Atlantic coast of Morocco throughout much of the third millennium.

Another luxury commodity exploited by the elite of the Tagus region was callaïs—a fine-textured green or greenish-blue stone which takes a high polish and was popular in the region for the manufacture of beads. Callaïs beads were frequently found in pre-Beaker and Beaker contexts in the Tagus region and in broadly contemporary grave assemblages in the Alentejo, but is virtually unknown in the later Palmela phase which implies that supplies were no longer available after the middle of the third millennium. The origin of the stone has not been certainly identified, but no sources are known in Iberia. The most likely occurrence is in southern Brittany, somewhere, now submerged, off the coast of Morbihan where the appropriate lithography has been identified. Callaïs beads and other items of the same stone have also been found in some quantity in the Morbihan region, and the probability remains that the stone may have been trans-shipped direct to the Tagus. That regular contact between the two areas was maintained in the early third millennium is further indicated by the large quantities of Maritime Bell Beakers found in both regions and by the discovery of two Iberian Palmela points close to the mouth of the Loire (6.10, 6.11). It is quite possible that Maritime Bell Beakers were introduced into southern Brittany at this time as a direct result of the maritime contacts between the two regions, but we will return to this question later (p. 234).

The final luxury commodity to be considered is gold. A few small items of gold were found in pre-Beaker contexts in the Tagus region, but gold becomes more plentiful in the Beaker period, occurring as basket-shaped earrings, spiral finger- or toe-rings, and small sheets perforated for attachment to fabrics. Even so the actual quantity available does not seem

6.10 The distribution of Palmela points in western Europe.

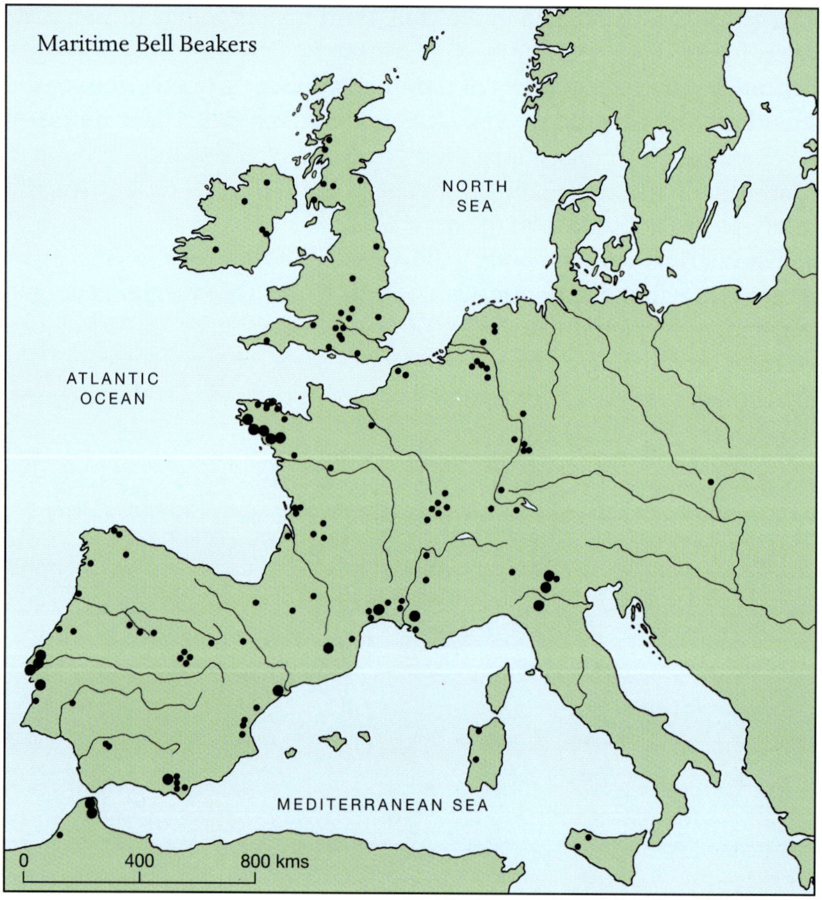

6.11 The distribution of Maritime Bell Beakers in western Europe.

to have been large. Where the gold came from is uncertain. Alluvial gold is recorded in the gravels of the Guadiana, but more plentiful supplies would probably have been available at this time from further north, from Galicia or from Brittany.

The position of Galicia in the maritime exchange networks of the early third millennium is not yet clear. By virtue of its focal position in relation to the sea routes one might have expected the region to have played a significant role, but relevant finds are not plentiful, although a number of Maritime Bell Beakers have been found which may have come from the Tagus region. At the large cemetery of Puentes de García Rodríguez, near Cape Ortegal, Maritime Beakers accompanied two burials while a third produced a gold diadem and four Palmela points. The local elites commanding the ports of Coruña midway between the Tagus and the Morbihan seem to have been able to benefit from the need of the maritime entrepreneurs to break their long journey. The collection of callaïs beads from the tomb of Monte da Mora, Savinâo, in the valley of the Miño is another reflection of the movement of goods along the Atlantic routes. Together, these finds from the north-western corner of Iberia show that the region was integrated into the exchange networks, but recognizable imported material is rare. While it could be argued that this indicates a low intensity of activity, it could simply be that other commodities, no longer recognizable in the archaeological record, were more acceptable to the local elites.

Finally, we should mention here the high concentration of Maritime Bell Beakers, All-Over Cord Zoned Beakers (AOC), and the Cord Zoned Maritime type (CZM) from around the Golfe du Lions between the Rhône valley and the flanks of the Pyrenees. The majority of the beakers were found in megalithic tombs. Several of the contexts have also produced beads of callaïs. Although it is conventional to argue that these groups reflect maritime contact with the Tagus, it seems more likely that the callaïs and the early Beaker component may have been the result of exchange systems at work along the long-established Garonne–Aude route linking direct to Brittany. The journey from Morbihan to the Golfe is only 700 kilometres by coast and river compared with 1,800 kilometres, entirely by sea, from the Tagus. Later in the Beaker period the Languedoc and Provence developed direct contact with the Mid-Rhine from where the standard Beaker package of archers' equipment, V-perforated buttons, and tanged knives was introduced.

Armorica

The appearance of beakers in Brittany in the third millennium coincided with the gradual demise of the megalithic burial tradition, but that there was an overlap between the two traditions is amply demonstrated by the fact that most of the Breton beakers have been recovered from megalithic tombs, and sometimes considerable numbers of beakers have been found in a single tomb. At Men-ar-Romped in the Côtes-d'Armor, for example, thirty-nine beakers were recovered from a single gallery grave and numbers of between five and ten are not uncommon. Since it is highly unlikely that such numbers would accompany a single burial, we may be reasonably certain that they represent the continuation of the collective burial tradition.

There are, however, examples of typologically early beakers found with similar burials accompanied by items of central European inspiration. In one of the chambers of the megalithic tomb at Goërem an All-Over Cord Beaker (AOC) was found in association with flint arrowheads, a copper awl, and four thin plaques of gold. At Kerouaren, Plouhinec, in the Morbihan a burial in a cist was accompanied by an All-Over Ornamented Beaker (AOO), a number of gold items including a diadem, and a stone wrist-guard, while at Penker, Plozevet, in Finistère, a Maritime Beaker was found with a stone wrist-guard, a tanged copper knife, and a V-perforated button.

There are several possible explanations for the occurrence of these rich Beaker graves. The simplest would be to suppose that they came fairly late in the sequence, the typologically early beakers simply reflecting a conservatism in the Beaker tradition in Brittany. Such a view is supported by the absence of 'developed' beakers from the region. This might suggest division into two phases, an early phase when beakers were used in traditional funerary rituals, followed by a later stage when single burial and the artefacts associated with the central European package were beginning to be adopted by the local elites. But in the absence of a reliable series of radiocarbon dates it is difficult to test the hypothesis.

The principal types of beakers found in Brittany—the classic Maritime type, the AOC, and the AOO types—have very similar patterns of distribution, occurring in two major concentrations, one focusing on the coast of Morbihan, the other on the coast of the Penmarc'h peninsula in the extreme south-west. There is also a scatter of find-spots along the north coast. The Morbihan littoral has by far the largest number of finds. The strictly maritime distribution is particularly interesting because it is at variance with the distribution of the broadly contemporary gallery graves, which are found not only in the coastal regions along with the earlier passage graves but inland as well. The implication would seem to be that the new value systems were accessible only to the coastal communities, and in particular to the long-favoured elites of the Morbihan.

How did the Beaker tradition arrive on the Atlantic coast? We have already shown that Brittany was involved in exchanges with the Lisbon area, and that it was probably here that the classic Maritime Bell Beaker type evolved. It is reasonable, therefore, to suggest that the Maritime Beaker may have been introduced from Portugal along the Atlantic sea routes possibly as early as 2700–2600 BC. We have also argued that the Morbihan was bound to a Loire exchange system with well-established links extending as far north-east as the Netherlands (p. 220). It is a possibility, therefore, that the cord-decorated styles of beakers were introduced to the Morbihan along this network, and that the same route also saw knowledge of the classic Beaker artefact assemblage transmitted to the Atlantic seaboard a century or two later. In support of the significance of the Loire route we should note the site of Ancenis on the Loire between Nantes and Angers, where dredging recovered a large collection of beakers of AOO type, including a number of cord-decorated examples very reminiscent of the earliest Netherlands types. While these scraps of data are sparse they do offer support to the idea that the Loire corridor remained a significant axis of communication in the third millennium, and they hint that knowledge of the early beaker styles developing in the Netherlands was being rapidly transmitted to the Atlantic coast.

Thus, the communities of coastal Morbihan and Loire Atlantique, by virtue of their long-established exchange networks, were able to absorb new ideas associated with elite display from both the Atlantic seaboard and the Middle Rhine. It could be argued, therefore, that this region became an important nexus—a melting-pot of ideas—and a focus through which concepts as well as materials could rapidly be transmitted. This said, it has to be admitted that the precise details remain obscure. One theoretical possibility would be to argue that it was through this region that the entire range of beaker forms reached the Atlantic seaboard from the Mid-Rhine, some being transmitted further to Portugal. A more likely suggestion, and one in accordance with the radiocarbon dates, is that the Morbihan acted as a zone of exchange receiving and transmitting traditions from both the Lisbon region and the Mid-Rhine. It was also well placed to have been the focus from which ideas spread to the Golfe du Lions via the Garonne route. Its relationship northwards to Ireland and Britain is an issue to which we will return (p. 246).

We saw, in the last chapter, how some time around the middle of the fourth millennium the tradition of building passage graves in Brittany gave way to the construction of gallery graves which, over the next five hundred years or so, were to spread to most areas of the peninsula. Collective burial rites continued in many of the old passage graves and in the gallery graves throughout much of the third millennium until about 2200 BC, by which time the long tradition of collective burial, going back to the fifth millennium, was at an end. Such a change signals a significant break with the past—the end of one set of value systems and its replacement by another.

That the change was structured rather than casual is shown by the fact that a number of the megalithic tombs were deliberately sealed. This was done in a variety of ways. At Île Carn, Ploudalmézeau, in Finistère, three passage graves incorporated in a long cairn were put out of use at the same instant when the entire early monument was incorporated in a massive circular cairn. The precise date of this act of closure is not known, but the latest material from the sealed passage graves dates to the first half of the third millennium. At Gavr'inis, in the Morbihan, the entrance to the tomb and part of its façade were obscured by rubble probably about 3000 BC or a little before. At a third passage grave, at Ty-Floc'h in Finistère, a similar blocking took place a century or two earlier. Taken together these three examples show that passage graves had begun to be closed in the period *c*.3200–2700 BC, that is, *before* the new Beaker burial traditions started to reach the region. During the next five hundred years or so many more tombs were blocked. Frequently tips of rubble were deliberately piled up to cover the entrances. In other cases, for example, at Crec'h-Quillé, St-Quay-Perros, in Côtes-d'Armor, stone blocking walls were built. Some of the closed tombs were sealed after Beaker items had been used in the latest burial rituals. The evidence, then, is of gradual change, with tombs being sealed over a period of a thousand years. While the process of change began before the appearance of beakers it may be that the local elites quickly adopted the 'Beaker package' as a means of displaying status, thus exacerbating the demise of the collective burial tradition. As the collective tombs—markers of territorial legitimacy—were abandoned the new elites chose to display their status with portable wealth, some tiny fraction of which was buried with them.

Other quite significant changes were now in the air. It is in the second half of the third millennium that the first significant signs of the 'hoarding' of metal become apparent in the region. It used to be thought that collections of objects buried in the ground were essentially utilitarian deposits buried at a time of stress or simply to keep valuable material safe for later recovery and reuse, but it is now believed that most, if not all, of the hoards were depositions confined to the ground, or to watery contexts such as rivers or springs, as gifts to the deities; that is, they were offerings of very considerable value taken out of circulation and placed in the realms of the gods with no intent to recover. To some extent the burial of valuable items with the dead is a related belief, but now new groups of items, most notably of valuable metal, are found deposited in isolation.

In the third millennium objects of copper and copper alloy will have had a high value because of the rarity of the metal and the labour and expertise required to produce even a small quantity. In Brittany the earliest items to be made were daggers and flat axes. Only a few daggers are known, and these were regarded as personal equipment and buried with the dead. On the other hand, over 180 axes have been recorded from the region: none come from burials, but a significant number were found in hoards. Clearly the axe was held to be in some way different in that it was an item appropriate for dedication to the deities. In this practice we may be witnessing the continuation of the ritual significance of the axe, a belief which can be traced back in the region to the fifth millennium.

Another example is provided by the treatment of gold lunulae. These are large, crescent-shaped sheets of gold designed to be worn around the neck as a decoration on the upper chest (6.12). The type is probably of Irish origin. Five have been found in Armorica in contexts which suggest that they were deliberately buried, but none were found with human burials. Here again, considerable wealth was being given to the deities. The lunulae raise a number of interesting questions, not least their function. One suggestion, that they adorned wooden statues of the deities, has much to commend it. It is possible that in the stone statue menhirs from Le Trévoux and Kermené in Brittany and Le Câtel in Guernsey (6.13), all with some form of crescentic chest or neck decoration, we are seeing rare stone versions of a more common type of wooden figure. Similar necklace motifs were also carved on the walls of some of the later gallery graves. Leaving aside the possible context of their use, the dedica-

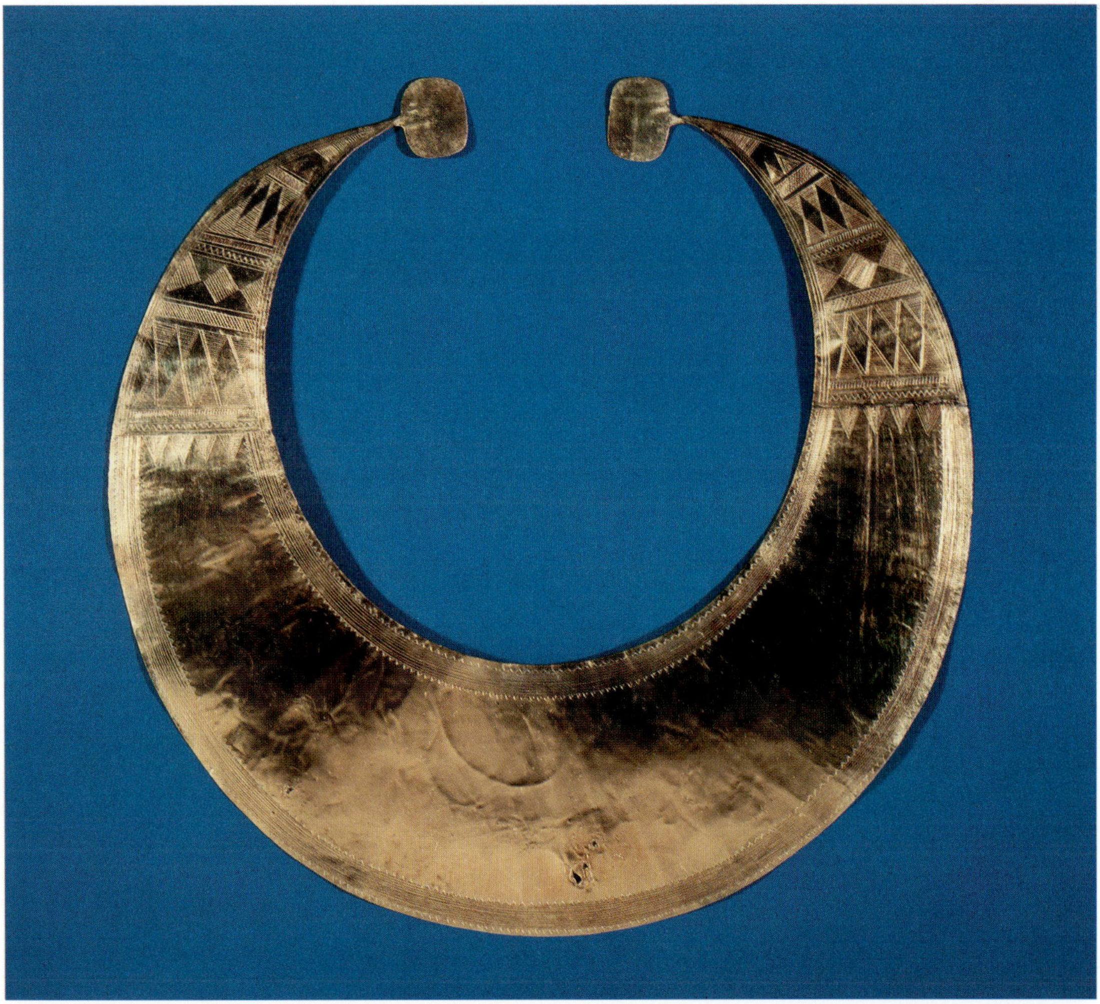

6.12 Gold lunula from Blessington, Co. Wicklow, Ireland.

6.13 Statue-menhir standing in the grounds of Câtel Church, Guernsey. The stylized figure appears to be wearing a neck ornament, possibly a lunula.

tion of the lunulae to the deities through deposition is another way in which the elite could demonstrate their power by controlling wealth.

The occurrence of beakers around the coasts of Armorica, with the concentration in the Morbihan, is sufficient to indicate that Brittany played a significant role in the intensifying networks of exchange which developed in the third millennium. Its favoured position, in the centre of the Atlantic sea lanes and close to the Atlantic end of the Loire and Garonne routes, meant that the peninsula was optimally sited to benefit from all the major exchange networks. We have already identified callaïs as one of the raw materials which the communities of the Morbihan contributed to the network, and Grand Pressigny flint as one which they received, but what of the metals copper and gold which played an increasingly important part in the elite systems of the peninsula? Both were probably extracted locally at the time, but it is doubtful whether local yields could have met consumption: importation is therefore likely.

Gold provides some clues. The lunulae, or at least some of them, were probably made in Ireland of gold from the Wicklow Mountains (6.14). One from Kerivoa in Côtes-d'Armor is almost identical to a Cornish find from Harlyn Bay, and both must be Irish exports. Gold also seems to have been imported from Iberia in the form of massive collars, like those found at Rondossec, Morbihan, which are comparable to Iberian collars known as *gargantillas*. These isolated comparisons hint at the complexities of the exchanges. Materials endowed with foreign symbolism would be highly acceptable even in regions able to produce the same materials. It was not only the value of the material but the added value of the labour that worked it that made an item socially acceptable, especially if, like the lunulae and *gargantillas*, the form was emblematic of elite status.

It is doubtful whether the more humble copper moved in this way, but gifts of axes, whether from Ireland or Iberia, would surely have been

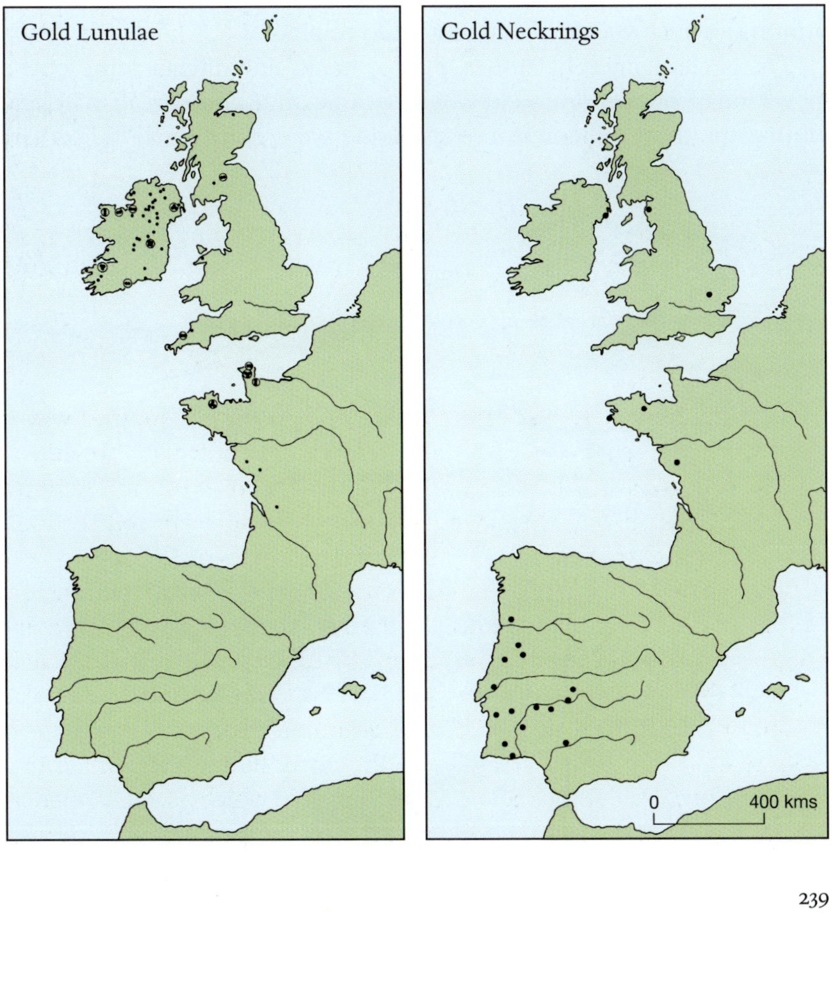

6.14 The distribution of gold neck ornaments: lunulae manufactured in Ireland, and Berzocana neck rings made in south-west Iberia.

acceptable. In this way metals moved through the system, and the various forms into which they were made inspired imitation.

Ireland and the Irish Sea

The third millennium was a time of rapid change in Ireland as it was in Brittany, and in many ways there are close parallels between the two—the passage grave tradition came to an end, simpler regional tomb types evolved, and new value systems emerged centred around the use of metals.

The end of the passage graves in Ireland seems to have come about in the first half of the third millennium, though precise dating evidence is lacking. But that the great monuments continued to be revered is well demonstrated by Newgrange, where a circle of standing stones was erected around the mound well clear of its kerb, some time in the later part of the third millennium. It is possible that at this time, or a little later, the cairn facing may have been thrown down as a deliberate act of closure. A rather similar delimiting took place at one of the satellite tombs (tomb 2), which was encircled by a series of pits.

The circle defined by stones, pits, or banks and ditches represents a new kind of ritual monument which became quite widespread in Ireland during the third millennium (6.15). Some were quite small, but others

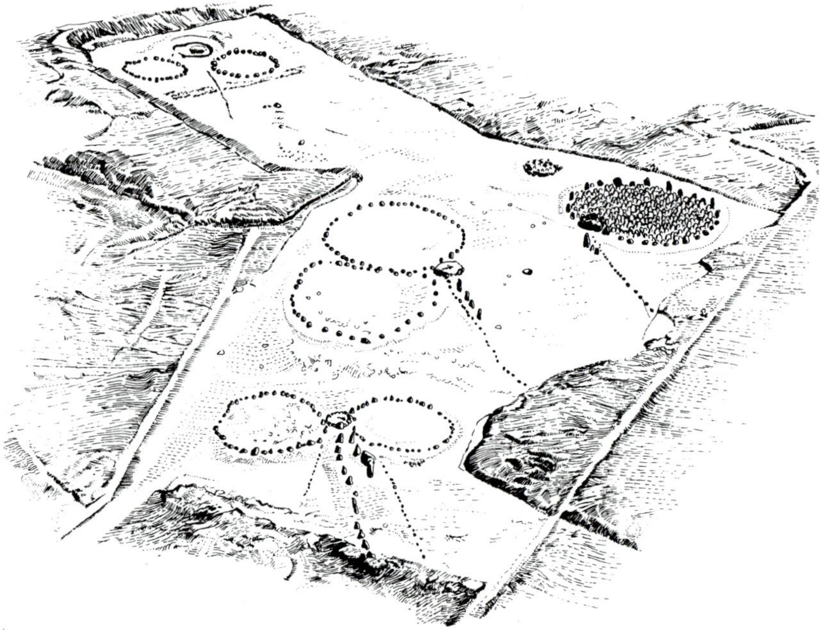

6.15 The stone circles and alignments at Beaghmore, Co. Tyrone, Ireland as they may once have appeared.

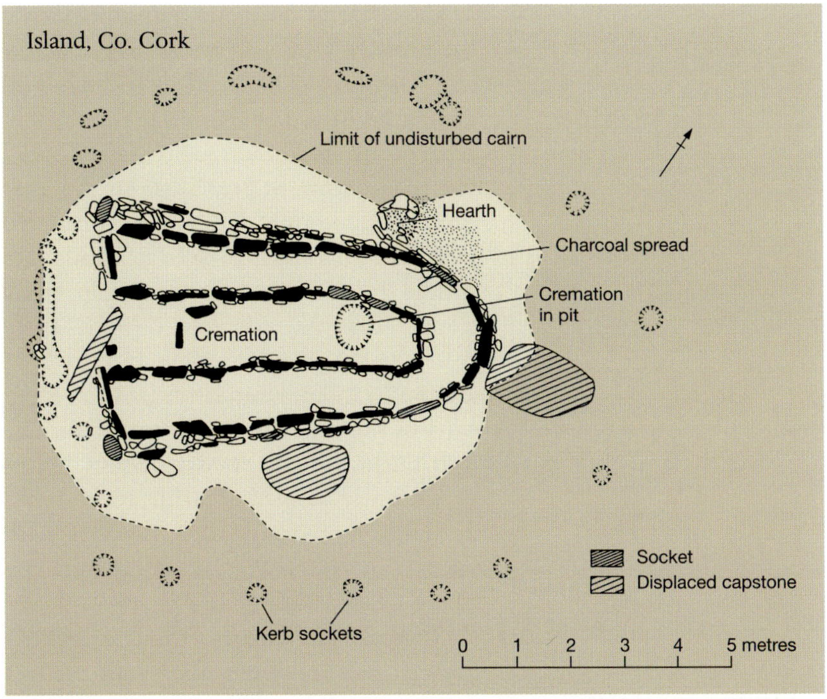

6.16 The wedge-shaped tomb at Island, Co. Cork, Ireland.

reached considerable proportions like the Giant's Ring at Ballynahatty—a roughly circular earthwork with an internal ditch measuring some 225 metres across. They fall within the general class of henges which we saw in Orkney and Wessex, beginning in the century or two before 3000 BC, in Wessex developing to colossal proportions in the next seven hundred years. In Ireland the exact relationship between the earthwork henge monuments and the circles of standing stones is difficult to define, but it would seem that the stone circles continued later and some may not have been erected until the second millennium. Ireland, then, seems to have been sharing in a general shift, evident throughout much of Britain, away from great burial monuments to defined circular spaces, at first embanked with limited access and later (the stone circles) open to approach from any direction. At a very simple (possibly too simple) level of interpretation one might see the progression from enclosed tomb to embanked circle to open circle reflecting a change in belief systems from chthonic/secret to sky/public. It is always tempting to read such things into the inanimate remains, but speculations such as these are impossible to test. At the very least, however, the third millennium saw a very dramatic change in the ritual structures associated with belief.

There is little evidence to suggest that the two other major types of megalithic tombs in use during the fourth millennium—the court tombs

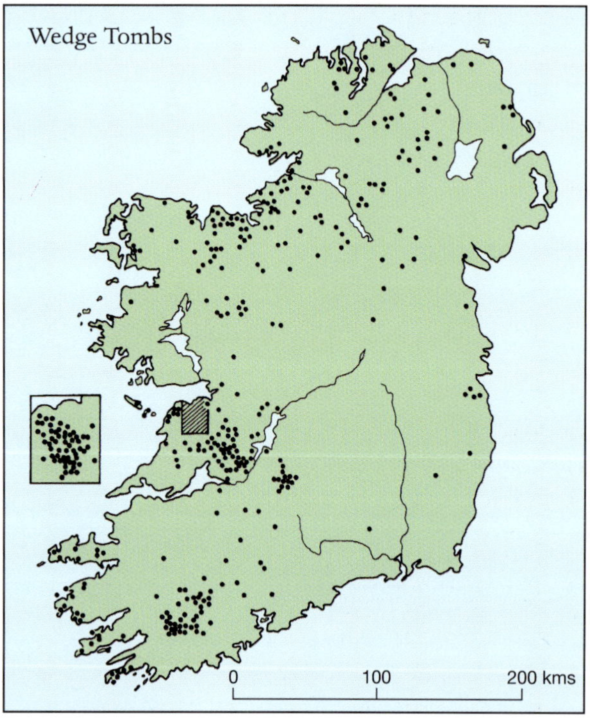

6.17 Distribution of wedge-shaped tombs in Ireland.

and the portal dolmens—continued into the third millennium, but another distinctive category—the wedge tombs—was evidently a third millennium monument type. None are known to pre-date 3000 BC, but many were in active use in the later third millennium and some continued well into the second. Wedge tombs are simple megalithic galleries set in small trapezoidal mounds edged with kerbstones (6.16). That over five hundred are known in Ireland demonstrates the longevity of the collective burial tradition. The distribution of the wedge tombs differs significantly from the earlier tomb types in that it is predominantly western, with particular concentrations in Cork and Kerry, Clare and Sligo (6.17).

General similarities to the gallery graves of Brittany, together with the fact that some of the wedge tombs have produced barbed and tanged arrowheads and Beaker pottery, have led to the suggestion that they reflect direct Breton influence, perhaps associated with prospecting for metal. While contacts with Brittany are likely (and there is reasonable evidence to support this), it seems unnecessary to derive the Irish tombs from abroad when they could equally well have been a local development specific to the Atlantic periphery of the island.

While the wedge tombs continued the old megalithic collective burial tradition in the west and north of the country, more complex and diverse burial rites were emerging elsewhere involving single burial in cists, pits, or graves, usually accompanied by highly decorated funerary pottery. Inhumation tended to be earlier, belonging to the later third millennium, with cremation becoming more common in the second millennium. These traditions, including the pottery styles, are shared between eastern and northern Ireland and southern Scotland, particularly the west coast, and clearly indicate a broad zone of contact and cultural interaction extending over a long period of time. Thus, in the third and second millennia Ireland seems to crystallize into two broad cultural groupings, one facing outwards to the Atlantic and retaining its old collective burial rites, the other facing inwards to the Irish Sea and western Scotland and sharing in the escalating social changes which were gripping Britain at the time.

The apparent insularity reflected by this sharp regionalization must be seen against a pattern of more distant contacts along the Atlantic seaways to the south. In this context the development of copper metallurgy in south-western Ireland is of crucial interest. As we have seen above, the earliest evidence at present available comes from Ross Island on the eastern side of Lough Leane, where extraction and smelting of the arsenic-rich ore can be dated to the period 2400–2000 BC and is associated with Beaker pottery. The workings at Mount Gabriel are later, dating to about 1700–1500 BC. The question which, inevitably, arises is who initiated the mining? While independent invention cannot be ruled out, it would seem simpler to suppose that knowledge of metallurgy spread through the networks of contact that for generations had linked Ireland to other communities along the Atlantic seaways. It is not difficult to envisage how fascination for the new desirable metal, already long-available in the south, spread, encouraging the search for the brilliant green- and blue-coloured ores which signalled its presence. Once located, others, experienced in mining and pyrotechnology, may have been brought in to begin exploitation. In such a scenario there is no need to suppose active prospecting by foreigners, when the lively curiosity and entrepreneurial flair of local people, sharing in the knowledge-base of the Atlantic world, would have been sufficient. That such overseas contacts were indeed in operation is indicated by the presence of beakers at the Ross Island working site.

It is unlikely that, at least in the early stages, the production of metal would have been on a sufficient scale to have satisfied more than the local exchange networks, but as more ore sources were found the resources of the south-west could have begun to supply much larger areas. To give some indication of scale, of the earliest copper axe type (belonging to the Knocknagar phase), dating to the period 2400–2200 BC, some two thousand are known. This can be only a tiny fraction of those manufactured. There is, however, no certainty that all were made of locally produced metal.

At present, then, the earliest metallurgy seems to be coeval with the appearance of the earliest beakers. Unlike Brittany, beakers are rare in Ireland, but in common with Brittany those that are found are largely restricted to the two earliest types, the All-Over Cord Zone (AOC) and other All-Over Ornamented (AOO) types, including the characteristic Maritime Bell Beaker. Beakers have been found on Dalkey Island (an important point of entry off the east coast), at the passage graves of Newgrange and Knowth, at the settlements of Lough Gur and Ballynagilly, and at a few other sites, including some of the wedge tombs. Thus beakers were used in Ireland in a variety of contexts but entirely within the local cultural milieu, in much the same way as they are in Brittany, but unlike the situation in Britain where the beakers are usually found in single burial contexts along with other elements of the 'Beaker package'. This raises questions of the route by which knowledge of early beakers reached Ireland, whether via Britain or direct along the seaways from Brittany, perhaps with Cornwall as an intermediate landfall. In support of the latter route it is instructive to compare the distribution of gold lunulae, evidently an Irish concept. Over eighty-five have been recorded in Ireland. Five sites have produced lunulae in Cornwall and six in Brittany and Lower Normandy (6.14). Three of the Cornish examples are closely comparable to classic Irish types, and one of the Cornish sites, Harlyn Bay, has produced a provincial type which can be paralleled at Kerivoa in Brittany. Although the lunulae probably date to the first half of the second millennium, the distribution clearly indicates the persistence of the Atlantic route at that time. It is not unreasonable to see this as simply a continuation of long-established contacts going back to the fourth millennium.

Britain

The situation in Britain during the third and second millennia is in many ways similar to that in Ireland, but differs from it in a number of significant respects, most notably the strong contacts which eastern parts of the country had with the Netherlands and the Rhine valley.

In common with Ireland the large burial mounds (in Britain mostly earthen long barrows) had gone out of use by about 3000 BC, and new ritual landscapes were beginning to emerge incorporating circular enclosures of varying kinds, usually grouped together under the name of henge monuments. The outermost bank and ditch at Stonehenge is one of the earliest of these, and together with a smaller structure nearby at Coneybury and another at Flagstones near Dorchester, Dorset, seem to date to about 3000 BC or a little before. Henge monuments of this kind became widespread in Britain during the third millennium, stretching, as we have seen, across the whole length of the country from the Wessex coast to Orkney and also to Ireland.

In Wessex these early ritual landscapes became increasingly elaborate and more monumental over time. At some time, probably about 2800–2700 BC, the remarkable collection of 'blue stones' from the Preseli Mountains in south-west Wales was transported to the centre of Wessex and erected within the early henge at Stonehenge, and at about the same time the colossal mound of Silbury Hill was constructed. In the middle of the millennium monumentalization had reached its peak, with the construction of the huge ditched enclosures at Mount Pleasant, Knowlton,

Durrington Walls, Marden, and Avebury, and a century or so later the achievement was capped with the erection of the sarsen trilithons and circle at Stonehenge. Over a period of six hundred years or so the Wessex landscape had been transformed by this cluster of ritual complexes stretching in an arc from the Dorset coast to the Kennet valley. The phenomenon is without parallel in prehistoric Europe and represents an enormous expenditure of labour harnessed by the coercive power of the elite to serve its socio-religious imperative. These monuments represent the culmination of the process which began in the late fifth millennium with the building of the first long barrows.

The sheer size of the ritual complexes and the spectacular uniqueness of the perfected Stonehenge were, whatever else, symbols of social power. It is tempting to believe that Stonehenge became a focus of pilgrimage bringing in visitors from afar. The very existence of Welsh blue stones in the centre of Wessex is enough to demonstrate the extent of the network to which Stonehenge belonged. The great henges, each dominating a natural route, define the heartland of Wessex, which was to remain a centre of wealth and power for another thousand years.

Other changes became apparent in Wessex in the third millennium. By the time the long barrows had become obsolete in the early centuries of the millennium the rite of single burial had begun to take over. At Amesbury, in barrow 71, a single inhumation was deposited within a circle of stakes surrounded by a ditch. The barrow was later enlarged for a new central burial about 2500 BC. The sequence shows that the classic rite of interment beneath a round barrow was already well under way in the first half of the third millennium. Within the next thousand years many thousands of round barrows had been constructed, of which six thousand are still extant in Wessex. Even though the number is far too small to account for all the dead, it is evident that barrow burial, covering first inhumations and later cremations, had become the normative rite for at least one sector of the population.

The general trends, so clearly demonstrated in the development of social and religious systems in Wessex, were broadly similar to what was happening elsewhere in Britain and in the eastern parts of Ireland, but only in Yorkshire and parts of eastern Scotland were the ritual monuments and the intensity of burial comparable in scale to Wessex.

It was upon these indigenous trajectories of change that the Beaker phenomenon impinged. The number of beakers found in Britain is impressive. Over 1,240 inhumations and forty cremations are known to have been accompanied by beakers, and from among this collection there remain more than eight hundred complete beakers for study. The material is rich and varied and has invariably generated many systems of classification. A great majority of the beakers are clearly indigenous developments, belonging to a number of regional styles and local varieties, but at the beginning of the sequence rather more generalized types can be recognized, including the ubiquitous All-Over Cord Zone Beaker (AOC) and a variety of All-Over Decorated Bell Beakers, among which the Maritime Beaker is prominent. Given the proximity of eastern and southern Britain to the Netherlands and the Mid-Rhine, where these early types developed, it would seem reasonable to suppose that the fashion for beakers, as an accoutrement to single burial, together with other artefacts of the northern/central European package such as arrows, wristguards, occasional battleaxes, and V-perforated buttons, was learnt from the Netherlands. That the later developments in the British sequence maintain cousinly links with later Dutch types adds support to the view.

The distribution of the AOC and Maritime Beakers in Britain has an eastern coastal bias, with concentrations along the Thames, the Humber, and the Firth of Forth as well as a very distinct focus in Wessex. In fact the early beakers were evidently being accepted by the more active innovating societies linked together by the east and south coast shipping routes. Once established in these regions the fashion for beakers flourished. Although the distribution clearly implies the movement of people by sea along the eastern coasts of the island and from Britain to and from the Dutch coast, there is no need to think in terms of the immigration of populations, least of all of invasion. The networks along which the knowledge of the Beaker package passed were already long established and the communities already shared many of the same beliefs and social systems. What we are seeing is a new, and archaeologically visible, means of displaying status being fed into existing networks of communication. Like a dye injected into a plant, it travelled along the capillaries and concentrated where the chemistry attracted it. The widespread distribution of late regional types shows that these same networks were still active well into the middle of the second millennium.

One of the densest concentrations of Beaker burial in Britain is in Wessex, in just the area where the great ritual monuments were built. The sequence begins with AOC types and continues with various types of European Bell Beaker. Although there is no reason to separate this group from those of eastern Britain on grounds of typology, it might be asked whether the location of Wessex, looking southwards to the Channel, might not have made it more open to contact with northern Brittany and the Channel Islands where similar early types of beaker are known. The possibility that the early Wessex beakers were derived from Brittany has been carefully considered by archaeologists and rejected. The comparisons made, however, were with the dense concentrations of beakers on the south coasts of the Amorican peninsula. Another possibility, worthy of consideration, is that the beakers found on the Channel Islands and the north coasts of Armorica were derived from Wessex through a cross-Channel network, reflecting the early stages in a system of exchange that was to intensify in the early second millennium when both regions developed parallel elite systems.

The Emergence of Elites in Wessex, Armorica, and Ireland

In the first half of the second millennium the elites of Wessex and Armorica were buried with increasingly rich grave sets, implying not only command of an expanding array of exotic prestige goods but also the social will to 'consume' wealth conspicuously by burying it with the dead. In both areas the act was commemorated by constructing a circular barrow above the grave, visible for all to see. The arrangement of these mounds in cemeteries created a 'history' of the lineage, and where barrows were arranged in linear fashion it is quite possible that some sense of the progression of time was being communicated. While the old collective tombs celebrated the timeless continuity of the lineage, the barrow cemeteries proclaimed the place of the individual in the parade of time passing (6.18).

The emergence of an elite in Wessex, recognizable now through archaeological remains, was the culmination of a series of processes which

6.18 The barrow cemetery at Winterbourne Stoke crossroads to the south-west of Stonehenge. The Bronze Age round barrows are laid out in relation to the Neolithic long barrow at top left.

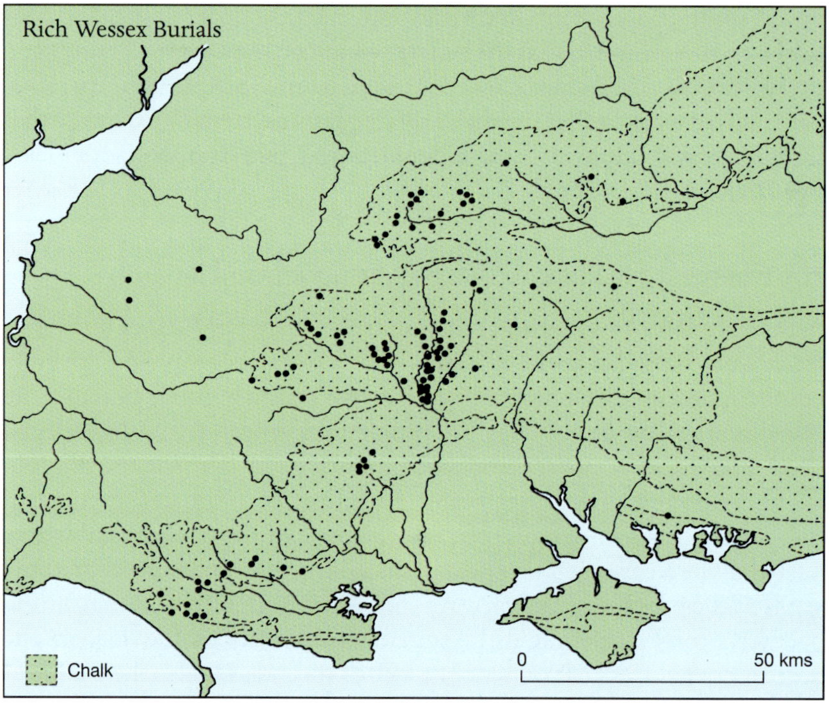

6.19 The élite Bronze Age burials of Wessex.

had begun long before, and it is no accident that the hundred or so rich burials coincided with the broad band of chalkland where, in the earlier third millennium, the great complexes of ritual monuments had begun to take shape (6.19). The social energy which had been channelled into monument building for the community was now directed to celebrating the power of certain individuals among the elite. The adoption of the 'Beaker package' around 2400 BC was simply a stage in this process of social transformation.

The hundred rich graves known through excavation used to be considered to constitute a separate intrusive 'Wessex culture', but it is now realized that they are only the richest of a much larger series of burials of the indigenous Early Bronze Age community. The rich burials span a period of some six hundred years, from *c.*2000 to *c.*1400 BC, divisible on the basis of the typology of bronze implements into two phases, centred around 1700 BC. Two examples give an idea of the richness that was available to command. At Bush Barrow, near Stonehenge, the male body was accompanied by three bronze daggers, the hilt of one inlaid with gold studs. Nearby were two sheet-gold lozenge-shaped plaques, a gold belt hook, a stone mace-head, a staff decorated with bone fittings, and a bronze axe wrapped in cloth (6.20). Not far away, at Upton Lovell in the Wylye valley, a female was buried with a decorated gold plaque, an amber necklace made up of five strands of beads separated by spacer plates, a gold-plated shale cone, gold studs and beads, and a bronze knife and awl, as well as two accompanying pots. These two burials are the richest known, but they give an idea of the range and quality of the prestige goods available at the time. In addition to the gold, amber, copper alloys, and shale found at Bush Barrow and Upton Lovell, jet and faience were regularly in use,

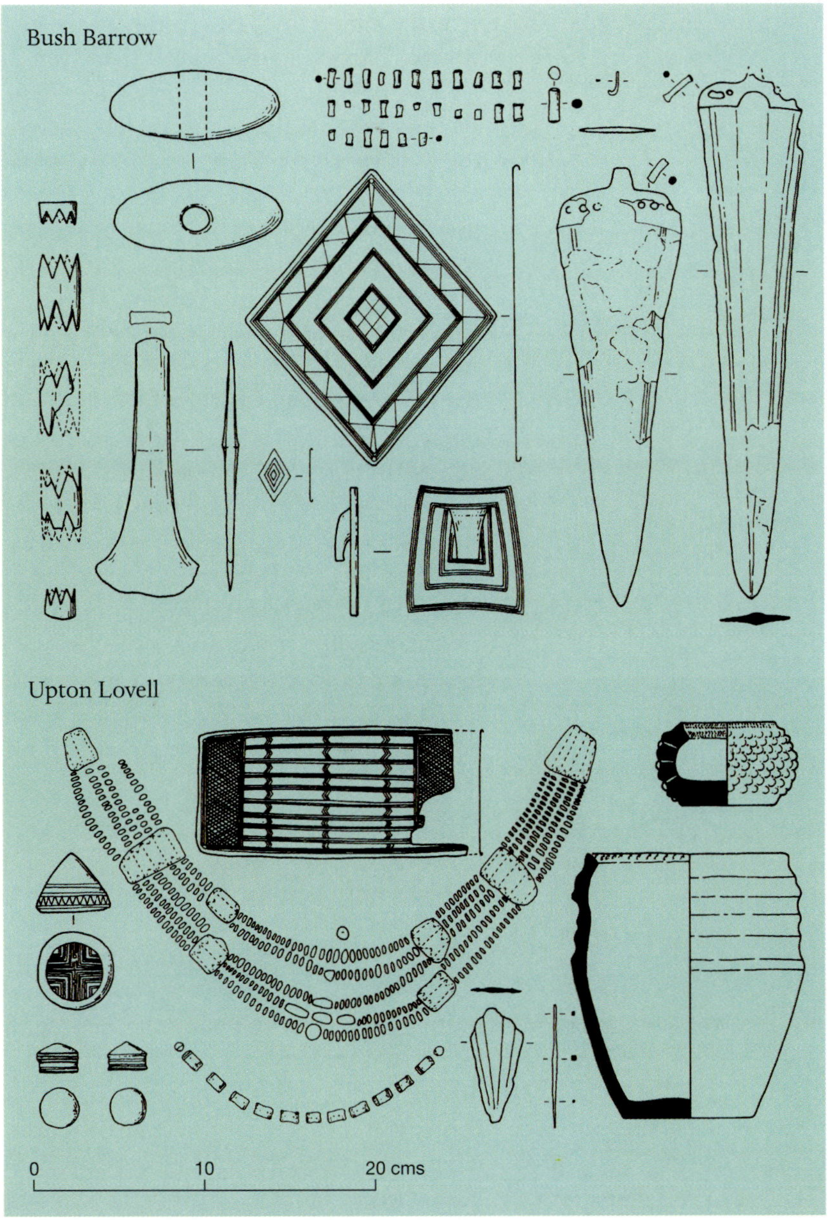

6.20 The contents of two of the élite Bronze Age burials of Wessex, the male burial of Bush Barrow, Wilts. and the female burial of Upton Lovell, Wilts.

nor should we forget the fine cloth, furs, and other organic materials that would surely have been available but no longer survive in the archaeological record.

How the elites of Wessex came to have access to such a variety of commodities in the early second millennium can, in part, be explained by geography. Wessex was crucially sited to command the major routes across southern Britain. It lay at a hub. To the south the rivers Avon, Stour, and Frome led to the ports of the Solent coast. To the west there was easy access to the Severn river system leading to Wales and the north. The Jurassic hills provided land routes right across the country to the Humber estuary, while the River Kennet gave access directly to the Thames and thus the east coast. No region of Britain was better located to articulate the intricate network of routes which threaded the island. As demand for commodities grew to serve increasingly complex social needs of the various developing communities of Europe, so those commanding route nodes like Wessex could benefit. But in addition to being a central place within a route network, Wessex was also a ritual centre of interregional importance. The great henge monuments crowned with Stonehenge, reaching its final lithic form about 2400 BC, cannot have failed to have gained a reputation spreading far and wide. It is not too fanciful to see these sites, and in particular Stonehenge, as centres of pilgrimage. As the history of medieval Europe shows, any town able to attract pilgrims had within its power the facility for growing rich.

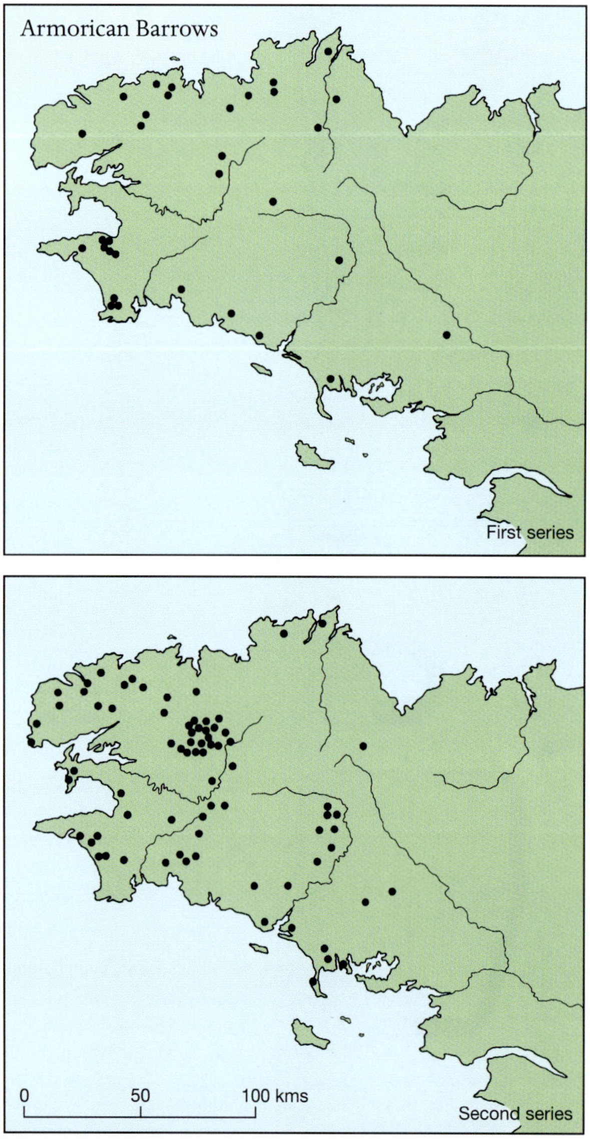

6.21 The élite Bronze Age burials of Armorica.

In Brittany a comparable series of barrow burials arose in the second millennium (6.21). Their similarities and differences to the Wessex tradition are particularly interesting. The first point of some significance is their distribution, which concentrates in the west of Brittany—west of the rivers Blavet and

Trieux—with a particularly dense clustering on the southern flank of the Monts d'Arrée. Although barrow burials do occur to the east of this line they are few. This is in stark contrast with the distribution of the earlier megalithic collective tombs which, as we have seen, had a south-eastern focus, particularly in the southern Morbihan. What we are presumably witnessing here is a change in political geography, with new centres of power emerging as the old declined. The beginning of this shift is first signalled by the distribution of the gallery graves of the later third millennium. The reasons for the change in focus are beyond recovery, but one contributory factor may have been ease of access to metals: the barrow concentrations reflect the more readily available sources of alluvial tin ore and gold.

The Armorican barrow burials were usually single burials placed in stone-built cists beneath barrows of modest size the largest being 50–60 metres in diameter. Two series have been identified. The first-series graves contain a quantity of stone items, in particular arrows represented by finely made barbed-and-tanged flint arrowheads, as well as items of copper alloy and gold. The second series contained burials accompanied by pottery vessels, occasional copper alloy implements, but never arrows. The first-series barrows are comparatively few (only about thirty have been identified) and concentrate in the northern coastal zone of Léon and Trégor, and in Penmarc'h in the south-west. They tend to be earlier than the second series, but the chronological division is not as significant as it was once thought to be. Unlike Wessex, where the indigenous single-grave tradition was later enhanced by the fashion for Beaker burial styles, there is very little evidence of the acceptance of the Beaker package in Brittany other than the early beakers themselves, which were used in traditional collective burials. Thus the emergence of the barrow burial rite in Brittany was either a purely indigenous development or it was influenced by contemporary belief systems already established across the Channel in Wessex. In support of this latter possibility, we have already suggested that the early beakers along the north coast of Brittany and on the Channel Islands might indicate exchange networks in operation in the later second millennium. The northern coastal concentration of the first-series barrows also points to the importance of maritime activity. This said, the Breton tradition has its own distinctive character.

The grave from Kernonen, Plouvora, in Finistère is a good example of a rich first-series grave (6.22). The burial was laid on a wooden floor in a rectangular stone chamber covered by a cairn and a mound 6 metres high and 50 metres in diameter. The grave goods, some placed in three oak boxes, included four bronze axes, two bronze daggers, and a short sword, all of which had wooden hilts inset with gold pins, a bronze dagger with

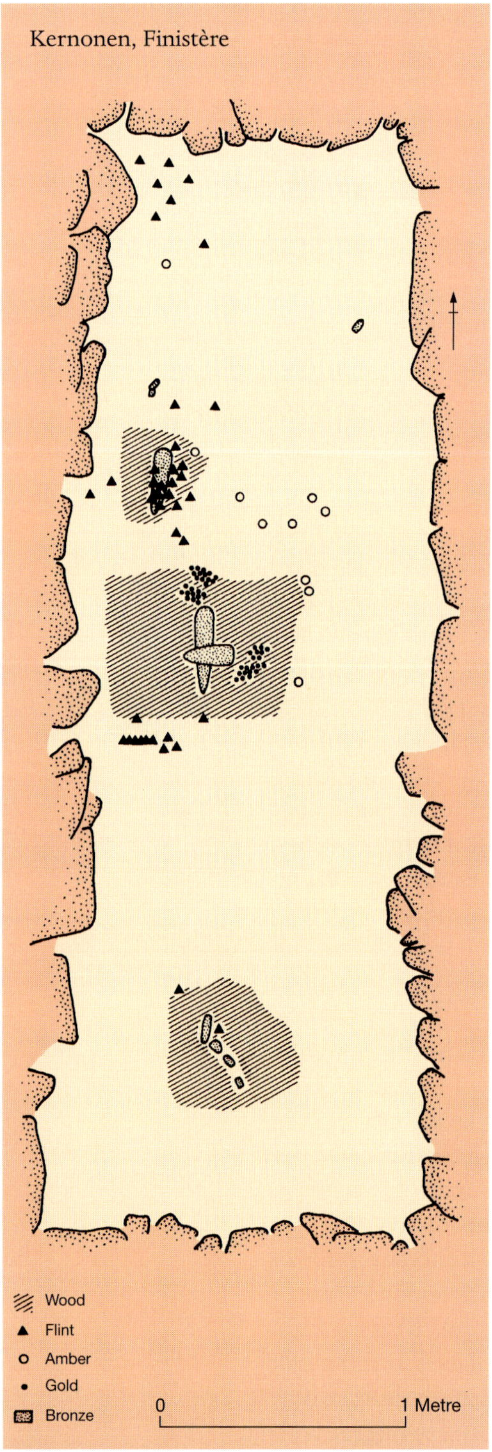

a bone pommel, sixty flint arrowheads, and twelve amber pendents. In another rich first-series burial, at Saint-Adrien, Côtes-d'Armor, the body was accompanied by two daggers, one with a wooden handle inset with gold pins, two short swords, forty-five flint arrowheads, a bronze axe, and a silver single-handled cup (6.23). Rich burials are also found in the second series, one of which, at 'La Motta' near Lannion, Côtes-d'Armor, produced, among other items, a decorated gold 'box' (6.24), while another, at Saint-Fiacre in Morbihan, was accompanied by a large plaque of amber.

Sufficient will have been said to show that while the Armorican elite graves have their own distinctive characteristics, in their choice of prestige goods Wessex and Armorica share much in common. Daggers with very finely ornamented hilts inset with tiny gold pins, of the kind found at Kernonen and Saint-Adrien, have turned up on about a dozen sites in Brittany and two in Wessex (including Bush Barrow) (6.25). In all probability these items were made in Brittany, in which case the two British finds might well have been gift exchanges between neighbouring elites. The gold box from La Motta, on the other hand, is thought to be a British product and therefore nicely reflects reciprocal exchanges.

The Armorican rite, however, remained significantly different from that of Wessex. The preference for finely made arrows serves to distinguish the Armorican elite. So too does the appearance of short swords and axes among the grave goods. The axes are often very large and non-functional, echoing the symbolic importance of the axe in Brittany going back to the fifth millennium. What we are presumably observing is the emergence of elites in the two regions sharing many of the prestige goods and symbols available through the cross-Channel exchange networks, but still maintaining their own cultural identities rooted in their different pasts.

In Ireland at this time it is rather more difficult to identify an elite in the archaeological record, large-

6.22 (*facing*) Plan of the élite Bronze Age burial at Kernonen, Finistère, Brittany.

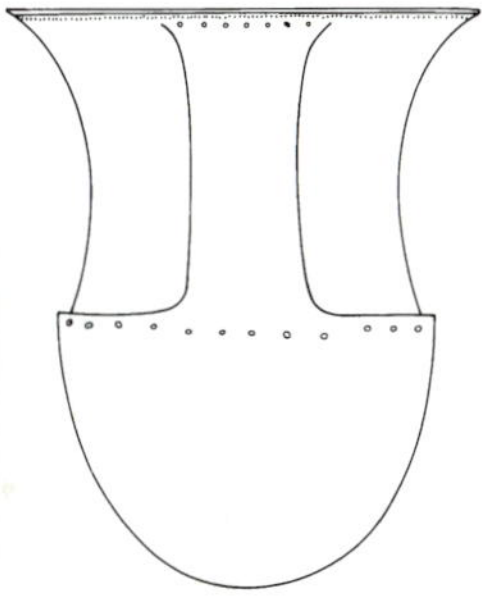

6.23 The silver cup from the Bronze Age burial at Saint-Adrien, Côtes-d'Armor, Brittany.

ly because burials do not appear to have been chosen as the means for conspicuous consumption. Yet the amount of luxury metalwork in circulation was very considerable. Axes, halberds, daggers, and spears were made in copper alloy, while gold was used for lunulae, earrings, and discs of various kinds. The sheer quantity of gold that has been recovered is staggering (in Ireland alone eighty-five lunulae are known), and this can only be a fraction of what was once in circulation. Where details of the find locations have been recorded, the bronze and gold has nearly always come from hoards or from watery contexts such as bogs and rivers. In other words, it had been taken out of circulation and placed in the realms of the chthonic deities. Although hoards are also known in Britain and Armorica at this time, the contrast in the disposal of prestige goods

between Ireland on the one hand and Britain and Armorica on the other is dramatic and must reflect very different value systems. The Irish elite may have chosen to display their status by making offerings of conspicuous wealth direct to the deities rather than indirectly, accompanying their dead. It was a practice soon to become more widely popular.

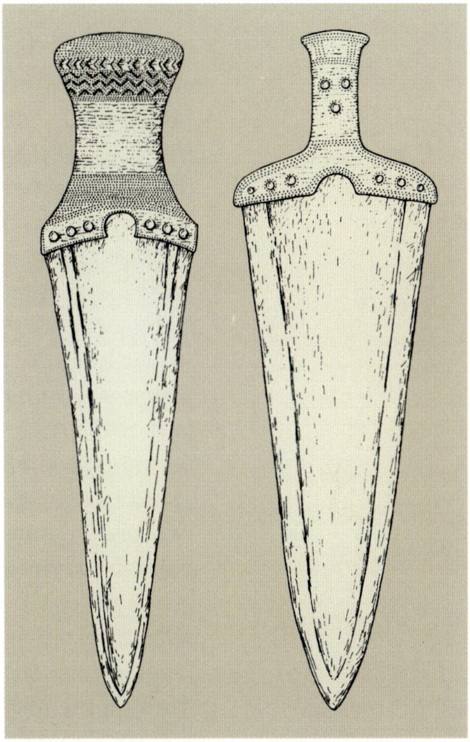

6.25 Bronze daggers with wooden handles inset with gold pins. Left, from Bush Barrow, Wiltshire and right, from Kernonen, Finistère, Brittany. Both may have been made by the same Armorican craftsman.

The Elite of Western Iberia

In the south-west of Iberia, as the second millennium progressed, the old tradition of communal burial was replaced by one of single burial, usually in simple stone-built cists or in pits covered with stone slabs and surrounded by kerbs of upstanding stones. The grave goods were generally unremarkable. The elite were provided with riveted daggers, but other items were generally rare except in the vicinity of the Tagus and Sado estuaries where small gold ornaments tend to cluster, reflecting the continued importance of the region.

In the Baixo Alentejo region, concentrated in the districts of Beja and Setúbal, a number of stone stelae have been found dating to the second half of the second millennium. They are carved with depictions of weapons, including short swords, hafted axes, and an item usually referred to as a double axe. These may be interpreted as symbols of power reflecting, perhaps, the authority of an elite. This same tradition carries on in south-western Iberia into the first centuries of the first millennium, but covering a more extended area.

There is sufficient evidence, in the form of exported gold, to show that the exchange of elite items was taking place along the Atlantic seaways. Incised and decorated gold neck rings, named after the site of Berzocana in Extremadura and found quite extensively in south-west Iberia, reached Armorica and Ireland, while Irish gold bar torcs and decorated discs moved in the opposite direction. These luxuries no doubt represent the more visible part of continued maritime interactions between the coastal elites.

6.24 (*facing*) Grave finds from the Bronze Age burial at 'La Motta', Lannion, Côtes- d'Armor, Brittany, including a whetstone, five bronze daggers, two bronze axes, two flint arrowheads and a gold box.

The Developed Atlantic Network in the Second Millennium

It is always necessary to remember that the archaeological evidence can provide only a weak and partial reflection of the distant past. Yet with all its imperfections the picture that emerges of the exchange networks operating in the second millennium is sufficient to show how intricate and powerful were the links forged between communities often separated by huge distances. The movement within these networks of commodities, concepts, beliefs, and values was on a massive scale. The developed network grew, as we have seen, out of earlier exchange networks going back into the fifth millennium or even earlier, but what is different is the sheer volume of rare materials now being moved together with the technical knowledge and skilled craftsmanship necessary to fashion each finished item.

The quantity of gold moving in various directions along the Atlantic seaways must have been considerable. Much of the gold in the northern part of the Atlantic zone surviving in the archaeological record from this period is in the form of lunulae which, from their distribution, would appear to be Irish products. The smaller items found in the Wessex and Armorican graves, spectacular though they are, in total could have been made from the gold of only four or five lunulae. To what extent these burial goods were reworked by local craftsmen from imported items it is difficult to say, but the Wessex master who made, among other things, the Bush Barrow plaques and the Lannion box had to get his raw materials through the exchange networks. His counterpart in Brittany who inset the wooden dagger handles with tiny gold pins was probably using local gold, but the presence of Iberian-style neck rings in Brittany reminds us that the networks were extensive and many sources of rare materials were available (6.14).

The scale and complexity of the exchanges are well demonstrated by a small group of gold- and silver-handled beakers. One of the most famous is a corrugated gold cup from Rillaton in Cornwall. It was very probably made in the same workshop as a plainer version found at Fritzdorf in Germany. Another ornamented cup from Eschenz in Switzerland shows many similarities, though is not necessarily by the same hand. The discovery of broadly similar vessels, but made in shale and in amber, from south-western Britain hints at a possible British origin for the gold vessels. From Armorica two silver cups of broadly similar form have been recovered from burials at Saint-Adrien and Ploumilliau. Whilst the silver could have come from local Breton sources, there is no evidence that the complex process of cupellation, involved in the extraction of silver from silver/lead ore, was known in Brittany at the time, and it may be that the silver was imported from Iberia where, in the Argaric period, very similar forms to the Breton cups were in use, although usually made in pottery. Could it be, therefore, that the gold, amber, and shale cups made in Britain were in some way inspired by silver vessels imported from Iberia?

There is no certain answer, but to ask the question opens up a vision of the intricate nature of the exchanges that may underlie the very partial archaeological distribution.

Another rare commodity of great value was amber—a fossil resin occurring naturally in the eastern Baltic and in north and west Jutland and also found washed up by the sea as far afield as the Norfolk coast, where lumps can still be found among the beach pebbles. Amber was used to make multi-strand necklaces, like that from Upton Lovell, and a range of beads and other trinkets. In the Breton grave at Saint-Fiacre a large plaque apparently served as an archers' wrist-guard of the type often found in Beaker burials. More spectacular still is the superb handled cup, 90 millimetres in diameter, from a grave at Hove, Sussex. While it is quite possible that some of the amber which found its way into graves in Britain was collected as beach pebbles from Norfolk, larger items like the Hove cup are more likely to have been made from raw materials imported through the North Sea networks, possibly via the Lower Rhine.

Another popular material for making multi-strand necklaces, buttons, and pendents was jet, most of which came from the cliffs of Whitby in northern Yorkshire. Its fine black, shiny appearance and electrostatic properties gave the stone a particular appeal. Jet necklaces (6.26) are found in some number in eastern Britain, demonstrating the vitality of east coast maritime traffic, but the material was widely distributed beyond this primary zone, to the western coasts of Scotland, to Ireland, and to Wessex. In southern Britain shale from Kimmeridge Bay in Dorset substituted for jet. Occurring in large blocks, it was also used to make handled cups like the example from Farway Down, Devon.

Finally we must consider a synthetic substance—faience. Faience is a composite material consisting of a core created by fusing fine quartz grains, covered with a separately applied glaze made from a soda–lime–quartz powder to which copper compounds have been added to impart a bright blue colour. The glaze powder would have been sprinkled over the core, which may already have been fired, and was fused into a glassy mass by heating to temperatures of about 1,000°C. In Britain many hundreds of faience beads have been recovered from second-millennium graves. They fall into two broad categories, quoit- and star-shaped beads found mainly in Scotland and Ireland, and cylindrical segmented beads found mainly in southern Britain with a concentration in Wessex. A few examples have also been found in the Channel Islands, Brittany, the Netherlands, and Denmark. Other concentrations appear in the Czech Republic, Poland, and Hungary. The question, which is still unresolved, is were the beads imported from the Near East, where the earliest faience is found, or were they made in other centres as well, and if so was the

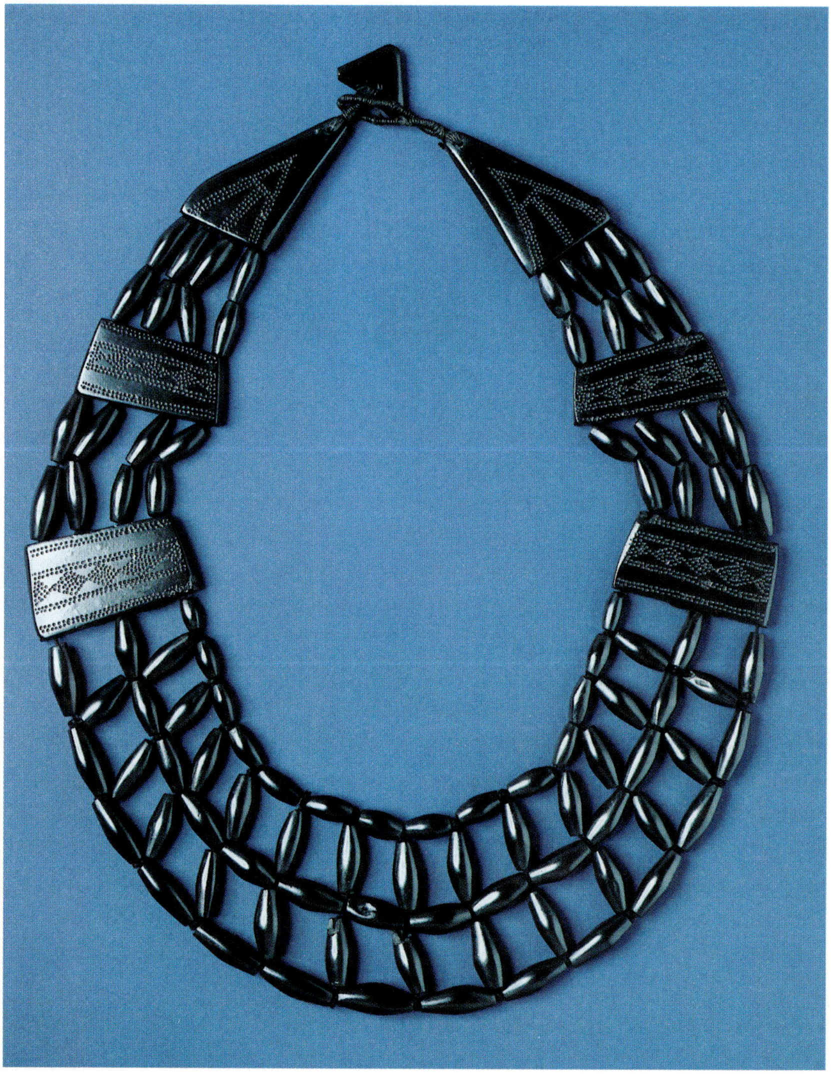

6.26 Jet necklace from a Bronze Age burial near Pitkennedy, Aberlemno, Angus, Scotland.

technique independently invented? On balance it seems more likely that production was carried out at a number of different sites. Given the complexity of the exchange networks spanning Europe it is quite possible that knowledge of the technology was passed from place to place. In Britain the distribution patterns of the two different kinds of bead would suggest that there was at least one centre at work in Scotland and one in southern Britain. Faience did not penetrate along the Atlantic networks further south than southern Brittany.

To this brief review of rare commodities—gold, silver, amber, jet, shale, and faience—must, of course, be added the more ubiquitous copper and tin produced and distributed in considerable quantities on quite a different level to the luxury goods. Alloyed together as bronze, these metals were used to make weapons such as daggers, short swords, halberds, spears, and axes employed by the local elites as symbols of status in life and in death and dedicated to the deities in increasing quantities through burial in the ground or deposition in watery contexts.

6.27 The developed exchange network by the middle of the second millennium BC showing the possible direction of influences of the All-Over Cord Beakers (AOC) and the Maritime Bell Beakers (M).

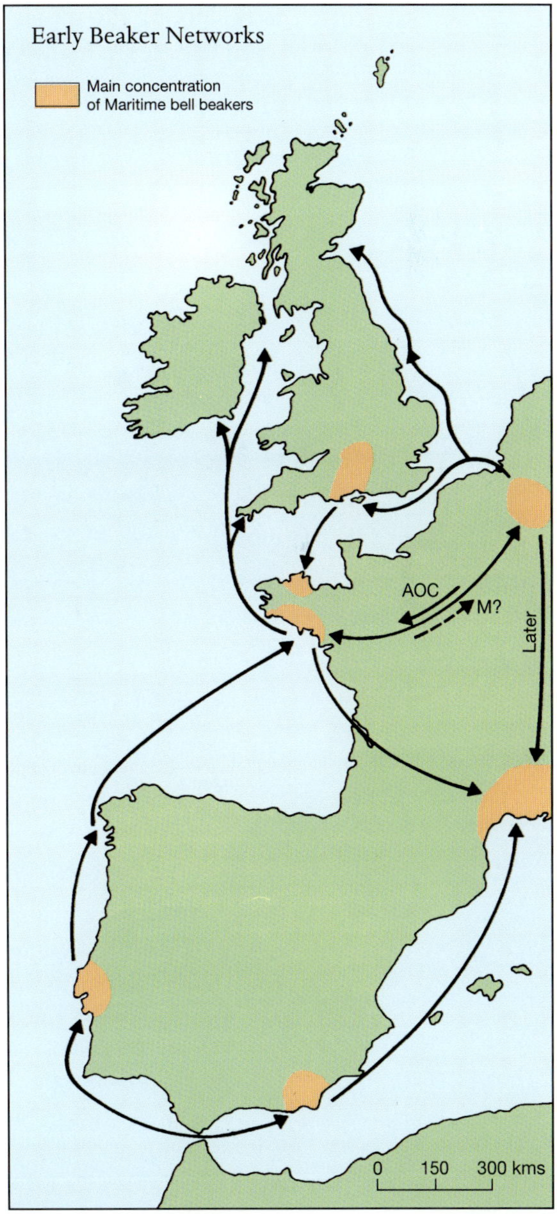

All of these commodities flowed through the Atlantic networks, concentrating in the nodes where the powerful elites were dominant, but two of the Atlantic resources, tin and gold, together with amber from the Baltic were comparatively so rare elsewhere in Europe that they would have been drawn into the wider European networks, ultimately reaching the Mediterranean polities. During this time the Mycenaean chiefdoms of the Aegean reached the peak of their power, their elite systems demanding massive quantities of luxury goods to fuel the expectations of the social hierarchy. The existence of such a consuming society cannot have failed to stimulate production and acquisition in the immediate hinterland, and this will have fed back deeper into the peripheries of Europe, creating demands to which the long-established networks were able to respond. In this way cycles of exchange escalated and the bulk and variety of goods on the move increased dramatically.

The Atlantic systems, until the late third millennium largely self-contained, were now drawn inextricably into Europe (6.27). The North Sea and Channel networks articulated through the Netherlands to the Rhine and beyond, while the Rhône–Paris Basin–Loire route gave access to the northern shores of the Bay of Biscay. Another route linked this same region, via the Garonne, to the west Mediterranean, while the Atlantic shore of Iberia was bound by the sea to the Spanish Levante and the Golfe du Lions. By the middle of the second millennium the many systems were working at pace and the elites of the Atlantic seaboard were enjoying rare materials and craftsmanship in no way inferior to those enjoyed by the chieftains of the Aegean.

With the collapse of the Mycenaean world in the twelfth century and the folk movements which ensued, the second-millennium economic infrastructure was disrupted. The harmonies which had built up over the centuries were thrown out of balance, but so vital were the Atlantic seaways linking the fringes of the world that the networks of contact were soon to re-form in the very different world that emerged.

7. Sailors on the Two Oceans: 1200–200 BC

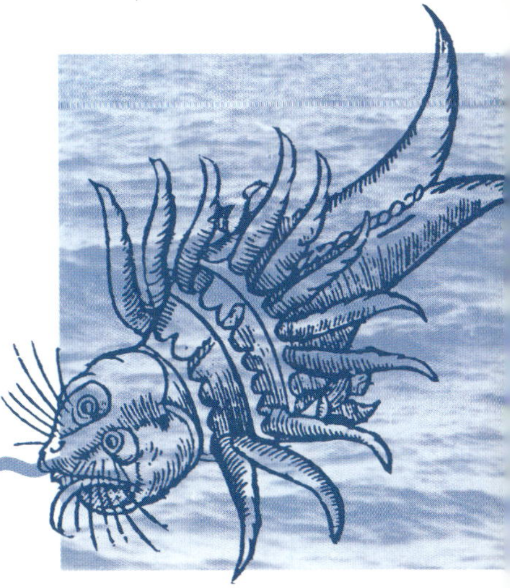

Some time towards the end of the fourteenth century BC a small trading vessel sank off the southern coast of what is now Turkey, near Ulu Burun, with its cargo intact. It was carrying 6 tonnes of copper ingots, ingots of tin, bronze swords, ostrich eggshells, ivory, slabs of blue glass, logs of exotic wood, amphorae of aromatic resin, amber, various items made in Syria and from along the Canaanite coast, and pottery of Mycenaean design. From the range of goods on board it is possible to work out something of the circular route the vessel tramped around the eastern Mediterranean from Cyprus, down the coast of the Levant, along the North African shore calling at the Nile delta on the way, before turning northwards to Crete then to the Greek mainland and finally through the islands and westwards along the shores of southern Turkey. The vessel picked up goods along the way and no doubt offloaded cargo wherever there was a market. It would have been one of many ships plying the sea routes during the summer sailing season: the only remarkable thing about it was that its wrecked cargo survived largely intact to be discovered by archaeologists.

The cargo carried by the Ulu Burun vessel gives a vivid idea of the range and volume of rare raw materials that were being moved around the eastern Mediterranean in the fourteenth century to satisfy the rapidly developing urban communities of the region—ostrich shells and ivory from Africa, amber from the Baltic, copper from Cyprus, glass from Syria, and tin from Etruria or possibly from as far afield as Cornwall or Galicia. Reviewing the array of material brought up from the wreck leaves no doubt about the complexity, and the intensity, of the trading networks that bound Europe and the Mediterranean together as a single interdependent system.

By the fourteenth century, when the Mycenaean kingdoms of the Greek mainland were reaching the peak of their power, ships from the Aegean were penetrating further and further west in search of raw materials. The distribution of distinctive 'Mycenaean' pottery provides some idea of the extent of these ventures. Ships were frequently visiting Sicily and Malta and were sailing up the western coast of Italy to the island of Iscia in the Bay of Naples, a convenient stepping-stone to Sardinia, rich in copper, and the array of metals, including the much sought-after tin, which could be had in Etruria. Once established these routes remained in operation, attracting increasing interest. Early in the eighth century settlers arrived from the Greek island of Euboea and established the earliest known Greek colony in the central Mediterranean at Pithecussae on Iscia. It was the culmination of the phase of exploration initiated by the Aegean traders from the Mycenaean world five hundred years earlier and was the beginning of a process of colonization that, by the sixth century, was to turn southern Italy and Sicily into an extension of Greece.

How far the late-second-millennium entrepreneurs extended their operations into the west Mediterranean beyond Sardinia is difficult to say, but it is clear, as we shall see later, that long-established maritime exchanges linked all parts of the region. Quite probably ships from the Aegean explored the western seas, if only on a sporadic basis, and if metals were an attraction it is likely that the south and east coasts of Iberia were visited. A hint of this comes from the discovery of sherds of Mycenaean pottery from Montoro, a settlement in the Guadalquivir valley, upriver from Córdoba. Perhaps the exotic pots were carried from the coast through the Sierra Navada to Montoro in exchange for silver from the Sierra Morena to the north. Whatever the true context, these few scraps of pottery are sufficient indication that the maritime systems of the east and west Mediterranean were interlinked.

The thirteenth century BC saw the collapse of the complex social networks that had evolved in the eastern Mediterranean. This was the time of the 'sea raiders' mentioned in Egyptian texts—it was a period of mobility and disruption. Empires like that of the Hittites fell apart and the Mycenaean kingdoms shrank into insignificance, but out of the chaos gradually there emerged a new order. Around the fringes of the Aegean Greek speakers began to establish stable communities that centuries later were to emerge as small city states, while along the maritime strip of Syria and Palestine the old Canaanite territory was transformed, after about 1200 BC, into what became universally known as the land of the Phoenicians.

The Phoenicians

The Phoenicians were an urban maritime people of the littoral occupying the interface between the Mediterranean and the developing civilizations of the Near East. Through their great ports of Tyre, Sidon, Byblos, and others they articulated the trading systems that serviced the growing needs of their eastern neighbours, and in doing so they maintained a hold on the maritime networks of the Mediterranean, building on the experience and detailed knowledge that had accumulated throughout the second millennium. They were the heirs of the entrepreneurs of the Mycenaean period. It is no surprise to find them established, and archaeologically visible, as far west as Sardinia as early as the ninth century.

As a great maritime people they were accomplished shipbuilders. To carry merchandize they used 'round' ships called *gauloi* (7.2), capacious vessels four times as long as they were broad, usually 20–30 metres long and 6–7 metres broad with a draught of about a metre and a half. The stern was rounded and terminated in a high, decorated sternpost. The bows were similarly treated, ending with a horse's head, hence the name *hippoi* sometimes used to distinguish them. The vessels had a main mast taking a rectangular sail hung from a yard: steering was by a large oar attached to the port side close to the stern. The internal arrangements varied, the main aim being to create maximum stowage space for cargo, but there was usually a quarterdeck at the stern to provide sheltered accommodation for the crew. Vessels of this kind, heavily laden but in a

7.1 Wall-relief from the palace of Sennacherib (705–681), Nineveh, Iraq, drawn after A. H. Layard, showing two types of Phoenician ship.

7.2 (*facing*) Wall-relief from the palace of Sargon II (722–705) at Khorsabad, Iraq showing river-craft, *hippoi*, carrying logs.

fair wind, would probably have achieved speeds of 2–3 knots, making them capable of travelling up to 50 nautical miles a day. The Phoenicians also developed warships that were sleeker and faster and could attain speeds of 5 knots (7.1). Special features included a bow strengthened to incorporate a battering ram, and a raised deck, or forecastle, for the bowmen and catapults needed during engagements at sea. To provide the necessary manoeuvrability the vessels had two masts, one in the centre to take the main sail, the other in the prow, the sail flexibly hung to catch the crosswinds. There was also provision for rowers to give extra speed or propulsion in adverse winds. These are, of course, generalized descriptions and there was, inevitably, much variation on the two basic themes to meet specific needs, such as fishing or the bulk haulage of large timbers, or to improve the fighting efficiency as naval engagements became more frequent.

The fleets were crucial to the well-being of the Phoenician cities, to bring in the basic resources for the needs of the urban communities, and to provide the prestige goods, and later the tributes demanded by their increasingly powerful neighbours, the Assyrians. These demands became more focused after the beginning of the eighth century. Assyria now required iron, copper, and, more particularly, silver, which the empire had begun to use as a medium for internal and external exchanges. In search of these materials the Phoenician shipmasters began to explore the far west, perhaps having heard talk of the silver mountains of Iberia from west Mediterranean sailors putting into the ports of Sardinia.

Phoenicians in the West

The exact chronology of Phoenician expansion into the west Mediterranean is much debated (7.3). The archaeological evidence, however, is sufficient to suggest that there was a Phoenician presence at Nora, on the south coast of Sardinia, at least as early as the ninth century, and by the eighth century the Phoenicians were well established in south Iberia with their main trading port on the island of Gadir (now Cadiz) on the Atlantic side of the Pillars of Hercules. Yet uncertainty arises as to when the first Phoenician landings took place here. The first-century AD writer Velleius Paterculus, referring to ancient traditions he had gathered, tells us that Gadir was founded by settlers from Tyre eighty years after the fall of Troy, which would imply a date of just before 1100 BC, while Utica, on the coast of Tunisia north of Carthage, was founded a few years later. A third city, Lixus, on the Atlantic coast of Morocco was also believed to be an ancient foundation of about this period. Carthage itself, later to become the focus of Phoenician/Punic power in the central Mediter-

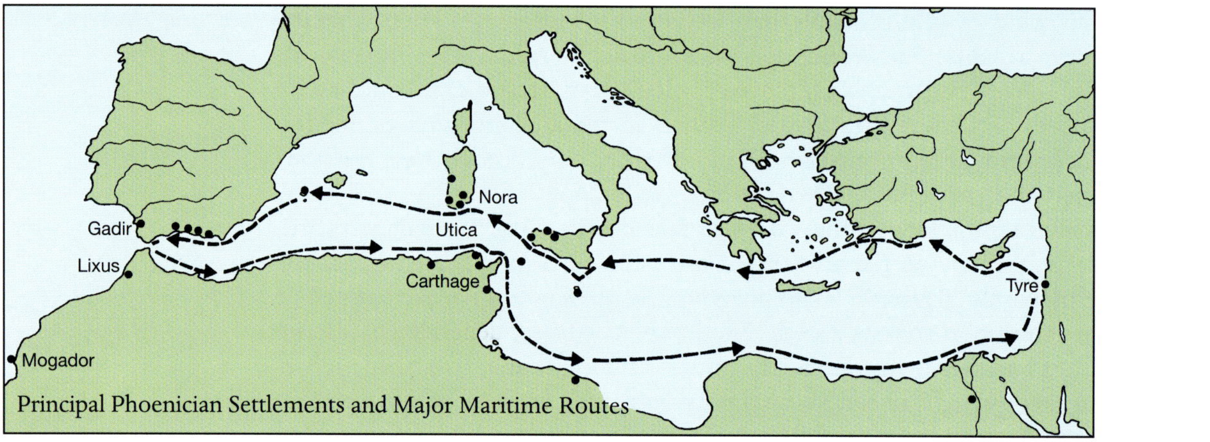

7.3 The principal Phoenician settlements and major maritime routes in the Mediterranean.

ranean, was not established, according to tradition, until as late as 814 BC.

An interesting account of the founding of Gadir is recalled by Strabo, probably quoting the Greek ethnographer Posedonius who had visited Gadir about 100 BC. According to the tradition an oracle had ordered the Tyrians to found a settlement at the Columns of Hercules. 'Those sent to explore arrived at the straits next to Calpe [the rock of Gibraltar], and thought that the promontories that formed the straits were the boundaries of the inhabited earth . . .' They landed and offered a sacrifice, but the omens were not propitious so they returned. A second expedition was sent and sailed through the Straits, arriving at 'an island dedicated to Hercules that lies close to Onoba' (Huelva). They too offered a sacrifice, but again the omens were unfavourable so they returned home. A third time, having landed on the island of Gadeira (Gadir), the gods were presumably satisfied and the colonists proceeded to erect a temple on the eastern part of the island and to build their city to the west. The story is interesting in that it hints at something of the processes of exploration that must have preceded the final choice of a site for settlement. It is not impossible that in this traditional account we have a reflection of a long, pre-colonial phase of contact during which traders visited southern Iberia in the spring, returning home again at the end of the season. During this time networks of friendship and obligation would have been created and a detailed knowledge of the local geography built up. The final decision to found a colony—that is, for one part of the visiting group to remain—would thus have been based on experience and undertaken in an atmosphere of mutual trust to the benefit of both the host country and the 'colonists'. It is quite possible that this pre-colonial phase was spread over time, with clusters of visits interspersed with long periods without contact. In such a situation it is easy to see how the first arrival could have preceded the formal establishment of the settlement by several centuries. That the decision to set up a permanent port-of-trade on Gadir was finally made in the eighth century may well have been the result of Assyrian pressure on the cities of the Phoenician motherland, requiring them to find and bring back regular supplies of silver and other metals.

The study of the Phoenician colony of Gadir is hampered by the brilliance of the founders' choice of site. So good was it that Gadir has remained a thriving port city throughout history to the present day (7.4). What little of the early settlement may remain lies deep beneath many metres of more recent overburden. Moreover, reconstruction of the early topography is not helped by the fact that there have been significant coastal changes over the last two and a half thousand years. The early accounts suggest that there were three islands in the estuary of the River

7.4 Cadiz from the air. The rocky reef (foreground) flanks the entrance to the channel that divided the small island of Erytheia from the larger island of Kotinoussa.

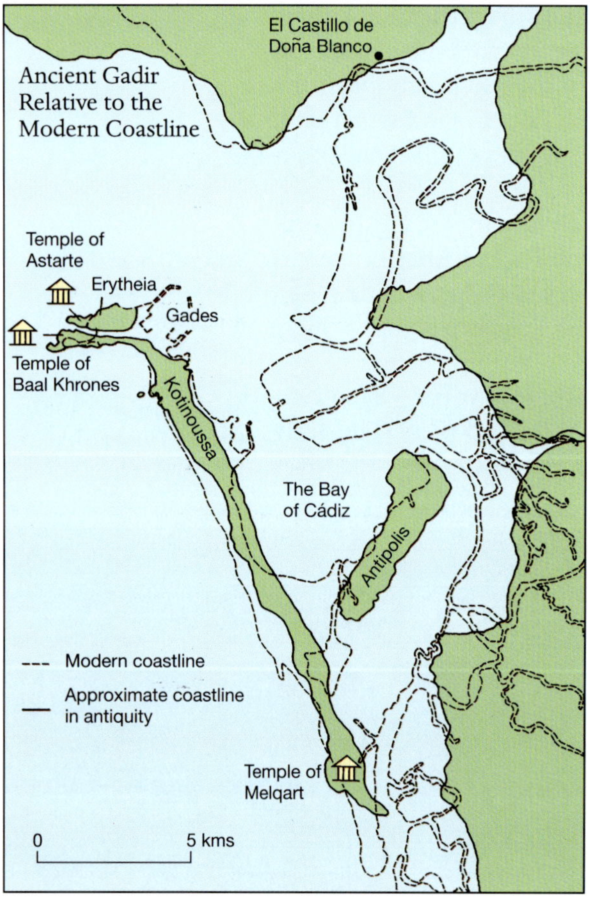

7.5 Gadir as it was in ancient times in relation to the modern coastline.

Guadalete which together were known as the Gadeira or Gedeiroi (Gardes in Latin) (7.5). The ancient city was established on the smallest island, Erytheia, at the extreme western extremity of which was the temple of Astarte. This was separated by a narrow channel from the long, narrow island of Kotinoussa where the main cemeteries lay. At its western tip, opposite the temple of Astarte, was a sanctuary dedicated to Baal Khronos, while at the far end of the island was the famous temple to Melqart (Roman Hercules). The third of the islands, Antipolis, lay between Kotinoussa and the mainland.

The siting of a port-of-trade on an offshore island was a common enough practice among Phoenicians and Greeks. An island was a distinct territory easily recognized as such by everyone. It was little threat to the indigenous, land-based population and yet was a safe place for foreign traders to establish themselves. Moreover, it was convenient for both partners in trade since it lay at an interface, easy to access by land and sea. Gadir was particularly well sited, not only with respect to the two important inland routes, via the rivers Guadalete and Guadalquivir, but also in that it was only a short journey from the estuaries of the rivers Tinto and Odiel which gave direct access to the metal-rich zone presided over by an important native settlement and port which lay at the confluence of the two rivers beneath the modern city of Huelva (7.6). It is quite possible that this settlement was the 'Tartessos' so frequently, but obscurely, referred to by classical writers. From Tartessos and the other native outlets produce for trade could be brought to the island of Gadir and there exchanged for the Mediterranean luxuries shipped in by the Phoenician merchants.

Some feeling for the nature of the exchange is provided by the Greek writer Diodorus Siculus, who was very probably using a lost text of Posedonius written early in the first century BC and local knowledge. Diodorus gives a fanciful account of how the silver was first discovered as the result of massive forest fires. 'Much silver trickled from the fiery ground and, as they melted, the silver-bearing ores formed countless rivulets of pure silver.' The natives, he claimed, did not know how to exploit it, but

> once the Phoenicians heard of the affair, they bought the silver in exchange for objects of negligible value. The Phoenicians took the silver to Greece, to Asia, and to all the other countries then known, thus obtaining great riches. It is said that such was the cupidity of the traders that they replaced the lead anchors of their ships with silver ones after there was no more room for silver in the vessels, and there was still a great quantity of the metal left over. This commercial traffic was long the source of a great increase in the power of the Phoenicians, who founded many colonies . . . (Diodorus 5. 35. 4–5).

The significance of the text is that it makes clear that silver was available in quantity and was avidly acquired by the Phoenicians. This much is well

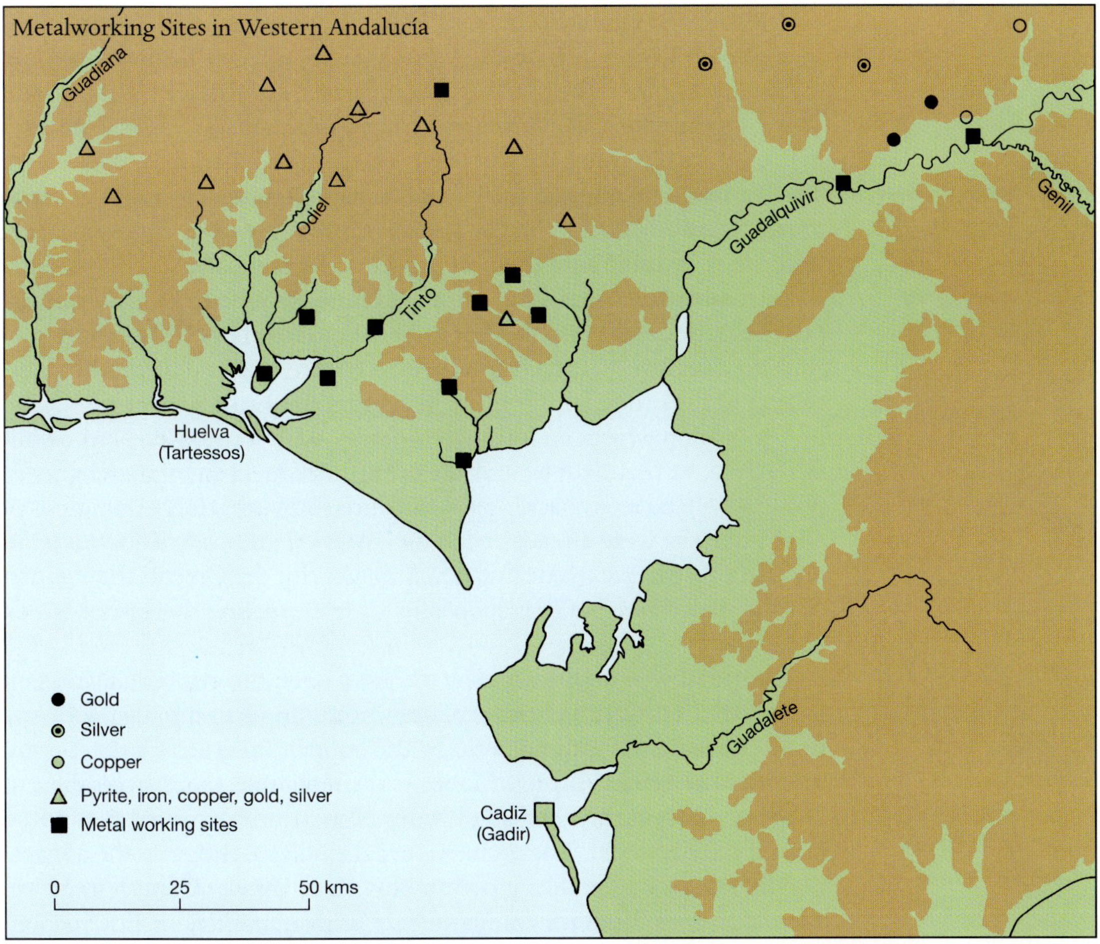

7.6 The coastline between Gadir (Cadiz) and the Tartessian settlement on the promontory between the Odiel and Tinto (now Huelva) as it was in the mid first millennium BC, showing the distribution of metalworking sites.

borne out by the archaeological evidence, which shows that silver production began to be undertaken on a large scale in many of the native settlements from the eighth century onwards. At one site, Cerro Salomón, which developed in the seventh century as a mining settlement, silver, gold, and copper were worked, the native population being engaged in all stages of the process from mining the ore to purification of the metal. Ore from other mines was transported to the port at Huelva and smelted there. While there can be little doubt that the Phoenician presence at Gadir was the stimulus for the dramatic increase in production, there is no need to follow Diodorus in assuming that the natives were unable to exploit it: they had long been extracting copper and gold. It becomes worthwhile to produce a commodity in surplus only if there is a market for it—and that the Phoenicians were willing to provide.

It cannot have been long before knowledge of Tartessian silver spread among the other entrepreneurs of the eastern Mediterranean. Herodotus records an interesting story about a shipmaster called Kolaios who, sailing south from Samos to Egypt, was caught in a gale from the east and driven the length of the Mediterranean, 'past the pillars of Hercules, and at last, by some special guiding providence, reached Tartessos. This trading town was in those days a virgin port, unfrequented by merchants. The Samians, in consequence, made by the return-voyage, a profit greater than any Greeks before their day . . .' When they returned safely home they invested a tenth of their profits in having an elaborate bronze vessel made to dedicate at the temple of Juno on Samos. The story has its problems, not least the inherent unlikelihood of there being a storm of such consistency that the ship was driven from one end of the Mediterranean to the other. It is far more likely that this was a deliberate voyage of exploration which, on internal evidence, must have taken place about 630 BC. But at that date to find the port 'unfrequented by merchants' is puzzling when the archaeological evidence shows that large quantities of Greek pottery were already reaching Huelva. Perhaps Kolaios was simply claiming to have opened up a new market for the Greeks, the Phoenicians already there being responsible for transporting the earlier Greek pottery.

The metal wealth of Tartessos will have been the principal attraction to east Mediterranean entrepreneurs—not only silver but also gold and tin from the hinterland and perhaps also copper. In return for these commodities the traders brought 'objects of negligible value' according to Diodorus, or 'oil and other small wares of maritime commerce' as noted in an unascribed text. The archaeological evidence supports the suggestion that oil was a significant commodity since Greek oil amphorae have been found; so too have comparatively large quantities of fine painted

Greek pottery. The 'other small items' will have included glass and metal vessels, furniture, musical instruments, fabrics, perfumes, and jewellery collected together by enterprising shipowners in the east Mediterranean and Italian ports. The disparaging remarks of Diodorus suggest that the benighted natives of Tartessos were being swindled by the wily Phoenicians—this is probably nothing more than ill-considered stereotyping. Exchanges will only have taken place if they were beneficial to both partners. To own mountains of silver is not much good unless it is possible to use the resource to acquire desirable commodities in exchange. The value of what was acquired—a fine Greek pot for example—will have been quite different in Tartessos than in, say, the Greek ports of Sicily. In Tartessos it could, perhaps, have been used in social exchanges in cycles of reciprocity or as a prestige gift signalling a hierarchic structure. Values are all relative, and commodities will not flow unless there is a positive desire to acquire them.

The early Phoenician traders impinged upon a native society that was still essentially Late Bronze Age in its technological development. Its hierarchical structure was well developed, with elites displaying their positions in the hierarchy by manipulating symbols of status. This much is well demonstrated by elaborate carved stelae depicting the accoutrements of power which we will consider again later (p. 284). To this society the traders brought a new range of prestige items and new value systems for the local elites to select from.

The most spectacular of the prestige goods which came into circulation in the seventh century were items of elaborate jewellery made from gold. Most of those so far known are concentrated in three collections, El Carambolo near Seville, Ebora in Cadiz, and Aliseda in Extremadura. The Ebora 'hoard' included ninety-three individual gold items and forty-three carnelians, while the Aliseda 'hoard' numbered some three hundred pieces, including a diadem, necklaces, bracelets, earrings, finger rings, and sheet decoration for sewing to cloth (7.7). In all probability these 'hoards' were from rich burials. There has

7.7 Gold jewellery from what was probably a rich tomb at Aliseda, Cáceres, Spain. The gold items were probably made by Phoenician craftsmen working in southern Iberia. The finger ring (centre, bottom) incorporates an amethyst seal of Syrian workmanship.

been much discussion about the origin of the pieces, but it is now generally agreed that much, if not all, of it was made by Phoenicians or Phoenician-trained craftsmen working in Iberia, most likely in Gadir. Much the same can be said of the elaborate ivory-work like the decorated combs found in the elite tombs at Carmona. An ivory-carving workshop has been identified in the native town at El Castillo de Doña Blanca at the mouth of the Guadalete just opposite Gadir. The ivory was probably imported to Gadir from one of the Phoenician trading posts established along the Atlantic coast of Morocco.

Other items of east Mediterranean inspiration adopted by the elites of Tartessos included bronze ewers (7.8), braziers, and sometimes tall incense burners. These objects are best regarded as belonging to sets used in the social or ritual systems adopted by the elites and thought appropriate to symbolize status in death. Though undoubtedly of eastern inspiration, they, like the gold and ivory work, were probably made by Phoenicians in Gadir or Huelva. Some found their way into local burials like the rich grave of La Joya at Huelva, where the bronzes were part of a grave set which also included a wheeled vehicle and an ivory box, but others were dispersed throughout western Iberia well beyond the territory of Tartessos (7.9). It is tempting to see these items as prestige gifts from Tartessos to the native elites who controlled metal production and the transport routes along which tin and gold would have passed. The distribution of these goods stretches northwards from Tartessos along the metal-rich pyrite zone, with a concentration in the valley of the Guadiana across which traffic would have had to have passed. There are also isolated examples on the Atlantic coast near the mouths of the Tagus and the Mondego, perhaps reflecting maritime commerce.

7.8 Bronze jug from the cemetery of La Joya, Huelva.

The brief anecdotes left by classical writers and the rich body of archaeological evidence together provide a remarkably detailed picture of the direct

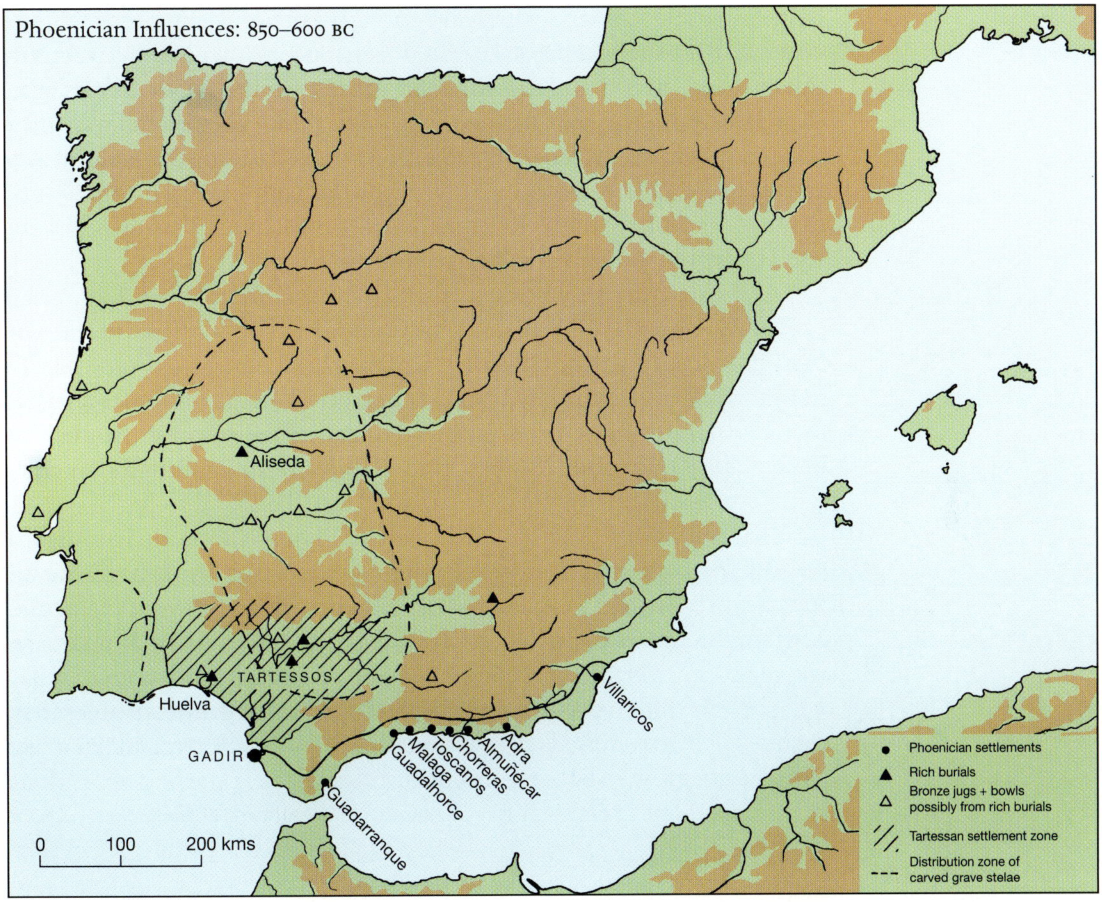

7.9 Phoenician settlements, Tartessos and the élite burials of the hinterland in the eighth and seventh centuries BC. The distribution of the carved native grave stelae indicates the approximate extent of a social territory through which gold and tin from the north were exchanged with Tartessos.

impact of Mediterranean civilization on a barbarian Atlantic society. What we see is not colonial exploitation of the kind many parts of the world experienced in the seventeenth to nineteenth centuries, but the subtle interaction of two systems articulating through a port-of-trade to the benefit of both.

The establishment of Gadir and the initial networks set up by the Phoenician traders with the elites of Huelva and the communities of the hinterland were essentially the first phase in a long and developing process of interaction. The next stage saw the establishment of a number of coastal colonies densely spaced along the narrow coastal fringe of southern Iberia between the Mediterranean and the high Penibaetic sierras (7.10). On present evidence the earliest was founded in the second half of the eighth century, but most of the rest do not seem to begin until the seventh century. These settlements, thought to be real colonies in the sense that they were established by communities of Phoenicans seeking land to settle and work, were very carefully sited, usually where a river coming from the mountains created a fertile alluvial zone between the uplands and the sea. Behind, the river valleys provided easy access to the rich intermontane plateaux and beyond them to the valley of the Guadalquivir and the silver-rich Sierra Morena flanking the valley to the north. In front of the colonies lay the ocean with its rich resources and ease of communication. In other words, the colonies were optimally sited to exploit a wide variety of resources.

The most extensively studied of the colonies is Toscanos, 30 kilometres east of Malaga. Here excavation has exposed a large warehouse containing Phoenician and Greek storage amphorae in which oil from the east Mediterranean would have been transported. Other imported goods included painted Phoenician pottery. For export the colonists would have been able to offer copper, silver, and gold from the hinterland together with local products like corn, wine, dried fish, dyes, and so on.

What motivated people to leave their Phoenician homeland in the seventh century is difficult to say, but social stress brought about by increasing pressures from the east might have been sufficient to encourage families to brave the long journey to seek their livelihoods on the far fringe of the civilized world. The colonial adventure was not an unqualified success, and in the first half of the sixth century most of the settlements were abandoned. A few continued, but only two, Malaka and Almuñécar, grew to become important centres.

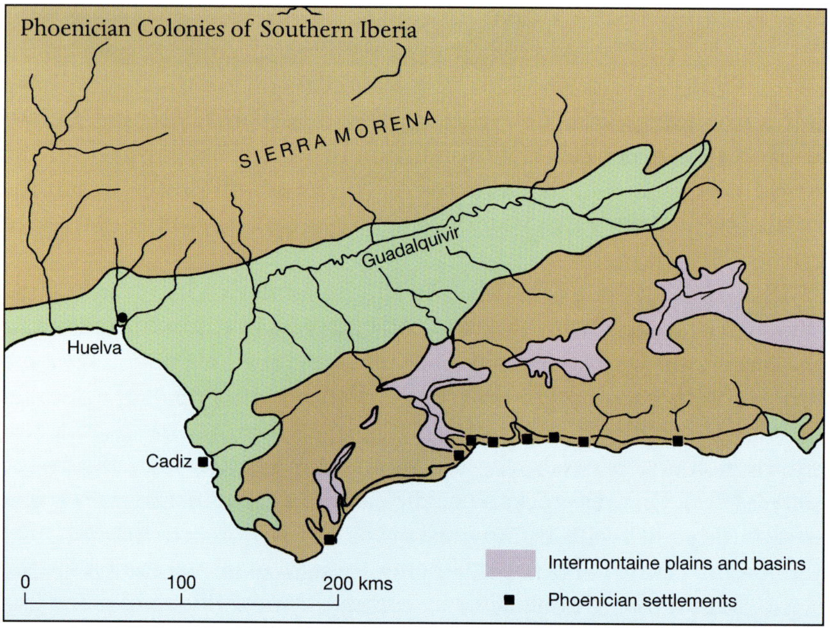

7.10 The Phoenician colonies of the southern Iberian coast in relation to the geomorphology of Andalucía.

The period from 600 to 550 BC was a time of significant change in the area, resulting from a combination of factors. The siege of Tyre by the Babylonians from 586 to 573 BC was a major disruptive event, but by this time it seems that the more easily accessible silver ores had been worked out and other sources of supply, for example in Attica, were beginning to come on stream. Another unsettling factor was the growing influence of the Greeks arriving from Phocaea on the Aegean coast of Anatolia to set up colonies in the western Mediterranean. Around 600 BC they founded a colony at Massalia (Marseilles) and soon another at Emporion (Ampurias). From here trading expeditions probed the old Phoenician preserve and, judging by the volume of Greek pottery from Huelva, it seems that Greek entrepreneurs were active in the early decades of the sixth century. The situation was stabilized again by the middle of the century, by which time the Phoenician city of Carthage had established itself as master of much of the western Mediterranean. Thereafter the coastal regions of southern Iberia began to share the Punic culture of Carthage, and the way between the Mediterranean and the Atlantic became the preserve of the Carthaginian fleet. So it was to remain until 208 BC when the Roman armies finally entered Gadir in triumph.

Much has been made, by ancient historians, of the 'Carthaginian control' of the Straits of Gibraltar in the period 550–208 BC, the assumption being that the general hostility that developed between the Carthaginians and the Greeks would have meant that the Straits were closed to Greek shipping. While this may have been true for periods of particular tension there is no reason to assume that Greek explorers and traders were forbidden access to the Atlantic and could only slip through the blockade at rare moments. For much of the time it is likely that a more *laissez-faire* attitude prevailed, not least because the political allegiance of cargo vessels and the ethnic origin of the crews were probably quite blurred.

The Atlantic Networks: 1200–600 BC

The establishment of Phoenician interest in southern Iberia and the creation of a permanent port-of-trade on the Atlantic island of Gadir in the eighth century brought the Mediterranean systems of trade and exchange directly into contact with Atlantic systems. Gadir/Huelva was the pin that held the two systems together, but each impinged upon the territory of the other: Atlantic bronzes flowed into the north-west Mediterranean, while the Phoenicians established colonies along the coasts of Portugal and Morocco (7.28). The benefit was to both. The Atlantic seaways provided access to unlimited supplies of copper and tin

for the Phoenicians to collect and feed into their own networks, while the demand for metals which they created may well have been a significant stimulus to the Atlantic cycles of exchange. Indeed it could be argued that the massive increase observed in the production and movement of bronze along the Atlantic façade was the direct result of the Mediterranean demand. The matter is difficult to prove, but the possibility is worth entertaining.

It is not our purpose in this chapter to look in any detail at the different Atlantic communities who were involved in the production and distribution of bronze, but simply to focus on the processes by which huge quantities of metal came to be generated and circulated along the Atlantic sea lanes in the six hundred years or so that constitute the Late Bronze Age.

The archaeological evidence for this is considerable. It consists for the most part of tens of thousands of bronze objects, mainly weapons, most of which had been deliberately deposited either by burial in the ground or by throwing them into watery contexts such as rivers, lakes, bogs, and the sea. Only a very small percentage of what constitutes the archaeological record of production and distribution comes from settlement or cemetery contexts. It could, therefore, be argued that most of what is available has been selected for deposition in accordance with ritual constraints and may not, therefore, be typical of material in daily use. This may be so, but the selection factors are not likely to have had much effect on the broad distribution patterns. The usual way to translate this evidence into usable archaeological documents is to plot the spatial distribution of distinctive types and from these maps to gauge the core area of 'home' distribution, distinguishing it from the total distribution which indicates the direction in which the items travelled and the intensity of the movement. Mapping contemporary artefacts made in different centres contributes to an appreciation of the overall trading network, while a series of plots of items of successive dates enable changes in the exchange network over time to be distinguished. It is a complex and time-consuming process, but the work of many scholars over the last century or so has laid a firm basis for interpretation, while the increasing availability of radiocarbon dates and a better understanding of the way in which they should be used mean that it is usually possible to offer dates to the nearest century or so.

7.11 (*facing*) The late prehistoric settlement of Dún Aonghasa on the Aran Islands in Galway Bay, Ireland. The air view shows the excavation in progress exposing a Late Bronze Age settlement. The enclosing wall, in its present form, is later but may incorporate a contemporary Late Bronze Age defensive work.

To gain a better understanding of the broad patterns which emerge, it is worth looking first at a few specific examples. Excavations on two remote Atlantic islands, Aran off the coast of Co. Galway, and Shetland, far to the north of Scotland, illuminate the theme at its simplest level. At the spectacular cliff edge site of Dún Aonghasa (7.11) excavations have uncovered part of a simple settlement dating to the period 1300–800 BC, existing before the visible wall of the great stone fortification, for which the site is famous, was built. Amid the occupation rubbish trampled into the floor of hut 1 were found fragments of two crucibles and lumps of baked clay moulds used for casting a bronze sword, a spearhead, and bronze rings or bracelets. Unimpressive though these scraps are, they show that the occupants of this remote slab of limestone, surrounded by the crashing Atlantic, had among them someone skilled in the manufacture of bronzes, a person who had access to the necessities of his craft—refractory clay, beeswax, and bronze scrap—and who carried with him a knowledge of the artefact shapes which tradition demanded should be adhered to. Over 1,000 kilometres away to the north-east, on the even more remote island of Shetland, similar evidence has been recovered from the settlement site of Jarlshof at the south end of the island. Here, within the confines of a modest settlement, production was on a larger scale. Sufficient mould fragments were recovered (7.12) to represent the manufacture of eight socketed axes, seven swords, a decorated pin of Irish type, a gouge, and a number of rods of various kinds.

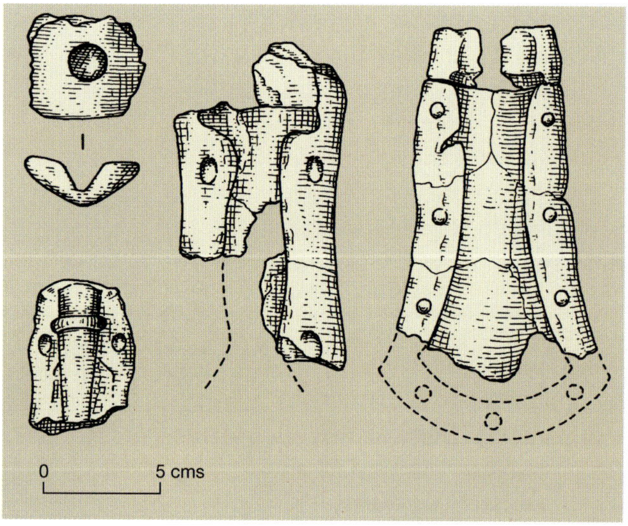

7.12 Baked clay moulds for casting bronze implements from the Late Bronze Age settlement at Jarlshof, Shetland.

What the evidence from Dún Aonghasa and Jarlshof shows is that by the Late Bronze Age even the most remote places had access to a variety of bronze weapons and tools. But particular interest lies in the fact that the communities' needs were met, at least in part, by local production. It is impossible to say whether the bronze smiths were resident members of the local communities able to acquire their materials by boat, or were itinerants moving from place to place with their bags of scrap metal, clay, and wax, offering their skills to those who could bestow patronage. Whichever was the case, we are witnessing production at its most basic level and the movement of technologies carried across the seas.

Direct evidence for Late Bronze Age shipping is sparse in Atlantic waters, but two finds, lying off the shores of southern Britain, are informative: both appear to be debris scatters resulting from shipwrecks. The largest is a collection of 189 bronzes found at the foot of Langdon cliff just to the east of Dover Harbour in 7–13 metres of water. The items were scattered on the seabed mostly within a radius of about 50 metres. The second 'wreck' was represented by seven bronzes found on the seabed off

Moor Sand, 3 kilometres east of Salcombe estuary in Devon. In neither case was there any trace of the vessel, but this is hardly surprising given the exposed nature of the seabeds and the constant scouring both sites had experienced. It is fortunate that so much of the cargo has survived to be discovered. What is of particular interest is that the bronzes found at both wreck sites are northern French in origin, and some of the items from Langdon Bay had been cut up to facilitate packing and handling. The conclusion must be that the vessels were bringing scrap bronze from the Continent to Britain where, we may assume, it was to be melted down and recast into local types.

The two wreck sites provide a fascinating insight into the complex networks of exchange that must have been the norm in western Europe at this time. The transport of scrap metal warns against arguing in too much detail from the distribution of individual types, since scrap dumps could be assembled and redistributed in a variety of ways which had little to do with regular exchanges of functioning artefacts.

The famous Huelva hoard presents a different range of interesting problems. The 'hoard', comprising over four hundred artefacts, was dredged from the River Odiel, just off the Tartessian city of Huelva, in 1923 (7.13). The collection included seventy-eight swords, of which fifty-five were of the distinctive carp's-tongue type (below, p. 280), twenty-two short swords or daggers, eighty-eight spearheads, some of which were of Irish manufacture, fibulae of a distinctive elbow-shape of east Mediterranean origin, fragments of a helmet, and a number of other items. The exact date of the deposition has been in some doubt, but a series of radiocarbon assessments from wood associated with the bronzes has finally tied the deposit down to the mid-tenth century BC. But what exactly the 'hoard' represents is open to debate. For a long while it was believed that the bronzes came from a shipwreck, but more recently other possibilities have been put forward, the most likely being that it is a votive deposit consigned to the sea in a single act of dedication. An alternative view, that the items were grave goods deposited with the body of a powerful member of the elite, has less to commend it. The votive-deposit hypothesis gains its support from the fact that in the Late Bronze Age the deposition of bronzes in 'watery'

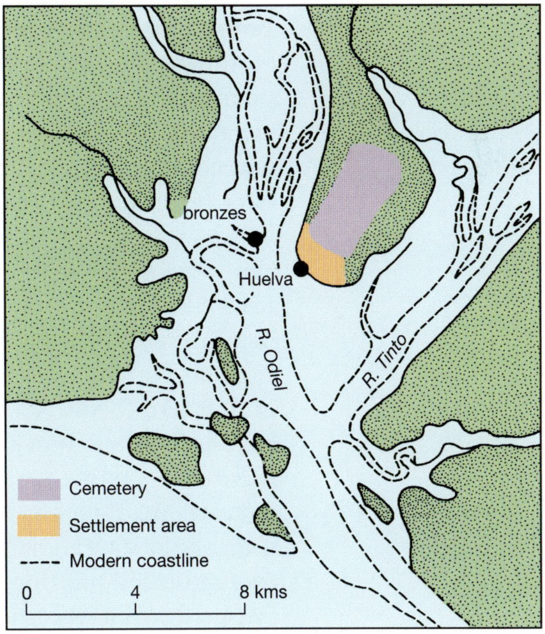

7.13 The estuary of the Odiel and Tinto as it was *c.*900 BC showing the position of the first millennium BC settlement and the location of the Huelva 'hoard'.

contexts was a widespread rite throughout Atlantic Europe. Why certain locations were selected is unclear, but one may suppose that the Odiel estuary was of huge significance in the tenth century since it marked the interface between the rich, metal-producing hinterland and the two metal-distributing seas—the Atlantic and the Mediterranean. The items deposited here symbolized the three zones which articulated at this one spot. The Huelva estuary was a gateway—a liminal place through which one passed from one world to another. As such it is little wonder that the gods were acknowledged by a major act of sacrifice.

The Huelva hoard is a good point from which to explore some aspects of the Atlantic bronze trade. One of the most distinct of the artefact types deposited there was the Irish type of spearhead with basal loops. These elegant weapons, some of them up to 40 centimetres long, were part of the parade gear of the elite. They occur widely in Ireland and in Britain, with significant numbers reaching France and extending south as far as Huelva. Their highly distinctive form and skilled craftsmanship will have made them desirable items in long-distance exchanges.

Another highly recognizable form was the carp's-tongue sword—a long sword with a slotted hilt to facilitate the attachment of the hilt-plates, and a distinctive long narrow point. It is this that reminded a British nineteenth- century antiquarian of the shape of a carp's tongue (with which he would have become familiar on his many fishing expeditions interspersed with his antiquarian exploits). Carp's-tongue swords are north-western French in origin but are found in eastern Britain (largely as scrap) and along the Atlantic seaways (7.14). Various subtypes have been identified and named after hoards where they were first recognized—Vénat in the Charente, Huelva in Iberia, and Monte Sa Idda in Sardinia—giving an idea of geographical extent. Several examples reached northern Italy. While most of the north-western French and British examples were probably of Breton origin the range of variation suggests that other centres were copying the basic form, and at two sites in southern Iberia, Ronda (Málaga) and Peña Negra (Alicante), moulds have been found showing that the Monte Sa Idda types were being made locally. This rather complex picture is particularly interesting in that it indicates the different ways in which objects and ideas of objects were transmitted. Over north-western France the swords themselves were distributed, no doubt for use, but in eastern Britain, which had its own favoured sword type, they occur only as scrap metal. Elsewhere, in southern Spain the type was considered to be of sufficient interest to be copied and traded in the western Mediterranean.

Another highly characteristic artefact to be recovered from the Huelva deposit are safety-pin brooches known as *fibules coudées*. These fibulae, probably of Cypriot origin, were distributed extensively in the east and central Mediterranean in the eleventh and tenth centuries and are known sporadically throughout Iberia and France. Their presence in the Huelva deposit is an indication that eastern Mediterranean artefacts were reaching Iberia in the 'pre-colonial' period, possibly in the ships of the earliest Phoenician explorers. Two other eastern artefacts are of interest in this

7.14 The distribution of carp's tongue swords.

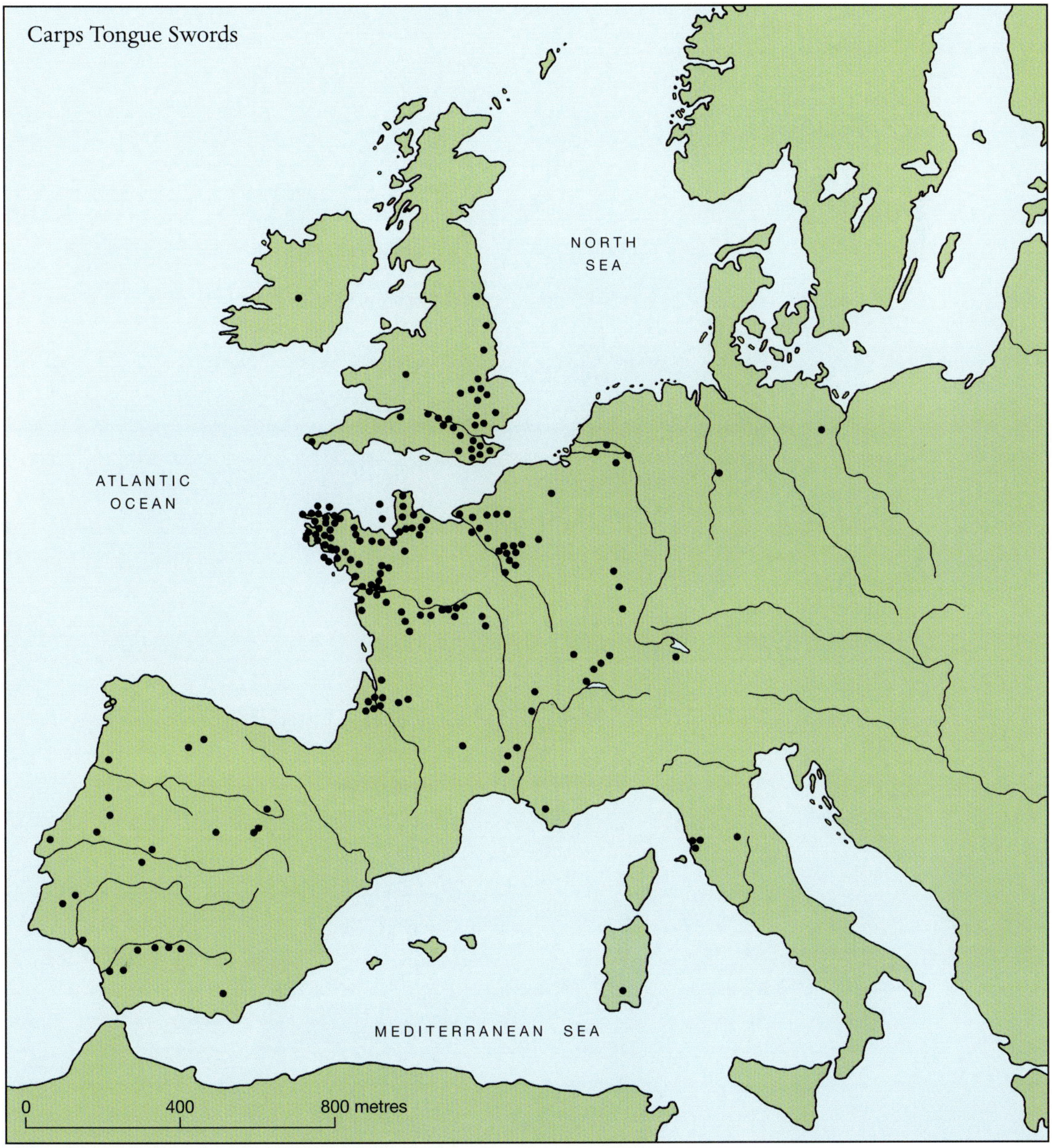

context: articulated spits for roasting meat and small bronze cup-like bowls—both accoutrements of the elite feast. Examples of both were introduced into Iberia in the tenth century and the articulated spits seem to have been accepted into Atlantic culture, occurring in some numbers in western Iberia, western France and eastern Britain.

The acceptance of the Mediterranean roasting spit by Atlantic communities is understandable since the feast was an important bonding rit-

7.15 Bronze cauldron from the River Thames at Shipton, near Oxford. Tenth or ninth century BC.

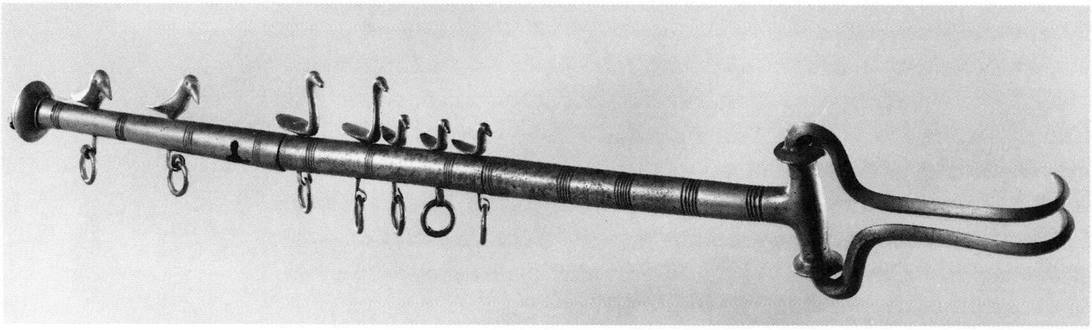

7.16 Bronze flesh hook from Dunaverney, Co. Antrim, Ireland.

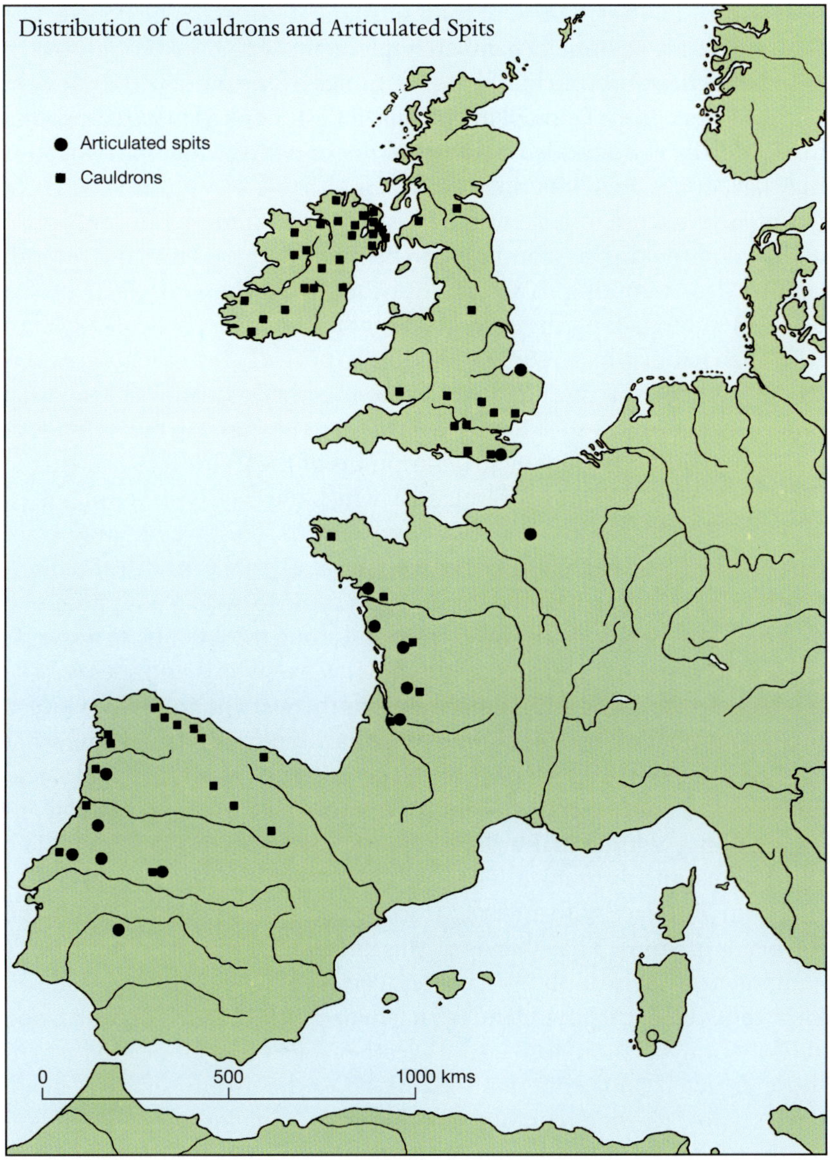

7.17 The distribution of cauldrons and articulated spits, two of the essential pieces of equipment of the Late Bronze Age feast.

ual in Atlantic society. Evidence for feasting is provided by the large bronze cauldrons (7.15) and flesh-hooks (7.16) and roasting spits discovered along the Atlantic seaways, with concentrations in Ireland, south-eastern Britain, Brittany, and north-western Iberia (7.17). The cauldrons are round-bottomed vessels made from bronze sheets riveted together, with the rim strengthened to take two rings by which the vessel would have been suspended over the fire. Their average capacity was in the order of 30–40 litres, sufficient for a substantial carcass to be boiled. The flesh-hooks are essentially handled implements with hooked ends which could have been used to lift the boiled hunks of meat out of the stew. In one discovery, from Feltwell in Norfolk, a flesh-hook was actually found in a cauldron, giving added credence to the suggestion that the two items may have functioned together.

Cauldrons seem to have originated in Ireland in the tenth century BC and, in different forms, continued to be made and used into the seventh century. It is tempting to see the distribution of these artefacts of the feast, stretching along the Atlantic, as indicators of a particular kind of social behaviour which required the elite to provide communal occasions when members of the hierarchy came together to reaffirm the social order. Echoes of just such a system are later to be found in the writings of Strabo and others in their vivid descriptions of the Celtic feast, and in the early vernacular literature of Ireland in which the feast is sometimes used with deadly effect to assert status. Given that the feast was an important part of elite social behaviour in the west, it is easy to see how the Mediterranean idea of the articulated roasting spit came to be so readily adopted.

A high percentage of the bronzes found along the Atlantic seaways, as indeed over much of Europe at the time, were swords and spears—the functional and symbolic accoutrements of the warrior. In south-western Iberia a number of inscribed stone stelae have been found depicting what appears to be the personal gear of the elite. The sword, spear, and shield are recurring motifs, and attempts have been made to identify the icons of weaponry with actual bronze types found in the region (7.18). The shields are quite distinctive. They are circular with concentric ribs interrupted in one place with a V-notch. Some also indicate what appear to be the heads of studs. That shields of this kind were a part of the warrior's equipment is not in doubt. What is less certain is what they were made of. Here the evidence from Ireland is particularly informative, for from a bog at Cloonbrin, Co. Longford, came a leather shield very similar in form to those depicted on the Iberian stelae even to the groups of 'rivet head' bosses (7.19). The find is unique, but that leather shields were not uncommon is suggested by the discovery, also in Ireland, of two wooden moulds for making shields of this kind. There are also two actual shields made in wood, but they may be more symbolic than functional.

The similarities between the Irish shields and the south-west Iberian representations are particularly striking and suggest that we may be seeing here a patchy reflection of a once widely distributed Atlantic type—the shield made of leather for lightness and resilience. A radiocarbon date for one of the Irish wooden moulds suggests that these V-notched shields may begin as early as the middle of the second millennium. It used to be

7.18 Carved stela from Solance de Cabañas, Logrosán, Cáceres, Spain. The warrior is shown with his spear, sword, shield, wagon, bow brooch, and an item that may be a mirror. Eighth or seventh century.

7.19 Leather V-notched shield from Clonbrin, Co. Longford, Ireland. The skeuomorphic rivet heads suggest that the shield is copying one made in bronze.

thought that the Atlantic tradition developed after local craftsmen had seen bronze shields imported from the eastern Mediterranean, but the evidence (two fragments of bronze shields from Cyprus and Greece, pottery votive models from Samos, and another representation from Crete) is not convincing. The revised dating for the Atlantic examples would suggest that the eastern Mediterranean finds may well have been brought from the west, possibly as trophies to be dedicated to the classical gods.

So far in discussing the Atlantic Bronze Age network we have selected the rather more exotic objects which tend to emphasize the long-distance nature of the exchanges, but it would be wrong to give the impression that this was the norm. It was, in fact, far more usual for an artefact type to have a comparatively limited distribution serving an essentially local market. To take just one example: in the Lower Douro valley of northern Portugal a distinctive axe type—a single looped palstave—was manufactured. The map of its distribution shows that it was concentrated in a restricted territory of western Iberia between the Miño and Tagus, with a few axes reaching northern Spain and odd examples scattered across the rest of the peninsula. This kind of pattern is indicative of restricted down-the-line trade, with the bulk of the axes being distributed from one community to the next within a defined territory. The few that reached the north were probably carried in mixed cargoes by coastal shipping working a regular circuit from the home territory on the Douro. The other isolated occurrences would have reached their more distant find spots after many exchanges, possibly ending up as scrap. Simple local systems of this kind formed an overlapping patchwork throughout the length of the Atlantic province from southern Iberia to northern Scotland (7.20). Through this kind of network bulk raw materials and cargoes of scrap were constantly being moved and with them, inevitably, ideas would be transmitted. Occasionally specialist gifts, like an Irish cauldron, might be carried over greater distances. New and exotic innovations could also be introduced. Some, like the articulated roasting spit, found favour because the item enhanced elite rituals; others, like the Sicilian shaft-hole axe, of which three or four have been found along the Atlantic seaways, were probably regarded as little more than curiosities, technically no better than the indigenous socketed axes and certainly not worth copying.

Nothing has yet been said of the changing intensities of contact in terms of the volumes of metal produced and exchanged in the period 1200–600 BC. This is a difficult question to approach archaeologically because the actual quantity of material found, mainly in hoards or other types of votive deposits, while a fair reflection of material deposited, need not in any way be proportional to the amount of metal originally

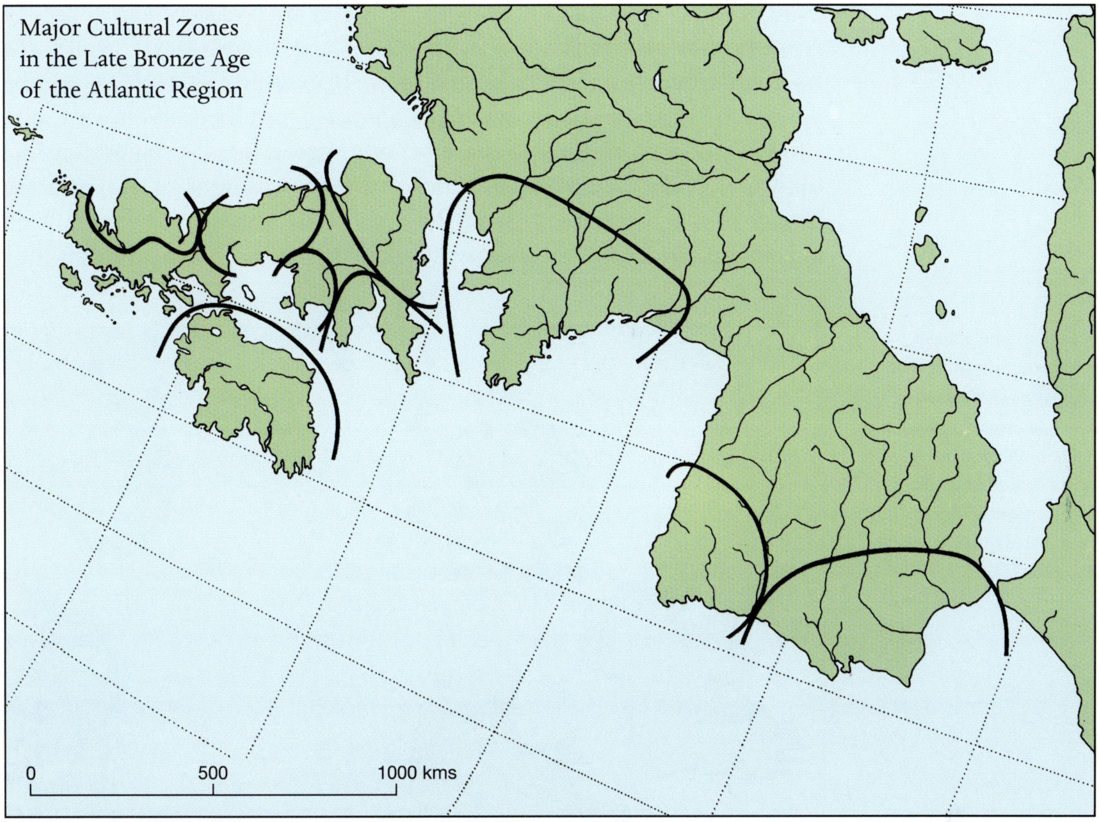

7.20 In the Late Bronze Age each area of the Atlantic zone produced a distinctive assemblage of bronze implements. The map shows the major regions. There was much interchange between them.

produced or in circulation. In other words, the fact that the number and size of hoards increase throughout the period need mean nothing more than that there was a greater desire to make more impressive offerings to the deities in the later period. This said, there does seem to be a general intensification of activity after about 1000 BC. By this time all parts of the Atlantic community were locked into complex networks of exchange and the extraction of metal must have now reached an unprecedented scale. While it is evident that some of that product was fed back into the earth as offerings, very considerable quantities will have flowed eastwards from the Atlantic to fuel the growing demands of the Mediterranean states and the powerful polities now developing in barbarian Europe.

One example will suffice to give some idea of the volume of metal extracted. In Brittany, at the end of the Late Bronze Age, a distinctive type of straight-sided socketed axe was made in considerable numbers. Most of those known have been found in Armorica (i.e. Brittany and Lower Normandy), but isolated examples were dispersed widely across Europe from Ireland to Poland and from Scotland to the Pyrenees (7.21). In Armorica the axes are known mainly from large hoards (7.22). In all some 315 hoards incorporating 38,000 axes have been found to date. Taking the figures for Brittany alone, where 25,000 axes have been recovered, and allowing a total production three times as great, it is estimated that the total metal involved was 5–6 tonnes of lead, 2 tonnes of tin, and 7–8 tonnes of copper. As the figures show, the alloy used was unusually high in lead (and indeed some axes were made in lead). This means that they

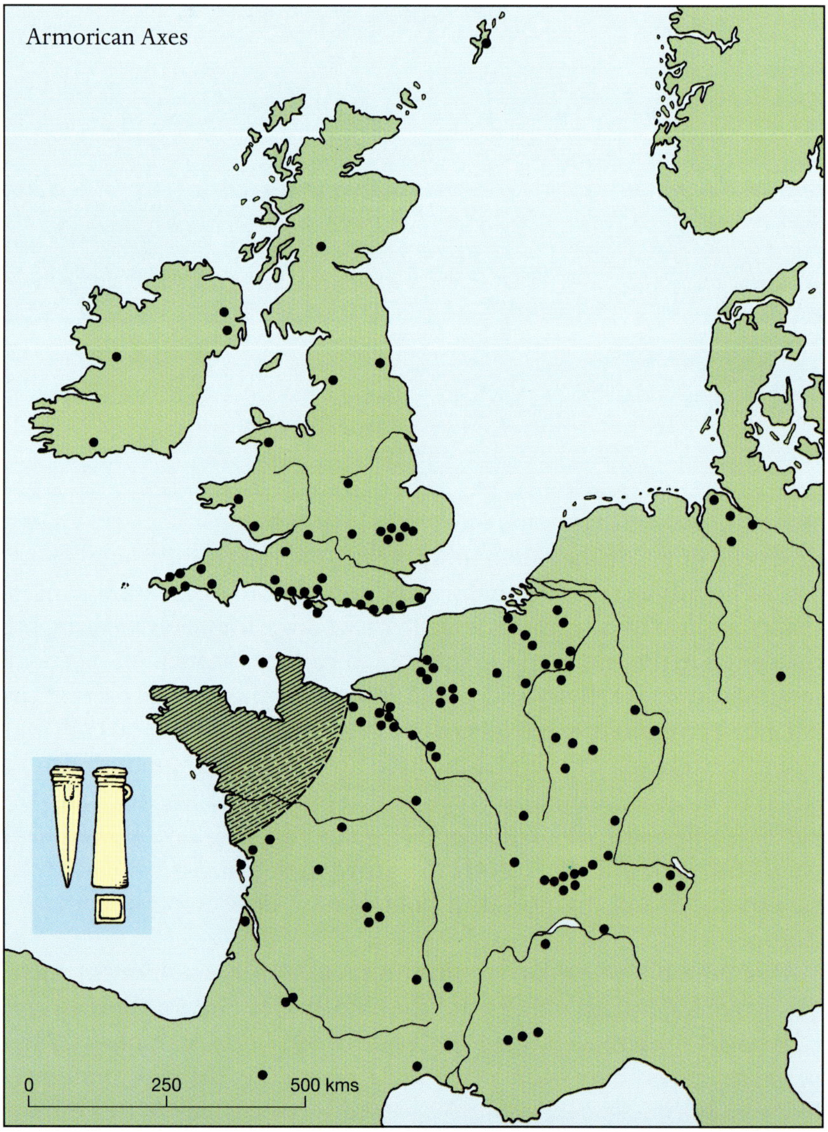

7.21 Distribution of Armorican socketed axes throughout western Europe. Tens of thousands were produced but most were buried in hoards in Brittany and Lower Normandy (the shaded zone).

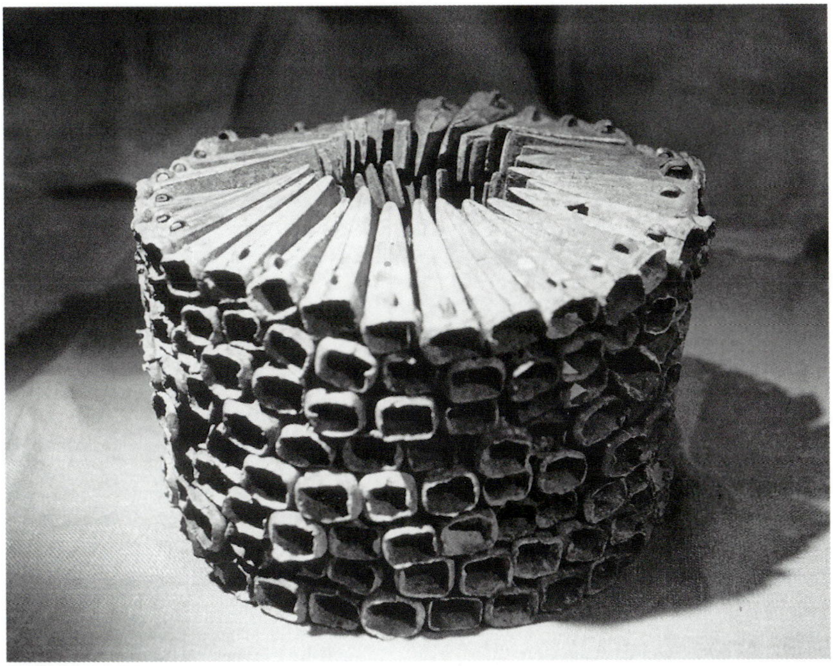

7.22 Hoard of Armorican axes from Langonnet, Morbihan stacked now as they were originally found in a hoard buried in the ground. Seventh century BC.

were barely functional, and the state of many of them when buried shows that they were never used. Taking all these factors together, it has been suggested that the Breton axes functioned as a kind of currency. An alternative, and perhaps more plausible, suggestion is that they were being made specifically for deposition, the increasing use of lead in the alloy, and the actual lead examples, reflecting the transition from functional to symbolic. Whatever the explanation, the fact remains that by the seventh century huge quantities of metal were being removed from circulation and deposited in the realms of the deities. It is quite possible that the increase in the number of hoards throughout Atlantic Europe as the Late Bronze Age progresses is indicative of the growing imperative to propitiate the religious powers. The process of burying hoards which we noted first in the first half of the third millennium had, after two thousand years, reached a crescendo.

New Contacts with Continental Europe

The discussion so far has concentrated on the Atlantic bronze industry, but this was only one of a series of major socio-cultural zones into which temperate Europe can be divided in the early first millennium BC. Much of western middle Europe formed part of a single province, which can be styled the *Rhine–Danube zone*, while to the north lay a separate, highly innovative *Nordic zone*. Britain, by virtue of its geographical position, occupied the interface between all three zones and, as it had done at various times over the previous three millennia, it was able to absorb cultural influences from northern and central Europe, transmitting them selectively to the west. The island also served as an intermediary for material exported from Ireland. These generalizations can be demonstrated by considering the distribution of a range of items. In the thirteenth century, for example, an area of south-western Britain (focusing on the counties of Somerset and Dorset) developed a highly distinctive range of ornaments, including bronze torcs and various kinds of bracelets. The inspiration for many of these items was northern Europe, and ideas were

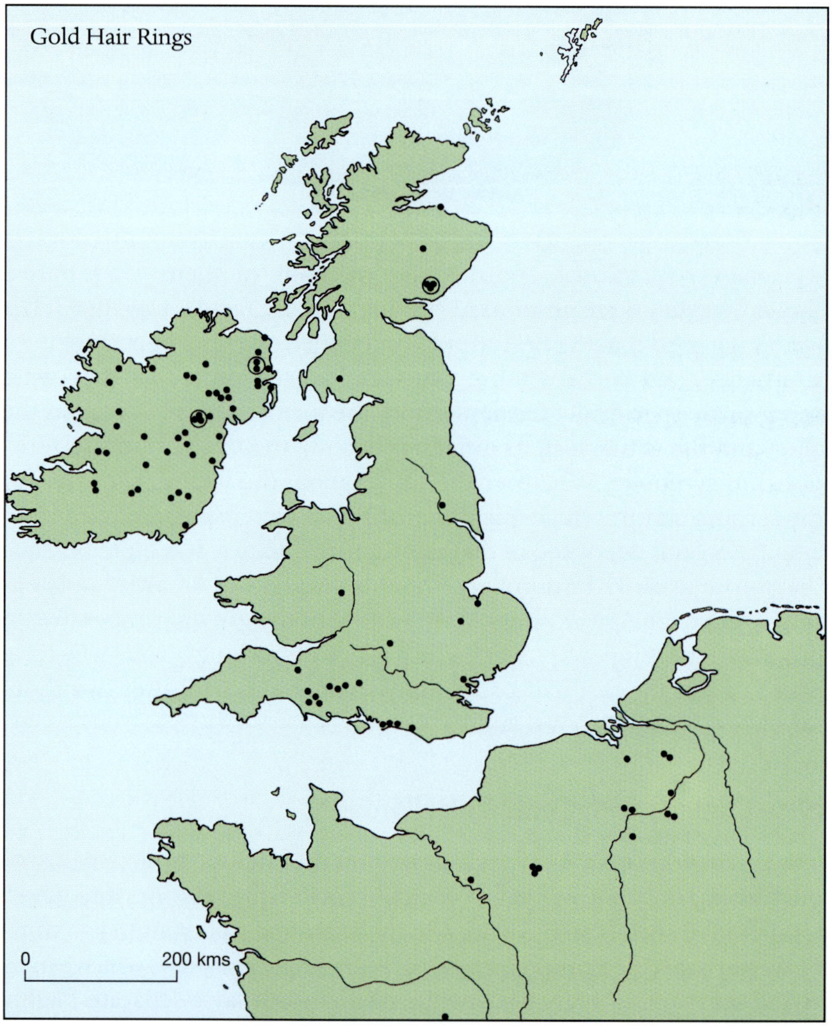

7.23 Distribution of Late Bronze Age gold 'hair rings' made in Ireland. It is possible that Wessex may have served as a transmission zone in the dispersal of these items from Ireland to northern Europe.

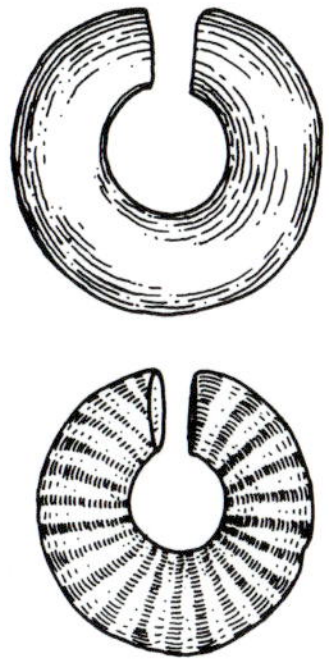

7.24 Gold hair rings of the Late Bronze Age from Ireland.

passed on to contemporary Irish cultures. It is quite possible that at this time Dorset and Somerset lay astride a route linking the Irish metal-producing sites to the English Channel and the Continent beyond. Some further support for this maritime link comes from the discovery of characteristic ornaments scattered along the southern coast and into Kent. That the same route may have persisted into the early first millennium BC is nicely demonstrated by the distribution of Irish gold hair-rings, which reach as far as the Seine and Lower Rhine (7.23, 7.24).

The one elite item which best illustrates the east–west network is the sword. One of the earliest leaf-shaped swords to be used in the British Isles was the Ballintober sword, named after a bog find in Co. Mayo. It dates to the twelfth century BC and is found in the northern part of Ireland, across southern Britain, and along the Seine valley. Another cluster in the Loire valley shows that some of the swords entered the Atlantic system (7.25). On the Continent the technology of producing fine bronze swords developed apace and a few eventually found their way into eastern Britain. One Late Bronze Age type—the Hemigkofen sword—was popular in western central Europe. A few seem to have been passed along the Loire, with at least one reaching Brittany, while the Rhine and the Seine may have been the routes along which the small group from the Thames region and East Anglia were trans-shipped.

In the seventh century BC a new sword type—the Gundlingen sword—came widely into use in western central Europe. These had large pommels and convex-sided hilts: the blades were long and narrow and quite thick in cross-section, providing the weight necessary for an effective

7.25 The distribution of swords of Ballintober-type. These were made in the north of Ireland in the twelfth century BC. It is possible that a variant was also made in the Loire valley.

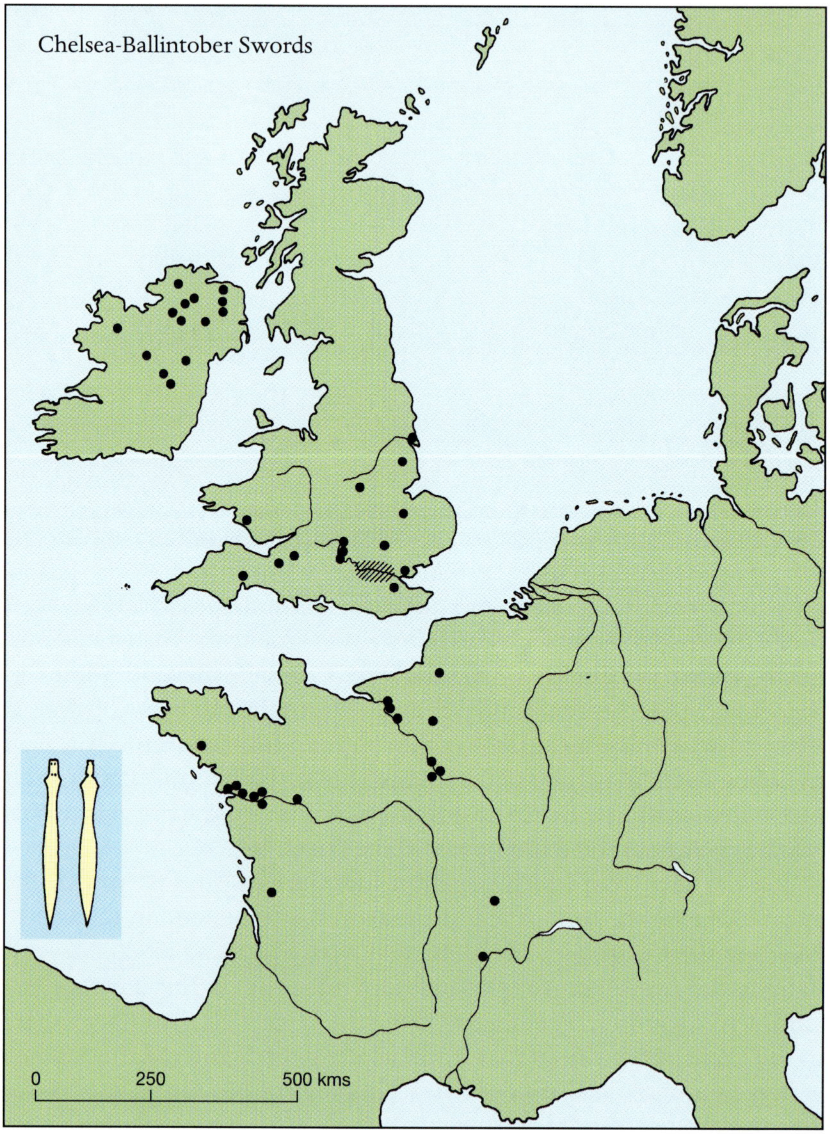

slashing stroke. Swords of this type became very popular in Britain and Ireland in the seventh and sixth centuries and were copied and modified by local bronze smiths. Their distribution shows that Britain and Ireland were now closely linked to Continental networks. Other Continental items, including a wide range of horse gear and cart fittings, found over the whole of Britain as far north as the Tay, suggest that the British elites were now receiving gifts of horses and the four-wheeled vehicles so popular among the paramounts of western central Europe. It is quite probable that knowledge of ironworking was introduced into Britain and Ireland at about this time.

The seventh and sixth centuries BC saw the culmination of these east–west exchange networks, with Britain, and to a lesser extent Ireland, now apparently more closely integrated with northern Europe than with the Atlantic system. It is the first time that this alignment appears so strikingly in the archaeological record. The fast-developing chiefdoms of western central Europe had by now established wide-ranging contacts with eastern Britain involving the exchange of elite equipment. It may be that Britain now occupied a middleman position, facilitating the transport of Irish metals direct to northern Europe, diminishing the need for Ireland any more to play an active part in Atlantic systems. The situation was, however, short-lived, for after about 600 BC Ireland entered a period of isolation and remained cut off from both British and Atlantic developments for several centuries. After the mid-fifth century Britain too seems to have lost its European networks. In Brittany, on the other hand, there is some evidence to suggest that links were maintained with west central Europe by way of the Loire route, as we shall see in the next chapter.

The period from *c.*700 to 400 BC seems, then, to have been a time of disruption, when the growing power of the chiefdoms of eastern France and southern Germany brought about readjustments in the traditional networks weakening the northern Atlantic system. Meanwhile, in the south, around the coasts of Portugal and Morocco, the establishment of Phoenician colonies created a new entrepreneurial dynamic which may further have undermined the contacts between Iberia and the north. The three centuries or so from 700 to 400 BC represented a period of transition, bringing an end to the old order and drawing the Atlantic zone closer into the affairs of temperate and Mediterranean Europe.

Talking To Each Other

By the end of the Bronze Age the communities of Atlantic Europe had maintained a high level of contact along the seaways for more than four thousand years. Over much of that time, as the archaeological evidence so vividly demonstrates, the links were persistent and sometimes intense. Large quantities of bulk commodities, in particular metals, were transported in ships, and this inevitably brought people of different ethnic origin into contact. These people needed to communicate. With such a complex and long-lived network in operation it is inevitable that a lingua franca would have developed, not just to facilitate the exchange of commodities, but also to allow technological knowledge and belief systems to be communicated. What, then, can be said of that language?

By the middle of the first millennium BC the languages spoken throughout much of western Europe were a closely related branch of Indo-European. The similarities were first recognized by an Oxford museum-keeper, Edward Lhuyd, at the end of the seventeenth century. By studying the languages still spoken at that time in Ireland, Scotland, Wales, Cornwall, and Brittany, Lhuyd was able to identify them as part of a single language group, which he called 'Celtic'. Subsequent studies of

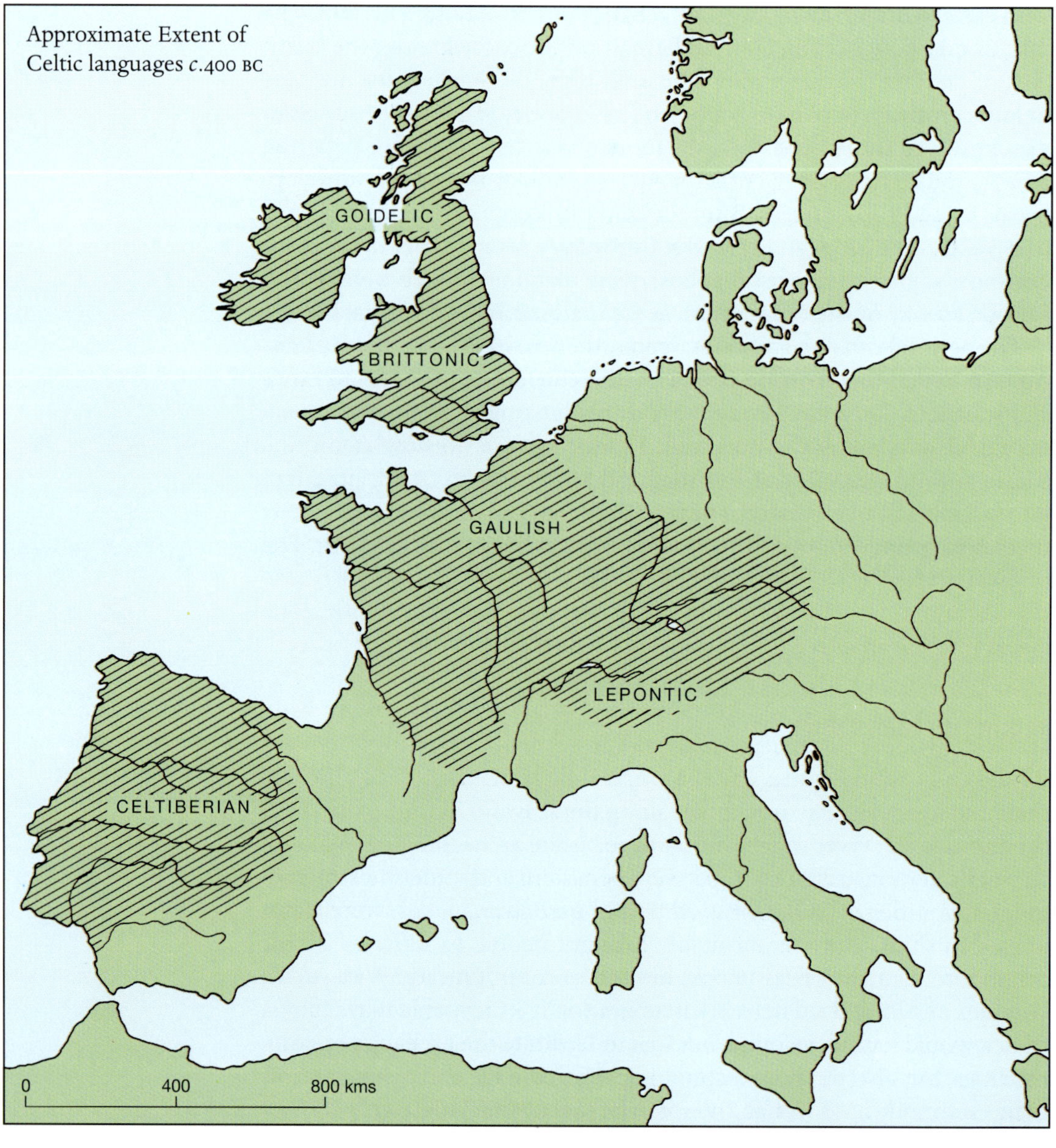

7.26 The 'Celtic' languages of western Europe.

epigraphy and place-names have shown that the languages spoken in the later first millennium in France, central and western Iberia, and the south-western Alps belonged to the same 'Celtic' family: these are generally known after the ancient tribal names of these areas—Gaulish, Celtiberian, and Lepontic (7.26).

A great deal has been based on this linguistic evidence. Lhuyd's 'Celtic languages' have generally been regarded as the languages spoken by the peoples described as Celts by classical authors. In some areas, such as central and western France, this is certainly so, but to insist that the Celtic languages, called such by a seventeenth-century antiquarian, represent Celts as loosely defined by Greek and Roman writers involves a circular argument. The simple fact is that no classical writer ever referred to the inhabitants of Britain and Ireland as Celts.

To complicate matters still further, the linguistic model was soon taken as the basis for constructing a historical model. Thus, of Britain, Ireland, and Iberia the inevitable question to be asked is, 'When did the Celts arrive?' Inherent in the question are clearly several unsubstantiated assumptions—among them that the languages of the west were the languages spoken by people described by Greek and Roman writers as Celts and that the 'Celtic' language was introduced by migrants from continental Europe. To some scholars the migrants soon became invaders. Archaeologists, eager to substantiate the invasionist model, endeavoured to find assemblages of artefacts by which the 'invaders' could be identified, and linguists used these suggestions as support for their own assumptions. In this way the circularity of the argument was complete. It is not difficult to see how this edifice came to be constructed. The classical texts gave lively descriptions of the movements of Celts from north of the Alps to the Po valley and down into Italy in the fifth and fourth centuries BC and into Greece and Anatolia in the third century. These were significant folk movements involving settlement, raiding, and mercenary activity. It was not illogical, therefore, to use the same model to explain cultural and linguistic similarities in the west. And so thick black arrows, representing waves of invading forces, appeared on all the maps.

Since 1960 invasion hypotheses have become *démodé*, but the 'arrival of the Celts' still remains embedded in some archaeological writing as it does in most of the popular literature. There has, however, been a movement away from the belief that Hallstatt and La Tène warriors braved the sea to conquer Britain and Ireland or crossed the Pyrenees into Iberia, setting up their ascendancy over the indigenes and imposing their language. Considerable continuities in the archaeological record in the west have argued strongly against any sudden change in the first millennium BC. In response, some archaeologists have looked to earlier periods for evidence of immigrants, favouring the period when Beakers became fashionable over large parts of Europe. In this model Beaker prospectors were the carriers of the Celtic language. Other archaeologists have taken a more radical line, in considering the Celtic languages to have been carried to the west much earlier by Neolithic cultivators.

The questions surrounding language are not easy to resolve, but if one divorces the linguistic evidence from the archaeological, and from pseudo-historical preconceptions, the simple picture which emerges is of a similarity of language over much of western Europe by the sixth century BC. Within this 'Celtic' family (to retain Lhuyd's terminology) there were a number of regional variations, with some suggestion that 'isolation' may have led to some regions retaining rather more archaic forms than others. Thus Lepontic, Celtiberian, and the languages of Ireland and Scotland exhibited 'early' characteristics, while Welsh, Cornish, Breton, and Gaulish were more 'developed'. Whether this apparent chronology has any significance, other than reflecting regionalism, it is impossible to say. If the linguistic evidence really can be taken to suggest that the languages of Wales, Britain, Cornwall, and France had evolved and exhibited a significant similarity then all this need reflect is a degree of interaction between these regions in the latter part of the first millennium BC.

The surviving, and recently surviving, 'Celtic' languages of the west, taken together with what is known of similar languages once in use in central and western Iberia and France until the time of the Roman occupation, are sufficient to suggest that closely related languages were spoken along the Atlantic seaways from Portugal to Britain by the middle of the first millennium BC. It is not unreasonable, therefore, to conclude that 'Celtic', as defined by Lhuyd, was the lingua franca of the Atlantic community. It could further be argued that the language had developed gradually over the four millennia that maritime contacts had been maintained, perhaps reaching its distinctive form in the Late Bronze Age when communication along the sea lanes was at its most intense, and when many aspects of the elite system, technology, and beliefs had coalesced to create a broadly similar cultural continuum. The archaeological and linguistic evidence support each other without being dependent. This does, however, raise the question of terminology. To speak of the 'Celtic' language is misleading, since it takes with it a package of hypotheses and assumptions many of which are wrong. But since the word is too embedded in three hundred years of scholarship to abandon, it might be better simply to qualify it by using the phrase *Atlantic Celtic*. This will distinguish it, conceptually, from the language which is generally assumed to have been spoken by the historical Celts whose migrations were recorded by the classical writers. The suggestion takes with it no implication that the two languages were different. Such were the complexities of the exchange networks which linked the Atlantic to western central Europe from the early third millennium BC, when metals became a significant item of exchange, that it would be surprising if a common language had not developed over the entire region from the Atlantic to west central Europe where the rivers Loire, Saône, Seine, Rhine, and Danube come together. This region was a major centre of innovation in the Late Bronze Age and, from the seventh century, saw the emergence of a powerful elite. It was from here, three centuries later, that bands of Celts, so described by the classical writers, were to burst out into southern and eastern Europe.

The Phoenicians and the Atlantic

It seems highly probable that the Phoenician entrepreneurs, exploring the southern coasts of Iberia, made their first tentative moves through the Straits of Gibraltar and into the Atlantic some time just before or just after 1000 BC. By the eighth century, with Gadir firmly established, their knowledge of the Atlantic coasts of Morocco and Iberia would have grown apace and regular trading ventures probably became the norm. According to Pliny, the earliest establishment on the African Atlantic coast was Lixus, founded, he believed, about 1000 BC. The site was well chosen. The settlement lay on the side of a hill overlooking the fertile plain at the mouth of the River Loukkos where there was a fine natural harbour—one of the few good harbours along an otherwise inhospitable coast (7.27). The river was navigable for some way and provided a route into the Atlas Mountains along which ivory, gold, and copper would have been shipped to the estuary. The settlement flourished and became a thriving town in the Hellenistic and Roman period. Limited excavations into the earliest levels take the occupation back to the seventh century BC, but nothing earlier has yet been identified.

Lixus was one of many settlements which grew up along the Atlantic coast of Morocco (7.28, 7.30). Seventh-century pottery, including Attic and Ionian amphorae carried by the Phoenician shippers, has been found at Sala close to the mouth of the Oued bou Regreg (near modern Rabat) and much further south on the little island of Mogador (between Casablanca and Agadir) opposite the mouth of the Oued Ksob. The island is typical of the situation favoured by the early Phoenician settlers. Mogador lies almost 600 kilometres south of Gadir at the southernmost limit of the regular coastal trading route (7.29). At one time there would have been a large number of coastal settlements between the two pro-

7.27 The town of Lixus on the River Loukkos, Morocco. The settlement was founded by the Phoenicians and continued in use throughout the Roman period.

viding havens for ships, but by the Roman period, by which time the land routes had become well established, many of these coastal sites had been abandoned. The situation is neatly summarized by Avienus: 'On this shore frequent cities formerly stood and many Phoenicians held these lands of old. The deserted earth now extends inhospitable sands. The lands bereft of crops lie neglected' (*Ora Maritima* 438–42). Recent work has shown that Phoenician settlements dating back to the eighth century were established northwards from Gadir along the coasts of Portugal. The three best-known sites are at Cerro da Rocha Branca (Faro), Abúl at the estuary of the Sado, and Santa Olaia at the mouth of the Mondego. A number of other sites, notably Lisboa and Santarém on the Tagus, have also produced early pottery of Phoenician type. Excavations have not been extensive at any of the sites but at Cerro da Rocha Branca rectangular buildings of the eighth century were overlain by a defensive wall with bastions built in the sixth century. Given the extent and density of the Phoenician entrepôts of Morocco it would not be surprising if more ports were to be found along the Atlantic coast of Portugal, sited at the river mouths to enable the rich resources of gold and tin more easily to be exploited. Further north scattered finds of Iberian–Punic pottery show that by the fourth–third centuries BC the coastal settlements of western Galicia were receiving visits from southern shipping. At this time there

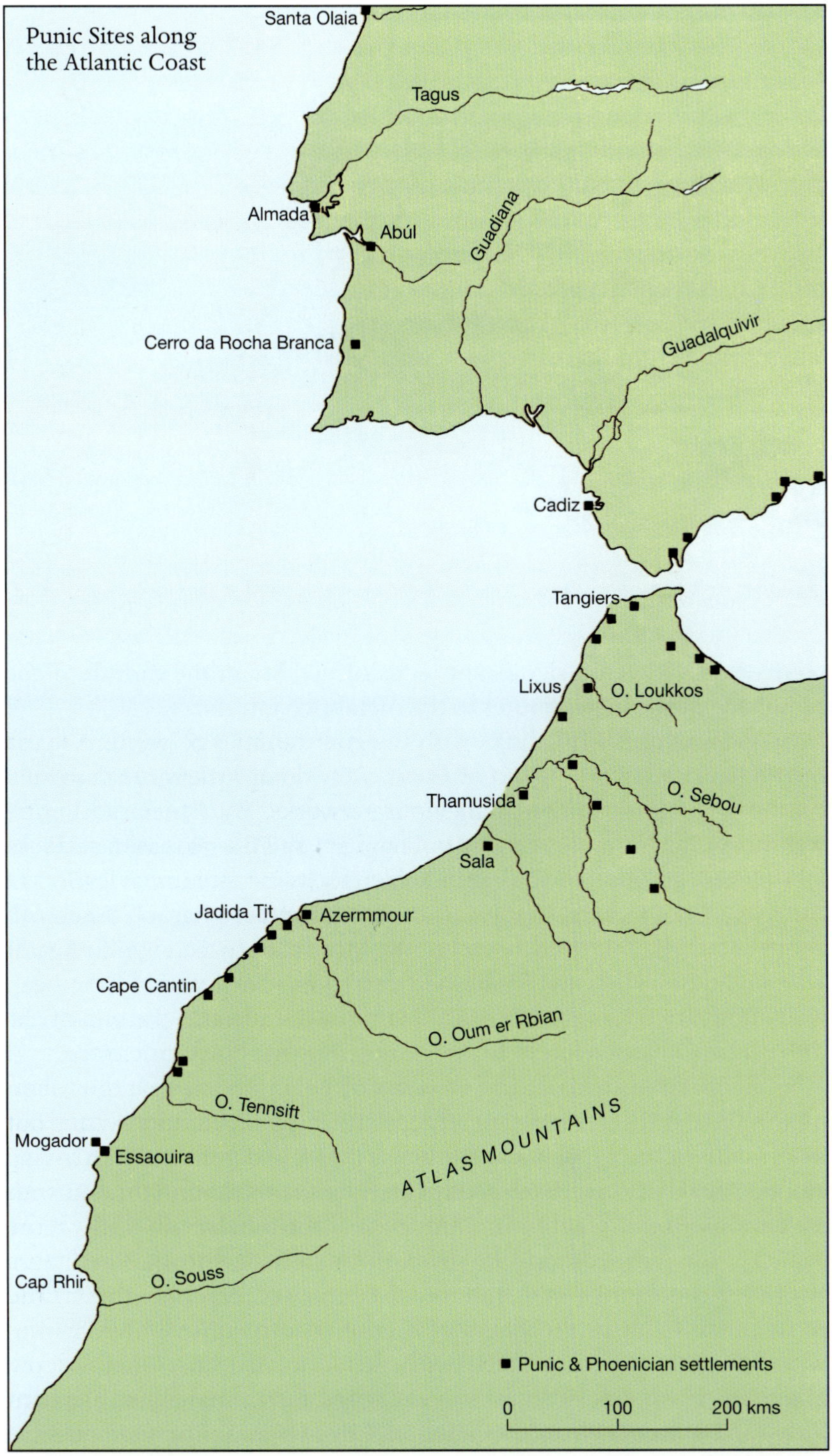

7.28 Punic material found along the Atlantic coast of Africa and Iberia. The principal settlements are identified by name.

7.29 The island of Mogador off the coast of Morocco was the site of one of the Punic trading stations established along the Atlantic route. The settlement lay on the sheltered (inland) side of the island. The shore of the mainland is lined by sand dunes but a river, the Oued Ksob, provided access to the hinterland.

seems to have been a significant focus of activity at the mouth of the Miño, one of the major routes to the metal-rich interior.

In opening up trading links with the communities of western Iberia the Phoenicians, working out of Gadir, were doing little more than infiltrating the long-established indigenous networks. The African adventure was more pioneering. As we saw in Chapter 3, there is no reason to doubt Herodotus' account of the remarkable clockwise circumnavigation of Africa by Phoenicians, employed by the Egyptian pharaoh Necho II, about 600 BC. By this time, however, the Moroccan coast down to Agadir was already serviced by established entrepôts. They would have been well known to other explorers like Hanno who, towards the end of the fifth century, reached Sierra Leone or possibly even the Cameroons.

In the wake of these deliberate feats of exploration came the fishermen and the traders. There are records of fishing expeditions setting out from Gadir in the small boats known as *hippoi* and in four days arriving among shoals of tuna. Even today the tuna shoals around the Canaries are famous for the quality and abundance of the fish. Details of the more distant trading expeditions are given in two classical texts. The first, a Greek *Periplus* dating to the mid-fourth century BC, describes the African coast as far south as the island of Cerne (also mentioned by Hanno) where the Phoenicians traded with the local Africans. They offered unguents, glass, and Attic pots in exchange for animal skins, elephant tusks, and wine. The exact location of Cerne is in doubt. One possible

identification is Herne Island off the coast of Spanish Sahara, but it is thought more likely that it lay at the mouth of the River Sengal in modern Gambia.

The second account is provided by Herodotus, writing in the fifth century BC, quoting a Carthaginian source:

> They no sooner arrive but forthwith they unload their wares, and, having disposed them after an orderly fashion along the beach, leave them, and, returning aboard their ships, raise a great smoke. The natives, when they see the smoke, come down to the shore, and, laying out to view so much gold as they think is worth the wares, withdraw to a distance. The Carthaginians upon this come ashore and look. If they think the gold is enough they take it and go their way, but if it does not seem to them

7.30 Satellite map of the Atlantic coast of Morocco. The snow-covered peaks of the Atlas Mountains are clearly distinguishable. The prominent cape where they reach the sea is Cape Rhir, to the south of which is the port of Agadir at the mouth of the Oued Souss.

> sufficient, they go aboard ship once more, and wait patiently. Then the others approach and add to their gold, till the Carthaginians are content. Neither party deals unfairly by the other: for they themselves never touch the gold till it comes up to the worth of their goods, nor do the natives ever carry off the goods till the gold is taken away (*Histories* 4. 196).

The account provides a vivid example of 'silent trade' of the kind well known to anthropologists. Once again the importance of gold is emphasized. Gold, ivory, skins, and slaves would have been the most sought-after of the African products.

Little is known of the exploitation of the Atlantic islands at this time. The Canaries were close enough to the main coastal shipping to be well known. There is also an account given by Diodorus Siculus (possibly quoting the fourth-century BC writer Timaeus) which describes how a ship from Gadir was blown off course and ended up on a large island with a pleasant climate far out in the ocean. The most likely candidate is Madeira. Diodorus goes on to say that the Etruscans wanted to colonize it but the Carthaginians were uncooperative. Further out in the ocean lay the Azores. In 1749 a hoard of coins, including Punic and Cyrenaean coins of the fourth and third centuries, was found on one of the islands. Given the maritime skills of the Carthaginian explorers there is nothing inherently unlikely in the find being a genuine ancient deposit. If so, it is not known whether the contact was ever repeated.

The Quest for Tin

The subject of Atlantic tin and its acquisition by the classical world has long been one of fascination to archaeologists and the general public alike. It is as well to remember, however, that the classical texts referring to tin-producing lands are fragmentary, ill-understood, and to a large extent contradictory. At best they are anecdotes quoted at many removes from the original source and without significant context. Add to this the factual and transcription errors which invariably accompany frequent copyings and something of the state of the documentary evidence will be apparent. Yet herein lies the fascination that has claimed the critical attention of many scholars, each more erudite and inventive than the last.

It was common knowledge in the ancient world that tin came from the west (7.31). Herodotus, writing in the middle of the fifth century, honestly sums up the situation when he admits: 'Of the extreme tracts of Europe towards the west I cannot speak with any certainty . . . nor do I know of any islands called the Cassiterides whence the tin comes which we use' (*Histories* 3. 115). The positive implications of his otherwise negative statement are interesting, for he is making the explicit point that the Greeks

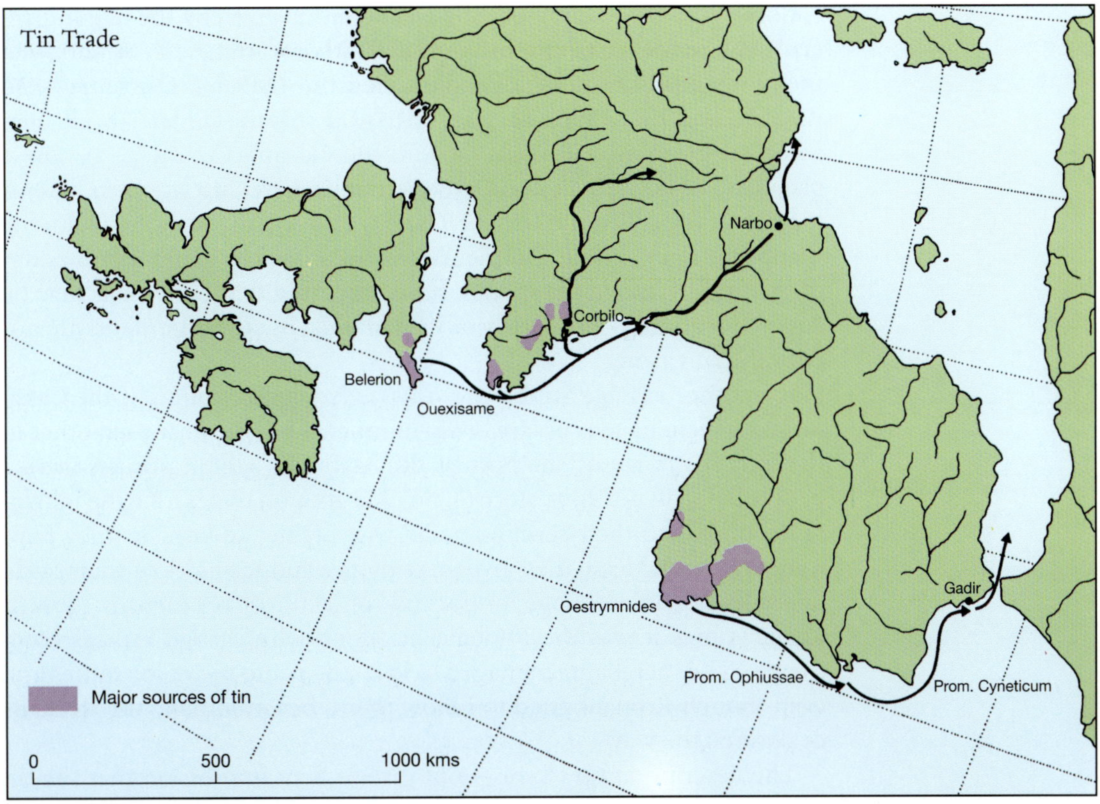

7.31 The Atlantic tin resources. Galician tin was probably transported to the Mediterranean by sea via the port of Gadir and was thus largely under Punic control. The tin from Britain and Armorica was carried via the river routes to the Greek ports of the Golfe du Lions. The names are those given in various classical sources.

used tin from the extreme west. Although a majority of the classical authors believed that the Cassiterides lay somewhere to the west of Iberia, there was much imprecision and confusion: the name simply means 'tin islands' and was probably applied generally rather than with geographical precision.

More specific stories of tin trading are provided in several of the surviving texts. In Avienus' poem *Ora Maritima*—a paste-and-scissors compilation using all the archaic sources that the author could muster—there is one fragment of direct relevance. It describes a lofty headland ancients knew as *Oestrymnis* facing the warm south wind. In the bay beneath islands called *Oestrymnides* 'stretch themselves out. They lie widely apart and are rich in tin and lead. The people are hard-working and sail in boats of leather' (*Ora Maritima* 92–106). There is nothing in the context of the piece to suggest where, geographically, *Oestrymnis* was thought to be. A statement a little later in the poem that the Carthaginians 'came to these seas' does not necessarily relate to what had gone before, and therefore cannot be claimed as proof of Carthaginian involvement in the tin trade as is frequently done.

Some possible help in locating *Oestrymnis* is given by the late-fourth-century Greek explorer Pytheas, quoted rather scathingly by Strabo, who mentions promontories, a people called the *Ostimioi*, *Ouexisame*, and islands (*Geog*. 1. 4. 5) and later goes on to note that the *Ostimioi* dwelt 'near a certain promontory thrust far into the Ocean' (*Geog*. 4. 4. 1). These places are usually understood to be Brittany where, in a later text, Caesar locates a tribe called the *Osismii*. *Ouexisame* is usually identified with the island of Ushant. Some commentators, impressed by general similarities of geography and in the names, have suggested that *Oestrymnis* may be equated with the promontory of the *Ostimioi*, but the arguments are not entirely convincing.

In another passage Strabo (3. 5. 10–11) gives a description of the Cassiterides which, he tells us, are ten in number. They 'lie near each other in the high sea north of the port of the Atabrians' (the Atabrians were a people living in north-western Spain). He goes on to describe the inhabitants' dress and their semi-nomadic way of life, adding, 'as they have mines of tin and lead, they give these metals and the hides of their cattle to sea-traders in exchange for pottery, salt, and copper utensils. Now in former times it was the Phoenicians alone who carried on this commerce.' The merchants managed to keep the route secret for some time even though Romans tried to follow them, but eventually the Romans discovered the way.

The description up to this point gives a firm impression that the tin islands are off the coast of north-west Iberia, but Strabo's final passage confuses the issue: 'After Publius Crassus crossed over to these people, and saw that the metals were being dug from only a slight depth, and that the men were peaceable, he forthwith laid abundant information before all who wished to traffic over this sea, albeit a wider sea than that which separates Britain from the Continent.' The distance (even if only compared with that from Dover to Calais) seems too great to refer to the islands off the coast of Galicia. Nonetheless Strabo reminds us of our geography in his concluding sentence: 'So much then for Iberia and the islands that lie off its coast.'

To sum up so far: if the link between *Oestrymnis* and *Ostimioi* is not accepted then it would not be unreasonable to conclude that the tin-rich *Oestrymnides* of the *Ora Maritima* and the Cassiterides described by Strabo were one and the same place and were located somewhere along the ria coastline of north-western Galicia, within easy reach of Phoenician merchants sailing up the coast. It is in just this region that Punic pottery has been found.

There are two other texts which specifically refer to British tin. The fullest account comes from Diodorus Siculus (5. 22):

> In Britain the inhabitants of the promontory called Belerion are particularly friendly to strangers and have become civilized through contacts with merchants from foreign parts . . . They prepare the tin, working the ground in which it is produced very carefully . . . They beat the metal into masses shaped like astragali (7.32) and carry it to a certain island lying off Britain called Ictis, for at the time of the ebb-tide the space between the island and the mainland becomes dry and they can take the tin in large quantities over to the island on their wagons . . . On the island of Ictis the merchants purchase the tin of the natives . . . whence it is then taken to Gaul and overland to the Mediterranean.

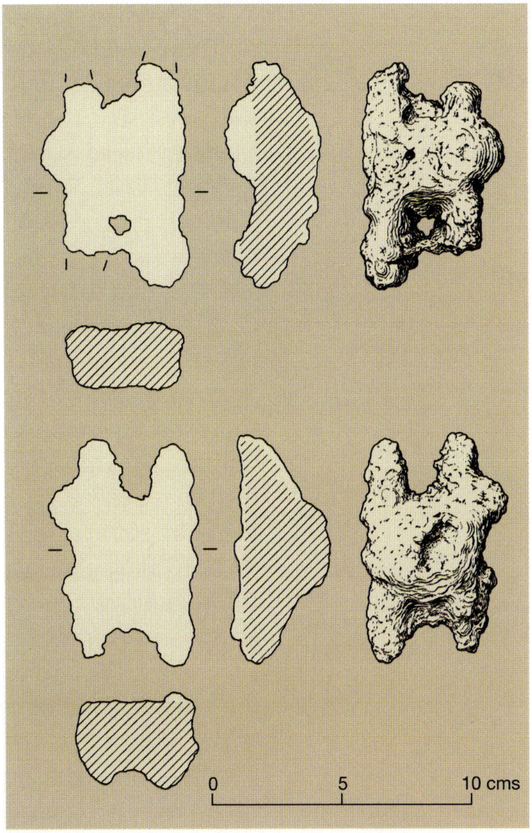

7.32 Tin ingots in the shape of knuckle bones (astragali) found on the site of a wreck in Bigbury Bay, south Devon, England. The vessel seems to have foundered on West Mary's rock in the bay at the mouth of the river Erme. The wreck is undated, and while it could be of Dark Age date it could equally well belong to the late prehistoric period.

Belerion is positively to be identified with Cornwall, in which case the location of Ictis would most reasonably be St Michael's Mount or Mount Batten in Plymouth Sound.

The second text, from Pliny (*Nat. Hist.* 4. 30. 104), records that: 'There is an island named Mictis lying inwards, six days' sail from Britain, where tin is to be had and to which the Britons cross in boats of osier covered with stitched hides.' Attempts to make the two texts compatible have absorbed a great deal of scholarly ingenuity. Ictis/Mictis has been identified by some commentators as the Isle of Wight, but it seems more likely that two separate islands are involved, with Mictis lying much further south, perhaps even between the Loire and the Garonne, though it must be admitted that the texts are too corrupt and garbled for us to be sure. The central point, however, remains—that the tin from south-west Britain was being traded on a regular basis to 'foreign merchants'.

Pliny notes that his source was the Greek historian Timaeus, who may also have been the source used by Diodorus. Timaeus was an armchair historian who culled the works of others. For his descriptions of the curiosities of the Atlantic he may well have used the writings of Pytheas. If so, the description of British tin extraction would date to the late fourth century BC.

There are some similarities between the description of *Oestrymnis* in *Ora Maritima* and the account by Diodorus of Belerion, most notably in the use of hide boats. While this might suggest that these two texts were based on the same source, it is simpler to accept that hide boats were a common feature of maritime culture along the Atlantic coasts.

The fascinating problems posed by the texts dealing with tin production have been set out in some detail here partly as an example of the difficulties inherent in dealing with textual anecdotes, but mainly because they represent the first cohesive accounts of the interactions between Mediterranean society and the prehistoric communities of western Europe. They suggest a degree of sophistication in the interaction between producer and entrepreneur and are in marked contrast to the more primitive dealings along the African coast.

Given that many uncertainties remain in the interpretation of the tin-trade texts, what seems to emerge is that there were two principal tin-producing regions known to the Mediterranean world, north-western Iberia and south-western Britain. There is no positive textual evidence to suggest that Breton sources were exploited at this early stage, but as we shall see later (pp. 322–3), the archaeological data suggest that the Breton communities were trading at this time with west-central Europe along the Loire route using long-established indigenous networks.

The Galician tin from north-west Iberia was most likely the preserve of the Phoenician / Punic enclave of Gadir, who would have found the direct coastal route preferable to having to pay high prices to middlemen controlling the overland routes. The development of entrepôts along the Atlantic coast of Iberia in the seventh century BC is a firm indication of this. Pliny offers an enigmatic scrap of potentially interesting information in noting that 'tin from the island of Cassiteride was first acquired by Midacritus' (*Nat. Hist.* 7. 56. 197). Midacritus was a Greek who was probably active before 500 BC, but it is not clear from the text whether he actually went to the Tin Island to pick up a cargo of tin or simply collected his supply, brought from the Tin Island, at some more convenient port like Gadir. The more romantic alternative, of an expedition into the Atlantic, is usually preferred but is impossible of proof. At any event it shows that the Greeks were aware of Atlantic tin by the middle of the first millennium. It may be that the large quantities of Greek pottery found at Huelva dating from the early sixth century reflect active Greek interests in the Atlantic at this time.

The growing hostility between Greeks and Carthaginians in the fifth century may have made it increasingly difficult for the Greeks to acquire Atlantic tin or even to gain access to the Atlantic all the time that the Carthaginians controlled the Straits of Gibraltar. This makes the Atlantic journey of Pytheas, a Massiliot traveller who explored Brittany and Britain about 330 BC, all the more interesting (7.33). It is generally believed that Pytheas began his voyage at Massalia using a Greek ship and sailed through the Straits of Gibraltar. Circumnavigating Iberia, he eventually arrived in the Bay of Biscay where his exploration began. There is, however, a plausible alternative—that he crossed southern France (Keltiké) by the Garonne route and picked up a local vessel in the Gironde for his northward sea journey. Such an itinerary would have had many advantages: it removes the need for him to confront the Carthaginians at Gibraltar; the short overland route of some 350 kilometres saved a sea journey of 3,200 kilometres; and once in the Gironde he would have had access to local vessels familiar with Atlantic sailing conditions and the local ports and harbours. There is ample archaeological evidence to show that the Aude–Carcassonne Gap–Garonne was a major channel of com-

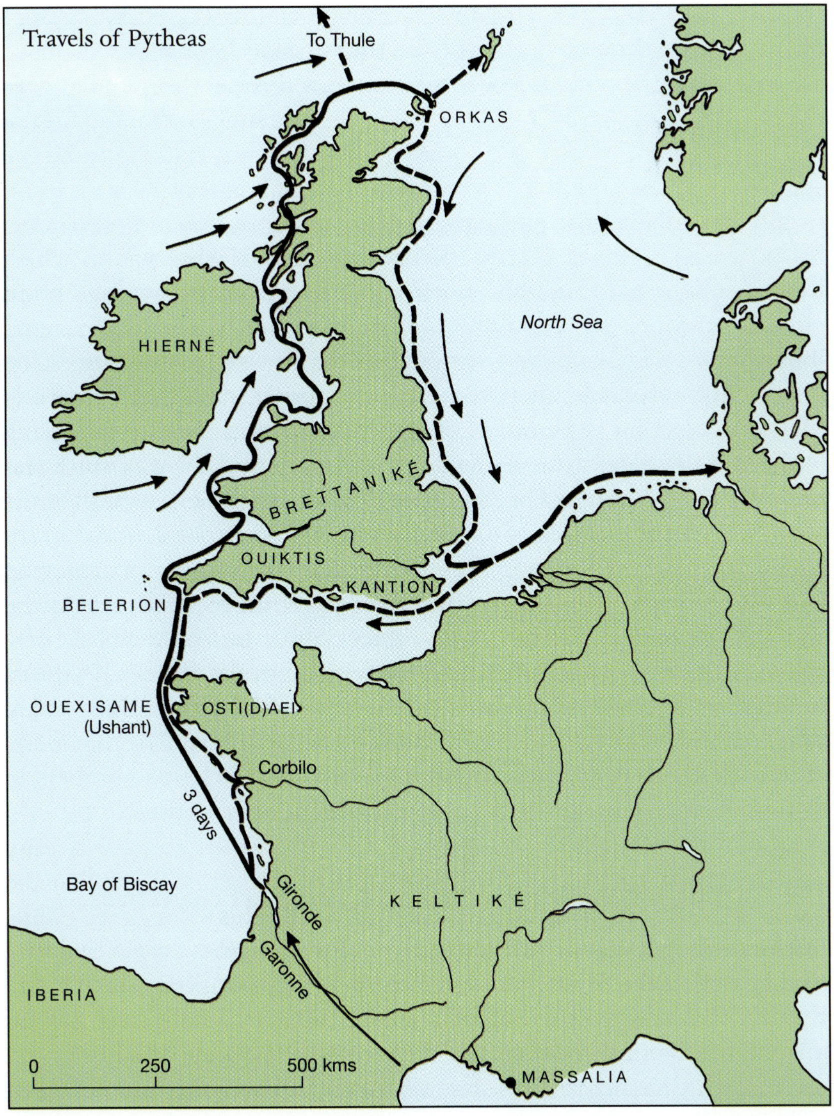

7.33 The travels of Pytheas in the late fourth century BC. He may have reached further north to Shetland. His journeys are likely to have been made in local vessels.

munication and commerce at this time, and it was probably already the way by which Atlantic tin was reaching the Mediterranean. By opting to take the overland route to the Gironde, Pytheas would simply have been following the tin back towards its source. This also makes sense of an observation, ascribed to Pytheas, which Strabo quotes and clearly does not understand. Writing of the Atlantic coastline of Europe, he refers to various headlands, 'particularly that of the Ostimians which is called Kabaion, and also the islands there along, the last of which is Uxisamē', [which] Pytheas says is distant three days sailing' (*Geog.* 1. 4. 5). The 'three days sailing' does not make any sense in the context in which Strabo places it, but Pytheas is correct in recording that the westernmost capes of Brittany are three days sailing from the Gironde, a journey which, we are suggesting, he may well have taken in a local vessel well familiar with the passage.

There is only one observation ascribed to Pytheas relating to Iberia, again quoted disparagingly by Strabo: 'The north part of Iberia is more readily accessible by way of Keltikē than by sailing by way of the Atlantic' (*Geog.* 3. 2. 11). This is exactly the sensible kind of observation which Pytheas might have thought worth recording from his vantage point on the Garonne. It is certainly not evidence that he sailed all around Iberia.

It seems reasonable, then, to accept the simple view that Pytheas of Massalia began his exploration of the Atlantic from the Gironde using local ships. If so, his achievement was no less heroic but was much less hazardous. If his aim had been to chart the waters and to establish direct contact with the sources of tin and amber, so much in demand in his native city, he chose the most appropriate and efficient way of achieving it. As far as the tin is concerned, by tracing its source to Belerion (Cornwall) he was opening up the way for direct contacts to be established by traders working out of the Gironde: the ten-day return journey (Pytheas' timings) would have posed little problem. It is likely that, once established, other Greek entrepreneurs followed and it may well be that many of the Mediterranean coins found in Britain, and in lesser numbers in Brittany, are the tangible archaeological evidence of this trade.

The Atlantic and the Mediterranean: Changing Perspectives

Before the beginning of the first millennium BC there is ample evidence to suggest that the Atlantic trading networks were working much in the way that they had been for two millennia or more, internally strong along the entire Atlantic façade but with links via the Garonne, the Loire, and the English Channel to the more inland area of western and northern

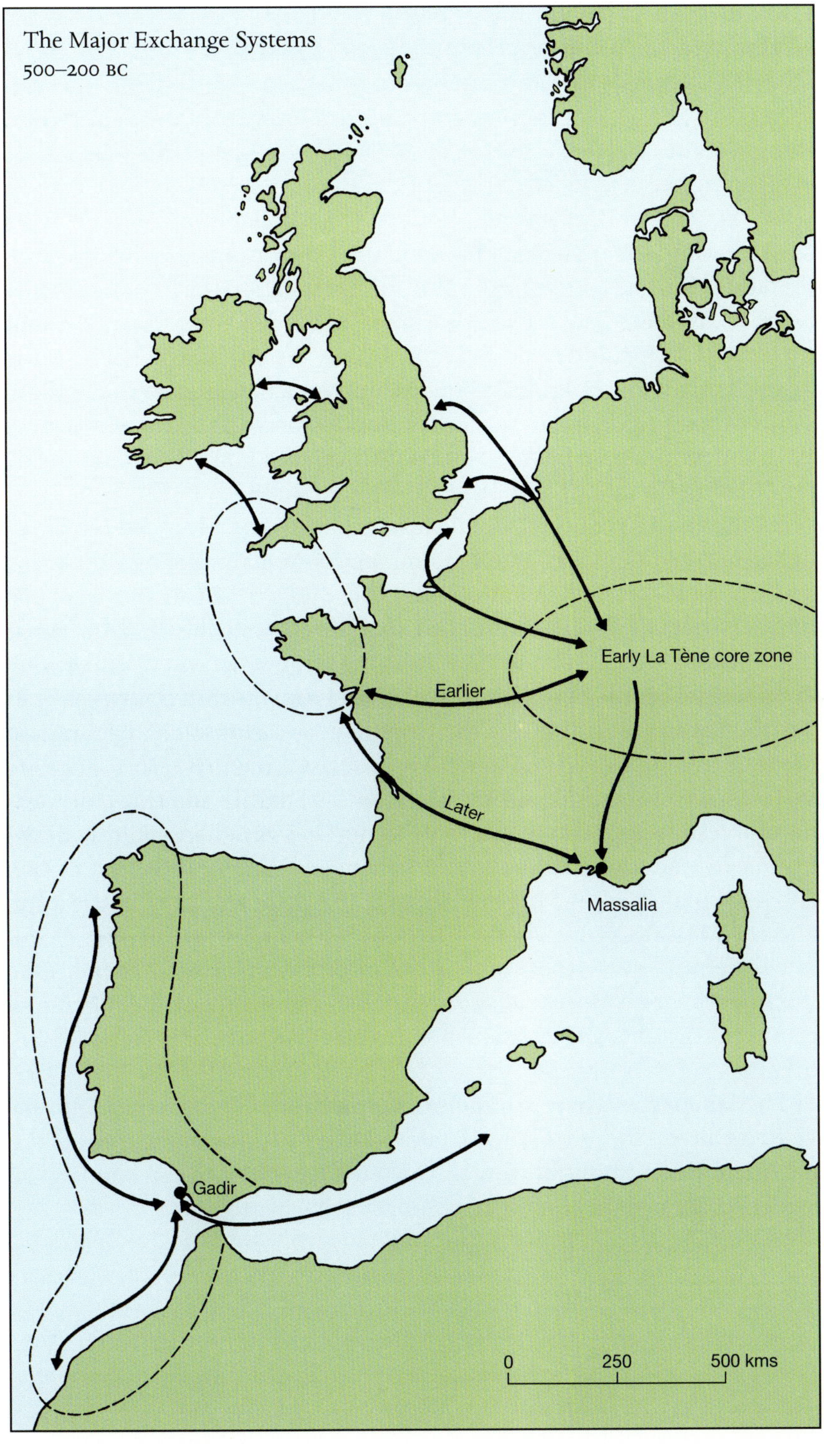

7.34 An indication of the principal exchange networks in operation in the first half of the first millennium BC.

Europe. Around 1000 BC things began to change. Developments in the Mediterranean, in western central Europe, and in the Nordic region created new demands for raw materials to feed their elite systems. This distorted the old networks, strengthening ties between the Atlantic communities and the new centres of innovation while at the same time weakening some parts of this Atlantic system.

By the end of the seventh century (7.34) Ireland and Britain were closely bound to northern France and the Low Countries while western Iberia and Morocco were now tightly integrated into the Phoenician network focused on Gadir. The position of Armorica is less clear. It seems that an insularity developed and may, at least in part, have been the cause of the remarkable hoarding phenomenon which caused so many thousands of axes to be made simply for burial—perhaps the breakdown in the old networks precipitated a crisis which could only be overcome by propitiating the deities with larger and larger gifts.

From the sixth century, while western Iberia and Morocco remained linked into a Phoenician / Punic-dominated system producing gold, ivory, and tin in increasing quantities for the Mediterranean markets, the northern part of the Atlantic zone experienced further shifts of orientation. Ireland seems soon to have become largely detached, embarking upon several centuries of relative isolation. From the fifth century the ties between much of Britain and the Continent were loosened. Brittany, on the other hand, revived and its networks spread, via the Loire, to the elite systems of west-central Europe. It may well be that, in addition to its own natural resources, Brittany was able to develop a middleman role drawing in new materials from southern Ireland and the south-west of Britain and passing them down the line, first via the Loire and later, as the influence of Massalia grew, via the Garonne. Eventually, by the end of the fourth century BC, Pytheas and no doubt others in his wake, penetrated the Atlantic networks to see for themselves the reality of the metal-rich promontories and islands where before there had been only rumours and myths.

The perspective, here so briefly sketched, is tolerably sound. It provides the broad framework to enable us better to understand the individual Atlantic communities who, through the wealth of the archaeological evidence, are now beginning to come into sharper focus.

8. Restating Identity: 1200–200 BC

In the last chapter we focused on the ocean as a means of communication used by the Atlantic communities themselves in traditional cycles of interaction and by entrepreneurs from the Mediterranean intent on exploring the commercial potential of the ocean fringe. In this way Atlantic Europe, for the first time, confronted Mediterranean civilization face to face, but while these brief encounters were taking place a more radical social and economic restructuring was under way among the peoples occupying the inland regions of western Europe. These processes, and the economic needs which they generated, were to have a significant impact on inhabitants of the maritime regions. It is as if the agents of change were now converging by land and by sea.

In the Heart of West Central Europe

One of the most geographically favoured areas of Europe is the broad arc of land extending around the north side of the Alps from Burgundy to Bohemia (8.1). Besides being temperate, fertile, and well resourced this great swath of land sits astride all the main routes which bind peninsular Europe north to south and east to west. Within a radius of barely 200 kilometres the headwaters of the Saône, Loire, Seine, Moselle, Rhine, and Danube converge. Through this area a traveller from Marseilles would pass to reach the North Sea or, deviating via the Danube and Morava, the Baltic. *En route* he might pass another journeying from the Atlantic to the Black Sea. Someone wishing to access this great route nexus from the east Mediterranean could do so via the Adriatic, the Po valley, and the Alpine passes. This is not to say that such monumental journeys were likely at this time, but simply that the routes existed and along them commodities passed over considerable distances, carried, one suspects, in a series of short-haul operations by those working their own familiar territories. Within this favoured zone of west central

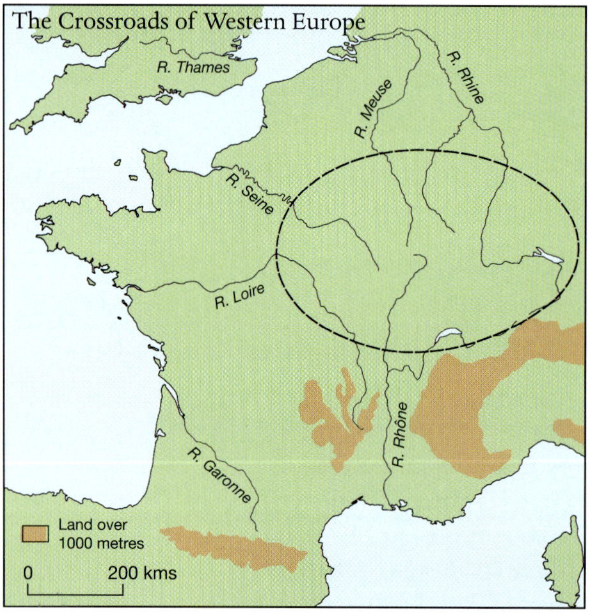

8.1 West central Europe and the favoured central focus to which the valleys of the great rivers give easy access.

Europe rapid social and economic change took place during the period from 800 to 400 BC. It is as if the region pulsated with energy, its dynamism spreading out to the west and north impacting upon the communities which lay within its extensive periphery.

It is necessary at this point to introduce some archaeological terminology. Much of it dates back to the nineteenth century but is so embedded in the literature that it is difficult not to continue to use it. Simply stated, much of the Late Bronze Age and the first part of the Iron Age, from *c.*1250 to 500/450 BC, is referred to as the Hallstatt period, named after a large cemetery and salt-mining site in Austria which were extensively excavated in the latter half of the nineteenth century. The second part of the Iron Age, from 500/450 BC until the time when the different territories were conquered by Rome, is called the La Tène period, after a site on Lake Neuchâtel in Switzerland from which a substantial collection of artefacts, probably ritually deposited in a lake, were recovered over many years of investigation. These two great collections provided nineteenth-century antiquaries with their basic data for classification. The Hallstatt and La Tène periods have been subdivided, usually on the basis of typology, into a number of phases identified by letters or numbers, and much effort has been spent refining these classifications to make them suit regional sequences and in arguing precise chronologies. For the purposes of the present discussion it is sufficient to note that the period which concerns us can be divided into the Hallstatt C, dating to about the eighth and seventh centuries BC, Hallstatt D to the sixth century, and La Tène A to the fifth. While there is continuing debate about exact chronology, and variation from region to region, this broad-brush approach enables the main story to be set out. It must, however, be stressed that the Hallstatt/La Tène terminology is nothing more than an artificial archaeological nomenclature—it takes with it no implication of ethnicity nor of major cultural continuities or dislocations.

In the Late Bronze Age the west-central region of Europe shared a broadly similar culture which had evolved from indigenous origins over the centuries, but in the eighth and seventh centuries a certain differentiation began to become apparent in the burial evidence within part of the region extending from southern Germany to Bohemia. Here distinctive warrior burials can be identified by sets of artefacts including a long slashing sword, the bronze trappings from horse harness, and in a few cases the elaborate four-wheeled vehicles upon which the deceased had been conveyed to the grave. Other luxury objects include finely decorated pottery and, more rarely, items of gold, glass, amber, and coral. What we are seeing here, in the archaeological record of the Hallstatt C period, is the coming into focus of an aristocracy using the horse and the vehicle as symbols of status. The concept of the vehicle burial may have been learned from the east, from the Pontic Steppes, where the tradition goes back to the third millennium, and it is quite possible that the actual horses were brought in from the east as items of exchange. In other words the aristocracy were identifying themselves as an elite, through their privileged access to exotic commodities and by adopting distinctive rituals.

About 600 BC the Phocaean Greeks established a colony at Massalia (Marseilles), close to the mouth of the Rhône. From here trade contacts were established along the Mediterranean coast of Iberia and in the immediate hinterland around the colony. Gradually Mediterranean goods such as painted pottery from Attica, bronze vessels made in the Greek workshops in southern Italy and in the Etruscan cities to the north, and wine produced along the Mediterranean littoral east of Massalia began to enter the exchange networks extending northwards up the Rhône valley. After the middle of the fifth century the quantity of exotic goods passing north into Burgundy and southern Germany increased and began to include spectacular items like the bronze gryphon-headed cauldron from Sainte Colombe and the huge ornate krater found at Vix. For the most part these exotics found their way into the graves of the elite, but imported pottery was certainly used in the defended hilltop settlements where the aristocracy presumably resided and entertained their clients.

The burials of the elite of this Hallstatt D period retained many of the characteristics of the earlier aristocratic tradition, most notably the use of the four-wheeled vehicle, but warrior equipment like swords and spears are no longer found. Instead what is emphasized is the feast, requiring that the dead person be provided with all the accoutrements necessary for the drinking of wine or mead whether they be native drinking horns, like those hung in the grave chamber at Hochdorf, or the set of vessels appropriate to the Greek symposion interred with the burial at Vix. There was also a westerly shift in the focus of distribution of rich graves, most of which are found in a restricted zone from Burgundy to the Rhine coinciding with the distribution of 'princely residences' (8.2).

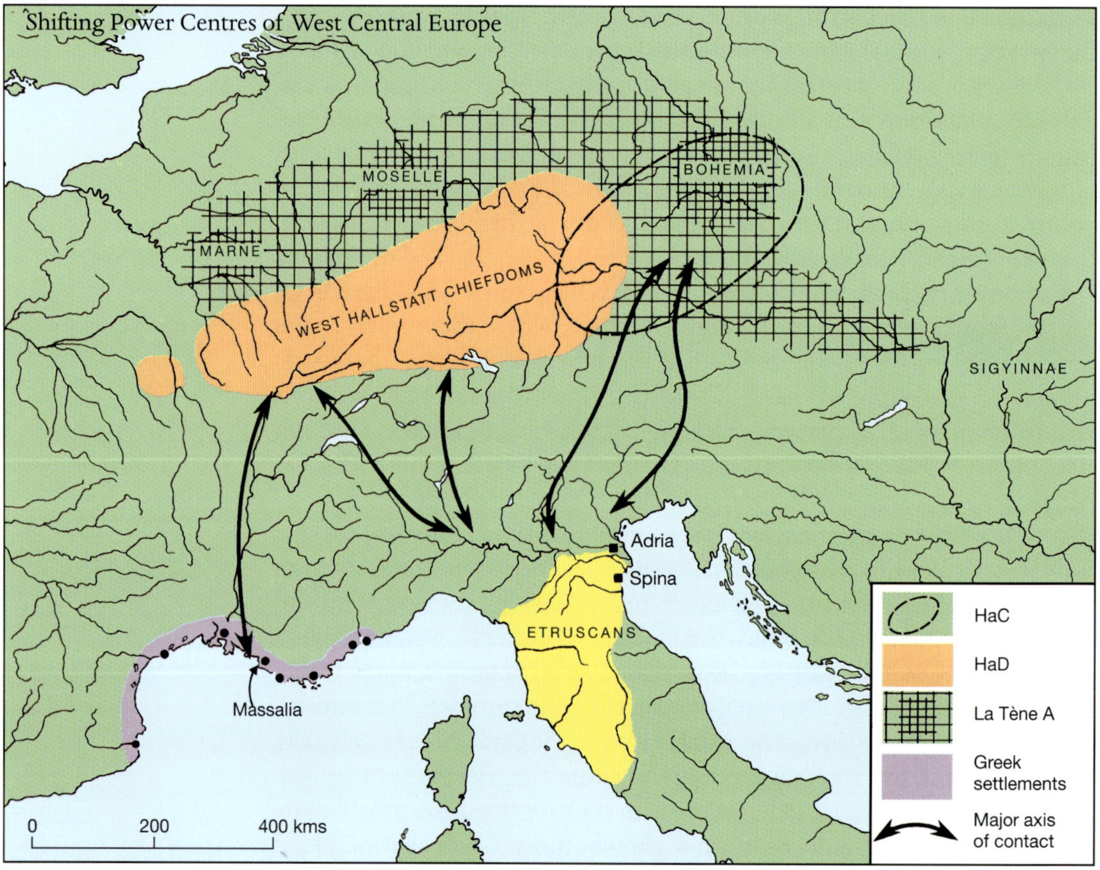

8.2 The shifting power centres in west central Europe between 700 and 400 BC. The initial focus of élite burials in Hallstatt C lay in a region from the Upper Danube to Bohemia. In Hallstatt D the focus of élite burial moved westwards, possibly partly in response to exchanges with the Mediterranean through Massalia. In the Early La Tène period the aristocratic zone lay to the north with the Marne, Moselle, and Bohemia becoming centres of innovation.

The shift may, in some part at least, have been caused by the growing importance of the Rhône route at this stage, as the way by which the luxury goods penetrated the north.

The elite system of west central Europe in the Hallstatt D period is often referred to as a prestige goods economy—that is, a social system based on the careful control, by paramount chieftains, of rare exotic goods which they used selectively as gifts to subordinates within their domains, to maintain the social hierarchy. In such a system we may envisage the paramounts articulating the flow of commodities by controlling the exchanges between the exotic prestige goods coming in and the raw materials going out. Some such explanation would account for why the warrior symbolism in the burials of the earlier Hallstatt period was superseded by a consumer symbolism in those of Hallstatt D. In exchanges of this kind there is no reason to suppose that the elite of west central Europe were manipulated by Greek traders for their own commercial ends. What the Mediterranean world had to offer were prestige commodities highly acceptable to native societies who needed such things to maintain their social hierarchies. Indeed it could be argued that, inspired by the desire for prestige goods, the agents of the west Hallstatt paramounts actively sought out consumer durables from the south, offering a range of raw materials sufficient to persuade the Greeks to comply. In any event the exchanges had to be socially beneficial to both communities. Only in such circumstances could exchanges of this kind flourish.

What kind of commodities were acquired by the west Hallstatt elite for trans-shipment south is unrecorded, but metals (gold, tin, and perhaps copper and iron) together with amber and furs would have been acceptable; so too were slaves. These various products could have been acquired from the territories to the west and north of the west Hallstatt zone through indigenous exchange networks. In other words, the west Hallstatt elite may have developed the function of middlemen in an economic system that embraced much of western Europe extending as far afield as Britain and Ireland. Given the volume of the commodities flowing and the length of time when the system was operating (*c*.530–450 BC), it is hardly surprising to find that those communities occupying the territory immediately to the north-west of the prestige core zone, stretching from the Loire valley through the Marne and Moselle regions to Bohemia, began to assume elements of elite behaviour, emulating those of the west Hallstatt paramounts but interpreting them within their own cultural milieu. In the Marne and Moselle regions significant new power centres developed in the fifth century, their culture now characterized as La Tène A. The new elite burials were accompanied by vehicles, but unlike those of the Hallstatt D graves these were two-wheeled, while swords and spears signifying warrior status were usually present. Another defining feature was the appearance of a new and hugely original art style, applied to decorating metalwork and pottery. The motifs at first rely heavily on Greek and Etruscan inspiration, as well as traditional geometric forms and concepts of animal art possibly derived from the east. Moulded together by local craftsmen, the new decorative concepts became the hallmark of the La Tène period and are often referred to as Celtic Art.

Some of the factors which gave rise to the development of the La Tène A elite zone are hinted at in the archaeological record. Simple emulation of the west Hallstatt chiefdoms and the growing ability of this inner periphery to control the flow of goods south will have played a part, but there may also have been some element of competition generated by new exchange systems being set up direct with the Mediterranean. Striking evidence for this is provided by the distribution of bronze beaked flagons, made in Etruscan cities like Vulci. They are found in some number in the Po valley and clustering around the southern ends of the Alpine passes, but with a significant concentration in the mid-Rhine–Moselle region where they are the type fossil of the rich La Tène graves of the early fifth century. The distribution strongly suggests that a new trading axis had been set up linking the Moselle chieftains direct to the Etruscan cities of the south. It is tempting to see in this some reflection of economic competition, with Greek influence via Massalia to the west Hallstatt zone being eclipsed, some time about 500 BC, by Etruscan influence via the Alpine passes direct to the fast-developing La Tène periphery. Whether the driving force in the new system was the Etruscans or the barbarian elites is far from clear. By the middle of the fifth century, however, the centre of innovation in western Europe had moved decisively away from the old Burgundy–southern Germany focus of the Hallstatt D period to the more northerly Marne–Moselle–Bohemia arc where the new La Tène A culture flourished (8.2).

It was from this zone, in the second half of the fifth century, that outward migration, apparently on a large scale, began, culminating in a massive flow of population southwards through the Alpine passes to the Po valley, and eastwards along the Upper Danube into the valley of the Middle Danube and beyond (8.3). These folk movements of whole populations, accompanied by raiding war-bands spreading even further outwards, were, from the beginning of the fourth century, to impact with some violence on the classical world of the Romans and the Greeks. To them the migrant peoples were Celts, and it is from the classical writers that we are given vivid descriptions of the Celts at war and the alien behaviour that distinguished them from their Mediterranean neighbours.

The classical writers were generally agreed that the prime cause of the migrations was overpopulation and the stress which it engendered. The archaeological evidence goes some way towards supporting this, in that excavations of the cemeteries of the Marne and Moselle regions suggest that populations were increasing throughout the fifth century but suddenly declined at the end of the century. The picture provided from the classical sources and from archaeology is consistent but ill-focused. The size and duration of migrations are difficult to gauge. All that can safely be said is that the later part of the fifth century was a time of social and economic disruption in west central Europe, with large numbers of people migrating to the south and east. During this time of upheaval long-established exchange systems were fractured and there may have been ripples of movement affecting many of the surrounding regions to the north and west. These are matters to which we shall return.

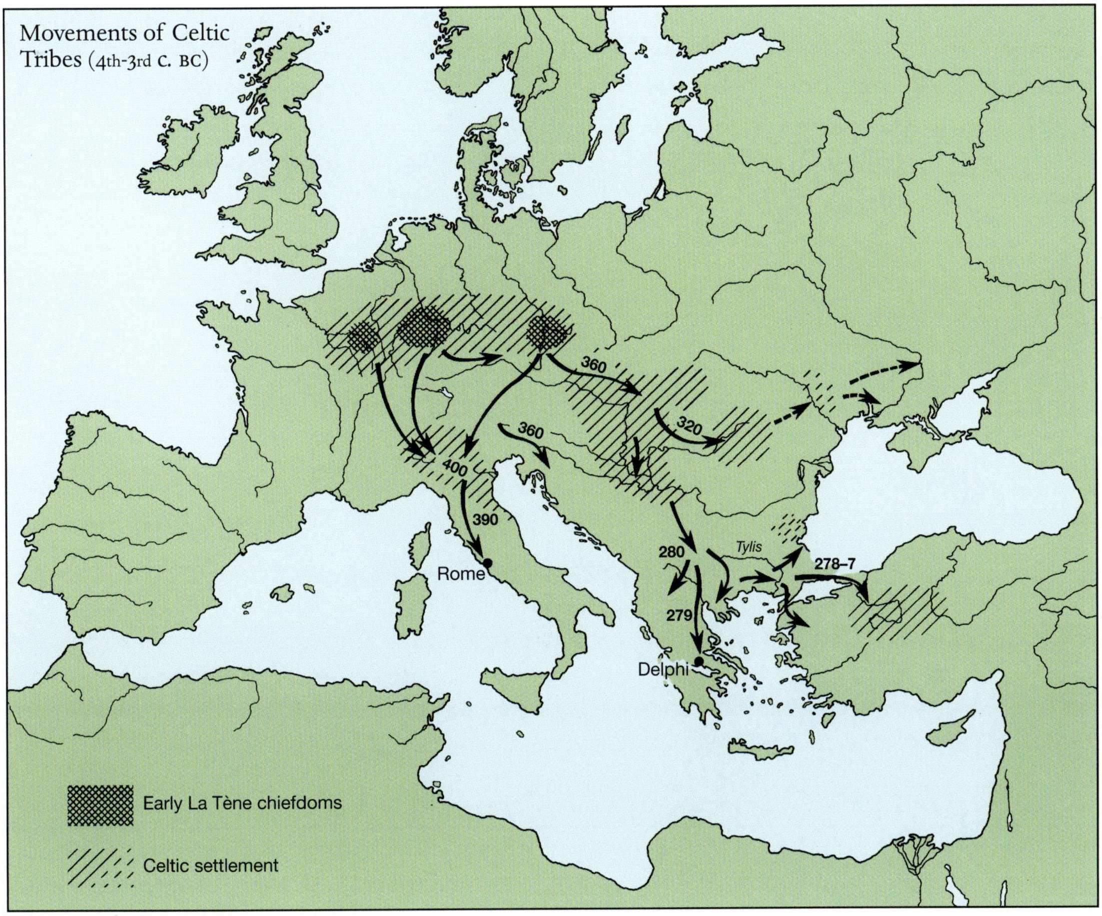

8.3 The principal movements of Celtic tribes in the fourth and third centuries BC.

Iberia

The Iberian Peninsula was separated from the rest of Europe by the Pyrenees but joined to it by its two seas coasts, one facing westwards and northwards to the open Atlantic, the other southwards and eastwards to the contained Mediterranean. The two long maritime zones developed distinct cultures (8.4). In the south and east the indigenous population, absorbing influences from Mediterranean 'civilization'—Phoenician, Carthaginian, Greek, and Etruscan—over many centuries of contact, emerged as a highly distinctive culture with its own art style, language, and semiurbanized settlement pattern. The different tribal groupings had individual names, but to classical writers the people were known collectively as Iberians—a term adopted by archaeologists to describe the cultural developments of south-eastern Iberia from the Pyrenees to the Guadalquivir. Along the west and north coasts of the peninsula a quite

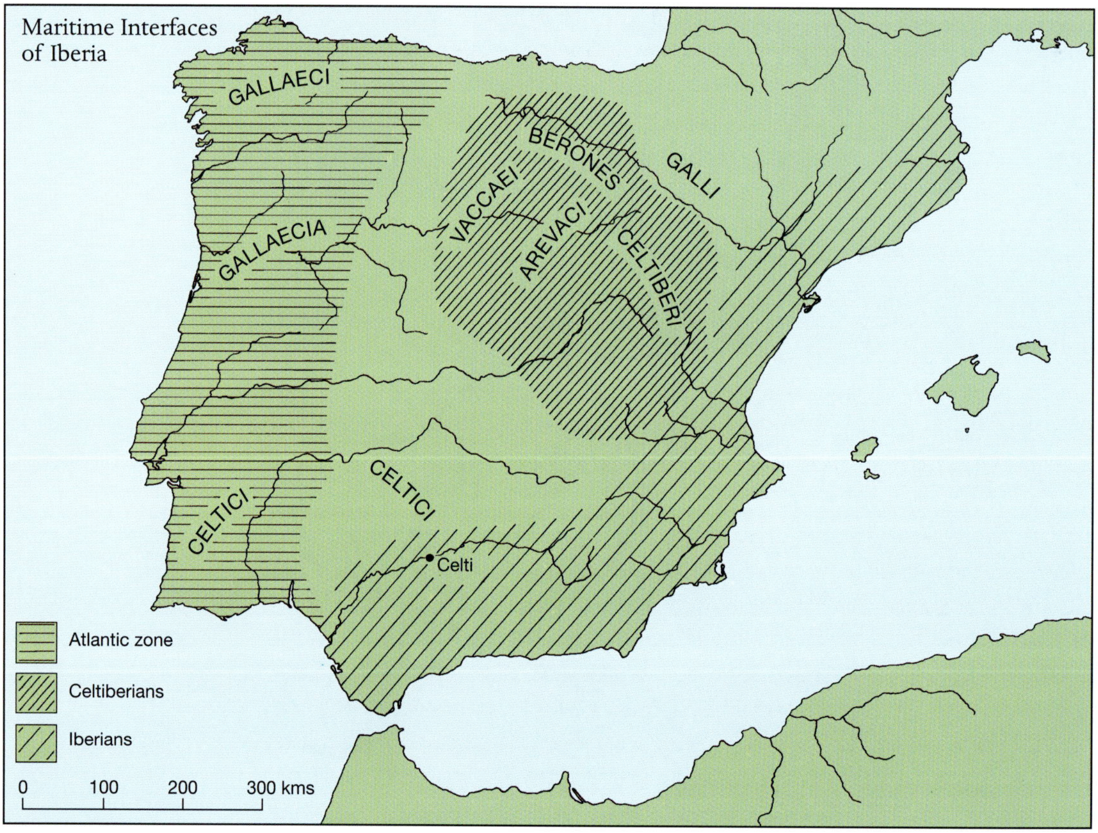

8.4 The two maritime interfaces of Iberia developed very different cultures. The Atlantic zone maintained its distinctive indigenous culture while the Mediterranean zone absorbed influences from the Phoenician, Punic, Greek, and Roman world to give rise to a sophisticated Iberian culture.

different Atlantic culture emerged, bound, as we have seen, by coastal traffic and quite possibly, from an early date, speaking a version of the 'Celtic' language.

The north-east of the peninsula, including the valley of the Ebro and the coastal region of Catalonia, was in close contact with southern France throughout the Late Bronze Age and shared much in common with the Urnfield culture of south-western Europe. The similarities in culture, on the two sides of the Pyrenees, have suggested to some commentators that actual movements of population may have occurred in the late second and early first millennia, incomers merging with the indigenous peoples to create a distinctive version of the Urnfield culture. After about 600 BC Greek influence, spreading from the coastal colonial settlements such as Emporion (Ampurias), brought the littoral zone into the western Greek sphere, but there is little evidence to suggest that the communities of the hinterland were much affected.

Over a large area of the interior of Iberia, from the southern flank of the Ebro valley to the eastern Meseta, there emerged, during the sixth and fifth centuries, a highly distinctive culture dominated by a warlike elite, which is generally referred to as Celtiberian. The Celtiberi were indeed one of the tribes known to have inhabited this region, but others—the Arevaci, Vaccaei, and Berones—near neighbours of the Celtiberi—shared much the same material culture and lifestyle. The presence of 'Celts' in Iberia is noted, though somewhat obliquely, by several classical writers beginning with Herodotus in the fifth century, but it is not until the second century that Celtiberes or Celtiberi come into prominence. Diodorus Siculus, who was probably using Poseidonius as a source, believed that the Celtiberi were a hybrid group resulting from the coming together of Celts and Iberians 'after long and bloody wars', and such beliefs persisted among Romanized locals like the poet Martial. Whether this view was based on folk memory or was simply a historian's rationalization is impossible to say.

The origin of the Celtiberi has been long debated by archaeologists. Some still adhere to the view that 'Celts' from west central Europe migrated en masse in the sixth century or earlier, but a more reasonable explanation is that the Celtiberi were essentially a group of indigenous peoples, sharing a broadly common culture, who emerged in a favoured region of Iberia benefiting from their proximity to both the metal-rich Atlantic west and the more socially advanced Iberian society of the Mediterranean littoral. By the sixth century the Celtiberian warrior elite was distinguishing itself in burial by the use of a recurring grave set comprising short swords, spears, round shields, and sometimes horse gear. Elaborate gold torcs were also widely in use but did not feature in the burial rituals. Thereafter Mediterranean influences became more apparent. By the fourth century the Celtiberi were making wheel-turned pottery, were using the rotary quern to grind their grain, and had learned to commit their Celtic language to writing. Many of them were also living in large defended hilltop enclosures, taking on the appearance of towns.

Some, rather scattered, evidence survives to suggest that bands of Celtiberi may have moved away from the homeland to settle in the south and west. Pliny records as a fact that some reached Baetica and established themselves to the north of the Guadalquivir, where they were called Celtici. Other tribal, personal and place-names incorporating *Celti* or *Galli* may indicate similar settlements in various parts of the west of the peninsula (8.4). How extensive these movements were is unclear, but there is nothing in the archaeological record to suggest that they were on the scale of the Celtic migrations from west central Europe.

There are interesting similarities between the development of the Celtiberi and the broadly contemporary Hallstatt D–La Tène A chiefdoms of west central Europe in that both lay on the interface between the more complex consuming societies of the Mediterranean littoral and the less-developed, resource-rich communities of the Atlantic zone. In both cases they commanded the principal routes which linked the ocean-facing extremes. The interactions between these two well-separated zones of elite dominance and the Atlantic region were instrumental in giving the maritime communities their distinctive character.

The Hallstatt/La Tène Chiefdoms and the West

One of the defining artefacts of the Hallstatt C warrior aristocracy was the long slashing sword of iron or bronze which usually accompanied the warrior to his grave. These swords, known after the cemeteries of Gundlingen and Mindelheim (the Mindelheim type being larger and more elaborate), were distributed throughout western Europe in the eighth and seventh centuries. The iron swords tend to be restricted to the west central zone from Burgundy to Bohemia, but the bronze types were more widely distributed in the west, occurring in some concentration in the Rhône valley, the Garonne region, and in lesser numbers in the valleys of the Loire, Seine, Somme, and Moselle—a pattern which suggests that the swords may have been items of exchange passing along the main riverine routes. Gundlingen swords were also found throughout Britain and Ireland (8.5), though a number of these are most likely local products made by indigenous swordsmiths copying imported styles. The other characteristic set of artefacts, so frequently found in the warrior graves, was bronze fittings for horse harness. These too are distributed throughout western Europe and occur in some number in Britain but not in Ireland.

The simplest interpretation of these artefact patterns is that the goods symbolizing elite status—the sword and trained horses with their tackle—were distributed through exchange networks reaching the western extremities of Europe north of the Pyrenees. The sword, presumably because of its lesser value, travelled the furthest, while the more valuable horses were restricted as gifts.

The overall pattern suggests that Britain, at this stage, was closely linked to the northern coasts of Gaul, between the Seine and the Rhine, with the Atlantic seaways playing a much less significant role. It was probably by way of Britain that the swords reached Ireland. That the more valuable horses (represented by horse gear) appear not to have been trans-shipped across the Irish Sea is an interesting reflection of the value gradient that can appear across an exchange network. In practical terms a commodity like, for example, Irish gold exchanged with the British for swords might, when further exchanged between Britain and the Continent, have commanded horses in exchange. This is, no doubt, a grossly simplistic caricature of what must have been highly intricate patterns of reciprocity, but it gives some idea of how distance may have played a part in changing values.

The other clusters of Hallstatt C swords in the west hint that the Loire may have played some role, albeit a subsidiary one, in linking the west central European chiefdoms to the Atlantic. A more significant cluster in the region of the Lot, Dordogne, and Garonne might reflect the growing power of the communities controlling the Aude–Garonne route.

Taking the distribution of Hallstatt C material at its simplest suggests that many of the long-established trade routes across western Europe remained active during the eighth and seventh centuries, and it was in this

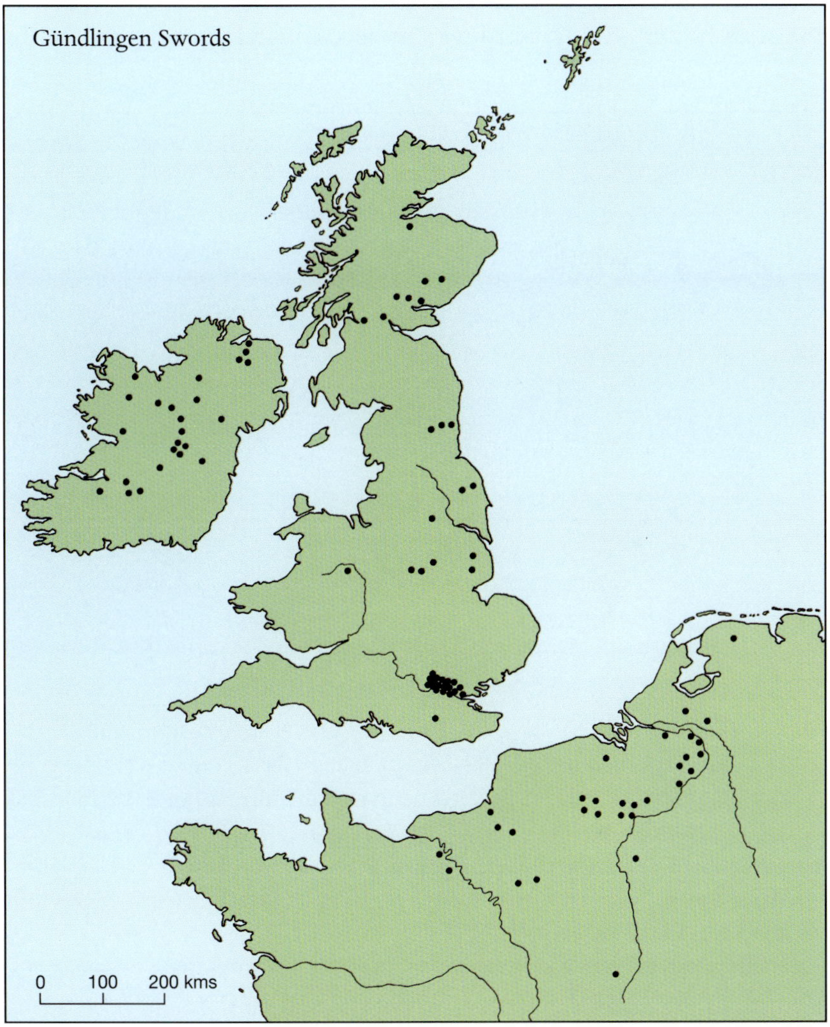

8.5 The distribution of bronze Hallstatt swords of Gundlingen type suggests that Ireland and Britain were at this time bound in exchange networks with north-west Europe across the southern North Sea.

way that raw materials from the Atlantic zone were drawn into the economic system which supported the Hallstatt elites.

The reorientation towards the Mediterranean, which came about in the sixth century, seems to have lessened the dependence on western resources. This much is implied by the artefact distributions. In Britain swords and daggers of Hallstatt D type are few compared with the numbers present in the Hallstatt C period, and in Ireland none are known at all. A significant number of those found in Britain come from a restricted part of the Thames valley, and most of them were of local manufacture copying Continental prototypes. Thus, while Continental styles were known and valued in Britain the actual number of imports must have been small and may have been restricted to the Thames valley.

There is an increasing body of evidence to show that by the middle of the sixth century the Loire route was becoming important (8.6). In the

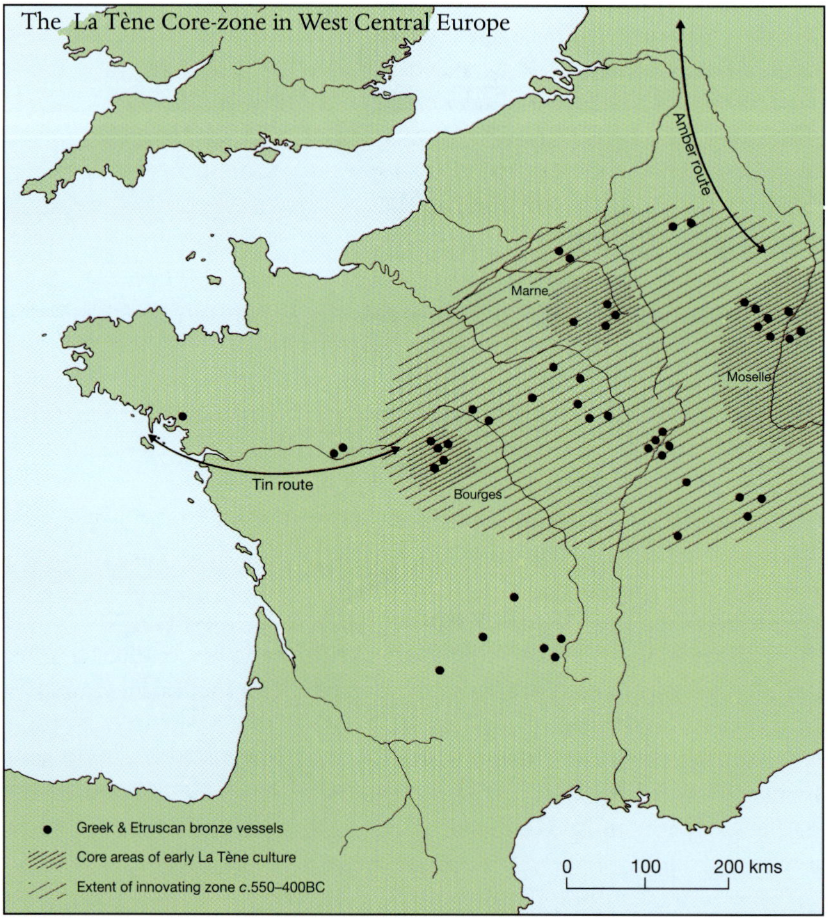

8.6 The Loire provided a convenient route linking the metal-rich Armorican peninsula to the innovating centres of La Tène culture in the Marne region and beyond. The enclave dominating the route in the region of Bourges prospered.

vicinity of Bourges, at the confluence of the Auron and the Yèvres, a tributary of the Cher, a centre of elite power developed in the period 540–450 BC. From the town itself have come Black and Red Figured Attic pottery together with Massaliot wine amphorae, while in the surroundings four cemeteries have been identified producing imported Mediterranean bronze vessels such as beaked flagons, stamnoi, and cordoned buckets. Clearly the elite of Bourges was able to obtain a range of luxury goods from the Mediterranean. Their power may well have lain in the fact that they commanded the short land route joining the Rhône–Saône system to the Loire and thus the Atlantic. In other words, they were optimally located to control the flow of metals from the Atlantic to the Mediterranean. The rise of the Bourges elite may reflect the growth in importance of the Loire route.

In Brittany too there are signs of developing contacts with the Mediterranean world. Two cemeteries in the Morbihan have produced imported bronze vessels of the late sixth and early fifth centuries, while at Kernavest, Quiberon, also in the Morbihan, an unusual inhumation burial in a cist under a tumulus was accompanied by an iron dagger in a highly ornamented bronze mount which may well have been imported from west central Europe. These few luxury imports, surviving in the archaeological record, may be representative of a much greater volume of exotics brought in from Continental Europe in exchange for tin and other commodities. Some hint of this is provided by changes in the locally made pottery, which now begins to imitate the form of metal vessels and is decorated with elaborate impressed decoration inspired by metalworking techniques prevalent in west central Europe. Taken together, the evidence from Brittany suggests renewed 'international' contacts very probably with the Loire valley serving, as it had done so many times in the past, as the main artery along which the long-distance exchanges were articulated.

The second half of the fifth century saw the emergence of major foci of elite power in the Moselle and Marne regions and the continuation of the elite centre around Bourges, each controlling one of the major river routes to the ocean—the Rhine, Seine, and Loire. It was in the Marne and Moselle regions that highly distinctive aristocratic art of the La Tène period emerged. Whilst much was shared between the skilled craftsmen of the two regions, stylistic preferences emerged. In the Moselle there was, from an early date, an emphasis on the three-dimensional. Imported Etruscan beaked flagons provided models inspiring masterpieces like the pair of early-fourth-century flagons from Basse-Yutz in Lorraine and the intricate goldwork so much in evidence in the Rhine / Moselle graves. In the Marne region the products are less flamboyant. There is a greater

8.7 An Etruscan flagon, now in the Musée des Beaux-Arts, Besançon, France, was elaborately decorated by a local Gaulish craftsman in Celtic style in the early fourth century. Knowledge of the art style may have spread west, to Armorica and beyond, along the Loire route.

concern for plant motifs worked in two dimensions and for openwork designs. Among the high points of artistic achievement we may list the fine bronze helmet from Berru in the Marne, the brilliant floral designs engraved by a local artist on an Etruscan flagon now at Besançon (8.7), and the bronze repoussé-decorated disc covered in sheet gold and inlaid with coral found at Auvers-sur-Oise in the Val d'Oise.

In parallel with the art of the metalworker ceramic art was developed to a peak of achievement in the Marne region in the late fifth and early fourth centuries. Not only were the forms of the vessels elegant, with their high pedestal bases, bulbous bodies, and slender necks, but the black-and-red painted designs which enhanced the bodies showed consummate skill in transposing complex tendril designs to a three-dimensional form. The painted Marnian pots serve to remind us of the importance of colour and the use of pigments in transmitting art styles. Fabrics, wood, and stone would all have been enhanced in colour, while the decoration of the human body is a commonly recurring theme across time throughout the world. Knowledge of an art style could be spread by the travels of a tattooed individual as well as by a traded bronze vessel.

The relationship of a society to its art is invariably complex. At one level the creation of a decorated item, involving rare materials and the skills and time of a craftsman, imparts value in the sense of rarity and consolidated work, and it is understandable that elites would use their command of such items to demonstrate their status. There are, however, likely to have been other levels of significance well understood by people at the time but inaccessible through archaeological remnants. Motifs might have had a ritual or magical significance or, as symbols of status, might have been restricted in their accessibility. Thus, a pair of dragons engraved on a sword scabbard may have endowed the sword with magical powers while the wearing of a torc might have been taboo for all but those of a special status. In the transference of art styles from one culture to another we may well be seeing the adoption of the beliefs and values which accompanied them.

The spread of La Tène art styles throughout Europe was a remarkable phenomenon. Indeed, it is not unreasonable to argue, as some have done, that La Tène art was the first truly pan-European art style. Its spread to the south and east of the Marne–Moselle region was, no doubt, accelerated by folk movement, but its adoption in the west and north, as far as the Atlantic coasts of Ireland and Scotland, was a more complex phenomenon involving many levels of acculturation, from the movement of actual objects by exchange to the selective emulation of motifs by local craftsmen.

8.8 Pottery vessel from the barrow at Kernevez near Saint-Pol-de-Léon, Finistère, France. The style of decoration is derived from decorated metalwork of the fourth century BC.

In Brittany the new art style was avidly adopted by the local potters. Vessel forms developed from the high-shouldered, narrow-based jars of the fifth century, and to this repertoire of shapes were added smaller open bowls, suitable for drinking from, which were evidently modelled on bronze bowls, a few examples of which have been found in western Britain and in Ireland. Both types of vessel were, in the fourth century, decorated with linear motifs closely derived from the metalworker's art of the Marne region. One of the most notable of these, the jar from Saint-Pol-de-Léon, Finistère (8.8), adopted motifs which closely echo those of the Besançon flagon and the Auvers-sur-Oise disc. The La Tène decorated pottery of Armorica, found mainly along the southern coastal zone and also along the north-west coast, shows that the motifs of La Tène art were widely adopted by the communities of the peninsula, no doubt as a result of the continued contacts with the Marnian region along the Loire which were under way by the beginning of the fifth century.

It may well have been by way of Brittany that knowledge of La Tène art spread to western Britain and Ireland. We have already mentioned that bronze bowls, of the type copied by the Armorican potters, are known in the west of Britain and in Ireland. Examples have been found at Youlton (Cornwall), Rose Ash (Devon), Birdlip (Gloucestershire), and Bulbury (Dorset), with one example in the north of Ireland at Keshcarrigan (Co. Leitrim) (8.9). This, essentially Atlantic, distribution is a reflection of maritime links. To these should be added the decorated metal vessel (or vessels) found in a cist grave at Cerrig-y-Drudion in Clwyd, north Wales which, though possibly a local product, was evidently inspired by the repertoire of the craftsmen of the Marne and Ardennes regions, as was the Saint-Pol-de-Léon pot.

There is also some evidence to suggest that other parts of Britain received their concepts of La Tène art styles by way of the southern North Sea, impacting upon the eastern coastal areas of Britain. In the Thames valley the school of craftsmen responsible for producing the British version of the Hallstatt D dagger was, by the fourth century, adopting the techniques of sword manufacture developed on the Contin-

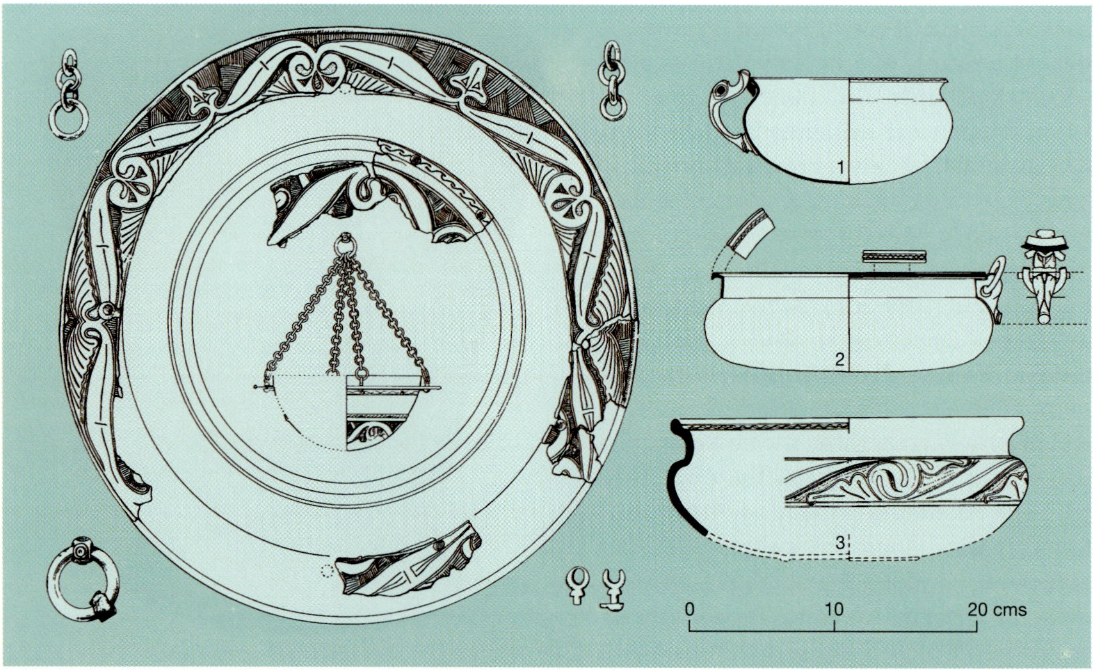

8.9 Metal vessels from Ireland and western Britain and a pottery vessel from Brittany. The highly decorated vessel (or vessels) once thought to be a hanging bowl was found in a cist at Cerrig y Drudion, Clwyd, Wales and closely copies Continental La Tène style of decoration. The two metal cups were found in bogs, 1 from Keshcarrigan, Co. Leitrim, Ireland and 2 from Rose Ash, Devon, England. The pottery vessel, 3, is from Hénon, Côtes-d'Armor, Brittany and clearly copies the metal types and the art style of La Tène metalworkers.

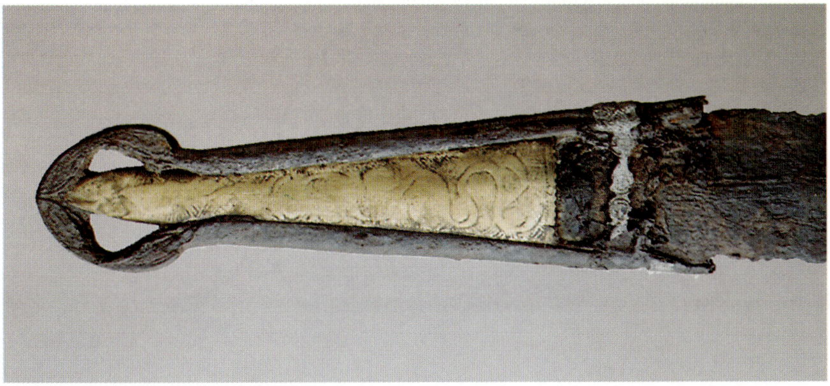

8.10 Bronze sword scabbards from, 1, Wisbech, Cambridgeshire, England and, 2, from the river Thames at Standlake, Oxfordshire, England. Both demonstrate local attempts at copying La Tène art styles in the fourth and third centuries BC.

ent in the early La Tène period. The earliest examples of La Tène art in eastern Britain are also found on sword scabbards, from Minster Ditch and Standlake (Oxfordshire) and Wisbech (Cambridgeshire) (8.10). Thereafter a range of items decorated in La Tène style were made, including the famous shield from the river Witham in Lincolnshire, the shield bosses from the Thames at Wandsworth, and the horn terminals and pony cap found together at Torrs in Kirkudbrightshire in Scotland. The exact date of these items is debatable but must lie between the fourth and second centuries. What is notable is the eastern distribution, many of them coming from east-flowing rivers, and the fact that the items are the parade gear of warriors.

The difference between the two manifestations of early La Tène art in Britain and Ireland—the Irish Sea and the North Sea—should not be overemphasized, since the items are few in number and accidents of recovery can distort patterns, but that there were probably two distinct routes by which the concepts were first introduced into Britain and Ireland need occasion no surprise: the two routes were, as we have already seen, of some antiquity (8.11).

8.11 The principal routes by which knowledge of La Tène art styles spread to Britain and Ireland.

From what has been said it will be clear that the pattern of contact between west central Europe and the maritime west varied over the period 800–300 BC. At the beginning the principal direction of contact lay across the southern North Sea to Britain and thence to Ireland, but by the middle of the sixth century the intensity of the contact seems to have diminished, with Ireland being left isolated. At about this time the Loire axis shows signs of invigoration, with contacts being developed with Armorica. This pattern was maintained or intensified during the fifth and into the fourth centuries, extending from Brittany to south-west Britain and the Irish Sea. In parallel with this, the pace of exchange across the southern North Sea began to pick up again.

8.12 (*facing*) Antennae-hilted sword from Alcacer do Sal, Portugal. Swords of this general type were widely used in northern Iberia and south-western France in the sixth to fourth centuries BC.

It will be evident from the discussion that our knowledge of these patterns is based entirely upon the style and distribution of artefacts and the reasonable interpretations which these may support. There are weaknesses in the method, but these can only be acknowledged and accepted. What emerges, however, is a coherent picture of gradually changing relationships as needs and energies of the centres of innovation in west central Europe changed over time. Whether or not the period of migration, which began in earnest at the end of the fifth century, had a significant effect on existing networks of exchange it is difficult to say, but there is some evidence in the western fringes of Europe of a greater isolation and regionalization from the fourth to the end of the second century.

Celtiberia, Iberia, and Beyond

The development of Celtiberian culture in the homeland between the Ebro and the eastern Meseta was, according to the archaeological evidence, continuous and unbroken from at least 600 BC, and probably for centuries before, until the Roman conquest in the second century BC, but during this time there were shifts in the locations of the most powerful elites. By the end of the fifth century, for example, the focus moved to the Upper Douro, the territory of the Celtiberian tribe the Arevaci. It is quite possible that this represents the growing importance of the Douro as a means of easy communication with metal-producing areas of Galicia to the west, whence came the gold torcs found throughout the Celtiberian region.

Direct archaeological evidence for the existence of exchange networks between the Celtiberian zone and the Atlantic communities is surprisingly sparse. The only elite item to travel far from the Celtiberian homeland is a type of dagger with a characteristic 'biglobular' handle (8.12). A few are found in the west of the peninsula in the foothills of the Central Sierras (between the Tagus and the Douro) and in the southern Meseta between the Tagus and the Guadiana. Another Celtiberian product—fibulae (brooches) in the form of a horse or a horse and rider—have much the same west-

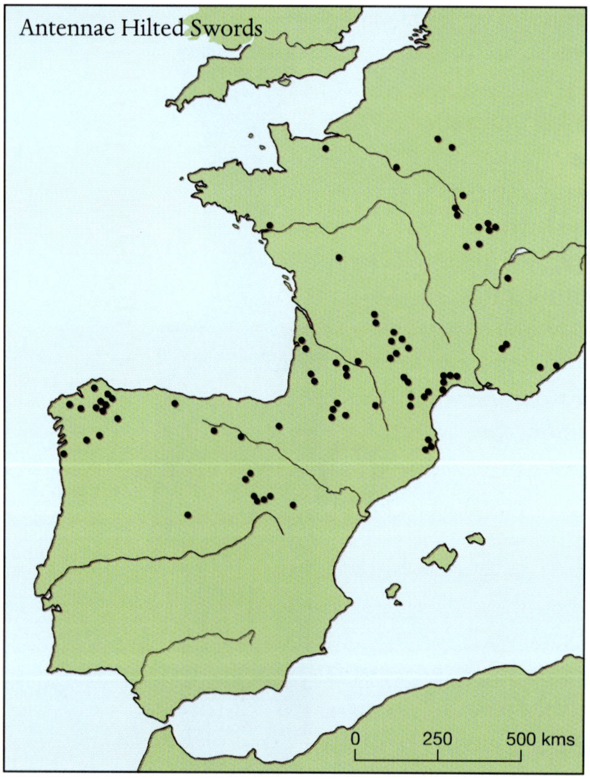

8.13 The distribution of antennae-hilted swords. Several different regional variations are included.

erly distribution, though they are more numerous particularly in the Upper Douro valley. The evidence for exchanges with the west is not impressive and need reflect little more than localized transactions along transhumance routes across the Meseta. Taken on its face value it would be possible to argue that the communities of western Iberia remained largely isolated from Celtiberia—a point to which we shall return later.

There is better evidence for there being links between Galicia, Celtiberia, and the communities on the north side of the Pyrenees, in Aquitania and Languedoc. All four areas have the antennae-hilted sword in common as the weapon of the elite warrior (8.13), and there are close similarities in detail between those of Celtiberians and the various southern French varieties, suggesting that contacts existed between the two regions around the west end of the Pyrenees and through the passes of the east. This raises the interesting possibility that the two areas may have developed in parallel over a long period of time, exchanging elite goods to maintain their social interactions. As part of these processes a few weapons of La Tène type were passed south to end up in the graves of the Celtiberian elites. Elite goods belonging to the panoply of the warrior were also finding their way to the Celtiberian territory from the Iberian region to the south and east. One such item is a large bronze breastplate with smaller plates attached to protect the top of the shoulders and the shoulder blades. It was found in the cemetery of Aguilar de Anguita in Guadalajara. A close parallel to this form of body armour can be seen on sculptures of Iberian warriors in action found at Porcuna in Andalucía. Iberian warriors also used circular shields, as did the Celtiberians, but the type was common throughout Iberia in the Iron Age and may have developed widely throughout the peninsula from Late Bronze Age antecedents.

The Celtiberians stand out as being a largely self-contained people occupying a central position within the peninsula. From their territory the different tribes could command gifts and traded commodities from neighbours through local exchange networks. So rich was the landscape that there appears to have been no need to develop long-distance networks of the kind in operation in west central Europe. Another difference lay in the relationship of the Mediterranean consumer societies to the Celtiberians and to the Atlantic coast metal resources. While it is quite possible that some metals may have passed through the hands of Celtiberian middlemen, the almost total absence of Greek pottery and other Mediterranean luxury goods in Celtiberia would argue that trade between the two was negligible. In all probability the gold, silver, tin, and copper produced in the west of the peninsula continued to be transported to the Mediterranean by sea, via the Carthaginian port of Gadir, as the various classical sources imply, cutting out the need for difficult cross-country transport and the increase in cost which would inevitably have accrued. It was for this reason that the communities of Galicia were able to turn their backs on the Celtiberians, except perhaps for the exchange of diplomatic gifts, and face their markets along the Atlantic shores.

The Major River Routes to the Atlantic

The Greek writer Strabo, in his wide-ranging *Geography* compiled at the beginning of the first millennium AD (he died about AD 26), discusses the main arteries giving access through Gaul from the Mediterranean to the Atlantic. His message is clear: the four great west-flowing rivers, the Garonne, Loire, Seine, and Rhine, were all used, the last three linking eventually to the Rhône which gave final access to the Mediterranean. He was, of course, compiling his work in the decades following Caesar's conquest of Gaul and would have been mindful of the burgeoning Roman trade of that period, but there can be little reasonable doubt that the riverine routes were by then communication axes of great antiquity. Since we have had cause to refer to their importance earlier in this chapter it is necessary now to review what the archaeology of the first millennium BC has to tell.

The shortest of the routes, via the Garonne, is summed up succinctly by Strabo: 'from Narbo traffic goes inland for a short distance by the Atax river [the Aude], and then a greater distance by land to the Garumna river [Garonne]; and this latter distance is about eight hundred or seven hundred stadia. And the Garumna, too, flows to the ocean' (*Geog.* 4. 1. 14). In terms of modern geography the first leg of the journey would have been along the River Aude as far as Carcassonne, where the river turns away south to the Pyrenees (8.14). From Carcassonne to Toulouse the overland haul was just under 90 kilometres, which might have taken four or five days to accomplish. At Toulouse, ancient Tolosa, the Garonne is reached

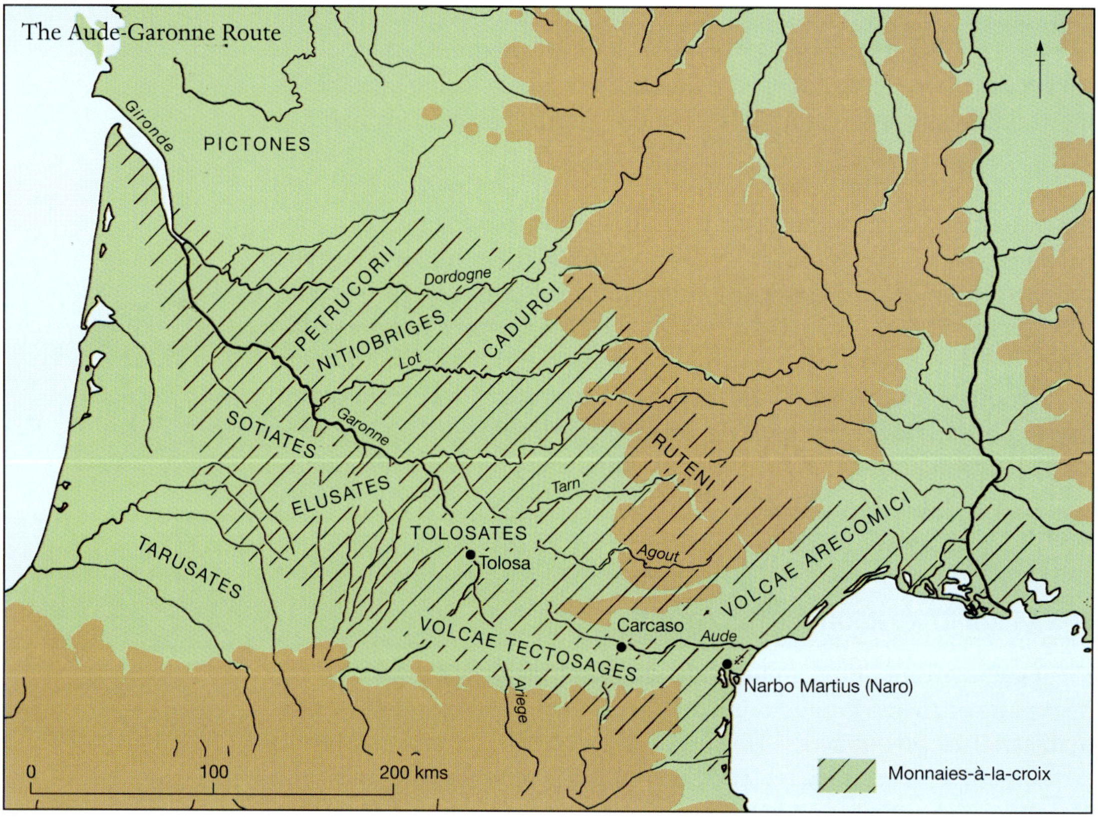

8.14 The Aude–Garonne route between the Atlantic and the Mediterranean showing the distribution of native coinage (monnaies-à-la-croix) copying the issues minted in the Greek colonies of Emporion and Rhode.

and from there is navigable all the way to the sea. At its confluence with the River Dordogne, 22 kilometres downstream from Bordeaux, the Garonne enters the wide estuary of the Gironde. From Narbo, close to the mouth of the Aude, to Bordeaux the journey would have taken between fifteen and twenty days.

Several ancient authors refer to the important port of Naro or Narbo at the trans-shipment point between the Mediterranean and the Aude. The ancient site is almost certainly to be identified with the oppidum of Montlaures, 4 kilometres from the later Roman settlement of *Narbo Martius* established at the end of the second century BC. The settlement covered some 18 hectares and produced ample evidence of intensive occupation, beginning at least as early as the fifth century BC. At that time a higher sea-level meant that ocean-going ships could come close to the oppidum, benefiting from a large and well-protected harbour. Later a change of sea-level, combined with silting, left the old settlement isolated as the shoreline retreated. The Roman foundation of *Narbo Martius* was sited to be as close as possible to the new harbourside facilities then functioning. Excavations at Montlaures have demonstrated the importance of the pre-Roman settlement as a major Mediterranean port from the fifth to second centuries BC, producing large quantities of imported pottery, including Attic Black and Red Figured ware, Etruscan and Punic pottery, and wares of western Greek type coming from the colony of Emporion (Ampurias) on the Golfe du Lions 100 kilometres or so to the south.

Of the other focal points on the route less is known of their occupation in the early period, but both Carcaso (Carcassonne) and Tolosa (Toulouse) were in use as early as the sixth century BC. Both have produced Attic Red Figured pottery of the late sixth–early fifth centuries, and Black Figured ware of a few decades earlier has come from Tolosa. Imported material is at present sparse, but it is indicative of active exchanges at least as early as the sixth century.

Further evidence for the growing importance of the route comes from a consideration of the locally issued coinage of the region. Two principal classes have been identified, one based on silver drachmas produced by the Greek colony of Emporion, the other on issues minted by the nearby colony of Rhode (now Rosas). The earliest copies of the Emporion prototype spread wide into Limousin, Poitou, and Berry, while the early copies of drachmas from Rhode were more limited in their distribution, being restricted to the Aude–Garonne and their immediate tributaries. These gave rise to a long tradition of local coinages known collectively as *monnaies-à-la-Croix* (8.15). The name derives from the cross-like motif which all of the varieties adopted on their reverses. This is a rendering, simplified and eventually reduced to a mere symbol, of the rose proudly displayed on the original Greek colonial prototypes.

The earliest copies of the Greek issues, of both Emporion and Rhode, found in south-western France probably date to the fourth century BC, with the *monnaies-à-la-Croix* developing in the early third century as the coinage of the Aude–Garonne corridor including the valleys of the Tarn, Lot, Dordogne, and Ariege. These types remained in use up to the time of the Roman conquest. Within this broad zone it is possible to distinguish the different coinages of many of the individual tribes making up the local population at the time of the conquest in the late second and early first centuries BC.

The adoption of Greek models for the local coinage does not mean that Emporion or Rhode held hegemony over the native tribes, but it does suggest that in the fourth century the Greek coinage was available and its value system, at least partially, understood in the region. The metal quality and weight of the earlier local copies were equivalent to the prototype coins, which suggests that the intention may have been to create a coinage acceptable in international exchange.

8.15 Monnaies-à-la-croix from Western France. The coins copy Greek coins issued by the city of Rhode on the Mediterranean coast of Iberia.

Taken together, the archaeological evidence shows that the Aude–Garonne route was in active use for exchanges with the Greeks of the west Mediterranean as early as the sixth century, following close upon the founding of the colonies, and by the fourth century the intensity of the contact had increased. By this time it may well be that regular trade was under way. The mountains on either side of the route were rich in metals. The Montagne Noire and the Pyrenees had ample resources of copper, silver, and iron, and there is evidence of large-scale silver production in Aveyron, where there are also sparser sources of tin which may have been exploited. In addition, gold from the Tarn and from the territory of the Tarbelli near the Atlantic is referred to by classical writers. There is also the strong possibility that Atlantic tin was channelled this way. Given the high economic potential of the region and its evident links with the Mediterranean world, the suggestion offered above, that the explorer Pytheas travelled the route to reach the Atlantic, is not unreasonable.

One final issue is worth considering. The Garonne does seem to have been something of a cultural divide. Caesar, in the famous opening paragraph of his *Commentaries* to the Gallic War, explicitly states that 'The Celts are separated from the Aquitani by the River Garonne', and the same point is repeated by Strabo, though in this he may have used Caesar as a source. The archaeological evidence lends some support to the idea, in that large defended oppida, typical of the Celtic Gauls, are not found south of the river, where the settlement pattern appears to be different. While there is no reason to suppose that the river itself was a precise frontier line, the corridor of communication which the Aude–Garonne provided will have been a zone of much movement, creating a broad interface between the two ethnic groupings.

The Loire valley provided an alternative route between the Atlantic and the Mediterranean (8.6). For this we again have the testimony of Strabo, who tells us that, since the Rhône was fast flowing and difficult to sail up, wagons were used for traffic up the valley and across to the Loire where river transport was used to reach the ocean. The easiest route between the two rivers, across the Montagne du Lyonnaise, would have been via the valley of the Gier, a distance of about 40 kilometres. The total journey, following the main course of both rivers, is about 1,000 kilometres which, even at the rate of 25 kilometres a day, would have taken forty days on foot. By taking a shorter route overland via Bourges and allowing that greater speeds could have been achieved by sailing down the Rhône, it would have been possible to cross France in about thirty days—the estimate which Diodorus Siculus gives for the time taken for the tin from Britain to be carried across Gaul to the mouth of the Rhône.

On the Loire, at or close to its estuary, was a major native trading port called Corbilo (Korbilon in Greek). Our knowledge of it derives from Strabo (*Geog.* 4. 2. 1), who records that Corbilo was mentioned by Pytheas (and was thus in active use in the fourth century) and that merchants from Corbilo and Narbo were present at Massalia in about 135 BC, for (Strabo is here quoting Polybius) men from the ports were questioned about Britain by Scipio (probably Scipio Aemilianus) but could, or would, tell him nothing of the island. Since no mention of Corbilo is made by Caesar, it is usually assumed that the port was no longer in operation by the mid-first century BC. No trace of it has been identified archaeologically, but of the several possibilities proposed a site beneath the Roman city of Nantes is the most likely. The place was clearly of some significance, for not only was it one of the few places named by Pytheas, but its traders were enterprising enough to have reached Massalia in the second century.

Moving upriver from the estuary, it is probable that the most widely used route followed the Cher, which joins the Loire below Tours, and that from somewhere in the vicinity of Vierzon a land route was taken south of the Collines du Sancerrois, through Bourges, to join the Upper Loire near Nevers. A scatter of Italic and Etruscan bronzes along the river route offers only a pale reflection of the volume of trade which there must once have been.

Bourges occupies a crucial point on the cross-land passage and it was here, as we saw above, that an elite emerged in the late sixth century able to acquire luxury bronze vessels, pottery, and wine coming from the Mediterranean world. Excavations within the city have produced sufficient imported pottery to suggest that a wealthy and sizeable settlement existed here at an early date. The town continued to flourish, and by the middle of the first century BC, known as Avaricum, it had become, according to Caesar, 'the largest and best fortified oppida in the territory of the Bituriges and one lying in an extremely fertile part of the country' (*Gallic Wars* 7. 13). Caesar proceeded to destroy it and slaughtered most of its inhabitants.

The journey between the Upper Loire valley and the Rhône probably joined the Rhône at or close to Vienne. Little is yet known of the earliest phases of occupation beneath the Late Iron Age and Roman city, but in one deep *sondage* the earliest layers produced sherds of Attic Red Figured ware of the fourth century, and thereafter imported Mediterranean pottery increased in quantity. Vienne occupied an important route node not only on the westerly route but also on the more northerly route via the Saône to the valley of the Seine.

Although Strabo mentions the Seine in his list of important river routes through Gaul, there is little reason to suppose that it played any significant part in the exchange systems which drew commodities from the western seaways and shipped them through to the Mediterranean: the westerly routes were more direct. But the Seine valley did provide a convenient way for the populous communities of the Champagne to gain access to commodities available in the Channel for their own use. The rich early La Tène population of the Marne region, stretching from just south of the river Marne to just north of the Aisne, required a range of raw materials not only for their own direct needs but also to exchange with neighbouring elites (8.6). The Seine will have allowed them to tap directly into the western maritime systems. Since there is little direct archaeological evidence of this and no major trading site has been identified, it is possible that such exchanges that took place did so in the context of gift exchange between neighbouring elites in the traditional prehistoric manner, rather than in the more controlled 'commercial' way which seems to have been applied along the Loire and the Garonne routes. Much the same processes may have brought the commodities, available throughout the southern part of the North Sea zone, along the Rhine route into the sphere of the elite dominating the Moselle–Mid-Rhine region in the early La Tène period.

That active communication did take place between the chiefdoms of the Marne–Moselle and the southern North Sea networks is shown by the transmission of early La Tène cultural concepts to eastern Britain. This is manifest in the occurrence of La Tène weapons in Britain and the adoption of many of the elements of the Continental burial rite by the communities living on the Yorkshire Wolds. Clearly a range of shared knowledge was circulating between the coastal communities of the southern North Sea.

This brief survey of the major river routes highlights the two different systems in operation in the second half of the first millennium BC: the essentially 'native' systems of the north-east and the more sophisticated Mediterranean-dominated systems of the south-west.

Atlantic Communities of the First Millennium BC

Until the beginning of the first millennium BC physical evidence for settlement sites along the Atlantic zone is somewhat limited. This is not to imply that settlement was sparse but simply that it was seldom of the form to leave easily recognizable field monuments. Society's desire for monumentality was instead channelled into other directions, like the erection of large burial structures or the massive production of bronze implements for deposition. There were, of course, some 'monumental' settlements—the great shell middens of the coastal Mesolithic hunter-gatherer bands and the complex stone fortifications of the third-millennium metal-using societies of the Tagus region are examples of this—but for the most part the settlements were simple and without lasting structures.

From the beginning of the first millennium BC many of the communities of western Europe began to build substantial settlement structures. Usually they were in some way defended and, more often than not, they were sited in prominent positions on hilltops or at the ends of ridges. For this reason they are frequently referred to in the archaeological literature by the general-purpose term 'hillfort' or whatever the local linguistic equivalent for fort or castle is. Although such terms are convenient in discussion, their use should not obscure the fact that these enclosed or defended settlements varied considerably in size, complexity, and presumably therefore, in socio-economic function.

While enclosed settlements are found throughout western Europe at this time, they are particularly in evidence in the extreme west, along the Atlantic fringes, and often occur densely packed in the landscape. At one level this must be a reflection of social organization but there are other factors to consider, not least that the settlements survive better in areas where they were built of stone and where the landscape and climate mitigate against more recent large-scale clearances for agricultural purposes. Factors such as these tend to distort the archaeological record and may make the remote Atlantic coastal regions appear more extreme and different than they are, but this said, the Atlantic zone does stand out as a region of defended settlements and homesteads built to be seen and to impress. To give some idea of both the similarities evident throughout the zone and the highly distinctive regional differences that occur, a brief survey of the different communities will be given before we return to the question of whether or not an Atlantic identity can really be claimed (8.16).

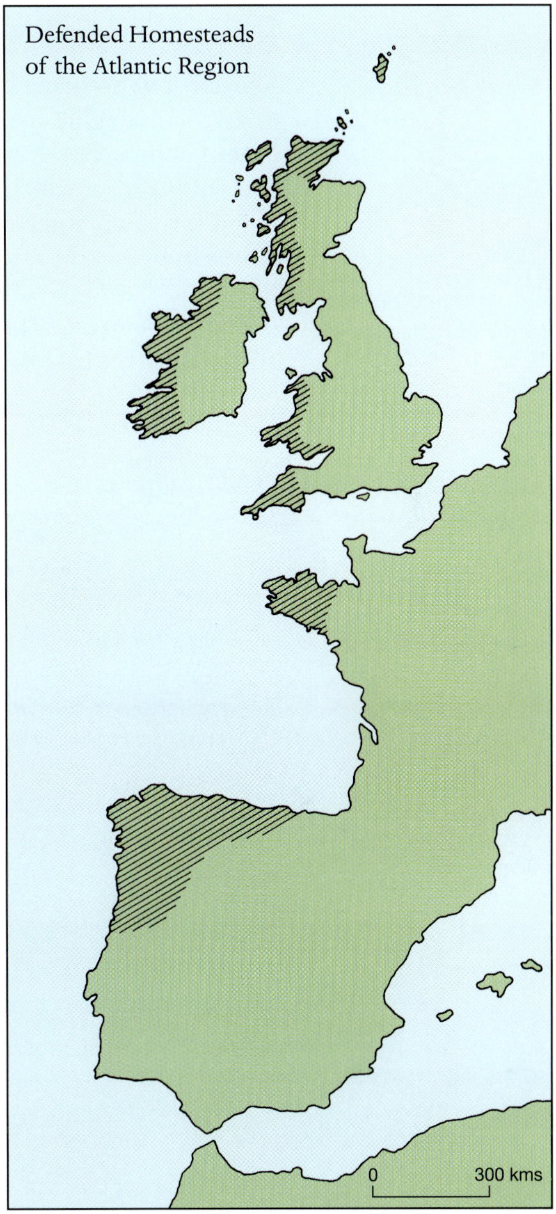

8.16 Atlantic communities with distinctive settlement forms in the first millennium BC.

The Castros of Galicia

The north-west corner of the Iberian Peninsula has long been recognized to have had a highly characteristic culture, distinguishing it from the rest of the country. Simply stated, the landscape is packed with defended settlements (*castros*) which occur in their many thousands between Coimbra in the south and Santander in the north (8.17). The density is at its most extreme in the north-west corner, in the Spanish province of Galicia.

The settlements represent occupation over a long period of time, beginning in the Late Bronze Age, at the start of the first millennium, and

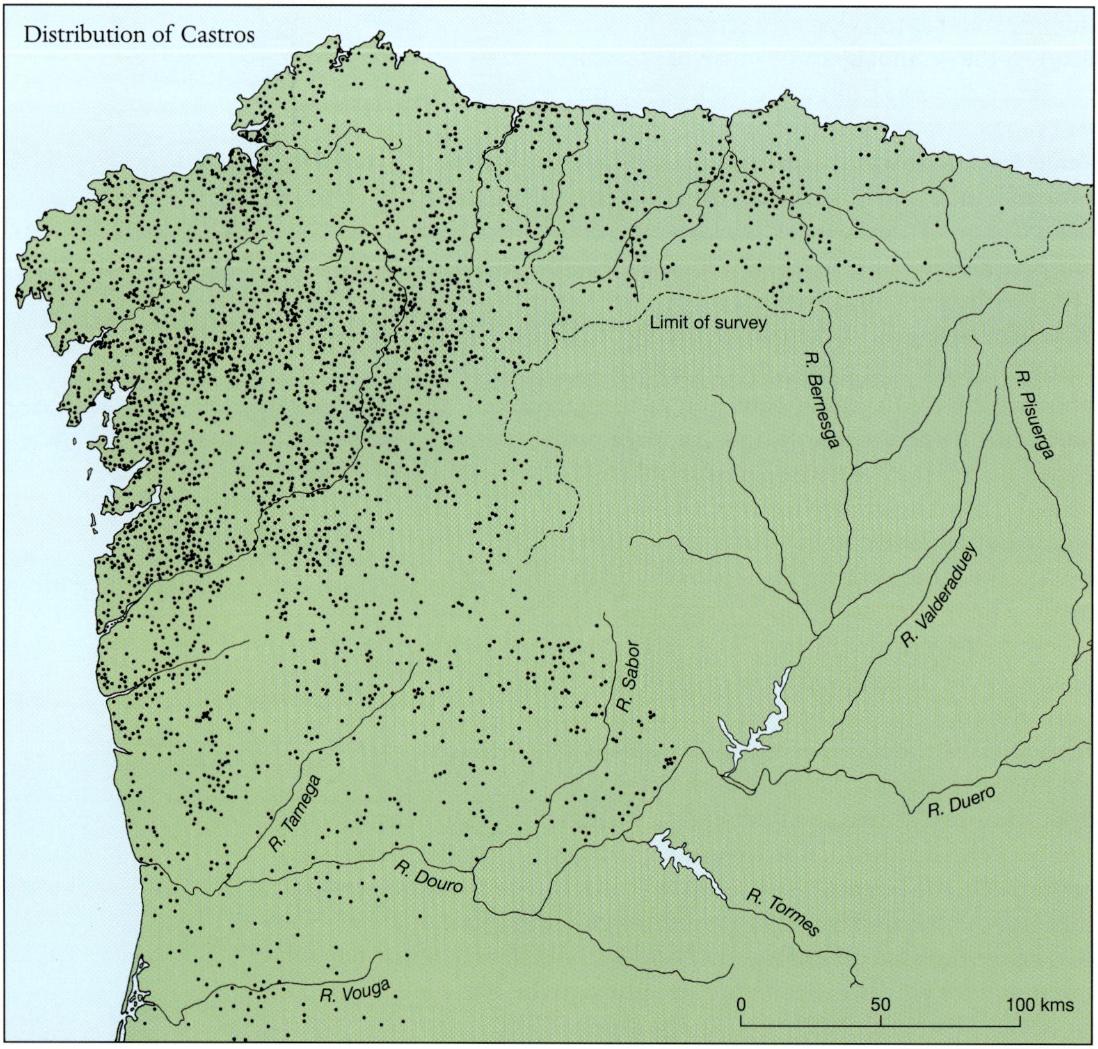

8.17 The distribution of castros in north-western Iberia.

extending to well into the Roman period to the early centuries of the first millennium AD. This long time-span can be divided into three broad phases. The first, from *c.*1000–*c.*500 BC, covers the end of the period of widespread maritime contact, reflected by the extensive exchange of bronzes, to the development of trading relationships with the Phoenician and Punic ports of the south. The second period, from *c.*500–*c.*140 BC, is a time of intense regional development when the highly distinctive local culture emerges, absorbing ideas continuing to come from the Punic south by sea and from the Celtiberian culture to the east yet maintaining a strong regional character. Towards the end of this period the effects of Roman contact begin to be felt as the Roman armies became engaged in wars against the Lusitanians to the south (194–138 BC). The third period begins with the Roman military expeditions of Decimus Brutus, who campaigned through the southern part of the region in 138–136 BC. This was followed by Julius Caesar's more wide-ranging expeditions in 61–59 BC, during which he penetrated Galicia and captured the native town of Brigantium (La Coruña). The conquest of the north-west was finally completed by Augustus and his generals in the so-called Cantabrian wars of 29–19 BC. Thus, over a period of 120 years or so, the communities of the north-west were brought progressively into contact with the Roman world, and the influences of this can be traced not only in material culture but also in the adoption of concepts of Roman urbanization evident in the plans of the larger castros.

Although the broad periodization is clear, there have been comparatively few scientific excavations in the region and in consequence the processes of social and economic change have yet to be worked out in detail; but what does emerge is the impression of a vigorous regional culture with a strong internal dynamic such that even by the second century AD, after two centuries of romanization, the indigenous social system was still largely intact. Attributes of Roman culture were absorbed but were used in a native milieu in a way that best suited native society. The persistence of indigenous institutions was remarkable. While it would be possible to present all this as a backwardness born of geographical isolation, it is more in harmony with the evidence to see it as the result of internal vigour, creating and maintaining deeply embedded social systems and the material and structural symbols that supported them. Being physically isolated, and against the ocean, may have provided the incentive to remain culturally distinct.

The principal characteristics of the castros are well known from several large-scale excavations, of which the most famous are Citânia de Briteiros, Citânia de Sanfins and Sabroso, in the region around Guimaraes in northern Portugal, and Monte Tecla near Pontevedra in

Galicia. All share the characteristics of hilltop location, multiple defensive walls, ordered internal settlement of high density, and the dominance of circular houses, at least in the phase before Roman influences begin to impact. These are all large nucleated settlements which went on in use well into the Roman period, but castros vary considerably in size, and more common would have been smaller examples like Castro de Baroña on its sea-girt promontory overlooking the Ria de Muros y de Noya on the rugged west coast of Galicia (8.18).

8.18 (*facing above*) The fortified coastal settlement of Castro de Baroña, on the Ria de Muros e Noia, Galicia, Spain.

8.19 (*facing below*) Gold torc from Vilas Boas, Vila Flor, Portugal.

Many aspects of the material culture of the north-west serve to distinguish it from neighbouring regions. At the elite level elaborate gold ornaments like bracelets, earrings, and torcs symbolized paramount status (8.19, 8.20). Here value lay not only in the quantity of metal employed and the craft skills used in making the item but in social restrictions on its use. A careful analysis of the styles apparent among the gold torcs shows a regional variation in their distribution, suggesting that the different styles may represent different ethnic groups. In other words, the torc was used to define membership of a discrete social entity.

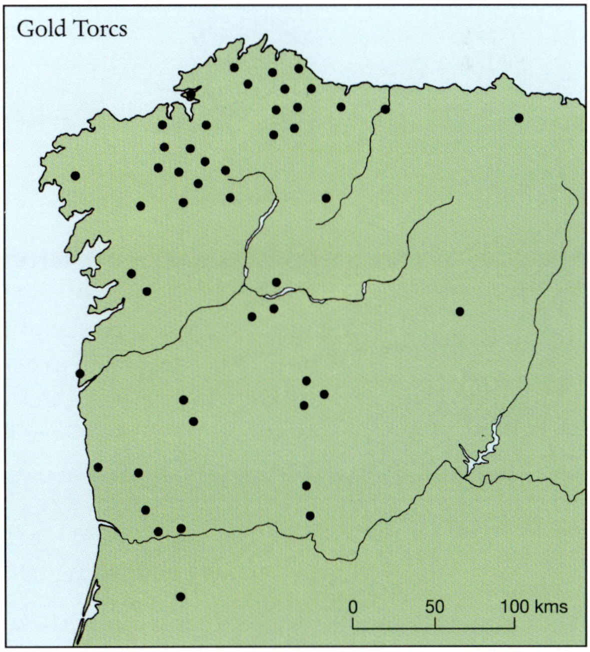

8.20 Distribution of gold torcs in north-western Iberia.

The highly decorated pottery of the Castro culture, using mainly stamped and incised motifs arranged in linear patterns (8.21), helps to identify the culture in contrast to neighbouring regions of Iberia. It is likely that the selection and combination of motifs were used as a means of defining social allegiances on a more local level.

In sculpture, too, the Castro culture stands out. Over much of the western Meseta of Iberia large stone quadrupeds known as *verracos* have been found. They are thought to represent bulls, and may have been used as territorial markers delimiting tracts of pasture land. In the southern part of the Castro cultural area similar zoomorphic markers are found, but they are usually restricted to heads. The most distinctive of the regional sculptures are the remarkable massive warrior figures carved in the round (8.22, 8.23). Stylistically they adhere closely to a single model. The warrior wears a tight-fitted, ornamented short-sleeve shirt and a short kilt kept up by a belt. He invariably holds a circular shield across the stomach and his right hand rests on the hilt of a short dagger. It is tempting to see these

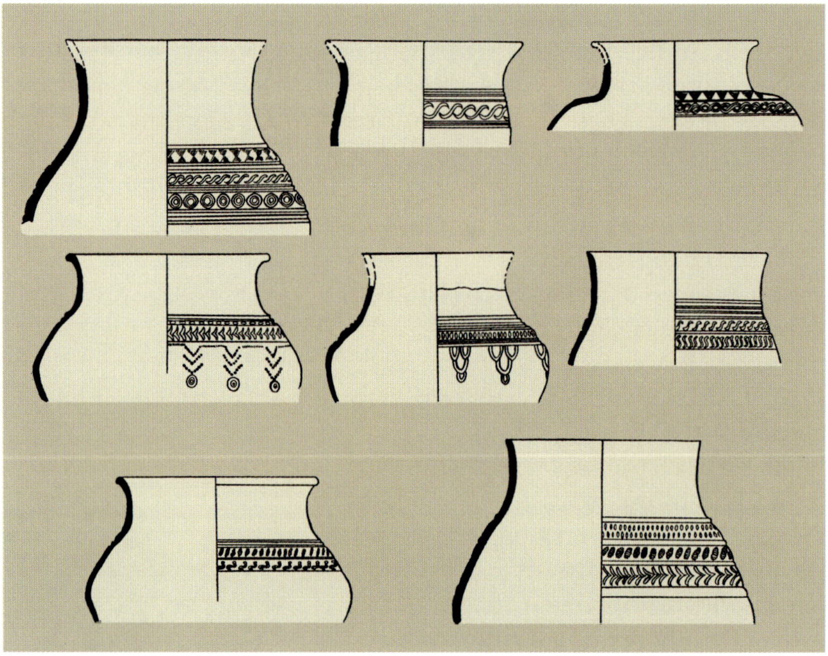

8.21 Selection of stamp-decorated pottery from castros in north-western Iberia.

icons as some kind of territorial marker signifying the power of a lineage over land.

In the context of sculpture we should consider a characteristic structure, best interpreted as a subterranean sauna bath, of which a number are known (8.24, 8.25). Various suggestions have been offered for their significance, from ritual/medical use to being places of initiation for warriors. It was presumably to these structures that Strabo was referring when he wrote that 'some of the peoples who live next to the Duro, it is said, live after the manner of the Laconians—using anointing-rooms twice a day and taking baths in vapours that arise from heated stones, bathing in cold water, and eating only one meal a day' (*Geog.* 3. 3. 6). The vertical entrance slabs are often elaborately carved with a variety of motifs which, it has been suggested, may symbolize the three elements, *fire*, *water*, and *wind* (8.25). However these structures may have functioned, it is evident that they were central to ritual life of the community and remained so into the Roman period.

There is comparatively little direct evidence for exchange between the Castro culture zone and the wider world, though there can be no doubt that gold and tin were exported on a large scale in raw form by sea. The discovery of Galician gold torcs in Celtiberian regions to the east is also an indication of the exchange of elite items between neighbouring polities.

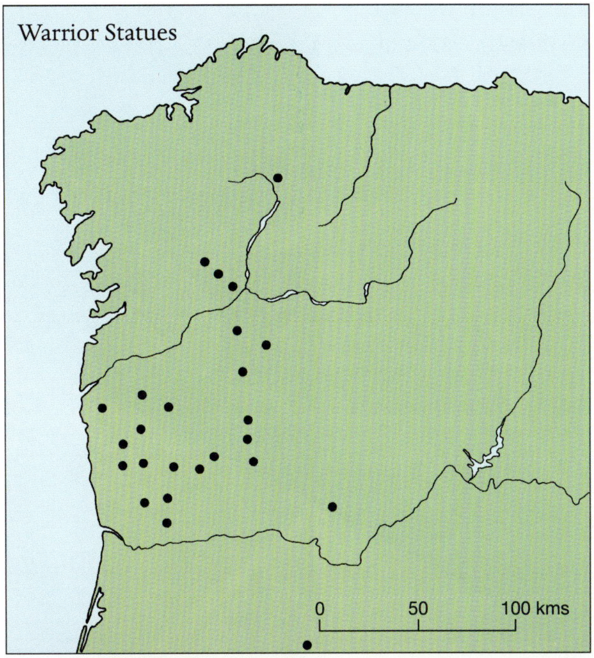

8.22 (*left*) Statue of a warrior from Lezenho, Portugal. He wears a torc around his neck and carries a dagger and circular shield.

8.23 (*top right*) Distribution of warrior statues in north-western Iberia.

8.24 (*above right*) Sauna bath at the castro of Citânia de Sanfins, Paços de Ferreira, Portugal.

8.25 Decorated slabs from the front of sauna baths at Citânia de Briteiros, northern Portugal.

Maritime trade with the south is attested by a scatter of imported materials including Greek and Ibero-Punic coins, Punic pottery, Greek pottery, and rare items of glass, but the volume is slight and little of this material penetrated far from the coast. It remains a strong possibility, therefore, that the imported goods, acceptable to the local population, were of the kind that have left no archaeological trace—things such as fabrics, perfumes, and perhaps spices. That maritime links were maintained along the northern coasts of Iberia as far as Aquitania seems likely. Some evidence for this comes from the distribution of distinctive fibulae with the upturned foot ending in a decorative disc. Fibulae of this general type have been found in some numbers in north-western Iberia and Aquitania. A few also reached the extreme south-west of Britain. Examples, though perhaps local copies, have been found at Mount Batten in Devon and Harlyn Bay in Cornwall. The discovery of dress-fastenings such as these in distant places invites the suggestion that the exchanges might have involved brides.

The overall impression given by the rather scattered data is of a society maintaining itself in a stable but evolving state over a long period of time, little influenced by external contacts. The warrior aristocracy seems to have become important in the later period, but this need not necessarily imply widespread aggression since warrior symbolism might simply be the means of expressing status. In his general description of the peoples of the north-west Strabo says nothing of internecine warfare, but stresses more the competitive nature of warrior existence.

The Armoricans

The Armorican peninsula can be divided into two broad geomorphological zones, the inland regions or Argoat, and the coastal lands or Armor. It was the coasts, with their rich variety of resources, that attracted the largest populations in the first millennium BC. First-millennium settlement in Brittany is still incompletely known, but aerial photography is beginning to show how densely settled the landscape once was. The principal settlement type seems to have been a banked enclosure, sometimes with a ditch outside, of the size that could have protected a family or an extended family. Much larger oppida are known, but those which have been examined are probably no earlier than the middle of the second century BC and are therefore more appropriate to the theme of the next chapter. A special type of enclosure, the cliff castle, is well represented, and its function as a place of refuge in the first century BC is described by Julius Caesar. As the name implies these sites were located on headlands projecting into the sea, and were usually defended by banks and ditches built across the neck of the promontory to prevent unrestricted access from the land. There is no firm evidence for their dating in Brittany, but in the British Isles similar sites were in use in the second half of the first millennium. The rather exposed nature of many of the cliff castles has led to the suggestion that they may have been sited more for religious reasons than for purely domestic purposes.

The material culture of Armorica suggests a stable population evolving gradually over a long period of time and developing its own highly distinctive culture. We have already seen how local potters responded to metalwork imported from west central Europe in the sixth to fourth centuries, copying the general shape of the metal vessels and adapting the decorative motifs of metalwork to suit the ceramic medium. These elegantly ornamented vessels were in use from the sixth to the second centuries throughout much of Lower Brittany and stand out, in contrast, to the styles current in the more easterly regions of the peninsula.

8.26 Stelae of Iron Age date from Brittany.

Two other cultural characteristics—stelae and souterrains—display exactly the same distributional pattern as the decorated pottery. The stelae are standing stones, the surfaces of which were worked, sometimes finely, before the stones were erected to serve as markers in the countryside (8.26, 8.27). Many thousands are known in Brittany, concentrating mainly in the coastal zones. They fall into two main shape categories—tall columnar and squat hemispherical. A small percentage of the surviving columnar stelae were decorated with deeply pecked geometric designs. Eleven are known, concentrating mainly in a restricted area in south-western Finistère. The majority share the same basic decorative concept, with the body of the stone divided into three zones. The top and the base were encircled by repetitive motifs, usually Greek key and running spirals, but sometimes involving chevrons, while the main body of the shaft was variously treated with vertical bands of zigzags and chevrons. A rather different decorated type, involving no less input of effort, are the fluted stelae which are found in much the same region of southern Finistère.

8.27 (*facing*) Iron Age stela at Croas-Men, Lampaul-Ploudalmézean, Finistère. A Christian cross added in the Middle Ages claimed the ancient pagan stone for the new religion.

These remarkable monuments raise a number of fascinating questions. Standing stones are a phenomenon which can be traced back to the Neolithic period, and it could be argued that the basic concept had continued unchanged since then, but the formal style of the decoration is intriguing. The fluted stelae have been compared to the fluted columns of

8.28 (*top*) The souterrain at Lauban, Kerfourn, Morbihan, Brittany. The two shafts led to chambers dug out of the bedrock probably for the purpose of storage.

8.29 (*bottom*) Distribution of souterrains in Brittany.

the classical world, while a decorative zone around the tops of several of the stelae, incorporating Greek key and spirals, is highly reminiscent of the treatment of Ionic columns in Greek temples and in particular the temple at Metapontium in southern Italy. Whilst these formal similarities might well be entirely fortuitous, seen in the context of Greek-inspired trade for tin, the question of there having been direct Mediterranean influence must remain open. Putting aside these provoking uncertainties, the worked stelae of Brittany represent a highly distinctive local response to the desire to control the landscape through monumentalization. Their function is beyond recovery. Some may have been grave markers, but a more likely explanation of their primary function is that they were territorial markers, indicating boundaries of ownership. The fact that many have been moved subsequent to their erection makes detailed locational studies of dubious value. Whatever the contemporary meaning of these remarkable symbols, the fact remains that it would have been difficult to travel far without being very aware of their presence.

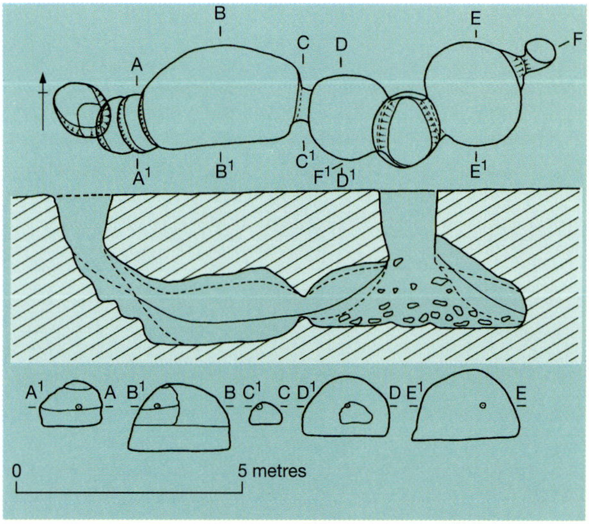

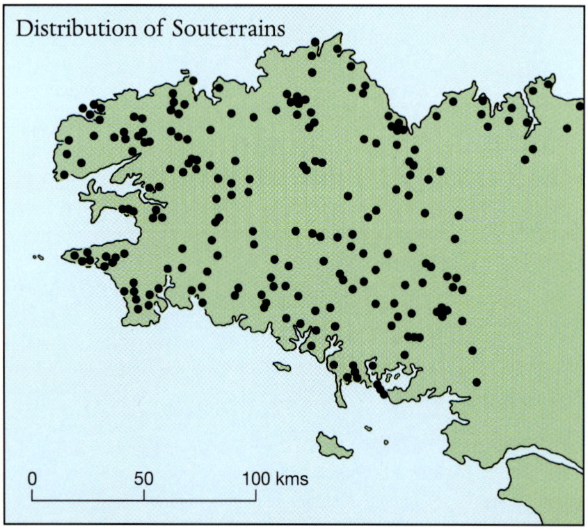

The other distinctive 'artefact' of Iron Age Brittany was the souterrain—an underground chamber associated with settlements (8.28, 8.29). Souterrains were usually tunnelled out of the natural granitic sand by digging a shaft and expanding from the bottom of it by hollowing out a succession of lateral chambers. The precise function of these structures is undefined, but storage, refuge, and ritual have all been considered. The most satisfactory suggestion is that they were constructed primarily for storage of seed grain, placed underground during the liminal period between harvest and sowing to be in the protection of the chthonic deities. If so, then the souterrain would be the western equivalent to the storage pit found extensively in northern France and south-eastern Britain.

Sufficient will have been said to show

that the western part of Armorica—later known as Lower Brittany—was culturally distinct from eastern areas. With their enclosed homesteads, stelae, souterrains, and decorated pottery, the communities living west of the line from the Vilaine to the Baie de Saint-Brieuc shared a lifestyle and visual symbols that gave them a close cultural coherence while distinguishing them from their landward neighbours. Rather like the peoples of north-western Iberia, they were a community apart.

The South-West of Britain

It is convenient to consider the communities of the south-western peninsula of England and south-west Wales together. The two territories were essentially promontories flanking the approaches to the Bristol Channel and the river system of the Severn, the one separated from the mainland by the Cambrian mountains, the other given a degree of isolation by the extensive upland moors of Dartmoor and Exmoor and the forested clay lands between (8.30).

The two peninsulas shared much in common, most notably their settlement patterns. The countryside seems to have been densely settled, the basic units being the family or extended family, each living in a compact defended enclosure. In Cornwall many of these enclosures survived as earthworks and are generally known as 'rounds'. In south-west Wales, where the pattern is similar, they are often called 'raths'. Where excavation has taken place it can usually be shown that the settlements were in continuous occupation over a considerable period of time, usually several centuries. In a few cases, for example at Trevisker in Cornwall, settlements can be shown to have begun in the second millennium BC, while there are many examples of raths and rounds being occupied well into the Roman period and possibly even later. The settlement pattern remained stable over hundreds of years: even the Roman occupation of Britain had very little effect on the indigenous native systems. Another highly visible component of the settlement landscape is the cliff castle (8.31, 8.32) of the type we have already seen in Brittany. They are particularly numerous, in southwestern Britain, and where excavation has taken

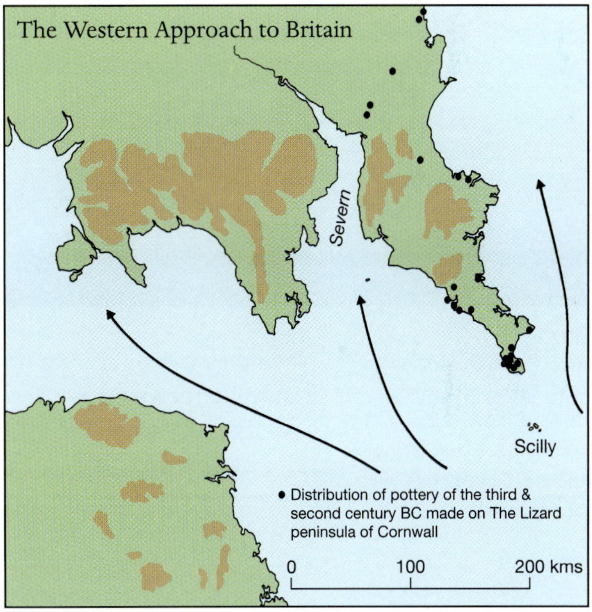

8.30 The peninsulas of south-western Britain, isolated by high land from the rest of the country, and the distribution of Iron Age pottery made on the Lizard peninsula.

8.31 The cliff castle of The Rumps, St Minver, Cornwall—a rocky promontory cut off from the mainland by two lines of earthworks.

8.32 (*facing*) The cliffs at Caerau, St Davids, Dyfed. Three of the headlands are separated from the mainland by banks and ditches. Even allowing that there has been erosion it is difficult to see these 'cliff castles' as defended settlements. It is more likely that the headlands were liminal places between land and sea.

place they can be shown to have been in use during the latter half of the first millennium BC.

Cornwall can also boast underground structures similar to the souterrains of Brittany. They are called *fogous*, but differ from the Breton examples in that they are constructed of stone walls and capstones set below ground in trenches and covered over except for the entrance. The same debates as to function have taken place and uncertainty remains, but an explanation involving the ritual protection of stored agricultural surpluses seems the most likely.

The material culture of the two regions is not particularly rich or distinctive. The Cornish communities made a limited range of pottery. Some of the earlier wares of the fifth–fourth centuries were stamped in a manner closely reminiscent of the contemporary Armorican wares. From the fourth century or thereabouts there emerged a locally made curvilinear ornamented pottery—usually referred to as South-Western Decorated ware—which was manufactured on the Lizard peninsula and widely distributed across south-western Britain. The same style, but with local variations, was adopted by potters working in Devon, Somerset, and elsewhere in the south. The widespread acceptance of the South-

Western Decorated style is interesting in that it suggests a degree of integration between the Cornish communities and the rest of the south-west rather than an exclusivity. The coastal distribution of the Cornish-made vessels outside the cultural territory shows that coastal contacts were maintained, linking the metal-producing area of the south-west to central southern Britain where surpluses of grain and wool were available for exchange.

The evidence, such as it is, suggests that the two south-western peninsulas were culturally distinct from neighbouring areas in terms of their socio-economic systems, but there is nothing to indicate an aggressive desire to symbolize their separateness. It may simply be that the natural geographical divides were sufficient to provide the assurance of isolation.

The North-West of the British Isles

The north-west of Britain, from the coasts of Galloway, through the Western Isles, to Caithness and Sutherland and on to the islands of Orkney and Shetland, was densely settled in the first millennium BC (8.33) and many of the sites, by virtue of their being stone-built, survive today as recognizable monuments in the landscape. It has for some while been conventional to divide them into two broad categories, duns and brochs, duns being drystone-walled enclosures of somewhat irregular plan, while brochs were more usually of circular plan, often with walls in excess of 3 metres in height and with cells built into their thickness. At this simple level of division the duns concentrated on the west coasts and Western Isles while the brochs were the common settlement type of the extreme north-west of Scotland and the Northern Isles. There is, however, a wide overlap between the two in form and distribution, and it is probably simpler to regard them both as varieties of complex round houses.

Sufficient excavation has been carried out in the area to show how the settlements of the region have developed. At the beginning of the millennium, in the Late Bronze Age, the houses tended to be roughly oval in shape, divided internally into a number of cells separated by projecting partitions. Structures of this kind are well represented at Clickhimin and Jarlshof (8.34) on Shetland and are very much within the local tradition which can be traced back to the Neolithic period. What is significant about them is that the emphasis is on the internal space, little trouble being taken to make the outside imposing in any way. From about the sixth century BC structures began to be more impressive and were built to dominate the landscape, the exterior appearance taking on a new impor-

8.33 (*facing*) The distribution of brochs and duns in northern Britain.

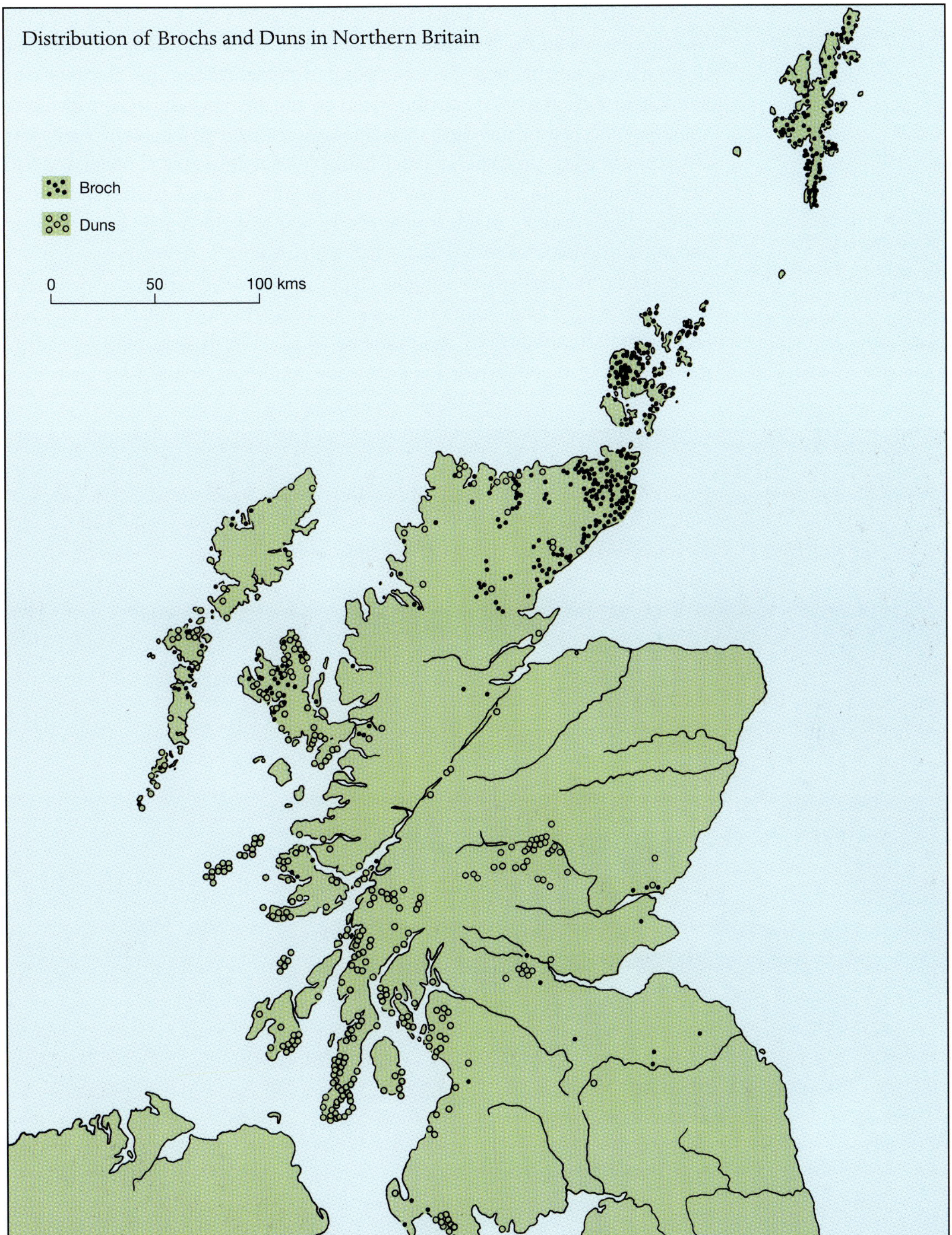
Distribution of Brochs and Duns in Northern Britain
Broch
Duns
0
50
100 kms

tance. Some of the brochs reached tower-like proportions, like the famous broch on the tiny island of Mousa off the mainland of Shetland (8.35) which far outgrew the basic need to provide adequate family living space and a degree of security. Most of the brochs, though impressive structures in their own right, are unlikely to have reached the functionally unnecessary proportions of Mousa. The origin of the broch is still a hotly debated subject, but early examples on Orkney have been dated to 600 BC. At Crosskirk in Caithness the broch was not erected until about 200 BC. Some brochs were still in use centuries later.

Another recurring settlement type is the wheel-house, a circular structure with radial walls or piers dividing the interior into cells and facilitating the roofing of the building (8.36). The type is really a monumentalized and regularized version of the earlier cellular structures of

8.34 Aerial view of Jarlshof at the southern end of Shetland. The promontory was probably continuously occupied from the Late Bronze Age to the late Middle Ages—a period of 2,500 years.

the Late Bronze Age. At Quanterness on Orkney an early house showing many of the characteristics of a wheel-house was dated to *c.*700 BC, but the classic wheel-houses tend to be later, flourishing in the first and second centuries AD.

8.35 The broch on the small island of Mousa off the mainland of Shetland. The broch tower still stands to its original height.

Over much of the region these various types of complex round houses stand in isolation, showing that settlement was dispersed, each house representing a single family, but on Orkney at several sites, most notably the brochs of Gurness and Howe, clusters of houses developed around the outside of the broch tower, the entire complex being protected within an outer wall. At Gurness the settlement could have housed between thirty or forty families by the time of its completion in the late first century BC or early first century AD (8.37, 8.39). The nucleation of settlement evident on Orkney may in part have been a response to a growing population, encouraged by the comparative fertility of the island. Nothing like it is found in the Western Isles or west coast of Scotland.

8.36 The inside of the wheelhouse at Jarlshof, Shetland showing the radial piers and the central area with its large rectangular hearth.

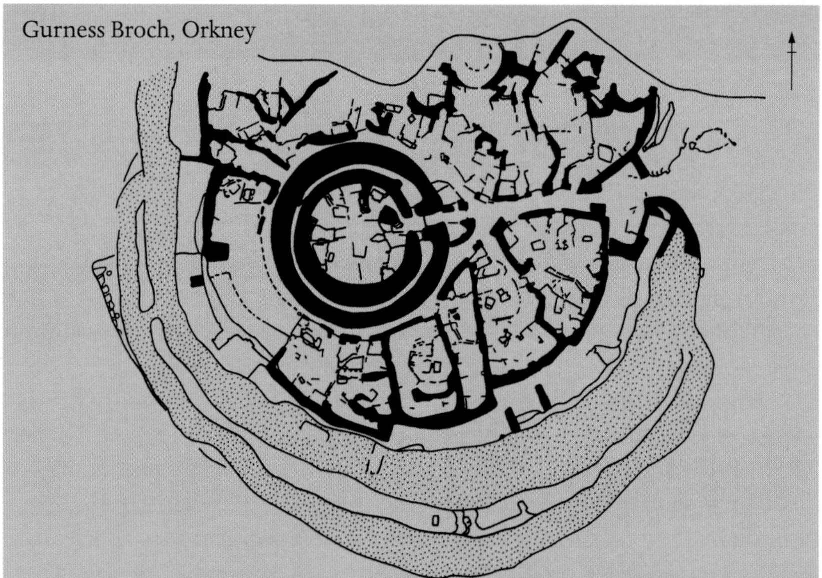

8.37 The broch of Gurness on Orkney is surrounded by a close-packed settlement defended by ramparts. Compare with 8.37.

8.38 Midhowe broch on the island of Rousay, Orkney. The broch is one of several built along the shore of Eynhallow Sound, a resource-rich stretch of protected water.

The general change from inconspicuous cellular buildings, sometimes buried in accumulations of sand or midden material, to upstanding dominant structures, prominently sited, suggests a widespread and socially deep-seated transformation in this part of the Atlantic region in the middle of the first millennium, with dominant structures being the norm until the second century AD. But how should it be interpreted? Aggression or warfare, once considered, seems no longer acceptable as the motivation. Not only are weapons virtually unknown, but the analyses of settlement patterns and landscape potential in areas such as Shetland, where the evidence is well focused, show that the land could have supported a substantially larger population without difficulty. In other words, there was no significant economic stress. The complex round houses are, at their simplest, symbols of dominance in signifying the ability of the family to mobilize labour to create a permanent presence in the wildness of the landscape (8.38). They also proclaim the identity of the

social group by presenting a set of physical structures as a manifestation of values. Seen in this perspective, the great round houses of the north-west perform many of the same functions as the megalithic monuments of the third and second millennia and the even earlier shell middens of the Mesolithic hunter-gatherers.

8.39 (*facing*) The broch of Gurness from the air. Compare with 8.37.

The care lavished on the houses contrasts noticeably with the apparent paucity of the material culture of the region. A basic set of tools, a few beads, and some bronze trinkets are all that survive apart from pottery. However, the pottery of the western part of the region is technically competent and much of it is quite elaborately decorated. Since it is all locally produced the different decorative styles no doubt reflect the expression of identity of the various lineage groups who made and used it. Although there are always dangers in arguing from absence of evidence, the impression given by the surviving material culture of the north-west is that artefacts were not used as significant symbols of identity or status: the efforts of the community were put into architectural expressions.

The Enigma of Ireland

The situation in Ireland in the first millennium BC is unclear. Large numbers of artefacts have been recovered, but usually without details of their contexts surviving. Weapons feature largely, as do luxury items of various kinds, and gold was widely used. From a study of this material it appears that Ireland was in contact with the north-west European exchange networks throughout the Hallstatt C period, but after about 600 BC and until the concepts of La Tène art were introduced around 300 BC there is little evidence that regular exchanges were maintained. After about 300 BC a range of La Tène-inspired artefacts appear, including horse gear, decorated sword scabbards, and other elite items. Stylistic comparisons can be made with contemporary developments in northern Britain, particularly in Yorkshire, but there are hints of some inspiration coming direct from the Continent. What is significant, however, is that vigorous schools of craftsmanship developed, producing finely made prestige goods to fuel the elite systems. A very high percentage of these items ended their lives as ritual deposits in lakes, rivers, or bogs.

The range and quality of elite metalwork available throughout the first millennium BC and into the first millennium AD are sufficient to suggest that much of eastern, central, and northern Ireland was under the domination of an aristocratic warrior elite, and it is within this broad central and eastern zone that the great ritual sites, Tara, Navan, Rathcroghan, and Dún Ailinne, are to be found. The Atlantic-facing lands from Co.

8.40 (*facing*) The spectacularly sited stone fort of Dún Aonghasa on the cliff of Innis Mór, the largest of the Aran Islands in Galway Bay. The wide chevaux-de-frise can be seen outside the outer (third) wall of the fort.

Donegal to Co. Kerry in the west and from Co. Cork to Co. Wexford in the south lie, for the most part, outside this zone of elite dominance and, apart from a few scattered exotic artefacts emanating from the elite zone, lack a distinctive material culture. Thus, although the artefactual evidence is disparate and contextually lacking, it does suggest that Ireland, in the later first millennium BC, divided into two distinctive socio-economic zones.

Within the Atlantic zone there is very little to be said of the contemporary settlement pattern. Two types of settlement potentially belong to this period—cliff castles and stone forts—but dating evidence is sparse in spite of strenuous efforts by Irish archaeologists to resolve the problem. More than 250 cliff castles have been identified. Not one has been satisfactorily dated, but comparisons with south-west Britain and Armorica would suggest that some, at least, are likely to belong to the first millennium BC. The stone forts, mainly found in Co. Clare and Co. Galway, are substantially stone-built homesteads. Many of those which have been excavated were in use in the first millennium AD and may have been built then, but the possibility that the tradition began substantially earlier remains.

At the dramatically sited Dún Aonghasa, high on the cliffs of Aran (8.40), excavations have shown that occupation began in the Late Bronze Age and continued (though not necessarily without a break) into the first millennium AD. The earliest settlement was probably enclosed by a stone wall, rebuilt and modified on a number of subsequent occasions. The present innermost fortifications, 5 metres thick and of equivalent height, representing the final rebuilding, may encase earlier structures going back to the Late Bronze Age. Dún Aonghasa shows something of the complexity of the stone forts which has become apparent only after extensive excavation.

There is much variation among the stone forts of the west, and the distinction between them and sites classified as hillforts in the region is blurred. The hillfort of Mooghaun in Co. Clare, overlooking the Shannon estuary, was a substantial structure with three well-spaced concentric walls, the outermost enclosing 12 hectares. Recent excavations have shown that this outer wall post-dates the beginning of the first millennium BC, but other than that there is little indication of the chronology of the structure or, in the absence of significant traces of occupation, of its function. Its dominant position, commanding the approaches along the Shannon, and the unusually large number of gold artefacts of Late Bronze Age date found in the immediate region, suggest that Mooghaun may have been the focal site in an elite system dominating the area for the first few centuries of the first millennium BC, but thereafter there is little

in the archaeological record to distinguish the region from other parts of the Atlantic zone in Ireland.

The lack of chronological clarity in the settlement archaeology makes generalizations difficult, but if it is accepted that the cliff castles and stone forts began in the first millennium BC, as seems not unreasonable, then the pattern of settlement would be broadly similar to that of south-western and north-western Britain. The lack of an elite, or even a distinctive material culture, suggests that status was proclaimed in other ways: it is tempting to think that the strong, visually-dominant enclosure was one. The nature of the relationship between the Atlantic zone and the zone of elite dominance in the centre, east, and north of the island is yet undefined.

Remote Places and Identity

Sufficient will have been said to demonstrate that there were broad similarities between the settlements of the different regions of the Atlantic zone from Portugal to Shetland. Most notable is the emphasis on strongly defended homesteads and the use of stone to create dominant and monumental structures. While there is much variation from one region to the next, two rather distinctive forms, the cliff castle and the *chevaux-de-frise*, are found throughout the Atlantic zone.

The cliff castles, as we have seen, are little more than natural sea-girt promontories divided from the mainland by one or more systems of banks and ditches. It could be argued that they are obvious places to defend, and wherever there are such promontories defence might be expected. But these places are quite often remote and inhospitable, exposed to extremes of weather and distant from productive land. Yet they were chosen in their hundreds and some were certainly occupied. Could it be that there was some imperative, other than ease of defence, which attracted communities to these places? Perhaps it was the sense of being at the interface between land and ocean where the powers of both could be harnessed: it is not too fanciful to regard cliff castles as liminal places giving access equally to the land and the sea. Such matters are difficult to pursue using only the archaeological data, but continuity back into the Neolithic period, demonstrable at several sites on the Channel Islands and in Brittany, might suggest that such places had a special significance, recognized and respected across time. Similarly, the number of major promontories along the south and west coasts of Iberia were specifically noted by various classical writers as being sacred to the gods. As landmarks for mariners they would have had a special part to play in helping to ensure safe passage. In the medieval period the siting of crosses and even small chapels on promontories served to guide sailors and provided places where propitiatory offerings to the local saint could be made by the fearful and the grateful. It is possible, therefore, that the cliff castles were special places used by the Atlantic communities to help articulate their relationship with the sea.

Another type of distinctive defensive structure appearing throughout the Atlantic region was the *chevaux-de-frise*—a zone of long, angular stones embedded in the ground close together to form an obstacle at the approach to a settlement. Examples are most numerous in north-west Iberia (8.41) but the phenomenon is also known in Wales, Scotland, and Ireland, one of the most dramatic examples being at Dún Aonghasa on Aran. While there can be no doubt that the *chevaux-de-frise* provided an effective deterrent both to horses and to men on foot, greatly slowing their approach, it is quite possible that the boundary may have been more symbolic than functional. The very distinctive nature of this feature and its widespread distribution would suggest that some exchange of specialist knowledge took place between the Atlantic communities. We are, of course, recognizing only the visible stone examples: many more of wood, now rotted, may have once existed throughout western Europe.

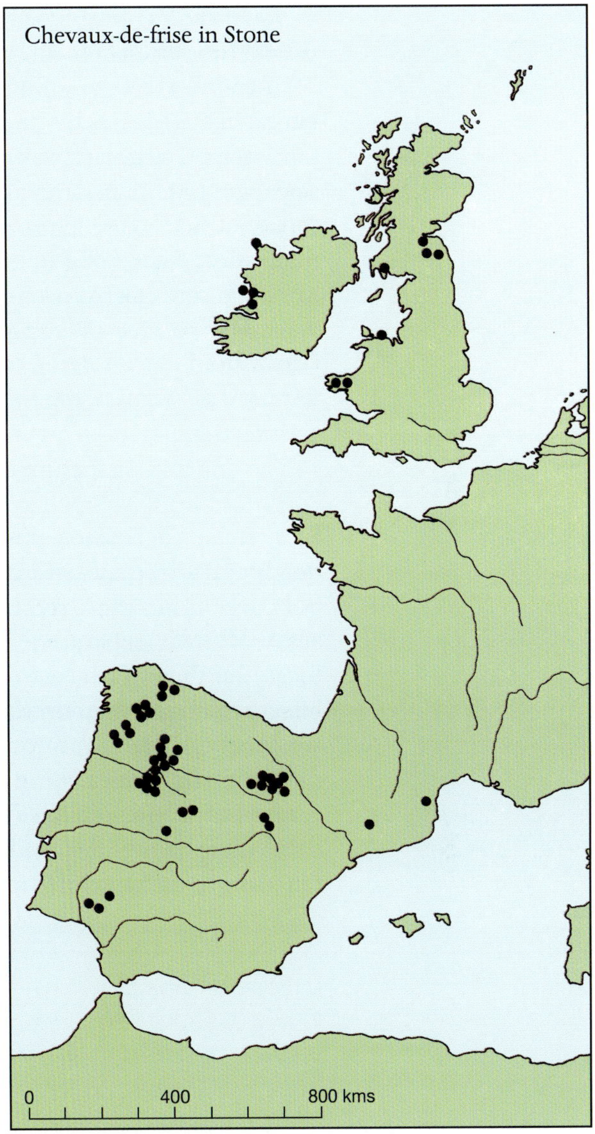

8.41 The distribution of chevaux-de-frises in Europe.

Another similarity of a more subtle type, dimly discernible in the general settlement pattern evidence of Cornwall, south-west Wales, and Caithness in the extreme north of Scotland, is the apparent pairing of settlements—that is, there are recurring instances where two settlements are found close together within larger territories with no other settlements nearby. Without knowing the precise chronologies it is difficult to interpret such patterning, but if these settlements were broadly contemporary it would suggest that we are witnessing a physical manifestation of landholding or inheritance systems comparable to the practice of partable inheritance which was recorded in much later times in Wales.

In addition to the similarities across regions there were also differences. In Galicia a warrior elite system was in operation, and settlement nucleation evidently took place, some of the larger castros becoming sizeable settlements made up of a number of families living closely together. Elsewhere in the Atlantic region, with the exception of limited nucleation developing in Orkney in the first century BC or first century AD, large settlements are not in evidence nor is there any indication of warrior elites. For the most part the settlement in these regions reflects family holdings scattered quite densely in the landscape, the only manifestation of status being the ability of the group to invest in its domestic architecture.

The one linking feature to stand out is the way in which these Atlantic communities developed symbols of their identity—dominant architecture, stelae, decorated pottery—to distinguish themselves from their neighbours. In their comparative isolation they accentuated these symbols over time, their remoteness intensifying the outward and visible signs of their separateness. Thus, it was their common geography, located as they were at the end of the world in like environments, and the effect which that had on social development, that led to the similarities we observe. There was not one identity but a number of identities. This said, the similarities were such that adjacent communities along the Atlantic façade would have found neighbours across the sea more akin in their values, and safer to deal with, than neighbours adjacent on land. Once more the sea joined and the land divided.

9. The Impact of Rome: 200 BC–AD 200

The Roman naval victory over the Carthaginians at the Aegates Islands in 241 BC marked the end of the First Punic War and, with the annexation of Sicily which followed, the beginnings of the empire. The sack of the city of Rome in AD 410 by Alaric's Visigoths, following a long period of decline was its symbolic end. In a brief 650 years Europe had changed out of all recognition. From the wastes of North Africa to the forests of the North European Plain and from the deserts of the East to the Atlantic a single rule of law had been imposed and a network of roads built to facilitate travel from one end of the empire to the other, cutting across natural barriers which had hitherto constrained movement, and drawing all regions, however remote, into a single economic system. Geography had briefly been subdued.

The Conquest of Western Europe

Rome's success in the First Punic War set in train a number of processes which led, with an awful inevitability, to almost four hundred years of aggressive expansion, briefly to be followed by an interlude of comparative peace before the chaos of the final disintegration took hold (9.1).

The immediate effect was on Carthage. Crippled by an oppressive indemnity imposed by the Roman victors, the Carthaginian leadership was unable to give the African mercenaries who had fought with her the rewards they were expecting. The result was a bloody and protracted rebellion. For nearly four years vicious internal wars raged while Rome, as a price for staying neutral, took over the islands of Sardinia and Corsica without opposition. Having lost its Mediterranean possessions, and being restricted on the African continent by powerful native tribes, the ambitious Carthaginians had to look elsewhere to rebuild their fortunes. Where better than Iberia? Close trading relations had been under way with the southern Spanish entrepôts for more than five centuries, and the

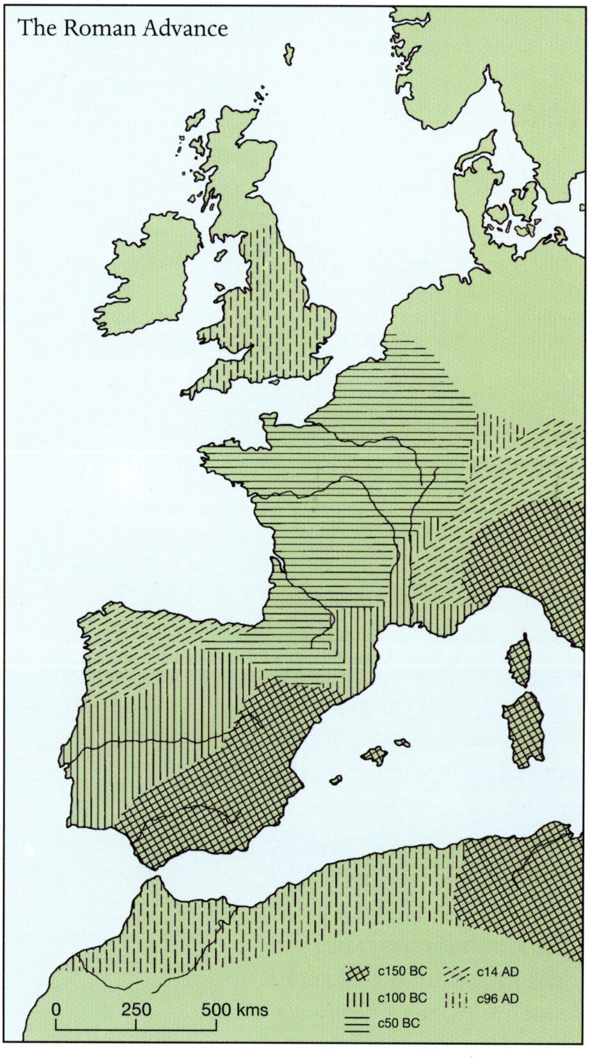

9.1 The progress of the Roman advance across western Europe.

shipping lanes around the Straits of Gibraltar, with Gadir as the focal port, were virtually a Carthaginian monopoly. The long-established intercourse will have left Carthage in no doubt of the mineral wealth of the Peninsula and the great fertility of the Guadalquivir valley. It was a land ripe for conquest.

In 237 a leading Carthaginian general, Hamilcar Barca, was chosen to head the expedition, and in the summer of that year, accompanied by his 9-year-old son Hannibal and his son-in-law Hasdrubal, he sailed for Gadir, taking with him what the historian Polybius has called 'a force adequate for the conquest of Spain', which included, we are told, a hundred elephants. The conquest proceeded apace, but in 229 Hamilcar drowned while covering a retreat following a defeat at Elche near Alicante. Leadership now passed to Hasdrubal, and in the years that followed, with an army of 50,000 infantry and 6,000 cavalry, now supported by two hundred elephants, most of Iberia from the Ebro to the Tagus was brought, either directly by military force or indirectly by means of negotiated treaties, under Carthaginian control. Of crucial importance to the enterprise was the early creation of a naval base and port at Carthago Nova (Cartagena), strategically sited both to be close to the massive silver resources of the south-east and to provide Carthage with a major outlet on the Mediterranean.

The growth of Carthaginian power in the Peninsula was a potential threat to Rome, now intent on establishing dominance of the west Mediterranean. It was also of direct concern to the Greek cities of the Golfe du Lions, led by Massalia which had recently concluded a treaty of mutual friendship with Rome. As the tension began to rise Rome and Carthage signed an agreement to accept the River Ebro as the effective frontier between their two spheres of influence. That was in 226 BC. In 218, as the result of the Carthaginian sacking of Saguntum—a city allied to Rome though in the Carthaginian sphere—war broke out. This, the Second Punic War, was to last in Iberia for twelve years, during which time successive Roman armies engaged the forces of Carthage and in doing so began to learn something of the benefits and difficulties of the Iberian Peninsula.

The end came in 206 when the Roman army commanded by Scipio decisively dispatched the Carthaginian force at Ilipa (Alcalá del Rio) on the Guadalquivir and established the first Roman colony in Iberia at Italica, not far from Seville. The capitulation of Gadir soon after was the symbolic end of Carthaginian hopes in the west, though the war was to drag on for four more years in Africa.

Rome, now the controlling imperial force in Iberia, had been in the Peninsula for only twelve years; it was to take two hundred before the entire land mass was firmly under Roman control. We will return to some aspects of this process as they affect the Atlantic provinces later, but for the moment it is the relevance of the Spanish involvement to the developing story of conquest that concerns us.

By 197 BC Rome commanded the coastal zone of south and east Iberia—a strip between 100 and 200 kilometres wide stretching from the Guadalquivir to the Pyrenees divided, for administrative convenience, into two provinces, Citerior and Ulterior. To maintain the provinces and to conduct the almost continual wars on their inland frontiers it was essential for there to be safe land routes between northern Italy and the Pyrenees through southern France. The dominant power in this crucial corridor lay in the hands of the Greek cities, and with each of these Rome maintained good relations. The route, however, was none too safe, particularly where the western Alps came close to the sea in the vicinity of Nicaea (Nice). For the hill tribes living there Roman convoys using the narrow coastal route were welcome prey. In 189 BC a Roman governor travelling to Spain with a force of 7,000 men was attacked and killed. Another governor died, possibly in similar circumstances, a few years later, in 173. During this time Ligurian pirates menaced the seas, and so serious was the threat that a Roman squadron of ten ships had to be dispatched to deal with them. The problems gradually got worse, with Massalia calling increasingly on Rome's help. The successive interventions culminated in a major military campaign mounted between 125 and 121 BC against the Celtic tribes of the Rhône valley. It was a turning point: thereafter Rome stayed, to set about annexing the entire coastal zone and large tracts of the hinterland from which they created the province of Gallia Transalpina. As a result the whole of Gaul was opened up to Roman entrepreneurs, and the great natural routes, along the Rhône to the north and the Aude / Garonne to the Atlantic, became busy corridors for Roman commerce. The next sixty years saw the consolidation of the Roman hold over trade, with further territorial expansion along the two major routes (below, pp. 385–6).

It was during this time that the ever-present threat of barbarian attack from the north, a fear seared on the Roman soul after the devastation wrought by the Celts in 390 BC, became frighteningly real. A confederation of tribes from the North European Plain, led by the Cimbri and Teutones, having caused havoc in central Europe burst into southern Gaul in 109 BC, to be joined by several dissident Celtic tribes. Over the next four years successive Roman armies were severely mauled while Rome itself trembled at the prospect of imminent attack. In the event, a reorganized army led by Gaius Marius managed to contain the situation in the north and in two successful battles, the first near Aquae Sextiae in Provence in 102 and the second at Vercellae in northern Italy in 101, the Teutones and Cimbri were successively beaten. It had been a damaging period for Roman commercial interests in Gaul and a frightening reminder to Rome that a new northern barbarian threat could suddenly emerge at any time. The fear offered a powerful tool to those with the wit to manipulate it.

Such a man was Julius Caesar. For a number of reasons, among them personal financial problems, political expediency, and pure ambition, Caesar needed a theatre of war in which to operate. Given such an opportunity he could mould a large and loyal army, demonstrate to an admiring populace his already proven skills as a military commander, and add new territories to the empire. More to the point, in doing so he could acquire a personal fortune. In 59 BC he used his consulship to engineer for himself a five-year command in the provinces of Cisalpine Gaul and Illyricum; from either of these regions, as close to Rome as it was possible to be, he could find the action he craved.

The opportunity came in 58 BC. The Helvetii from Switzerland were planning to migrate to western France, and at the same time news came that a Germanic force from the Upper Rhine led by Ariovistus was threatening a Gaulish tribe, the Aedui, who were allies of Rome. Caesar was able to present this as a direct threat to the security of Rome, playing on the Mediterranean fear of the northern barbarians and arguing that the movement of the Helvetii would cause instability in the region, allowing Germans to flood in. His own summary of the situation, which no doubt he proclaimed forcefully to the senate, was that Gaul was poised—the only way to prevent it from becoming German was to make it Roman. His opinion carried conviction. In spring he moved with his army into Transalpina to engage first the Helvetii, then Ariovistus. Thereafter he was to campaign annually in Gaul, with short sorties into Britain and Germany, until 51, by which time he could claim the territory conquered.

The conquest of Gaul took a surprisingly short time given the size of the country—about the same area as Iberia—but the landscape was far less divided and the through routes more accessible. Moreover, the tribes of Gaul, at least of the centre, had been softened up to Roman ways through decades of contact. At first the only serious opposition came from the maritime tribes (as Caesar refers to them) stretching from Armorica to the Rhine, and from the Belgae between the Seine and the Rhine, but in 52 a serious revolt broke out in the centre, and for a while everything was in balance until Caesar was able to destroy the focus of resistance at Alesia and take the Gaulish war leader Vercingetorix captive.

After eight years of war, during which hundreds of thousands of Gauls had been slaughtered or sold as slaves, the country was exhausted. Its assimilation into the Roman empire was not completed until 12 BC.

In 49 BC the Roman world was plunged into civil war by Caesar's defiance of tradition in leading his army across the Rubicon. Five years later, on the Ides of March 44 BC, he was stabbed to death at the base of Pompey's statue in Rome, unleashing a terror which was to last for another fifteen years. Eventually, in 31 BC, of the various contenders for power only Octavian remained. Four years later, in 27 BC, he assumed the title of *Princeps* and the name of Augustus.

As post-war reconstruction got under way Augustus turned his attention to the frontiers. The first priority was that the remaining north-west corner of Iberia should be brought under control. This done, Augustus could begin to consolidate Gaul. Roads were built and a census taken as a prelude to imposing an efficient tax system. Finally, in 12 BC, when all was in place, at Lugdunum (Lyons) at the confluence of the Rhône and Saône, an altar was dedicated to Rome and Augustus symbolizing the birth of the newly organized provinces.

Caesar's brief campaigns in Britain in 55 and 54 BC are open to various interpretations. At one level he was playing to the Roman gallery by crossing the ocean and setting foot in a land of mystery, but curiosity, not least about the rumoured mineral wealth of the islands, may have provided an incentive. Limited conquest might have been an option, but in the event he left after having established some kind of treaty relations with the Trinovantes, and probably other tribes, in the region north of the Thames.

There matters rested throughout the Civil War and its aftermath, and by the time Gaul had been reorganized Rome's acquisitive attentions had turned to Germany and elsewhere. It was therefore not until AD 43, at the command of the Emperor Claudius, that the legions landed in southern Britain to complete what Caesar had begun ninety years before. The initial intention seems to have been to take control only of the more socially and economically advanced south-east. This was achieved within a year or two of the landing, and a frontier zone established along the Severn–Trent axis backed by a military road—the Fosse Way—running from Lyme Bay to the Humber estuary. But troublesome tribes in the west Midlands, Wales, and the north caused recurrent problems requiring continuous military intervention. Gradually the armies were drawn into Wales and further and further into the north, until by AD 84 the military grip had reached the foothills of the Grampian Mountains. Only the north-west of Scotland, the Western and Northern Isles, and Ireland remained free. Within a few years of 84 the withdrawal of troops from the Province required a retreat from the far north to more easily managed frontiers alternating between the Tyne–Solway line (Hadrian's Wall) and the Clyde–Forth line (the Antonine Wall).

The Roman conquest of the Atlantic provinces had begun in 218 BC and ended in AD 84. As the devastation of conquest passed on so the wounds healed, though seldom without recurring revolts, and peace ensued. The disparate parts of the empire were held together as a single system by the power and authority of Rome, and Roman ways were everywhere adopted. But for some, living in the remote fringes against the Atlantic, the façade of romanization was slight. In these regions indigenous systems remained strong, requiring little from the Roman world. Their means of communication remained the sea.

Iberia: The Conquest of the West

The varied geography of Iberia has created dramatic contrasts between regions, and this in its turn has affected social and economic development. Contrast, for example, the energetic urban life of the Guadalquivir valley, with its roots in the Late Bronze Age or even earlier, invigorated by contact with Phoenician and Greek culture and benefiting from the lush productivity of the plain, with the remote, mountainous north. At the beginning of the first century AD the south and east had enjoyed the benefits of Roman urbanism for two centuries. Poets of international standing had been reared here and soon the area was to produce an emperor. Yet of the opposite end of the Peninsula at this time Strabo could write: 'Northern Iberia, in addition to its ruggedness, not only is extremely cold, but lies next to the ocean, and thus has acquired its characteristic of inhospitality and aversion to intercourse with other countries; consequently it is an exceedingly wretched place to live in' (*Geog.* 3. 1. 2). This is, admittedly, seeing geography through the jaundiced eyes of a Mediterranean, but like all caricatures it has an element of truth. The contrasts between Atlantic-facing and Mediterranean-facing Iberia were stark, and

9.2 (*facing*) Stages in the Roman conquest of Iberia.

greatly affected both the progress of the Roman armies and the veneer of romanization that followed in their wake.

The conflict between Carthage and Rome in Iberia left the Romans in full control of the culturally advanced Mediterranean coastal zone, and in particular the highly fertile valley of the Guadalquivir which was to become the province of Baetica under the early empire—one of the most productive regions in the whole of the Roman world (9.2). To the north-west, roughly from the valleys of the Guadiana to the Douro, with the Tagus as its centre, lay the territory of the Lusitani, while in the north-east, from the Ebro to the Eastern Meseta, the various tribes known collectively as Celtiberi held sway (9.3). These two powerful tribal groupings were the neighbours of Rome's first Spanish provinces, but many more smaller units, known by their individual tribal names, existed around the still-vaguely defined frontiers. It was from this unstable periphery that attacks came, prompting many engagements, from skirmishes to significant campaigns, as successive Roman governors attempted to gain control in the fifty years or so following the defeat of the Carthaginians.

Rome's involvement in the west began almost immediately with an attack by the Lusitani in 194 BC. The Roman army counter-attacked and a temporary peace was established, but it was ineffective and in 179 a major campaign had to be mounted. The army thrust north, across the Guadiana and Tagus, and heavily mauled the Vaccaei occupying the Middle Douro valley. The aim of the operation seems to have been partly to display Rome's strength but principally to drive a

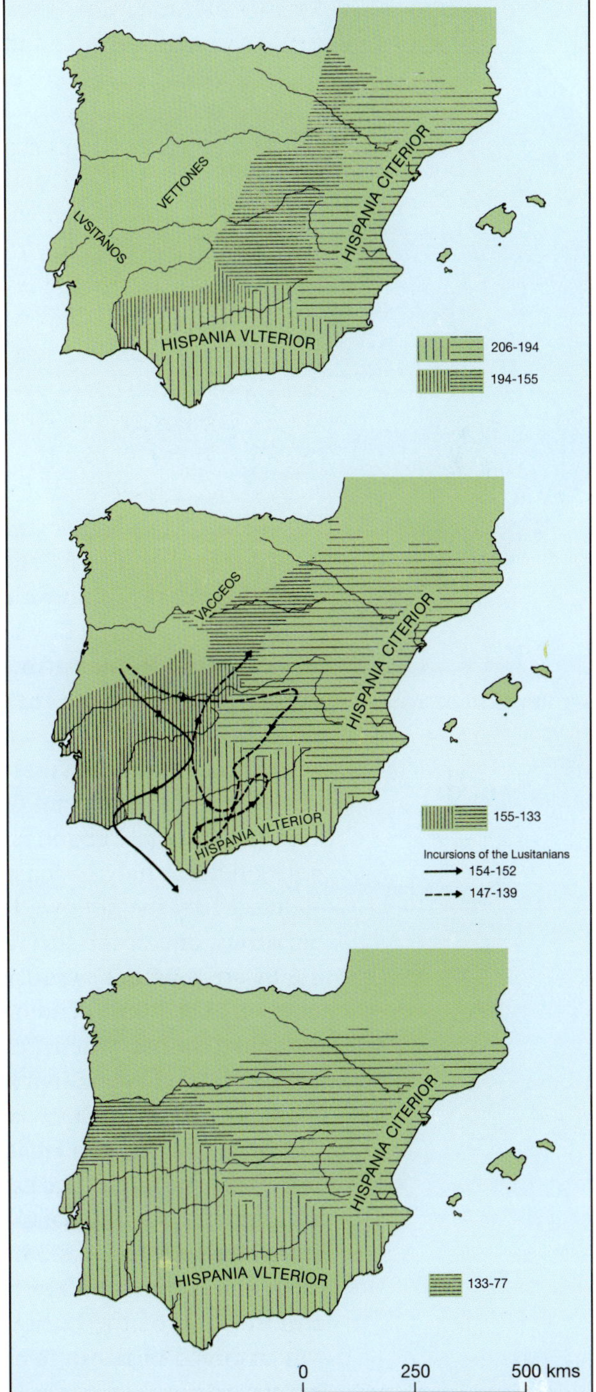

The Roman Conquest of Iberia 206–77 BC

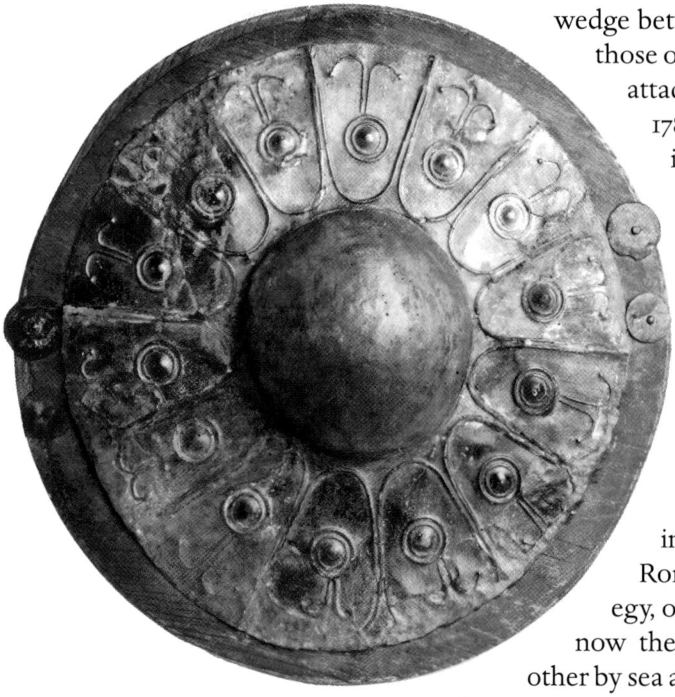

9.3 Iberian shield from the cemetery of Griegos, Teruel.

wedge between the maritime tribes of the west and those of the interior. This done, the Lusitani were attacked and some kind of treaty concluded. In 178 a similar treaty was signed with the Celtiberi in the east, establishing an uneasy peace lasting for more than two decades.

From 155 to 133 BC Rome was almost constantly at war with both the Lusitani and Celtiberi—a bloody conflict which ended only with the capture of the Celtiberian stronghold of Numantia. The Lusitani began their raids again in 155. This time they were the more effective by being better co-ordinated and did much damage to the Romans, culminating in the defeat of the governor in 151. The Roman response was to develop a pincer strategy, one force moving by land through what are now the provinces of Badajoz and Cáceres, the other by sea along the Algarve coast—the first time that the Roman army ventured on the Atlantic. The campaign was successful and brought the Lusitani to negotiate a peace. But, on the pretext of offering them new land to settle, many tribesmen were rounded up and slaughtered. Other acts of Roman duplicity followed, with the result that 9,000 Lusitani died and some 20,000 were sold as slaves. The treachery of these actions shocked even Rome, and on his return as a private citizen to Italy, Galba, the governor responsible, was impeached.

In the fury that followed the Lusitani were led by a brilliant war leader Viriathus, one of the survivors of the massacre. From 147 to his death in 138 by an assassin's sword Viriathus conducted a highly successful campaign against Rome, leading raids deep into the province of Ulterior. The Roman response, when it came, was to force the theatre of conflict north between the Guadalquivir and the Guadiana and to separate the Lusitani from the Celtiberi who were now also in revolt against Rome. This they did by constructing a military road between the upper reaches of the Guadiana and Tagus and then thrusting north, devastating the territories of the Vettones and Callaici, while another Roman army moved south from the Upper Douro. Mindful of the importance of the sea, ports like Chipiona at the mouth of the Guadalquivir were made ready. The effective isolation of the Lusitani from allies to the east was a serious blow which forced Viriathus to negotiate. It was at this moment that the assassin struck.

With Rome victorious the political geography of the west began to change. Large numbers of tribesmen were trans-shipped to other parts of Spain and settled there, while Lusitanian territory as far north as the Guadiana was added to the province of Ulterior. The huge tract of land north of the Guadiana to the Douro was maintained under a lighter hold as a buffer against the still-hostile, and largely unknown, north. It was a temporary measure while preparations were made for a new northern campaign.

In 138 BC the governor Decimus Brutus took to the field, having first established a major supply port at the mouth of the Tagus at Olisippo (Lisbon). His prime aim was to attack the Callaici of Galicia who had sent support to Viriathus, but there can be little doubt that the mineral wealth of the region provided an added incentive. His success was marked by the enormous value of the spoils which he acquired and the fact that during his brief campaigns he claims to have taken 6,000 prisoners and killed 50,000 tribesmen. All the land south of the River Mondego in central Portugal was now in Roman hands, and through middlemen and traders the gold and tin of the north-west could easily be accessed.

The year 133 BC, when Numantia fell, marks a lull in the Roman annexation of Iberia and is the beginning of an intensified period of economic and social unrest in Rome which was to last for a century, until Octavian emerged triumphant from the Battle of Actium in 31 BC. Although Iberia was drawn into the international strife of this protracted period of upheaval the west remained remote from the main theatre of activity in the south and east of the Peninsula, but it did not remain at peace.

A decade of raiding in Lusitania culminated, in 61 BC, when the new governor, Julius Caesar, decided to take an active hand. His initial campaign against dissident tribesmen between the Tagus and the Douro was successful in restoring order, and led to an interesting minor action when he was forced to use ships from Gadir to help dislodge dissidents who had taken refuge on the Ilhas Berlengas off the Portuguese coast. Once the situation had been stabilized Caesar thrust northwards into Galicia. Using the fleet in support he reached the extreme north-west and took Brigantium (La Coruña), before returning with a welcome volume of booty. No attempt seems to have been made to establish a hold on the territory. The continued instability of the west is witnessed by the fact that there were three Lusitanian revolts in the next thirty years, in 54, 36, and 35 BC, though how serious the disturbances were is unclear.

One of the first tasks which Augustus took on after becoming *Princeps* was to complete the conquest of the north-west. To do this effectively would greatly reduce the number of troops needed there for use elsewhere, and would lessen the potential danger of revolt among the Aquitani north of the Pyrenees with whom the tribes of northern Iberia maintained contact, no doubt using the sea as the principal means of communication.

The two main tribes in the northern mountains were the Cantabri and the Austores. Campaigning began in 29 and 28 BC with attacks deep into enemy territory and a determined attempt to subdue the Vaccaei, one of the powerful tribes immediately to the south. The difficult mountain warfare continued, including an advance into Galicia, until 24 BC, by which time Augustus felt justified in claiming a triumph. But the tribes were far from cowed and revolts broke out in 24, 22, 19, and 16 BC. The troubles in 19 were sufficiently serious to require the firm hand of Agrippa, one of Augustus' top generals, to bring the recalcitrant rebels to submission.

The conquest of the west and north of Iberia took a long time to achieve. In many ways it is surprising that there was little sustained effort to bring these distant regions under control and to make the ocean the frontier, especially in view of the mineral wealth of the region. No doubt pressing events elsewhere were given priority. Had the Romans been more prepared to use the Atlantic conquest could have been achieved with less effort, but their lack of experience of tides, combined with the fierceness of the ocean in these parts, made them reluctant to develop the full potential of the sea as a major line of advance in spite of tentative efforts to do so. Roman commanders were happier to trust their troops to the certainties of land travel than to the impetuous ocean.

The Mineral Wealth of North-West Iberia Under the Romans

The Elder Pliny served as procurator of the province of Citerior in about AD 72–4. During this time it is probable that he visited the gold-mines of Asturias which, he tells us, produced the bulk of the gold coming from Spain (9.4). His long description of gold-mining (*Nat. Hist.* 33) may well have been based on his first-hand observation of the mines of Las Médulas, where vivid evidence of the activities still survives (9.5, 9.6). One of the principal methods of bulk extraction involved the driving of deep tunnels beneath the gold-bearing alluvial terraces so that the rock, gravel, and sand collapsed into the voids beneath, fragmenting the compacted material and freeing the flakes of native gold. On the hills above large water tanks were constructed fed by springs and aqueducts, while below, funnelling away from the tumble of smashed rock, was a battery of plank-lined channels filled with heather. At the appropriate moment the sluices of the upper tanks were opened and water gushed through the broken deposits, washing out the gold which was captured in the vegeta-

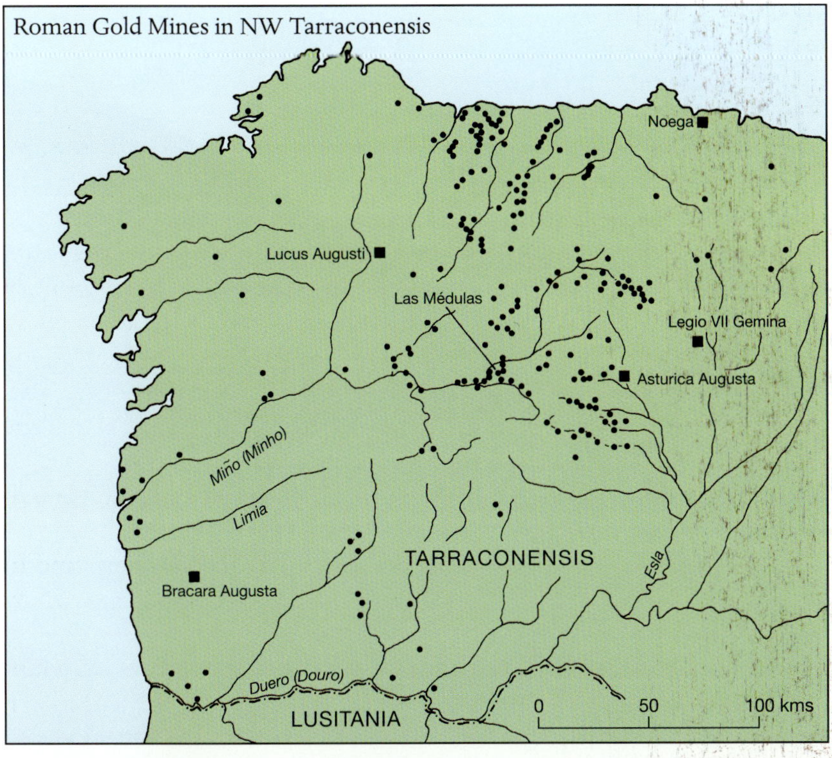

9.4 Roman gold mines in north-western Iberia.

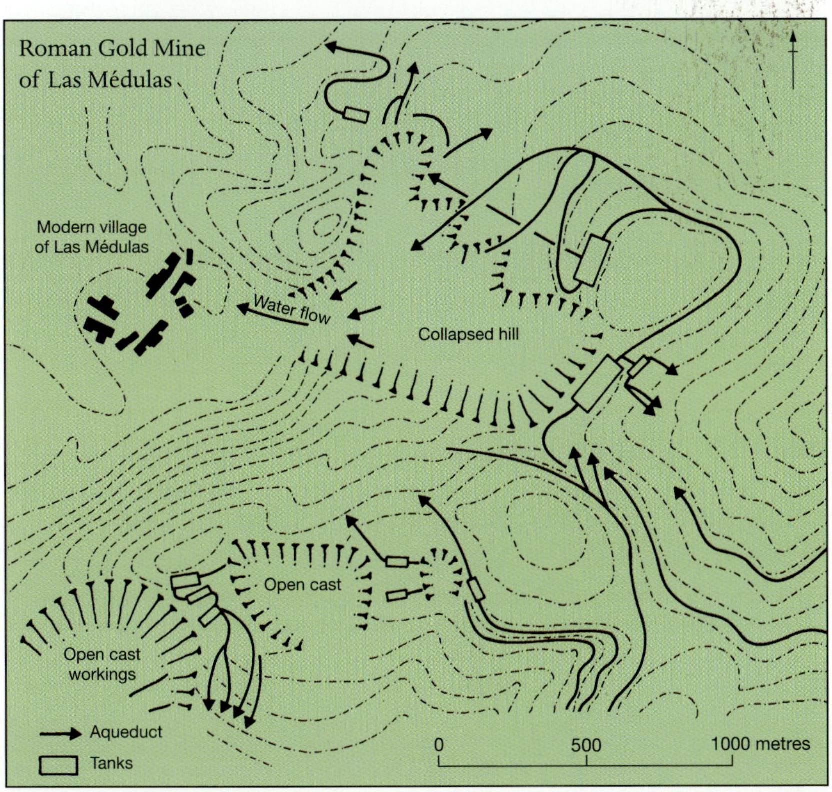

9.5 The Roman gold mine of Las Médulas showing the mine workings and the water tanks and aqueducts constructed to provide a flow of water to wash out the gold.

tion-filled channels. After drying out, the plant material was burned and the resulting ash washed on a bed of turves to concentrate the flakes of pure gold. Pliny also mentions that gold was recovered from deep mines where nuggets were found, some weighing as much as 10 pounds. The extracted rock from these workings was crushed, washed to concentrate it, and fired so that the gold would melt and gather in the furnace.

9.6 (*facing*) The Cabrera valley in the Cantabrian mountains of northern Spain. The site of one of the prolific gold mines worked in the Roman period.

Pliny concludes his detailed account by noting that, 'according to some authorities Austuria, Galicia, and Lusitania produce twenty thousand pounds weight of gold in a year, the former supplying the largest amount'. This is hardly to be doubted given that archaeological survey has identified more than 230 individual mining sites. So rich were the deposits that to prevent the market being flooded the senate placed restrictions on annual production levels. The gold from the region was taken to the provincial capital of Asturica Augusta (Astorga) and thence was transported by a road (still known as Camino de la Plata) through Emerita and Hispalis to the port of Gadir for trans-shipment to Rome.

By the time that Pliny was writing the mines had been under Roman control for ninety years, and it is clear that Roman mining and hydraulic technology was being used. Nonetheless many of the technical terms used in his description are evidently native words reflecting a continuity of tradition which must go back to Bronze Age times, if not before.

Silver was also obtained from the western regions from Galicia and from workings at Vipasca in Lusitania, where copper was mined as well under imperial authority. The most prolific deposits of silver, however, were found in the Sierra Morena and near Carthago Nova in the south.

Little is known of the production of tin, though Pliny writes of it being found in many parts of Iberia, particularly in Lusitania and Gallaecia (the north-west). While tin may have been obtained from alluvial deposits, as it was in the prehistoric period, mines are also known in Cantabria and Asturia. Production must have been on a massive scale, since Spain was the main tin-producer for the empire at least until the third century.

Finally we must mention iron. Cantabrian ore was famous. Pliny writes of a mountain composed of ore and Strabo tells us that ore from Cantabria was transported down the Ebro to Dianium, where it was smelted and forged.

How metal production was organized in the pre-Roman period is impossible to say, but the communal effort required to produce the sheer quantity that came from the region implies some form of control, perhaps at clan level. Once Rome had established authority over the area all rights to metal resources were claimed by the state, which then arranged for the deposits to be worked. An example of this is provided by the mines of Vipasca (Aljustrel) in Lusitania, where a series of bronze plaques record the organization of the silver and copper workings at the time of Hadrian. It appears that the mines and their installations, as well as the town, all belonged to the state and were under the direct control of the imperial procurator. A person who wanted a mining concession could obtain one after first paying an occupation tax. The value of the ore deposit was assessed and the lessee had to undertake to guarantee the state half of the agreed value either by paying over the cash or by giving some other form of security. If he then worked the mine for a continuous period of six months his licence was confirmed. In this way members of the local population, whose ancestors may have worked the lodes for generations before the Roman occupation, were able to retain a stake in their land. The regulations also contain other details of the organization of the mining works, including penalties for theft of ore by slaves or freemen. Most of the facilities of the town, including the baths, the fulling works, the barber's shop, and so on, were also run by individuals under state concessions.

The organization of the Metallum Vipascene offers a fascinating example of how even remote areas were brought firmly within the Roman administrative system. Even the most isolated community was subject to Roman taxation and Roman law, and the infrastructure necessary to both was put firmly into place. Thereafter it was up to the local population how much of the Roman value systems to accept and adopt. Outside the newly established towns, created as an essential part of the state infrastructure, the degree to which romanization penetrated the west varied considerably from region to region.

Romanization in Western Iberia

Under Augustus Iberia was divided into three provinces, Tarraconensis, Baetica and Lusitania, which were further subdivided into a number of *conventi* (judicial districts), each with an urban centre where the systems of taxation and justice were administered. In western Iberia (9.7) the Douro formed the provincial boundary between Lusitania in the south and the north-western extremity of the much larger province of Tarraconensis.

The principal town of the west, and the capital of Lusitania, was Augusta Emerita (Mérida), founded by Augustus as a veteran colony following the conquest of Galicia. Its great strategic and economic importance lay in its position commanding the crossing of the main north–south road—the Camino de la Plata (which effectively marked the inland limit of western Iberia) and the Guadiana. Of the other *conventus* capitals, Pax Iulia (Beja) and Scallabis (Santarém) were probably established by

Julius Caesar, the latter on the site of a native settlement overlooking the Tagus, while the three northern towns Lucus Augusti (Lugo), Bracara Augusta (Braga), and Asturica Augusta (Astorga) were all, as their names imply, Augustan foundations. After the initial Augustan impetus the towns developed gradually. It was not until the Flavian period, in the late first century, that a new wave of urban regeneration can be seen which manifests itself in a campaign of monumental building throughout the west.

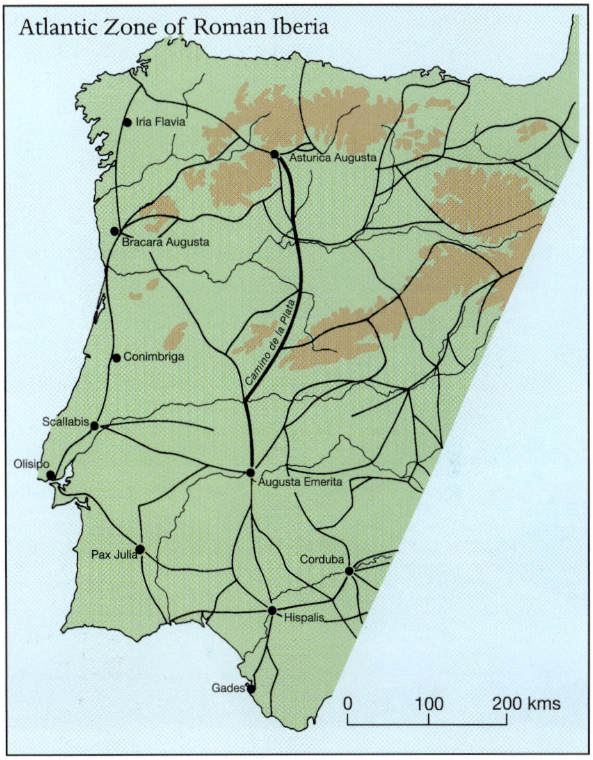

9.7 The Atlantic zone of Roman Iberia.

It is not yet possible to offer a balanced assessment of the impact of Roman urbanization in western Iberia, largely because few of the towns have been excavated on any scale, but at Conimbriga near Coimbra, in the valley of the Mondego, the Roman city is uncluttered by more recent building and extensive excavations have been possible (9.8). As the *-briga* element in its name implies, the site was probably a native settlement beginning in the pre-Roman period. In Augustan times a new urban plan was imposed, which was modified in the Flavian period when a number of the buildings, including the forum, were reconstructed on a much grander scale. The public buildings, including the public baths built in the early second century and the private houses with their fine mosaics and elaborate gardens well supplied with flowing water, leave little doubt that the inhabitants eagerly embraced all the luxuries which Roman urban life had to offer.

It was in the north-west, in the region where the castros had dominated the landscape for many centuries, that the old ways persisted. Hilltop enclosures continued to be principal forms of nucleated settlement, but changes brought about by contact with the Roman world are now evident. New urban settlements, owing much to large established native traditions, developed to provide social, administrative, and religious functions for the larger community, evenly spaced within the landscape about a day's journey from each other. The Citânia de Sanfins is an extensively excavated example of such a site (9.9). It is more than 15 hectares in extent, with its interior divided by a fairly regular grid of main streets. Each *insula* was subdivided, often into four plots each of some 200–300

9.8 (*above*) The Roman town of Conimbriga. In the centre (right) is the temple reconstructed in the Flavian period over the early Augustan temple. The baths at the top left are Trajanic. The baths in the centre below the temple are late Roman. Left of them are rich houses with peristyle gardens.

9.9 (*right*) The hilltop town of Citânia de Sanfins, Paços de Ferreira, Portugal. The defences enclose an area of 15 ha. The ordered internal planning divides the settlement into eighteen rectangular insulae each divided into household units. Although the regularity of the planning was inspired by Roman practice the individual houses are, for the most part, built to the native circular plan.

square metres containing four or five domestic buildings, usually circular, arranged around a communal yard. These complexes probably represent extended family units. The ordered grouping of four such family groups to an *insula* and the arrangement of the *insulae* in larger 'neighbourhood' groupings seem to reflect the lineage system made manifest in the urban plan. If each extended family numbered between ten and twenty persons then the population could have been as large as 3,000.

In Citânia de Sanfins no evident public buildings have been identified, but several public open spaces were provided. At Citânia de Briteiros, however, an unusually large circular building, 11 metres in diameter, was set apart from the family units. Stone benches built around the interior walls suggest that it might have been a meeting-house of some kind, possibly for an assembly of elders. Many of these urbanized castros continued to serve as central places throughout the Roman period. Citânia de Briteiros was still in active occupation at the end of the fourth century.

The urban arrangement within Citânia de Sanfins vividly demonstrates that the lineage system of the pre-Roman period survived throughout Roman times. This is also clear from epigraphic evidence. Over three hundred inscriptions are known recording the names of clans (*gentes*, *gentilitates*), invariably ending in *-um* or *-on*. These clans were subdivisions of a larger social group, the *gens*. An inscription from Asturica Augusta, referring to AD 27, records the names of two *gentilitates* and that of the *gens* to which they belonged. Other inscriptions naming individuals often add the name of the *gentilitas* after the person's filiation, thus Segontius Talavi filius Talabonicum. It may have been names of this kind that Pliny was recalling when he commented on the barbarous names of the peoples of the north-west.

9.10 A *tessera hospitalis* in the form of a hand. These small inscriptions record contracts of friendships between families. From Botorrita, Zaragoza.

Another pre-Roman social survival was *hospitium*—that is, reciprocal hospitality agreed between two communities and formally recorded on inscribed tablets exchanged between the participants (9.10). The inscription from Asturica Augusta noted above was one such. This pattern of formal binding hospitality clearly goes back far into the pre-Roman period. The treacherous use which Roman commanders made of native reliance on the bond of hospitality is ample witness of this. The persistence of *hospitium* into the second and third centuries AD in the north-west is a firm indication that pre-Roman social systems and traditions remained strong centuries after the conquest.

To what extent the persistence of native social structures and a marked preference for traditional settlement forms in the north-west were the result of a deliberate rejection of the attributes of romanization or were simply a feature of remoteness is unclear. The region seems to have received no significant influx of population from the Mediterranean world, and so long as taxes were paid and the population remained placid there was no need for provincial administrators to take much interest in the region: it could simply be left to generate a steady flow of valuable metals. Thus the remoteness of the region and the native disinclination to embrace the Roman value system combined to ensure that the traditional ways remained strong throughout the Roman period.

While it is true that the road system was of crucial importance for the movement of raw materials and personnel throughout the Peninsula, there is ample evidence to show that the Atlantic remained an important thoroughfare. Gades (as Gadir was called by the Romans) was still the major Atlantic port. 'Here', wrote Strabo, 'live the men who fit out the most and largest merchant-vessels, both from Our Sea and the outer sea' (*Geog.* 3. 5. 3). Among the commodities which they carried would have been the huge quantities of olive oil produced in the valley of the Guadalquivir between Cordoba and Seville. Baetic oil was transported throughout the Roman world, carried in its distinctive globular amphorae (known as Dressel 20 after the scholar who classified them). Much of the output went to Rome, where a mountain of sherds, called Monte Testaccio, on the banks of the Tiber mark the spot where some 40 million amphorae were offloaded and decanted. The same type of amphorae, presumably once carrying oil, are found throughout western France and Britain. Some oil may have been transported to Narbo and then overland to the Gironde, but for the bulk of the trade it is more likely that ships from Gades sailed direct to the western Gaulish and British ports. Interesting support for this comes from an inscription from Oducia (Tocina) on the banks of the Guadalquivir in the centre of the production zone. It records the presence of Cassius Sempronianus, a *diffusor olearius* (an oil distributor) from Olisippo (Lisbon). He may have been in Baetica on a business trip arranging trans-shipments of oil to his home town, whence it could have been shipped by river barges inland or taken onwards in seagoing vessels perhaps as far as Britain.

Another desirable local product was fish sauce (*garum*), made by marinading fish in brine and concentrating the liquor produced. It was widely used in cooking throughout the Roman world. Garum production is attested at many sites around the coast, but they are particularly numerous along the Atlantic shores from Lixus in Morocco to Cape St Vincent in Portugal where the mackerel and tuna, preferred for making it, were readily available. Packed in distinctive amphorae (Beltrán forms I, II, III, and IV), the ships of Gades transported the liquor to markets as far afield as Italy and Britain.

The Atlantic routes used for long-distance shipping at the time would have involved several ports of call. From Gades the first stopping-off point would probably have been Olisippo (Lisbon). From there Flavium Brigantium (La Coruña) could have been made in a single haul. After this it was a choice of either sailing along the north coast to the Gironde or braving the Bay of Biscay to make for a port somewhere in south-western Armorica. If shorter sea passages were preferred a stop could be made in the estuary of the Douro, at or near Oporto, and along the coast of Cantabria, perhaps at Santander. In addition to long-distance traffic there would, of course, have been coastal cabotage linking all the smaller estuaries and inlets. It was in this way that pottery and a range of other items from Baetica and beyond found their way into the coastal settlements of Galicia.

9.11 The Roman town of Brigantium (La Coruña) developed on a protected harbour on the side of a rocky promontory joined to the mainland by a sand bar. The Roman lighthouse, La Torre de Hércules, was built at the north-west extremity of the headland.

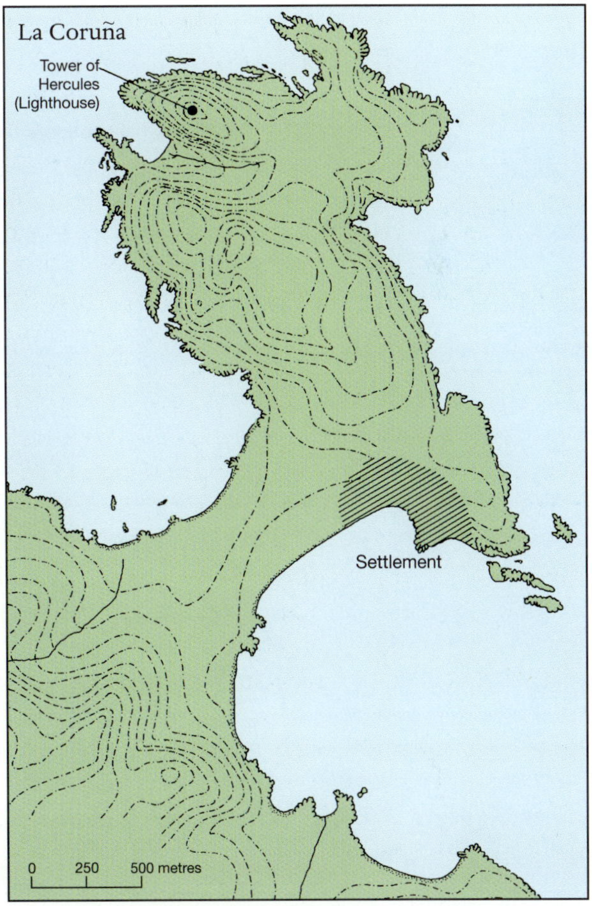

In all this maritime traffic the port of La Coruña was a vital link (9.11). Here what was once a rocky island had become joined to the mainland by a wide sandbar creating, on either side, two well-protected harbours. On the eastern harbour the Roman port of Flavium Brigantium developed. No remains earlier than the first century AD have been identified on the site but two castros are known nearby. One of these, Elviña, was occupied from the third century BC to the first century AD, and the discovery of Greco-Italian amphorae of the second or first century BC from the harbour shows that long-distance trade was under way before the Roman invasion. The main Roman town developed rapidly after it had been granted municipal status in the Flavian period and it continued to flourish well into the second century. During this time the famous lighthouse, the Torre de Hércules, was built on the north-west promontory of the island (9.12). Much of the Roman structure is incorporated in the present lighthouse—still vital to the port's livelihood. The presence of the lighthouse on this remote corner of Iberia ensured that all Atlantic mariners, in the Roman period and thereafter, have cause to remember Galicia.

Gaul: The First Foothold

The Roman military engagements in southern Gaul between 125 and 121 BC brought to an end a period of uncertainty for the Greek cities of the Mediterranean coast, who could now continue their lives in peace safe from the threat of attack by barbarian hill tribes. They welcomed Roman military intervention and gave direct encouragement to it. Even so Cicero was probably overstating the case when he said that without the help of Massalia Rome could never have triumphed over the Transalpine Gauls (9.13).

The prime concern of the annexation was to secure the land route

9.12 The Roman lighthouse of La Coruña refaced and heightened in the late eighteenth century and modified again in the nineteenth.

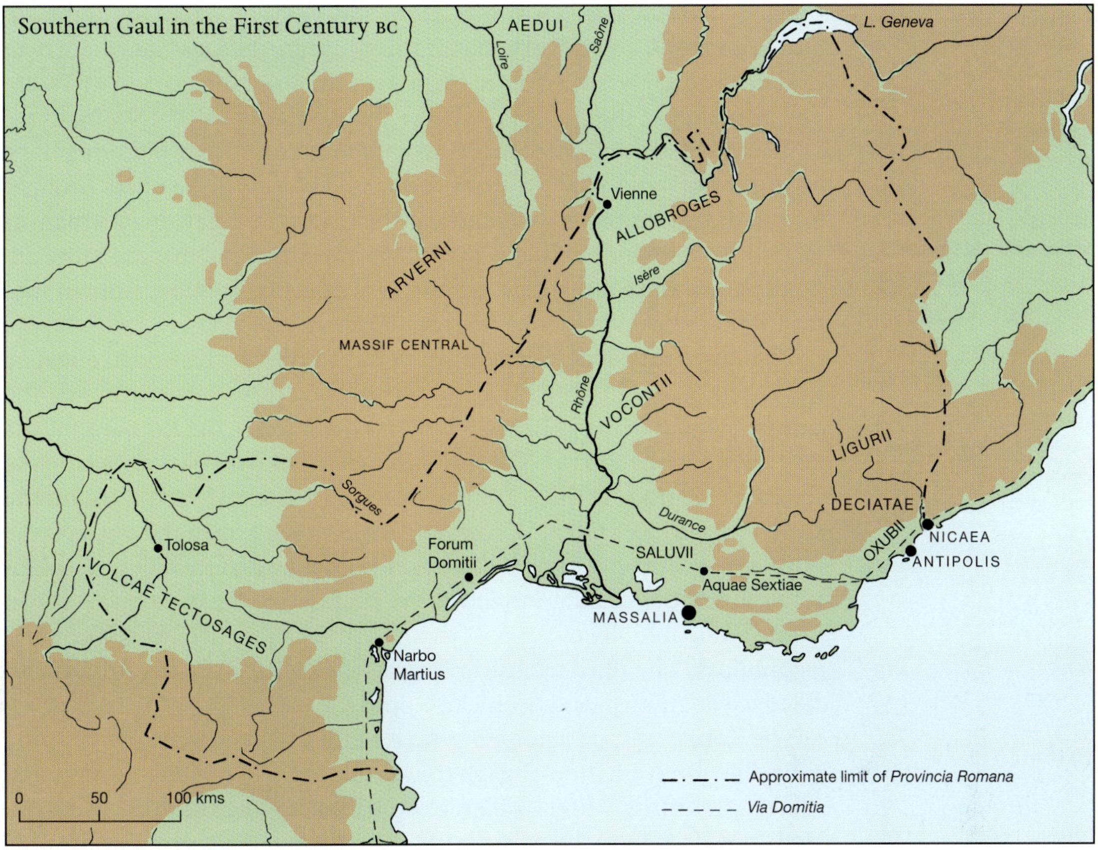

9.13 Southern Gaul in the first century BC.

between northern Italy and Spain. The road, which must have existed for centuries, was improved by military engineers during the consulship of Cn Domitius Ahenobarbus and was thereafter known as the *Via Domitia*. Domitius is also credited with the establishment of the new port town of *Forum Domitii*, but it was the foundation of the citizen colony of *Narbo Martius* around 118 BC, replacing the ancient trading post of Narbo, that was to signal Rome's determination to command the trade routes to the west along the Aude–Garonne route. To ensure that trade through the still-barbarian lands was well regulated Rome negotiated with the native town of Tolosa (Toulouse), persuading them to accept a Roman garrison. The purpose of this force was to maintain peace in the area and to give traders, many of them now Roman, a degree of security so encouraging further investment. It also served a valuable function as an early-warning system in case the Roman province was threatened with trouble from the neighbouring tribes. But the arrangement was short-lived. During the chaos that ensued as the Cimbri and Teutones rampaged through

9.14 (*facing above*) North Italian amphorae used to transport wine.
Left, Dressel 1A type; right, Dressel 1B. The 1A type was in use from the mid second to mid first century BC but declined thereafter, being replaced by the 1B type in the second half of the first century BC.

9.15 (*facing below*) A Roman ship wrecked off Giens in southern France, with part of its cargo of Dressel 1 wine amphorae still in position.

the area, two local tribes, the Tigurini and Volcae Tectosages, joined in and, after the Romans had suffered a devastating defeat somewhere near Bordeaux in 107 BC, the Volcae turned on the Roman garrison at Tolosa and slaughtered them. The next year the Romans took their vengeance and sacked the city, destroying its ancient temple and appropriating huge quantities of gold pillaged from the sacred places. Tolosa was brought within the province, as was much of the Garonne valley downstream as far as the confluence with the Tarn. This move ensured that the more difficult part of the route to the Atlantic was now firmly under Roman control.

The other major river route, along the Rhône to the north, engaged the attention of the Roman armies from the outset. After bringing the Saluvii, who lived in the hills above Massalia, to heel, the Romans moved quickly along the Rhône. The intention seems to have been to secure the crucial route node at the confluence of the Rhône and the Saône. To the west, in the Massif Central, were the Arverni who from the outset were hostile to Rome, but beyond them, commanding the vitally important land routes between the Saône and the Loire, were the Aedui who saw in Rome a valuable ally to support them in their constant battles with their neighbours. The third tribe dominating the valley were the Allobroges, allied to the Arverni and hostile to Rome.

The Roman response to this complex political geography was to send a sizeable force north to engage the combined army of the Arverni and Allobroges in the Rhône valley close to its confluence with the Isère. Here the Romans achieved a notable victory against great odds. As a result the Allobroges became subject to Rome, the Aedui were protected, and the Arverni contained. Roman merchants now had unrestricted access eastwards along the Rhône to Lake Geneva, northwards via the Saône to Burgundy and beyond, and westwards to the Loire valley. The ancient trading settlement at Vienne became the hub of the network.

The initial thrust to the north was effective, but there were subsequent disquiets to contend with. The Saluvii rebelled in 90 BC but were soon put down. Later, discontent flared among the Allobroges, first in 67 and later in 62 BC, but on both occasions rapid response by the Roman army was sufficient to stifle the revolts. Disrupting though these sporadic uprisings were, trade with the barbarian north developed apace.

Wine for the Barbarians

The one trade commodity that has a high archaeological visibility is wine, since at this period it was transported in near-indestructible pottery amphorae. Many different forms of these containers are known, reflecting changes over time and also the region of origin of the products carried (9.14). Typological considerations together with recent advances in the petrographic analysis of the clays from which the amphorae were made make it possible to pin down places of manufacture with some precision, enabling the changing patterns of trade to be worked out in fine detail. Further information of trading systems is provided by the names which some producers stamped on their amphorae. Given that so much data are available, it is hardly surprising that studies of trade in the early Roman period have focused on the transport of wine. Important though it was, however, it is as well to remember that wine was only one of the surplus commodities that the Mediterranean entrepreneurs were anxious to exchange with the barbarian world.

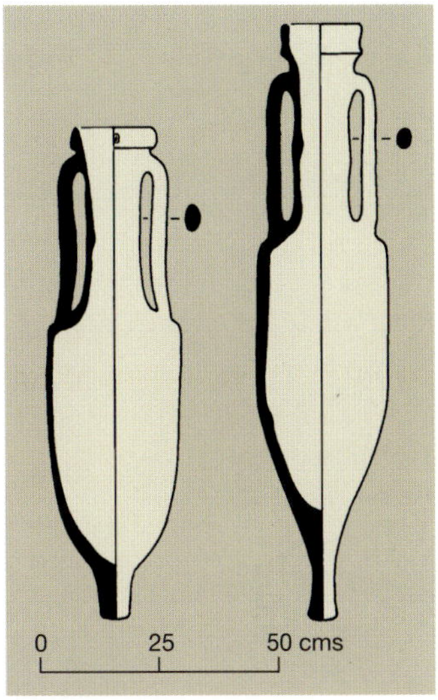

For the north Italian producers working their vast estates with slave labour, the exploitation of the European hinterland beyond the coastal strip of the province of Transalpina offered unlimited opportunities. The ports were only a short and comparatively safe sea journey from the north Italian outlets, the province was safe and well provided with roads, and, more important, the indigenous populations were avid for wine (9.15). The situation is neatly summed up by Diodorus Siculus in his account of the Gauls, derived largely from the first-hand observation of Posedonius:

> They are exceedingly fond of wine and sate themselves with the unmixed wine imported by merchants; the desire makes them drink it greedily and when they become drunk they fall into a stupor or into a maniacal disposition. And therefore many Italian merchants with their usual love of cash look on the Gallic craving for wine as their treasure. They transport the wine by boat on the navigable rivers and by wagon through the plains and receive in return for it an incredibly high price, for one amphora of wine they get in return a slave—a servant in exchange for a drink. (5. 26. 3)

The text is fascinating. At one level it enforces the usual stereotype of the unstable, drunken Gaul or Celt as 'different-from-us', but at another it offers an insight into the mechanisms of the exchange system and the nature of the transport involved.

For the Roman entrepreneur the Gaulish love of wine was a godsend. To a Gaul the availability of Mediterranean wine provided a new way of expressing status through traditional systems of conspicuous consumption. Thus, a member of the elite, wishing to demonstrate his status, could acquire large quantities of wine from a Roman trader and offer it to his followers in orgies of feasting. The more the host was able to provide the greater was his status. An actual example was recorded by Posedonius (and quoted by Athenaeus). A chieftain of the Arverni, named Louernius, in an attempt to gain status, 'made a square enclosure one and a half miles each way, within which he placed vats filled with expensive liquor and prepared so great a quantity of food that for many days all who wished could enter and enjoy the feast prepared, being served without break by the attendants'. Anthropologically such an event, in which the chieftain is essentially publicly destroying wealth, is known as a potlatch. One characteristic of this kind of system is that it tends to generate a momentum as other contenders for power seek to emulate and outdo each other in order to acquire larger and larger entourages of clients. Louernius was evidently successful, since he could boast 'tens of thousands' of followers.

Here, then, was an exchange system of mutual benefit to both partners. The Romans were able to dispose of surplus wine while the Gauls could use this highly desirable consumable to maintain their elite systems.

If the rate of exchange, of an amphora of wine for a slave, recorded by Diodorus was the actual rate in operation it might appear that the Gauls were getting a raw deal, since in the Roman market a decent-quality Gaulish slave would have been worth five or six times that amount. But in Gaulish society raiding—a socially embedded practice—provided ample opportunity to acquire captives, and since slavery does not appear to have been of particular importance locally, the facility to exchange these spoils of war for something more socially desirable was clearly to be welcomed. It is in this context of mutual benefit that the intensity of the wine trade in the first century BC can be understood.

Quantifying ancient trade is always difficult, but the order of magnitude may be grasped from the quantities of amphorae found at various sites in Gaul (9.16). At two locations, Toulouse and Châlon-sur-Saône, huge numbers have been recovered. At the site of Vieille-Toulouse the amphora sherds were so thick in the ground, an eighteenth-century observer noted, that although 'the labourers there cart them away to clear the earth . . . the plough-shares are continually blunted by the

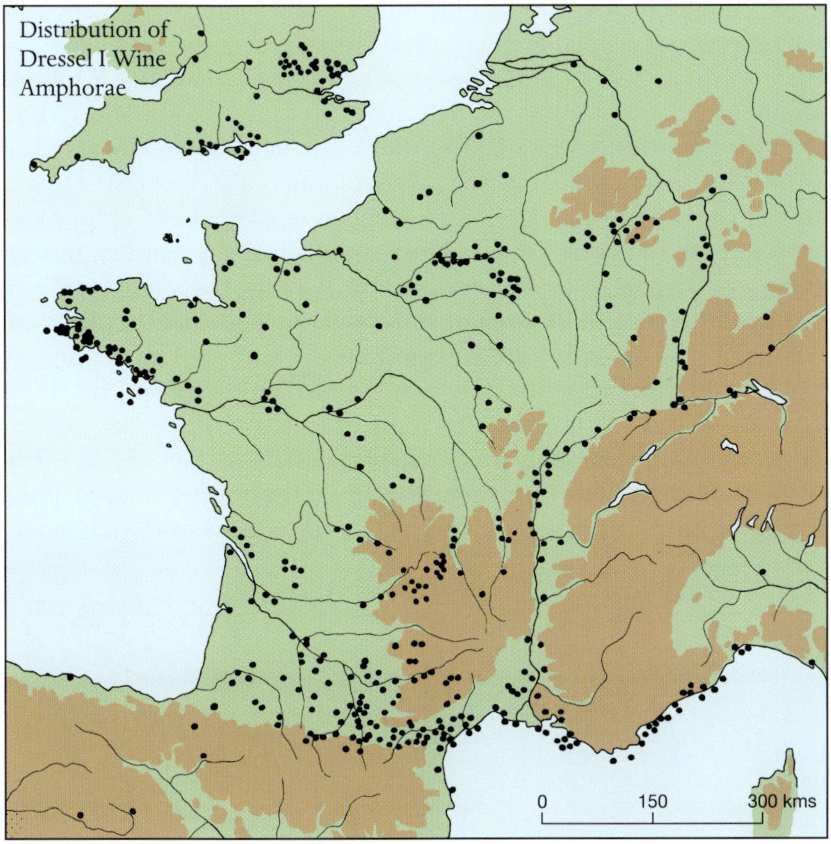

9.16 The distribution of Dressel 1 wine amphorae in western Europe.

impact of this pottery'. At Châlon nineteenth-century dredging of the Saône produced an estimated 24,000 amphorae, and it is reasonably suggested that the total thrown into the river could have been between a quarter and half a million. Numbers of this kind suggest that Toulouse and Châlon were probably the major trans-shipment points on the two routes, where a percentage of the wine was decanted into barrels for onward passage into the hinterland. At other native oppida like Montmerlhe, Essalois, Jœuvres, and Bibracte, all within barbarian territory, the numbers of amphorae recovered run into hundreds or thousands. These sites may well have been served by more enterprising traders taking their wares direct to the local elites. At these centres the wine was either consumed or passed as gifts down the hierarchy and thus out into the landscape.

Viewing the evidence as a whole, one scholar has suggested that the volume of Italian wine transported annually to Gaul may have been as much as 100,000 hectolitres per year. This is by no means an unreasonable figure when compared with the estimate of half that figure for the annual production of the Cosa district in northern Italy—just one of many production centres supplying the market. Over the century or so when the trade was at its peak export at this scale would have generated 40 million amphorae.

In the last century and a half of the first millennium BC north Italian wine was transported in two basic types of amphorae, known as Dressel 1A and Dressel 1B (9.14). Dressel 1A was in use mainly from 150 to 50 BC, with Dressel 1B taking over in the second half of the century, though there was a degree of overlap in the currency of the two varieties. When the distribution of these amphorae throughout western Europe is plotted the trading patterns stand out quite clearly, with the two major river routes being dominant (9.16). The densest distribution is along the Aude–Garonne route. This is largely the result of local exchanges, not only for slaves but also presumably for metal, particularly copper, mined extensively at this time in the Montagne Noire and the northern slopes of the Pyrenees. But it also reflects the through trade which saw the amphorae

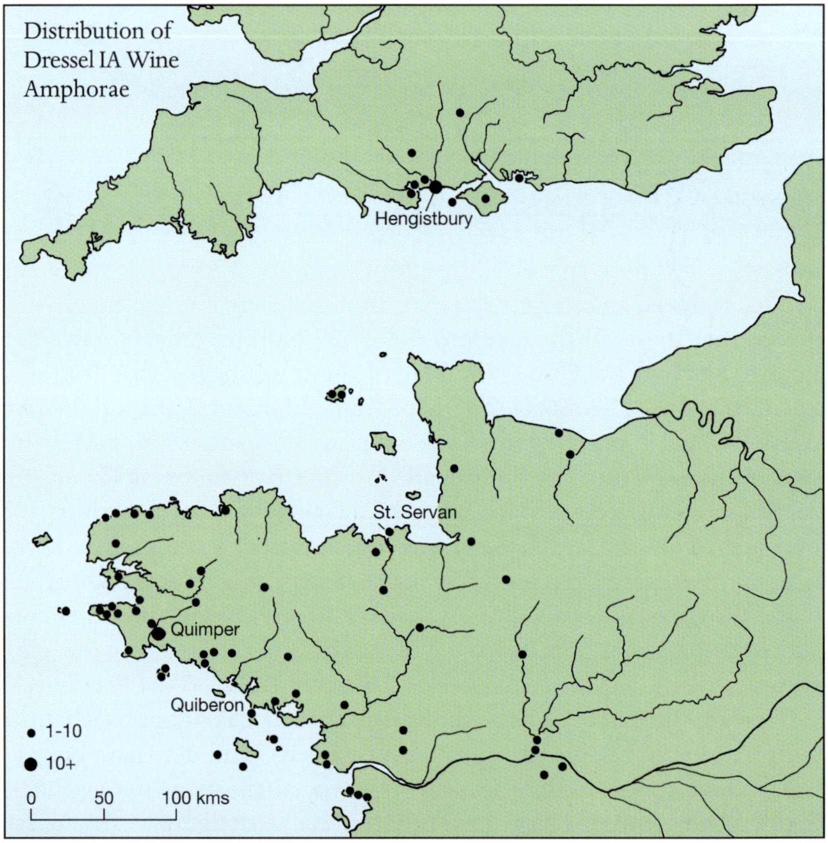

9.17 The distribution of Dressel 1A amphorae in Armorica and southern Britain.

re-embarked at Bordeaux for shipment to Armorica, whence some were taken on even further, possibly in local boats, to central southern Britain. Amphorae found in the sea around Belle Île, off the coast of Morbihan, and near the Isle of Wight show that not all of the trading ventures met with success.

When the amphorae found in Armorica and central southern Britain are looked at in more detail (9.17) it appears that the majority of them are of the Dressel 1A type, which suggests that the bulk of the wine trade along the Atlantic sea routes pre-dated the Gaulish campaigns of Julius Caesar in the middle of the first century. Thereafter it seems to have tailed off quite dramatically. How much of this Atlantic trade was in the hands of Roman entrepreneurs it is impossible to say. The simplest explanation of the observed facts is that Roman wine was only one of the luxury commodities picked up by local shippers, together with the other profitable goods that were moved along the Atlantic cabotage routes. In other words, the Roman amphorae give archaeological visibility to long-established indigenous patterns of coastal exchange. What commodities, other than slaves, flowed back to the Roman world we can only guess. Metals, corn, and hides would have bulked large, and Strabo specifically mentions salted pork as one of the delicacies coming from eastern Gaul. Other imports may have included resins, amber, woollen fabrics, furs, salt, and honey. Nor should we forget wild beasts for spectacles in the amphitheatre. Gaul was a large and productive region with easy access to Britain and Germany: the Roman entrepreneurs made good use of their privileged position in Transalpina to pursue the possibilities of growing rich with some vigour.

Caesar and the Maritime Tribes

Caesar's activities in Gaul began in 58 and lasted until 51 BC. The commentary on his last campaign, written after his death by Aulus Hirtius, ends with the words 'Gaul was exhausted by so many defeats. Caesar was able to keep it peaceful by making the terms of subjection more tolerable' (*De Bello Gallico* 8. 49). Gaul must indeed have been exhausted if Plutarch's estimate of war casualties is correct. During the eight years of campaigning, he said, 1 million Gauls had been killed and another million sold into slavery.

Caesar had fought across most of the country and by the end must have known it well. We may therefore accept as a reasonable generalization his assessment that ethnically Gaul was divided into three parts, the Aquitani south-west of the Garonne, the Celts in the centre, and the Belgae north-east of the Seine and Marne. When he writes of the maritime

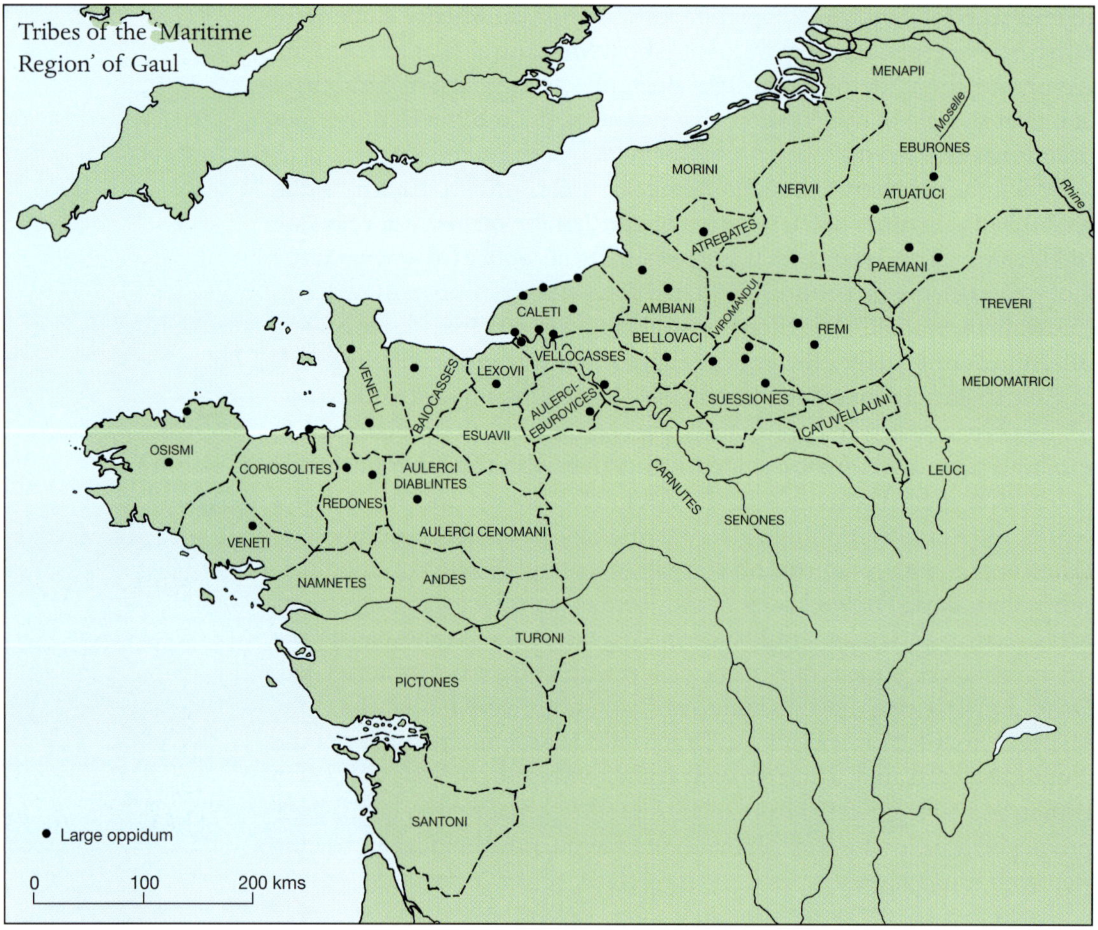

9.18 The tribes of the 'maritime region' of Gaul at the time of Caesar.

9.19 (*facing*) Caesar's Armorican campaigns in 57 and 56 BC.

regions (9.18) he includes the coasts of Armorica from the Garonne to the Seine and of Belgica between the Seine and Rhine.

His first contact with the coast came in the second year of campaigning (57 BC). While he was involved in fighting the Belgic tribes he sent his general Publius Crassus with a legion 'to deal with the tribes of the Atlantic seaboard' (9.19). Those named lay between the Loire and the Seine. No further details are given, but Crassus, it seems, had received their submission. With the campaign at an end the legions were overwintered in camps spaced along the Loire, a deployment suggesting that Caesar appreciated how volatile the situation was. During the winter embassies were sent to the Coriosolites and Esubii to acquire grain for the army. This act sparked a revolt spearheaded by the Veneti, who lived in the area roughly coincident with the *département* of Morbihan. The rest of the story, told in vivid detail by Caesar (*De Bello Gallico* 3. 7–27), can be briefly summarized. Caesar was in Illyricum when he received the news, but immediately ordered that ships be built on the Loire and crews recruited in Transalpina. He then deployed his legions widely. Labienus was sent to keep an eye on the Belgae while Crassus was dispatched to Aquitania to stop reinforcements from being sent to the Armorican tribes. This done, Decimus Brutus was put in charge of the fleet, composed of specially built galleys augmented by vessels requisitioned from the Pictones and Santones who occupied the coastal region between the Gironde and Loire. Sabinus was then sent with one force into Lower Normandy and Upper Brittany while Caesar himself moved against the Veneti in the south.

Sabinus was able to bring his opponents to a set-piece battle which he won, apparently with ease, but Caesar had far more difficulty persuading the Veneti to meet him. Every time he besieged an oppidum, usually sited on the ends of cliffs, the tribesmen escaped by ship and re-formed (9.20). The only solution was to lure their vessels to fight the Roman fleet. In the end this was done and a sea battle took place somewhere in the Bay of Quiberon involving an armada of 220 Venetic ships. The outcome was a Roman victory, precipitating the surrender of the tribe. Caesar acted decisively to end the rebellion, as his succinct summary makes clear: 'I decided that they must be punished with particular severity, so that in future the Gauls would have a greater respect for the rights of envoys. I put all their elders to death and sold the rest into slavery' (*De Bello Gallico* 3. 16). Meanwhile in Aquitania Publius Crassus seems to have had serious difficulties with the recalcitrant local tribes supported by Cantabrians from northern Spain, but eventually, by the end of the summer, he had managed to restore the situation.

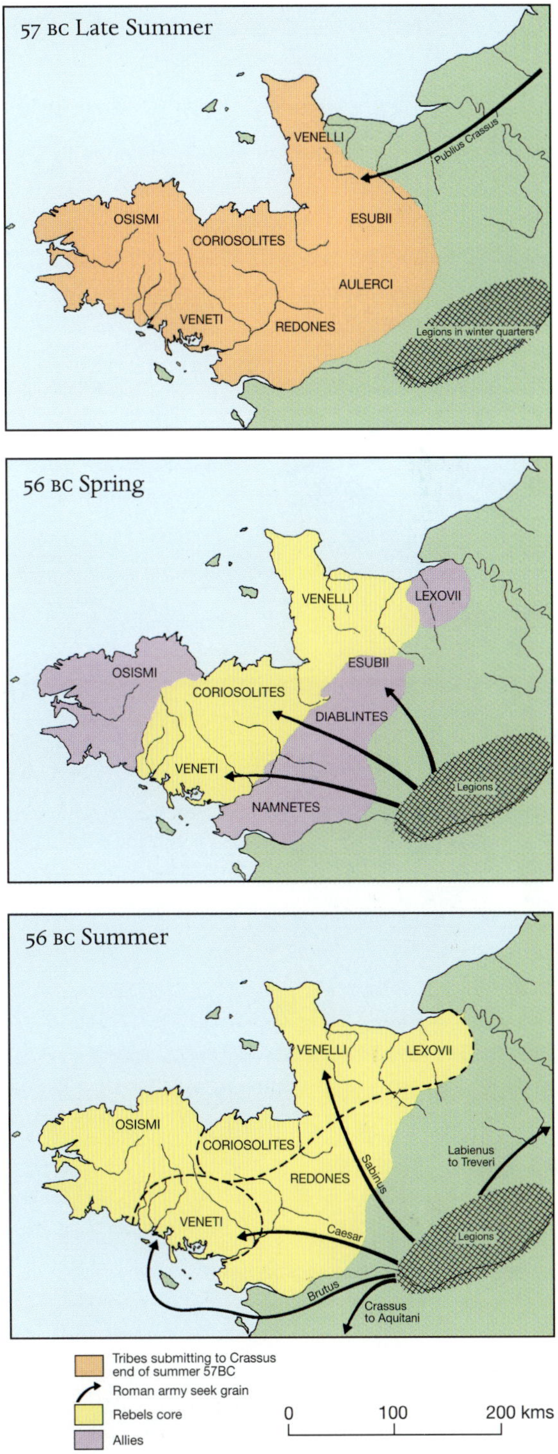

The whole Armorican episode is particularly interesting, not least because Caesar provides an unusual amount of detail about the Veneti. They were, he claims,

by far the strongest. They have a great many ships and regularly sail to and from Britain. When it comes to knowledge and experience of navigation, they leave all the other tribes standing. The sea on that coast is extremely violent and open and the harbours few and far between. Since the Veneti control these they are able to exact tolls from amongst all who regularly use those waters (*De Bello Gallico* 3. 8).

Taken on its face value, the description presents the Veneti as middlemen in the coastal trading networks. The distribution of the Dressel 1A amphorae goes some way to supporting this, but there is little evidence of Venetic contact with Britain (below p. 402).

Caesar's famous description of the Venetic ships (*De Bello Gallico* 3. 13) is a brilliant evocation of a sturdy Atlantic vessel honed to perfection by centuries of hard experience gained from plying the rugged, storm-beaten coasts of Armorica. Solid though the Venetic vessels were, they relied entirely on sail and thus were no match for the Roman galleys with their well-trained rowers: it was an uneven contest from the outset. Only scant mention is made of the vessels of their southern neighbours, the Pictones and Santones, requisitioned by the Romans: there is nothing to show if they were built on lines similar to the Venetic craft or followed a different tradition.

The campaigning year ended with Caesar's rapid intervention against the Morini and Menapii, tribes who occupied adjacent coastal territories between the Somme and the Rhine. His efforts were inconclusive, and because of the lateness of the season he withdrew and settled his army for the winter 'among the tribes who had recently fought against us', concentrating them in Lower Normandy. The events of 56 BC had brought the Roman army to the maritime limits of Gaul. In a single year the Roman troops had penetrated all parts of the coastal zone from the Pyrenees to the Rhine, and Caesar had experienced the Atlantic for himself—for the second time in the space of five years.

What followed suggests that Caesar had already had it in mind to lead an expeditionary force across the Channel to Britain. It is quite possible that he had planned this for 56 BC and that the revolt of the Armorican tribes was a deliberate attempt to deflect him. At any event, his move against the Morini and Menapii, dangerously late in the campaigning season of 56, looks very much as though he was intent to prepare his ground for an invasion in the spring of the coming year. In the event he was distracted by Germanic insurgents, and it was not until the end of the summer that he was ready to sail to Britain.

9.20 (*facing*) The dramatically sited cliff castle of Castle Meur, Cléden-Cap-Sizun, Finistère, France. Several lines of banks and ditch cut off the promontory from the land. The 'pock marks' on the surface may be hut sites of Iron Age date.

By way of preparation he sent Gaius Volusenus in a warship to reconnoitre the British shores and 'gave orders that ships should assemble there from the neighbouring districts together with the fleet built the previous summer for the campaign against the Veneti'. Altogether he amassed eighty vessels. The crossing was not easy, nor was the landing. A few days later storms and misjudgment about tides led to the loss of some ships. After some limited campaigning the army returned to Gaul, wiser now about the dangers of the Channel crossing.

In the next year, 54 BC, a more determined invasion was mounted. Caesar had already ordered that new ships should be built designed to suit the Channel, 'slightly lower than the vessels we usually use in the Mediterranean' and slightly wider. 'I ordered that all these vessels should be suitable for both rowing and sailing, an arrangement made all the easier because of their low freeboard.' Caesar reached Boulogne to oversee the final preparations, but adverse weather held up the invasion for nearly a month. Eventually the huge armada of 800 ships set sail and was able, though not without navigational difficulties, to land unopposed. The land campaign in Britain was moderately successful but the return across the Channel hit unforeseen (and unexplained) difficulties, although in the end the troops were disembarked safely.

The two cross-Channel adventures showed how difficult the Romans found these waters. Unused to dealing with the combination of swift currents, strange tides, and rapidly changing weather, disasters were only narrowly averted. Even Caesar's careful and selective presentation of the events does not obscure the many errors of judgement that were made.

The rest of Caesar's campaigns were concerned largely with the recalcitrant Belgic tribes in the north and with putting down the rebellion that broke out in the centre of Gaul. We know of no further major actions in the maritime regions, but there are many hints that the west was by no means subdued. In the winter of 54 BC a legion based somewhere in Lower Normandy, under the command of Lucius Roscius, came under threat from a large force assembled by the Armorican tribes. Roman successes in Belgica and Caesar's diplomacy managed 'to keep a large part of the country loyal', but Caesar's selective presentation of the situation suggests that the west was still unstable. When, in 52, a general uprising orchestrated by Vercingetorix got under way, 'all the tribes on the Atlantic coast' joined in what they hoped would be the rout of the Romans. Among the Atlantic communities sending troops to bolster the rebellion Caesar lists the Santones (sending 12,000 men), the Pictones (8,000), the Lexovii (3,000), the Redones, Veneti, Osismi, Coriosolites, Venelli, Caleti, and other Armorican tribes (some 30,000 altogether). In all, the Atlantic coastal communities contributed 53,000 troops to the rebel force of nearly a quarter of a million men which marched to engage Caesar. The confrontation, when it came, ended with the Romans triumphant. There was, as Caesar so coolly records, 'great slaughter'. Large numbers of those who survived were captured and sold into slavery, while the remnant fled, 'making off to their various tribes'.

In the mopping-up operation that followed Caesar's great victory in 51 BC the Atlantic tribes still posed a threat. We learn that a large enemy force had assembled south of the Loire in the territory of the Pictones, but the resistance was overcome and the Gauls were dispersed by Caesar's generals. Towards the end of the year Caesar himself, in a rapid show of strength in Aquitania, received the submission of all the tribes between the Garonne and the Pyrenees. When, in the late summer, the legions were being dispersed to winter quarters Caesar felt it expedient to station two of his ten legions, in the territory of the Turones, in the valley of the middle Loire, to 'secure all that part of the country that reached the Atlantic coast'. Still, it seems, he was wary of the maritime communities.

The Consolidation of Gaul

The exhausted people of Gaul were gradually brought under firm Roman control over the next forty years. This was a period not entirely without its problems, and sporadic local revolts are recorded, including one among the Aquitani in 28 BC, which may have been linked to the Cantabrian revolt in the previous year. The decision of Augustus, in 26 BC, to conquer the northern Spanish tribes may have been influenced by the realization that the Cantabri and the tribes of Aquitania in alliance presented an unacceptable threat to both Iberia and Gaul.

These difficulties apart, the romanization of Gaul continued apace. The country was divided into administrative regions. The original province of Transalpina now became Gallia Narbonensis, while the rest of Gaul was divided into three, roughly along the ethnic boundaries suggested earlier by Caesar: Aquitania, Lugdunensis and Belgica; the only real difference being that Aquitania now included the territory from the Pyrenees to the Loire. Crucial to the development of the new provinces was an efficient system of communication (9.21). The major river routes continued to be important arteries, but to augment them a network of new trunk roads was laid out from the centrally located city of Lugdunum (Lyons), founded at the confluence of the Rhône and Saône. From here it was possible to travel due west to Mediolanum Santonum (Saintes) and to the Atlantic coast beyond; north-west, via Paris or Reims, to the Channel port of Gesoriacum (Boulogne); or north-east to the military centre of Colonia Agrippina (Cologne) on the Rhine, which now formed the northern frontier of Gallia Belgica. On the estuaries of the Garonne, the Loire, and the Seine major ports developed: Burdigala (Bordeaux), Condevicnum (Nantes), and Rotomagus (Rouen). The main Channel port was established at Gesoriacum (Boulogne) where, in the early first century AD, a lighthouse was built, later known as the Tour d'Ordre, to guide ships into the sheltered estuary of the Liane (9.22). But all around the coast innumerable smaller ports grew up at places like Quimper, Avranches, and Cherbourg and many others.

The new communications system and the greatly changed political geography had a dramatic effect on trade. The Roman entrepreneurs were still intent on developing the northern markets, but much of the territory of Gaul to which before Caesar's time they had had free access, to exploit in any way they wished, was now under state control as part of the empire and it was therefore far less easy to make quick and substantial profits. But beyond the Rhine and the Channel lay barbarian territories receptive to trade. The Rhine and the land to the south of it very soon developed as a military zone, providing a firm frontier and a springboard for the advances into Germany. As such it consumed a wide range of

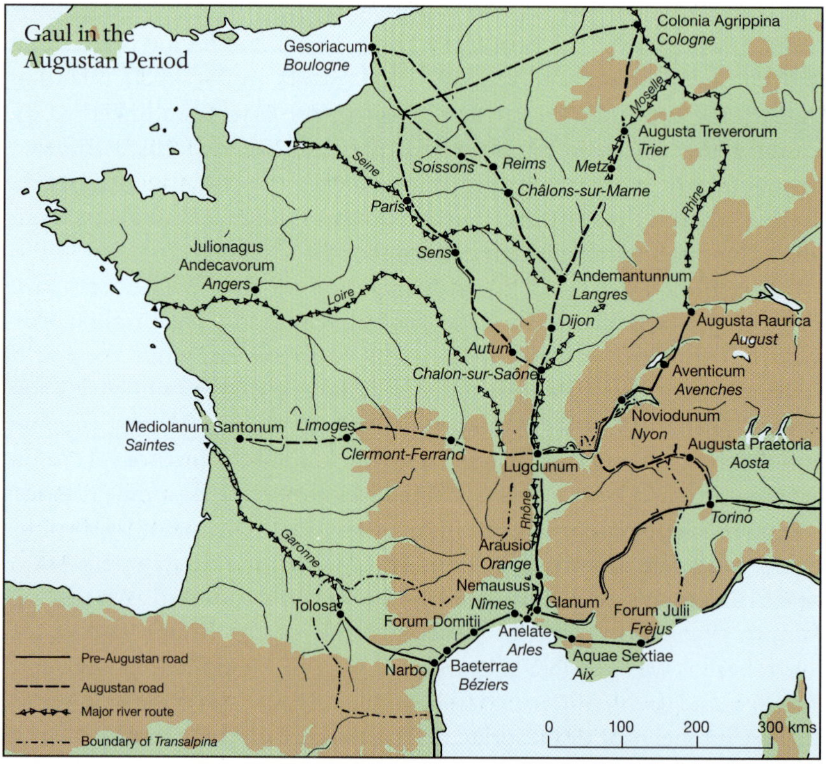

9.21 Gaul in the Augustan period showing the principal routes enhanced by the new road system.

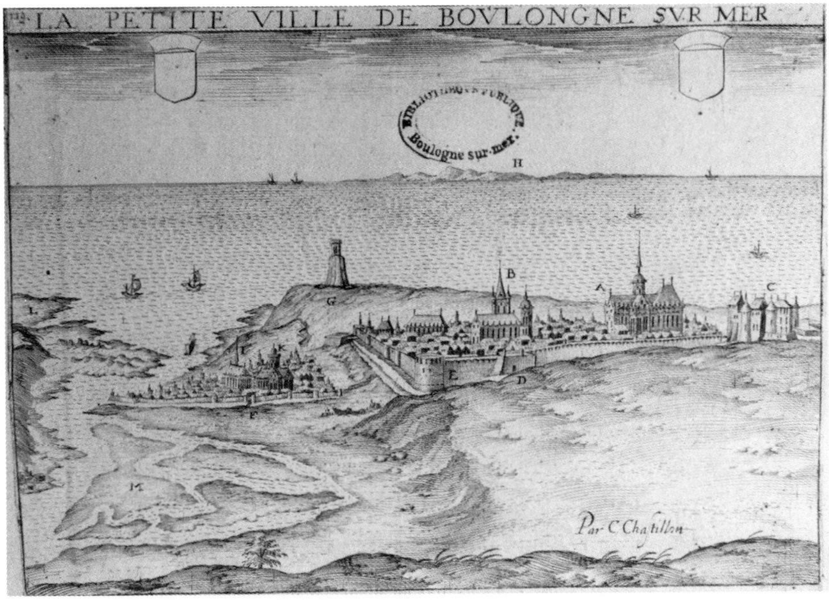

9.22 Boulogne-sur-Mer, from a print by Chastillon (1648). On the hill above the harbour is the Roman lighthouse, the Tour d'Ordre, guiding ships to the estuary of the Liane. The lighthouse no longer stands.

commodities and had to be kept in constant supply. This encouraged the development of an intensive trading network using the Rhône and the new road system to Cologne, while the Rhine itself and the supply roads running along it enabled goods to be quickly dispersed. It seems that this route became, in the post-Caesarian period, the way by which the markets of eastern Britain were now brought into the ambit of Rome. The Rhine–Thames axis, which becomes evident as a major commercial axis in the late first century BC, was to remain in active operation in the century to come. As knowledge of the Channel improved and Roman merchants established themselves on the coasts of Gaul, other ports like Gesoriacum (Boulogne) will have come into their own.

The rapid build-up of trade across the southern North Sea seems to have had a direct effect on the volume of material passing along the Atlantic route. This is shown by the dramatic decline in the amount of wine exported, reflected in the low number of Dressel 1B amphorae found in Armorica and central southern Britain when compared with the earlier Dressel 1A. It is difficult to resist the conclusion that the overland routes through Gaul to the southern North Sea ports now took the bulk of the trade, leaving the Atlantic sea lanes to shrink back to local cabotage. It could be that the destruction of the Venetic fleet exacerbated the decline, but the prime cause must have been the desire of the Roman traders to use routes which they were more easily able to control.

The new Roman structure took with it the need to establish towns to serve as capitals of administrative regions closely based on the original tribal territories. Thus in Armorica new cities were built at Vogium (Carhaix), Darioritum (Vannes), Fanum Martius (Corseul), Condevicnum (Nantes), and Condate (Rennes) as the cantonal capitals of the Osismi, Venetes, Coriosolites, Namnetes, and Reidones respectively. Where sufficient archaeological evidence survives, these towns seem to have been deliberately laid out with regular street grids in the reign of Augustus and developed all the attributes of comfortable Roman cities. Among the towns of Atlantic Gaul, Mediolanum (Saintes), capital of the

9.23 The Roman arch at Saintes (*Mediolanum Santonum*) erected in honour of the Emperor Tiberius and his sons before AD 19 to mark the entry to the town.

Santones, was particularly well endowed with elaborate monuments represented now by a triumphal arch and an amphitheatre. The arch (9.23) was set up by a romanized Gaul in honour of the Emperor Tiberius and his sons some time before AD 19, at the point where a bridge across the river gave entry to the city. The amphitheatre, erected at the western limit of the settlement in the middle of the first century AD, is only a little smaller than the famous amphitheatres of Arles and Nîmes. Nothing of this grandeur has been found in Armorica, hinting that, after their auspicious start under Augustus, the urban communities of the north-west failed to develop to the same extent as many of the other more centrally located cities of Gaul.

Economically the west had much to offer. The land was of sufficient fertility to produce surpluses, while the mineral wealth continued to be exploited. The alluvial tin deposits at Saint-Renan in north-west Finistère and at the mouth of the Vilaine continued to be worked in the Roman period, while at Abbaretz-Nozay there is evidence that tin ore was extracted by digging sizeable trenches following the lode. Lead mines are known at Plélauff in Côtes-d'Armor and Donges-Crossac in Loire Atlantique, while iron ore, both magnetite and haematite, is widespread in Armorica and there is ample evidence of extraction, although the workings are not well dated. To what extent metals were won on a sufficient scale for export is unclear, but the rarity of tin elsewhere in Europe suggests that some effort will have been made to maximize Armorican production.

One new consumable which seems to have come into production as the result of romanization was fish sauce (garum) and possibly fish paste. Before the conquest salt-works, where salt was extracted from seawater, were found all round the coasts of Armorica. Salt continued to be produced, but in some areas, particularly around the Bay of Douarnenez, new installations comprising batteries of fish-salting tanks make their appearance from the second century onwards (9.24). Analysis of the debris found in these establishments shows that the fish used were almost exclusively small sardines which could be obtained in plenty in offshore waters, as indeed they still can. Fish sauce, fish paste, and perhaps even the salted fish themselves would have been packed in barrels and trans-shipped to the major markets. The scale of production, and the desirability of garum, point to a major export trade, the barrels

9.24 Roman tank for steeping fish in salt to make fish sauce (*garum*) exposed on the edge of the Bay of Douarnenez at Le Caon, Telgruc, Finistère, France.

no doubt finding their way along the Loire and the Garonne and by ship northwards to Britain. The Armorican garum producers may even have been in competition with the south Iberian and Moroccan factories for the more distant Mediterranean markets.

It is difficult to assess the degree to which Atlantic Gaul, and in particular the Armorican peninsula, remained isolated from the development of the rest of Gaul during the early empire. Its very remoteness, being well away from the major through routes, would have ensured that the region was left much to itself. This said, farmsteads adopting the Roman manner of building, with luxuries such as baths and mosaic floors, were quite numerous in the coastal region where the bulk of the population lived. Many of the more affluent readily embraced the trappings of Roman culture while, no doubt, relishing the freedom that comes with isolation.

Britain and Gaul: Cross-Channel Exchanges

The relationship between Britain and Gaul before the Caesarian conquest remained close and seems to have intensified at the beginning of the first century BC. The clearest manifestation of contact is provided by the distribution of the Dressel 1A wine amphorae which, as we have seen, were being carried along the Garonne to the Atlantic. Many of them ended up in Armorica, but a significant number were trans-shipped across the Channel to central southern Britain (9.17). Caesar quite specifically identifies the Veneti as the tribe conducting trade with Britain but the archaeological evidence suggests that it may have been more complicated. Venetic coins are rare in central southern Britain, but coins of the Coriosolites, living on the north side of the Armorican peninsula, are relatively numerous, indicating that the Coriosolites are likely to have been the main trading partner of the southern British tribes. This is not surprising given that the two territories faced each other across the Channel. Further evidence comes from the discovery of distinctive Armorican pottery, made in the region of the Baie de Saint-Brieuc, on the Channel Islands and in some quantity at Hengistbury Head, the major port of entry on the Solent coast. On Guernsey and at Hengistbury the Armorican pottery occurred together with sherds of Dressel 1A amphorae. The simplest explanation for all this is that the Coriosolites transported Italian wine, together with local products carried in locally made pottery, to Hengistbury, using Guernsey as a port-of-call en route. The Italian wine reached the Coriosolites from Venetic territory on the opposite side of Armorica, either by sea or across the peninsula using the river routes.

Hengistbury Head, on the Dorset coast, was, both in its topography

9.25 Hengistbury Head, Dorset protecting the tranquil waters of Christchurch Harbour (*right*). In the Iron Age the volume of water from the rivers Avon and Stour would have kept the harbour clear of silt. Since then there have been some changes in coastal topography as a comparison with 9.26 will show. A long sand bank has formed (*bottom right*), behind which a marsh has developed.

and siting, an ideal port-of-trade (9.25, 9.26). It is a prominent headland, readily recognizable from some distance out to sea, protecting a large sheltered harbour (now Christchurch Harbour) into which flow two major rivers, the Stour and the Avon, allowing easy access into the heart of densely populated Wessex. Hengistbury was located in a region producing iron, salt, and Kimmeridge shale (used for making bracelets), and within easy reach of the Wessex chalkland offering surpluses of corn and wool. Moreover, excavations there have shown that extensive trading links were maintained with south-western Britain from where lead, copper/silver ore, and probably tin ore were acquired. There is ample evidence that these commodities were brought together on the headland, presumably for the purpose of trade (9.27). The goods shipped in from across the Channel, in addition to the amphorae of wine and Armorican pottery, included bronze tableware, ingots of purple and of yellow glass, and also figs. The range of commodities assembled on the headland for exchange, and recognizable in the archaeological record, is impressive, but it is no doubt a partial list. In writing of British exports at the end of the first century Strabo notes that the island produced for export grain, cattle, gold, silver, and iron, together with hides, slaves, and dogs 'that are

9.26 Hengistbury Head, Dorset as it is assumed to have been in the Late Iron Age when the harbour settlement was flourishing.

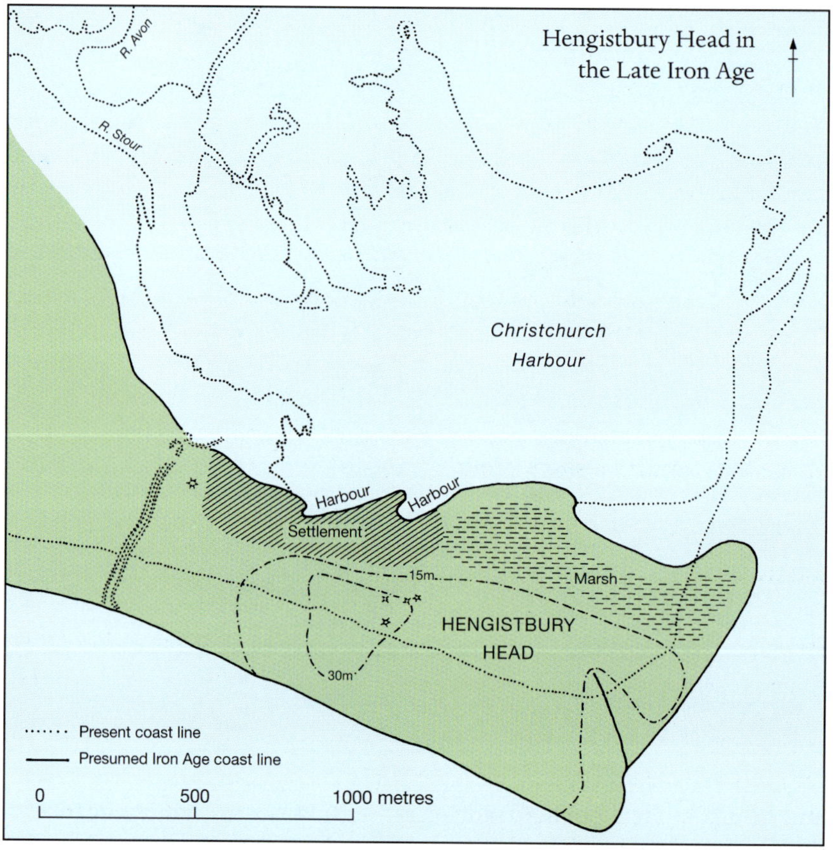

9.27 Hengistbury Head provided the main port for trade with Armorica in the early first century BC. It formed the focus of a 'contact zone', prolific in its own right, to which commodities were brought for exchange by land and sea from south-western Britain.

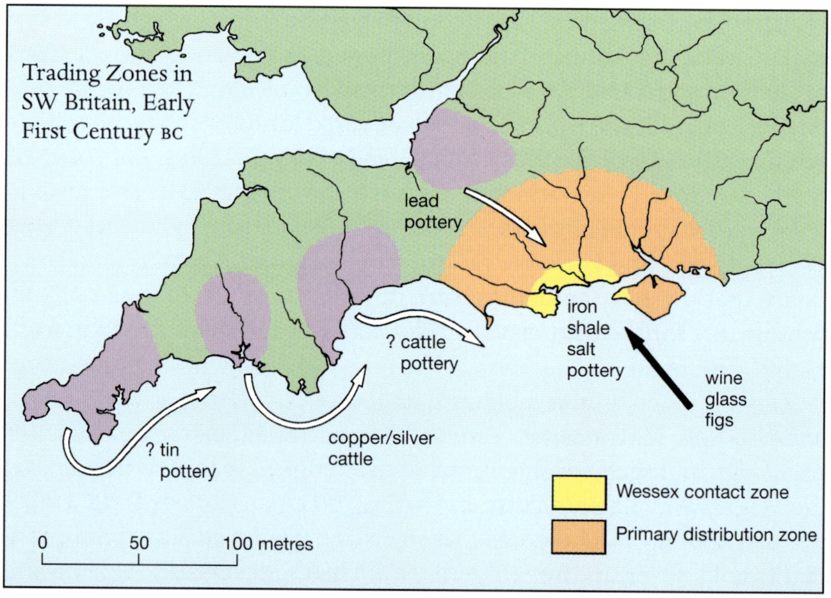

by nature suited to the purposes of the chase'. In return the Britons imported 'ivory chains, necklaces, amber gems, glass vessels, and other pretty wares of that sort' (*Geog.* 4. 5. 2–3). Although these lists refer to the post-Caesarian period, together with the archaeological evidence they give some idea of the nature of trade in the first century BC: from Britain came manpower and raw materials, for which the natives received Mediterranean luxuries and ornaments.

Judging by the distribution of the Dressel 1A amphorae in Britain the pre-Caesarian trade with Armorica was tightly focused on Hengistbury, and it was to the headland that people from south-western Britain came, probably by boat along the coast, bringing commodities for exchange. This does not mean that direct contact between south-western Britain and the rest of Armorica was in abeyance, but simply that in the first half of the first century a single trading axis dominated the flow of goods, if only for a brief decade.

Elsewhere along the Channel coast long-established contacts between the tribes of Belgica and those living in the south-east of Britain were maintained and may well have intensified. In the late second century coins minted by the Gallo-Belgic polities began to appear in Britain in quite large numbers. For the most part they were staters and quarter staters of gold, and therefore were of considerable value. It is better to see them as items of wealth circulating within patterns of gift exchange rather than money used for commercial transactions, and their appearance in Britain must reflect social relationships between tribes on both sides of the Channel. The fact that the British tribes began copying and modifying the Gallo-Belgic versions is a measure of their prestige. Caesar provided an interesting insight into trans-Channel relationships when he mentioned that King Diviacus of the Suessiones, whose domain focused on the Aisne valley, was the most powerful ruler in Gaul some time about 80 or 70 BC, and had control not only over a large part of northern Gaul but also of Britain. From this it sounds very much as though Diviacus was a paramount king to whom other tribal leaders acknowledged allegiance. In such a relationship gifts of valuable coins might well be expected to change hands. Given allegiances of this kind, it is hardly surprising that Britain sent troops to support the Gauls in their struggle against Caesar.

Finally there is a different kind of relationship to be considered. In a tantalizingly brief passage Caesar mentions that some time in the recent past Belgic raiding parties had attacked the coast of Britain and some of the Belgae had decided to settle. Precisely when is not stated, but it may have been around 100 BC. A clue as to where the settlement took place is provided by the early Roman geographers who, in the second century

AD, identify the Belgic tribal territory as occupying an area of central southern Britain—roughly Hampshire and West Sussex—with its capital at Venta Belgarum (Winchester). Some added support is given to this by the story of the Atrebatic chieftain Commius, who fell foul of Caesar and escaped to Britain to 'join his people already here'. He seems to have made for the Solent and crossed southern Hampshire to establish his new domain, henceforth known as the Atrebates, in northern Hampshire and Berkshire. It would appear, then, that the early invading Belgae entered Britain through the Solent shores, carefully choosing a no man's land between the Armorican trading axis and the eastern Channel zone where complex social relationships and allegiances were already actively in force.

The example of cross-Channel contacts in the first half of the first century BC is informative. The high quality of the archaeological evidence and the few historical scraps provided by the classical sources together enable us to glimpse the complexity and to tease out some of the individual threads. What emerges is a variety of contact—a direct trading axis, a network of social allegiances, raiding, immigration, and the flight of political refugees. It is a not-unexpected complexity and may well have been quite typical of what had been happening for centuries before and was to pick up again after the Roman interlude.

Caesar's conquest of Gaul changed all this. As we have seen, the second half of the first century BC saw Rome gradually increase its administrative hold, with Roman entrepreneurial imperatives now taking over right up to the Channel coast of Gaul. One immediate effect was the decline in volume of trade along the Atlantic axis. Trade did not cease altogether, as the scatter of imported amphorae and fine tablewares in central southern Britain shows. In Britain Poole Harbour now becomes the main entry point, and local products, in particular armlets made of Kimmeridge shale, begin to appear on contemporary sites in Armorica heralding the return to local trading patterns that were to continue throughout the Roman period.

As the Roman presence along the southern North Sea coast of Gaul became established so Roman trade with the north Kent and Essex coast developed apace, bringing to the British shores Italian wine, now in Dressel 1B amphorae, north Italian bronze tableware, and a range of fine pottery from factories in northern Gaul. These luxury goods were avidly received by the local elites and are now most frequently recovered from the rich burials of the aristocracy. The social and economic pattern in many ways reflects that of five hundred years earlier, when Greek luxury goods were used by the Hallstatt paramounts of west central Europe to maintain the hierarchic structure. There is a geographical logic to the development of this southern North Sea axis. The sea-crossing is comfortably short: Strabo tells us that ships from the Rhine mouth region sailed south along the coast occupied by the Morini (roughly from the Somme estuary to the Belgian / French border) before taking to the open sea and crossing to Britain. But there is also a political element to be considered. Caesar had established treaty relationships with the tribes of Essex, and this may well have involved trading agreements. Fifty years later Strabo noted that these arrangements still held. New treaties had been agreed with Augustus and British embassies paid court to the emperor in Rome, dedicating offerings in the Capitol. They 'have also managed to make the whole of the island virtually Roman property. Further, they submit so easily to heavy duties both on exports . . . and on imports . . . that there is no need to garrison the island' (*Geog.* 4. 5. 3). It is overstating the case to say that the whole island was tied to the Roman economic system, but the archaeological evidence leaves little doubt that a substantial part of the south-east certainly was.

The Conquest of Britain and its Aftermath

Almost ninety years after Caesar's expeditions, that is, after four generations of arm's-length romanization, the Roman army landed in southern Britain and rapidly established the province of Britannia behind a frontier zone running from Lyme Bay on the Dorset coast to the Humber estuary. The Claudian invasion of AD 43 was politically motivated to meet the aspirations of the new emperor, but it may be that local factional squabbles threatened to disrupt lucrative trade, providing an acceptable excuse to unleash the legions on the island. Gradually the army was drawn further inland to the west and north until a frontier was established from the Tyne to the Solway at the beginning of the second century.

The invasion fleet used by Claudius' general Aulus Plautius had been built a few years earlier under the authority of Gaius (Caligula), and assembled at Gesoriacum to mount an invasion, but rebellion among the troops led to the plan being aborted. Once the Claudian army had landed, the vessels would have been vital in supplying the advancing force and moving troops by sea to bring up reinforcements close to the battle front. As the zone of military operations moved further west and north, the fleet—the *classis Britannica*, as it was soon to be called—settled down in its Channel bases to guard the shipping lanes and provide services for the military. The two principal fleet bases were at Gesoriacum (Boulogne) and Dubris (Dover), where permanent forts to house the marines have been identified and partly excavated. The establishment at Gesoriacum (9.28) was significantly larger than at Dubris, and is therefore most likely

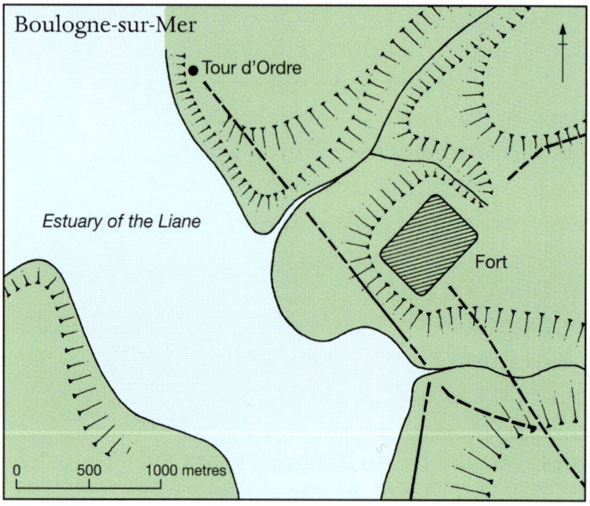

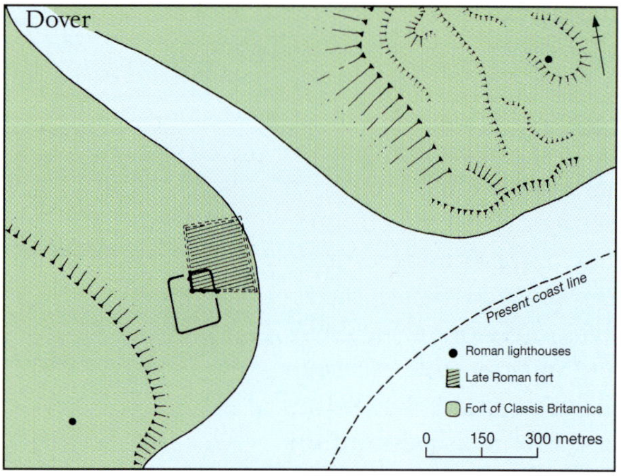

9.28 (*above*) The location of the Roman *classis Britannica* fort at Boulogne-sur-Mer. It served as the headquarters of the Channel fleet in the early second century AD and was rebuilt in the late third century on the same site.

9.29 (*below*) The location of the Roman *classis Britannica* fort at Dover in the second century AD. The military base was resited in the late third century.

to have been the headquarters of the operation. Its harbour was already well established and had been provided with a lighthouse, probably by Gaius. The port at Dubris was also well signed by two lighthouses, one on each of the flanking heights (9.29). The one that still survives in the grounds of Dover Castle is in a remarkable state of preservation (9.30). Evidence from elsewhere around the Kentish coast suggests that there might have been ancillary bases at Richborough and Reculver, guarding the Wansum Channel, and at Lympne controlling the river access to the Weald, at this stage a vitally important iron-producing zone. At or near Lympne Aufidius Pantera, a prefect of the *classis Britannica*, set up an altar, appropriately to Neptune, in about AD 140.

The *classis Britannica*, in addition to its function in guarding cross-Channel shipping and supplying the military, would have carried out a number of tasks involved with creating and maintaining the infrastructure of the new province. It may well have been employed to build and look after roads and harbours, and an inscription from the fort of Benwell on Hadrian's Wall records the presence there of a detachment involved in construction work. There is also some evidence to suggest that men from the fleet were engaged in running the ironworks in the eastern Weald. It may even be that this Wealden iron was supplied to the army in the north, whose consumption of iron for building purposes and weapons was prodigious.

The romanization of Britain was by no means even throughout the island. Towns were built on the Roman model and villas sprung up in the countryside, many of them with baths and mosaics, but both are a feature of the south-east of the island—that part which had already developed a complex socio-economic system in the pre-Roman period. The Roman towns were the successors of native oppida, while many of the villas were simply embellishments of rural establishments going back into the first century BC or even earlier. In other words, the physical

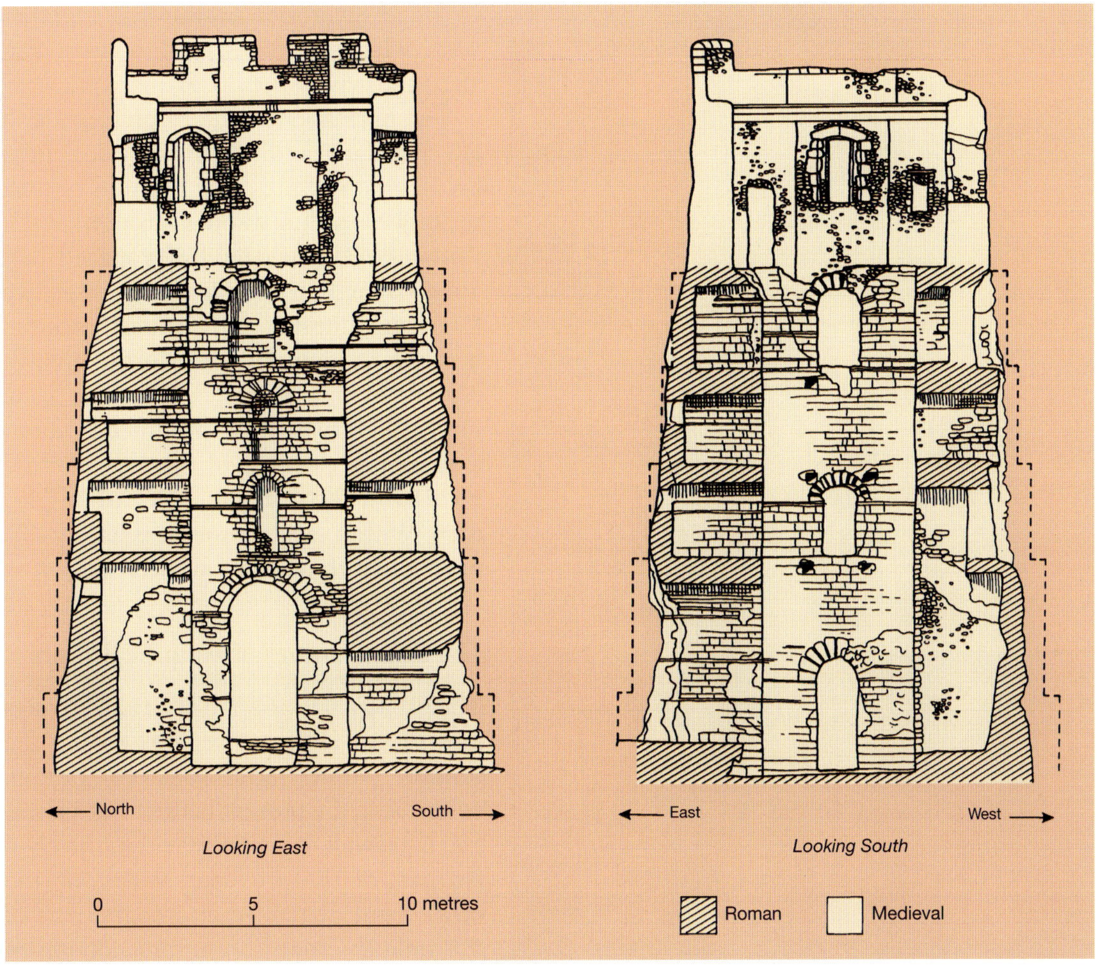

9.30 The Roman lighthouse at Dover Castle heightened in the medieval period.

manifestations of romanization were adopted by the native urban and rural elites where the new model proved socially acceptable. There was, of course, a new administrative and judicial system imposed, and official encouragement was given to those communities or individuals who wished to embrace the new ways, but for the most part the indigenous social structure remained strong beneath the veneer of romanization.

One of the most significant changes to come about as the result of Britain's integration into the Roman world was an intensification in production and exchange. Trade flourished, and with it London grew as the principal port through which the bulk of the traded goods passed. Less than twenty years after the invasion Tacitus describes London as 'teeming with traders and merchants', and the archaeological evidence

9.31 First-century harbour works at the port of Roman London exposed in excavations near Fish Street. The massive timbers front the river wall. They are tied back with bracing timbers and are supported in front by buttress posts.

of huge quantities of imports together with wharves, jetties, warehouses, and ships adds vivid support to this (9.31).

The permanent military presence also affected the island. Much of Wales and a broad swath of northern Britain from sea to sea were military zones throughout the Roman period, held by closely spaced forts linked by military roads to fortresses like Caerleon, Chester, and York set back behind on the interface within the civilian region. In the second century the zone under military control amounted to about a quarter of the total of the province and involved a force in the order of 125,000 men. Within this territory it is hardly surprising that romanization barely began.

The Communities of Atlantic Britain

The broad Atlantic zone of Britain divides into several different regions during the Roman period. South-western Britain, comprising the present counties of Devon and Cornwall, lay wholly within the civilian part of the province. Wales, on the other hand, remained an integral part of the military zone throughout. North of Hadrian's Wall, up to the Forth– Clyde line, the southern uplands were only lightly held by the military on a sporadic basis, while further to the north lay an area beyond the military grasp. In each of these regions, irrespective of the presence or absence of the army, native culture remained strong.

Perhaps the most surprising of all the Atlantic territories was south-western Britain—the region belonging to the tribe known as the Dumnonii whose eastern boundary with the neighbouring Durotriges was marked by the rivers Parrett and Axe. In the early years of the occupation a legionary fortress had been established at Exeter and a string of small forts were set up through the middle of the peninsula, but the area remained untroubled and the military presence was withdrawn about AD

75, the site of the fortress at Exeter being taken over as the administrative centre for the region. What is remarkable is that the native pre-Roman social and economic system seems to have continued virtually without change. The normal type of settlement continued to be the bank and ditched enclosure, known more recently as rounds, which had been common throughout the first millennium BC. In many cases pre-Roman sites simply continued in use, but a number of new rounds were built during the Roman period. One of the best-studied of these, Trethurgy near St Austell, was not constructed until the late second century AD (9.32). The only difference which it shows when compared to its Iron Age precursors is that the houses inside are oval in plan rather than round and the material culture used by the family included a few Roman artefacts and pots. At the western extremity of the peninsula a rather different type of building—the courtyard house—developed. These were cellular structures comprising a central open area surrounded by a number of small cells set

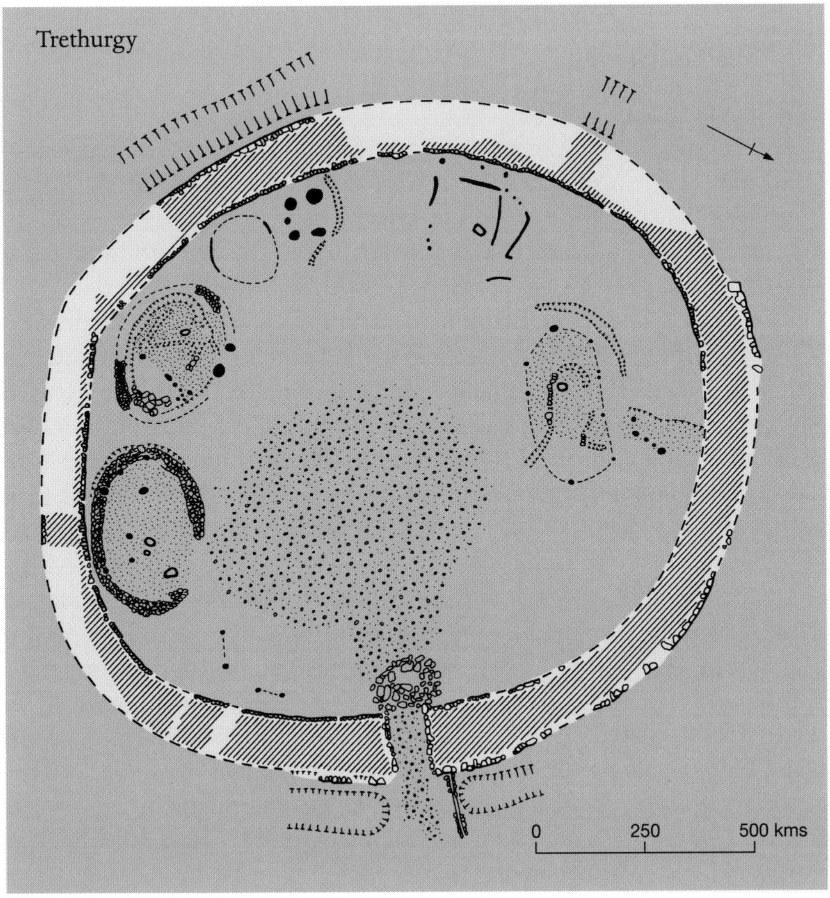

9.32 The early third century AD settlement at Trethurgy Round, Cornwall.

into the thickness of the enclosing wall. The best-preserved example of houses of this type are the eight houses arranged along a street at Chysauster in Penwith, surrounded by small paddocks and set within a system of fields (9.33). These courtyard houses may have originated late in the pre-Roman period but they were certainly in active use in the second and third centuries AD. One further point is worth noting. Coins are rare in the south-west in spite of the comparatively large number of excavations which have taken place. The implication would seem to be that the native economic system remained largely unaffected by the Roman monetary economy.

Taken together the evidence from Dumnonia shows that the inhabitants of the region adhered rigorously to the native way of life and native value systems. Whilst this could be presented as backwardness springing from their remote location, the sharpness of the divide along the tribal boundary between Dumnonia and the highly romanized Durotriges looks far more like the deliberate rejection of Roman values by the tribe. By adhering to their native system the Dumnonii were setting themselves apart from the rest of the province. It is hardly surprising, therefore, that their native language—a version of Atlantic Celtic—has remained in use until recent times.

South Wales was the preserve of two tribes in the pre-Roman period, the Demetae of the extreme south-west and the Silures of the south. The boundary between the two, in the vicinity of the Loughar valley or the hills to the east, remained a significant social divide throughout the Roman period, though both regions lay within the military zone.

The Silures were provided with a cantonal capital at Venta Silurum (Caerwent), but also had within their territory the legionary base at Caerleon and a number of permanent forts guarding the roads through the mountains. Here, especially along the more fertile coastal plain, a thin overlay of romanization can be seen in the adoption, by some of the local elite, of Roman building styles, resulting in a thin scattering of villas. The reality of this process is nicely demonstrated by the farmstead excavated at Whitton, west of Cardiff, where a native farmstead, set within a rectangular enclosure, was built in the early years of the first century AD and continued to be modified throughout the Roman period by successive rebuildings. It was not until the end of the second century that the first, very simple masonry building was erected. At the end of the next century it had begun to take on the characteristics of a small villa. Here we are witnessing the very gradual adoption of Roman values as successive generations of the resident family became affluent enough to build in the Roman manner. This seems to have been the general pattern throughout the more fertile part of Silurian territory.

9.33 *(facing)* The Roman village of Chysauster, Cornwall. The stone-built cellular houses were arranged in pairs along a main street with adjacent garden plots and fields beyond. The house plan is a development of the native round house.

In the extreme south-west, in the territory of the Demetae, the situation was different. A small cantonal capital was established at Carmarthen as the administrative centre of the region, but in the countryside around life continued in the pre-Roman manner with enclosed homesteads—the raths—remaining the principal settlement form. As in Dumnonia, a number of the pre-Roman establishments continued throughout the Roman period and new enclosures were built in native style. The only acknowledgement of the Roman world was the adoption, by one or two households, of the rectangular house form. The persistence of the native social system echoes the situation in the south-west peninsula, and it is tempting to argue that here again the Demetae maintained their traditional ways deliberately rather than by default.

The north-west of Wales, the territory of the Ordovices, was a mountainous region sparsely populated but for the coastal strip some 10 to 20 kilometres wide. The region was held by a number of Roman forts linked by roads to the legionary base and later colonia at Deva (Chester). Once

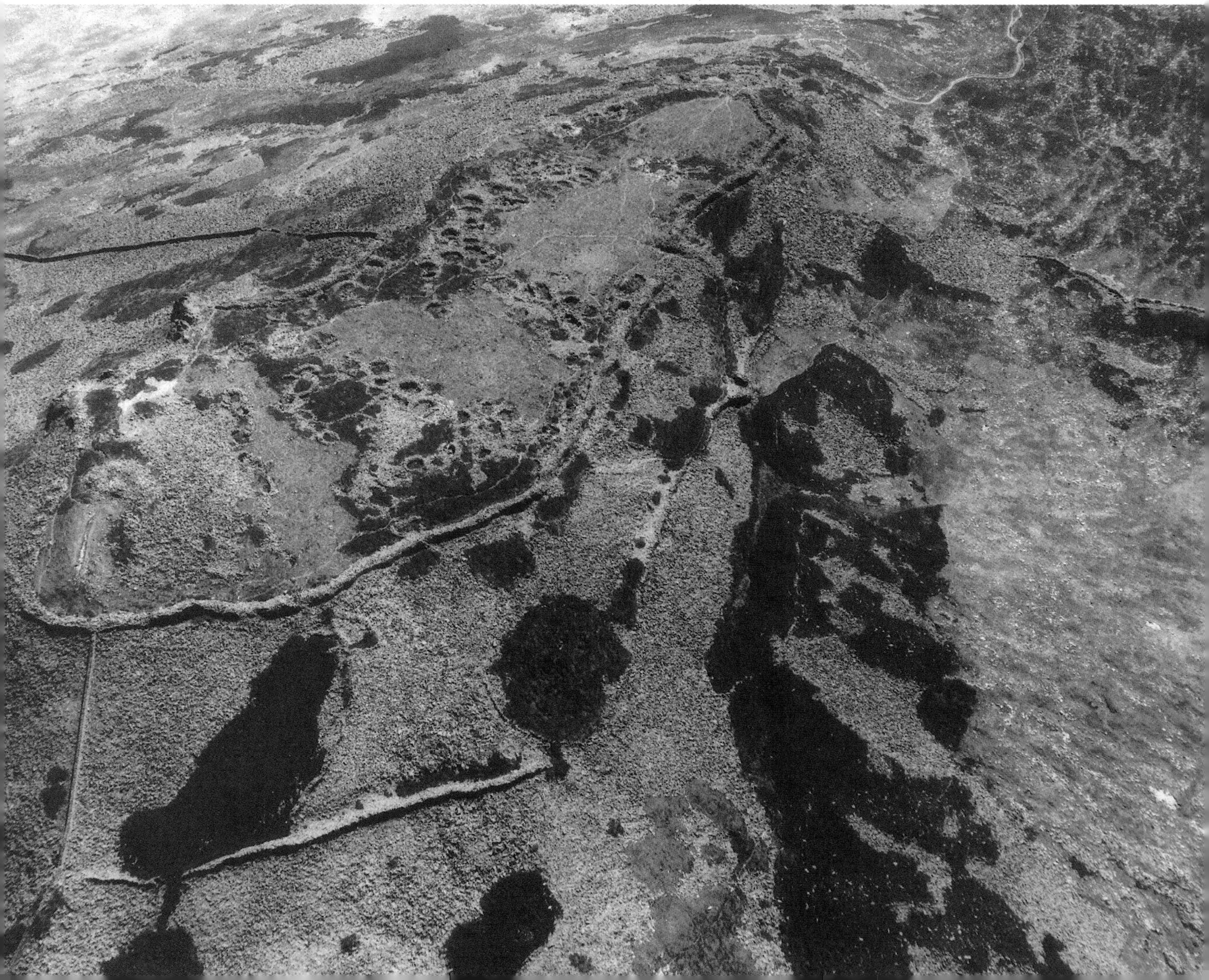

9.34 The Iron Age hillfort of Tre'r Ceiri on the Lleyn peninsula of north-west Wales. The fort continued to be used throughout the Roman period and it is to this period that many of the small circular houses inside belong.

more the native pre-Roman settlement system predominated, the principal type of settlement being the single family farmstead built in drystone construction. Within the enclosure wall circular houses clustered, sometimes set close together in cellular style. The only effect which romanization appears to have had is that some of the enclosures and a few of the houses take on a rectilinear plan. A number of the hillforts also continued to be occupied throughout the Roman period, the prime example being Tre'r Ceiri in Gwynedd where some fifty individual cellular buildings have been identified (9.34).

Outside the network of Roman forts there is no trace of romanization of any significant kind: the Ordovices remained socially and economically in the Iron Age.

Finally, turning to the north-west of Britain we find a zone that remained outside the Roman world. Even the western part of the southern uplands between the walls of Hadrian and Antoninus—the territory of the Novantii—was largely untouched by the Roman military. In the whole of the west and the north of Scotland, including the Western and the Northern Isles, the native system of settlement continued, the duns, brochs, and wheel-houses of the late first millennium BC continuing in use throughout the first half of the first millennium AD. The Roman commander Agricola had sent a detachment of the Roman fleet to explore the north seas in AD 84 and it seems that they sailed as far as Orkney, but it was little more than a desire to establish the limits of the island and nothing came of it. During the four centuries or so of Roman occupation a few trinkets penetrated the exchange systems of these remote parts, but native life continued without deflection.

Sufficient will have been said to show that much of the Atlantic region of Britain, whether under Roman control or not, maintained social and economic systems that were deeply rooted in the past. Such aspects of Roman culture as were accepted were absorbed into the rhythm of native life without changing it in any noticeable way. Geographical remoteness was, no doubt, a significant factor in all this, but so too was the strength of the local social systems which, over many generations, had established a fine equilibrium with the challenging Atlantic environment. By facing the sea these communities, deliberately or inadvertently, turned their backs on Roman culture. In doing so they retained not only their lifestyles but also their language and, in varying degrees, their independence.

Ireland: Beyond the Empire

Strabo, writing at the beginning of the first century AD, admitted that he had nothing much to say about Ireland other than the unconfirmed hearsay that its inhabitants were more savage than the British, practising both incest and cannibalism. But Tacitus, writing forty years or so after the conquest of Britain, was more informative. He notes that its soil, climate, and its social systems were much like those of Britain, and adds that Ireland's approaches and harbours were reasonably well known from information brought back by the merchants who traded there. The implication to be drawn from these two contrasting texts is that, following the Roman invasion of Britain in AD 43, a lively trade had sprung up with Ireland. The remarkable extent of the geographical knowledge available to the classical world is shown by the 'map' which can be constructed from the series of latitude and longitude co-ordinates recorded by the astronomer Ptolemy in the late second century. Altogether some fifty-five locations are listed, including capes, rivers, islands, tribes, and 'cities', giving an accurate approximation to real geography. The 'map' leaves little doubt that the coasts, other than the western Atlantic coast, were well known and a surprising amount of detail was available about the more inland regions. This can only have come from the personal observations of sailors and traders.

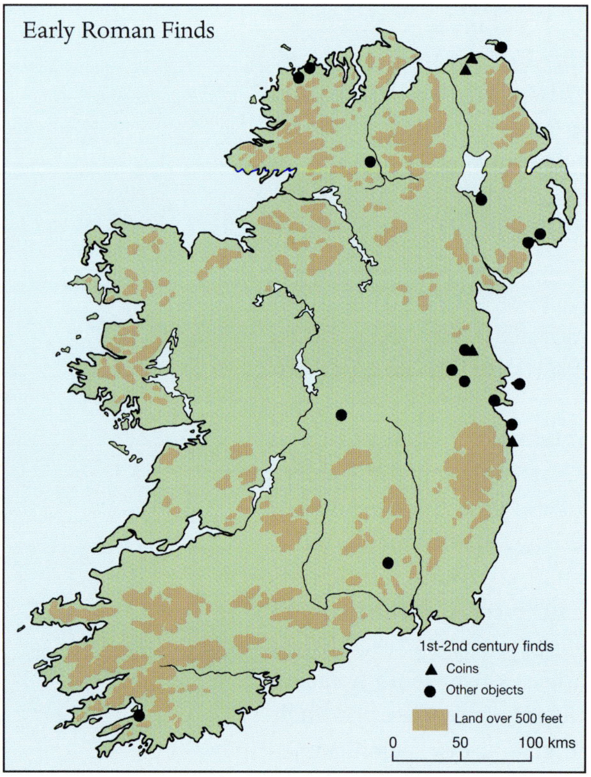

9.35 The distribution of Roman coins and other items of the first and second centuries AD in Ireland.

The archaeological evidence confirms that contacts were maintained during the first and second centuries AD (9.35). Most of the finds of material of this date occur along the east coast and its hinterland between the Liffey and the Boyne and along the north coast, suggesting the existence of two main axes of contact, one directly across the Irish Sea possibly coming from Deva (Chester) or the Severn estuary, the other emanating from the Solway Firth or the Firth of Clyde, instigated perhaps by merchants supplying the frontier garrison.

The Irish Sea traders may well have used the defended promontory of Drumanagh, 6 kilometres north of the mouth of the Liffey, as the principal port-of-trade. A large quantity of early Roman and native Irish material has been found here, including ingots of copper, coins, and pottery, but details are still inaccessible. Drumanagh, by virtue of its geomorphology, location, and well-protected harbours, would have been an ideal location for traders from the Roman world to meet their Irish counterparts. Another possible location for a port-of-trade in the area was Lambay Island in Dublin Bay opposite the mouth of the Liffey. A cemetery was found here comprising a number of inhumation burials with grave goods including a sword, a shield, and various ornaments, among them brooches, a torc, and bracelets of jet and bronze. Cemeteries of this kind are unknown in Ireland and, given that the grave goods are of northern British type, it has been suggested that the individuals may have been Brigantes escaping from the Roman advance. Another possibility is that Lambay was a location used by traders from Britain to articulate exchanges with the Irish in the decades before the more convenient site of Drumanagh became the agreed port.

Together, the evidence from archaeology and the classical sources is sufficient to show that Ireland became well known to Romano-British entrepreneurs in the early Roman period. It may be that Irish mercenaries joined Roman auxiliary regiments, returning home with a knowledge of the wider world. This said, there is little evidence that the proximity of Rome had any significant effect on the development of Irish society. The intricate social system, the laws, and the remarkable vernacular oral tradition, which survived into the early Middle Ages, were a legacy of its prehistoric past undimmed by the shadow of Rome.

East or West: Rivers or the Sea

Huge volumes of trade goods reached Britain from the Continent during the Roman period. The results of bulk import are readily to be seen in the hundreds of thousands of pottery and glass vessels recovered from excavations, but these are only the visible tip of the iceberg. Bales of valuable cloth, barrels of wine and fish sauce, and crates of spices will have flowed into the ports, while from Britain wool, in its raw state and as finished garments, and corn were the principal exports. That the volume of trade increased out of all proportion with the Roman occupation is clear: the question that remains is, by what routes were the goods carried?

We saw that in the first century BC the patterns of importation of Italian wine showed a significant shift, the Atlantic route to central southern Britain giving way to the southern North Sea route to the Thames estuary, and we argued that the prime, though not necessarily the only, reason for this was the rapidly developing importance of the Rhine frontier as a zone of intense consumption and production (9.36). The coming into existence of such a zone led to the creation of an efficient infrastructure of road and river communications, with the necessary posting stations, markets, and subsidiary production centres to support it. This will

9.36 Major routes through Gaul in the Roman period showing their changing emphasis.

inevitably have encouraged the flow of goods, the Rhine acting as a magnet.

The advantage of this route over the Aude–Garonne–Atlantic or the Rhône–Loire–Atlantic route was that the sea crossing was much shorter and considerably safer than the long and potentially dangerous haul around the Armorican and Cherbourg peninsulas. Moreover, in the Roman period the crossing from the Rhine to the Thames ensured that the goods were delivered to the economic heart of the new province and the hub of its communication system. While there is no doubt that sea transport was cheaper by the mile than land or river transport, the danger of shipwreck in Atlantic waters was an ever-present reality, with the potential for wiping out profits.

The preference for the Rhône–Rhine route over the Atlantic routes is demonstrated by the trade in Massiliot wine which, in the latter part of the second century AD, was transported in characteristic flat-based amphorae known as Dressel form 30. The type is fairly widely distributed in Britain, and when the find spots are mapped it is abundantly clear that the Rhône–Rhine route was used to the total exclusion of the Atlantic routes (9.37).

9.37 The distribution of Dressel 30 amphorae manufactured in southern Gaul to transport wine. The map shows clearly the dominance of the Rhône–Rhine route.

Not only did Mediterranean products favour the northern route, but Gaulish products like *terra sigillata*—the fine red tableware used throughout the empire—made in southern, central, and later eastern Gaul were also fed into the same commercial transportation system.

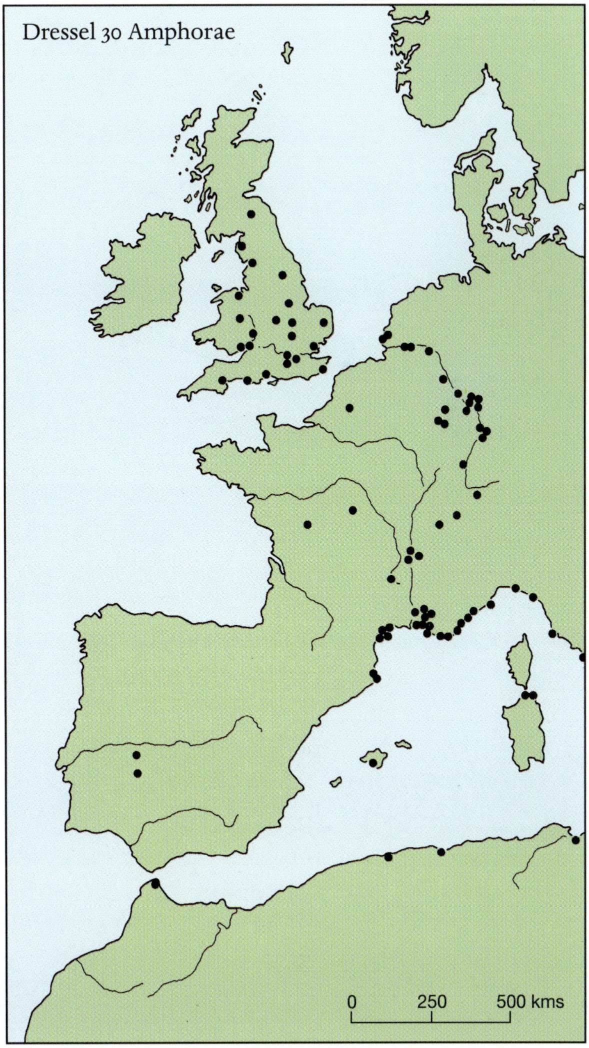

There is ample evidence from the Rhine and its subsidiaries that river transport was well organized, and a significant number of river vessels have been found. One of the principal routes to the sea from the Rhine in the Roman period was via the Waal to the estuary of the Scheldt. At this time the river-mouth lay between the mainland and a large island and was flanked by two temples, at Colijnsplaat and Domburg, dedicated to the goddess Nehalennia. The temples are likely to have been sited at harbours used by the traders of the southern North Sea, and it might well have been here that goods from the frontier zone, brought via the Rhine, and from Gallia Belgica, via the Scheldt, were trans-shipped from river barges to seagoing vessels. At any event, a number of traders engaged, so the inscriptions inform us, in the export of salt, wine, and pottery felt it expedient to dedicate altars to the deity as thanks for, or in anticipation of, safe and profitable voyages (9.38). From here locally built vessels, navigating their familiar home waters, sailed for the ports of eastern Britain.

What, then, of Atlantic trade during the Roman period? That Mediterranean boats sailed in Atlantic waters is demonstrated by the discovery, near Porth Felen in the Lleyn peninsula of north Wales, of a Greco-Roman lead anchor-stock (9.39). From its position, 30 metres off a dangerous rocky shore in 15 metres of water, it would appear that it came from a vessel that had got into serious difficulties. The anchor-stock is difficult to date but probably belonged to the second or first century BC or just possibly the first century AD, and it shows that at least one Mediterranean vessel was prepared to face the perils of Cardigan Bay at this time, but how rare it was for Mediterranean shipping to penetrate the Atlantic sea lanes it is impossible to say. The wreck found in St Peter Port harbour on Guernsey, carrying pitch possibly from western France, was built in the native tradition and was clearly a local vessel engaged in coastal cabotage. The same may be true of the ship carrying British lead ingots that came to grief on the treacherous Septs Îles off the north coast of Armorica. These two wreck sites reflect a lively trade involving the short-haul transportation of local products from port to port, but there is no evidence, either from the known wrecks or from archaeological distribution maps, to suggest that the Atlantic routes were used for the bulk transport of Mediterranean commodities. In other words, the impact of the Roman commercial world on the Atlantic seaways appears to have been negligible. Shipping continued as before, with local shipmasters continuing to work the seas in much the same way as their ancestors had done. Some will have carried Roman goods between Atlantic ports, and it is possible that cargoes of Spanish products, such as olive oil or garum, might have been picked up in the ports of western Iberia by more entrepreneurial shippers, but that Mediterranean trading fleets regularly braved the Atlantic seems, at least on present evidence, highly unlikely.

9.38 (*facing*) Roman altar to the goddess Nehalenia, set up by a salt merchant (*negotiator salarius*), Marcus Exgingius Agricola of the Treveri, at the temple of Colijnsplaat in the estuary of the Rhine.

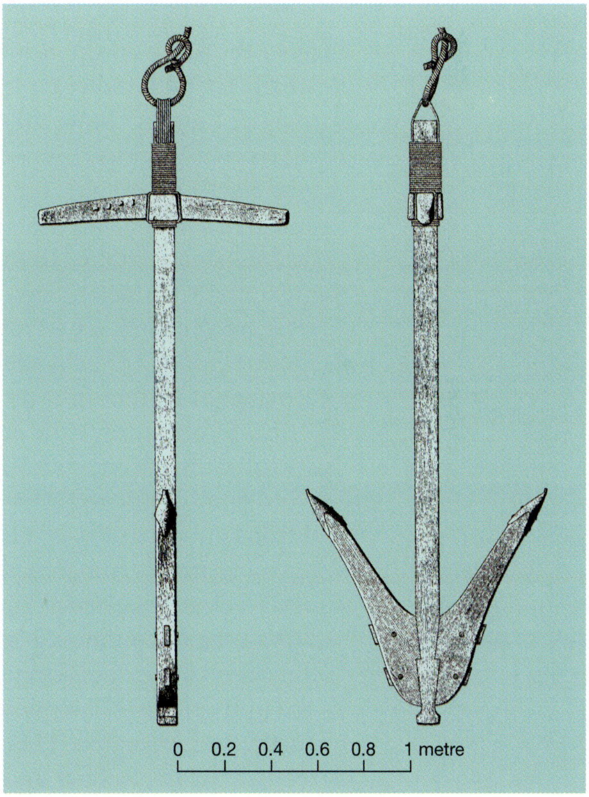

9.39 Lead anchor stock from Porth Felen, north Wales with the full anchor reconstructed after contemporary Roman examples.

10. Migrants and Settlers in the Early Middle Ages AD 200–800

On 4 February 211 the Roman emperor Septimius Severus died at York. Nearly six hundred years later, on Christmas Day 800 at Rome, Charlemagne, king of the Franks and Lombards, was crowned by the Pope *imperator et augustus*. Severus had spent the last years of his life in the wild north of Britain, campaigning against the barbarian Caledonians and Maeatae in an attempt to stabilize the crumbling northern frontier of his still-pagan empire. To those present at Charlemagne's coronation the great event marked a new beginning—the rebirth of the empire in the west, resplendent in its vestments of Latin Christianity. The face of Europe had totally changed, and yet Rome was still looked to as the provider of legitimacy.

In western Europe the end of the ancient world, dominated in its last centuries by Mediterranean culture, and the emergence of the Middle Ages greatly enriched in ethnic and cultural variety can, very crudely, be divided into two phases. The first, from about 250 to 450, witnessed a systems collapse accompanied by population mobility on a scale probably never before experienced in Europe, while the second, from 450 to 800, was a time of continuous readjustment and consolidation. What caused the massive social dislocations, which reached their peak in the fourth and fifth centuries, is a question which has been, and will continue to be, energetically debated. There is, of course, no simple answer. Many interrelated factors, feeding upon each other, led rapidly to the crescendo of collapse. Yet behind it all lay the dynamics of demography.

The Roman empire in its early years thrust steadily outwards, bringing within its boundaries territories that could provide the manpower, food, and other raw materials necessary to sustain its non-productive and heavily consuming core. All the time that outward expansion was possible the empire retained an equilibrium, but once the geographical limits had been reached, beyond which the still unconquered territories were unable to sustain the infrastructure of a provincial Roman economy, tensions began to appear. That limit was reached in the early decades of the second century during the reign of Hadrian. At this time the boundaries of the empire were fixed and in Europe a firm frontier was established using, for most of its length, the line of the rivers Rhine and Danube. The frontier was drawn across a demographic gradient, and its prime function was to control movement. It put a stop to what had been happening for centuries, possibly millennia—the continuous, and usually gradual, flow of population from areas of high population growth in the north to areas of low population growth in the south. Once the frontier had been set, the declining population within the empire and the rising population outside created a marked, and increasing, disparity along a fracture line, thinly manned by the army. And so the pressures built. Other contributory factors—rising sea-levels and deteriorating climate, the barbarian predisposition to raid to sustain their elite systems, the social dislocation created by the Roman market for slaves, and many others—exacerbated the pent-up energies of the barbarians. Meanwhile, to the south, the rotten core of the empire began to disintegrate as the birth rate declined to dangerously low levels. What followed was a natural biological readjustment.

The Disintegration of Roman Authority: AD 250–450

Some forewarning of what was to come was given in AD 162 when a German tribe, the Chatti, made an attempt to cross into Roman territory. It was the beginning. A few years later we hear of Marcomanni and Langobardi crossing the Danube into Hungary, to be followed by more massive movements of Marcomanni, Quadi, and Iazyges, some of whom managed to penetrate as far south as the head of the Adriatic. For Rome it was the recurring nightmare of the northern barbarians made stark reality. Although the immediate threat was effectively dealt with, the underlying causes remained.

In the seventy years or so following the Roman wars against the Marcomanni great changes were taking place north of the frontier and new confederations were emerging from the smaller tribal entities of earlier times. In the west the two most powerful were the Franks and the Alamanni (10.1). The Franks, taking their name from the word *Franci* meaning 'bold, fierce', came together from the disparate Germanic groups living north and east of the Lower Rhine in what is now the Netherlands and north-western Germany, while the Alamanni, meaning 'all the people', emerged in the awkward re-entrant in the frontier between the River Main and the Danube. Gradually, with the growing strength of the new

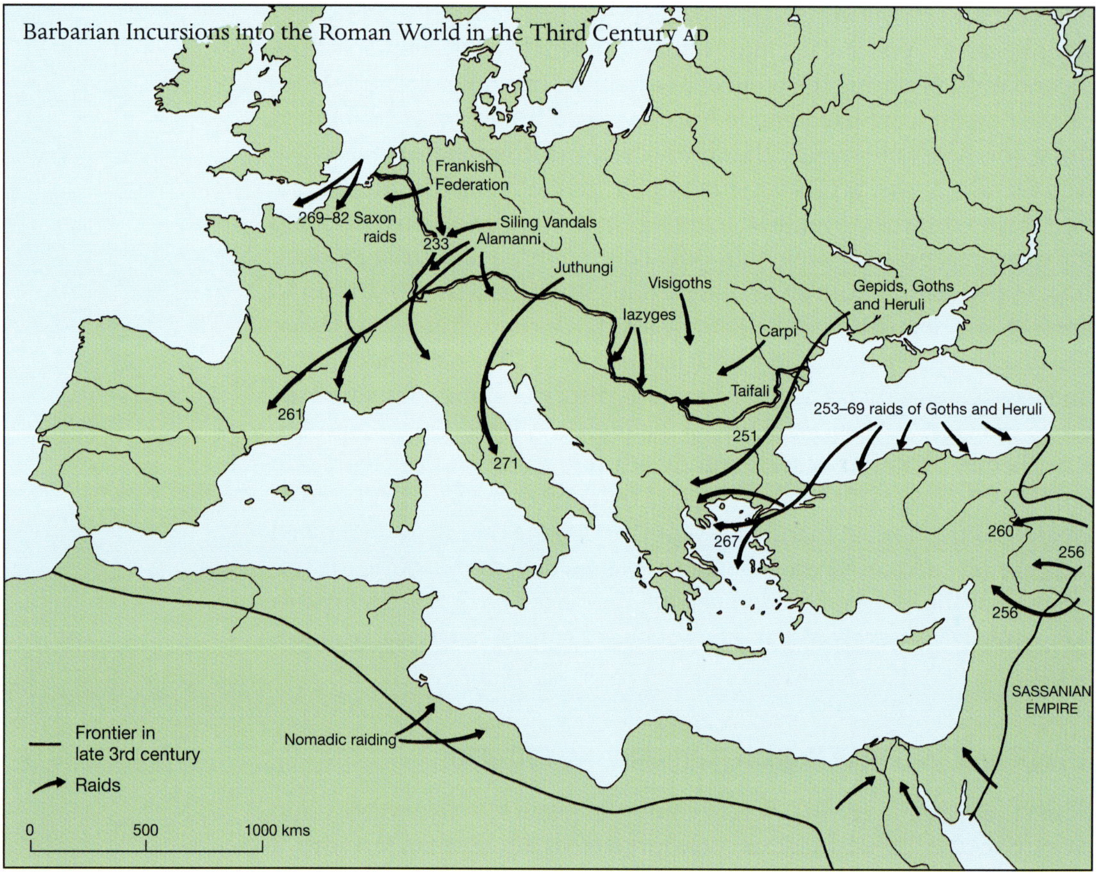

10.1 Barbarian incursions into the Roman world in the late third century AD.

confederacies, the pressures on the frontier mounted. In response existing Roman forts were strengthened and new ones built, but the preparations were inadequate and in the decade 250–60 the land east of the Upper Rhine was abandoned as the Roman army fell back to the safety of long-abandoned forts on the west bank of the river. In 260 or 261 the Alamanni, taking advantage of disarray in the Roman command, swept across the frontier and through Gaul, raiding and destroying as they went. In the next year the Franks followed and, having plundered Gaul, they moved into Spain, sacking Tarragona, and then took ship to Africa, where it seems one group set up a successful pirate base which operated until 272, disrupting shipping in the west Mediterranean and Atlantic.

The growing crisis on the Rhine led to the governor, Postumus, setting himself up as emperor in the west in 260, creating a separate Gallic empire which was to last until 274. One of the prime tasks of this new regime was to restore order in the west and this, it seems, was successfully accomplished. But the barbarian threat remained, and in the turmoil that followed the restoration of the west to central rule in 274 a more massive incursion took place. This time the Franks and Alamanni were joined by Vandals and Burgundians. One contemporary source tells us that sixty Gallic towns—about half of the total in the Gallic provinces—were badly damaged and in need of restoration. At this time Frankish ships were active in the Channel, using the rivers to penetrate deep inland. The situation was serious, and the very large number of coin hoards of this period found throughout Gaul and Britain shows that panic was widespread, exacerbated by unrest and brigandage in the countryside.

The Emperor Probus (276–82) dealt effectively with the crisis, rebuilding towns and restoring the Rhine frontier, and although the situation remained highly unstable the land frontier held. In the Channel, however, Frankish and now Saxon pirates continued to create serious trouble for the coastal communities in Gaul and Britain. To cope with the threat a Menapian marine, Carausius, was appointed with the specific brief of ridding the seas of pirates, but falling foul of the central administration in 286 he proclaimed himself emperor of Britain and he and his successor retained their breakaway island empire until it was recaptured and returned to the central authorities in 296. The events of the late third century in the west had shaken the empire, and although a semblance of stability was restored behind the toughened frontier it was only a temporary respite.

The campaigns fought against the Germanic tribes in the frontier region at the end of the third and beginning of the fourth centuries, though limited in extent, appear to have been successful. Of the large numbers of prisoners and other displaced persons resulting from these activities many were settled within the empire, usually in the frontier zones, as *laeti*—that is, prisoners of war who were granted land to farm in return for military service. There were several advantages to such a system. By giving potentially troublesome prisoners a stake in the land the Roman authorities were returning to productivity territory abandoned by the frightened and dwindling provincial population, at the same time peopling it with seasoned fighters who would defend their livelihood against further barbarian attack. In simple demographic terms surplus population from north of the frontier was being siphoned off to fill the population vacuum to the south. Another method of readjustment that became increasingly popular from about this time was the use of contingents of Frankish and Alamannic troops in the Roman army. To begin with they were recruited as regular auxiliary units and are listed as *cohortes* and *alae* in the traditional manner, but as their number increased throughout the fourth century these confederate troops (*foederati*) were organized more loosely. By the end of the century the army had become heavily Germanized. Detachments of Franks, for example, are known to have served not only in Gaul and Spain but also in Asia Minor, Egypt, and Mesopotamia, and some Franks, Alamanni, and Vandals aspired to the highest military ranks.

The settlement of successive groups of *laeti* in northern Gaul throughout the fourth century is reflected in the appearance of distinctive weapon graves scattered throughout much of the region from the Rhine to the Loire. Stationed throughout the same area were officials—*praefecti laetorum*—whose job it was to oversee the immigrant families and arrange their military service (10.2). The evidence is sufficient to suggest that the number of settlers was large, and by the end of the fourth century the gradual ethnic change that was taking place must have begun to be quite noticeable.

Whilst all this was in progress a new phase of Germanic raiding began in 350 but was contained by the Emperor Julian and culminated in a Roman victory near Strasbourg in 357. Further groups of Germans were brought into the empire and settled in the frontier region, including a branch of the Frankish confederacy—the Salini—who were given land just west of the Rhine mouth. It was the Salini who, in the mid-fifth century, were to assume the leadership of the Franks in northern Gaul. Julian's victory in 357 did not stem the tide, and throughout the 360s suc-

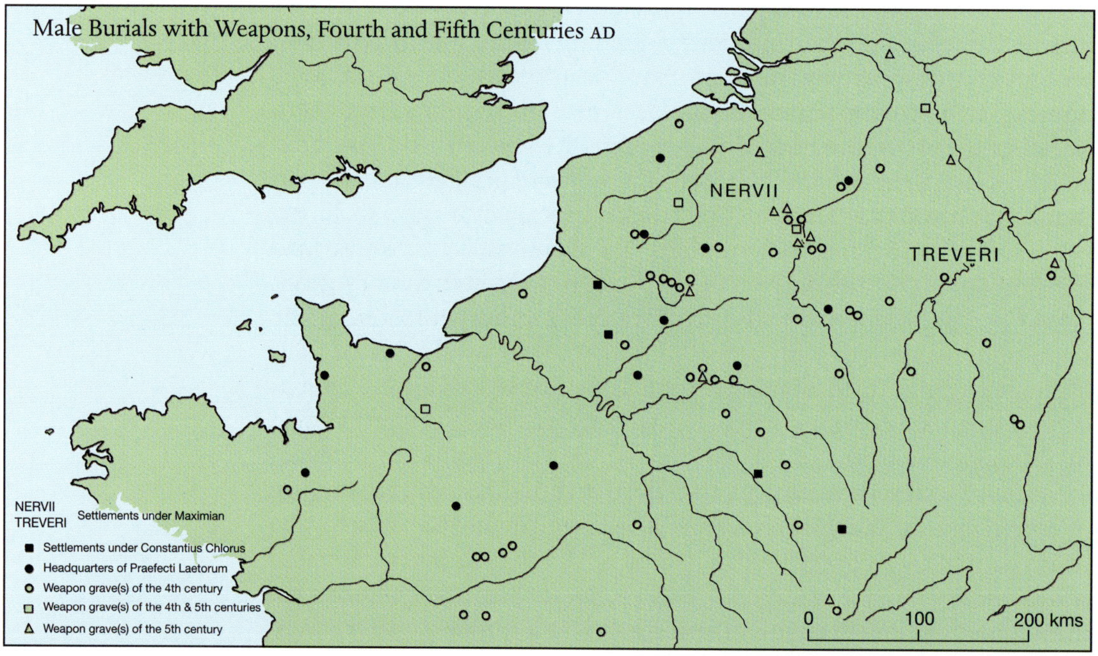

10.2 Male burials with weapons of the fourth and fifth centuries AD in northern Gaul indicate the extent of the settlement of *laeti* under the control of *Praefecti Laetorum*.

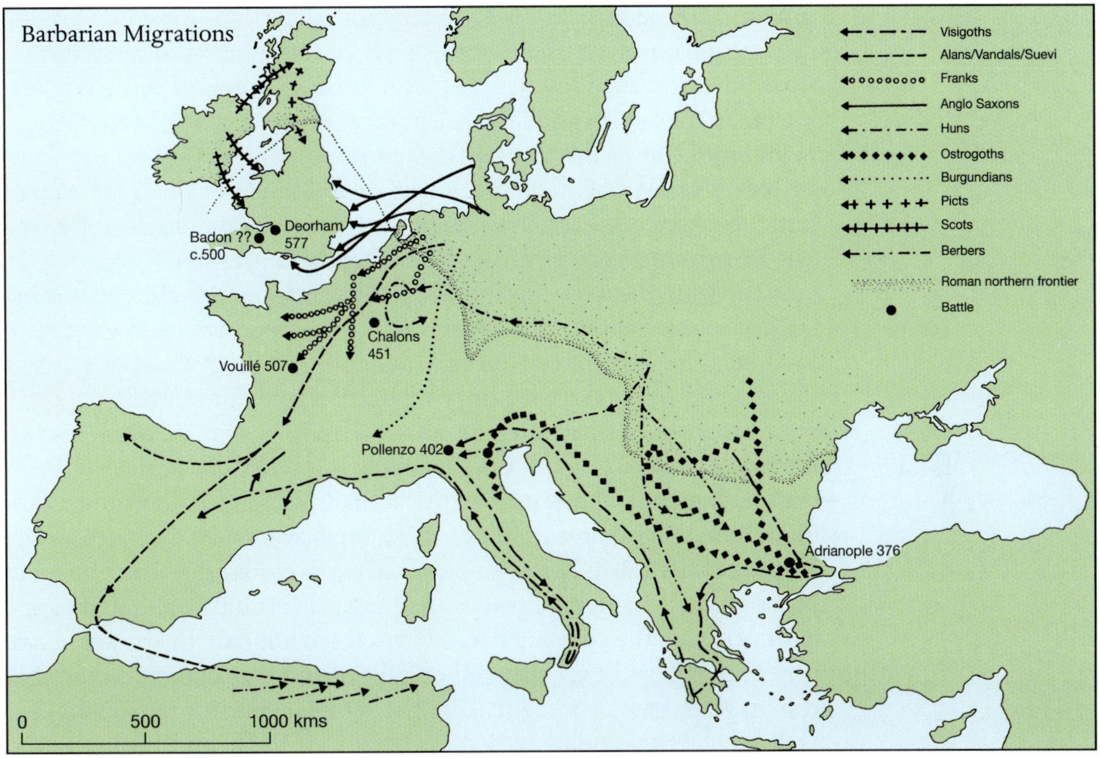

10.3 Barbarian migrations in the late fourth to early sixth centuries.

cessive Roman armies were actively engaged along the Rhine. Nor was Britain free of these problems. Early in 360 the Picts of central Scotland and the Scots (at this time living in Ireland) began to cause serious trouble in the northern frontier region. Five years later further attacks were recorded, this time including Attacotti, from the Western Isles or Ireland, and Saxons from northern Germany. Matters reached a head in 367 when a concerted attack was launched (a *barbarica conspiratio*) involving Picts, Scots, Attacotti, Saxons, and Franks during which much of the province was thrown into confusion and the Roman fleet commander killed. Peace was not restored until 369, but even then it was only a temporary respite.

From 370 to 410 the political confusion deepened and the Roman empire sank quickly into anarchy (10.3). Britons, beset by raiders on all sides and deserted by successive military commanders, whose interest lay in leading armies to the Continent to fight their cause, turned to their own defence. In Gaul the Franks both inside and outside of the province were engaged in negotiations and bound by treaties of mutual support, while the Roman military fought to plug holes in the rapidly disintegrating Rhine frontier. Meanwhile, in the east the Visigoths, employed by the

Emperor Theodosius in his campaign for leadership, were now totally out of control. In 392 the Bishop of Constantinople in desperation recorded that they had many times 'overrun huge tracts of our lands, setting fire to the countryside and seizing the towns. Instead of returning to their homes, like drunken revellers they mock us.' It was a short step from the Balkans to Italy, and by the winter of 408–9, under the leadership of Alaric, the Visigothic army was besieging Rome. When, in the following year, no ransom was offered the city was sacked.

By this time the west was in turmoil. In the winter of 406–7 the Rhine had frozen over, allowing huge numbers of Alans, Suebi, and Vandals to flood into the Roman provinces. Gaul collapsed into chaos as peasant revolts broke out in the west and rival Roman generals used the opportunity to stake their claims to the imperial throne. One of these was an obscure army officer from Britain calling himself Constantine III. With what remained of the British army he made a dash for Gaul and established himself at Arles, creating a new breakaway Gallic empire which lasted until his defeat by the imperial army in 411. By this time the main thrust of the Germanic invasion had passed through Gaul, and in the autumn of 409 the combined force of 200,000 Vandals, Suebi, and Alans were in northern Spain engaged in 'pillage and massacre without pity'. Roman resistance disintegrated in the familiar bids for personal glory, while the Siling Vandals settled in Baetica, the Alans in Lusitania, and Suebi and the Asding Vandals in Gallaecia. The situation in Iberia was further complicated when in 415 the Visigoths, who had previously sacked Rome, crossed the Pyrenees and, from their court established at Barico, proceeded to wipe out the Siling Vandals in Baetica and the Alans in Lusitania. As a result of this impressive feat the Visigoths were persuaded by the imperial authorities to return to Gaul in 418 and were given land to settle in Aquitania in return for military services. Of the Germanic groups remaining in Iberia the Asding Vandals, led by Gaiseric, quit Europe in 429, crossing the Straits of Gibraltar into Africa, leaving the Suebi still based in Gallaecia as masters of the Peninsula. The return of the Visigoths in 456, at the instigation of Rome, marked the beginning of a long struggle for domination, the Visigoths upholding what remained of Roman values.

In Gaul the early fifth century was an equally confused period. In the north the Salian and Rhineland Franks were in firm control, and we hear of raids against the rump of the Roman province in 413, 420, and 428, but equally some groups of Franks joined the Roman side against the Vandals while others became involved in squabbles between contending Roman generals. In the south two large confederate groups had been settled, the Visigoths in Aquitania in 418 and the Burgundians in the south-east in 443. Both groups were under the command of their own kings and held these lands with the agreement of the Roman government in return for military services. In Armorica, Britons from the south-west peninsula and Wales had already begun to settle, while in other parts of the maritime region small bands of Saxons had established themselves, in the Pas-de-Calais, Lower Normandy, and the Loire mouth.

That part of northern Gaul that remained was still nominally under imperial control. In the 430s and 440s it was commanded by a Roman general, Aëtius, who maintained a delicately balanced relationship with his encircling barbarian neighbours. His renown was such that the exhausted inhabitants of Britain appealed to him to send help against the inflow of Saxon settlers, but it was no good—the situation in Gaul was now too pressing. Aëtius was on good terms with some of the Frankish elite, and his careful diplomacy paid off when in 451 Attila and his massive Hunnish army attacked the west. Among the forces arrayed on the Roman side at the Battle of the Catalaunian Fields were Salian Franks, Burgundians, and Visigoths. Their active involvement contributed in no small part to Attila's defeat. But the great victory was almost the last gasp of the exhausted empire. Three years later Aëtius was assassinated by order of the emperor, and within a few decades what remained of Gaul was swallowed up by the rapidly growing Frankish state.

Sufficient will have been said in this brief outline to give some idea of the speed and magnitude of the changes which gripped western Europe in the two hundred years or so after 250. The first barbarian incursion caught the Roman world ill-prepared yet still able to respond effectively, but a century later it was very different and the slide into chaos was astonishingly fast. The principal participants were Germanic peoples from the North European Plain, and if the numbers given by contemporary historians are reliable the size of the populations on the move was frighteningly large. But the fact that Picts, various tribes from Ireland, Welsh, and south-western Britons were also taking to their ships to seek new lands shows that much of western Europe was caught up in the restlessness of the times. Nor should we forget the many, though obscure, references to peasant revolts in Britain, western Gaul, and Spain: it is as if the whole countryside was on the move. Against this quickly sketched background we can begin to look in some detail at Atlantic Europe.

The Gallic Empire

When Philip the Arab celebrated the millennium of Rome in AD 247 anyone familiar with the Rhine frontier would have been aware that here lay the empire's Achilles heel. The build-up of Germanic tribesmen—the confederacies of the Franks and Alamanni—was serious enough, but an equal danger lay in the power of the Roman frontier army to make or break emperors. Would-be contenders for the throne, popular with the troops, would be tempted to carry off what forces they needed to support their cause. So it was in 253. The result was that Franks and Alamanni broke through the depleted frontier, causing havoc in Gaul as far south as Arles. It was the most devastating attack on the empire since the rampage of the Cimbri and Teutones 350 years earlier.

To make good the damage his actions had caused the new emperor Valerian sent his son Gallienus (10.4) to the frontier to restore order. Although matters were stabilized sufficiently to allow Gallienus to claim the title *Restitutor Galliarum*, the lands east of the Rhine were lost and the Germanic tribes had tasted blood.

What follows is not entirely clear, but Gallienus quit the German frontier about 258, leaving things in the hands of his commander-in-chief, Postumus. Two years later Postumus (10.4) was proclaimed emperor by his troops and sent a message to Gallienus announcing that he intended to remain in Gaul as protector. By this act he was claiming the independence of Gaul—the new Roman empire of the Gauls—which was soon to include Britain and Spain as well. His murder, by his own troops in about 268, was followed by a period of increasing instability—four emperors rose and fell in quick succession. The last of these, the governor of Aquitania, P. Esuvius Tetricus (10.4)—a man who, judging from his middle name, was proud of his Celtic ancestry—eventually bowed to the inevitable and surrendered to the legitimate emperor, Aurelian, in 274. In Aurelian's triumph Tetricus marched in full Gallic dress before being allowed to return to his civilian career.

The immediate result of the collapse of the Gallic empire was a massive attack on Gaul by the Franks and Alamanni in 275–6, far more devastating than the events twenty years before, and it was only by the strenuous efforts of the new emperor, Probus, that the situation was

10.4 Coins of Gallienus (253–68), Postumus (259–68) and Tetricus (270–3).

restored. By now most of the cities of Gaul had adopted a siege mentality, building massive defensive walls to create protected inner enclaves.

It is difficult from the terse and distorted scraps of contemporary writing to judge the ethos of the brief Gallic empire—to what extent it heralded a resurgence of Gallic nationalism or was simply part of the game-play of would-be emperors. In all probability it meant different things to different people, but nationalists would not have been slow to take advantage of the new opportunities.

Armorica, deeply conservative and adhering to its traditional rite of cremation burial throughout, provides a well-studied example of how the communities of Atlantic Gaul reacted to the dramatic events of the late third century. Throughout the history of Roman Armorica there is an undercurrent of unrest dimly visible but ever present. The first known incident, recorded on an inscription dated to the late second century found in Croatia, mentions trouble in Armorica sufficiently serious to require a force to be sent from Britain to restore the situation. It is possible that this may have been a specific uprising in the general unrest recorded in the west in the 180s, during which peasants and deserters 'overran the whole land of the Gauls and Spaniards, attacking the largest cities, burning parts of them and plundering the rest before returning' (Herodian 1. 10. 3). A century later, in 282–4, a widespread peasant revolt gripped the maritime regions between the Seine and the Loire foreshadowing a far more serious peasant uprising in the early fifth century (below, pp. 460–2). These historical scraps should not be built into too grand a scheme, but together they hint at an undercurrent of social discontent that could erupt from time to time. It may well be that the interior of the Armorican peninsula, away from the more prosperous coastal zone, harboured a large peasant population that adhered to traditional, pre-Roman values.

The coastal regions seem to have been none too safe in the late third century. During the Gallic empire a significant number of coin hoards were buried in the maritime zone from Pas-de-Calais to the Loire, and Postumus is known to have fought against pirates in the North Sea. There is also evidence that villas were burnt at this time. Taken together, these facts suggest that coastal raiding, presumably by Franks, must have been an increasing hazard.

It may have been in this context that two extensive fortifications were built on the north coast, Alet at the mouth of the Rance and Le Yaudet on the estuary of the Léguer (10.5, 10.6). Both sites were promontory locations with excellent harbours guarding river routes to the interior, and both had been major oppida in the Late Iron Age at the time of the Armorican revolt against Caesar. The excavation at Le Yaudet shows that

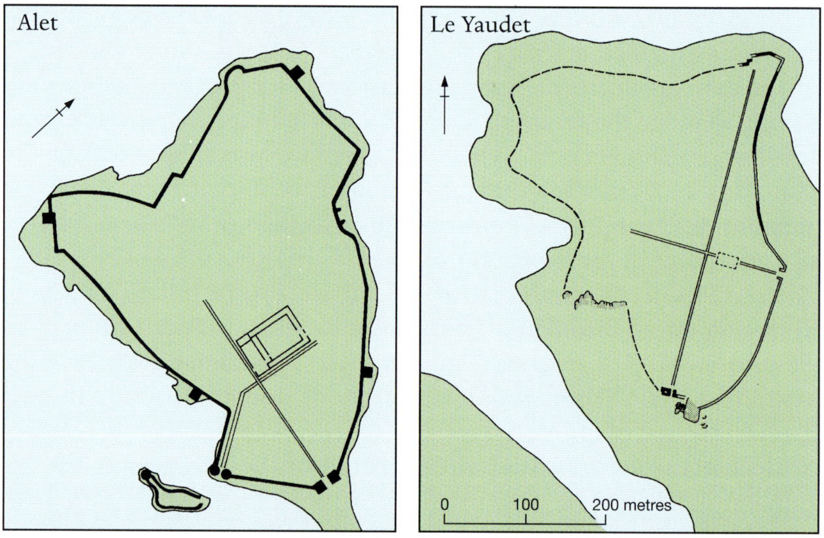

10.5 Defended settlements of the late third century on the north coast of Armorica.

10.6 The promontory of Le Yaudet, an Iron Age fortification refortified in the late third century AD, commanding the estuary of the Léguer.

the new Roman defensive wall replicated exactly the line of the Iron Age defences last used three hundred years before, and the same may well be true of Alet. The building of these two major fortifications during the period of the Gallic empire raises a number of interesting questions. Their locations add support to the suggestion that sea raiding was now a serious problem, but the choice of ancient Gaulish sites and the careful way in which the Roman wall exactly follows the earlier fortifications (at least at Le Yaudet) hint that there may have been a conscious returning to the past—the new order perhaps laying claim to a Gaulish legitimacy. The abandonment of both sites for decades after the end of the Gallic empire also adds some support to the suggestion, since it is clear from other evidence that the pirate threat was undiminished.

The restoration of Gaul to the control of the legitimate emperor did not bring an end to the changes now under way in Armorica. That none of the villas destroyed in the late third century were rebuilt suggests a retreat from the economic system that fostered villa estates—a possibility that gains some support from palaeobotanical evidence from central Finistère, which shows a dramatic decrease in cultivation accompanied by forest encroachment at the end of the third century. At the same time the garum industry, so important to the local economy, had ceased by the century's end.

The towns of Armorica (10.7), which might be expected to reflect the fortunes of the region in the later empire, have as yet produced little of direct relevance to the question, but the two inland towns of Carhaix and Corseul remained undefended and in decline, and at Carhaix the city's aqueduct had broken down by the late third century and was not repaired. Rennes, Nantes, and Vannes, on the other hand, were all fortified with substantial walls provided with forward-projecting bastions. At Nantes the defences date to the reign of Constantius (305–6). The picture which is beginning to emerge, then, suggests that while eastern Armor-

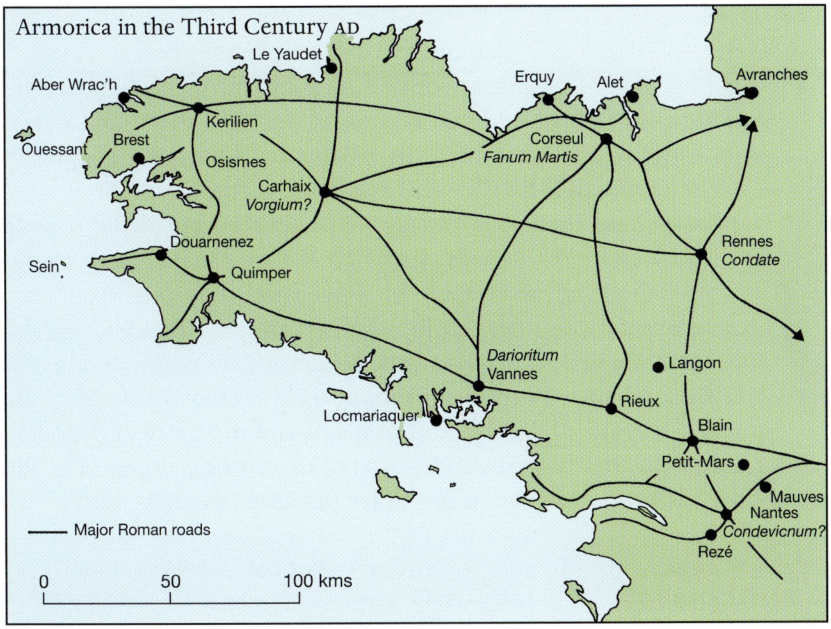

10.7 Armorica in the late third century AD.

ica followed the pattern of the rest of Gaul, defending its cities to provide protected administrative enclaves in an increasingly unstable countryside, the western part of the peninsula, remote from the area where the new order was being shaped, was left to itself. We saw the same east–west divide in the immediate pre-Roman era and will see it again from the fifth century onwards. It was as if the three hundred years of Roman rule was little more than an interlude.

Britain and the Defence of the Seaways: AD 250–350

From its headquarters at Gesoriacum (Boulogne) the British fleet (*classis Britannica*) patrolled the Channel and southern North Sea throughout the second and third centuries, keeping the seas safe for Roman shipping. At some stage, probably in the late second or early third century, it had been thought advisable to bring up detachments of troops from the northern frontier and place them in new forts built at Brancaster and Reculver to guard the Wash and the Thames estuary. The *cohors I Aquitanorum* was stationed at Brancaster while the *cohors I Baetasiorum* was assigned to Reculver. Whether or not these deployments were the result of increasing threat of raids it is impossible to say.

The first clear signs of increased naval activity came during the Gallic empire. Two coin types issued by Postumus, bearing the legends *Neptuno Comiti* and *Neptuno Reduci*, probably record naval victories against Frankish pirates off the Gaulish coast and will certainly have involved the *classis Britannica*.

Late in 285 Carausius, a Menapian by birth from the coastal region of what is now Belgium, was appointed to rid the seas of Belgica and Armorica of Frankish and Saxon pirates (10.8). His command would certainly have included the *classis Britannica*, though it is not specifically named, but he was also assigned an additional force comprising nine legionary detachments, probably totalling some 9,000 men in all. He was clearly an experienced military leader with a thorough knowledge of the sea and an impressive record as a land commander, having recently suppressed a widespread peasant revolt in Gaul. From the beginning his command, based on Gesoriacum (Boulogne), would have included not only the northern region of Gaul from the Rhine to the Loire but probably Britain as well. But within a short time of assuming command he fell foul of the authorities. As a contemporary historian records,

10.8 Coin of Carausius (287–93).

> although he caught many barbarians, he did not give their spoils back intact, either to the provincials or to the imperial treasury, and when he began to be suspected of

allowing the barbarians in so that he could intercept them sailing past with their spoils and thus become rich, under sentence of death from Maximian he assumed the imperial power and seized Britain. (Eutropius 9. 21)

This was probably in 286. What truth there was in the accusation it is impossible to say, but it presents a not-unlikely scenario. However, an equally plausible interpretation of events is that Maximian invented the charge to rid himself of a potentially dangerous rival.

Once established in Britain, and with his Gaulish command still intact, Carausius was in a strong position. Nonetheless he extended his fleet by enlisting Gallic merchantmen and Frankish pirates. In the winter of 288–9 the Emperor Maximian ordered a new Roman fleet to be built on the Rhine and Moselle, presumably with the intention of attacking Carausius' coastal installations by sea. The preparations came to nothing. Bad weather was blamed, but this might obscure a defeat at the hands of Carausius or his allies, somewhere in the vicinity of the Rhine mouth. There matters rested for four years while Carausius consolidated his position in Britain.

The next attempt to oust him was led by Constantius Chlorus in 293. In a rapid thrust from the imperial base at Trier Constantius reached Boulogne and proceeded to blockade the port with a barrier of piles and rubble. Incarcerated with no hope of relief the headquarters garrison surrendered, and with it the maritime regions of Gaul passed into the hands of the imperial government. For Carausius and his supporters the setback was serious and unsettling, and not long afterwards, he was assassinated by his finance officer, Allectus, who took over the role of emperor of Britain.

Over the next three years Constantius built ships in the coastal ports and estuaries of Gaul, and when all was ready the invasion began. While Constantius caused a diversion in mid-Channel, his troop-carriers, commanded by Asclepiodotus, slipped into a Solent port unnoticed: 'just at the right moment a mist covered the surface of the sea so thickly that the enemy fleet, watching in ambush near the Isle of Wight, was bypassed without realizing it' (*Panegyrici Latini* 8 (5). 15–1). On landing, Asclepiodotus burned his boats and marched towards London. En route he met and routed Allectus' force. Allectus died in the battle and the rump of the defeated army, composed largely of Germanic mercenaries, fell back towards London, intent on sacking the capital. But the timely arrival of Constantius and his troops sailing up the Thames saved the day, providing him with the occasion later to issue a commemorative medallion showing the grateful city personified welcoming the conquering hero (10.9).

The brief Carausian episode is a fascinating affair, revealing much

10.9 The Arras medallion issued by Constantius to commemorate the liberation of Britain from the rebels. The reverse side of the medal shows the grateful citizens of London personified welcoming Constantius I as he rides to the relief of the city.

about the later Roman world. Carausius in his youth on the Belgian coast had taken to the sea, serving as a steersman. At this time the detachments of Frankish *laeti* living in the countryside would have been a familiar sight. It is hardly surprising that Frankish 'pirates' were later to serve in his fleet and Germanic mercenaries in his army. There must have been occasions when allegiances and loyalties were more than a little confused in the ethnic and cultural melting pot of the Channel and North Sea coasts. But this said, Carausius was by no means making a stand for native independence. He was first and foremost a Roman with a strong desire for official recognition, determined to acquire a share of imperial power. Nothing could be clearer from the placatory propaganda coinage he had minted, culminating in an issue showing three heads, his own and that of the co-emperors Maximian and Diocletian, under the legend *Carausius et fratres sui*, 'Carausius and his brothers'.

The most stark reminders of this period of turmoil in the late third century are the gaunt fortresses that fringe the British coastline from Southampton Water to the Wash—large enclosures with strongly built masonry walls strengthened at intervals with forward-projecting towers to take heavy artillery (10.10, 10.11). These are something entirely new—a military architecture redolent of defence rather than aggression—a style that was rapidly being adopted on the Continent by the urban authorities and the military alike in the wake of the barbarian inroads.

There has been continuous debate about the date and significance of the British forts over the last century or so, but uncertainties still remain. Already by the middle of the third century a system of coastal defences had begun to evolve. The principal bases of the *classis Britannica* were still, as we have seen, at Dover and Boulogne, with another establishment near Lympne and possibly other smaller installations at Richborough and Reculver. Later two military detachments had been moved down from the northern frontier and installed in new forts at Brancaster and Reculver. Other defended sites, which may have functioned as part of a unified system, were Brough-on-Humber and Caistor-by-Yarmouth, while at Richborough a strongly defended signal station was set up. There is also the possibility that coastal erosion has destroyed other installations. The system, if such it can be called, evidently functioned to guard the shores of eastern Britain, from the Straits of Dover to the Humber, a coast vulnerable to raid by pirates working the North Sea. One of the latest forts to be added to this early system was Burgh Castle on the River Yare. It is a curious transitional structure, begun in the style of the typical second-century forts, with rounded corners, internal rampart, and towers, but completed in the later style with forward-projecting bastions. The simplest explanation would be to see it as a construction in progress overtaken by events. In its completed state Burgh Castle belongs to the late-third-century reorganization of the coastal defences. At this time the existing installations at Richborough, Dover, and Lympne were replaced by entirely new forts, two additional forts were built on the east coast at Bradwell and Walton Castle, while the Channel coast was given protection for the first time with forts at Pevensey, Portchester, and Clausentum (near Southampton). Where dating evidence is available all of the forts with bastions best fit in the late third century, though some could be later. All that can safely be said by way of detail is that Portchester cannot be earlier than the reign of Carausius, and Pevensey was built in or after the time of Allectus. Such is the tantalizing imprecision of the archaeological evidence.

Standing back from the detail, it is clear that the British coastal defences were being continuously, if sporadically, updated and that in the late third century, under the impetus of intensifying raids, at least nine

10.10 The third- and fourth-century coastal fortifications along the channel coasts of Britain and Gaul.

new forts of the most up-to-date design were put up. Although it is tempting to suggest that these structures were added by Carausius and Allectus to protect their island empire from the legitimate forces of Rome (and the evidence as we know it would just accommodate such a view), it is safer to allow that the late forts may have been built over as much as seventy years (*c.*260–*c.*330), starting with Burgh and ending with Pevensey. At any event, by the early fourth century, when a semblance of peace had been restored, all the installations were in place and available for use as the threat from the sea began to build to alarming proportions. These are matters to which we will return (pp. 450–2).

10.11 (*facing*) Portchester Castle, at the upper reaches of Portsmouth Harbour, was built, probably under the authority of Carausius, in the late third century. Thereafter it was used almost continuously until the early decades of the nineteenth century. The outer wall is entirely of Roman work though refaced in places.

What all this meant to the inhabitants of south-eastern Britain it is difficult to say. Large numbers of late-third-century coin hoards and evidence of the destruction of villas in coastal regions are sufficient to show that the area was unsafe, but once Carausius had established himself there is every reason to think that stability was restored. Carausius certainly reformed the monetary system and minted good-quality coinage, while supporting the provincial infrastructure in other ways like maintaining roads. Canterbury was enclosed within a defensive wall some time in the late third century, though not necessarily under the auspices of Carausius, while at London the riverside defensive wall was erected in or soon after 294, either by Allectus in preparation for the imperial attack or by Constantius after 296. Whatever the precise chronology, it is clear that at least some of the towns of south-eastern Britain were following the Gallic communities in beginning to look after their own defence. With its shore defences and fortified cities Britain was beginning to develop the visible signs of a siege mentality. Yet the trauma passed, and the early decades of the fourth century were to see the elite of the south-east indulging in an almost reckless spending spree, adorning their country residences with figured mosaics and other luxuries on a scale never before experienced.

The Irish Sea: *c.* AD 250–350

The west coast of Britain, from the Severn estuary to the Solway Firth, with its innumerable inlets and havens, was far more difficult to defend against threat of seaborne attack than the south-east, yet some defensive precautions were put in hand (10.12). The most impressive of these is the fort with regularly spaced towers at Cardiff, sited to guard the upper reaches of the Severn estuary and its rich hinterland. Further north, existing forts at Caernarvon and Lancaster were rebuilt and a small fortlet was installed at Caer Gybi on the west coast of Anglesey to guard a landing beach. Many of the other earlier military installations along the coastal

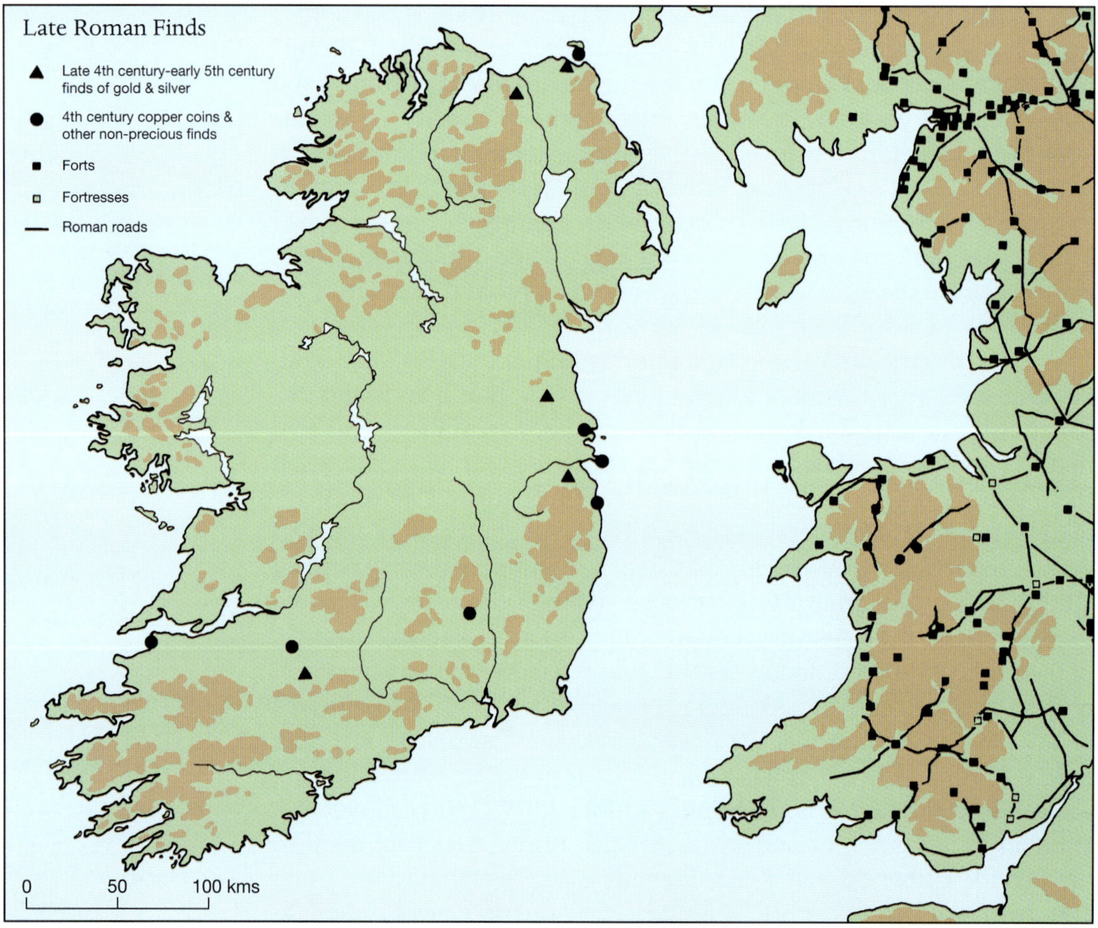

10.12 Ireland and the Irish Sea in the fourth and early fifth centuries. The defences of western Britain seem to have lacked the co-ordination of those of the Channel and North Sea coasts. The fourth-century coins and other finds are shown only for Ireland.

zone from Chester north to the west end of Hadrian's Wall remained in use throughout the late third and fourth centuries. Although these scattered sites can hardly be called a system, they did offer some degree of protection to the vulnerable coasts facing Ireland.

The archaeological evidence is sufficient to show that there was regular intercourse between Ireland and western Britain. Much of it, at least in the first and second centuries, would have been normal commerce organized by local entrepreneurs on both sides of the Irish Sea, little more than had been practised for generations before, but by the late third century the mood seems to have changed, with the Irish taking a more proactive stance. Some may have offered themselves to Roman recruiting officers; some, no doubt, took advantage of the sea to make quick raids on the richer parts of the province; while others migrated to Wales to find new lands. To distinguish between these activities and to offer a chronology is not always easy, given the fragmentary nature of historical and archaeological sources.

One of the clearest of the historical traditions for Irish settlement in Britain is preserved in a saga—*The Expulsion of the Déisi*—which tells of the migration of the Déisi from Co. Meath to Munster and Leinster and of the further migration of part of the tribe to Dyfed in south-west Wales. One of the leaders named was Eochaid son of Artchorp, whose name occurs in Welsh genealogies. This has encouraged some scholars to work back from known dates in an attempt to date the initial settlement. By this method it has been suggested that the first migrants arrived in the late third century. However, others have dismissed the detail of the early sagas as largely invented and prefer to date the earliest Irish settlement in Wales to the late fourth century, possibly after the province had been stripped of troops by Magnus Maximus in 383. That large numbers of Irish had settled in the south-west and north-west of Wales by the fifth century while others had crossed to Scotland, establishing themselves in Argyll, is not in doubt, but how early these movements began is unclear. The building of the fort at Cardiff, probably in the late third century, might be thought to suggest trouble from the Irish Sea at this time, while the comparatively large number of coin hoards buried in the late third century in south Wales, together with the violent destruction of the villa at Ely near Cardiff, add some support to the view that these were troubled times.

There is nothing unlikely in there having been small-scale movements of Irish into Wales as early as the late third century. The two primary areas where Irish settlement is later attested—the extreme south-west and the Lleyn peninsula in the north-west—were both regions where the native tradition remained strong throughout the Roman period (above, pp. 412–15). They are both close to Ireland—less than 90 kilometres away. It is highly likely that the two regions were linked by exchange systems and allegiances going back for many generations. In the increasing chaos of the late third century people may well have migrated. Once the foothold had been established, more would have followed. It is quite conceivable that during the fourth century the Roman administration accepted some of the immigrant groups as *foederati*, and settled them in strategic locations with the intent of repelling further comers.

What is possible for Wales is also possible for Cornwall and western Scotland, where Irish communities were certainly established by the fifth century. Earlier penetration remains a possibility, but an unproven one.

Settlers with links to their homeland and mercenary soldiers returning home from service in the Roman army could be the explanation of the scattering of late-Roman finds in Ireland, distributed not only in the same

10.13 Part of a hoard of Roman silver of early fifth-century date from Ballinrees, Co. Derry. The hoard may have been loot from Britain or bullion payment for mercenary services.

regions as the first- and second-century material in the centre east coast and the north coast, but now also inland across the south (10.12). But nor should we forget that much of this, not least the great silver hoards from Ballinrees, Co. Derry (10.13), and Balline, Co. Limerick, are quite likely to have been spoils from successful raids on the vulnerable coasts of the fast-disintegrating province. These late raids, beginning in the late fourth century, and the population movements associated with them will be considered in more detail later (pp. 456–60).

Atlantic Iberia: *c.* AD 250–350

To what extent western Iberia suffered during the barbarian inroads of the late third century it is difficult to say. The horde of rampaging Franks who crossed into Tarraconensis in AD 262 is said to have sacked Tarraco before sailing to North Africa. Some time later, in AD 297, Franks from the pirate bases on the African coast were still a nuisance in the west Mediterranean, where their raids extended to the Spanish coasts. There is no record during this time of the intervention of the *Legio VII Gemina*, stationed at Legio (León) in the north-west. Its prime purpose was to guard the gold-mines, and it seems to have remained steadfastly at its post. Large numbers of coin hoards of this period suggest extensive unrest. The concentration of hoards along the Atlantic coasts of Lusitania and Gallaecia is an indication that disruptions had spread far from the Mediterranean fringe, and hints at quite separate troubles now affecting the distant Atlantic shores. Perhaps it was the awareness of these problems which lay behind Diocletian's decision to split the unwieldy province of Tarraconensis into smaller, more manageable units in 298. As a result of this administrative readjustment the north-west corner of the Peninsula was separated to become the province of Gallaecia, with its capital at Bracara Augusta (Braga).

Atlantic Trade Before the Deluge

Surprisingly little is known from documentary sources about trade in general in the Roman west in the late Roman period, but there are recurring references to the export of British wool and woollen cloaks, and in the fourth century British corn was regularly trans-shipped to the Rhine to feed the army when local harvests failed to meet the military demand. These two commodities, together with tin and lead, may well have been the staples which Britain supplied to the empire throughout the Roman period. Much of this trade would have followed the southern North Sea route linking London and other Thames estuary ports to the Rhine mouth. The persistence of this route, after the troubles of the late third century, is well documented in the archaeological record by the discovery, in southern Britain, of imported Continental pottery, produced at Mayen in the Rhine valley and in the Argonne region between the Meuse and the Aisne (10.14). These imported wares are found, as might be expected, at sites around the Thames estuary, with the largest concentrations being at London and the port of Richborough in Kent. The reverse pattern shows British products from the Oxfordshire kilns, and other production centres, scattered along the coastal regions of Belgica. These distributions are sufficient to show that the southern North Sea route remained active throughout the late third and fourth centuries in spite of the insecurities caused by pirate activity, but of the intensity of trade and the interruptions which sporadic upsurges in raiding may have caused there is little to be said.

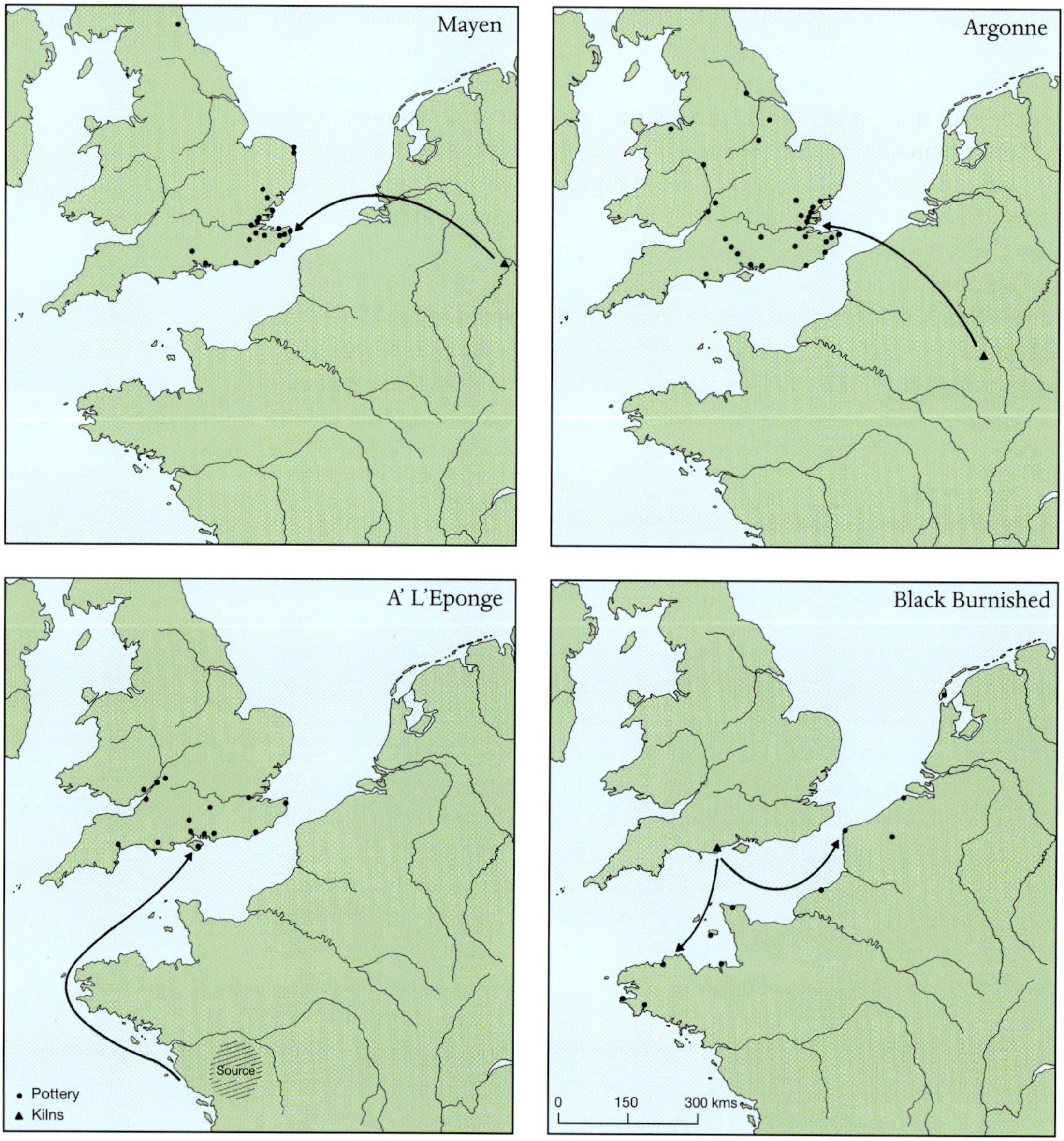

10.14/15 The distribution of pottery imported to and exported from Britain in the late third and fourth centuries AD.

Activity along the Atlantic routes is also reflected in ceramic distributions (10.15). The most revealing is that of a distinctive type of pottery known as *ceramic à l'éponge*, a finely made tableware with a glossy yellow-orange slip sometimes further ornamented with a darker marbled slip. The exact location of the production centre has not been identified, but it must lie somewhere in western France between the Loire and the Gironde. From here vessels were traded northwards along the long-established Atlantic route to Armorica and to central southern Britain, occurring in largest quantity at the Solent port of Clausentum (near Southampton). That Clausentum was the main point of entry is shown by the fact that 70 per cent of the *à l'éponge* in Britain has been found within a radius of 80 kilometres from the port. But finds at Exeter and around the upper estuary of the Severn suggest that other, more westerly points of entry may have been in use as well. The reverse pattern can also be traced. British pottery from the New Forest pottery kilns and from the major centres around Poole Harbour, producing Black-burnished pottery, occurs widely in north-western Gaul at Cherbourg, Alet, and Le Yaudet in significant quantity and at other Armorican sites in lesser amounts. These products were no doubt trans-shipped through the south coast ports of Clausentum and Hamworthy (near Poole). The pottery evidence is sufficient to show that the Atlantic routes were in active operation, but we should remember that, useful though pottery is to an archaeologist as an indicator, this ceramic trade is unlikely to have been of much commercial value at the time. At best the pots are surrogates for trade in other commodities of which little record survives.

10.16 Ingots of lead from the Roman vessel wrecked on Les Sept Îles, off the north coast of Armorica.

More direct evidence of late Roman trade along the Atlantic seaways is offered by two shipwrecks, one from Les Sept-Îles off the north coast of Armorica near Ploumenac'h and the other from St Peter Port on Guernsey. The Sept-Îles vessel was carrying a cargo of lead ingots of which 271 were recovered, totalling 22 tonnes of metal in ingots varying in weight from 28 to 150 kilograms (10.16). Inscriptions on some of the ingots mention the Brigantes and Iceni, presumably indicating the place of origin of the metal. The Brigantian region of northern Britain was, indeed, lead-producing, but the Iceni possessed no lead in their territory. This apparent difficulty could, however, be overcome by supposing the lead to have been exported through one of the Icenian ports where a local *negotiatore* stamped it. If so, the vessel had made a long journey before it met its violent end.

The St Peter Port wreck was comparatively well-preserved in the sheltered waters of the harbour, and in consequence a range of finds was recovered in addition to a substantial part of the vessel itself. The cargo which the ship was still holding when it caught fire in the harbour some time in the 280s included blocks of pitch derived from pine trees, quantities of grain, and an unknown commodity carried in barrels. It is impossible on present evidence to say where these items came from. The pitch could have been produced in western France or Armorica, where pine trees are prolific, while it is tempting to suggest that the barrels may have contained Armorican garum or western Gaulish wine. Pottery found in association with the vessel was probably used by the ship's crew but is an eclectic collection, including Dressel 30 amphorae from Marseilles, *à l'éponge* bowls from western France, Black-burnished jars from Poole Harbour, a cup from the Nene valley, and mortaria from East Anglia. It would have been possible to pick up the entire consignment in any major port like London, but it is not impossible that the pots were bought as and when needed in various ports around the coasts between the Gironde and the Wash.

While the two wrecks add fascinating details to our all-too sketchy knowledge of trade along the Atlantic routes in the late third and fourth centuries, it is impossible, on evidence of this kind, to assess the volume of trade in comparison with the early Roman period or with contemporary late Roman trade across the southern North Sea. Atlantic trade is certainly of high archaeological visibility in the later period, and it could be argued that the pirate threat to the Rhine–Thames trade encouraged a greater use of the western routes. This is not unlikely, but the matter is incapable of proof.

Trade along the Atlantic coasts of Iberia remained active throughout the late third and fourth centuries, but there is no direct evidence of contact between Iberia and the systems north of the Garonne. Mediterranean commodities are more likely at this time to have used the river routes through Gaul than to have risked the much longer sea journeys around Iberia, in spite of the fact that sea transport was cheaper. This does not, however, preclude local cabotage linking the two systems in short-haul hops or a few more enterprising shipmasters facing the journey across the Bay of Biscay.

The 'Folk Wanderings' of the Germanic Tribes in Continental Europe: AD 350–500

At the beginning of this chapter we considered in broad outline the massive migration of Germanic tribes—Franks, Alamanni, Saxons, Suebi, Vandals, Burgundians, and Visigoths—that broke through the Rhine frontier, first to rampage and loot and later to settle in the western Roman provinces in the 150 years after the middle of the fourth century. Here we will look in a little more detail at the immigrants who ended up along the Atlantic coasts of Europe.

The story of the Franks is one of progressive dominance over northern Gaul, culminating about AD 500 in a massive expansion under Clovis south and east into the territory of the Visigoths, Burgundians, and Alamanni. The Franks' presence in northern Gaul began with intermittent raids on the Roman provinces and soon turned into the licensed settlement of communities of *laeti* well within the provincial boundaries. To judge from the headquarters of the officers charged with their administration—the *praefecti laetorum*—the settlements were particularly dense between the Seine and the Meuse but occurred throughout Lower Normandy across to the borders of Brittany. By the beginning of the fifth century much of Gaul north of the Loire and west of the Rhine was settled by Frankish groups, both *laeti* and *foederati*, some still on active service with the Roman army. The presence of these groups is well represented in the archaeological record by graves accompanied by weapons.

After 350 troubles along the Rhine intensified, and it was as the result of campaigns in 357 and 358 that Salian Franks were settled within the empire south of the Rhine mouth, where they were to remain at peace until they assumed leadership of all the Franks in the middle of the fifth century.

In the aftermath of the barbarian invasion of 406–7 the many different Frankish groups entered the mêlée, some fighting on the Roman side, others against the Romans. In the famous battle fought by Aëtius against Attila and the Huns in 451 the Salian and Rhineland Franks fought with the Romans, but others, called Bructeri, sided with the Huns. At this stage the Salian Franks' principal town was Tournai, while that of the Rhineland Franks was Cologne.

Thereafter the expansion to the Loire began, with decisive battles at Orleans in 463, and Angers and at Soisson in the north in 486. Under the leadership of Clovis (*c.*481–511) the Franks were unified and the conquest of the south began, reaching the Mediterranean in the 530s–40s but leaving Brittany untouched.

Although Frankish pirates were a menace in the southern North Sea in the late third and fourth centuries, the Frankish communities appear to have paid little attention to the Channel coast, leaving it to be settled by small isolated bands of Saxons. One Saxon community is attested largely by place-name evidence around Boulogne, another is known from cemeteries in the zone from Bayeux to the Cotentin peninsula, while another group settled around the Loire mouth. The distribution is distinctly coastal, implying that the settlements were established by raiders coming in from the sea. These peoples were in all probability part of the movement that was impacting more strongly on the coasts of eastern Britain in the first half of the fifth century (below, p. 453). The size of the Saxon migrant groups in Gaul was probably quite small, and with the growth of Frankish power, by the mid-fifth century, they had ceased to be visible.

The settlement of the Visigoths in Aquitania in 418 was a deliberate Roman policy. Well aware that the rapid Germanization of northern Gaul was an inevitable result of the collapse of the frontier, and scared that the large-scale uprising of the peasants—the *bagaudae*—in Brittany and the Loire valley would spread to the still-prosperous area of Aquitania, the invitation to the Visigoths to settle in the region was a logical solution. The Visigoths had become thoroughly aware of the benefits of Roman civilization over the previous fifty years and this, combined with their abilities as fighters, was sufficient assurance that they could be relied upon to protect Aquitania as their own land. The exact details of the treaty arrangements are not known, but the Visigoths seem to have been given land to settle and farm and remained under the authority of their own king with the right to own slaves. It may even be that they were granted the privilege of collecting taxation. At any event, the arrangement worked and Aquitania prospered. One contemporary writer, Salvian, referred to Aquitania as the best part of all Gaul and a veritable paradise. Thereafter the Visigoths gradually assumed political authority, as links with Rome weakened and disappeared. That the experiment was judged a success by the central authorities is shown by the actions of Aëtius who, having destroyed the Rhine kingdom of the Burgundians in 437, settled the tribe in the south-east of Gaul six years later.

The Visigothic kingdom in Aquitania lasted until 507, when the Frankish army led by Clovis defeated the Visigoths at Vouillé near Poitiers and killed the king, Alaric II. In the aftermath Clovis proceeded to pillage the Visigothic treasury at Toulouse. After this, although the culture of Aquitania remained largely unaffected, the Frankish kings became the new overlords.

Some idea of the complexity of the situation in the Iberian Peninsula (10.17) in the fifth century has been outlined above (p. 428). In the west Gallaecia was held by the Suebi, while the south-west corner was the preserve of Alans and Siling Vandals, most of the rest of Lusitania being a region of disputed authority, much fought-over. The situation was to remain highly unstable until 475, by which time the Visigoths had established a new order in Iberia.

The Suebic enclave in Gallaecia, secure in the remote corner of the Peninsula and in control of the gold-mines, was a powerful force in the fifth century. They minted their own gold coins in the name of the reigning Roman emperor and maintained much of the Roman administrative infrastructure. From their safe haven successive armies were led against neighbouring territories. In 429 the Suebi campaigned south of the Tagus

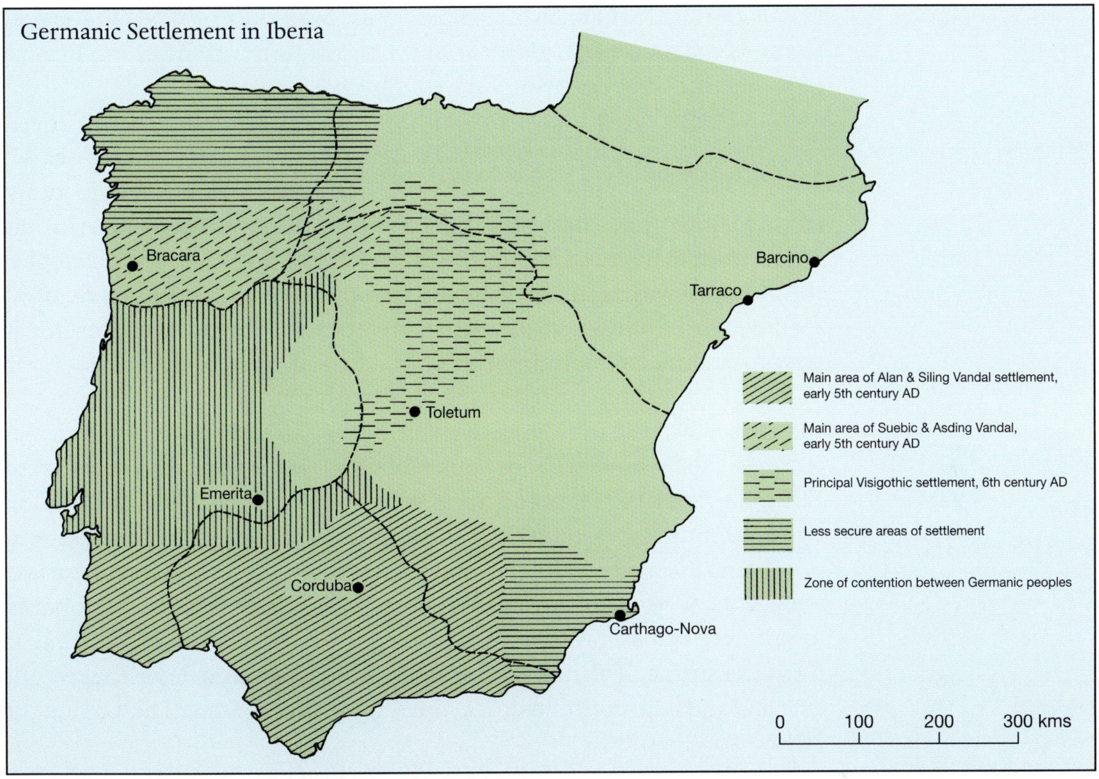

10.17 Germanic settlement in Iberia in the fifth and sixth centuries.

deep into Lusitania, and throughout the next twenty years, from the new royal capital in the Roman town of Emerita (Mérida), raiding forces were sent out in all directions. In 455, in an attempt to stabilize the situation, the Roman emperor encouraged the Visigothic king, Theoderic I, to intervene in western Iberia. Moving against the Suebi he quickly captured Asturica (Astorga) and went on to sack Bracara (Braga), where the Suebic king was caught and executed. The royal capital at Emerita was then taken, and the campaign ended with the widespread massacre of several urban communities, temporarily checking the power of the Suebic kingdom. In 468 the Suebi once more began sacking towns in Lusitania including Conimbriga, but were again driven back into Gallaecia by the Visigoths, who by this time had established their authority over the whole of the rest of the Peninsula. Thereafter the Suebi were left in obscurity, safe behind the Duero, protected by mountains to the east and the ocean to the north and west. Once more the remoteness of the region had played its role in history. Here the ancestors of the 80,000 Suebi who had crossed the Pyrenees in 409 merged imperceptibly with the indigenous population, making the last significant contribution to the gene pool of the region. By the end of the fifth century it is unlikely that the immigrant population had retained much of its Germanic culture. The elite simply took over what remained of the symbols of authority from the Roman past, the thread of continuity remaining ever strong.

Raiders and Settlers in the North Sea: *c.* AD 350–500

In 350 Magnentius, a barbarian born in Gaul as a *laetus*, seized the throne. He seems to have been popular with the British, and it is highly likely that the province was depleted of troops to support his cause. His reign, however, was brief, and after his death in 353 reprisals were taken against those who had supported him in Britain. The loss of troops and the suspicion and demoralization caused in the aftermath will have greatly weakened the province at the moment when the barbarian threat was building.

In 360 the first record of serious raiding mentions only Picts and Scots. Five years later the Picts and Scots were joined by Attacotti and Saxons, and in 367 Franks were added to the list of aggressors. Clearly Britain was now being assailed on all sides, and if our reading of Ammianus is correct the events of 367 were devastating since the barbarians were now operating together in some kind of conspiracy. We will consider the raiders from the north of Britain and from Ireland separately later (below, pp. 456–60), and here concentrate on those from the Continent first named as Saxons and Franks.

The disaster of 367 was serious. For the first time barbarians had overrun Hadrian's Wall when it was fully garrisoned and they had rampaged through the country causing chaos south to the Thames, capturing the military commander of the province (the *dux Britanniarum*), and killing the *comes maritimi tractus*—the senior officer in charge of the naval defences of the south and east coasts. So dangerous was the situation that an imperial force commanded by Count Theodosius was sent in 369 to restore order. As a result forts were built or rebuilt (10.18), town defences were strengthened with wide ditches and projecting towers, and the military command was augmented. The reorganization was far-reaching and effective and held Britain together for four more decades.

The military situation in the late fourth and early fifth centuries is reflected in a document known as the *Notitia Dignitatum*, which was a handbook of military units maintained by the authorities for administrative purposes such as the organization of pay and supplies. Among the commands included are those of the Count of the Saxon Shore, the *dux tractus Armoricani et Nervicani*, and the *dux Belgicae secundae*. The three commanders shared responsibility for protecting the north and west coasts of Gaul and the south and east coasts of Britain. The Count of the Saxon Shore was in command of nine coastal units stationed in forts

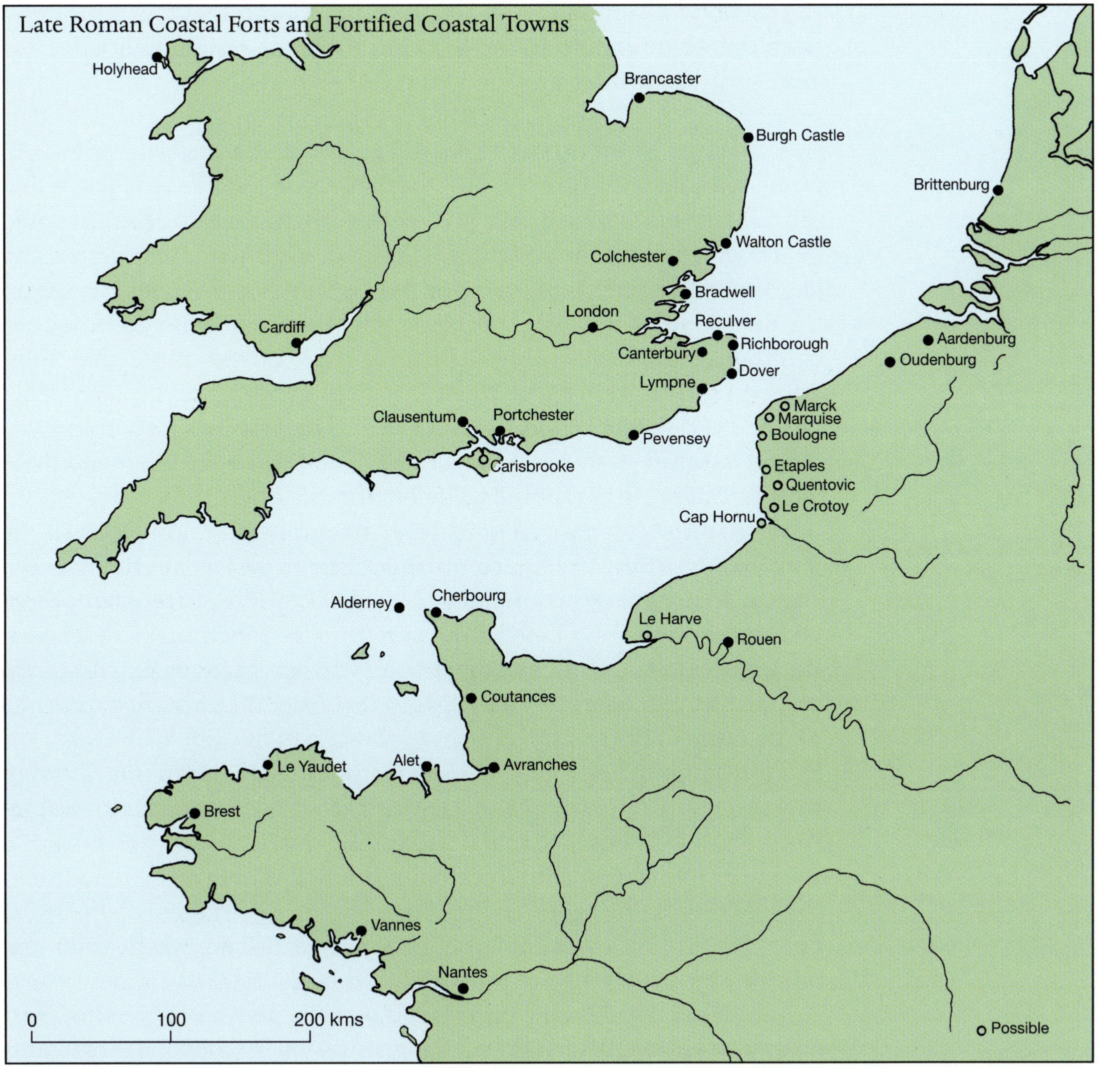

10.18 The Roman defences of the Atlantic and North Sea coasts at their greatest extent in the fourth century AD.

stretching from Brancaster to Portchester, all of which had probably been built by the begining of the fourth century. In addition he controlled two Continental units, *Grannona* in the *tractus Armoricani* and *Marcis* in the *tractus Belgicae*. Neither site has been convincingly identified. That the British command had Continental outposts presumably reflected the need to have active patrols sweeping the Channel for potential raiders and reporting back so that concerted action could be arranged. Just such ships—called *pictae*—are mentioned by Vegetius: they were small, fast, forty-oared vessels painted sea-green for camouflage. Continental outposts would have been essential to maintain an operation of this kind. Of the other two commands, the *dux Belgicae secundae* controlled the coast from the Rhine mouth to the Somme, while the responsibilities of the *dux tractus Armoricani* stretched from Rouen in the Seine valley to Blaye overlooking the Gironde. Together the three commands provided effective coverage of an extensive coastal region and a massive expanse of pirate-infested sea. From the sites that have been identified it is clear that the military units were based anywhere that appropriate defences could be found, whether it be antiquated forts built more than a century before, like Brancaster and Reculver, or towns like Nantes and Vannes founded in the first flood of imperial enthusiasm by Augustus and reduced by circumstances to encircle only their urban centres with protective walls. Rarely, it seems, were entirely new installations built, like the little fortlet on the tiny offshore island of Alderney. The empire's last attempt to defend its western shores was redolent of the make-do-and-mend mentality prevailing in the moments before the collapse.

In Britain events moved quickly. In 383 a rebellion broke out led by Magnus Maximus, an able commander intent on leading the western empire. In pursuit of his ambitions he sailed for Gaul taking a large force with him, only to be killed five years later. Stripped of its defenders, Britain became increasingly vulnerable. Further forces were withdrawn by Stilicho in 401 to protect Italy against the Visigoths, and what remained of the resident Britons still able and willing to fight were finally taken off by a usurping soldier, calling himself Constantine III, in 407 in an attempt to restore Gaul after the devastating inroads of the barbarians in the previous winter. After some initial successes Constantine III was forced to surrender to the imperial forces and was killed. That was in 411. Writing of these events, the historian Procopius succinctly summed up the situation: 'The Romans were never able to recover Britain, which from that time onwards continued to be ruled by tyrants.'

Another contemporary historian, Zosimus, puts an interesting gloss on events. He tells us that the barbarian invasion brought the inhabitants of Britain and Gaul to the point of revolt against Roman rule:

> The Britons took up arms and, braving danger for their own independence, freed their cities from the barbarians threatening them; and all Armorica and the other provinces of Gaul copied the British example and freed themselves in the same way, expelling their Roman governors and establishing their own administration as best they could. (Zosimus 6. 5)

This revolt against the central administration took place in the aftermath of a devastating Saxon raid on the province in 408. In 410 the Emperor Honorius, unable to intervene, accepted the *fait accompli* and wrote to the British civic authorities telling them to look after their own defence.

Until the beginning of the fifth century there is no reason to believe that the attacks of the Franks and Saxons were anything but raids with intent only to plunder, but the Saxon attack of 408 may have been the first of a series of folk movements of whole communities fleeing from the low-lying coastlands of Germany and Denmark, where deteriorating environmental conditions caused by rising sea-levels were making life impossible. In these regions the archaeological evidence shows widespread desertion by 450: in eastern Britain this is precisely the period when the first Saxon communities were establishing themselves.

The process of the settlement of England in the fifth century is referred to in a number of near-contemporary and later texts, often difficult to interpret. But when considered against the background of the rich and well-studied archaeological record, the outlines of a coherent picture begin to emerge.

The earliest settlements, beginning as early as 410–20, are found in eastern Britain, in East Anglia, the east Midlands, Lincolnshire, and east Yorkshire, and are represented by cremation cemeteries in the Saxon and Anglian cultural tradition (10.19). It seems likely that these communities came into a landscape depleted of population, and it may well be that they were allowed to settle in some kind of federate status on abandoned lands clear of the romanized enclaves that still existed around towns like Lincoln and Verulamium (St Albans). A rather different kind of Germanic settlement can be detected along both sides of the Thames, from the estuary to the middle reaches of the river in the Oxford region. Here the burial practice adopted certain aspects of Roman funerary tradition, such as the rite of inhumation. Men were buried with their weapons and fifth-century versions of late-Roman military belts, while the women often wore brooches of north Germanic origin. Ethnically these peoples were Saxons and Franks and may well have been recruited by the British authorities from the disintegrating field armies or units of *foederati* of northern Gaul and the Rhineland. They were evidently settled strategically to block further entry along the Thames and to protect the south and south-west from the settlers flooding into eastern Britain north of the Thames. A different group from Jutland seems to have been settled at about this time in Kent. These federates were probably the people who, the sixth-century British historian Gildas tells us, were invited in by the British leader Vortigern. The policy soon backfired, the protectors rebelling against the British authorities and inviting more of their countrymen in to settle. The breakdown in the treaty probably took place in the late 440s, when the British towns are known to have pleaded with the Roman general Aëtius for assistance but received no response.

One of the immediate results of the rebellion was the foundation of

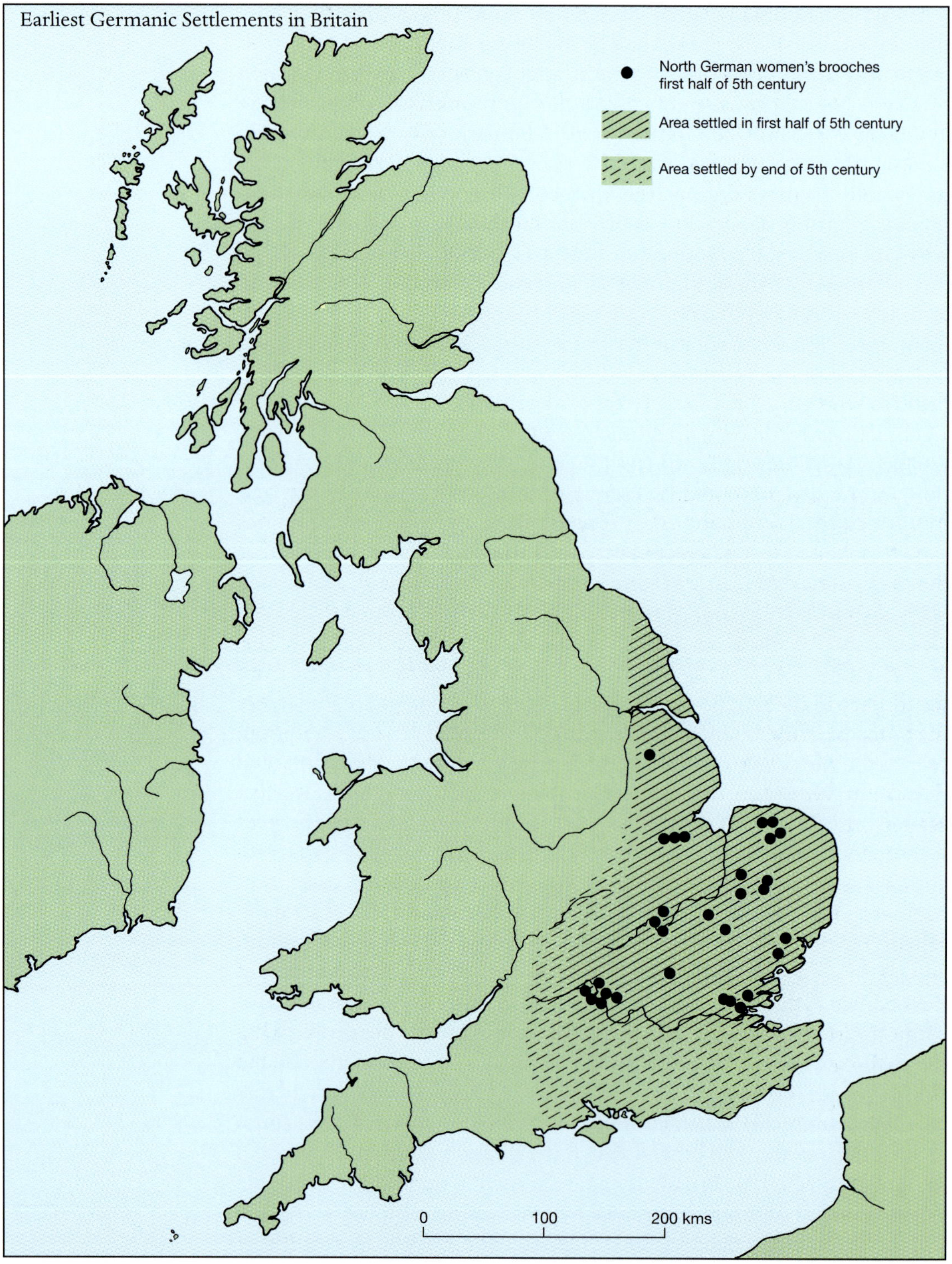
Earliest Germanic Settlements in Britain
North German women's brooches first half of 5th century
Area settled in first half of 5th century
Area settled by end of 5th century
0
100
200 kms

the kingdom of Sussex by a mixed group of Saxons and Franks some time around 450. They seem first to have taken the old Roman shore fort at Pevensey before spreading along the coast towards Chichester, which was still, at this time, a Roman enclave. North of the Thames new immigrants settled in the Cambridge region and in the Upper Thames valley.

The first stage in the Saxon migration came to an end towards the end of the fifth century, with the settlement of Hampshire by groups who may have been sent out from the kingdom of Sussex. The earliest penetration seems to have focused on the Saxon shore fort of Portchester. From here and other landfalls in the Solent the settlers moved inland along the river valleys. The discovery at Portchester of pottery made in a fabric which seems to have come from the Cotentin peninsula is a reminder that the Saxon communities of southern Britain and Normandy maintained contact with each other across the Channel. It is not inconceivable that Saxons from Normandy took part in the initial settlement of Hampshire.

By AD 500 the westward thrust of the Saxons had come to a temporary halt (10.19). In the south the Test valley marked the effective western limit of penetration, the middle Thames valley was heavily settled, while to the north Saxon and Anglian communities had reached almost to the Trent. Some time about AD 500 Gildas records a great battle at *Mons Badonicus* at which the Britons were victorious, the Saxon advance was halted, and after this peace prevailed for several decades. There has been much debate about the location of the battle, and while doubt will always remain, one of the strongest contenders, supported by both topographical and linguistic evidence, is the Iron Age hillfort of Badbury Castle in Dorset overlooking the major land route to the west and the line of advance inland from Poole Harbour or along the River Stour. Whoever commanded the hill was in a strong position to control movement.

The fifth century, which saw the establishment of Anglo-Saxon England, saw also the consolidation of British resistance in the north and west. The influx of Germanic and Scandinavian settlers will have caused disruptions among the local populations, and while many stayed and eventually merged with the newcomers, others will have fled westwards. By 500 the ethnic dividing lines were beginning to be drawn. Those living in the west did so under the authority of their own war leaders in small kingdoms or chiefdoms not at all unlike those of their ancestors five hundred years before. The rapid reversion to the past was made even more evident by the reuse of long-abandoned Iron Age hillforts. Defended enclosures like South Cadbury and Cadbury–Congesbury once more became the homes and rallying places of local elites. With the whole east of the country dominated by the Saxons and the east and south-east

10.19 (*facing*) The earliest Germanic settlement in Britain in the fifth century AD.

coasts inaccessible, the remaining Britons now looked west to the Atlantic as their own safe world.

Raiders and Settlers in the Irish Sea: 350–500

In the second half of the fourth century there seems to have been an upsurge in pirate activity and raiding in the Irish Sea. The Scotti, who at this time lived in the north-east of Ireland, were much in evidence throughout the 360s, attacking the north-west coasts of Britain alongside the Picts from north of the British frontier and the Attacotti. Where the Attacotti came from is unclear. The name is Celtic in origin, but it is generally supposed that they lived in western Scotland or northern Ireland. They were evidently mobile, for St Jerome records having seen a band in Gaul indulging in a cannibalistic feast, while the *Notitia Dignitatum* lists three units of Attacotti serving in the Roman army, one in the imperial bodyguard. The *Notitia* also mentions a *gens Scoti* in post on the Continent. How many of these north-western raiders saw service in the Roman army, and of those, how many returned to Ireland cannot be estimated, but the large hoards of Roman silver found in Ireland at Ballinrees in the south-west and Coleraine and Balline in the north could quite conceivably have been loot acquired while on active service in the early fifth century rather than during raids on Britain, though it is equally likely to have represented the pay of mercenaries.

The scale of the raids is difficult to estimate, but St Patrick writes of thousands of Britons killed or captured in the Irish attacks on Britain. While panegyrics composed in praise of prominent commanders are renowned more for the exuberance of the language than for the accuracy of their facts, it is worth recalling that one written at the end of the late fourth century in praise of Stilicho tells us that all of Ireland rose up against Britain and 'the sea foamed to the beat of hostile oars', while at news of Roman successes 'ice-bound Hibernia wept for the heaps of slain Scotti'. The scale of the raiding clearly caught someone's imagination. Some confirmation that raiding had become endemic comes from the Irish sources. In one poem the high king of Ireland, Niall of the Nine Hostages, is credited with having led seven expeditions across the sea to Britain in the early fifth century, and it was said that his mother, Cairenn, had originally been brought to Ireland as a British captive.

10.20 (*facing*) St Patrick talking to an unknown king. The miniature comes from the manuscript of the Golden Legend of Jacopo da Voragine of *c.*AD 1260.

Perhaps the most revealing anecdote reflecting on these times comes from the *Confessio* of St Patrick, written in the saint's old age after the mid-fifth century as an *apologia* (10.20). While there is still much debate concerning Patrick—whether there were two people conflated into one legend and what was the real chronology of the mission to the Irish—we

may accept the basic facts presented in the *Confessio* as a reasonably accurate reflection of conditions in the early fifth century. Patrick tells us that as a boy he was brought up in the still-civilized world of Roman Britain but was captured by an Irish raiding party and carried off to Ireland, there to spend six years in a remote rural area looking after the flocks of the man who had acquired him. Eventually he decided to escape. He writes of heavenly voices speaking to him on the mountainside telling him to travel two hundred miles to the sea where he would find a ship waiting. This he did. The ship was a merchant vessel carrying a cargo of dogs—hunting dogs perhaps—to Gaul. The journey took three days, but when they arrived they found the countryside in chaos. Eventually, after many adventures, Patrick managed to get back to Britain and rejoined his family. It was then that he had his famous vision and heard 'the voice of the Irish' crying out 'we beseech thee, holy youth, to come hither and walk among us'. The story thus far gives an entirely believable account of conditions in the west in the early fifth century. That trade with western France was still going on may at first sight seem surprising, but as we shall see, it is amply demonstrated by the archaeological evidence.

The Irish raids of the late fourth and fifth centuries no doubt occurred throughout the length of Roman Britain from Cornwall to the Solway Firth, but certain areas were likely to hold greater attractions than others. Raiders penetrating the Severn estuary would have found the towns and rich villas of south Wales, north Somerset, and Gloucestershire readily accessible and highly vulnerable. Evidence of widespread destruction in the region in the late fourth century hints at raiding deep inland along the Avon and Parrett. Another profitable point of entry would have been by way of Chester to the Welsh borderland. Extensive destruction occurred in the centre of Wroxeter in the late fourth century. While there is no direct evidence that the Irish were to blame for this widespread devastation, the possibility remains.

Alongside the raiding came folk movement and settlement. We have already seen that the settlement of the Déisi in south-west Wales may have begun somewhat earlier, and was probably a largely peaceful event that may even have been encouraged by the Roman authorities. Once established, other settlers followed throughout the fourth and fifth centuries and even into the sixth, creating a large and well-established Irish community that remained in contact throughout with its homeland just across the water. The extent of this settlement is well demonstrated by the distribution of Ogam inscriptions throughout Dyfed (10.21). Other Irish settlers, probably Scotti, moved into the Lleyn peninsula of north-west Wales, quite possibly to fill the vacuum left by the withdrawal of Roman troops from the area by Maximus in 383. Their presence is attested

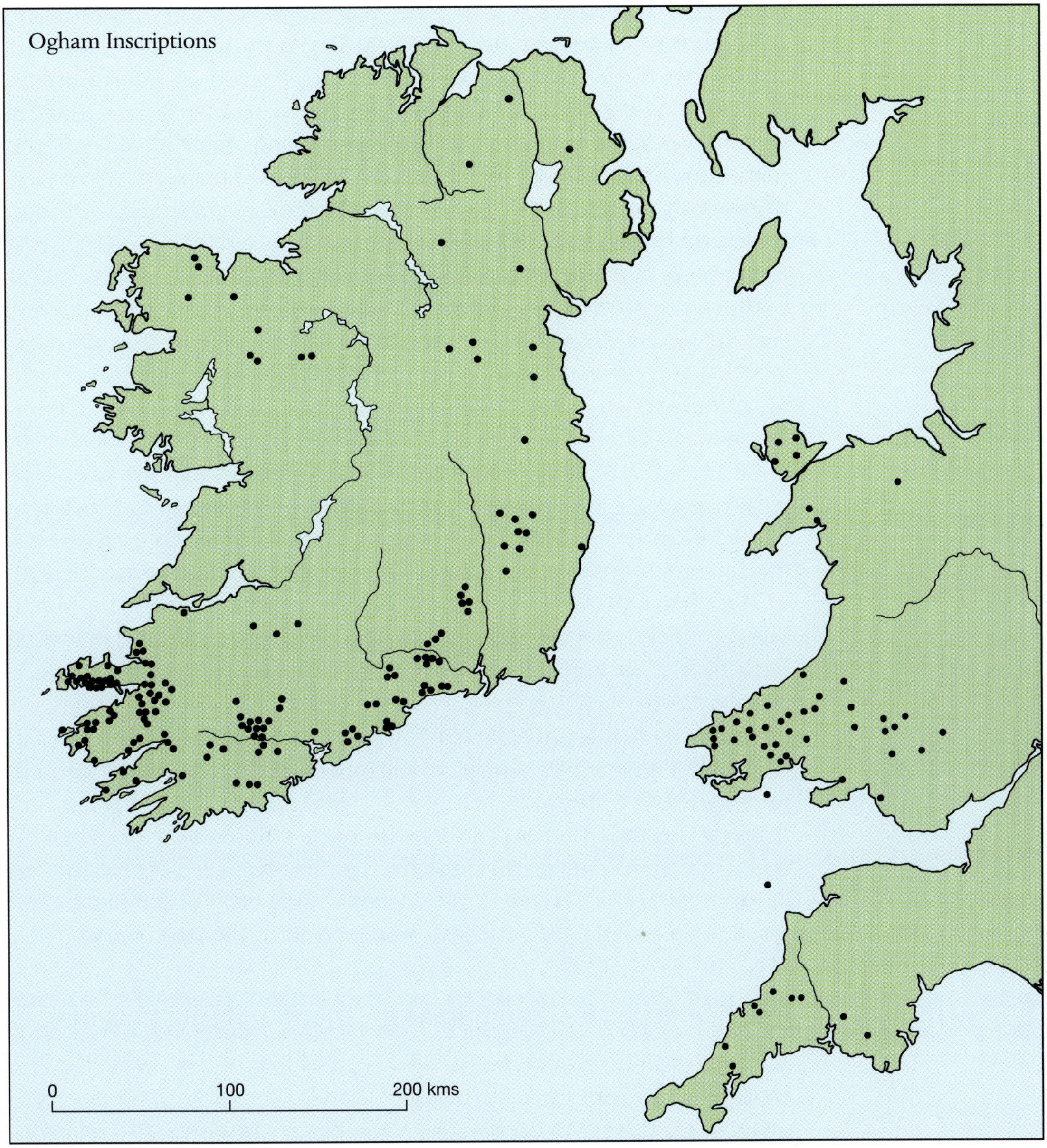

by place-name evidence and also by a Welsh historical tradition which records the expulsion of the Irish from the region by a force of Votandini, from southern Scotland, led by Cunedda some time in the early fifth century.

10.21 Irish settlement in western Britain in the fifth and sixth centuries AD indicated by the distribution of Ogham inscriptions.

In Scotland (which takes its name from the Irish Scotti who settled there) the *Life of St Columba* tells of the landing of a small band of 150 men from Dál Riata in Antrim, who crossed the North Channel and settled in Argyll in the late fifth or early sixth century. From this modest initial settlement grew the powerful kingdom of Dálriada, which held power on both sides of the sea. The settlement is well attested by place-names of Irish origin on the mainland and adjacent islands. Similar evidence also points to Irish settlement on the Galloway peninsula. That the settlers on the two sides of the north Channel should have been in close contact with each other in the fifth and sixth centuries need occasion no surprise. A community of common cultural ideas can be traced back to the Neolithic period when the region was closely linked by a common burial ritual, and throughout the Iron Age and Roman period the archaeological record shows that there was constant contact. The 150 settlers mentioned by St Columba's biographer were simply part of a continuing process of interaction.

Finally, what of Cornwall? While it is entirely possible that Irish communities settled in the south-west peninsula in the fourth and fifth centuries, the direct evidence of an Irish presence dates to the sixth century and later. However, given the degree of mobility that there was at the end of the Roman period it is highly likely that the Cornish were in contact with southern Ireland, and some movements of population may well have taken place at this time as a prelude to more extensive settlement a century or two later.

From what has been said it will be clear that the evidence for Irish raiding and settlement in Britain in the late fourth and fifth centuries is varied, imprecise, and scanty in the extreme, yet that there was much toing-and-froing across the Irish Sea cannot be in doubt. Raiding was a stark reality, and populations did resettle. Perhaps the most balanced way to see this apparent flurry of activity is as a comparatively brief and more violent series of episodes in the *longue durée* of transmaritime intercourse.

Britons and Bretons: Armorica in the Fourth and Fifth Centuries

At some time in the late fourth century the coastal defences of north-western Gaul from the Seine to the Gironde were put under the command of the *dux tractus Armoricani et Nervicani*, who controlled nine military garrisons spread around the coasts. The command lasted into the early decades of the fifth century, by which time the area was in turmoil. According to the historian Zosimus the barbarian inroads of 406–7 led to a breakdown of authority in Armorica culminating, in 409, in a rebellion of the local Armoricans against 'their Roman governors'. After this they administered themselves as best they could, but there is some circumstantial evidence to suggest that the region was brought back under central control by 417 following an expedition led by Exuperantius. Rebellion flared again in 435. It appears to have been a popular uprising of the disaffected peasants identified as *bagaudae*. The *Gallic Chronicle*, which notes the events, says that the Armorican uprising was followed by 'almost all the Gaulish peasants'. Two years later the insurrection was put down and its leader, Tibatto, killed. However, the Armorican *bagaudae* continued to present a serious problem. In 442 the Roman military command unleashed Gohar, *rex ferocissimus*, and leader of a band of Alani *foederati* against the Armoricans, but by this time the remnants of Roman authority in Gaul were fast disintegrating in the face of growing Frankish power. Whatever the extent and disruption caused by the peasant uprisings in Armorica, it is likely that the principal defended towns in the east, Vannes, Nantes, and Rennes, held out behind their strong defensive walls as bastions of Roman life. What happened to the various detachments guarding the coast under the *dux tractus Armoricani* is less certain—some may have been recalled to fight in the field army elsewhere in Gaul, while others may simply have drifted away to maraud through the rebellious countryside. It is against this background of social disintegration that the arrival of the Britons must be considered.

Before turning to the traditional account of the British migration, it is worth considering the possibility that regular military forces from Britain may have ended up in Armorica. Several Welsh traditions record that the remnants of the army taken by the British imperial pretender Maximus to Gaul in 383, and defeated five years later, settled in Armorica under their leader Conan Meriadec, who proceeded to found a dynasty of Breton kings. There is no historical proof of the story, but the suggestion that some of the defeated army, making their way back to Britain, decided to stay in Armorica is not entirely unreasonable. Nor should we overlook the possibility that *foederati* from Britain may have settled in Armorica in the troubled times of the late fourth or early fifth century. Since there is ample evidence of commercial traffic between Armorica and southern Britain throughout the fourth century, small-scale movements of people are quite likely.

The British monk Gildas, in his work *De Excidio* written about 540, provides the simplest account of the migration of Britons to Armorica. In a vivid and emotional passage he describes how, under pressure from the Anglo-Saxons arriving in great number in eastern Britain, some of the Britons in desperation 'made for lands beyond the seas'. As they sailed the air was full of lamentations, and instead of sea shanties they sang the psalm 'You have given us like sheep for eating and scattered us among the heathens'. The Byzantine historian Procopius believed that settlers from Britain were still moving to Gaul in the mid-sixth century because their homeland was overpopulated. It is he who first refers to Armorica by the name of Britannia, but the inhabitants of Armorica were called Britanni by Sidonius Apollinaris as early as 480 in a letter he writes about the trial, held in 468, of a prefect of the praetorian guard charged with treason for inviting the Visigothic king to attack the Britanni, who had established themselves in the estuary of the Loire under their king Riothamus. A later text confirms that Riothamus had a force of 12,000 'Bretons' who were to be used in support of the emperor against the Visigothic king who had invaded Gaul. What can reasonably be made of these near-contemporary texts? Together they show that settlers from Britain were arriving in Armorica in some number in the first half of the fifth century, and that movements were still taking place in the sixth. This much is reasonably certain. Gildas' description, despite its literary flourishes, implies that it was a folk migration of families and lineage groups, while the account of Riothamus and his force of 12,000 Bretons suggests that warrior bands under their own leaders may also have been involved, though whether Riothamus assembled his military force in Britain and sailed it to the Loire or gathered it from among Britons already settled in Armorica must remain undecided.

On linguistic grounds it is generally assumed that the immigrants came from south-western Britain, and possibly from south Wales since the Breton language in its developed form had close similarities to Cornish and Welsh. If so, Gildas' explanation for the exodus, that it was caused by pressure from the Anglo-Saxon advance, seems difficult to accept. But if Irish raids and settlement were a significant factor in the south-west then the migration is easier to understand. Perhaps a better way of viewing it is in more general terms as a response to the complete breakdown of the Roman system, exacerbated by raids and population pressures. Population mobility often accompanies situations of sudden political and economic disruption. Once under way it can suddenly escalate into mass migration and, after pioneering populations had established themselves, others would follow for some time after.

The linguistic evidence features large in discussions of the formation of Brittany, but there is by no means agreement as to how it is to be interpreted. The close similarities between Breton, Cornish, and Welsh are not in doubt. Where the debate focuses is on whether Breton was introduced from south-western Britain into a land where the indigenous Gaulish language had all but disappeared after four centuries of romanization, or whether the 'Celtic' language was still widely spoken in some parts of the peninsula and was simply strengthened by immigrants speaking closely similar dialects. There is no simple way to resolve the problem, but taking the broader perspective, the long-established contacts between Armorica and south-western Britain, especially during the latter part of the first millennium BC, will inevitably have led to a convergence of languages between adjacent areas, and there is now ample archaeological evidence to suggest that maritime contacts were maintained throughout the Roman period. In such circumstances it would seem highly unlikely that the common native language was not kept alive in everyday use. While, therefore, not dissenting from the view that Breton was revitalized by the influx of refugees, the actual numbers of immigrants need not have been large—in other words, there is no reason to suppose a significant replacement of population.

The distribution of place-names provides a further insight into questions of ethnicity (10.22). Place-names containing the elements Plou-, Tré-, and Lan- concentrate in the north and west of the peninsula, in what became two major political divisions of Brittany, Domnonée and Cornouaille, while names with the suffix -ac are to be found mainly in eastern Brittany, with a concentration in the southern coastal region around Vannes. This broad divide is roughly reflected in the dialects of modern Breton, the division being made between the language of Cornouaille, Léon, and Trégor (with Goëllo), known as KLT, and that of Vannetais. Once again, there is much debate about the interpretation of these differences, but a strong case has been made for suggesting that they reflect the linguistic situation in the pre-Roman period. The archaeological evidence which we considered above (pp. 345–9) adds considerable support to this in showing that the cultural divide existed at least as early as the fourth century BC, and that it was still evident in the fourth century AD is suggested by the fact that the last strongholds of romanization—the fortified towns of Rennes, Nantes, and Vannes and a number of surviving villas—clustered in the Vannetais region. If it is accepted that the linguistic division had its roots in the pre-Roman period, then it lessens the need to explain it in terms of large-scale influxes of population from Britain.

These fascinating issues have been laid out here in some detail because of the light they throw on difficulties inherent in studying migration, even when the historical evidence and the linguistic data are rich. While the linguistic debates continue, we can look to archaeology gradually to add a new range of evidence.

One final point may be made here about the folk wanderings of the Britons. Some time in the fifth century a community settled in Galicia in north-west Iberia. By the mid-sixth century they had established the abbey of St Maria de Bretona near Mondenedo, and in 572 Bishop Mailoc (a distinctive 'Celtic' name) attended a council in Braga. Thereafter they disappear from notice. It is tempting to believe that the colony resulted from a shipload or two of adventurous Britons sailing along the estab-

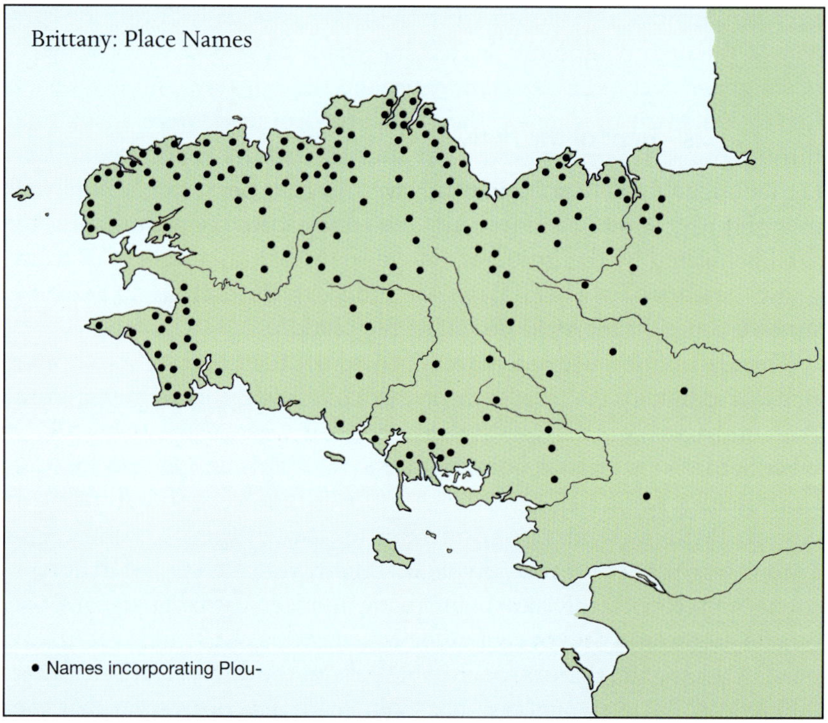

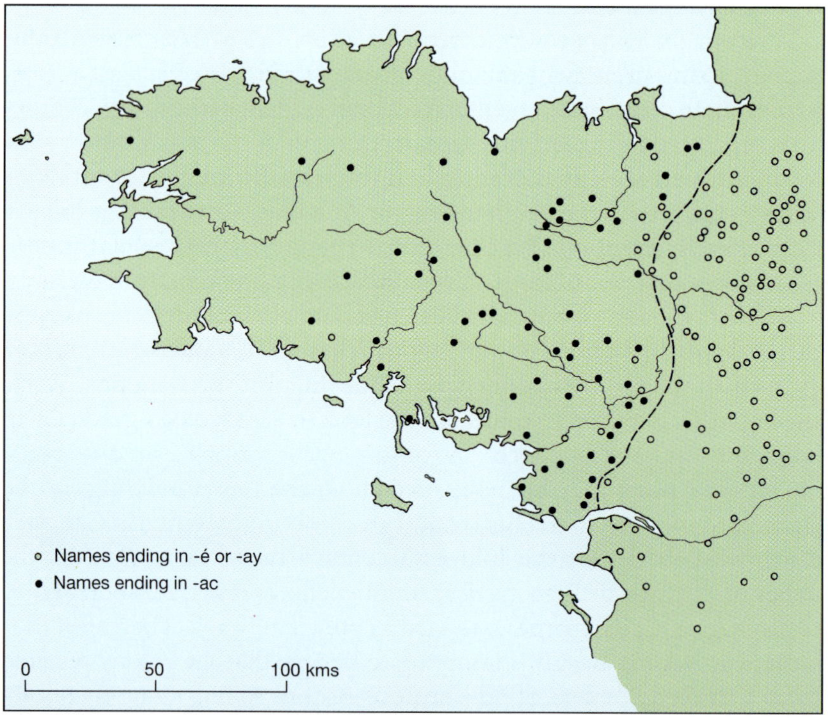

10.22 The settlement of Brittany: aspects of the linguistic evidence.

lished seaways to found a new home, secure in the knowledge that mercantile shipping would keep them in contact with their homeland.

The Establishment of the New Order: AD 500–800

The creation of a new order in north-west Europe began with the expansion of the Franks under the leadership of Clovis at the end of the fifth century and ended, at least symbolically, with the coronation of Charlemagne in 800. Charlemagne's empire at its greatest extent stretched from Navarre and Lombardy in the south to the borders of Bohemia and Denmark in the north, and except for Brittany, included within it the whole of the old Roman provinces of Gaul. Until the middle of the eighth century the Bretons lived in isolation and comparative peace on the fringe of the Frankish domain, but with the accession of Pippin the Short in 751 the Carolingian assault began. Vannes was taken and incorporated, with Nantes and Rennes, into the March of Brittany which served as a Frankish-held buffer zone against the more recalcitrant Bretons of the west. After an uncomfortable period of raiding and suppression the political situation was stabilized by the appointment in 831 of Nomenoë, a member of the native elite, as a ruler of the Bretons under the authority of the emperor. In this way Brittany was brought within the political and cultural ambit of the Carolingian world.

In Iberia the Visigoths continued to rule, preserving much of the administrative structure of the late Roman world. Under their, somewhat removed, leadership Hispano-Roman culture developed in comparative peace until the Arab invasion in 711.

The Arab advance through North Africa had been startlingly rapid. In 640 they had reached Cairo and only thirty years later they were establishing themselves at Kairouan in Tunisia. In 682–3 the Arab army had ridden triumphant through the Maghreb, reaching the Atlantic coast at Agadir in Morocco. It was here, it was said, that Oqba ben Nafi rode out into the sea, claiming that only the ocean had prevented him from carrying his conquests still further. The ease and rapidity with which the Arabs conquered Spain is in part a reflection of the looseness of the hold of the Visigothic elite over the local population. Only a small Christian kingdom in the mountainous country of Austurias managed to hold out against the Umayyad advance, defeating the Arabs at the Battle of Covadonga in 718. In the years to follow the Christians gradually beat back the invaders, until by AD 800 the kingdom of Austurias had managed to extend its boundaries south to the river Douro.

In the British Isles, after a pause in the early sixth century, the Anglo-Saxon advance to the west and north began in earnest until the entire country as far north as the Southern Uplands had been engulfed, leaving only Wales and Cornwall still free. The Pictish kingdoms still held sway over much of the east of what was to become Scotland, while the western coastal regions were divided into the British kingdom of Strathclyde and the kingdom of the Scots to the north. The Anglo-Saxon territories were divided into several separate kingdoms. Of these the kingdom of Mercia rose to dominance in the late eighth century under its king, Offa. By this time close diplomatic and commercial relations had been established with the Carolingian empire.

Around the Atlantic fringes of the emerging states—the kingdoms of the Anglo-Saxons, the Carolingian empire, and Umayyad caliphate—there survived enclaves from former times striving to maintain their independence. Facing their foes to landward, the sea provided their freedom and their means of communicating with each other.

The Scots, initially of western Scotland, traced their ancestry to King Erc, whose three sons with 150 warriors arrived from Ireland in the late fifth century to settle in Argyll and the adjacent Islands. Thereafter Dálriada's power increased until, by a combination of aggression and intermarriage, the Scots merged with their Pictish neighbours. The traditional date of the final union is 843, when the whole of the Highlands and Islands came under the rule of Kenneth mac Alpine. Throughout these four formative centuries the Scots retained a close relationship with their northern Irish forbears, and indeed much of their history as we know it comes from the Irish *Annals*. While the importance of the sea in linking the communities was crucial, it is doubtful if many travelled much beyond their immediate territorial sphere, though one of their kings, Aedán, is known to have led an expedition to the Orkneys in 590.

To the south of the Antonine Wall, which ran from the Clyde to the Firth of Forth, was a native enclave known as the kingdom of Strathclyde occupying much of the Scottish Midlands, except for Lothian where the Anglian kings of Northumberland held sway. The traditional links of the kingdom were with Wales, dating back to the time of the legendary Votandinian leader Cunedda who is credited with ousting the Irish from north Wales. The north Welsh sources recognized the kingdom as *Gwŷr y Gogledd*—'men of the north'—in the same way as they referred to the south Welsh as *Gwŷr y Des*—'men of the south'. The main lines of contact between the two regions would have been across the Irish Sea by way of the Isle of Man. The kingdom of Strathclyde maintained its independence until about 1015, when it fell to the Scottish king Malcolm II.

The divided and mountainous nature of Wales favoured the development of a number of different kingdoms, each maintaining its own dynastic succession unbroken over long periods of time. In the south-west lay Demetia, tracing its origins from its Irish settlers—the Déisi—and retaining its distinctly Irish character well into the tenth century. The kingdom of south-east Wales boasted of its Silurian origin and traced its dynasty back to Caratacus in the first century AD, while the royal dynasty of the Upper Wye claimed descent from Vortigern, one of the powerful war leaders who emerged after the collapse of Roman authority. Other stable and long-lived kingdoms included Powys, Gwerthrynion, and Brycheiniog. Of the many Welsh polities the one that rose to prominence was the kingdom of Gwynedd in north-west Wales. With its long coastline and many harbours it was able to dominate the sea lanes, benefiting from the varied cultural influences transmitted by the merchant shipping plying the Irish Sea.

Of Dumnonia, the kingdom of the south-west peninsula west of Exeter, little is known, though we may suppose it maintained close links with Brittany. By the eighth century a unified ruling house seems to have emerged, and Gerontius (Geraint) the last known king, led Dumnonian forces against the Saxons of Wessex in 710. But there seems to have been no concerted Saxon push against Dumnonia until 814, when Ecgbert of Wessex ordered a new advance culminating in a decisive battle in 838. After this Cornish kings became vassals of the Wessex dynasty.

Ireland, wholly free from Roman military intrusion, developed uninterrupted, emerging from its legendary past into history with the appearance of the high king Niall of the Nine Hostages early in the fifth century. Niall is credited with dividing Ireland into two regions, the southern region of Munster with its capital at Cashel, and the northern part which he and his sons took, dividing it into the southern Uí Néill, with Tara as the capital, and the northern Uí Néill. While the Uí Néill looked inwards towards the Irish Sea, the people of Munster regarded the broader Atlantic as their realm and looked south towards the many influences emanating from Atlantic Gaul and Iberia.

Brittany was divided into three kingdoms, Domnonia, Cornouaille, and Bro Erech. Domnonia accounted for the densely settled north side of the peninsula, with Cornouaille taking up much of the south-west. The third kingdom, Bro Erech, comprised the rest of southern Brittany including the inland area and the western part of Vannes. The Breton kingdom stood out against Frankish advances, but the defeat of a Breton force by Clovis about 490 somewhere in the region of the Loire mouth seems to have marked a significant change, for thereafter, according to Gregory of Tours, the Bretons came under the domination of the Franks 'and their rulers were called counts not kings'. While it is true that some of the Breton leaders acknowledged Frankish overlordship for some of the time the situation was confused. Waroc, one of the leaders of Bro

Erech, was constantly harrying the Marches. He attacked the Bishop of Nantes and succeeded in capturing Vannes at the end of the sixth century, yet fifty years later Judicael, king of Domnonia, was prepared to submit to the authority of the Frankish king Dragobert, exchanging gifts with him and acknowledging Frankish superiority. Behind the uneasy frontier lands, roughly coinciding with the valley of the Vilaine, local kings continued to vie with each other for power.

In northern Iberia that part of the tribe known to the Romans as the Vascones, who occupied the more mountainous areas of the western Pyrenees, developed a high degree of independence sandwiched between the Visigoths in the Ebro valley and the Franks in western France. Throughout the seventh century they were in constant conflict with their lowland neighbours—a conflict which intensified their own identity. By the beginning of the eighth century they had extended their control to include part of the Ebro valley to the south and Aquitania to the north. This latter area became known as Gascony (from the Latin Wasconia), and their ancient tribal name, Vascones, was soon to give rise to their more familiar name—Basques.

Linguistically the Basques come from a very ancient and distinctive gene pool, but it was an extended period of conflict with their lowland neighbours that welded them together into a people with a strong ethnic identity.

In north-western Iberia the ancient Gallaici, strengthened in the fifth century by the incursion of Germanic Suebi, who took over much of the existing Roman infrastructure, maintained their distinctive culture in their remote corner of the Peninsula. A further incursion, this time of Britons arriving by sea in the sixth century, added to the ethnic mix. Although very little is known of the magnitude of the British settlement or of the ability of the incomers to remain as a cohesive group, it is possible that their presence strengthened maritime links with the north, albeit only for a generation or two, and contributed to the folk belief of a shared 'Celtic' ancestry linking Galicia, Brittany, and western Britain.

In the remote regions facing the Atlantic society was made up of small polities ruled by competing elites. The murder of rivals was not infrequent and sometimes rivalry led to outright aggression. Even when high kings emerged, as they did in Ireland, their authority was superficial. Beneath it all lay a complex network of lineages and allegiances held within the grip of difficult landscapes, isolating communities one from another and nurturing an independence of spirit. When later some Atlantic communities came to acknowledge the overlordship of neighbouring states—the Dumnonians accepting West Saxon supremacy, the Bretons sporadically acknowledging the Frankish kingdom—geography ensured that the indigenous cultures remained largely intact. As the landward frontiers against the Anglo-Saxons, the Franks, and the Umayyads hardened and became marcher zones where the aspiring youth of the opposing worlds flexed their muscles and won prowess, so the sea took on an increasingly important role, becoming a core to the peripheral lands.

Christianity and Culture

The fourth century saw the Roman world embrace Christianity within its administrative system. Roman Christianity was essentially an urban-focused religion: the bishops were based in towns, while their dioceses became coincident with the units of civilian government which were being readjusted to meet the changing needs of empire. Outside the towns the country-dwellers—the *pagani*—for the most part adhered to their old religions. Yet Christianity did spread into western regions well beyond the limits of Roman urbanism during the fourth century, reaching as far afield as Ireland. The processes by which the new ideas were transmitted were varied. Traders still maintained constant links with the Irish Midlands and Irish raiding parties might well have found themselves in possession of Christian slaves. In such unwilling expatriate communities Christian beliefs will have flourished. At any event, in the early years of the fifth century Christianity was finally established well beyond the Roman frontier in Ireland.

In 431, so Prosper of Aquitaine notes in his *Chronicle*, the pope, Celestine, sent Palladius, a deacon in the church at Auxerne, to minister to 'those of the Irish who believed in Christ'. The eight dedications associated with the Palladian mission cluster around Co. Wicklow and tend to support the legend that Palladius landed at Arklow on the Wicklow coast. Other dedications in south-west Wales might suggest that he came by sea, stopping in the territory of the Déisi before making the Irish Sea crossing. We hear nothing more of Palladius, but the following year, according to the Irish *Annals*, Patrick returned to Ireland after his escape from slavery some years before and began his highly successful ministry in the north, making Armagh his base. He travelled extensively, 'even to outlying regions beyond which no man dwelt, and where never had anyone come to baptize or ordain clergy or confirm the people'. If, as seems likely, Patrick's original home was in the north of Britain, possibly in the romanized region of Dumbarton, his choice of the north of Ireland would have been entirely logical in that he would have been following the long-established and no doubt still-operative trade route across the North Channel.

10.24 The early Christian hermitage on Church Island, Valencia, Co. Kerry, Ireland. The surviving stone beehive hut and the oratory replaced earlier timber buildings.

In the absence of towns in Ireland Patrick organized his church not into dioceses but into *parochia*—that is, rural areas each provided with a church which served as a focus for the scattered religious communities in its territory. Typically, such an establishment would be a circular enclosure containing a church or oratory where Mass was said, a large house for the clerics, and a separate kitchen and refectory. These centres were governed by bishops.

The Patrician church was not monastic, but at about the time of Patrick's mission in the mid-fifth century monasticism was gaining a hold on western Christianity, spreading from its place of origin among the Desert Fathers of Egypt. The new belief system was widely adopted in Gaul in the latter part of the fourth century, and from here probably spread along the Atlantic seaways to western Britain and Ireland. There is some evidence to suggest that the impact of these Atlantic contacts was first felt on the south coast of Munster. On the island of Dair-inis in the Blackwater estuary a very early monastery was established where one of the earliest literary texts of the Irish Church—the *Collectio Canonum Hibernensis*—was composed. The work shows direct influence from Brittany, and the monastery was evidently in close contact with west Mediterranean culture. Another pointer to direct contact with Gaul was the early and widespread popularity of the cult of St Martin of Tours, the

10.23 (*facing*) The monastery of Clonmacnoise, Co. Offaly, Ireland was founded in the seclusion of a great system of raised bogs on the banks of the river Shannon.

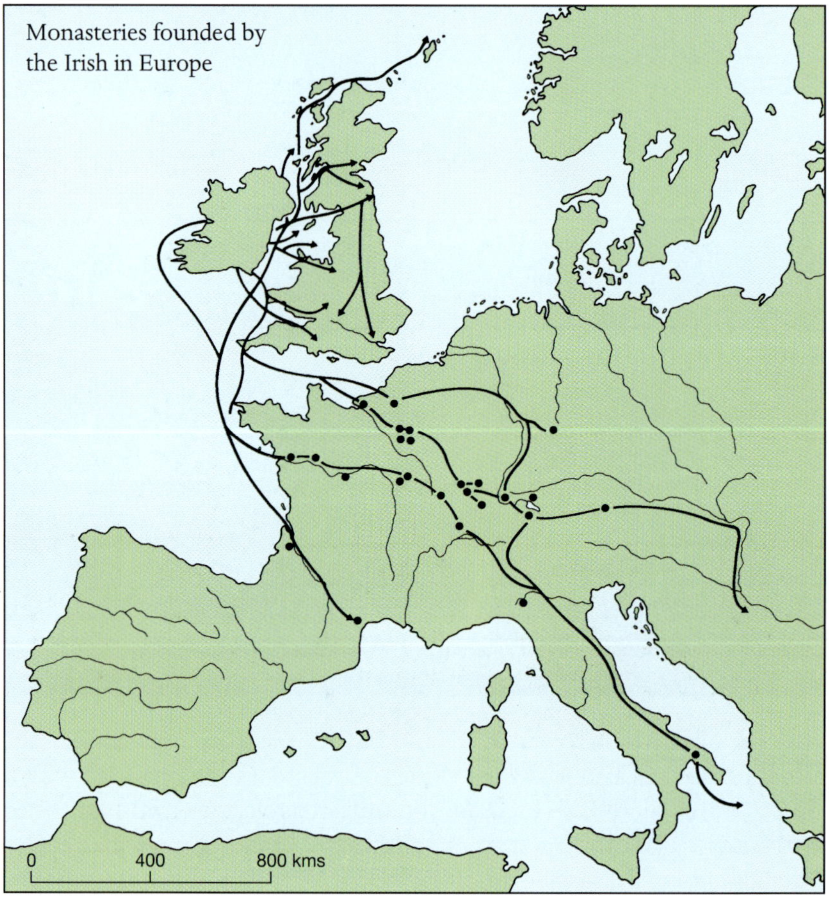

10.25 The travels of the Irish *peregrini* in the fifth to eighth centuries and the settlements and monasteries which they founded.

saint credited with the introduction of monasticism to the west. The version of his *Life*, included in the *Book of Armagh*, may have reached Ireland as early as 460.

As monasticism spread throughout Ireland in the sixth century the ecclesiastical organization set up by Patrick withered away and bishops ceased to have a significant role. In its place scattered monasteries, independent and following the rule of a single founder, spread across the face of Ireland (10.23, 10.24). By the end of the century the Patrician system had all but vanished.

10.26 (*facing*) Baile Mór with the abbey beyond on the island of Iona overlooking the ocean beyond. The early abbey was protected by an earthwork enclosure.

The readiness with which the monastic ideal was accepted in Ireland and western Britain may in part be explained by the nature of society in which the family provided a strong bonding focus. In such a social context the self-mortification and penance required of Christianity could most effectively be achieved by cutting oneself off from familial support and leaving home to live in isolation or to work among strangers.

Samson
Petroc
Pol de Léon
Guénolé
0
100
200 kms

The mood is nicely caught in the story of three Irish *peregrini* whose skin boat was washed up on the coast of Cornwall after drifting helplessly at the whim of the sea. When eventually they arrived at the court of King Alfred they told the king that they set sail because they were prepared to go into exile for the love of God but 'they cared not whither'. The great exodus of *peregrini* from Ireland and south Wales to remote and inhospitable places and to the lands of strangers was, therefore, more a response to the religious compulsion to remove themselves from the comfort and pleasure of the family than to the desire to seek converts (10.25). In their own phrase, their aim was to search for 'the place of one's resurrection'.

10.27 (*facing*) The dedications to saints who travelled the Atlantic sea-ways.

This said, some of the *peregrini* created monasteries of wide influence. In about 563 Columba (Columcille) sailed from northern Ireland with twelve followers to Dálriada in west Scotland, and two years later founded a monastery on the island of Iona where he died in 597 (10.26). The establishment flourished and became highly influential, both as the focus of a group of Columbian monasteries spread throughout the north of Ireland and as the centre from which the Picts were converted. In the seventh century the monks of Iona were invited by King Oswald of Northumbria to found a new monastery in his kingdom and to convert his subjects. In response twelve monks, led by St Aiden, set out and established themselves on Lindisfarne in the North Sea in 635. Another of the influential monasteries of the Scottish west coast was the monastery of St Ninian at Whithorn in southern Galloway in the British kingdom of Strathclyde. According to Bede, it was founded as early as 397 and was famous for its white-painted stone church, the *Candida Casa*. Bede claimed that St Ninian's followers were responsible for converting the southern Picts before the arrival of Columba and his mission to the northern Picts.

10.28 Thirteenth-century stained glass window in the Cathedral of Dol, Brittany, showing St Samson sailing towards Armorica.

Many of the *peregrini* travelled considerable distances by sea, as the large number of commemorations to Irish and Welsh saints in Brittany bears witness (10.27). One of these, for whom we have reliable evidence, is St Samson, whose *Life* is recorded in a text of the early seventh century written within fifty years of the saint's death. He grew up in south Wales and spent some time in a monastery on Caldy Island. After a visit to Ireland, where he acquired a cart, he sailed from Caldy, taking his cart with him, to Cornwall, landing near Padstow on the north coast. Here he stayed briefly before crossing the peninsula, probably to the estuary of the Fowey, where he took ship again (still accompanied by his vehicle). Landing in Brittany in the estuary of the Rance (10.28) he travelled eastwards to found his monastic bishopric at Dol. Later on his much-travelled Irish cart transported him to Paris. The story gives an interesting glimpse of travel arrangements in the late sixth century. Ships were evidently available in the major ports and long journeys at sea were taken with equanimity. However, the journey across the Cornish peninsula might indicate that sea passages were generally short-haul, and to make a long journey it was necessary to change vessels from time to time.

There is another revealing detail recorded in St Samson's *Life*. In Cornwall he came upon a pagan ceremony in progress, whereupon, having chastized the participants, he performed a miracle which encouraged them to be baptized. At the end of the ceremony he carved the sign of a cross on a megalithic stone that was evidently part of the pagan monument where the gathering was being held. The act of Christianizing megaliths was widespread and is represented by many monuments still extant in Brittany today. By making the sign of the cross on the ancient stones the power of the pagan monument was being captured for the new religion. Assimilation was more effective than outright rejection.

The importance of the sea to the travels of the Irish monks is self-evident. Once clear of the Irish Sea they sailed along the Channel to the Seine and the Somme and down the Atlantic coast of France to the Loire, the Gironde, and beyond, some reaching as far as Galicia. After landing they followed the main rivers into the heart of Europe. Their routes were, of course, the familiar ones of commercial exchange. The very fact that so many were able to travel overseas in this way is a reflection of the healthy maritime commerce operating at the time, for many of those travelling south would surely, like St Patrick, have negotiated a passage on a merchant vessel.

Those who travelled north were of more adventurous spirit, prepared to chance their lives by sailing into completely uncharted waters. St Cormac reached Orkney following good local advice given by the king of Inverness, but on a later voyage he sailed due north for fourteen days and nights, perhaps visiting the Shetlands or the Faroes. That such journeys were not exceptional is clear from the *Liber de Mensura orbis Terrae* written by the Irish monk Dicuil in 825. In it he tells of the Northern Isles, adding: 'There are many other islands in the ocean to the north of Britain . . . on these hermits who have sailed from our Scotia have lived for about a hundred years.' Here he is quite probably referring to the Faroes, which were settled by monks about AD 700, and to Iceland, where Irish monastic settlement was under way by the end of the eighth century. These brave northern ventures were true voyages of discovery carried out for no personal gain other than to find the solitude necessary for spiritual regeneration.

The Irish monastic diaspora of the fifth to eighth centuries was a remarkable phenomenon—an explosive energy generated by an insular faith. At home the cultural explosion was no less astonishing. In the monastic workshops and libraries items of exquisite quality were created, almost all for the glory of God: chalices, reliquaries, sculpted high crosses, and illuminated manuscripts. The art was highly original, though rooted in the traditional craft skills and styles of Iron Age Ireland and Britain, with inspiration coming from the eclectic Christian arts of western France and Spain. In the pagan Iron Age men of great skill lived in the courts of the elite, using their abilities to create fine works for their masters. Now, in the early medieval monasteries, their successors plied their even more refined skills for the glory of God. The hierarchic systems of patronage were much the same, but the Lord was infinitely more demanding.

Atlantic Trade: AD 400–800

The three Irish monks washed up on the Cornish coast in their little hide boat and the intrepid *peregrini* who sought solitude in the North Atlantic are representative of local maritime initiative which must have bound the Atlantic seaways tightly together in a network of criss-crossing voyages. But more entrepreneurial activities are also to be glimpsed in the scant historical sources and the rather fuller archaeological record.

In Adamnan's *Life* of Columba, in an account of one of the saint's prophetic revelations, a passing reference is made to 'Gaulish seamen arriving from the provinces of the Gauls' in a *barca*—a term not used for local vessels. The context in which the story is told suggests that this was no isolated occurrence—there was clearly the expectation that Gaulish vessels would arrive at a particular time of year. These visits took place during the saint's life at Iona (565–97). In another text, written in the 680s, Adamnan refers to the presence on Iona of a Gaulish bishop, Arculf. According to Bede, Arculf had been shipwrecked on the western coast of Britain and had eventually made his way to Iona. These two incidents are sufficient to show that ships from Gaul were not unfamiliar in the Irish Sea in the sixth and seventh centuries. Irish ships were also venturing south along the Atlantic sea lanes. The ship on which Patrick escaped in the 420s may have been an Irish merchant vessel, and when the Irish cleric Columbanus was returning from Burgundy via the Loire in 610 he encountered a ship at Nantes which had just offloaded a cargo from Ireland and was waiting to return. What the cargo was is not recorded, but the *Life* of St Philibert refers to Irish traders arriving in the seventh century at the monastery on the island of Noirmoutier, just south of the

Loire mouth, bringing with them to trade large quantities of shoes and clothes.

The archaeological evidence for a lively Atlantic trade comes largely, as is so often the case, from the study of exotic potsherds found during the excavation of settlement sites. The earliest group of post-Roman imports to be identified arrived in western Britain in the fifth and sixth centuries from the Mediterranean, and included fine tablewares from North Africa (African Red slipware) and from western Turkey (Phocaean Red slipware) together with a range of amphorae (called B wares) from North Africa, the coasts of Turkey, and Egypt (10.29, 10.30). Most of the amphorae were of types thought to have been used to transport olive oil.

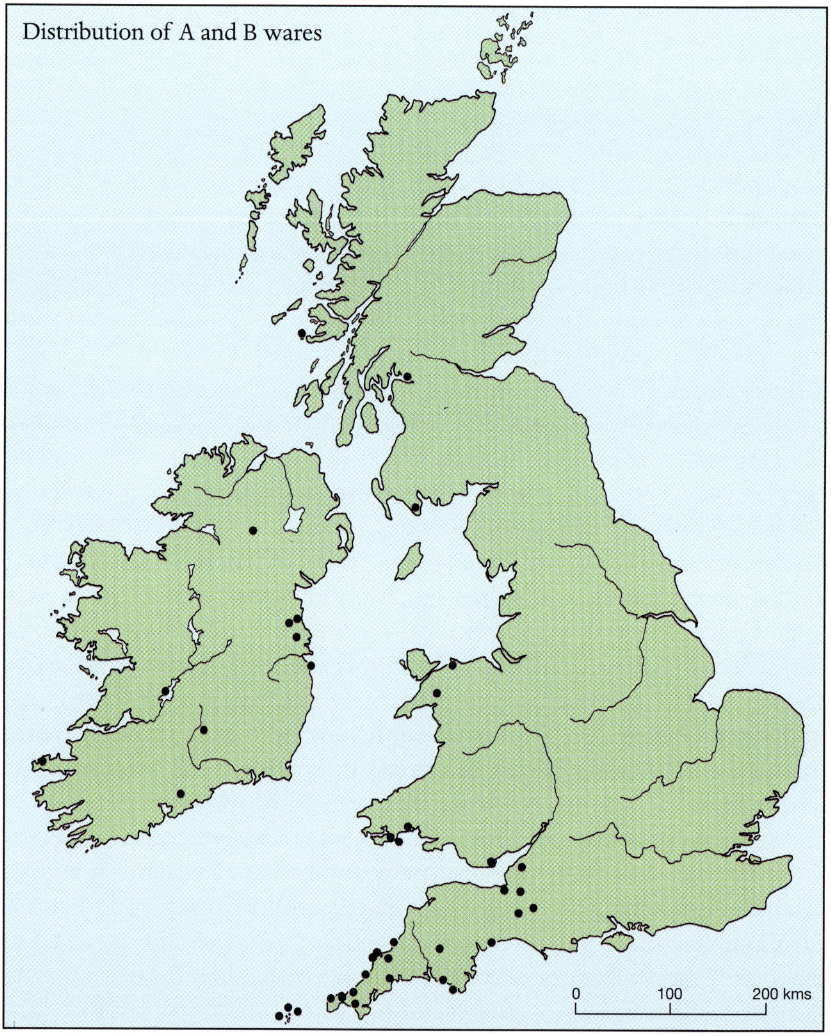

10.29 The distribution of Mediterranean pottery (A and B wares) in Britain and Ireland in the fifth and sixth centuries AD.

The cargoes from which ultimately these archaeological scraps derived were most probably carried by Byzantine vessels, loaded in the east Mediterranean but stopping en route at Carthage or another of the Tunisian ports to take on additional supplies. Once through the Straits of Gibraltar it seems that they made for Portuguese ports in the Tagus and Mondego estuaries, where concentrations of the imported pottery have also been found.

Interesting confirmation of these long-haul Byzantine voyages to the Atlantic comes from the historical sources. In one of the *Lives of the Saints* written near Mérida and referring to events in the late sixth century we learn of Greek merchants (*negotiatores*) coming by ship from the east Mediterranean and travelling upriver to visit Mérida. That such long-distance journeys were not unusual is further shown by the frequently mentioned sea journeys of St Martin in the mid-sixth century from the east Mediterranean to Galicia.

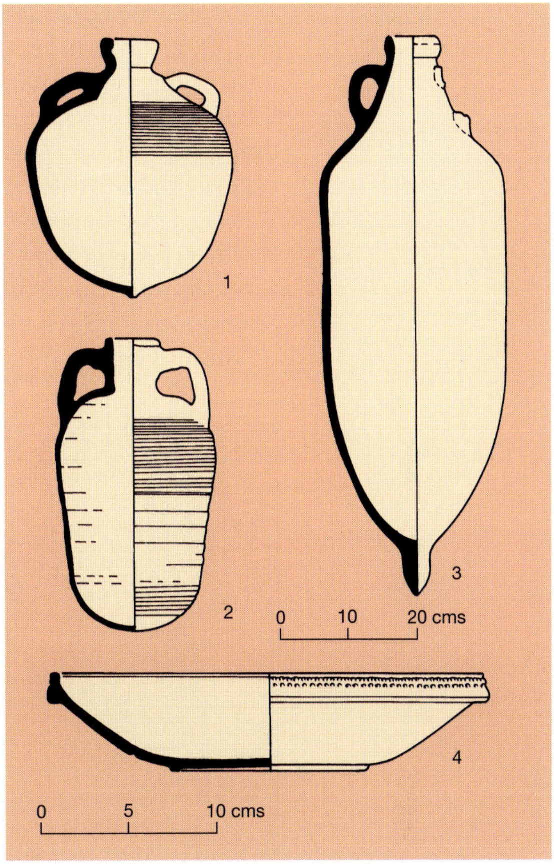

10.30 Imported Mediterranean pottery from Britain. The amphorae (1, 2, and 3) are from various sources: 1 is probably from the Aegean, 2 may be Syrian, while 3 is Tunisian. The bowl, 4, is Phocaean red slipware.

By what means the cargoes of Mediterranean goods were transported to western Britain is less clear. It is possible that the Byzantine vessels continued onwards, stopping perhaps at Scilly or Tintagel to offload, but a more likely scenario is that local vessels, used to the rigours of Atlantic sailing, picked up the cargoes in the Portuguese ports for the last leg of the journey across the Bay of Biscay, past Ushant to the havens of western Britain. By far the greatest quantity of the imports have been found in south-western Britain and south Wales, where the cargoes were probably offloaded. Scarcer finds in Ireland, north Wales, and western Scotland may have resulted either from a few more penetrating voyages or by redistribution through local shipping networks.

It is not possible, from the archaeological evidence, to estimate the intensity and duration of this 'trade' with the Mediterranean. One extreme would be to see the pottery distributions as resulting from a few boatloads of diplomatic gifts sent by the Byzantine state; the other would be to argue for regular commercial exchanges over an extended period of time. The question is incapable of resolution.

Long-distance contacts with the Mediterranean were at an end by the middle of the sixth century, but it was at about this time and lasting well into the seventh century that a new type of exotic pottery, called E ware, is found in western Britain (10.31, 10.32). E ware vessels are entirely domestic and were made somewhere in western France, possibly in the Loire valley or the Gironde region. Although there are prolific finds on western British sites it is unreasonable to suppose that the vessels were imported for their own intrinsic value. It is more likely that they were containers for some desirable foodstuff, and were packed in the interstices of a more bulky cargo such as barrels of wine.

The distribution of E ware differs significantly from that of the earlier

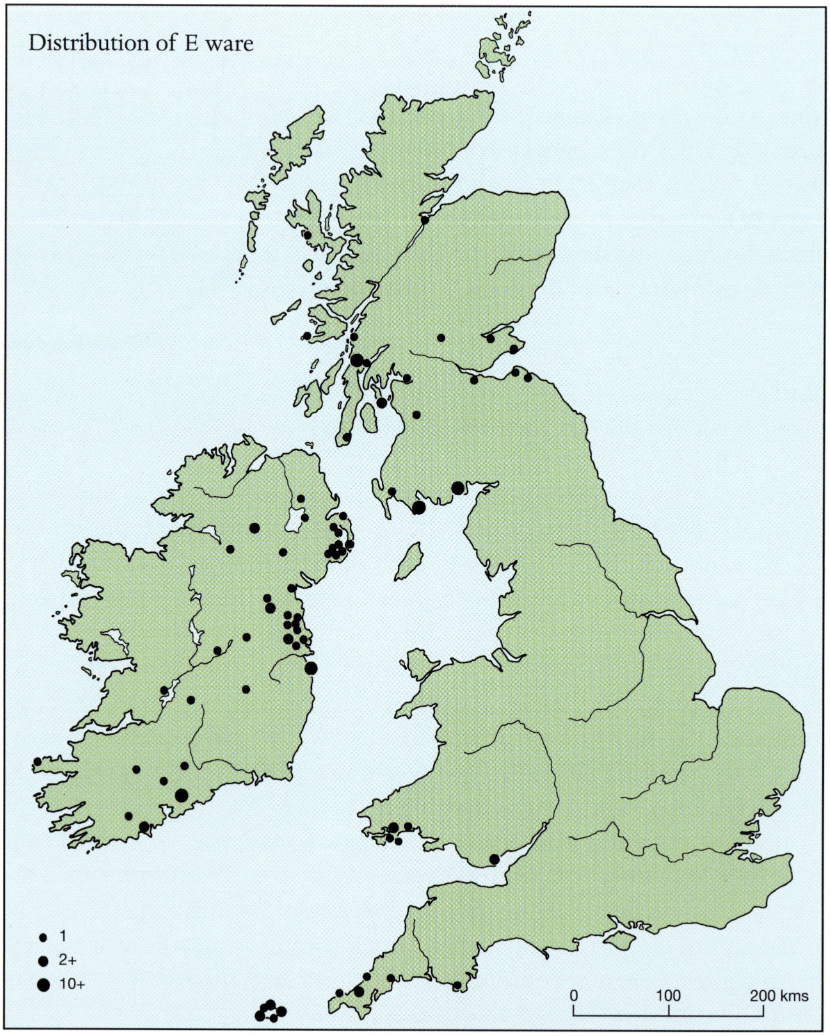

10.31 The distribution of western French pottery (E-ware) of the seventh and eighth centuries in Britain and Ireland.

Mediterranean imports in that, apart from the Scilly Isles, south-western Britain was no longer well represented, the bulk of the cargoes going now to the south and east coasts of Ireland and the west coasts of Scotland, carried no doubt by the Gaulish sailors in their *barcae*. It may have been a cargo of wine and western Gaulish relishes that St Columba was so eagerly anticipating on lonely Iona.

It is always necessary, in dealing with archaeological evidence, constantly to bring to mind how partial and potentially misleading it can be. At best it gives us episodic glimpses of systems which might well have been robust and long-lived. So it is with movement along the Atlantic seaways. The period from AD 200–800 saw many changes as the geopolitics of western Europe convulsed. For a brief period, *c*.250–450, trade was overshadowed by raiding, but thereafter the native rhythms seem to have reasserted themselves and the Atlantic seaways once more became the corridor along which a rich array of cultural ideas was transported between the innovating centres of Ireland, Atlantic France, and Christian Spain.

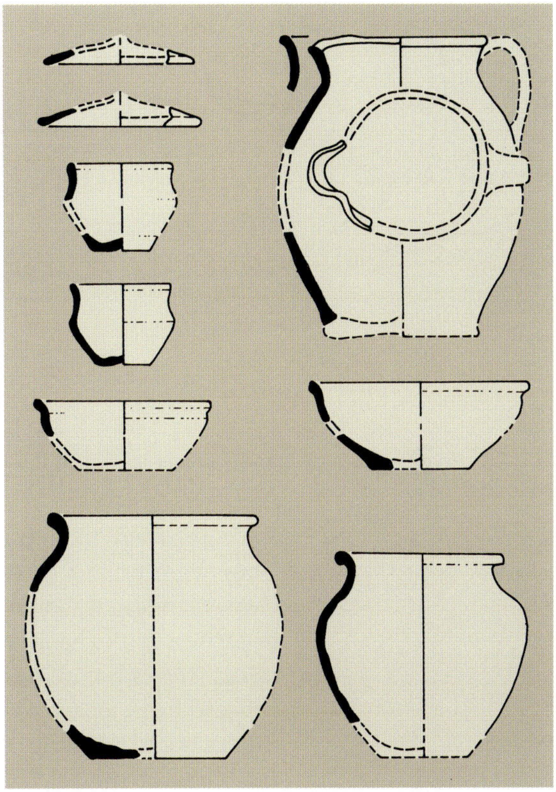

10.32 Pottery of 'E-ware' found in Britain.

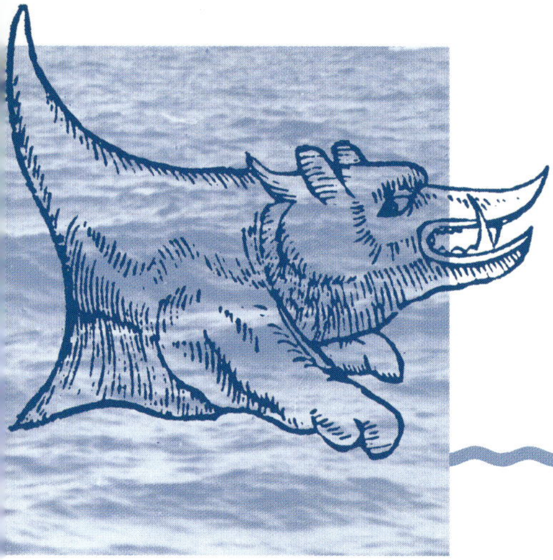

11. The Coming of the Northmen

About 790 Beaduheard, the king's reeve at Dorchester in southern Britain, got news that three foreign ships had landed at Portland and, assuming them to be traders, he went to welcome them. He was wrong. They were raiders from Scandinavia and he died for his mistake. The Dorset landing was a foretaste. A few years later, in 793, the raiding began in earnest with the attack on the monastery of St Cuthbert on Lindisfarne: 'Never before has such terror appeared in Britain as we have now suffered from a pagan race, nor was it thought that such an inroad from the sea could be made. Behold, the church of St Cuthbert spattered with the blood of the priests of God, despoiled of all its ornaments; a place more venerable than all in Britain is given as prey to pagan people.' So wrote the English cleric Alcuin at the court of Charlemagne. Many more raids followed around the coasts of Britain and Ireland (11.1). The Franks were soon to suffer, so too the Bretons. By the 840s Viking war bands were exploring further south along the Atlantic coasts. A vast fleet of 150 ships sailed up the Garonne and plundered almost to Toulouse. Then it moved onwards to attack Galicia and Lisbon before sailing into the Guadalquivir. Here, from their base on the Isla Menor, the Vikings pillaged Seville but were severely mauled by the Moors. Those captured were hanged from the city's palm trees, and two hundred Viking heads were sent by the Emir to his allies in Tangier as an effective witness to his military prowess. Undeterred, the Viking force continued through the Straits of Gibraltar harassing the coasts as they sailed to the mouth of the Rhône where, on an island in the Camargue, a base was established for raiding upriver into the heart of France and across the sea to the coasts of Italy. In 861 they returned to their base on the Loire. The expedition had been 'at once profitable and honourable'.

The Mediterranean venture, while a notable feat, was of little lasting consequence. But meanwhile, in the north, raids and settlement had reached significant proportions. Some indication of what was going on is given by the pained lamentation of Ermentarius, a monk at Noirmoutier, writing in the 860s:

> The number of ships increases, the endless flood of Vikings never ceases to grow bigger. Everywhere Christ's people are the victims of massacre, burning, and plunder. The Vikings overrun all that lies before them, and no one can withstand them. They seize Bordeaux, Périgueux, Limoges, Angoulême, Toulouse; Angers, Tours, and Orleans are made deserts. Ships past counting voyage up the Seine . . . Rouen is laid waste, looted, and burnt; Paris, Beauvais, Meaux are taken, Melun's stronghold is razed to the ground, Chartres occupied, Evreux and Bayeux looted, and every town invested.

Raiding soon gave way to settlement. North-west Scotland and the Northern and Western Isles were already a Norse homeland and commercial enclaves had been established around the coasts of Ireland, when the 'Great Army' landed in eastern England in 865 to begin appropriating land on a massive scale. At about the same time Iceland was being colonized. In the tenth century Northmen settled in Normandy and Brittany. In Britain Alfred the Great stemmed the Viking advance, and in doing so unified England under his command.

In the last decade of the tenth century Viking raids in the west were

11.1 Commemorative stone from Lindisfarne, Northumberland. The scene probably symbolizes Doomsday but it may well have been inspired by the Viking raid of 793.

renewed again in earnest along the entire length of the Atlantic coast from the Elbe to Spain. England was the main focus of attack, and by 1013 it had been conquered. Two years later King Knut established himself in the kingdom his father had gained, thus effectively protecting the island from further harassment. In the muddle over the succession following his death in 1035 William, Duke of Normandy, emerged triumphant. Threats continued and actual raids took place in the far north, but by 1100 the age of the Northmen was at an end.

The importance of the sea to the Viking phenomenon needs no emphasis. It led them to the Atlantic shores, initially for raiding but as time progressed also for trading and settlement. The estuaries of the great rivers were a favourite focus and islands in the estuaries often became safe havens for overwintering bands, the rivers themselves providing access for spring campaigns deep into prosperous inland regions.

The indigenous communities of Atlantic Europe interacted with Vikings in a variety of different ways. The Northern and Western Isles became a homeland from an early date, the lands of Northumberland, Anglia, and Mercia were brought under the command of Scandinavian lords, while intrepid settlers colonized the wastes of Iceland and Greenland. In Ireland merchant settlements grew up at the major ports on the east and south coasts, while on the Continent rivers like the Seine and the Loire provided points of entry for warlords prepared to intervene in the tangled politics of the time. Only in Spain were the raids of little lasting consequence. Perhaps the most significant effect of the Viking episode on the densely settled lands of western Europe was as a catalyst to changes already under way. In some areas, like England and France, it encouraged state formation; in others, like Ireland, Wales, Cornwall, and Brittany, it strengthened the sense of independence. But overall, the greatly increased maritime mobility accelerated the development of trade at all levels, firmly establishing the basis upon which the intensive trading enterprises of the early Middle Ages were to develop along the Atlantic seaways. The fury of raid, plunder, and slaughter helped to forge the new order.

Commerce in the North Sea Region in the Eighth and Ninth Centuries

In the last chapter we considered the changing patterns of trade along the Atlantic seaways in the four hundred years or so following the end of the Roman period, and now we must briefly turn to the southern North Sea to sketch in what was happening up to the time when the Viking attacks began.

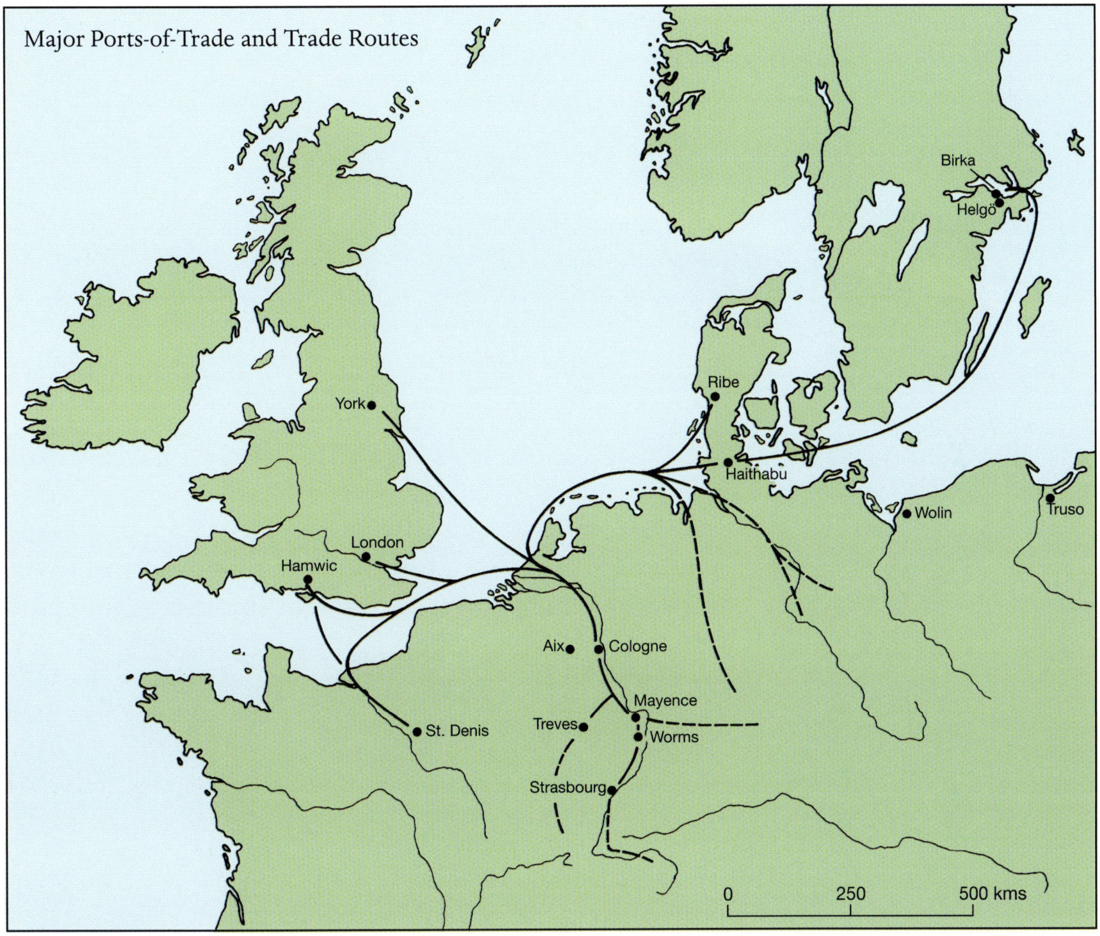

11.2 The major ports-of-trade and trade routes in north-west Europe in the seventh to ninth centuries.

As early as the early sixth century the Rhine corridor began to regain its former importance as a zone of productive energy and a route along which commodities flowed, and invariably the Rhine mouth once more became an interface between the rich riverine hinterland and the southern North Sea (11.2). One of the key locations in this region was Dorestad, lying at the confluence of the Lek and the Rhine on what had been the frontier zone between Frankish-dominated territory and the land of the Frisians. Some time about 680, as the result of conquest by Pippin, the settlement passed to the Frankish kingdom, and from this time onwards it began to develop as a major port, articulating trade both with Britain and the Baltic. By the middle of the eighth century Rhenish pottery was being traded across the North Sea (11.3) to the East Anglian port of Ipswich and the West Saxon port of Hamwih (Saxon Southampton). It was also through Dorestad that a range of trade goods, of Anglo-Saxon,

11.3 A selection of Middle Rhenish imported pottery from Dorestad in the Netherlands.

Frankish, and Frisian origin, were being trans-shipped to reach the Scandinavian ports of Kaupang in south-west Norway and Helgö, west of Stockholm.

That the peak of trading activity at Dorestad belonged to the period *c*.760–810 no doubt reflected the political energies and prestige of Charlemagne, and it was during this time that a treaty was arranged between the Carolingian empire and the Danes. The formal agreement is reflected in the large quantities of Rhenish goods which were traded northwards to the Danish ports of Ribe on the North Sea coast of Jutland just south of Esbjerg, and Haithabu near the mouth of the Schlei in the Baltic. It is less clear how far the Carolingian trade networks penetrated into the Baltic, but items of Rhenish metalwork reached the Swedish ports.

Other Continental ports which rose to prominence during the seventh and eighth centuries were St Denys, just outside the gates of Paris, Rouen, further towards the mouth of the Seine, Amiens on the Somme, and Quentovic towards the mouth of the River Canche near Étaples. Together these sites, which developed as major markets, controlled the movement of commodities in the Frankish domain and were the ports through which trade with England was articulated.

To begin with the principal links in the sixth and seventh centuries were with Kent and the Isle of Wight, but at the beginning of the eighth century a new West Saxon port was founded at Hamwih on the river Itchen, at the head of Southampton Water, across the river from the late Roman fort of Bitterne, 2.19. The first peak of trading activity through Hamwih came in the second quarter of the eighth century, at which time Wessex was under the hegemony of the Mercian royal house, but a renewed intensity can be seen at the end of the eighth and beginning of the ninth centuries, reflecting, as at Dorested, the upsurge of international trade encouraged by Charlemagne and the Mercian king Offa. An interesting reflection of the trading relationship between England and the Carolingian empire comes in correspondence between the two kings. Some time about 789 a quarrel developed between them over marriage negotiations for their offspring, and as a result Charlemagne closed all Frankish ports to English traders. But negotiations were soon reopened, both kings agreeing that traders would have the protection of each other's laws and the right of appeal to the king. In other correspondence 'black stone', possibly querns of Niedermendig lava, are mentioned as exports from Gaul, while Charlemagne complains to Offa that English cloaks (or perhaps lengths of woollen cloth) were too short and asks that Offa sees to it in future that fabric of the agreed length be sent. These trivial exchanges provide a fascinating insight into the complexities of administered trade as it was being formalized, perhaps for the first time, just before 800.

Of the English ports functioning at this period, we have already mentioned Hamwic and Ipswich. Others existed in Kent, possibly at Fordwich or Saare, and at London, while further north important commercial centres were developing at Norwich and York. At all of these English sites, and their Continental counterparts from the Seine to the Rhine, the bustle of production and the processes of exchange will have created concentrations of portable wealth both in terms of the coinage used to facilitate the transactions and the bulk materials being trans-shipped. It is, therefore, hardly surprising that in the first Viking raids of the early ninth century the ports became prime targets.

The rapid development of trade between the Frankish world and its neighbours in the eighth century created a demand for goods from the north, not least quality furs which were otherwise largely unobtainable. To meet the demand southern traders sailed to the northern markets, first to Ribe on the west coast of Jutland, and later penetrating the Baltic to Hedeby and Birka and to Wolin at the estuary of the Oder. Here they met traders from the Baltic region offering the desirable furs, together with feathers of the eider duck, skins of various kinds, walrus ivory, whetstones, and amber. A ninth-century text gives a detailed account of the tribute paid to a Norwegian nobleman by the Saami (Lapps): 'each pays according to his rank. The highest in rank has to pay fifteen marten skins, five reindeer skins, one bear skin, and ten measures of feathers, and a jacket of bear skin or otter skin, and two ship's ropes. Each of these must be sixty ells long, one made of walrus hide, the other from seal skin.' Tribute of this kind would eventually have found its way to the large emporia around the Baltic, where it would have passed into the hands of commercial traders.

Those able to control the trading posts, and the routes to and from them, would have grown rich. Denmark was particularly favoured in this respect, commanding as it does the land and sea routes between the Baltic and the North Sea. It was no doubt with the intent to cash in on the increasingly lucrative trade that the Danish king Godfred moved the entire merchant community of the Slavic town of Reric and transplanted it to create a new trading colony at Haithabu in 808. The new market was well sited to control the short land route across the Danish peninsula.

By the eighth century Frankish trade with Scandinavia was well under way, and Scandinavian traders had begun to visit Dorestad and other northern ports. One Frankish cleric travelling northwards through Frisia encountered a group of Northmen who 'knew the route and the harbours of the sea and the rivers that flowed into it'. Perhaps they were engaged in bringing northern products south to the Frankish emporia.

In the 770s the Carolingian armies began campaigning northwards through Saxony, and by 804 they had reached the Saxon–Danish border. An uneasy period of stand-off followed, culminating, in 810, in a Danish raid on the coasts of Frisia and the Frisian Islands involving a fleet of two hundred ships. It was the first time that the Frankish world had had to face the well-coordinated response of the emerging Danish state. The reasons for the conflict were twofold: fear of the relentless northern advance of Charlemagne interfering with Danish trading communities, and the inevitable attraction of the wealth of the Christian south. What started as a raid largely for defensive reasons soon escalated into a wild scrabble for wealth and plunder.

Why the Raids of the Northmen Began

The raids of the Danes and Norwegians began in the last decade of the eighth century, and over the next seventy years rose to a devastating crescendo. No single factor was responsible for unleashing the fury, but there can be little doubt that the overseas ventures became possible only after the longship had reached its peak of excellence by the middle of the eighth century. The Scandinavian landscape demanded good shipping. The long Atlantic coastline of Norway, with its deeply indented fjords, was accessible with ease only by sea, while the sounds and islands of Denmark had, for millennia, been bound together by boat. The Baltic, too, was a cradle for navigation—a great inland sea providing ease of access between the extensive littorals and their productive hinterlands, and to the river routes penetrating far south across the North European Plain. Throughout Scandinavia settlements favoured the sea coasts and the inland lakes and waterways. They faced the open water and kept their backs to the forest. Thus communities depended upon ships for their livelihood, their rulers able to maintain their power only by command of the sea. In such a world it is easy to see how the ship became a symbol of authority, honed to perfection to reflect the status of the elite. A ship, either real or symbolic, might also accompany its owner in his burial.

Sleek, elegant vessels of clinker-built construction, with planks sewn together, are known as early as the fourth century BC. By the fourth century AD the overlapping edges of the planks were clasped by iron nails, and paddles had been replaced by rowing oars (11.4). When the sail was introduced is still a matter of uncertainty. Saxon vessels of the late-fifth-century raiders in the North Sea are recorded to have been sailing vessels, but the earliest evidence yet available for the sail in Scandinavia is the Oseberg ship found to the west of Oslo fjord, dating to 820. By this time the coins issued by the trading colony of Hedeby regularly show sailing vessels (11.5). It is probable, therefore, that the sail became widely adopted in Scandinavia some time earlier, perhaps by the middle of the eighth cen-

11.4 The boat from Nydam in Denmark is dated by dendrochronology to AD 310–20. Seen here is an illustration by Magnus Petersen produced soon after the discovery in 1863.

11.5 Coins from the port town of Hedeby, Denmark minted in the early ninth century. They provide detailed images of Nordic ships of the period.

tury. Another sophistication of the Oseberg vessel (3.22, 11.6) is that, instead of having rowlocks on the gunwale to hold the oars, separate oarports were provided allowing the oars to hit the water at a lower and more efficient angle. The Oseberg ship shows that, by the early years of the ninth century, all the features characteristic of the classic Viking ship had been brought together, creating fast and highly efficient seagoing vessels suitable for carrying men across the ocean in search of land and plunder.

We have seen above how, in the course of the eighth century, trade between continental Europe and England developed apace, with well-established links leading northwards to the Baltic. In this way the volume of mercantile traffic in the southern North Sea increased dramatically, while the rulers of Denmark became increasingly aware of the wealth to be had to the south. Through the various traders who visited the Scandinavian ports they would also have learnt the political geography of western Europe—most notably the whereabouts of its rich, isolated monasteries and the distracting factional disputes endemic among its ruling households. To the Scandinavian elite there was much prestige to be had in leading a successful raid: the spoils would enrich the begetters and would bind followers closer to their leader. In the competitive emulation which accompanied the early raiding expeditions the number, intensity, and duration of the raids inevitably escalated.

Another, quite different, factor at work was the desire for new land to settle. With a growing population the narrow coastal zone of Norway was too restricted a territory to provide the social space needed for enterprising sons to establish themselves. The only solution was to find new territories overseas in Britain and Ireland, and further afield on the more remote islands of the north Atlantic. For the most part what was sought was new farmland, like the home territories, where families could set up new farms with plenty of space around for expansion by successive generations. It was this that the north Atlantic could supply in plenty. What England had to offer was rather different but no less acceptable—well-

11.6 The Oseberg ship seen here at the time of its excavation. It had been used for the burial of a high-status female in the ninth century and was preserved beneath a mound of clay.

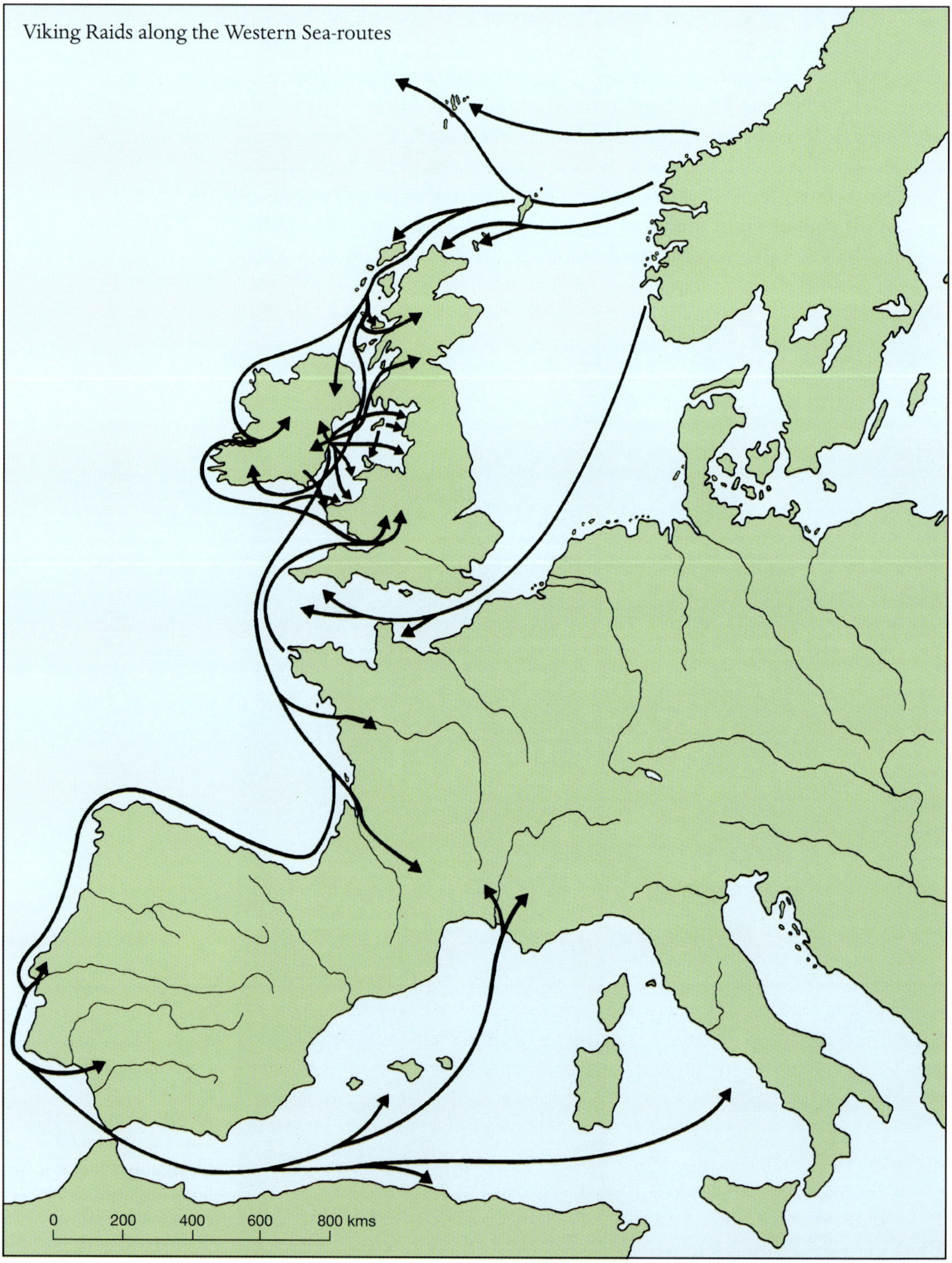
Viking Raids along the Western Sea-routes
0
200
400
600
800 kms

run estates which new Scandinavian lords could leave largely undisturbed, simply taking the profits.

Another incentive to moving overseas was the possibility of setting up merchant colonies emulating those that were so successful in the Baltic and along the eastern coasts of the North Sea. York, already a developing English market, was taken over by the Northmen in 866 and rapidly expanded to become the principal entrepôt in northern Britain, while an entirely new port-of-trade was established at Dublin and soon became a centre for Irish Sea commerce. In all of these ventures the ship was vital.

It would be wrong to give the impression that overseas activities were narrowly focused: trading could soon turn into raiding, while raiding could dissipate itself into settlement. One was never exclusive of the other. This is evocatively summed up in an account of the lifestyle of Svein Asleifarson recorded in the twelfth-century *Orkneyinga Saga*, no doubt referring wistfully to a long-gone era when Vikings behaved like Vikings:

> In the spring he had more than enough to occupy him, with a great deal of seed to sow which he saw to carefully himself. Then when the job was done, he would go off plundering in the Hebrides and in Ireland on what he called his 'spring-trip', then back home just after midsummer where he stayed till the cornfields had been reaped and the grain was safely in. After that he would go off raiding again, and never came back till the first month of winter was ended. This he used to call his 'autumn trip'.

The Vikings in the West: A Brief Progress

Accounts of Viking exploits in western Europe all too easily become lists of dates and raids, not least because this is how they were usually recorded in the chronicles of the time. In the brief account given here only an outline of the main events will be attempted, to serve as a background for the themes to follow (11.7). *Viking* is the word frequently used by the English sources to describe raiders and settlers from Scandinavia, while the Carolingian sources prefer *Northmen*. Both words include, without differentiation, Danes and Norwegians. Until the mid-ninth century it is possible to make a broad distinction between Norwegians, who settled northern and western Scotland and the Northern and Western Isles and were active in the Irish Sea, and Danes, who raided the North Sea and Channel coasts, but thereafter the distinction becomes blurred.

The progress of the settlement of north-western Britain by the Norwegians is unrecorded, but contact began as early as the seventh century and it is quite likely that the colonization was largely completed during the course of the eighth century. The newly settled areas provided the springboard for attacks on Ireland and the Irish Sea coasts, becoming

11.7 (*facing*) The major sea routes used by the Vikings in the ninth and tenth centuries.

increasingly widespread and frequent in the period 795–840. The rich and unprotected monasteries were the target. Iona was attacked three times, in 795, 802, and 806, in the first flush of activity. Thereafter raids thrust further and further south—821 Wexford, 822 Cork, and 824 the isolated monastery of Skellig Michael in the Atlantic off the Kerry coast. Having picked off the vulnerable coastal communities the attacks then began to penetrate inland, but usually no more than 30 kilometres or so from the safety of navigable water. These early attacks were opportunistic hit-and-run affairs, meeting no significant organized opposition.

Meanwhile in the North Sea the Danes adopted similar tactics. In 820 a massive Danish fleet of two hundred vessels threatened Saxony, and in three successive years, beginning in 834, the great trading port of Dorestad was devastated. Frisia became the immediate focus of contention. In 838 the Danish king Harik demanded of the Frankish king Louis that 'The Frisians be given over to him'—a request that was roundly refused. The vulnerability of the coast was vividly brought home when, in 835, the monastery of St-Philibert on the island of Noirmoutier south of the Loire estuary was attacked. England suffered only sporadic raids at first, but these intensified in the 830s. The Isle of Sheppey in the Thames estuary was ravaged in 835 and other attacks were recorded in the Severn estuary, on the north coast of Somerset in 836, and the south coast of Cornwall in 838. These two last attacks may possibly have been at the hands of the raiding parties who had previously attacked the Loire.

11.8 The island of Jenfosse in the Seine midway between Paris and Rouen where Viking raiding bands over-wintered in 853 and 856.

From 840 the attacks escalated in all areas, most particularly in the Frankish kingdom which was now weakened by internal dissent. The Seine valley suffered most to begin with. In 845 Paris was threatened and in 852/3 a Viking force overwintered on an island in the Seine near Rouen (11.8). Harrying attacks continued in the region for a decade from 856. Meanwhile the trading ports of Quentovic and Hamwic were sacked in 842 and the Thames estuary came under persistent attack. In 850/1 a fleet overwintered on the Isle of Thanet, and in 854/5 on Sheppey. Canterbury and London were both mauled in 851 by a Danish force commanding 350 ships. A few years later, in 859, raiders sailed from the Somme to the Solent to attack Winchester, but were defeated and returned to the Continent two years later. The concentration of the attacks on the profitable trading centres along the rivers on both sides of the Channel from the 840s to the 860s reflects the concerted effort of the raiders to profit from the unprotected cities, either by directly plundering them or by demanding huge bribes not to attack.

While all this was going on other bands were exploring the potential of the other rivers of western France. The Loire received the brunt of the attacks. The most serious were in the early 840s around Nantes and again in 855, when the raiders penetrated upriver to Tours where they attacked the monastery of St-Martin. Further south in Aquitania the Garonne was used by one group of raiders, who reached Toulouse in 844. Bordeaux fell after being besieged in 848 and other towns to suffer were Saintes and Périgueux, while Poitiers was burned in 865 by Northmen marching overland from their Loire-mouth enclave. The raiding party that had reached Toulouse in 844 went on to circumnavigate Iberia, as we have seen above, causing chaos on the way.

The events of 840–65 saw the Scandinavians working the full length of the Atlantic zone from the Rhine to Gibraltar and beyond, but they were at their most active and most persistent along the major rivers—the Seine, the Thames, the Loire, and the Garonne—feeding off the cities that owed their wealth and well-being to their command of the river routes. The rivers that brought them their commercial advantage through access to the sea now brought men who sought to take it for themselves.

The 860s saw a change of pace from raid to settlement, accompanied by intensified and co-ordinated opposition by those whose land the Northmen were intent on taking. The Franks were the first to come to terms with the new reality by building fortified bridges across the rivers Seine and Loire, by fortifying towns and monasteries, and by paying tribute to groups of Vikings in return for protection or military services. These tactics protected the heart of the kingdom while leaving the lower reaches of the two rivers to the roving bands of invaders who had now taken up residence in the areas. The strategy kept Frankia free from further incursions until a new wave of attacks began on Paris in 885. In the meantime the Vikings turned their attention to eastern England. In 865 a large invasion force landed in East Anglia and was soon joined by others to create what a contemporary called 'a great heathen army'. The army overwintered, and in the course of the next five years went on to conquer

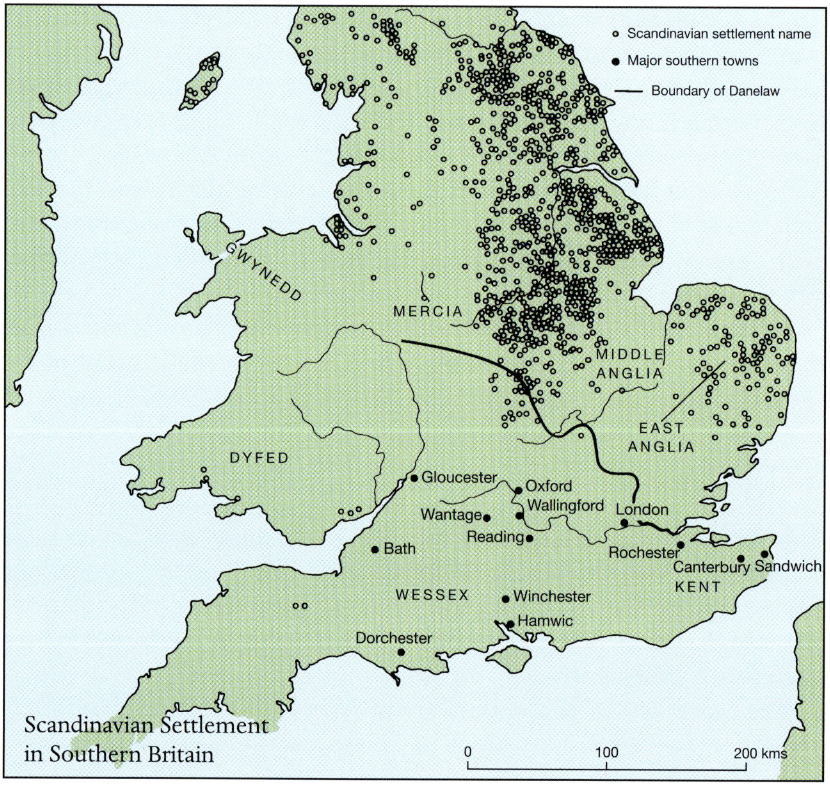

11.9 The boundary agreed by Alfred and Guthrum, about 880, between England and the Danelaw and the distribution of Scandinavian place-names.

East Anglia and Northumberland and much of Mercia. In 871, with their new domain firmly under control, the Vikings turned their attention to the kingdom of Wessex. A major battle was fought at Reading, after which the West Saxons agreed terms and the Great Army turned to the north, in 874/5 spending the winter encamped by the River Tyne. In the following year the conquest of Northumberland had been completed and the land shared out between the conquerors. Thereafter 'they proceeded to plough and to support themselves'.

In 875 another attack was mounted against Wessex, followed by a third in January 878, but later in the year, at Edington in Wiltshire, Alfred led the West Saxons to victory, forcing the attackers back beyond the northern boundaries of his kingdom. Throughout this period, in the eastern region of Britain that would become known as the Danelaw, the Northmen extended their authority, taking over what land they wanted to settle and farm (11.9). The boundary between the Danelaw and England was formally agreed in 879/80, and Alfred set about fortifying his kingdom and building a strong navy to protect its long and vulnerable shore line. All this was to good effect and when, in 892, a new invading force of some

250 ships arrived in Kent to be joined in the same county by another of eighty ships, the West Saxon defences were ready. In the ensuing conflict, lasting until 896, Wessex emerged triumphant, the Viking force eventually dissipating itself, some to East Anglia and Northumberland, others 'that were moneyless' taking ship for the Seine valley.

In Ireland, meanwhile, the comparatively small isolated Norse settlements were unable to make a united stand and in consequence came under increasing pressure from the Irish kings and were gradually defeated one after the other, culminating in expulsion of the Vikings from Dublin in 902. Many of those ousted from the island settled in the

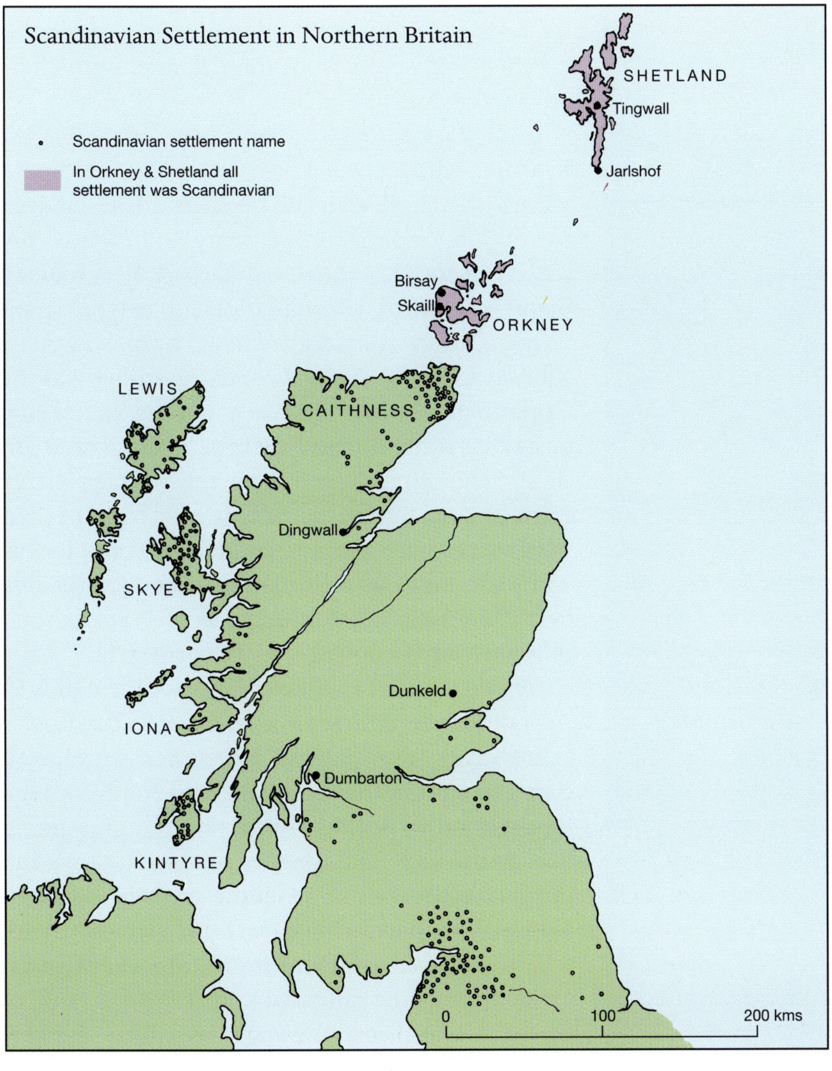

11.10 Scandinavian settlement in northern Britain.

Isle of Man and in Cheshire, while others took ship for Iceland where colonization by the Norwegians had begun in the 870s.

With much of Britain either settled by Northmen or strongly opposed to them under the leadership of Wessex, and the Irish elite now gaining the upper hand, the thrust of Viking aggression focused again on France. As always it was the two vulnerable river valleys, the Seine and the Loire, that posed the problem. The upriver areas were by now fairly well protected, but the estuaries lay open to attack. The Carolingian leadership took the only action possible in the circumstances—they invited bands of potential attackers to settle in the expectation that they would guard their new territories from further inroads and would thus form a buffer protecting the inland regions. By taking this action the Carolingians were distancing themselves from the Atlantic, with all its advantages and its dangers.

11.11 One of the ivory chessmen from the Isle of Lewis in the Outer Hebrides presenting a familiar image of a Viking raider.

In the Lower Seine valley a band of raiders led by Rollo, who had been defeated at Chartres in 911, were settled in Rouen and given extensive lands in the region. Under a formal treaty Rollo was recognized as a count of the Rouen district: he remained firmly in control, consolidating and extending his domain, and was succeeded in 927 by his son. At its fullest extent the duchy extended as far west as the Cotentin peninsula. The place-name evidence suggests that some of the Northmen who finally settled in the region came from the west, probably from Ireland. The settlement proved to be permanent, and extensive intermarriage soon led to complete cultural assimilation—the *Nor(d)manni* becoming a maritime principality of Frankia, their domain *Nor(d)mannia* giving its name to one of the *circumscriptions* of modern France—Normandy.

A similar settlement was allowed in the Lower Loire valley when, in 921, Northmen were given rights to land in the region around Nantes after a long period of Viking activity in the area going back to the 840s. The agreement of 921 followed an unsuccessful siege of a Viking enclave, based in Nantes, who had fortified the Loire estuary to protect their fleet. The token Viking capitulation came when they agreed to 'receive the faith of Christ'. The Loire Vikings remained actively

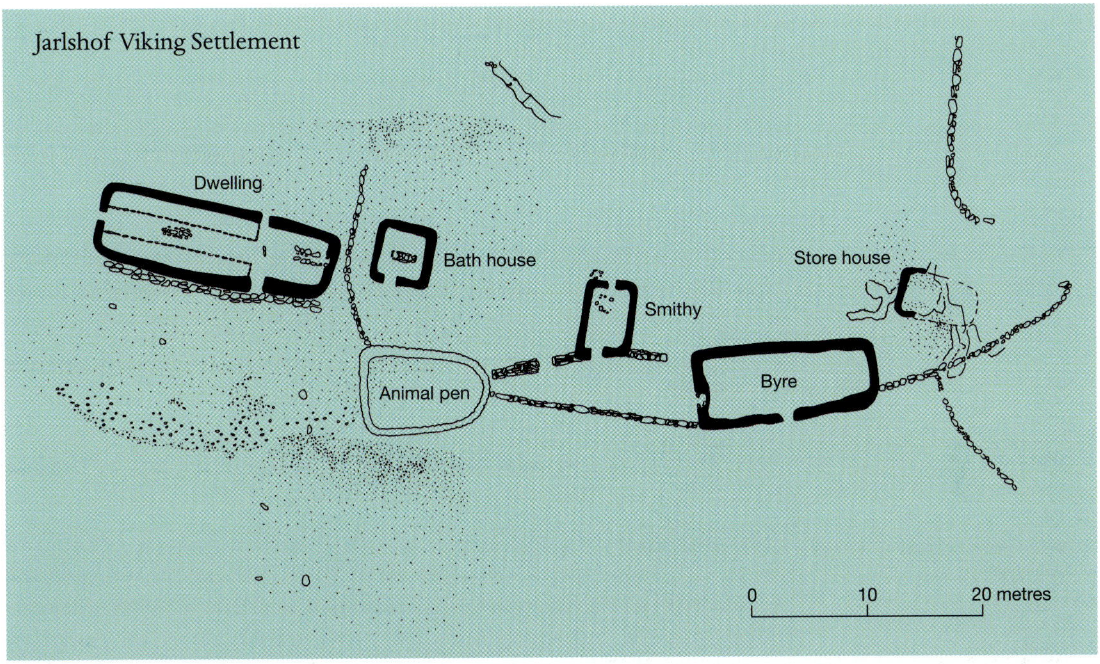

11.12 The earliest phase of Viking settlement at Jarlshof, Shetland.

aggressive, raiding the Seine valley in 923–4 and along the Loire penetrating as far east as Bourgogne in 924. Viking forces were also active throughout Brittany. But the occupation was short-lived, and in 937 a Breton force succeeded in ousting the Northmen from Nantes and two years later dispersed the remnant army in a battle north of Rennes. Although there were later raids by Northmen from the Seine valley in the 940s and again in 960, Brittany had been cleared of Vikings. The lack of Scandinavian place-names, even in the Loire valley, shows that the brief period of settlement had little lasting impact.

Towards the end of the tenth century, with the rise of a strong dynasty in Denmark under Harald Bluetooth and his son, Sven Forkbeard, a new phase of Viking raiding was initiated, and once more it was the Atlantic coastal regions as far south as Iberia that took the brunt of the attack. England was particularly vulnerable. In 991 Sven Forkbeard led his first raid against the English, his activities culminating in the conquest of the kingdom in 1013. Three years later, after his death, his son Knut was formally recognized as king of England. Dynastic squabbles and claims and counter-claims to the English throne rumbled on throughout the eleventh century, but the failure of the threatened Danish conquest of England to materialize in 1085 was the effective end of the Viking episode. Occasional Norwegian expeditions to the Northern and Western Isles were the last ripples, three centuries after the Viking wave first struck.

Scandinavian Settlement in Scotland and the Islands

In spring the prevailing east winds would take a ship comfortably, within the space of two sailing days, the 180 nautical miles from the Norwegian coast, in the vicinity of Bergen, to the Shetland Isles. When the first journey was made is unknown, but we can be tolerably certain that Norse settlement of Shetland and Orkney was well under way by the end of the eighth century, and thereafter the control of the west coast of Scotland and the Western Isles followed rapidly (11.10, 11.11). For Norwegians, restricted to the narrow littoral zone of their homeland, the new territories in the west provided much-needed space for expansion in a congenial and familiar environment. The fertility of Orkney soon made the archipelago the political centre of the Norse settlement. The earldom of Orkney was established towards the end of the ninth century, and by the late tenth century its authority extended over Shetland, the coastal mainland of Scotland, the Western Isles, and the Isle of Man.

The settlement in this broad Atlantic zone was based on the isolated, self-contained farmstead and would have involved the influx of pioneering family groups, but there must also have been a degree of intermarriage with the local population. The survival of Norse place-names throughout the region leaves little doubt that immigrant groups were numerous, and that once established the new culture became dominant.

Unlike Ireland, where the principal activity of the newcomers seems to have been the setting up of trading entrepôts, no centralized trading port

11.13 Reconstruction of the first Viking farmhouse at Jarlshof, Shetland.

11.14 (*facing*) The original farmhouse at Jarlshof with later additions.

has been identified. What exchanges there were (and there is ample evidence that timber was imported from Norway) would have been organized on a small-scale local basis, presumably with the merchants visiting individual coastal settlements. What stands out from the increasingly rich archaeological evidence is that the socio-economic level of the Norse settlement was much like that of the early-first-millennium settlements it replaced. In some cases, like Jarlshof (11.12, 11.13, 11.14) on Shetland and Udal on North Uist, the same settlement sites simply continued in use. On the island of Rousay Viking burials were found in a cemetery which had been established centuries earlier, the Viking graves carefully avoiding the earlier burials that had been marked by boulders.

11.15 Odd's cross slab from Kirk Braddan, Isle of Man carved in Jellinge style popular in Norway at this time.

The Northern and Western Isles and the adjacent mainland littoral zone can be regarded as the western homeland of the Norwegian Vikings, and it was from here that raids on Ireland and further afield were mounted in the slack periods during the agricultural year. For these activities the Isle of Man provided a perfect springboard, its location in the centre of the Irish Sea making it equally suitable for raiding to west, east, and south (11.15). Such cemetery evidence as there is suggests that the Scandinavian element was mainly male, the females being provided by the indigenous population. This would be consistent with the island functioning essentially as a base for maritime raids. It is surprising that the Galloway peninsula appears not to have been settled by Vikings (11.10). The place-name evidence and the distribution of distinctive hog-back tombstones show that there was a sizeable Scandinavian population in northern Cumberland and along the north side of the Solway Firth, but this is best seen as an extension of the settlement of northern England and not as part of the Norse Atlantic area. Thus the indigenous population of Galloway, maintaining its independence against the Scots and Angles, seems also to have formed a buffer between Norse settlement of the northwest and the Danish settlement spreading from the south-east.

The Settlement of the North Atlantic

To the land-hungry Norwegians the prospect of new land to settle in the west would have been attractive (11.16). How they came to gain the confidence to explore beyond Shetland we will never know, but it may well be that the existence of the Faroes, settled by Irish monks early in the eighth century, was common knowledge on Orkney and Shetland when the first Norse settlers arrived. When eventually Irish monks reached Iceland at the end of the eighth century news will have spread quickly to the Northern Isles. It is not unreasonable to suppose that the earliest exploration of the Faroes by Scandinavians was carried out by settlers from Orkney, and from the Faroes it was a comparatively short haul to Iceland. Once the basic routes and navigational rules had been established it was only a matter of time before a serious attempt was made to settle the new lands.

Norse settlement of the Faroes began about 800, and the first permanent settlements were being established on Iceland sixty or seventy years later. It cannot have been long before the sailing directions, recorded in the thirteenth-century version of *Landnámabók* (The Book of Settlements), became widely known. Sailing from Stad on the coast of Norway, passing north of Shetland and south of the Faroes, it took seven days to reach Horn in eastern Iceland. From Reykjanes in south-west Iceland to

11.16 The Viking conquest of the North Atlantic.

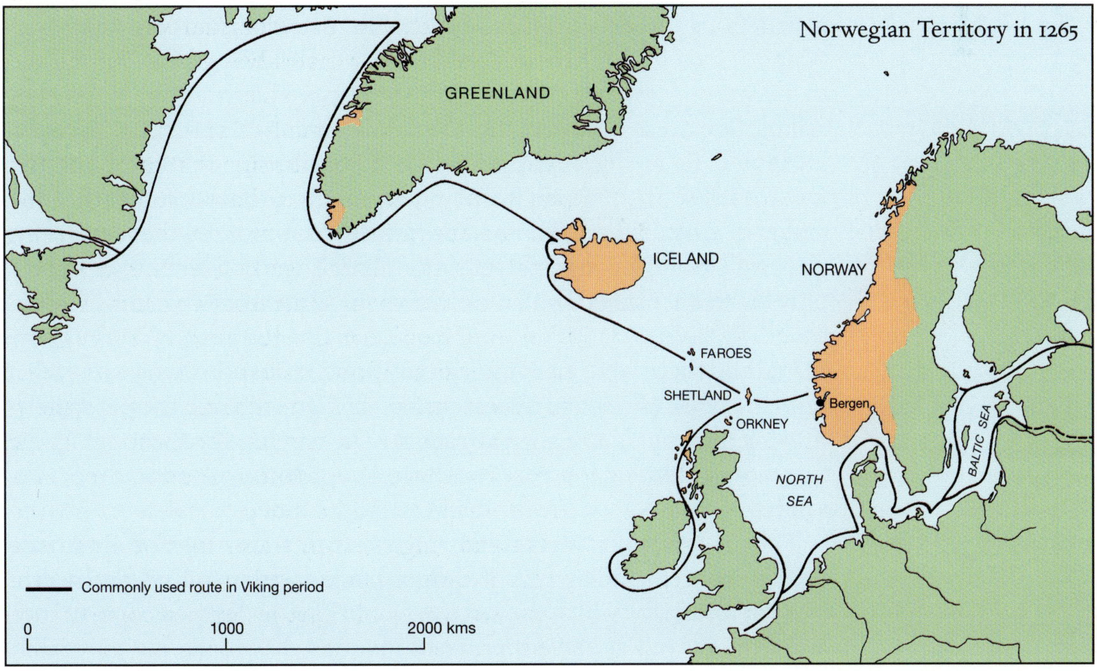

Slyne Head on the west coast of Ireland was a three-day sailing. The record may reflect the routes most commonly in use.

The *Landnámabók* gives a largely mythical account of the discovery and settlement of Iceland, but in its detail, if not in its characterization, lie some insights into the nature of the early voyages. One of the earliest explorers, Flóki Vilgerdason, we are told, sailed from Norway with his daughters and livestock. He went via Shetland, where one of his daughters was drowned, and stopped at the Faroes, where his second daughter was given in marriage. From there he made towards Iceland, setting free three ravens in succession. One returned home, one flew back to the ship, but the third flew straight ahead to the new land giving him the bearing to sail. The route taken and the use of birds to locate land are interesting insights into the methods of the earliest explorers.

The first settlers arrived between 860 and 870, and within sixty years or so all the inhabitable land had been taken. That the period of colonization corresponds with reverses experienced in Ireland, Wessex, France, and Brittany may be more than coincidence. The presence of 'Celtic' place-names among the four hundred recorded in *Landnámabók* has been thought to indicate an Irish element among the original population, introduced by Norse settlers coming from Ireland at a time when the Irish kings were ousting Viking communities. At any event Irish slaves and concubines are several times mentioned in the texts.

Greenland lay about 300 miles to the west of Iceland. The sailing instructions in *Landnámabók* say that the extreme southern tip, Hvarf (Cape Farewell), could be reached in four days' sailing from Snæfellsnes in the west of Iceland, but it could also be gained direct from Norway by sailing due west between the Shetlands and the Faroes. An account, attributed to an Icelandic priest Ari Thorgilsson, written about 1130 records the settlement of Greenland beginning about 985 under the leadership of Eric the Red, who had previously reconnoitred the west-facing coast and found it congenial for settlement. Twenty-five ships set sail but only fourteen reached land, the others being driven back or sunk. The discovery of the new land was opportune. Iceland was already densely populated and there were growing signs of land exhaustion. Ten years earlier there had been a serious famine and many had suffered: the prospect of moving on would have been attractive. The few hundred who set up the first pioneer settlements rose rapidly to a population of about three thousand.

The new territory was prolific, producing a wide range of commodities for export including furs of various kinds, hides, wool, oil, and walrus ivory in return for which the settlers would have welcomed corn, timber, and iron as well as the other small luxuries that made life agreeable.

Though remote and sometimes harsh, the west coast of Greenland, with its deeply incised fjords, was not at all unlike the homeland of Norway and there was habitable land in plenty. For the more adventurous spirits with a lust to explore, unlimited possibilities faced them a mere three or four days' sailing away. That some rose to the challenge and landed in the Americas archaeology is now beginning to show.

The Vikings in Ireland

For four decades, following the first devastating raids of 795, the coasts of Ireland were subjected to an increasing number of hit-and-run attacks by highly mobile maritime war parties sailing from their homelands on the Northern and Western Isles of Scotland. From the outset the raiders did not have it all their own way: in 811 one of the war-bands was slaughtered by the Ulaid, and in the following year two other raiding parties were defeated in the south. The invaders had taken on a country already in a state of military preparedness, whose warriors had become inured to fighting in interminable local dynastic feuds. As some measure of the reality of the times it is worth recalling that the Irish annals for the period 795–820 record twenty-six Viking attacks compared with eighty-seven outbreaks of violence among the Irish themselves, and in the 180 years *before* the first Viking attack there were thirty recorded burnings of monasteries, many of them, no doubt, instigated by Irish warlords. The situation in Ireland was very different to that in England and Scotland. Social instability was rife: the appearance of the Northmen simply added to it.

The intensification of the Viking raids after 830 was accompanied by the establishment of *longphorts*—defended enclosures for men and ships—which allowed the attacking forces to overwinter (11.17). The first were set up in 841 at Annagassan, in Louth, and at Dublin, and it was at about this time that collaboration between Viking raiders and Irish warlords is first recorded. Both factors were to become important themes in subsequent Hiberno–Norse relations.

As the number of *longphorts* increased, so more sedentary communities of Vikings became established around them, and what had started out as military installations began to take on the functions of trading and manufacturing enclaves. These new centres soon assumed many of the centralizing functions that had previously focused around the larger monasteries, but because they were sited at good anchorages, often on navigable rivers, and were in the control of highly mobile maritime communities, they quickly developed as active centres in a network of overseas trading which bound the dispersed Scandinavian settlements

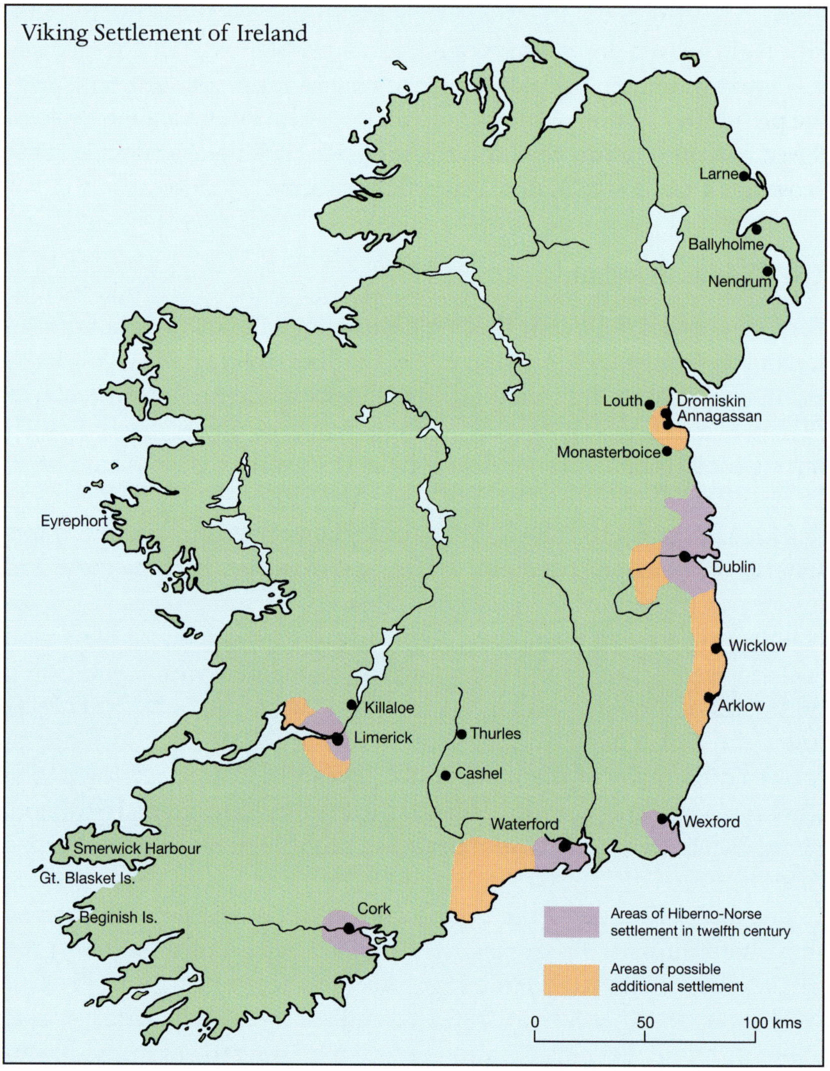

11.17 The Viking settlement of Ireland.

together. As a result the Irish Sea became a significant commercial focus. Nor were the attractions of the Viking trading stations overlooked by the Irish kings. Such places were convenient concentrations of wealth to be raided or controlled whenever opportunity allowed. These fixed and vulnerable Viking settlements provided easy prey for the mobile Irish warbands. Throughout the 840s the Irish kings were active and usually successful in their attacks against the Viking enclaves, a phase culminating in the ravaging of Dublin by Máel Sechnaill in 849.

The complex relationships between the Norse settlers and the Irish were further confused when new bands of Scandinavians, including

Danes from England, arriving in the period 849–53, caused internal dissent by attacking Norse settlers already in occupation.

For the rest of the century two major trends can be discerned behind the plethora of actions and counter-actions—the gradual elimination of the smaller Viking enclaves around the coast by Irish war leaders, and the growth in the political and economic importance of Dublin, which was now functioning much as an Irish kingdom with interests in expanding its dominance (11.18, 11.19). In 866 the rulers of Dublin began to be active in the affairs of Scotland, capturing the important centre of Dumbarton on the Clyde in 870, but thereafter internal dissension greatly weakened them, and in 902 a combined attack by the Irish kings of Brega and Leinster brought the Viking control of the now-flourishing town of Dublin to an end. Many of the Vikings, displaced in the constant attacks of the Irish throughout the second half of the ninth century, sought new lands overseas in Cumbria and in Iceland.

The Viking presence in Ireland in the ninth century was played out against a background of almost constant warfare among the competing

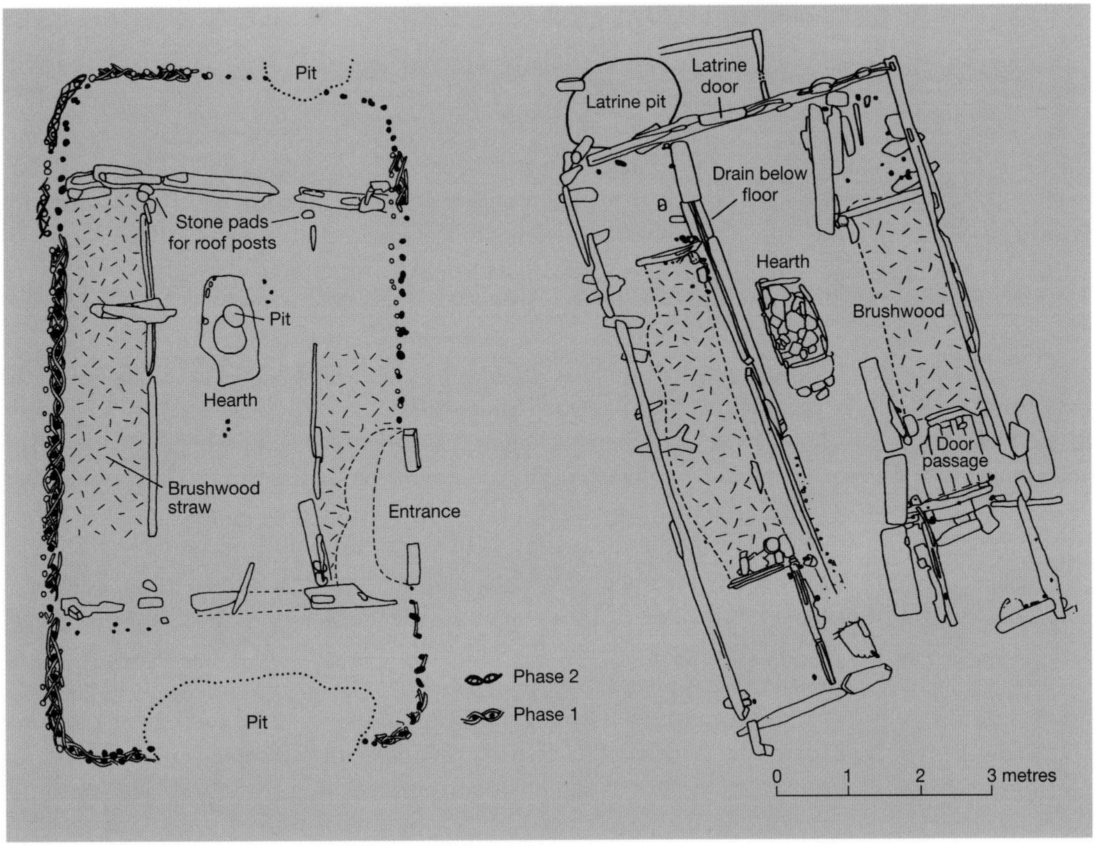

11.18 Viking houses in Dublin.

Irish dynasts, whose loyalties were divided between a multiplicity of small kingdoms and the authority of over-kings. In these internecine conflicts the Vikings played their part, both physically as participants and as a catalyst to the creation of larger confederacies. Out of the chaos of conflict of the early ninth century the over-king of the southern Uí Néill, Máel Sechnaill, emerged triumphant and on his death in 862 was referred to as king of Ireland by the contemporary annalists.

The beginning of the tenth century saw the Viking threat intensify once more, with large-scale raids beginning again in 914. In the turmoil that followed, the new invaders, the many existing Norse enclaves, and the Irish kings joined in the mêlée. In 944 a united Irish force fell on Dublin and sacked the city: 'its houses, house-enclosures, its ships and other structures were burned; its women, boys and common folk enslaved, its warriors were killed; it was altogether destroyed, from four persons to one, by killing and drowning, burning and capture, apart from a small number that fled in a few ships and reached Dalkey.' The city was to survive into the politically confused times of the late tenth and eleventh centuries, its control passing from one king to another as fortunes waxed and waned. It was now the principal commercial centre of Ireland, and as such was an essential appurtenance of Irish kingship. The Norse enclaves in Ireland, most notably Dublin, Wexford, Waterford, Cork, and Limerick, remained throughout this long period of internal conflict as the prime economic centres of the island, whether they were independent or under the rule of Irish kings, and were to emerge into the later Middle Ages as significant ports conducting international trade. From the middle of the tenth century long-distance exchanges began to flourish as never before. Some sense of this is given by the account of the wealth of Limerick, seized by the Irish in the attack of 968: 'They carried away their jewels and their best property, their saddles beautiful and foreign, their gold and their silver; their beautifully woven cloths of all colours and of all kinds; their satins and their silken clothes, pleasing and variegated, both scarlet and green and all sorts of cloth in like manner.' The list, if it can be accepted as actual rather than poetic, implies an extensive trading network, quite possibly extending along the Atlantic seaways to Iberia. One of the products generated by endemic warfare—a plentiful supply of slaves—would have been a valuable export commodity. Slave-raiding features large in motivation behind the Viking attacks of the late ninth century, and there is no

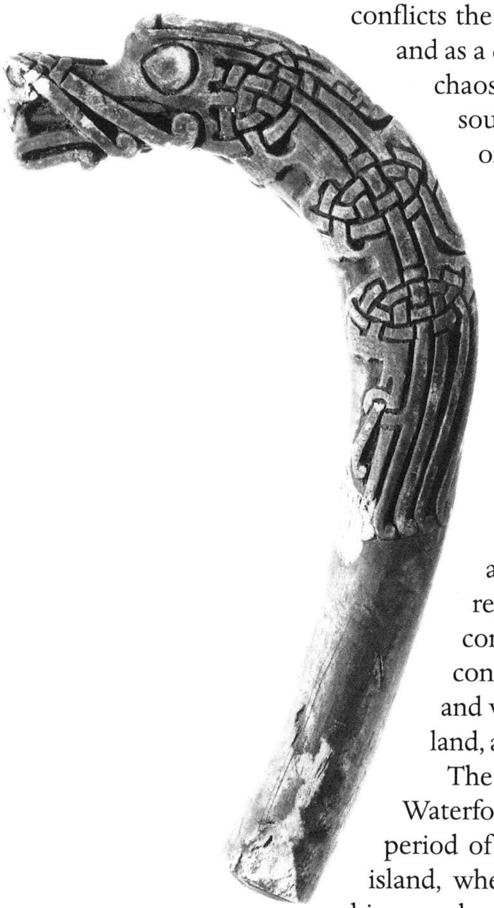

11.19 Carved wooden crook, possibly a whip handle, from excavations in Viking Dublin.

reason to suppose that the markets diminished throughout the next hundred years. Many of the slaves were taken to Scandinavia and Iceland, but others may well have found their way to the slave markets of Andalucía where Mediterranean luxuries were to be had in return.

The Norse contribution to shipping and seafaring cannot be overestimated. Although the Irish tradition of boat-building was well established and was efficient enough, as we have seen, to transport monks to Iceland, the Viking vessels introduced a new level of sophistication. That many of the words associated with shipping and with fishing found in the Irish language derive from Old Norse is sufficient to stress the impact of Scandinavian seafaring on the indigenous culture. Perhaps the greatest effect which the Viking episode had on Ireland came by way of the sea, for Ireland was now brought firmly into the broader world of western Europe. The Irish elite watched as English kingship developed apace. The successes of Athelstan against the Vikings in the north of England will not have gone unnoticed by the Uí Néill and their successors as they fought for control of the Viking trading enclaves. Of no less significance was the wealth which overseas trading ventures now brought within the reach of the Irish kings. The concentration of these riches in the hands of the powerful dynasts had a major impact on the hierarchization of power and the move towards a kingship of Ireland which gained momentum in the eleventh century.

The Welsh, the Cornish, and the Vikings

The Viking attacks on Wales in the ninth and tenth centuries mirrored those of the Irish four centuries earlier, reflecting the fact that the richest land lay in the Lleyn peninsula and Anglesey in the north and Dyfed in the south. Lleyn and Anglesey were perilously close to the Viking strongholds of Dublin and the Isle of Man, and inevitably became a prime target for raids in the later ninth and at intervals throughout the tenth centuries. Apart from Scandinavian names acquired by a few significant coastal landmarks and a small cluster of Scandinavian place-names around the Dee estuary, there is no evidence of any significant settlement.

In Dyfed the situation was different. Place-names suggest settlement at intervals all along the coast, from Fishguard to Newport, with a dense distribution in the extreme south-west around Pembroke. The Vikings are recorded to have wintered in Dyfed in 878, and it may well be that settlement began at this time. There were further attacks a century later from the Western Isles, Dublin, and from Limerick. The principal target was the cathedral of St David's, which was sacked four times in the space of seven years. Some of the raiders offered their services to aspiring local Welsh dynasts, but with little significant effect. Overall, the evidence from Dyfed suggests limited colonial settlement based around a port-of-trade at Pembroke, much like the trading enclaves around the south coast of Ireland.

The south-west peninsula of Dumnonia (Cornwall and Devon) was vulnerable to Viking incursions, both from the south along the Channel and from the north via the Severn estuary. The earliest Viking threat coincided with a major thrust westwards by the armies of Wessex, instigated in 814 by Ecgbert. As the result of this initiative Devon and part of Cornwall were brought to heel. A Cornish rebellion in 825 failed, but resistance flared up again in 838, encouraged by the appearance of a large Viking force who joined the rebels to oppose the West Saxons. Ecgbert moved rapidly to Cornwall and defeated the alliance, effectively bringing to an end the independence of Dumnonia. Thereafter the local kings of the south-west acknowledged the authority of Wessex. Forty years later, when Alfred was facing the Great Army, seaborne attacks by Viking bands on the coasts of Devon failed to kindle any spark of local resistance. Another spate of attacks towards the end of the tenth century was roundly resisted by local thegns and, except for one incident in 1001 when a local leader, Pallig, allied his forces with a Danish raiding party, the south-west remained steadfastly on the side of Wessex. Unlike Brittany, where the spirit of resistance to the Franks was still strong when the Vikings appeared on the scene, in Dumnonia the desire for independence was all but spent.

The Breton Fight for Independence

The sack of Vannes by the Frankish king Pippin III in 753 marked the beginning of a concerted attempt by the Franks to subdue Brittany, and by the end of the century the whole region had been overrun. Yet resistance remained, and on several occasions in the first thirty years of the ninth century expeditions had to be mounted from Rennes and Vannes to put down rebellions in the west. It was against this background of instability that the first Viking attacks impinged, introducing an entirely new factor into the conflict (11.21). Until about 840 the raids had focused on the coast of the Vendée and the island of Noirmoutier (11.20), but in that year the death of Louis the Pious created political instability, encouraging the Vikings to greater efforts. Attacks on the Loire intensified, and in 843 Nantes was attacked. The same interregnum saw the Breton overlord Nominöe taking the offensive against the Franks and campaigning far inland to Le Mans. The discomfort caused to the Frankish kingdom by

11.20 (*facing*) The mouth of the River Loire. To the south is the island of Noirmoutier joined to the mainland by a sand spit. It was first raided by the Vikings in 799. Vikings settled extensively around the Loire estuary.

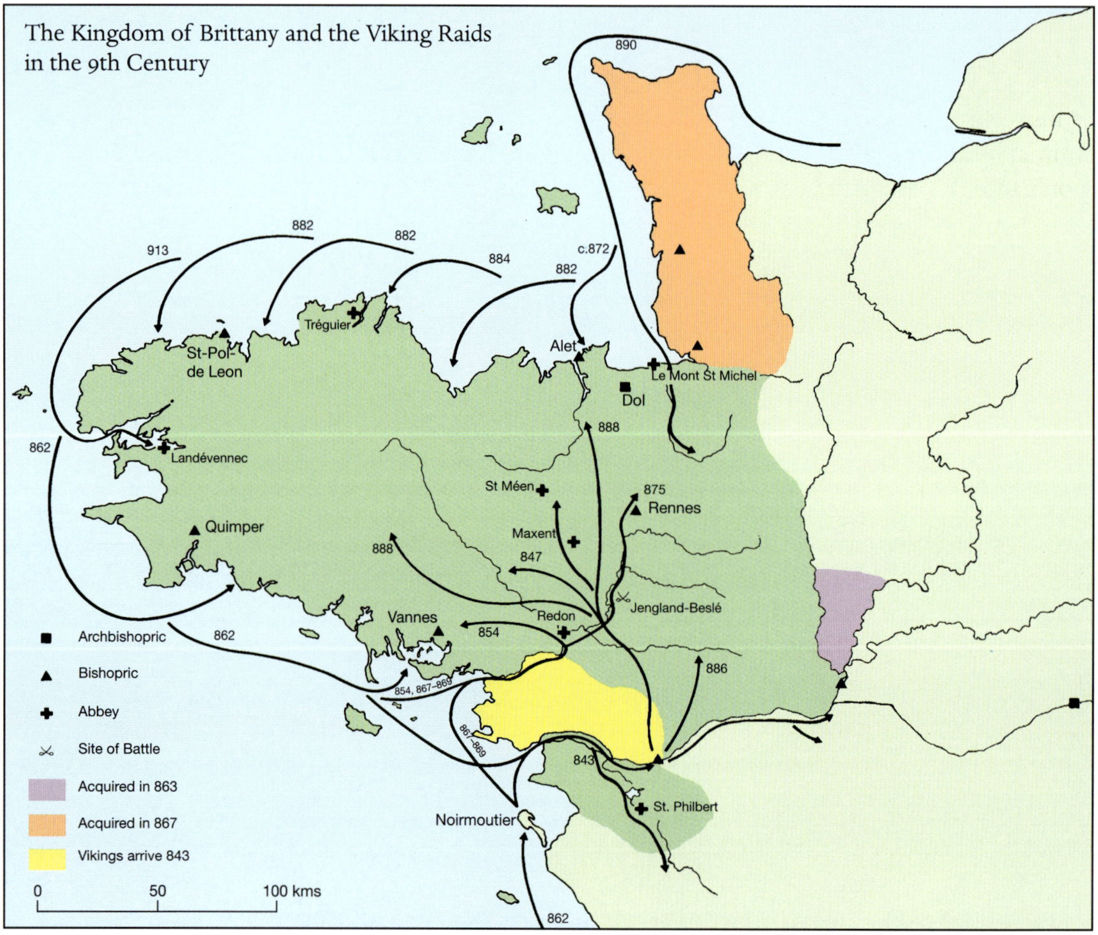

11.21 Brittany in the Viking period.

the Viking fleets on the Seine and the Loire gave Nominöe the opportunity to consolidate Breton gains. By 846 he had taken Rennes and Nantes and was raiding far into Anjou. Then followed an uneasy period involving both conflict and occasional allegiances between the Bretons and the different bands of Vikings in the Loire estuary.

The second half of the ninth century saw the Scandinavian assault on France intensify. In Brittany the new ruler, Salomon (857–74), seized the initiative and in 862 hired twelve Viking ships from the Loire in defence against the flotilla of Viking vessels from the Seine hired by Count Robert of Anjou and sent against him. The episode marked a serious escalation in the use of Vikings as mercenaries in the struggle between Brittany and France. In 866 a large force of Northmen working with the Bretons penetrated along the Loire valley and destroyed Le Mans, in a later engagement killing Count Robert. From this time until his death in 873 Salomon played a complex political game, sometimes strengthening his position with Viking assistance and sometimes co-operating with Charles the Bald to keep the Vikings in check. In this way he extended the boundaries of his Breton kingdom as far east as Angers and incorporated the Cotentin peninsula. The period of dynastic squabbling that followed Salomon's murder in 874 saw the various contenders for power sometimes relying on allegiances with Vikings, but more often fighting resolutely against them. So successful were they that, except for the enclave remaining on the Loire, by 892 Brittany had been cleared of invaders under the inspired leadership of Alain the Great.

Alain's death in 907 coincided with renewed Scandinavian attacks on a massive scale. Leaderless, the Breton resistance crumbled and the entire peninsula passed under Scandinavian domination until the country was again freed by the highly successful campaigning of Alain II between 936 and 939. The inactivity of the Franks during this period is partly a reflection of their concern for other parts of the kingdom, and partly relief that the Vikings were now containing their old Breton enemies (11.22).

By the time of Alain II's death in 952 the political geography of north-western France had changed dramatically, with the establishment of the Scandinavian Duchy of Normandy as a formidable maritime force. To consolidate his uncertain position the emerging Breton king, Conan I, signed a treaty with Richard I of Normandy establishing for the first time a Breton–Norman axis effectively controlling the entire seaboard from the Seine to the Loire, but the relationship was unequal and by the middle of the eleventh century the Bretons had become vassals of the Normans. Thus, after centuries of fighting for their independence from the Franks the Bretons had now been brought, reluctantly, under new masters.

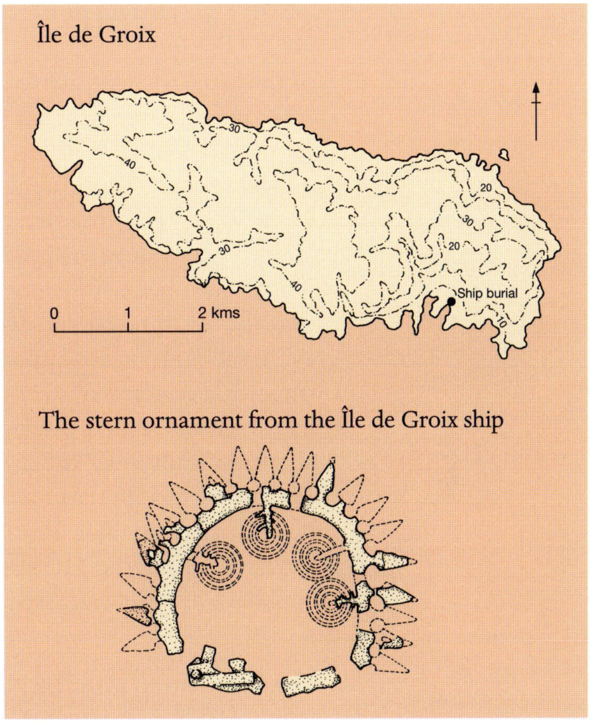

11.22 The Viking ship burial on Île de Groix, off the coast of southern Brittany. The stern ornament was all that survived of the vessel.

The Viking Impact on Iberia

The Viking penetration of the southern Atlantic seaways is mentioned in Arab sources, the Northmen being referred to as *madjus*—'heathen wizards'. Three separate expeditions were recorded. In the first, in 844, the red sails of the raiding vessels approached the port of La Coruña but were unable to take it, and sailed on to greater success at Lisbon and later Cadiz and Seville. Later, in 859, a fleet of sixty-two vessels set out from Brittany but found the western coasts of Spain well guarded, and only after entering the Mediterranean were they able to indulge in their customary plundering raids. On their return in 861 it seems that they met with some success on the north coast. Landing at Navarre they marched inland, taking Pamplonia and capturing the king, for whom they were able to obtain a ransom of 60,000 gold pieces.

The two raiding parties of the ninth century demonstrated the richness of the Iberian Peninsula but they will also have recognized the might of the Muslim defensive forces, and in particular the power of their fleets. The raiding force which set out in 844 met formidable naval opposition off the coast of Galicia, and went on to Andalucía where thirty ships were lost in a naval engagement. Later, at Gibraltar in 861, the second Viking force was severely mauled by the Moorish fleet: only a third of their original sixty-two ships made the return to the Loire. Experiences of this kind would have been sufficient to impress upon the Scandinavian venturers that the Arab naval vessels were more than a match for them. At any event the raids do not appear to have continued. This does not, of course, mean that contacts of a more commercial kind were not maintained. The list of goods seized during the attack on Limerick in 968, mentioned above, sounds very much like cargoes of finery that could have been obtained from Iberian markets in return for northern slaves. It has also been suggested that the clinker-built tradition of boat construction prevalent along the Atlantic coasts of Iberia from the tenth century may well have been learned from the observation of Viking vessels.

The Northmen and the Atlantic Communities

That the impact of the Scandinavians on the Atlantic communities was profound and lasting there can be no doubt, but sufficient will have been said to show that it varied significantly from region to region.

In lightly inhabited or empty lands like the Northern and Western Isles, the Faroes, Iceland, and Greenland, Scandinavian culture was directly transplanted in its entirety and flourished much in the style of the Norwegian homeland, but elsewhere the Scandinavian component fused with indigenous culture. In regions where the local systems were well established and comparatively stable, as in eastern England and the maritime region of France (soon to become Normandy), the new order emerged imperceptibly from the old with little disruption to the social or economic balance, but in other areas, like Ireland, where warfare between rival factions of the elite was endemic, the Scandinavian presence was a catalyst for widespread change. Here the ferocity of the Irish warlords matched their own. For this reason the small enclaves established at harbours around the coast remained small, developing as isolated trading colonies in an otherwise hostile landscape. Apart from certain areas of the north-east, large-scale land-taking and settlement was not possible. Much the same pattern can be seen in south-west Wales.

The Scandinavian settlements of the Irish Sea zone chose good docking facilities, initially to serve as protected anchorages for the vessels of the early raiders, but these quickly developed as trading centres, making the Irish Sea the major focus of exchange in the Scandinavian maritime system. From here ships might go south to Andalucía, north to Iceland and beyond, or around Britain eastwards to the Baltic. In this way the Irish Sea became the hub of a complex network of communications built upon the long-distance exchange systems which had already been established in the preceding centuries.

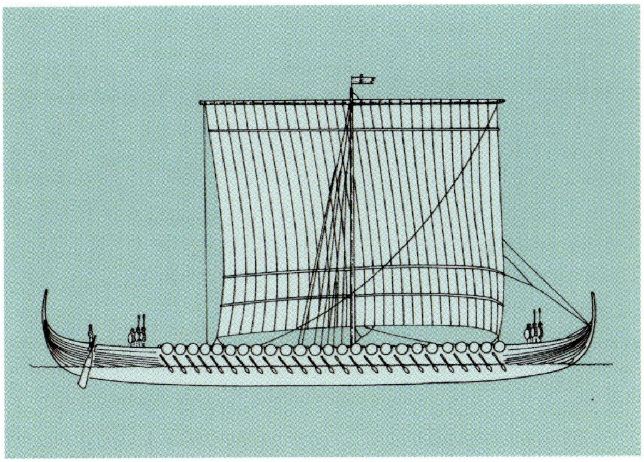

11.23 One of the vessels from Skuldelev, Roskilde, Denmark (wreck 2) sunk to block the mouth of the fjord in the late eleventh or early twelfth century. Dendrochronology shows that the ship was built about 1060 at or near Dublin.

In Brittany a rather different pattern of interaction emerged. Here the long-term hostility between the Bretons and the Franks provided a situation in which raiding and mercenary activity could profitably be maintained, while the internecine warfare that broke out in both kingdoms in the painful periods when succession was being contested offered the raiders further opportunities for easy intervention. Throughout this time the Loire formed the focus of Scandinavian activity and Nantes was often in their control, but there is, as yet, little evidence that a major trading enclave developed here. It may simply have been that the political turmoil in the region allowed warfare in its various modes to provide the necessary economic underpinning to sustain Viking society. From the Breton point of view the Scandinavian presence, disruptive though it was, was an important factor in helping to maintain their independence from the Franks.

South of the Loire, Viking military activity was sporadic and superficial, at least in so far as the historical record allows us to judge, but given their interest in trade it is difficult to believe that there were not regular visits by merchants to the Gironde and Garonne and along the Atlantic seaboard of Iberia. In this they would simply have been following the routes plied by their predecessors.

11.24 Section of the Bayeux Tapestry showing shipbuilders at work in Normandy preparing vessels for Duke William's invasion of Britain in 1066.

Some measure of the integration of the multifaceted maritime system that emerged is provided by a wreck (ship 2) excavated at Skuldelev in the Danish fjord of Roskilde (11.23). It was one of six that had been sunk to block the fjord from seaward attack some time in the late eleventh or early twelfth century. The vessel was a typical Viking longship suitable for carrying fifty to sixty warriors. Dendrochronology has shown that the ship had been built about 1060 at, or in the vicinity of, Dublin. What service it saw as a raiding vessel in the seas around Britain and France we will never know, but its final resting place 2,200 kilometres from the yard in which it had been built is a vivid reminder of the capacity of the sea in bringing the communities of Atlantic Europe ever closer together (11.24).

12. New Centres, New Peripheries: AD 1000–1500

At the beginning of the second millennium western Europe was at its most politically fragmented. In France and Spain what unifying powers there had been had all but collapsed. The empire of Charlemagne, divided on his death between his three sons, was by now a mosaic of fiefdoms ruled by princes (12.1), nobles, the holders of castles (castellans), and lesser knights—a mélange aptly described as a kind of aristocratic anarchy. All paid allegiance to a king, chosen by assembly and anointed by bishops, who served as the supreme lawgiver but had little territorial power except over the royal states in the Île de France. The feudal pyramid was a shaky structure. At its foundations were the knights—mounted warriors who were prepared to attach themselves as retainers to any household offering sufficient reward. In their mobility they often behaved as little better than mercenaries. The political situation resembled, in many ways, the archaic Celtic system that had prevailed in Gaul in the decades before Caesar's intervention a thousand years earlier.

Iberia, at this stage, was divided on religious grounds between the narrow band of Christian states in the north—the kingdoms of Asturias and Navarra and the Marches—and the Muslim Caliphate of Córdoba, but even the apparent unity of the Caliphate shattered when, in 1031, the last of the caliphs, Hisham III, was removed from power and al-Andalus broke up into twenty-four separate states (*taifas*) based on the cities and ruled by local nobility and war leaders.

Only in England was some degree of unity created by the Wessex kings in the mid-tenth century and appropriated first by the Danes and, after 1066, by William, Duke of Normandy. But Wales, Scotland, and Ireland still, at this date, retained their essentially tribal structure.

The next four hundred years or so saw this kaleidoscope of often-warring states coalesce into larger power blocs focused on Muslim Spain under the Almoravid emirs and the Almohad caliphs, Christian Spain

12.1 The political boundaries of western Europe *c.*AD 1000.

under the kings of Castile and Aragón, France led by the Capetians, and England by the Angevins. As the second millennium progressed the interfaces between these power blocs were zones of continual conflict—Christians against Muslims in Spain, English against French in France, and England against the kingdoms around its Atlantic periphery. Out of the centuries of conflict emerged the nation states of western Europe—Portugal, Spain, France, and England. By 1500 those who commanded the Atlantic façade had become assured enough to have embarked upon the first of their spectacular conquests across the ocean.

The Transformation of Western Europe

The history of these five centuries, in which archaic, tribal Europe was transformed, is a story of continual power struggles often erupting into long bloody wars. Active aggression was endemic, yet against this dominating political history many other histories were being played out: belief systems, intellectual enquiry, social systems, and economics were evolving fast. All underwent revolutionary change in the period 1000–1500. Within the confines of this book our focus is necessarily restricted to developments along the ocean fringes and to the ocean itself in its function as a catalyst, but by way of background we must begin with a brief sketch of the great political changes which transformed the west and gave new power to the ocean as a force for change.

In the extreme north-west corner of the Iberian Peninsula, distant from the focus of Muslim power in al-Andalus, so legend has it, a hermit, Pelago, was guided by a star to an overgrown place of burial. Calling in his bishop, the place was cleared and bones were found identified by an inscription as those of St James, son of Zebedee. For many this was hardly surprising, for as early as the fourth century AD the belief had grown up that St James had preached the Gospel in Spain three hundred years before.

The traditional date of the miraculous discovery of his bones was 812, a century after the Moors had crossed from Africa to Spain. The identification of the bones as those of the saint was an astute move, for it provided the Christian enclave in the mountainous north of Iberia with a rallying-point against the Muslim occupation engulfing much of the Peninsula. By the end of the ninth century the church built on the spot had become the focus of the prosperous town of Santiago de Compostella. So rich and powerful had the shrine become that in 997 the Umayyad army, led by al-Mansur, attacked Galicia and removed the great doors and the bells of the cathedral of Santiago, taking them to Córdoba and hanging the bells in triumph in the Great Mosque. The Arab advance in the late tenth and early eleventh centuries under al-Mansur and his son marked the peak of the Muslim bid to control the north. Thereafter the tide turned. The end to this particular story came in 1236 when the victorious King Ferdinand, having taken Córdoba, forced the defeated Moors to return to Santiago de Compostella all that had been pillaged from the shrine 240 years before.

The struggle for power in Iberia between the Christian north and the Muslim south was a long-drawn-out affair. The kingdoms of Astur-Leon, Aragon, and Navarra, together with the Spanish Marches established by Charlemagne, incorporating much of the Catalan counties, formed a solid buffer zone across the entire northern side of Muslim Spain, stretching from the Atlantic to the Mediterranean. Though divided between rival, and sometimes warring, kings these disparate territories were bound by adherence to the Christian faith and, more remarkably, by the busy pilgrim route to Compostella which ran the length of northern Iberia to the west end of the Pyrenees, from there fanning out, in a number of different routes, throughout France (12.2). The constant flow of pilgrims, bringing, as pilgrims so often do, great wealth to those who host them, was a major factor in providing strength and a degree of unity to the northern kingdoms.

From the tenth century onwards there was a gradual migration of people, mainly Cantabrians and Vascones, from the mountains of the north to the sparsely populated frontier zone between the upper reaches of the Duero and the Ebro. The tough mountain folk who settled and heavily fortified the region became known as Castilians and were to play an increasingly important role in what was to follow. Political rivalries and allegiances in the north, and lack of overall leadership in the south following the end of the Caliphate of Córdoba in 1031, combined to encourage a Christian thrust to the south, an effort crowned with success when, in 1085, the King of Castilla and León entered Toledo in triumph (12.3).

In the Muslim south the chaos of individual petty states was given a new coherence by a wave of crusading Muslims, the Almoravids, arriving from the region of the Atlas Mountains in Morocco in 1086. The Christian advance was halted and the *taifa* rulers were freed from the ignominy of having to pay tribute to Christian overlords. A few decades later Almoravid rule was replaced by the influx of another dominant group from the Atlas, the Almohads, who arrived in Spain in 1147. In a crushing victory over the Castilian king, Alfonso VIII, at Alarcos, in 1195 the Christian advance was halted and a *frisson* of panic spread through Christian Europe at the prospect of a Muslim revival. The shock brought a new reality to the politics of the north which helped forge success, and when,

12.2 (*facing*) The pilgrim routes to Compostella.

Pilgrimage Routes to Santiago de Compostella
Galway
Dublin
Dingle
Wexford
Waterford
Cork
Pembroke
Bristol
Southampton
Plymouth
Saltash
Paignton
Dartmouth
St. Ives
Penzance
Fowey
St. Michaels Mount
St. Austell
Paris
Chartres
Tours
Vézelay
Bourges
Nevers
Poitiers
Saintes
Limoges
Périgueux
Le Puy
Bordeaux
Cahors
To Arles
Toulouse
Santiago
de Compostela
Bilbao
León
Pamplona
Jaca
Logroño
0
100
200
300
400
500 kms

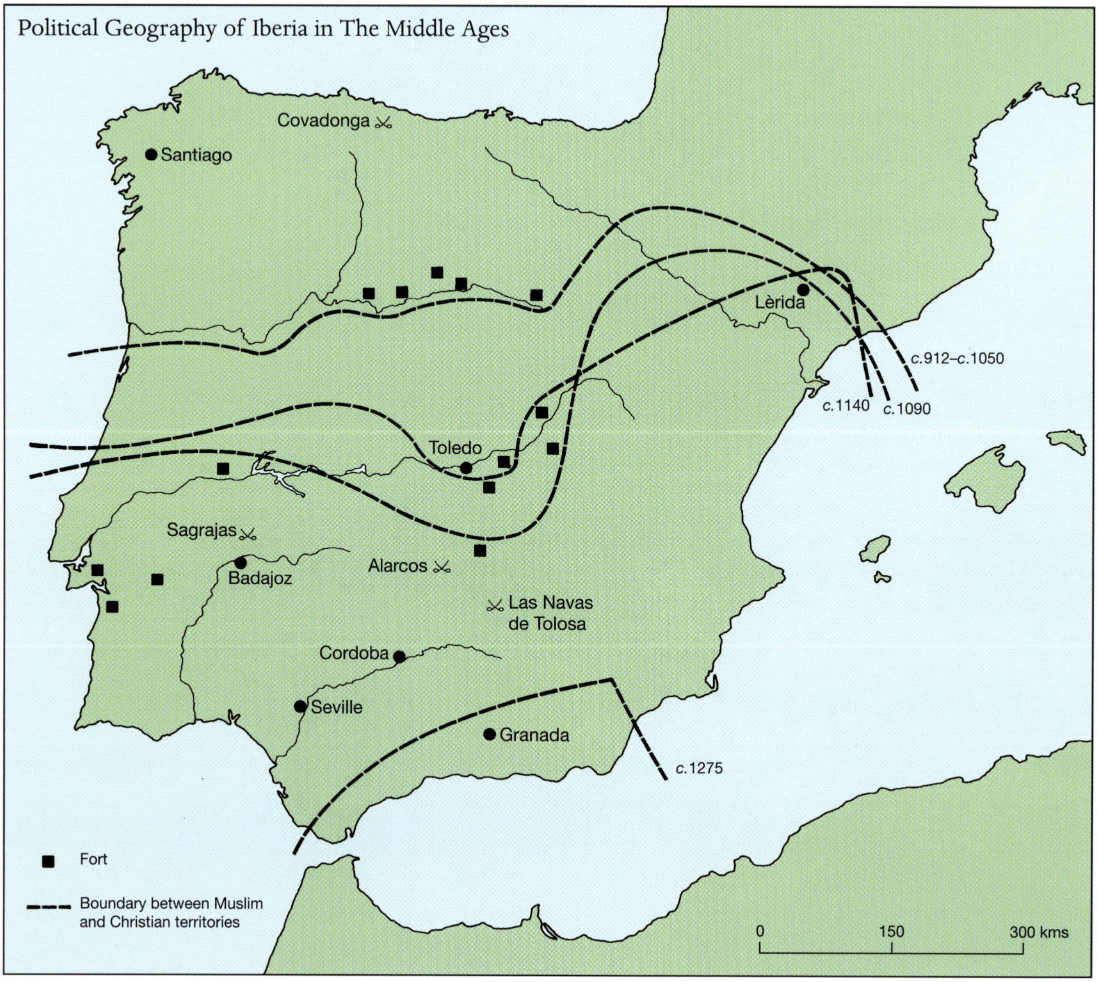

12.3 The changing political geography of Iberia, 1100–1300.

in 1212, the kings of Castilla, Aragón, and Navarra, together with detachments of French knights, marched against the Almohads at Las Navas de Tolosa, it was to a spectacular victory.

The prestige and power of Castilla-León was now considerable. Córdoba fell to the Christians in 1236, Jaén in 1245, and Sevilla 1246. All that remained of Muslim Europe was the much-reduced Nasrid kingdom of Granada, which was to survive for another 250 years. In the rest of the Peninsula three major power blocs emerged, Portugal, Castilla-León and Aragón, with the tiny kingdom of Navarra still maintaining its distinctive identity, sandwiched between its two massive neighbours but looking more to France and the Bay of Biscay than to the Peninsula.

The beginning of the final act came with the marriage of Isabella of

Castilla and Ferdinand of Aragón in 1469. The mutual support which they provided each other throughout long periods of civil war which preceded their accession to their individual thrones was crucial to Spain's increasing stability. Once firmly in power, Isabella in 1474 and Ferdinaud in 1479, they chose the conquest of the Muslim kingdom of Granada as a suitable enterprise to unite the factions of Christian Spain and to heal the wounds of civil war. The operation was to take ten years to complete, but in 1492 the royal couple were at last able to ride into Granada in triumph. It was later in the same year that, ever mindful of the successes of Portugal in gaining control of the Atlantic coasts of Africa, they decided to back a Genoese sea captain, Cristóbal Colón, better known as Christopher Columbus, who was attempting to sell his dream that the Indies could be reached by sailing westwards across the Atlantic.

While the kingdoms of Spain and Portugal were gradually crystallizing out of the political mélange of the Iberian Peninsula, an equally complex process of state formation was under way in France. When, in 987, Hugh Capet was nominated King of France, the territory he actually controlled—the Île de France—was only a narrow strip from Paris to Orléans, amounting to barely 200,000 square kilometres. The rest of the country under his nominal authority was ruled by counts or dukes many of whom were so powerful and independent as to be virtually of kingly rank. The feudal relationship of these men with the royal house (named Capetian after Hugh) was complex and unstable and, in the case of the Duchy of Normandy, was made the more so when one of the Norman dukes, William II, mounted a successful expedition of conquest in England, becoming its king in 1066. As William, Duke of Normandy he was subservient to the Capetian king, but as King of England he was his equal. In the long conflict which inevitably ensued divided loyalties and family rivalries were exploited on both sides as both ruling households vied for power.

The situation came into a sharp and dangerous focus in 1154 when Henry of Anjou (Henry Plantagenet) was crowned King Henry II of England. Henry had become Duke of Normandy in 1150 and the next year had inherited the territories in Anjou, Touraine, and Vendôme from his father. In 1152 the Duchy of Aquitaine and Gascony became his on his marriage to Eleanor. Acceding to the throne of England in 1154, he could also claim authority over the King of Scotland and the princes of Wales. Further territory followed (12.4). On the death of his brother Geoffrey in 1158 he invaded Brittany, and in 1171–2 he led an expedition to Ireland, receiving the submission of most of the Irish kings. The next year the Count of Toulouse paid homage to him. The creation of the Angevin empire by inheritance, marriage, and conquest was a spectacular achieve-

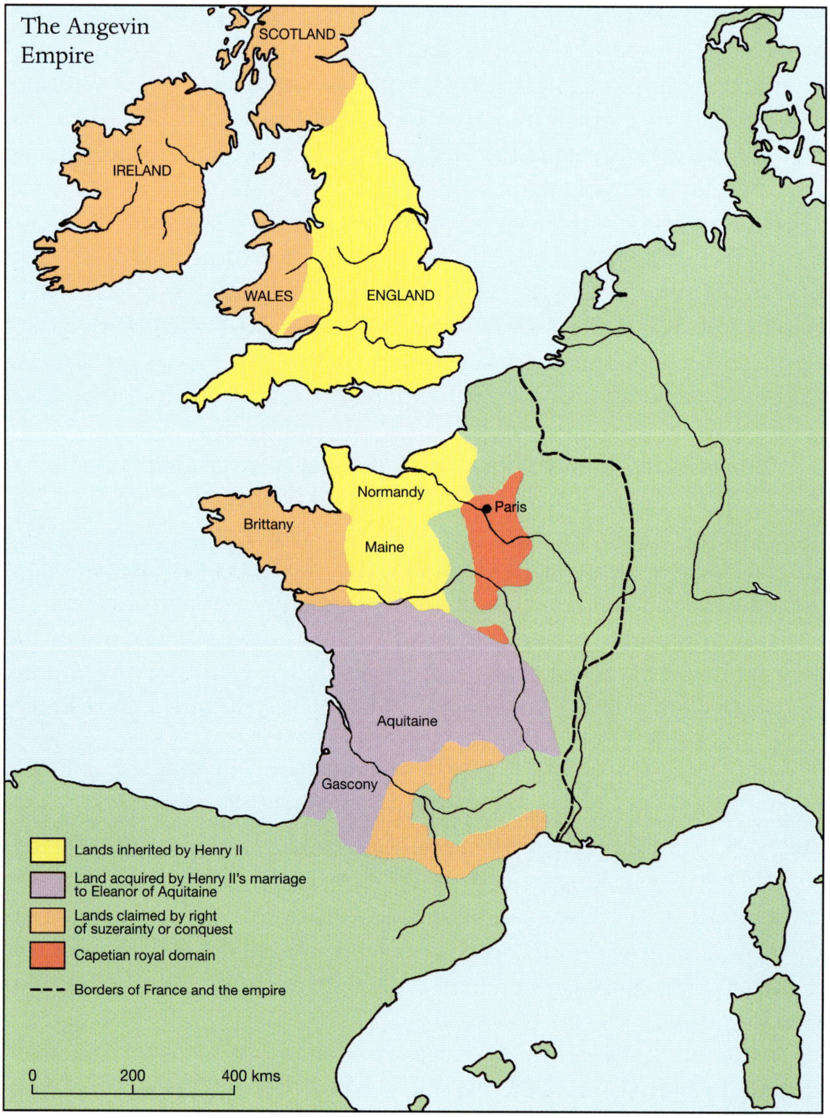

12.4 The Angevin empire.

ment. In the last quarter of the twelfth century the entire Atlantic seaboard from Scotland to the Pyrenees was under the command of the kings of England.

But it was not to last. The 'empire' lacked political coherence, and over all the French territories the French kings could claim feudal rights. This Philip II did, leading him to declare war against the English king, John. By the time of Philip's death in 1223 he had increased the French domain threefold, reducing the Plantagent holdings in France to Gascony and Béarn in the foothills of the Pyrenees.

In 1328 Charles IV, the last of the Capetian line, died leaving only a daughter. The throne passed to Philip VI of Valois but the succession was in doubt, one of the potential claimants being Edward III of England. Edward still held Gascony and at first was prepared to pay homage to Philip, but when, in 1337, Philip seized Gascony Edward responded by claiming the throne of France. Thus the long-drawn-out conflict which became known as the Hundred Years War began: it was to drag on, the fortunes of the two sides constantly changing, until 1453 when the English forces were defeated at the Battle of Castillon and were forced to give up Normandy. In the autumn of that year Bordeaux capitulated to the French, leaving only Calais as the last English enclave in France. The conflict, which really began with William's conquest of England in 1066, took nearly four hundred years to run its course, and throughout this time it was the inhabitants of France and their land that suffered most. As one French observer wrote a century later: 'From the Loire to the Seine, and from there to the Somme, nearly all the fields were left for a long time . . . not merely untended but without people capable of cultivating them . . . for the peasants had been killed or put to flight.' He goes on to say that he himself had seen vast areas of northern France absolutely deserted and uncultivated, 'devoid of all inhabitants, overgrown with brushwood'. Warfare, civil unrest, and the Black Death had decimated the landscape.

While the English kings attempted to defend what they claimed to be their legitimate rights in France, they frequently had cause to look over their shoulders at Wales, Scotland, and Ireland.

In Wales the penetration of the country by the Norman lords, settled in the Marches in Chester, Shrewsbury, and Hereford, was rapid and to a degree successful, although the native principalities were active in their resistance. But the freelance nature of the colonization posed problems for the Crown, not least because it empowered potential rivals. The uncertainty of the situation led Edward I to intervene with force in 1282–3 and to carry out large-scale reorganization, accompanied by the construction of a series of royal castles. From the beginning of the fourteenth century lands under royal control formed a Principality that was usually the prerogative of the king's eldest son.

In Scotland the situation was rather different. Here a successful small feudal kingdom emerged composed of a variety of elements, Gaelic, Saxon, Norse, and Norman, which came together under the authority of a line of native kings who owed allegiance to the Anglo-Norman monarchy. The situation, however, changed dramatically in the 1290s when Edward I began serious attempts to take over Scotland. Much of the resulting conflict took place in the south, in the region between Hadrian's

Wall and the Antonine Wall. Scottish successes under Robert I (Robert Bruce) won recognition of Scottish independence in 1328, but war began again four years later under Edward III, who managed to regain much of the south. Thereafter the gradual recapture of key fortresses by the Scots reduced the disputed zone simply to the border region. The close parallels between the English attempts to overrun Scotland and those of the Romans a millennium or more before provide a vivid illustration of the dominating effect that landscape can have on historical events.

Against the background of the English–Scots conflict on the mainland of Britain must be placed the fate of the Norse settlements in the Western and Northern Isles. The Western Isles and Caithness were incorporated into feudal Scotland during the thirteenth century, the last, Lewis and Skye and the Isle of Man, remaining in Norwegian hands until 1266. Orkney was not annexed to Scotland until as late as 1468–9.

English involvement in Ireland began with the entrepreneurial activities of barons who had earlier established themselves in Wales, but fear that they might become too powerful led Henry II to intervene with a royal army. By the beginning of the thirteenth century a patchwork of Anglo-Norman lordships had been established, but large areas were still held by Irish nobility, and by the fourteenth century the areas subject to Gaelic custom and lordship had greatly increased at the expense of the Anglo-Norman territories which lay in the hinterlands of the major urban centres of Dublin, Drogheda, Waterford, Cork, and Limerick. The importance of these port centres to the maintenance of the colonial settlement nicely mirrors the situation in the earlier Viking period.

To generalize from the dramatic political readjustments that were taking place in western Europe in the period 1100–1400 is not easy. It was, however, a period of widespread, endemic warfare. The marcher zones of Iberia, Wales, and southern Scotland were in continuous conflict and most parts of France were ravaged by warfare at one time or another. Yet within the framework of violence and upset large areas escaped devastation, and there were long periods of stability allowing social and economic institutions to develop. Trade along the Atlantic seaways flourished at all levels and, after the Straits of Gibraltar had been made safe for Christian shipping, new links were forged with the Mediterranean obviating the need to rely solely on the more cumbersome trans-Continental routes. The growth of the Atlantic ports like Lisbon, Oporto, Bordeaux, La Rochelle, and Nantes is a measure of the intensity of traffic now flowing along the seaways. And yet, with all this cosmopolitan activity, the maritime communities still maintained a high degree of independence. These are the issues to which we may now turn.

The Mediterranean and the Atlantic

The Islamic invasion of Iberia beginning in 711 effectively made the Straits of Gibraltar a Muslim preserve, and so it was to stay until the Christian advances of the early thirteenth century. Throughout this long period the ports of al-Andalus, most notably Almeria and Seville, served as the western termination of an extensive Muslim network of maritime trade which threaded along the southern side of the Mediterranean to its eastern ports-of-call at Alexandria and Cairo, which were themselves the western limit of more wide-flung routes leading to the Indian Ocean (12.5). With such a network before it, al-Andalus turned its back firmly on the opportunities offered by the Atlantic.

12.5 A Muslim ship depicted on a plate of the eleventh century probably from the Balearics.

Until the end of the eleventh century the vessels using the Iberian ports seem to have been exclusively Muslim, but thereafter there is increasing evidence of the involvement of Italian merchants from Genoa and Pisa. A Genoese vessel is recorded in Malaga in the late eleventh century and another at Almeria in about 1120. It was a small beginning. By the end of the century a contemporary Muslim writer speaks of Genoa as one of the greatest mercantile cities of Europe, trading throughout the Mediterranean from Syria to al-Andalus (12.6). In the second half of the twelfth century Genoa developed treaty relations with the Almohads guaranteeing safe conduct for shipping and favourable tariffs for Genoese merchants and, once established in the Iberian ports, the Genoese maintained their privileges throughout the political upheavals of the early thirteenth century. After Seville was taken by Ferdinand of Castile in 1248 their special rights were reaffirmed, subsequently to be extended throughout the newly won Christian territories. Thus the Genoese were in an extremely advantageous situation when the Straits of Gibraltar were at last opened to all shipping.

From the middle of the thirteenth century Seville and Malaga became the two principal ports for long-distance shipping. Already, under Muslim rule, Seville had developed all the facilities of an international port along the banks of the Guadalquivir (12.7). The installation and transactions were under the control of the city's chief judge (qāḍī). A contemporary document tells us that 'It is incumbent upon the qāḍī to watch over [this quarter] with the greatest care since it is the gathering place for mer-

LIGVRIA
BIFARIAM·DIVISA
IN·PLAGAM
NEMPE·ORIENTALEM
ET·OCCIDENTALEM
CVIVS·TERMINI·SVNT
FLVMINA·VARVS·AB
OCCASV·MACRA·AB
ORTV·HVIVS·REGIONIS
GENVA·CAPVT·EST
VRBS·MARITIMIS·OPIB
AC·NAVALI·GLORIA
PERPETVO·FLORENS
COMPLVRIB·Q·EGREG·VICTORIIS
ATQ·IMPERIO·IN·MVLTAS·ORIENTIS
PARTES·LATE·PROPAGATO·CLARA
LIGVSTICVM
I. di Spotorno
I. di Albenga
ALBENGA
SAVONA
NOLI
MONTI APENNINI

chants, travellers and others'. According to a late-thirteenth-century account, by then Seville had become a vibrant international centre:

> Ships come up the river every day from the sea, including *naves*, galleys, and many other seagoing vessels. They . . . bring all kinds of merchandise from all over the world: from Tangiers, Ceuta, Tunis, Bougie, Alexandria, Genoa, Portugal, England, Pisa, Lombardy, Bordeaux, Bayonne, Sicily, Gascony, Catalonia, Aragon, other parts of France, and many other regions of the sea, both Christian and Muslim . . .

Seville had become the crucial interface between the Mediterranean and the Atlantic.

Within the Mediterranean, Almeria, of prime importance under the Muslims, lost its pre-eminence to Malaga. Malaga had two particular advantages: it was well sited to acquire Granadan fruit and sugar for export, and it was a vital holding-port for those waiting for suitable wind conditions to allow them to sail westwards through the Straits of Gibraltar. As the volume of trade between the oceans increased so Malaga's fortunes rose.

The last quarter of the thirteenth century saw the Genoese expand into the Atlantic shipping lanes. One of the earliest pioneers was Nico-

12.6 (*facing*) Genoese vessel from an painting by Danti Ignazio (1536–86).

12.7 The city and port of Seville in the sixteenth century. By Alonso Sánchez Coello (1531–1588).

lozzo Spinola, who in 1277 sailed from Genoa to the port of Sluys on the coast of Flanders—the port providing access to Ghent. The following year two ships made the voyage, stopping at Southampton, Sandwich, and London *en route*. This was the beginning of the famous annual convoys of Italian galleys that were to be sent from Genoa and Venice to England, the Low Countries, and the north for the next two hundred years. The Italian vessels for the most part carried luxuries such as silks and damasks, elaborate metalwork, fruit, and spice but some transported raw materials such as alum from the east Mediterranean, so important for the processing of fabric. On their return they carried wool, cloth, and some tin. Some vessels stopped *en route* to collect salt from Guérande just north of the Loire mouth (12.8) or from Setúbal on the Portuguese coast, a commodity much in demand in the Mediterranean for salting meat and fish.

While many of the great galleys will have made their journeys in a series of long hauls, lack of space for the food and water necessary to sustain the considerable crews of rowers meant that the ships would have had to make calls *en route* to replenish supplies. Lisbon, La Coruña, La Rochelle, and Nantes were all favoured ports and here the agents of the large Italian shipping families had their bases, but Genoese galleys are also known to have used smaller Breton ports, including Quimperlé, Quimper, and Dinan, in the thirteenth century. There were, no doubt, many factors affecting choice of port, and in time of warfare compromises had to be made as the political situation demanded. There was also a desire for some degree of exclusivity. In the early fourteenth century the Venetian fleet were putting into the Galician port of El Ferrol deliberately to avoid the Genoese, who had adopted La Coruña.

The Genoese were the first to take advantage of the freeing of the Straits of Gibraltar, with the Venetians hot in their wake, and from the late thirteenth century until the end of the fifteenth they provided a consistent thread in the Atlantic maritime networks that were to develop, but others were soon to join in to take advantage of the new commercial opportunities that were fast opening up. Among these the best placed, geographically, were the Castilians, who commanded the entire north coast of Iberia from Galicia to the Pyrenees, and the Portuguese, who controlled much of the west coast. Both had established colonies in the Low Countries in the late thirteenth century and were in active competition with each other to dominate traffic crossing the Bay of Biscay.

12.8 (*facing*) The salt pans of Gúerande on the coast of Loire-Atlantique, still one of the principal salt-producing areas of the Atlantic coast.

Already in the early thirteenth century Castile was trading with the ports of Bristol, Southampton, London, Bruges, and Arras, but relations with England fluctuated in the thirteenth and fourteenth centuries depending upon the fast-changing political situation and the attitudes of

the Castilian rulers to Britain's enemy, France. The Portuguese, on the other hand, retained friendly relations with England and were able to benefit commercially. Both countries were involved in carrying goods from the Atlantic to the Mediterranean market. Ships from Santander, for example, transported English wool, textiles from Flanders, and iron from northern Castile to the Andalucían port of Seville, taking back local olive oil, spices, and Italian fabrics. But there was little attempt by the Castilians or Portuguese to ship their wares through the Straits of Gibraltar to the ports of the west Mediterranean, where the monopoly of the Italian, Catalan, and Provençal merchants made Atlantic ships unwelcome.

The friendly relations between Portugal and Britain existed from the twelfth century. They were formalized in 1386 by the Treaty of Windsor, which provided a firm basis for maritime commerce between the two countries throughout the fifteenth century. In the ports of Lisbon and Oporto English merchants enjoyed the same privileges as those from Genoa and Pisa. Portuguese wine was of good quality, comparing favourably with that of Gascony, and when Gascon wine became prohibitively expensive after the end of the Hundred Years War trade in Portuguese wine increased significantly. Other commodities included cork, from Portugal's famous cork oaks, sugar from its Atlantic colony of Madeira, fruit of various kinds, wax, and red dye derived from the bodies of insects inhabiting the oak trees. In return the English supplied cloth and corn and occasionally smaller quantities of lead and tin.

The volume of the Portuguese trade, though significant, was not great. In the period 1300–40, for example, seven Portuguese ships visited British ports compared with fifty-nine from Spain. Portuguese products exported to France in Portuguese ships were also at a comparatively low level. In the seven years from 1355 five Portuguese ships loaded wine at Bordeaux compared with 104 from the Basque region. After 1340 the number of Portuguese ships visiting Britain began to increase, and greater opportunities developed in the latter part of the fourteenth century after hostilities had broken out between England and Castile. It was during this period that the west coast port of Bristol began to be favoured. In the period 1379–80 ten ships are recorded, but this was the peak and throughout the 1390s only three ships in total are known to have visited.

While the figures are sufficient to suggest that the volume of Portuguese shipping sailing north in the fourteenth century was never very great, it is equally clear that the English merchants were active in exploiting Portuguese markets. In the period 1376–1400 two-thirds of the vessels leaving the port of Bristol were sailing to Portugal, though the yearly numbers fluctuated in reverse proportion to the number of Portuguese vessels plying the routes. In this period 24 per cent of British cloth exported went to Iberia, and of this more than half was destined for Portugal.

The trading links between the two countries increased during the fifteenth century. Most of the Portuguese shipping came from Lisbon and Oporto, while Bristol, London, and the West Country ports supplied by far the greater number of the English vessels. The peak of Portuguese shipping movements to England came in the 1430s and 1440s when there were up to a dozen ships a year in British ports, the most popular by far being Southampton. Thereafter numbers declined in the 1450s and 1460s but increased again at the end of the century, when the early stages of Portugal's colonial expansion began to introduce a new range of commodities into the system. Sugar from Madeira became a major import together with other exotics such as oranges, pomegranates, almonds, and parrots. The trade in slaves now also began to gain momentum.

Portuguese shippers developed links with many of the Atlantic ports besides those of England. Trade with Flanders generally exceeded that with England, but elsewhere the volume of shipping movements was less. The ports of southern and western Ireland were frequently visited, and trade with Normandy, most particularly Harfleur but also Rouen and Dieppe, was on a significant scale. Breton ports were also occasionally visited. Yet, taken over all, the volume of Portuguese shipping was never very great. Portugal was, after all, a comparatively small country, in part poor and mountainous. It probably did not generate enough capital to allow more than a limited investment in high-risk enterprises such as overseas trading. Moreover, in the fifteenth century royal investment in voyages of discovery leading to colonization deflected the interests of the maritime sector into these more lucrative ventures. The Portuguese remained a significant presence in maritime commerce, but it was foreign shippers, particularly the English, who carried the bulk of Portuguese goods.

Throughout the fourteenth and fifteenth centuries the Castilians were active in the Atlantic. Seville was the principal southern port, but the kingdom also commanded the ports of northern Iberia including those of the Galician rias and a number of havens on the north coast from Santander eastwards to the Pyrenees. From Seville and the southern ports came fruit, in particular figs, raisins, and dates, as well as large quantities of wine, oil, and salt. Other commodities included delicacies such as almonds, honey, licorice, saffron, and high-quality leather work. The northern ports specialized in raw iron from the Cantabrian mountains and manufactured goods of iron. Among the other exports may be listed wax, tallow, rosin, tar, woad, and cork. In return the English and Flemish

12.9 Bronze relief panel from the Sacristy of Saint Antonio, Padua, Italy, 1484–8. Jonah is being thrown into the sea from a typical carrack of the late fifteenth century.

ports provided cloth and corn. Other commodities exported from Bristol included herring, hake, tanned hides, lead, and tin, the fish and hides probably coming from the Irish Sea and Ireland. Much of the Castilian trade was in the hands of the Basque shippers who, working from Santander, Bilbao, and other smaller ports in the region, gained for themselves a reputation as reliable sailors able to transport bulk cargoes over long distances not only along the Atlantic seaways but also into the Mediterranean. Their ports were also easily accessible to the wine-producing areas of the south and the iron-rich Cantabrian mountains.

The Galician ports were more remote from the productive regions of Iberia. They were, however, valuable as ports-of-call, providing shelter, food, and water for vessels on long-haul voyages and, for the many pilgrims from England and Ireland making the journey to the shrine of St James at Compostella, the sea was the quickest approach. The ships of Bristol, sometimes stopping at Plymouth *en route*, might carry as many as a hundred pilgrims at a time, and for pilgrims from Ireland all the major ports from Dublin in the east to Galway in the west provided ships. So numerous were the pilgrims passing through Dublin that a special hostel was set up to provide accommodation for those who had to wait for a boat. The journey, which could take six weeks or more, was uncomfortable in the extreme. The boats were usually crowded and disease-ridden and the food and water stale. One English pilgrim travelling in the fifteenth century described how the sailors were constantly shouting at him to get out of the way, and so violent was the pitch and toss of the boat that he had no appetite and could not even hold a tankard to his lips.

The numbers of pilgrims converging on Compostella by sea, from Ireland, Britain, and the countries fringing the North Sea, were frighteningly large and at times must have posed considerable problems for the local population. On one occasion, in 1189, between ten thousand and twelve thousand pilgrims landed at La Coruña, having sailed from many parts of northern Europe. So potentially destructive was the invasion that the local townspeople turned them back without allowing them to visit the shrine.

The wines of Castile and Portugal, though an important part of the Iberian trade, could not compete in sheer volume with the export of French wines. England was one of the principal importers. Before the creation of the Angevin empire the main source of supply had been the Seine valley and possibly Burgundy beyond, the casks being taken on board at Rouen for the short journey across the Channel. But with the union of England and Gascony, Gascon wines became increasingly important, totally eclipsing exports from Rouen by the end of the thirteenth century. The chief town, Bordeaux, doubled in size in the early thirteenth century as its importance as a trading centre grew.

The English came to rely more and more on Gascon wines, allowing English vineyards to go out of production, while the agricultural land of the Bordelais was increasingly given over to viticulture at the expense of other agrarian production. In this way the English and Gascon economies became inextricably bound together. Gascony was now dependent on England, both as a market for its huge surpluses of wine and as a provider of foodstuffs such as grain, fish, and dairy products. English cloth was also a major export to Gascony. Something of the scale of the operation can be appreciated from figures computed for the mid-fifteenth century which indicate an annual import of Gascon wine to England amounting to 3 million gallons, which in cash terms was equivalent to nearly one-third of the value of all England's imports at the time.

The vicissitudes of the Hundred Years War caused quite violent fluctuations, especially as the war neared its end in the middle of the fifteenth century. But political restrictions, and also piracy, while making the fortunes of trade uncertain, were insufficient to break the centuries-old dependence of the two countries. After France had acquired Bordeaux it was in the interests of the new French masters that the trade should be allowed to re-establish itself. As soon as residual hostilities had been brought to an end by the Treaty of Picquigny in 1475 things returned to normal.

Throughout the long period of contact between Gascony and England the two principal Gascon ports were Bordeaux and Bayonne. The quantity of wine passing through Bordeaux was prodigious, but Bayonne, peripheral to the productive heartland, was of lesser importance, the more so after the middle of the fifteenth century when the harbour approaches began to be obstructed by sandbars and silting. Yet Bayonne remained a town of native sailors, while Bordeaux was content to rely on foreign shippers. In one year in the early fourteenth century, of the two hundred ships leaving the port of Bordeaux only five belonged to local shipowners. The men of Bayonne, on the other hand, not only shipped their own produce but were prepared to carry for others. They soon developed a reputation, along with the Basques and the Bretons, as reliable and fearless sailors.

The records of Bordeaux show that the local wine was transported by many different carriers: Bretons, men of Bayonne, Flemings, and above all by the English. At least thirty-five English ports from as far north as Newcastle and as far west as Milford Haven are listed as sending vessels to Bordeaux. In one year, 1409–10, of the two hundred ships that left Bordeaux twenty-seven were from Dartmouth, thirteen from London, eleven from Hull, and nine from each of Bristol, Fowey, and Plymouth, but this does not mean that the home ports were dependent on their own ships for wine. At Bristol, for example, only half the wine offloaded there came in Bristol ships, the rest being brought in the vessels of Bayonne, La Rochelle, and a number of other English ports. Most of the ships arrived either in the spring or at the time of the vintage, the average expedition taking about two months, although the actual sailing time from London to Bordeaux was about ten days. Journeys were also made in midwinter and midsummer to collect other commodities such as woad, essential for dying cloth, and dye fixatives like alum and potash. Other commodities carried at these times included wax and honey and a range of things brought in from Iberia for trans-shipment.

The well-researched example of the Gascon wine trade, with its copious contemporary documentation, gives an insight into the complexity of medieval trading systems. Any commodity could be carried, passed through any number of ports, and ships of any nation might do the carrying depending only on the political situation at the time.

Occupying a central place in the Atlantic system was Brittany. As maritime trade developed so the Bretons were inevitably drawn in, benefiting from their dominant geographical position. The coastal waters were not without their dangers, both from the treacherous coastlines and from predatory ships ready to pounce on unsuspecting traders. The Duke of Brittany made good use of this by instituting 'briefs' which provided foreign shipping with protection in convoys and guidance, when necessary, to safe anchorages for taking on food and water. In the early thirteenth century Breton maritime trade began to develop with England and with Santonge and Guyenne, the Breton ships often acting as the middlemen transporting goods between the north and the south. Of their own products, salt, from the mouth of the Loire and the Bay of Bourgneuf, and dried fish from the *sécheries* around the coast of Finistère were much in demand, particularly in Bayonne, and were sought by Italian merchants for their Mediterranean markets. By the fifteenth century Breton vessels themselves were sailing into the Mediterranean in small but increasing numbers, trading in salt and dried fish.

The Irish ports also played a significant part in regional trade, those of the west and south coast favouring Bristol as a port of entry to England. Waterford was the most important, but ships are recorded from Cork and Kinsale and others came from the many smaller harbours of the south coast. In the west Limerick, on the Shannon, was particularly prosperous as was Galway further to the north. These ports dealt directly with Spain and Portugal, Galway also serving as the focus for the pilgrim traffic from Ireland to Compostella. Exports from Ireland included herring, fresh or salted, as well as a range of other large sea fish such as hake, pollack, and cod, together with salmon caught in the fast-flowing rivers. After the fishing season was over the boats turned to carrying the other main product of Ireland—hides used to make a wide variety of manufactured goods, together with the skins of a variety of other animals from deer to squirrels. Irish oak was also highly prized, and by the fifteenth century Irish linen had developed an international reputation. In return Ireland acquired salt and iron as well as wine, much of which came direct from the wine-growing areas of France and Iberia. The productivity of Ireland and the intensity of its trade do not seem to have been adversely affected by the political turmoil of the time.

Many of the vessels bringing commodities northwards by way of the Atlantic seaways passed along the English Channel into the southern North Sea to offload at ports in Flanders or along the eastern coast of England at London, Hull, Newcastle, and a number of the smaller havens. Here they came into contact with a powerful mercantile confederacy—the Hanseatic League—comprising two hundred or so towns stretching from the Rhine to the Gulf of Finland (12.10). The League had branches even further afield in Bruges and Antwerp, London and York, and Oslo and Bergen. The focus of the confederacy was Lübeck, where the idea had been born in the middle of the twelfth century. To maintain order and compliance among its members the League relied entirely on economic constraints: in this way it came to dominate North Sea and Baltic trade. Such interests as the League had beyond Calais could be met through its agencies in Bruges and London, with the exception of one commodity—high-quality sea salt. Salt was needed to salt fish, especially herring, which after about 1300 became a major commodity in exchanges around the North Sea. To acquire salt of the right quality the Hanse annually sent large fleets of forty or fifty vessels to the saltworks of southern Brittany and the Bay of Bourgneuf. In the early fifteenth century the

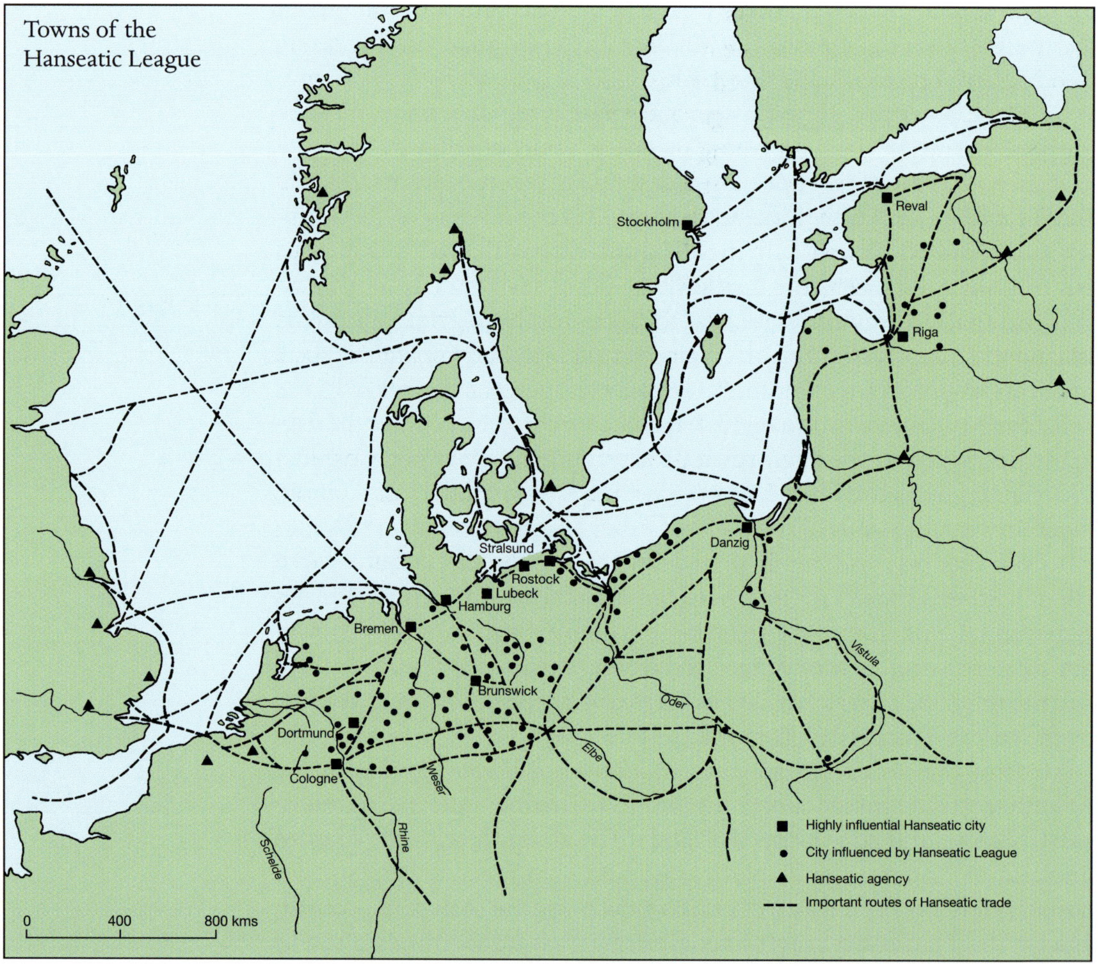

12.10 The towns of the Hanseatic League in the fifteenth century.

salt convoys (*Baienfahrt*) began venturing further south to the saltworks of the Setúbal estuary region, where salt of even higher quality was to be had. These vessels took south cargoes of grain which were offloaded at Lisbon for onward trans-shipment, together with smaller quantities of wax, wood, and tar. Along with their cargoes of salt they brought back smaller quantities of fruit, wine, and oil. The Hanseatic League was intent on dominating the Baltic and the North Sea, and in pursuit of this it successfully blocked the English advance to the Baltic and expelled the English from Bergen on the Atlantic coast of Norway. These events were to have a direct effect on English activity in the north Atlantic.

Throughout the fourteenth century English fishing vessels had been active in the coastal waters of Norway. The customary procedures demanded that aliens report to the Staple at Bergen to pay dues before exporting their catch. The system was cumbersome and costly, but for the most part it worked without serious problems. However, things changed in the early fifteenth century when the Hanseatic League began to dominate Bergen and to work towards excluding all foreigners from the profitable market. The response of the English fishermen was to look elsewhere for fish stocks, and the place they chose was Iceland.

Iceland, as we saw in previous chapters, was first settled by Irish monks and later colonized by Scandinavian settlers from Norway. In the early days, following the initial settlement, regular contacts were maintained with Norway and when, in 1262, the Icelanders agreed to union with Norway the mother country agreed to send no fewer than six ships to the island every year to provide the necessities of life in exchange for local products, almost exclusively fish. The decline in seafaring among the Scandinavians, however, soon saw the agreement lapsing, leaving the Icelanders in poverty and isolation. Thus, when the English began to explore the fishing grounds around Iceland they met with a friendly, even eager, reception.

In 1412 the Icelandic annals record that yet again no ships had arrived from Norway but a strange ship was seen bearing fishermen 'out from England'. The following year thirty or more English fishing vessels appeared in Icelandic waters (12.11) and some of the foreign sailors landed to buy provisions from the natives. In the wake of the fishermen came merchants. It was the beginning of an active, profitable, and for the most part friendly relationship that was to last for most of the century. Yet the political context for the direct relationship between England and Iceland was complex and constantly changing. The first traders had obtained permission from the Scandinavian king Eric, but this was later revoked as the volume of trade increased and the Scandinavian authorities, encouraged by the Hanse, began to be concerned for lost tax revenue caused by the flouting of the Bergen Staple. In spite of prohibitions, supported by the English Crown, trade flourished throughout most of the century, some of the vessels' owners buying licences to trade, others simply taking their chances of being caught and facing forfeiture and imprisonment.

The English fishing vessels congregated off the coasts of Iceland in the summer and with long line and many hooks brought aboard cod, ling, and keling to be salted and packed on board, the ships returning home in October or November. The size and number of the English fishing doggers soon took their toll, undermining the fishing activities of the Icelanders to such an extent that local endeavour wasted away. The English fishing fleets came from a variety of ports, mainly along the east coast. Lynn, Hull, and Grimsby feature large, but many of the smaller ports between the Tyne and the Thames sent ships. A few also came from West Country ports.

12.11 Bench ends from the chapel of St Nicholas, King's Lynn, Norfolk dating to about 1415. They show English fishing boats engaged in fishing for cod.

Along with the fishing doggers came the merchant vessels. Many sailed from the east coast ports, but the western route was also used. Bristol was particularly active and the thriving ports of western Ireland also joined in. A Bristol ship sailing westwards around the Atlantic coast of Ireland could reach Iceland in a week. The needs of the Icelanders were many, and accordingly the trading ships carried varied cargoes. Food was most in demand, and wheat, meal, butter, honey, and wine formed the bulk of the goods carried. Clothing and cloth were also eagerly sought, and the virtual absence of wood and metal in Iceland meant that timber and manufactured items of iron and copper found a ready market. In return the merchants acquired salted fish, mainly cod, hake, pollack, and salmon. The trading season differed from that of the fishing fleets. They arrived in early spring and remained to trade throughout the first part of the summer, returning home during August or September. The more enterprising could profitably use the rest of the year sailing south to the markets of Gascony or Portugal, where they might obtain a high return for their cargo of fish.

The trading system which had developed so quickly in the early decades of the fifteenth century was short-lived. The poverty of the Danish Crown and the increasing power of the Hanse combined to curb the activities of the English through rigorous trading restrictions and competition. From the 1470s merchants from the Hanseatic League began to move in in earnest: the English monopoly was broken, and what had been an easy market with rich pickings now became overcrowded and economically risky. Yet the demand for fish remained. It was time for the English entrepreneurs to find new fishing grounds. This is what John Cabot was to do in the closing years of the century by his discovery of Newfoundland and the coast of Labrador.

In this all-too-brief overview of maritime trade in the Middle Ages something of the complexity and intensity of the trading activities binding the Atlantic communities, from the Canary Islands to Iceland, has been laid out to provide some sense of the immensely rich texture of it all. It was a constantly changing kaleidoscope of closely interrelated parts, varying enormously in scale. At the one limit were the fleets of huge galleys sent annually to Flanders and London from Genoa and Venice. On the other were the many individual boat-owners, like the fishermen of Guernsey carrying their small loads of conger eels to Southampton and prepared to fetch anything back to make the journey worthwhile. What motivated it all was a fast-developing consumerism growing, at least in part, from a relatively more stable political situation which itself encouraged the emergence of a more hierarchic and more demanding elite. These forces, together with vagaries of geography, encouraged each region to become productive, concentrating on those desirable goods and raw materials it could most effectively generate. Thus Castile produced oil, Portugal fruit, Gascony wine, Brittany salt, England cloth, and Iceland fish, all in quantities far in excess of local needs. It was to redistribute these commodities—to equalize their spread—that traders came into their own and the sea routes became of crucial importance to the economic stability of western Europe.

There is another factor which deserves emphasis—the importance of the sea itself as a provider. Against the background of the changing trade routes, the varied flow of commodities, and transient political allegiances, the persistent sea with its annual cycles of fish migrations created its own rhythm and stability irrespective of time and politics. As population increased so fishing became more important until, by the Middle Ages, it was an essential prop to the economy. A significant percentage of shipping movements in the Atlantic were determined by the movement of the shoals. The all-important herring—the staple of medieval peasant diet—was avidly followed from the Northern Isles in June to the Normandy coast in January. The more expensive large stock fish were to be had in a brief summer season in the waters of Iceland and Norway, while the tuna-fishing season off the coast of Morocco was restricted to the period from May to August. At these crucial times the fishing fleets converged, only to disperse again with their salted catch to the coastal markets serving large hinterland populations. In slack periods during the year the fishing boats could be used to transport other goods for whoever cared to hire them, or the fishermen could return to the land to tend their fields or turn to make a quick profit by indulging in privateering—a popular pursuit, particularly in time of war. Such was the versatility of the sailor.

Remoteness and Identity

The intensity of the maritime trade during the Middle Ages brought about an integration of the coastal communities to a degree never before experienced. At any one time there were hundreds of people on the move and in every port there were foreigners, mostly in transit but in a few cases resident to oversee the interests of their own nationals. These coastal communities were bound together by common interests: they aspired to move cargoes and thereby to make profits, they shared a common knowledge of ships and navigation, and they feared and suffered the same dangers. The Atlantic community was a cosmopolitan brotherhood. But it was far more than a string of harbourside populations. Each port belonged to a hinterland, and the two were inextricably bound in a web of interdependence. Dendritic patterns of roads led back into the countryside, some linking productive zones to the port, others serving as the arteries along which could travel goods from more distant regions. The same systems of communications were used to distribute imported goods. In many regions rivers provided easily navigable routes deep into the hinterland (12.12). Thus, for much of the Atlantic coastline geomorphology conspired to create a broad zone dependent upon the sea. That dependence took with it a sense of identity and a feeling of separateness from the more inland regions, a separateness which often manifested itself in different forms of political expression.

The Iberian Peninsula provides a clear example of this phenomenon. The kingdom of Portugal, created as the Moors were gradually defeated in the course of the twelfth and thirteenth centuries, was finally recognized as a discrete and independent kingdom by the Treaty of Alcañices in 1297. Portugal is essentially the western coastal zone of the Iberian

12.12 River boats carrying casks of wine to the port of Paris .

Peninsula, extending inland little more than 170 kilometres from the Atlantic seaboard. The entire country looks to the Atlantic, with its back to the rest of the Peninsula. It is an example of medieval political pragmatism accepting geographical reality. Once the boundary was confirmed the Portuguese could begin to intensify their own language and culture, using both to distinguish themselves from their Spanish neighbours. Despite the climatic variation from south to north, creating quite different ecozones, and the varied ethnic background, the population was prepared to accept the unity of their national culture. In this case, the national boundary seems to have coincided with the perceived sense of territory of the inhabitants.

The northern coastal strip of the Iberian peninsula presents a somewhat different picture. Here the Cantabrian cordillera separates a maritime zone of varying width from inland Spain. The distinctive nature of this region was recognized in the definition of Galicia, Asturias, and the Basque provinces as separate administrative regions before the end of the fifteenth century. The peoples of these regions clearly felt their own distinctiveness, and this was to some extent reflected in local administrative arrangements. By the end of the fifteenth century the three Basque provinces, which acknowledged the sovereignty of the Crown of Castile, were largely independent, Asturias had its own regional government (*Junta Generale*), and Galicia was to be granted a similar privilege early in the sixteenth century. Yet unrest was never far below the surface. In Galicia there were peasant uprisings against the feudal lords in 1431 and 1467, and in 1485 the Count of Lemos led a revolt against the Crown which was contained only after the personal intervention of Ferdinand and Isabella.

Galician culture of the twelfth and thirteenth centuries was quite distinctive. In art a characteristic Galician-Romanesque style of religious sculpture emerged, and there flowered the extraordinary lyrical poetry of the itinerant minstrels (*cancioneros*) who wandered through Galicia and northern Portugal. The Galician language was also widely spoken and was used in drafting laws up to the end of the fifteenth century, after which Castilian was finally introduced as the language of the administration. A strong feeling of cultural identity and independence remained and became increasingly vocal after the middle of the nineteenth century. It was finally recognized in 1981, when Galicia was accepted as an autonomous region of Spain ruled by its own Xunta.

Asturias and the Basque provinces were more restricted in geographical area than Galicia. Populations were small, dispersed, and largely pastoral. Politically Asturias was part of Castile, and the Basque provinces, while being ruled by their own kings, also came under the authority of Castile. Asturias was a poor country and largely undeveloped, but the Basque provinces, by virtue of their easily accessible harbours stretching along the coast between Santander and Bayonne, and the through trade from Castile to the Atlantic, developed rapidly after the beginning of the twelfth century and experienced a degree of urban growth. This, together with the fast-expanding flow of pilgrims travelling between France and Compostella, ensured that the Basque region was locked into the broader European system. Even so it remained politically divided into small kingdoms with no evident feeling of nationhood, sharing only its highly distinctive language. Although widely used, there was little sign that the language was perceived to be a vehicle for developing a Basque identity until the later sixteenth century, when the first Basque historian, Esteban de Garibay, published a four-volume work arguing for the great antiquity of the language. It was the beginning of the movement to gain recognition as a separate polity that is still a very live issue today.

The Atlantic coastal region of western France between the Pyrenees and the Loire was inherited by Henry II of England after his marriage with Eleanor of Aquitaine in 1152. Thereafter much of the region remained in English hands for three hundred years. Close economic ties, depending largely on the production and export of wine by sea, ensured that the French communities looked outwards to the Atlantic rather than towards the Île de France. Something of the separateness of the Atlantic zone is reflected in the strength of Huguenot feeling in the region in the sixteenth century and the counter-revolutionary peasant rising of the Chouannerie which had its origins in the Vendée and spread rapidly throughout Brittany in the 1790s.

The very geography of Brittany gives it a distinct identity, moulded by the ocean and isolated by its remoteness from Continental Europe. In the Middle Ages Brittany sat politically between England and France and was inevitably drawn into the conflicts between the two states, but the dukes who led it maintained a considerable degree of autonomy. From the tenth to the mid-twelfth centuries the duchy managed to remain aloof, but the creation of the Angevin empire brought the English Crown onto the scene, with Henry II taking an active interest in Breton affairs. The marriage of Conan IV to Marguerite, sister of Malcolm IV of Scotland, in 1160 may well have been an act of mild defiance, but perhaps a more significant response to Angevin interference in Breton affairs was the growth of the Arthurian myth in popular imagination. Arthur, reflecting a golden age long past, became a focus for national identity—a freedom-fighter whose exploits were broadcast widely through a burgeoning oral tradition.

Inevitably, both Britain and France became embroiled in the Breton civil war which occupied the middle years of the fourteenth century. The conflict centred on a matter of succession between Montfort, who was defending his rights against the French-backed Blois. General distrust of growing French influence and economic reliance on the trade between Guyenne and England were significant factors in focusing popular Breton support around Montfort's cause. Montfort's eventual success in 1365 established his house, which thereafter remained in power until the end of the fifteenth century. During this period the emerging sense of identity was given further form and impetus by a succession of histories, compiled largely from ducal records. In focusing on the privileges of the dukes of Brittany, on customs, and on territory these volumes sharpened the distinctions that separated Brittany from France. Le Band's *Croniques et ystoires* (1480) provided Brittany with its first narrative history, and in using the earlier mythical histories of Geoffrey of Monmouth it was possible to present the legitimacy of the dukes as the inheritors of royal privileges independent of those of France. These medieval histories, together with the deeply ingrained folk culture of the region and of course its distinctive language, provided a strong sense of regional identity to sustain the population through the centuries of French rule following the loss of Breton independence in 1532.

In Britain and Ireland the Atlantic communities responded in different ways to the challenge of their geographical isolation. Each had its own culture and language, but their differing landscapes and histories generated different responses. In Wales, more open to direct Anglicizing influences than the others, the 'conquest' of the country was completed by Edward I at the end of the thirteenth century, by which time much of the best land was firmly in the hands of the Anglo-Norman lords and the

Crown. The population was small, probably not more than a quarter of a million, and scattered throughout an essentially pastoral landscape. Outside the manorial system, imposed discontinuously by the English, the social structure remained tribal. The manorial system and the gradual growth of commerce, albeit on a small scale, facilitated the purchase of land, causing the number of dispossessed tribesmen to increase. This, combined with the ravages of the Black Death, created widespread unrest, culminating in the revolt of Owain Glyn Dŵr at the beginning of the fifteenth century. One of the immediate consequences of the devastation and chaos caused by the uprising was that the English made a clear distinction in law between themselves and Welshmen, who were now carefully defined as second-class citizens: Welshmen had had their national identity defined for them. When, towards the end of the century, Henry Tudor fought his way to the English throne this part-Welshman (his grandfather had been pure Welsh), who had spent much of his life in exile in Brittany and France, was widely accepted by Welsh and English alike—he had had, after all, the foresight to carry the standard of Cadwaladr, a red dragon on a white and green background, on the field at Bosworth! By this time his deeds and ancestry were known throughout the Principality, proclaimed far and wide by the many bardic poems composed in his honour. A symbol of national identity had been created, only to be appropriated by the English.

In Scotland, on the other hand, the situation was somewhat simpler. The infiltration of the Anglo-Norman elite had been halted in 1286, and thereafter intermittent warfare between Scotland and England occupied the next 250 years, during which time folk heroes like Wallace and Bruce emerged to inspire a sense of national unity. The long period of hostility, and a close relationship with the French, together served to enhance the separateness of the Scottish and English peoples. The sense of national identity seems to have emerged much earlier here than elsewhere in Europe. In the Declaration of Arbroath (1320) it is the voice of an emerging nation we hear, not that of an elite or a tribe: 'For, as long as but a hundred of us remain alive, never will we under any condition be brought under English rule. It is in truth not for glory, nor riches, nor honour that we are fighting, but for freedom.'

In Ireland the fragmented and confused political situation that prevailed throughout the Middle Ages, with the country divided into a palimpsest of small polities ruled by Irish kings, Anglo-Irish lords, and the English Crown, provided little scope for the development of a sense of unity. The different components fought one with another, and the freebooting bands of Irish mercenaries were not particular to whom they hired their services. Added to this, the physical isolation of Ireland and the distractions of the Hundred Years War greatly reduced the interests of the English in Irish affairs. Pressure lessened and estates were sold off to residents. The Irish kings watched the changing situation with some hope, and in 1364 an imaginative ode could proclaim:

> Ireland is a woman risen again
> from the horrors of reproach . . .
> she was owned for a while by foreigners
> she belongs to Irishmen after that.

In this period of Gaelic renaissance in the fourteenth century the Anglo-Irish began to merge with the local population, adopting native values. They employed bards and historians to sing their praises and to stress their legitimacy through generations of intermarriage. In serving these 'new' masters the intellectual elite of Celtic society were simply plying the trade of their ancestors. The complex processes of interaction led to a blurring of ethnic differences. Safely distanced from a distracted England, the varied Irish community could turn its attention to perpetrating local feuds and rivalries in the time-honoured manner and in raiding and feasting, using the bards to broadcast their valour and to satirize their enemy. In this way they were maintaining a traditional culture of great antiquity.

Across the Ocean

By 1400 Europe had recovered from the ravages of the Black Death and was beginning to move out of the cycle of devastating warfare that had consumed so much energy in earlier centuries of the millennium. The volume of trade was escalating, and with it came new demands and new aspirations. Peninsular Europe was well endowed with raw materials and much of its land surface was productive, but the growing complexity of society created requirements that could not easily be met from within. Among these requirements were gold to fuel the monetary economy, slaves to provide manpower, and spices to make palatable the large quantities of meat that were now being consumed. Gold and slaves were to be had in sub-Saharan Africa, but these commodities had to pass through the hands of the Moorish traders of the north African coast and were therefore costly. Similarly, the much-needed spices—pepper, cinnamon, cloves, nutmeg, and mace—from India and the Indies were readily available but were made expensive by the profit-taking of many middlemen. Moreover, the increasing power of the Ottoman Turks was now beginning to take control of the crucial overland routes linking the East to the east Mediterranean ports. There was, therefore, a growing desire to develop maritime routes direct to the production centres of these much-desired resources.

The early fifteenth century saw a growing awareness of the world. It was already widely believed that the earth was spherical, but what lay on the other side was unknown and much debated, and how accessible the distant parts were was in doubt. Some believed that the Atlantic could not be navigated, others that anyone trying to cross the equator would be burnt to death. The publication in 1406 of Ptolemy's *Geography*—a text written in Greek in the second century AD—introduced the concept of latitude and longitude which meant that a particular location could be fixed on the globe and could, with appropriate navigational skills, be returned to at will. Although there were misconceptions and inaccuracies in Ptolemy's work, it opened up the mind to the possibilities of distant navigation. The publication, about 1470, of the text of Strabo's early-first-century AD *Geography* offered a direct and clearly focused challenge. He believed that the world was round, 'so that, if the immensity of the Atlantic Ocean did not prevent it, we could sail from Iberia to India along the same parallel over the remainder of the circle'.

12.13 A Portuguese caravel of the fifteenth century from a painting by Rafael Monleón, 1885.

The sense of the Atlantic as a barrier was, however, still stressed by the Arabs, and indeed it remained a barrier until navigational techniques and ship construction developed to meet the challenge. It was here that Portugal led the way. With its long maritime interface Portugal was forced to come to terms with the constraints and opportunities imposed by the ocean. Advances in ship design, combining the resilience of the square-rigged cob with the manoeuvrability of the lateen rigging of the slimmer Arab vessels, provided a new type of vessel—the caravel—which was robust enough to face the Atlantic but could sail much closer to the wind (12.13). At the same time significant improvements were being made in the art of navigation. Estimates of latitude by taking the angle of elevation of the Pole Star were certainly being made in the 1460s, and twenty years later Portuguese astronomers had developed a more reliable method by calculating the height of the midday sun, converting it to latitude by means of tables of the sun's declination. With the aid of a quadrant it was now possible to navigate with comparative ease and precision using the method known as running down the latitude—that is, by sailing due north or south to the required latitude and then following the latitude east or west to the desired landfall.

12.14 Prince Henry of Portugal from a painting by Nuno Goncalves.

In the early fifteenth century the Portuguese started to explore the Atlantic seaways to the south. To begin with their horizons were limited to the north and west coasts of Africa. In 1415 Prince Henry (12.14) led a successful expedition against the north African coast, capturing Ceuta—then a Muslim port situated opposite Gibraltar at the end of a series of caravan routes extending southwards deep into Africa. It was an important breakthrough, giving Portugal a firm foothold in Africa and providing direct access to travellers with precise knowledge of the resources of west Africa. Command of Ceuta was also of strategic importance in creating a shield to safeguard the maritime exploration of the Atlantic coasts of Africa. Once established, the Portuguese began their exploration in earnest (12.15, 12.16). Under Henry's direction, from his position as governor of the Algarve, ships reached and colonized Madeira in 1419, and within the next two years had penetrated down the west African coast as far as Cape Non, believed to be the southernmost limit of safe sailing. The cape was eventually passed in 1434, and by the time of Henry's death in 1460 the coast had been charted at least as far south as Sierra Leone. By this time ships sailing in a broad westerly arc had discovered the Azores. The Cape Verde Islands were reached a few years after Henry's death.

In 1470 a new phase of exploration began. Fernão Gomes explored a further 3,200 kilometres of coastline by 1475, and Diego Cão crossed the equator, sailing up the River Congo and reaching as far south as Namibia by 1483. Five years later Bartholomew Dias rounded the Cape of Good Hope. The sea route to the East was now established. In July 1497 Vasco da Gama set sail from Lisbon for India, arriving back home in September 1499 with a cargo of pepper and cinnamon. In the following year, 1500,

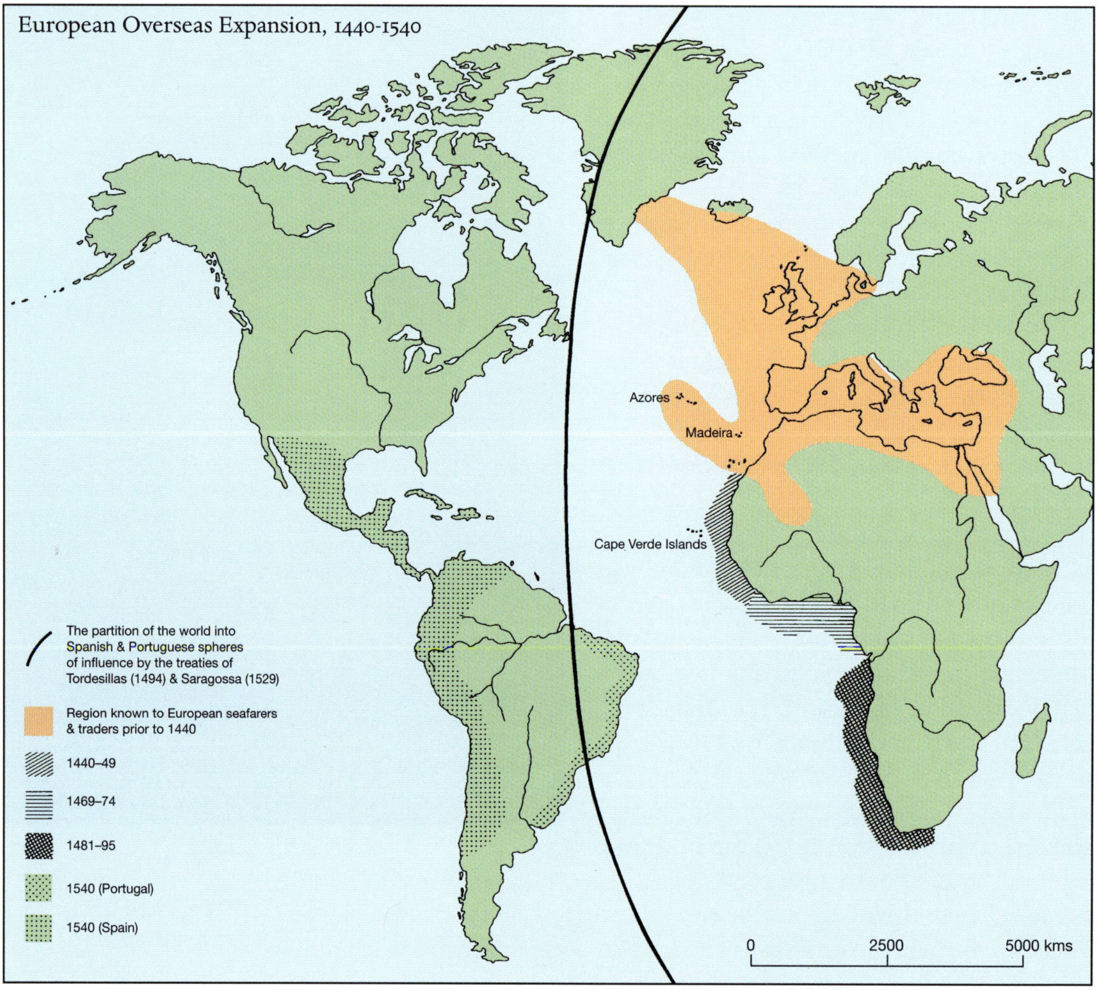

12.15 European expansion overseas, 1450–1550.

thirteen vessels set sail for the Malabar coast, discovering Brazil on the way, and so began Portugal's colonial and commercial empire in the East and the West.

There were many, like Strabo, who believed that a direct route westwards across the Atlantic was the most convenient way to India and the East. Cardinal d'Ailly, in his *Imago Mundi*, was optimistic. Writing of the Atlantic, he said, 'it is evident that this sea is navigable in a very few days if the wind be fair'. Christopher Columbus owned a copy of this book, and the text no doubt fuelled his obsessive belief in the Atlantic route to the East. Columbus, evidently an experienced Atlantic sailor who knew Madeira and even claimed to have visited Iceland, tried first to persuade the Portuguese king to sponsor his venture, but at this time the Por-

12.16 (*facing*) Predominant winds in the Atlantic in the first quarter of the year.

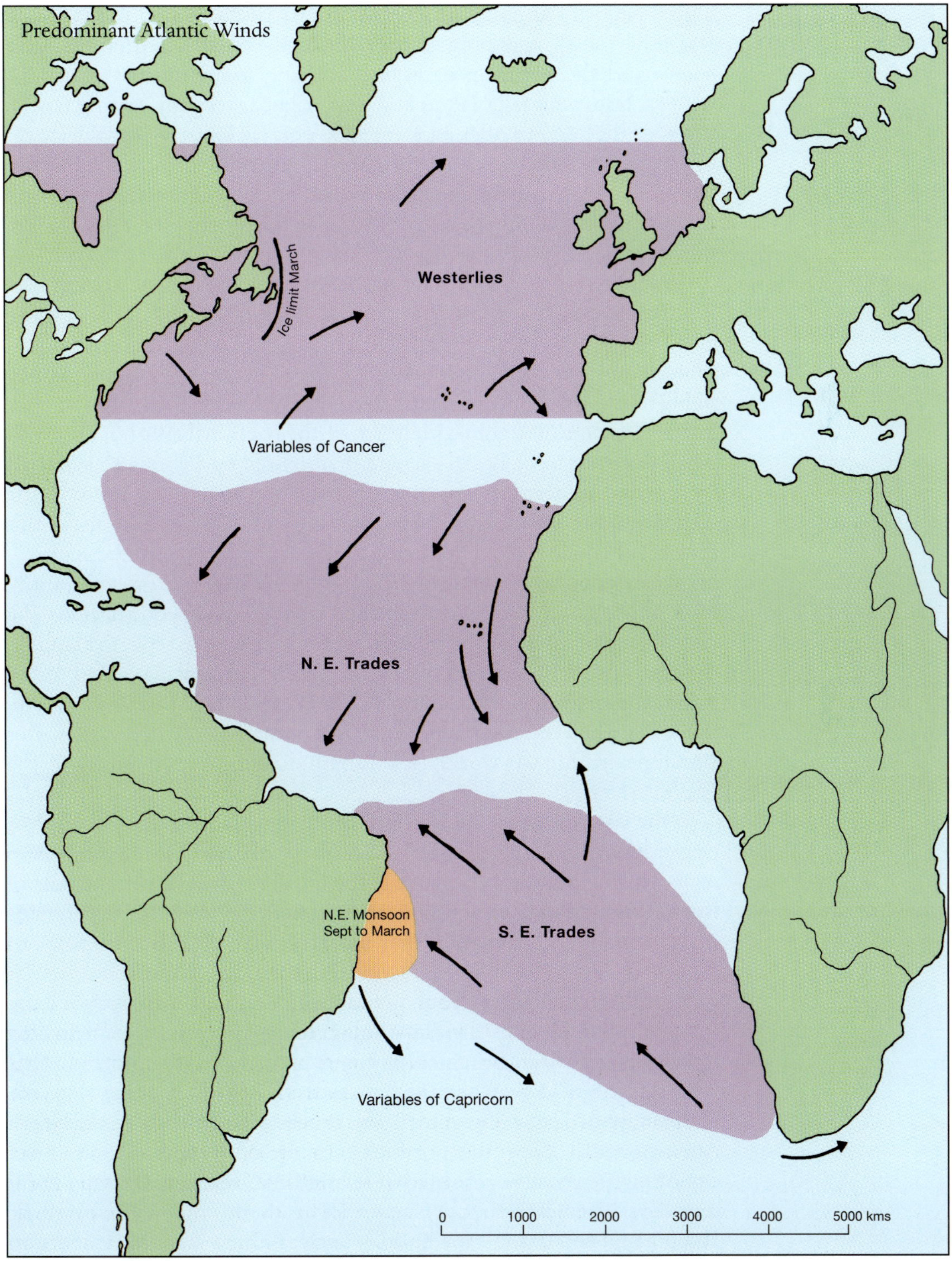
Predominant Atlantic Winds
Westerlies
Ice limit March
Variables of Cancer
N. E. Trades
S. E. Trades
N.E. Monsoon
Sept to March
Variables of Capricorn
0
1000
2000
3000
4000
5000 kms

tuguese effort was going into the southerly route around Africa which was now (1484) beginning to look distinctly possible. Attempts were made to sell the idea to Spain, France, and England, at first without much success, but eventually Ferdinand and Isabella, recently triumphant at Granada, decided to offer backing. The port of Palos in Andalucía was ordered to provide two ships, the caravels *Niña* and *Pinta*, while Columbus hired a larger vessel, the *Santa Maria*. The expedition left Palos on 3 August 1492, signalling the entry of Spain in the race to establish a sea passage to India.

Columbus's discoveries initiated a flurry of diplomatic activity, the Portuguese now becoming concerned to safeguard their sphere of influence. The result was an agreed line of longitude which recognized that Spanish interests could be exercised to the west while Portugal retained rights to the east. This was ratified in the Treaty of Tordesillas in 1494, leaving Portugal not only with much of the south Atlantic but also with what was to become Brazil—a land first sighted by Cabral in April 1500. By the end of the century Spain had firmly established itself in the Caribbean, but Portugal had won the race to India. It was at about this time that Juan de la Cosa produced the first map of the Americas, showing the extent of the discoveries made in the first decade of exploration: most of the coast from Newfoundland to Brazil had been charted. The cognitive geography of the time, however, still believed that the land on the east side of the Atlantic was part of a long peninsula joined to the Asian land-mass, and such a view still held even after Magellan's expedition of 1519 had rounded Cape Horn and returned to Seville in 1522 after circumnavigating the world, establishing *en route* the immensity of the Pacific Ocean.

In the last decade of the fifteenth century, which saw the Portuguese penetrating the Far East and the Spaniards establishing themselves in America, the English were active in the north Atlantic. It was the port of Bristol, with its long-established Atlantic trade between the extremities of Iceland and the Canaries, that took the lead. The first attempts to explore the north Atlantic are recorded in the 1480s, but without significant result. In 1496 John Cabot, probably of Genoese birth, received the sponsorship of Henry VII for his attempt to seek a northern route to Asia by sailing west from Britain. Nothing is known of his ventures in that year, but the next year he sailed again from Bristol in a tiny ship, the *Matthew*, with a crew of eighteen, this time reaching the shores of North America, most likely the north-eastern tip of Newfoundland. After exploring the coast he returned in record time, reaching Brittany in fifteen days. The next year, 1498, he set off again, this time with five ships. What happened to the expedition is unclear; there is some evidence to suggest that the vessels reached America and may even have got as far south as Florida, but John Cabot never returned. Thereafter several other voyages were made by Portuguese ships, but it was the expedition under English patronage led by Cabot's son, Sebastian, in 1508–9 that made the greatest contribution, exploring the American coastline from Labrador to Cuba.

The French came comparatively late to the scramble for transatlantic territories. The first expedition left Brittany under the command of a Florentine, Giovanni da Verrazzano, in 1524 for the Carolinas, then sailed northwards to New York Bay, the coast of Maine, and Newfoundland before returning to France. Ten years later, in 1534, Jacques Cartier sailed from St Malo, in the first of a series of expeditions which were to open up the St Lawrence river for eventual French colonization.

The brief span of 120 years between Henry's expedition to Ceuta and Cartier's sailing up the St Lawrence changed the world. From Atlantic ports like Seville, Lisbon, St Malo, and Bristol distant lands were being explored and colonized, creating, for the first time, a true world system. As the Mediterranean, for so long the centre of western civilization, became a backwater, the Atlantic façade of Europe took on a new role as the innovating interface between old Europe and the lands beyond the ocean. The Atlantic, once the end of the world, was now the beginning.

13. The *Longue Durée*

Those who face the ocean will always be in awe of the uncontrollable power of the waves and the swells, and the inexorable, reassuring, strength of the sea's rhythm. It is an ever-present force of raw energy which has to be contained by the belief systems and behaviour patterns of the people who live within its compass. However informed we may be of the nature of the sea in the terms of modern science, it is difficult not to recall, in some half-remembered way, deeply rooted ancestral beliefs in the personality of Ocean.

Those who are of the Atlantic inherit a mindset that is markedly different from that of the dwellers of the Continental interior. To distill the elements of that difference is not easy. Yet dominating all is the need to maintain an equilibrium with the fearsome natural force by competition and by propitiation. The ocean is an adversary to challenge, but one demanding deep respect. Then there are the tides, so much more impressive in the Atlantic than in the effete Mediterranean. Their changing magnitude and regularity add a different measure of time, both complex and subtle, to the day–night cycle and the changing seasons. Daily observation of tidal rhythms greatly enhances a community's awareness of the nature of time and its passage. In this, perhaps, may lie the desire to monumentalize aspects of time in lines and circles of stone and intricately contrived burial monuments. The ocean is also an energetic creature, always moving. Its very existence is a goad to travel and exploration. Thus, in so far as one can identify the elements of an oceanic mentality, they include challenge, awe, a heightened awareness of time, and a deep restlessness.

The richness of the Atlantic region has been a leitmotif running through this story. The land itself, so much of it of old, hard, and heavily mineralized rocks, contributes gold, silver, copper, and tin as well as a variety of fine stone for functional and decorative purposes, and there were amber and jet to be had from the North Sea shores. These fine, rare, attractive materials were the stuff of elite display and exchange, and their sparse distribution inevitably encouraged mobility. This the sea made easy.

The mingling of the warm Gulf Stream and the nutrient-rich Arctic flows spreading down the Continental shelf of Atlantic Europe from Iceland to Morocco encourages the growth of plankton, supporting a dense and varied biomass. In these enriched waters live enormous shoals of fish—sardine, herring, tuna, cod, hake, and many others—whose seasonal migratory movements can be followed and harvested by those willing to brave the seas.

Between the land and the sea lies the remarkably prolific littoral, composed of estuaries, marshes, and intertidal zones, presenting a huge range of food resources there for the gathering. The particular importance of this resource lay in its variety, and therefore its reliability were one component to fail, and in the ease with which it could be harvested as and when required by the very young or the very old. In short, the littoral provided a buffer of food reserves which could be utilized in a way that maximized the energy of the community as a whole. But it had even more to offer. It was a ready source of salt, an essential component in the preservation of surplus protein, whether fish or meat, and less obviously, it provided iodine through the ingestion of seafish, marine molluscs, and seaweed. Iodine is a mineral essential to maintaining fertility. It is not impossible that in this simple fact lay the explanation for the apparent sustained growth of population in coastal regions in the Mesolithic period. The varied diet of coastal communities and the balance of minerals available to them was an important factor in keeping the population healthy and productive.

The restlessness of the ocean, the seasonality of fish migrations, and the uneven distribution of elite resources together encouraged travel by sea along the Atlantic façade. It is easy to underestimate the skill-base of past communities. Early hunter-gatherers would have been intimately aware of their environment, and because of their mobility on land, following the migrating herds of their principal prey, their ability to navigate over large territories and find their way back to their base camp would have become highly developed. They would have come to use a variety of information, familiar land forms, the movement of sun, moon, and stars, the direction of flight of migrating birds, and a host of other indicators, observed, assessed, and passed on, all contributing to the mental map held in common by the group leaders. These same skills enabled the coastal communities to travel the seas with equal confidence.

The earliest of the maritime movements were inshore, but it cannot have been long before a developing knowledge of the migration of fish-stocks encouraged longer voyages. Once at sea, the need for fresh water would have required the boats to put in to foreign land from time to time. In this way each community established a network of landfalls around the limits of its ocean territory. It is easy to see how, in such a situation, stable social interactions soon developed, particularly as the hunter-gatherer groups of the littoral zone became increasingly sedentary. The system of gift exchange, which would inevitably have emerged in the interests of maintaining harmony, provided the mechanism by which technological innovations, and the knowledge associated with them, moved quickly from region to region. One can understand how polished stone axes, pottery vessels, seed grain, and even domesticated animals came to be trans-shipped. The speed with which the 'Neolithic package' initially spread through Armorica, Britain, and Ireland is more easily understood in terms of transmission by sea than by supposing step-by-step colonization across the land. By this time the essential infrastructure of maritime interaction had been establishing itself for over three thousand years.

13.1 A currach on Inis Mór, the largest of the Aran Islands in Galway Bay, made of tarred canvas stetched across a light wooden framework. It is the modern version of the hide boat dating back to prehistoric times

Maritime movements of the kind envisaged here, involving the transport of high-bulk cargoes like livestock, presuppose the existence of suitably sturdy seagoing vessels. There is nothing unreasonable in this. Communities used to working in timber, wattle, and skin would have had the skills to make log boats enhanced by side strakes and outriggers or the large skin boats made of hides stretched across a wicker framework for which the Atlantic seaways later became well known (13.1). Such vessels, propelled by paddles or oars, could well have been a familiar sight at the coastal settlements of the Mesolithic period, and no doubt continued in use without much modification for several thousand years, at least until about 1000 BC when new influences began to impact.

Through the developing maritime networks of the fourth and third millennia a wide range of rare raw materials were transported along the length of the Atlantic seaboard. Local networks, probably of great antiquity, overlapped in such a way that the entire coastal zone from Morocco to Shetland was loosely bound together, though it is highly unlikely that any vessel strayed much beyond its traditional restricted circuit. The materials which were moved in this way included axes, in stone and later copper alloy, ornamental stones such as callaïs, and gold ornaments. Such items were no doubt among the gifts which were exchanged in cycles of reciprocity, rather as in the *Kula* ring of the Trobriand Islands of Melanesia. Grand ceremonial exchanges of this type would also have provided the occasions when goods of a more mundane kind carried by the voyagers could be traded. Whilst the archaeological record of exchange tends to be focused on the commodities manipulated by the elites, the bulk of the goods which may have been transported—commodities such as foodstuffs, fabrics, and pigments—remain archaeologically invisible.

The one item which stands out prominently in the exchanges of the fourth and third millennia is the axe. We have seen how polished stone axes were made in considerable numbers in parts of the Atlantic region and widely distributed. Non-functional axes in rare stones were also used to adorn elite burials, and the axe, in various forms, featured prominently in megalithic art, particularly of Armorica. In the second millennium axes of copper and bronze, though rarer than the stone, were distributed widely from their various sources and are frequently found buried in 'hoards' or, less often, accompanying burials. It is difficult to resist the conclusion that the axe was a symbol of great potency along the Atlantic seaways in the Neolithic and Bronze Age: it remains a distinct possibility that axes featured large as the prime gifts in the cycles of exchange which bound societies together. If this is so, then the crescendo of axe-burying, which consigned tens of thousands of socketed axes to the earth in Armorica in the seventh century BC, may in some way represent the cataclysmic end of a long-established and deeply rooted system tracing its origins back to the end of the Mesolithic period. For convenience we can refer to the period up to about 800 BC as the *first cycle* of the Atlantic system.

During this time—a span of more than four thousand years—the communities of the Atlantic shared a common core of knowledge and a sophisticated belief system manifest in the development of megalithic tombs for collective burials (13.2) and the related alignments and circles of upstanding stones. Three aspects of this highly intricate system stand out: the emphasis on bringing ancestors together in burial, the use of large stone slabs standing on end, and a highly developed knowledge of some aspects of astronomy. How much of this, if any at all, is the result of the maritime heritage it is difficult to judge. Communal burials are known in the Mesolithic shell mounds of Armorica, and the phenomenon of burying the dead in these ancestral middens occurs around the coast from Scandinavia to Iberia. Perhaps in this practice we are seeing the desire of the hunter-gatherer communities to lay claim to the liminal territory at the edge of the land, the midden also representing the 'history' of the community going back to its ancestral beginnings. One could even go so far as to suggest that the mounds of the megalithic tombs may have been inspired by the physical form of the shell midden. The discovery of shell midden deposits in the chambers of a number of Neolithic burial mounds, most notably on the Channel Islands, is a tantalizing hint that the ancestry of the burial tradition might here be being symbolically acknowledged.

The astronomical knowledge embedded in the construction of at least some of the megalithic monuments is no more than might have been expected of people rooted in a tradition of sea travel, who used their close observation of the heavens to help them navigate and daily experienced the disappearance of the sun on the western ocean. That this highly specialist knowledge was given architectural form might in some way reflect the claim of the elite to have a spiritual relationship with the celestial powers who controlled the rhythm of the world.

It is difficult to know how to explain the desire to use massive stones in non-secular constructions. In constructing time-marks out of living rock society was demonstrating its power to alter landscape in a particular way. Is it too fanciful to relate this reverence for bare rock faces to the experience of sailors navigating rocky coasts? Probably, but the question is a reminder that in the distant past, when life was tenuous, the natural world in its untamed state would have been a focus of fear and reverence. To exert any form of control over it, however puny, gave reassurance.

It was, no doubt, during this first cycle of maritime contact that a lin-

gua franca developed allowing travellers by sea to communicate one with another. If, as we might reasonably suppose, the ships were the prerogative of the elite, then the language which evolved over the millennia would have become the language of the elite. In such a situation the disparate languages which might have been spoken before contact intensified would soon have converged to become a similar tongue, understandable throughout the lands of the Atlantic façade. By the first millennium BC the common language spoken across most of the region was a branch of Indo-European known, since the seventeenth century, as

13.2 The megalithic burial chamber of Le Couperon on the Island of Jersey overlooking Rozel Bay.

'Celtic'—the language which still survives, though in modified form, in parts of Scotland, Ireland, Wales, the Isle of Man, and Brittany.

The foundation of the Atlantic port of Gadir (Cadiz) by the Phoenicians about 800 BC offers a convenient point to begin the *second cycle*, characterized by increasing interaction with the Mediterranean. It remains a possibility, however, that Phoenician exploration of the Gulf of Cadiz may have begun two centuries earlier. If so, then the apparent increase in the volume of bronze implements being moved and deposited along the Atlantic seaways may, in some way, have been linked to this development. One plausible explanation of the processes at work would be to suppose that the Phoenician presence created a demand for bronze which encouraged the leaders of the maritime cycles of reciprocal exchange to generate a greatly increased volume of bronze items for trade. In this scenario the presence of the Mediterranean power provides the catalyst for internal readjustment within the native system. It must be admitted, however, that the interpretation is speculative and difficult to test.

By 800 BC, with the Phoenicians firmly established at Cadiz, the Mediterranean presence had become a reality. The impact was twofold: a new market was created for a range of rare consumer durables, including gold, silver, tin, and ivory, and an alien technology of shipbuilding was introduced into Atlantic waters.

The archaeological evidence is not of a kind that generally allows for accurate quantification to be made of production and distribution, not least because it is often difficult to identify and account for social processes which may have affected the surviving data. It does, however, appear that after 800 BC a marked decline becomes evident in the quantity and variety of the luxury goods moving along the Atlantic seaways in the traditional cycles of exchange. The simplest explanation for this is that the growth of the Mediterranean polities—Phoenician and, later, Carthaginian, Greek and Etruscan and, later, Roman—created such demands for manpower and raw materials that the exchange systems of 'barbarian' Europe were forced to readjust. The process, which began *c.*800 BC, was not over until the Roman empire collapsed *c.*AD 400.

One of the earliest effects on the Atlantic system seems to have been to draw into the Mediterranean ambit the Moroccan and western Iberian coasts along which trading enclaves were soon established by Phoenician entrepreneurs. Although the direct Phoenician impact does not appear to have extended much further north than the Tagus estuary, it seems that the metal-producing region of Galicia was now firmly linked into the Phoenician system and remained so during the following centuries. Further north the rivers of Gaul—the Garonne, Loire, and Seine—began to develop as major routes linking the Atlantic to inland Europe and eventually to the Mediterranean. These lines of communication had been active for centuries, but now the demands of the Hallstatt chiefdoms of west central Europe and the Mediterranean states seem to have caused an intensification of trade, drawing off more and more of the desirable surpluses of the Atlantic region and in doing so diminishing the vitality of the earlier maritime systems.

The archaeological evidence of the seventh to second centuries BC suggests that much of the British Isles was now linked with northern Europe across the southern North Sea, though the intensity of the interaction seems to have diminished after the end of the seventh century, by which time Ireland enters a period of isolation.

Armorica and south-western Britain are part of a separate system which was linked first, via the Loire, to the west Hallstatt region, but from the fourth century BC enjoyed increasingly strong relationships, by way of the Gironde axis, direct to the west Mediterranean. This is not to say that the Atlantic system failed to operate, but simply that its intensity seems to have diminished as the various regions of the Atlantic zone were drawn into the broader European sphere. In social terms, the system of gift-exchange cycles which had welded the communities of the Atlantic region into a series of interlocking social territories fragmented as each of the component territories, favoured by desirable natural resources, entered into new systems of exchange. The result was the realignment of some regions and the isolation of others.

By the late second and early first centuries BC it is possible to glimpse some of the local systems in operation. Most readily recognizable is the system linking the Garonne, Armorica, and the Solent, expressed archaeologically in the distribution of Roman wine amphorae. Yet the movement of wine, and many other commodities, along this route was, most likely, in the hands of a number of different shippers working only the sectors of the route familiar to them. Distributions of later Roman pottery of the third and fourth centuries AD, made in central southern Britain and western Gaul, show that the same shipping lanes were still active, though by this stage the transactions would have been purely commercial.

The appearance of Phoenician sailing ships in the Gulf of Cadiz introduced new techniques of shipbuilding to the Atlantic. It is possible that knowledge of the sail first spread to the outer ocean in this way but, given the extent of maritime traffic in the Atlantic before this, it could well be that the sail had already been independently invented in the previous four thousand years or so of intense maritime activity. Later the Roman military presence, first along the Atlantic coasts of Iberia and then, in the mid-first century BC, in the seas around Gaul and Britain, brought

Mediterranean shipbuilding techniques firmly into the consciousness of the Atlantic shipbuilder. Native traditions were highly conservative, but some ideas, of benefit in local waters, were adopted.

The second cycle, spanning the period 800 BC–AD 400, saw the Atlantic communities gradually drawn more firmly into a European-wide system of trade and exchange. As the traditional patterns of gift exchange died out, so large-scale production and entrepreneurial marketing began to take over. By the time of the Roman empire production on an industrial scale was under way in many parts of the region—gold, silver, tin, and copper mining in western Iberia, salt and fish-sauce production along the coasts of Armorica, and pottery production around Poole Harbour and in the nearby New Forest are among those most readily recognized. Throughout this period the sea as a means of transport retained its importance.

The *third cycle*, from *c.*AD 400 to 1500, saw the re-emergence of an Atlantic system but one significantly different from that of the prehistoric period. The cycle began with the catastrophic breakdown of the Roman economic system in the decades around AD 400, as much of the old infrastructure was torn apart by restless surges of population bound up in raids and land-grabbing. While it is possible that previous estimates of the scale of the population displacement may be too great, there can be no doubt that the social and economic disruption caused was massive. The entire edifice of united Europe crumbled into its constituent parts, many of them now, once again, isolated and remote.

Ships still threaded along the seaways. Mediterranean cargoes, possibly changing ship in the Tagus estuary, found their way to the Irish Sea, while trading vessels from Ireland reached Gaul. The seaways also provided the means by which large numbers of people moved, as raiders, migrant populations, or as individuals driven by their religion to search for solitude. The distances travelled were considerable. British populations crossed the Bay of Biscay to settle in Galicia while, some centuries later, Norwegians braved the north Atlantic intent on setting up home on Orkney and Shetland. Some ventured still further to reach Iceland, Greenland, and beyond. Although only scraps of evidence survive in the incomplete historical tradition, and the even more imperfect archaeological record, it is difficult to resist the impression that the seas were alive with shipping of all kinds. In all probability this was in no way different from the situation going back for at least a millennium and maybe much further.

The mainstream tradition of shipbuilding continued much as before. In the waters around Ireland the remarkably sturdy skin boats carried monks across the open seas out of sight of land for days on end, while in the Channel vessels plank-built in the Romano-Celtic tradition moved cargoes along familiar shipping lanes. It was the North Sea shores of Scandinavia that saw something of a revolution in shipbuilding with the addition of the large, square-rigged sail to long, sleek, plank-built native vessels. The resulting Viking warships carried fighting men throughout the length of the Atlantic seaboard and into the Mediterranean to raid and plunder, while vessels built in the same sturdy Nordic tradition transported their families to the new lands they had chosen to settle.

After the initial disruption caused by the migrations of the fifth and sixth centuries, a new economic structure emerged as trading centres began to develop at coastal ports and on major rivers, some on entirely new sites, others continuing already-existing settlements. A growing population and the new expectations of the emerging elite created increasing demands for raw materials and foodstuffs, and so trade grew to unprecedented levels.

It was now that the Atlantic seaways came into their own, facilitating the movement of bulk cargoes from one productive zone to another—southern commodities such as fruit, sugar, oil, and wine to the north and northern products including tin, cloth, wool, and fish to the south. One of the features of the developing economy was the emergence of a high degree of specialization in regional production. Thus, by the early Middle Ages Britain had become one of the prime suppliers of wool and cloth as well as providing smaller volumes of tin, while Gascony concentrated almost exclusively on wine production. Specialization of this kind inevitably took with it a degree of interdependency. Britain, having let its own vineyards decay, was wholly dependent on imported wine, mostly from Gascony, while, since much of the productive land of Gascony was given over to viticulture, the Gascons were reliant on imported food staples. Similarly, the huge demand for fish by the largely Catholic population of western Continental Europe meant that those able to harvest the vast shoals of cod and herring along the Atlantic edge and those who commanded the saltworks around the Loire estuary, together controlled a valuable monopoly. Large-scale production on an industrial scale, the development of a comparatively stable money supply, emerging monoculture, and the new consumerism together created an economic system of intricate complexity. Facilitating it all were the thousands of ships which braved the Atlantic sea lanes, shifting cargoes from place to place in search of profit or pursuing the fish stock into the more open ocean. These vessels and their crews, together with the infrastructure of ports, warehouses, chandlers, timber merchants, rope makers, sailcloth weavers, hauliers, merchant financiers, and the many others necessary to sustain the system, gave the ports of the Atlantic edge an intensity they had never before enjoyed. What had emerged was a highly distinctive maritime culture sharing a common store of knowledge and set of values and having the same fears, superstitions, and respect for the ocean. It was a bond that transcended mere geography.

The first half of the second millennium saw the maritime culture of the Atlantic communities still further enhanced. Knowledge of the magnetic compass spread, sailing instructions were committed to writing and passed from hand to hand, and charts began to be drawn, although at first they were rare and jealously guarded. The ship too was gradually improved. The square-rigged cog was a sturdy vessel, well suited to carrying cargo and fighting men through the familiar coastal waters, but it was not until lateen sails were adopted from Arab shipping that vessels could be made to sail close enough to the wind to begin to explore the more distant African shores with their difficult winds and tides.

By the early decades of the fifteenth century Atlantic Europe was ready, poised to face the challenge of the open ocean. Within a century the ocean had been crossed many times and the world circumnavigated.

The three simple cycles of Atlantic development we have outlined here are, of course, a broad generalization, but they do fairly reflect the changing situation as we have come to understand it through the archaeological and historical evidence. In the first, or prehistoric, cycle, the maritime movements were bound up in systems of gift exchange and reciprocity deeply embedded in patterns of social interactions. Later, in the second, or protohistoric, cycle, the old patterns were distorted and to some extent dislocated by the consumer needs of distant states. Finally, in the third, or historic, cycle the power of the ocean reasserted itself and the

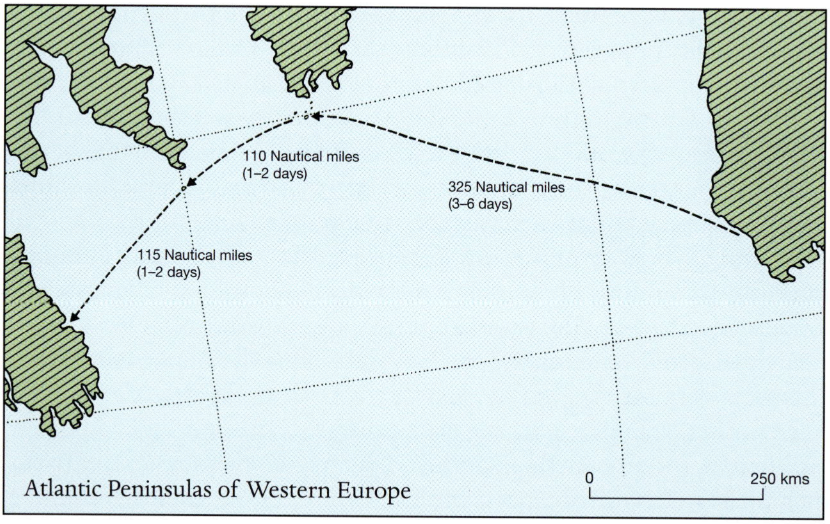

13.3 The maritime relationship between the Atlantic penninsulars of Spain, France, Britain, and Ireland.

maritime regions came together to create the most dynamic and productive commercial zone Europe had ever experienced. It was from the entrepreneurial communities of this Atlantic façade that the rest of the world was colonized.

To what extent was there a sense of community among the peoples of the Atlantic? Was there something, however ill-defined, that could be called an oceanic mentality? The ocean, as we have stressed so many times in this book, is one of the greatest ever-present natural forces that humankind can experience. Its savage energy and remorseless rhythm cannot fail to make a deep impression on anyone who comes within its presence. The ocean dominates. There is also the sense of limitlessness—of being on the edge of the world looking out across an infinity of ever-changing sea. These simple realities are part of the experience shared by all those who have faced the ocean. To contain this frightening vision, communities have constructed myths and peopled the sea with anthropomorphic powers demanding to be propitiated. Across time there has been the sense that anyone trespassing on Ocean's territory enters a state of unstable equilibrium with the powers. They become—as the Christian hymn puts it—'those in peril on the sea'. From time to time the ocean would take its toll of humanity. Such was the inevitable reality. Towards the sea, therefore, man has always been ambivalent.

The unifying bond created by the ocean, for those who have lived around its edges, should not be underestimated. Once journeys by sea had begun there can be no doubt that a brotherhood grew up among sailors. Experiencing the same dangers on alien Ocean, a degree of mutual support would have been essential. A sharing of landfalls and access to local resources would have created social interactions which developed, as we have suggested, into cycles of gift exchange, creating the basis for the more complex systems of exchange and trade that were to follow. In this way the varied resources of the Atlantic littoral were developed and exploited. With these maritime movements came the unrestricted spread of knowledge and beliefs and values. Thus the ocean facilitated the emergence of a shared Atlantic culture communicated through a lingua franca we have come to know as 'Celtic'.

The maritime zone of western Europe focused around an arc of peninsulas (13.3), all accessible within five to ten days' sailing of each other. Within and beyond this arc stretched an extensive, sinuous coastal region. Allowing land within 50 kilometres of the sea to be considered maritime, the map (13.4) shows just how extensive this region of Europe really is. For the most part the communities living within it will have looked to the sea before them, rather than the land behind. To this extent they belonged to the ocean and were remote from the Continent. It was

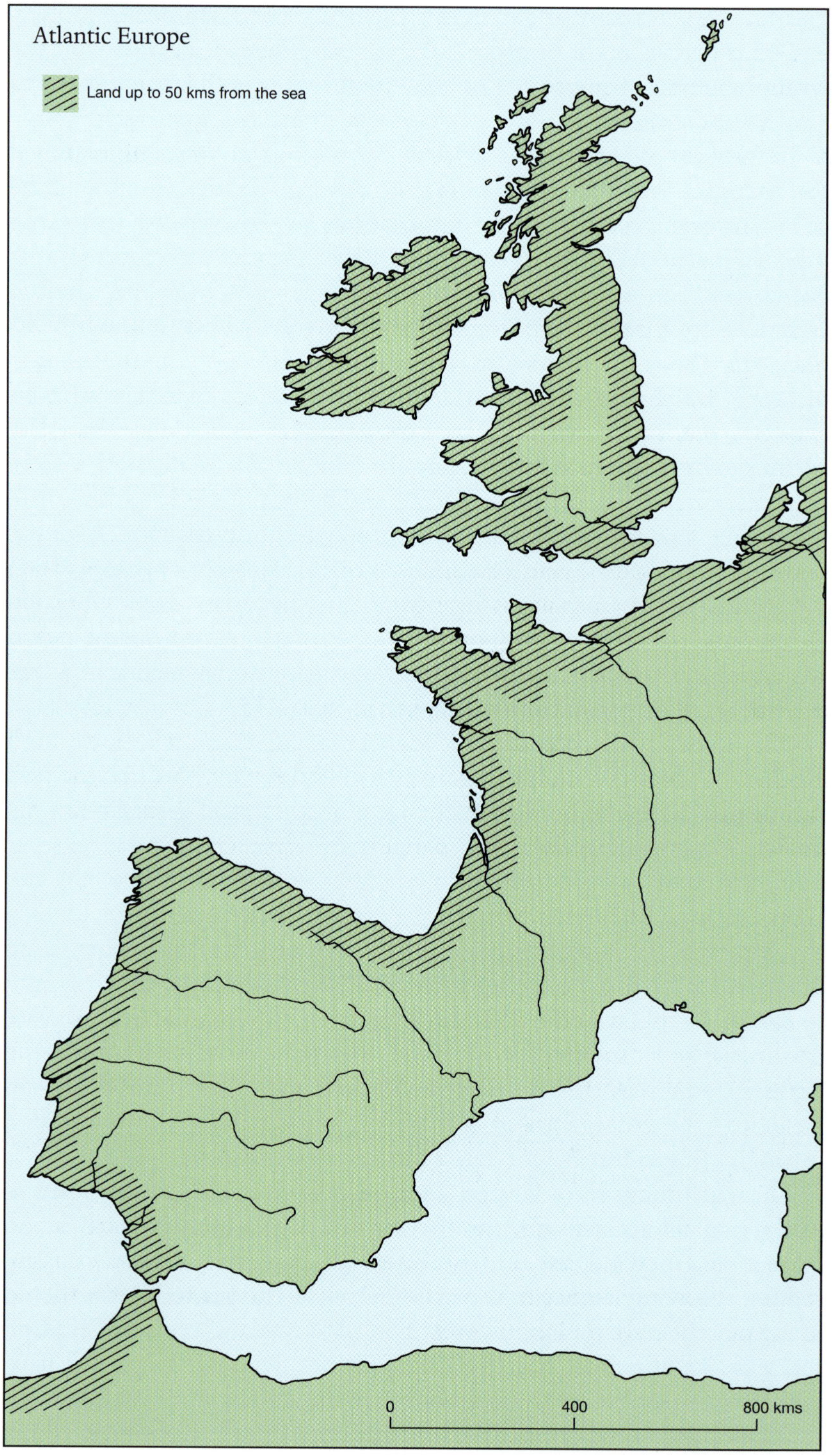

13.4 The Atlantic zone

a remoteness that nurtured independence. In times of stress the ethnicity of these regions might be strengthened by the development of cultural symbols—in architecture, art, dress, or behaviour—to distinguish them from inland neighbours. When, following the folk movements of the fifth and sixth centuries AD, new peoples speaking different languages settled the inland regions, the indigenous languages of the maritime communities became important manifestations of their 'otherness'. It was in this way that the 'Celtic brotherhoods' of the nineteenth century came into being as nascent resistance movements against Spanish, French, and English centralized authority. Between the coastal communities, securely protected by the sea from each other, the sea could be used as a means of building alliances: such was its ambiguity. This collaboration between maritime communities helped to intensify their distinctive oceanic culture and to set them apart.

In his novel *Pêcheurs d'Islande* Pierre Loti bases his story around the fishing fleets leaving the north Breton town of Paimpol each year for the fishing grounds of the north Atlantic. In the religious ceremonies which initiated the sailing season, and the sailors singing the hymn to the Virgin 'Salut, Étoile-de-la-Mer' as their vessels departed, in the long period of agonized waiting—the wives and mothers watching anxiously for the ships to return in the autumn—and in the death of the hero, Yann, taken back in a deathly marriage by the sea which had nurtured him through life, Loti exposes the timeless emotions of those who, through the millennia, have faced the ocean. The heroine of the story, Gaud, waiting for her husband's return goes up on to an exposed headland. She

> sat there, all day long at the foot of a lonely cross which rises high above the immense waste of the ocean. There are many of these crosses hereabouts; they are set up on the most advanced cliffs of the sea-bound land as if to implore mercy and to calm that restless mysterious power which drags men away never to give them back and in preference retains the bravest and noblest . . . At regular intervals the sea retreated and great spaces were left uncovered everywhere as if the Channel was slowly drying up; then with the same lazy slowness, the waters rose again, and continued their everlasting coming and going without any heed of the dead.
>
> At the foot of the cross Gaud remained surrounded by these tranquil mysteries, gazing ever before her, until night fell and she could see no more.

At the interface of sea and land the communities of the Atlantic façade have, throughout time, shared the same turmoil of emotions, unfailingly called up by the presence of the ocean. Only in small details—the theme of this book—have their responses differed.

A Guide to Further Reading

Providing a bibliographical background for a book of this kind is always likely to entail compromises. While it would have been possible to footnote heavily, or to lard the text with many hundreds of Harvard-style citations, the sight of pages made dense with scholarly apparatus is invariably off-putting. I firmly believe that it is the prime function of an author to create a work that can be read and, if possible, one that can be read with pleasure, rather than to try to impress the reader with the outward and visible symbols of erudition. But an unreferenced text can be frustrating to anyone wishing to follow up a particular point of interest. The compromise I have adopted here is to offer, chapter by chapter, some guidance on further reading following, as closely as possible, the main themes considered in each chapter. For the most part I have tried to quote recent books written in English which are themselves extensively referenced, but where suitable works do not exist I have suggested foreign-language works, restricting the list, as far as possible, to French and Spanish texts. Inevitably there are details or specific points of argument that are better covered in papers published in specialist journals. When so, the citations are provided. The rule has been to offer readers enough guidance to the literature to allow quick and easy access so that they may begin the further exploration for themselves. I hope the balance is about right and that the byways of the vast and endlessly fascinating subject area I have tried to cover are well enough signposted to indicate the points of entry. May your journeys be as enjoyable as mine have been.

Chapter 1. Perceptions of the Ocean

In many ways this is the hardest chapter to offer a list of background reading for, not least because perceptions of the ocean are to be found scattered through an enormous range of literature, but a good place to begin is with the writings of those who first encountered the ocean. Two books provide a thorough introduction to the classical geography: E. H. Warmington, *Greek Geography* (London, 1934) and J. O. Thomson, *History of Ancient Geography* (Cambridge, 1948). The religious context for the early beliefs is considered by R. Cadwell, *The Origins of the Gods* (Oxford, 1989), while E. S. Ramage, in *Atlantis Fact or Fiction* (Bloomington, 1978), provides a well-balanced guide to the still-popular sub-theme.

The rich folklore of the Atlantic seen through contemporary eyes is more difficult to root out. The Breton stories will be found in two standard works, Hersart de la Villemarque, *Barzaz-Breiz* (Paris: 2nd edn. 1845) and E. Souvestre, *Le Foyer Breton*, most recently republished in a 1947 edition (Paris). The Irish vernacular literature is more accessible. M. Dillon, *Early Irish Literature* (Chicago, 1948) is an excellent short introduction, as is M. Dillon and N. Chadwick, *The Celtic Realms* (London, 1967). There is also much to be gleaned from the rich array of texts brought together in K. H. Jackson, *A Celtic Miscellany* (Harmondsworth, 1971). The attitude of the early monks to the ocean is explored by T. O'Loughlin in his chapter 'Living in the Ocean', in C. Bourke (ed.), *Studies in the Cult of Saint Columba* (Dublin, 1997). The many myths surrounding Atlantic islands are conveniently collected by D. S.

Johnson in *Phantom Islands of the Atlantic* (New York, 1994), to which should be added T. J. Westropp, 'Brazil and the Legendary Islands of the North Atlantic: Their History and Fable. A contribution to the Atlantic Problem', *Proceedings of the Royal Irish Academy*, 30 (1912), 223–60. The journal *Folklore* contains much that has relevance to this chapter. Two particularly useful papers are J. Doan, 'The Legend of the Sunken City in Welsh and Breton Traditions', *Folklore*, 92 (1981), 77–83, and C. Hole, 'Superstition and Beliefs of the Sea', *Folklore*, 78 (1967), 184–9.

Turning now to the developing views of archaeologists, the classic pre-war works in order of their publication are: O. G. S. Crawford, 'The Distribution of Early Bronze Age Settlements in Britain' in *Geographical Journal*, 40 (1912), 184–203; H. J. Fleure and E. J. Roberts, 'Archaeological Problems of the West Coast of Britain', *Archaeologia Cambrensis*, 70 (1915), 405–20; E. T. Leeds, 'Excavations at Chun Castle in Penwith, Cornwall', *Archaeologia*, 76 (1927), 203–40; H. Peake and H. J. Fleure, *Corridors of Time VI: The Way of the Sea* (London, 1929); C. Fox, *The Personality of Britain* (Cardiff, 1932: 4th edn. 1959); and O. G. S. Crawford, 'Western Seaways', in D. Buxton (ed.), *Custom is King: Studies in Honour of R. R. Marett* (London, 1936), 181–200. The theme of the importance of the Atlantic seaways to the spread of 'megalithic' ritual and religion was explored by Gordon Childe in *The Prehistory of European Society* (Harmondsworth, 1958), especially in the chapter 'Missionaries of Megalithic Religion', 124–34, and by Glyn Daniel in *Megalithic Builders of Western Europe* (London, 1958). The two most influential and comprehensive works on the use of the Atlantic routes in the past are E. G. Bowen's two books, *Saints, Seaways and Settlements* (Cardiff, 1969) and *Britain and the Western Seaways* (London, 1972).

Finally, the new political mythology is explored in B. Tanguy (ed.), *Aux origins de nationalism breton* (Paris, 1977) and J. Martray, *Nous qui sommes d'Atlantique* (Rennes, 1991).

Chapter 2. Between Land and Sea

To understand the Atlantic coastline the prime requisite is a good map or a series of regional maps of the appropriate scale. These should be augmented by geological maps. The best maps are published by the appropriate national agent, in Britain by the *Ordnance Survey*, France by *Institut géographique national*, Spain by *Instituto Geográfico y Catastral*, and Portugal by *Instituto Geografico e Cadastral*.

An extremely valuable commentary on Atlantic coastal geography will be found in a source which, at first sight, may appear to be somewhat unlikely—the Geographical Handbook Series published by the Naval Intelligence Division during the last war throughout the early 1940s. The volumes on the *Netherlands* (1944), *Belgium* (1944), *France* (1942), *Spain* (1944), *Portugal* (1942), and *Morocco* (1941/2) cover the area treated here. Since they were prepared by geographers specifically to inform a military command, deeply concerned with details of maritime routes, ports, harbours, and their inland lines of communication, the emphasis of these volumes is of particular relevance to this chapter. More recent geographical accounts include J. A. Steer's *The Coastline of England and Wales* (Cambridge: 2nd edn. 1964), P. Pinchemel, *France: A Geographical Survey* (London, 1969), and F. Braudel, *The Identity of France*, Vol. I (London, 1988).

For the nature of the sea as a facilitator and inhibitor of movement the *Admiralty Pilots* and the *Tidal Stream Atlas* (Hydrographic Department) are invaluable. The subtleties of the sea are admirably presented in S. McGrail, *Ancient Boats in North-West Europe* (London: 2nd edn. 1998), especially chapter 13 on Seamanship (258–74). More specific studies, providing insights into particular sea lanes, include J. Purdy, *New Sailing Directory for the English Channel* (London: 9th edn. 1842) and S. McGrail, 'Cross-Channel Seamanship and Navigation in the Late First Millennium BC', *Oxford Journal of Archaeology*, 2 (1983), 299–338.

The intricacies of sea-level change are discussed in a variety of specialist scientific literature. A useful selection of papers have been brought together in F. H. Thompson (ed.), *Archaeology and Coastal Change* (London, 1980), including a helpful introductory chapter, 'On Sea-level Changes', by C. E. Everard (1–23). More specific studies include R. J. Devoy, 'Analysis of the Geological Evidence for Holocene Sea-level Movements in SE England', and A. Heyworth and C. Kidson, 'Sea Level Changes in South West England and Wales', both in *Proceedings of the Geological Association*, 93 (1982), 65–111, and M.-T. Morzadec-Kerfourn, 'Coastline Changes in the Armorican Massif (France)

During the Holocene', in C. W. Finkl (ed.), *Holocene Cycles, Climate, Sea Levels, and Sedimentation, Journal of Coastal Research*, Special Issue no. 17 (Fort Lauderdale, Fla., 1995), 197–203.

The individual ports and havens mentioned in this chapter will recur throughout this book and selected texts will be referred to where appropriate, but two examples of particular interest may be singled out for mention here: Cadiz, for which see M. E. Aubet, *The Phoenicians and the West* (Cambridge, 1993); and Southampton, treated in detail in C. Platt, *Medieval Southampton: The Port and Trading Community, AD 1000–1600* (London, 1973).

Chapter 3. Ships and Sailors

The literature on ships and shipping in the eastern Atlantic is prolific, but the essential standard work is S. McGrail, *Ancient Boats in North-West Europe* (London: 2nd edn. 1998). Two earlier books, B. Greenhill, *The Archaeology of the Boat* (London, 1976) and P. Johnstone, *The Sea-craft in Prehistory* (London, 1980), provide the broader background. Medieval vessels are specifically treated in G. Hutchinson, *Medieval Ships and Shipping* (Leicester, 1994) and I. Friel, *The Good Ship* (London, 1995). Two useful collections of specific papers, given at conferences, are R. Reinders and K. Paul (eds.), *Carvel Construction Technique* (Oxford, 1991) and S. McGrail (ed.), *Maritime Celts, Frisians and Saxons* (London, 1990).

Among the many works providing the broader historical context are J. H. Pryor, *Geography, Technology and War* (Cambridge, 1988), M. Mollat du Jourdin, *Europe and the Sea* (Oxford, 1993), and P. Butel, *The Atlantic* (London, 1999).

Turning now to individual vessels (and being highly selective), the following publications offer an idea of the range of archaeological evidence that is now available covering vessels from the prehistoric to the medieval period: E. Wright, *Ferriby Boats* (London, 1990); M. Millett and S. McGrail, 'The Archaeology of the Hasholme Logboat', *Archaeological Journal*, 144 (1987), 69–155; S. McGrail (ed.), *The Brigg 'Raft' and Her Prehistoric Environment* (Oxford, 1981); S. McGrail, *Logboats of England and Wales* (Oxford, 1978); G. Rosenberg, *Hjortspring fundet* (Copenhagen, 1937); F. Kaul, *Da våbnene tav Hjortspring fundet og dets baggrund* (Copenhagen, 1988); P. Marsden, *Ships of the Port of London: First to Eleventh Centuries AD* (London, 1994); M. Rule and J. Monaghan, *A Gallo-Roman Trading Vessel from Guernsey* (St Peter Port, 1993); V. Fenwick (ed.), *The Graveney Boat* (Oxford, 1978); R. Bruce-Mitford, *Sutton Hoo Ship Burial*, Vol. 1 (London, 1995); O. Olsen and O. Crumlin-Pedersen, *The Skuldelev Ships* (Copenhagen, 1967); O. Crumlin-Pedersen, *Viking-Age Ships and Shipbuilding in Hedeby/Haithabu and Schleswig* (Schleswig and Roskilde, 1997).

The subject of early navigation is thoroughly covered in S. McGrail, *Ancient Boats in North-West Europe* (London: 2nd edn. 1998), ch. 14 (pp. 275–85). Other works providing specific insights are P. C. Fenton, 'The Navigator as Natural Historian', *The Mariner's Mirror*, 79 (1993), 44–57; K. Oatley, 'Mental Maps For Navigation', *New Scientist* (1974), 863–6; and L. E. G. R. Taylor, *Haven-Finding Art* (London, 1971).

The classic example of early sailing directions, *Sailing Directions For the Circumnavigation of England and For a Voyage to the Straits of Gibraltar*, was edited by J. Gairdner and published in *Hakluyt Society*, 79 (1889). Early charts are discussed in P. Whitfield, *The Charting of the Oceans: Ten Centuries of Maritime Maps* (London, 1996), and M. Mollat du Jourdin and M. de la Roncière, *Sea Charts of the Early Explorers 13th–17th centuries* (London, 1984).

One of the most widely quoted accounts of early exploration is Pytheas of Massalia, *On the Ocean*. The text is edited, with commentary, by C. H. Roseman (Chicago, 1994). The poem *Ora Maritima* by Rufus Festus Avienus contains fragments of early accounts and is available in a version edited by J. M. Murphy (Chicago, 1977). For an intricate discussion of one scholar's interpretation of early Atlantic exploration it is difficult to better C. F. C. Hawkes, *Pytheas: Europe and the Greek Explorers* (Oxford, 1977). The explorations of the Phoenicians are carefully considered in D. Harden, *The Phoenicians* (London, 1962). Two comprehensive works charting the activities of later explorers are J. H. Parry, *The Age of Reconnaissance: Discovery, Exploration and Settlement 1450–1650* (London, 1963) and G. J. Marcus, *The Conquest of the North Atlantic* (Woodbridge, 1980).

Finally, for those unused to nautical terms, it is difficult to better Admiral W. H. Smyth's absorbing compilation, *Sailor's Word-Book*, more reassuringly subtitled, *An Alphabetical Digest of Nautical Terms*, first published in 1867 but reprinted more recently (Trowbridge, 1991).

Chapter 4. The Emergence of an Atlantic Identity: 8000–4000 BC

The questions of climate and sea-level readjustments after the last Ice Age are introduced in three general volumes each containing a number of specialist papers: F. H. Thompson (ed.), *Archaeology and Coastal Change* (London, 1980); A. Harding (ed.), *Climatic Change in Later Prehistory* (Edinburgh, 1982); and I. Simmons and M. Tooley (eds.), *The Environment in British Prehistory* (London, 1981). All three volumes have lengthy bibliographies giving access to the specialist literature.

As a general background to this chapter several broad regional surveys provide succinct introductions. Among these the most accessible are: J. Jensen, *The Prehistory of Denmark* (London, 1982); T. Darvill, *Prehistoric Britain* (London, 1987); J. Waddell, *The Prehistoric Archaeology of Ireland* (Galway, 1998); P.-R. Giot, J. L'Helgouac'h, and J.-L. Monnier, *Préhistoire de la Bretagne* (Rennes, 1999); F. Jordá, M. Pellicer Catalán, P. Acosta Martínez, and M. Almagro-Gorbea, *Historia de España Vol. 1 Prehistoria* (Madrid, 1986); and A. Coelho Ferreira da Silva, L. Raposo, and C. Tavares da Silva, *Pré-história de Portugal* (Lisbon, 1993).

For the Mesolithic period, the most accessible short introduction is S. Mithen's chapter in B. Cunliffe (ed.), *Prehistoric Europe* (Oxford, 1998), to which should be added the thoughtful long essay on the subsistence base of the early hunter-gatherers by D. Clarke, *Mesolithic Europe: The Economic Basis* (London, 1978). Two volumes of edited papers provide a rich array of detail: C. Bonsall (ed.), *The Mesolithic in Europe* (Edinburgh, 1989), and P. M. Vermeersch and P. Van Peer (eds.), *Contributions to the Mesolithic in Europe* (Leuven, 1990). Scandinavia is particularly prolific of Mesolithic finds. An overview is provided in J. G. D. Clark, *The Earlier Stone Age Settlements of Scandinavia* (Cambridge, 1975), updated by L. Larsson in 'The Mesolithic of Southern Scandinavia', *Journal of World Prehistory*, 4 (1990), 257–309. Reports on two comparatively recent settlement excavations directly relevant to our theme are to be found in the *Journal of Danish Archaeology*: S. H. Andersen, 'Tybrind Vig', in vol. 4 (1985), 52–69; and S. H. Andersen, 'Ertebølle revisited', in vol. 5 (1986), 31–86. For Britain and Ireland, A. Morrison, *Early Man in Britain and Ireland* (London, 1980), gives much of the background. Two classic Atlantic zone sites are published in monographs: P. Mellars, *Excavations on Oronsay* (Edinburgh, 1987), and P. Woodman, *Excavations at Mount Sandel* (Belfast, 1985). For Iberia see L. Straus, 'Epipaleolithic and Mesolithic adaptations in Cantabrian Spain and Pyrenean France', *Journal of World Prehistory*, 5 (1991), 83–104, and two papers: J. Roche, 'Spatial Organization in the Mesolithic of Muge, Portugal', and J. E. Morais Arnand, 'The Mesolithic Communities of the Sado Valley, Portugal, in their Ecological Setting', both in C. Bonsall (ed.), *The Mesolithic in Europe* (Edinburgh, 1989).

The subject of Mesolithic burial is assessed in G. A. Clark and M. Neeley, 'Social Differentiation in European Mesolithic Burial Data', in P. Rowley-Conwy *et al.* (eds.), *Mesolithic North West Europe: Recent Trends* (Sheffield, 1987). For three of the more informative cemeteries see: E. E. Albrethsen and E. B. Petersen, 'Excavation of a Mesolithic Cemetery at Vedbœk, Denmark', *Acta Archaeologica*, 47 (1976), 1–28; L. Larsson, 'The Skatholm Project—A Late Mesolithic Settlement and Cemetery Complex', *Meddelanden frau Lunds Universitets Historiska Museum* (1983–4), 1–38; R. Schulting, 'Antlers, Bone Pins and Flint Blades: Mesolithic Cemeteries of Brittany', *Antiquity*, 70 (1996), 335–50.

The Early Neolithic period in Europe is most conveniently summarized in A. Whittle, *Neolithic Europe: A Survey* (Cambridge, 1985), and in the same author's chapter 'The First Farmers', in B. Cunliffe (ed.), *Prehistoric Europe* (Oxford, 1998). For Denmark the evidence is reviewed in P. Rowley-Conwy, 'The Origins of Agriculture in Denmark: A Review of Some Theories', *Journal of Danish Archaeology*, 4 (1985), 188–95. In the Netherlands the impact of the first agriculturalists on native hunter-gatherers is considered in detail in L. P. Louwe Kooijmans, 'Understanding the Mesolithic/Neolithic Frontiers in the Lower Rhine Basin, 5300–4300 cal. BC', in M. Edmonds and C. Richards (eds.), *Understanding the Neolithic of North-Western Europe* (Glasgow, 1998), 407–26. The situation in western France is complex. A useful early review is given in a book by C. Scarre (ed.), *Ancient France 6000–2000 BC* (Edinburgh, 1983). Thereafter an intense debate has ensued which may be followed in a succession of five short papers: C. Scarre, 'The Early Neolithic of Western France and Megalithic Origins in Western Europe', *Oxford Journal of Archaeology*, 11 (1992), 121–54; C. Boujot and S. Cassen, 'A Pattern of Evolution for the Neolithic Funerary Structures of the West of France', *Antiquity*, 67 (1993), 477–91; S. Cassen, 'Material Culture and Chronology in the Middle Neolithic of Western France', *Oxford Journal of Archaeology*, 12 (1993), 197–208; M. Patton, 'Neolithisation and Megalithic Origins in North-Western France: A General Interaction Model', *Oxford Journal of Archaeology*, 13 (1994), 279–93; A. Sherratt, 'Instruments of Conversion? The Role of Megaliths in the Mesolithic/ Neolithic Transition in North West Europe', *Oxford Journal of Archaeology*, 14 (1995), 245–60.

The situation in western Iberia is no less complex. Some recent theories are presented in J. Zilhão, 'The Spread of Agro-Pastoral Economy Across Mediterranean Europe: A View From the Far West', *Journal of Mediterranean Archaeology*, 6 (1993), 5–63.

For Britain the problems surrounding the way in which the techniques of food production were introduced to the islands were elegantly summed up in H. Case, 'Neolithic Explanation', *Antiquity*, 43 (1969), 176–86, while the chronology has been considered by E. Williams, 'Dating the Introduction of Food Production into Britain and Ireland', *Antiquity*, 63 (1989), 510–21. The Irish evidence is presented in J. Waddell, *The Prehistoric Archaeology of Ireland* (Galway, 1998), where full references to recent work will be found.

Finally, for a thoughtful view of the importance of the Atlantic seaways and of fishing in this period see G. Clark, 'The Economic Context of Dolmens and Passage Graves in Sweden', in V. Markotic (ed.), *Ancient Europe and the Mediterranean* (London 1977), 35–49.

Chapter 5. Ancestors and Ritual Landscapes: 4000–2700 BC

The essential background to this chapter will be found in A. Whittle, *Neolithic Europe: A Survey* (Cambridge, 1985), R. Bradley, *Rock Art and the Prehistory of Atlantic Europe* (London, 1997), and in the chapters by A. Whittle (ch. 4) and A. Sherratt (ch. 5) in B. Cunliffe (ed.), *Prehistoric Europe* (Oxford, 1998).

The origin and development of megalithic tombs have generated a substantial literature, but much of the early work published before about 1975 is seriously out of date and is quite often misleading. Two useful overviews are provided by a series of regional surveys in C. Renfrew, *The Megalithic Monuments of Western Europe* (London, 1983) and in the general book by J. Briard, *Les Mégalithes de l'Europe atlantique* (Paris, 1995). The results of recent work have been brought together in the papers of an international conference edited by A. A. Rodríguez Casal, *O Neolítico Atlántico e as Orixes do Megalitismo* (Santiago de Compostella, 1997). Three short discussion papers which have had a significant effect on recent thought are: C. Renfrew, 'Megaliths, Territories and Populations', in S. de Laet (ed.), *Acculturation and Continuity in Atlantic Europe* (Bruges, 1976), 198–220; I. Kinnes, 'Megaliths in Action: Some aspects of the Neolithic Period in the Channel Islands', *Archaeological Journal*, 145 (1988), 13–59; A. Sherratt, 'The Genesis of Megaliths: Monumentality, Ethnicity and Social Complexity in Neolithic North-West Europe', *World Archaeology*, 22 (1990), 147–67.

The megaliths of Armorica are well known and much visited. A useful overview of Armorican and west French megaliths is to be found in C. Scarre, *Ancient France 6000–2000 BC* (Edinburgh, 1983), while the monuments of Brittany have been treated in detail in M. Patton, *Statements in Stone: Monument and Society in Neolithic Brittany* (London, 1993). To this should be added the papers dealing with the Breton Neolithic listed for the last chapter. Among the many guidebooks written on the subject, G. Bailloud, C. Boujot, S. Cassen, and C.-T. Le Roux, *Carnac. Les premières architectures de pierre* (Paris, 1995) and J. Briard and N. Fediaevsky, *Mégalithes de Bretagne* (Rennes, 1992) are to be recommended, not least for the quality of their illustrations.

The megaliths of Ireland have been extensively surveyed and published in detailed monographs, but a very convenient overview is offered in J. Waddell, *The Prehistoric Archaeology of Ireland* (Galway, 1998). Two of the most famous sites have been treated in well-illustrated books: M. O'Kelly, *Newgrange* (London, 1982) and G. Eogan, *Knowth and the Passage-Tombs of Ireland* (London, 1986). Among the many general discussions the following are of particular interest: A. Sheridan, 'Megaliths and Megalomania: An Account and Interpretation of the Development of Passage Tombs in Ireland', *Journal of Irish Archaeology*, 3 (1986), 17–30; A. ApSimon, 'Chronological Contexts for Irish Megalithic Tombs', *Journal of Irish Archaeology*, 3 (1986), 5–15; G. Eogan, 'Irish Megalithic Tombs and Iberia: Comparisons and Contrasts', *Problem der Megalithgräberforschung* (Madrid, 1990), 13–37.

North and west Britain is well endowed with megaliths and the Scottish tombs have been subject to systematic survey. A useful general work, resulting from a symposium, brings together several regional overviews: T. Powell (ed.), *Megalithic Enquiries in the West of Britain* (Liverpool, 1969), while the spectacular monuments of Orkney are fully treated in C. Renfrew, *Investigations in Orkney* (London, 1979). Well-illustrated general surveys of megalithic stone rings and alignments will be found in A. Burl, *Rings of Stone* (London, 1979) and the same author's *From Carnac to Callanish* (Yale, 1993).

The Iberian megaliths have been surveyed and published in a series of magisterial tomes of which V. Leisner, *Die Megalithgräber der Iberischen Halbinsel: Der Westen* (Berlin, 1965) is of most relevance. Among the general papers discussing broad themes may be listed F. Criado Boado and R. Fabregas Valcarce, 'Megalithic Phenomenon of North West Spain', *Antiquity*, 63 (1989), 682–96. There are also a number of regional papers relevant to western Iberia in A. A. Rodríguez Casal (ed.), *O Neolítico Atlántico*, quoted above.

Under the heading of shared beliefs comes the popular but difficult subject of 'megalithic astronomy' which has generated much literature, not all of which can be said to be firmly founded on fact. Fortunately the theme has been thoroughly reconsidered in a critical overview in C. Ruggles, *Astronomy in Prehistoric Britain and Ireland* (Yale, 1999). For the subject of megalithic art see E. Twohig, *The Megalithic Art of Western Europe* (Oxford, 1981) and J. L'Helgouac'h, C.-T. Le Roux, and J. Lecornec (eds.), *Art et symboles du mégalithisme européen* (Rennes, 1997).

The exchange systems which developed in the fourth and third millennia are made most visually manifest in the distribution of stone axes—a subject which has attracted many enthusiasts. There are two volumes of papers edited by T. H. McKClough and W. A. Cummings, *Stone Axe Studies 1* (London, 1979) and *Stone Axe Studies 2* (London, 1988). Among those presented, C.-T. Le Roux, 'Stone Axes of Brittany and the Marches' (in vol. 1, 49–56) is of particular importance to our theme. So too is M. Patton, 'Stone Axes of the Channel Islands: Neolithic Exchange in an Insular Context', *Oxford Journal of Archaeology*, 10 (1991), 33–44.

Chapter 6. Expanding Networks and the Rise of the Individual: 2700–1200 BC

This chapter spans a period of rapid change, the general nature of which is perhaps best grasped by reading chapters 5–8 (by A. Sherratt, K. Wardle, and M. Popham) in B. Cunliffe (ed.), *Prehistoric Europe* (Oxford, 1998). Armed with this perspective the reader is prepared for the detail to follow!

The Beaker phenomenon is difficult even for specialists to understand. R. Harrison, *The Beaker Folk* (London, 1980), offers a balanced introduction to the subject and was developed from the more detailed research published by the same author in *The Bell Beaker Culture of Spain and Portugal* (Harvard, 1977). An updating in the light of new evidence is given in R. Harrison, 'Bell Beakers in Spain and Portugal', *Antiquity*, 62 (1988), 464–71. A rather different perspective is provided by J. Lanting and J. Van der Waals, 'Beaker Culture Relations in the Lower Rhine Basin', *Glockenbeckersymposion* (1976), 1–80. For British Beakers the classic work is D. L. Clarke, *Beaker Pottery of Great Britain and Ireland*, 2 vols. (Cambridge, 1970). A new approach has been pioneered in H. Case, 'Beakers: Deconstruction and After', *Proceedings of the Prehistoric Society*, 59 (1993), 241–68.

The metal resources of the Atlantic zone are discussed in J. Briard, *Les Depôts bretons et l'âge du Bronze Atlantique* (Rennes, 1965); W. O'Brian, *Mount Gabriel: Bronze Age Mining in Ireland* (Galway, 1994), and the same author's 'Ross Island and the Origins of Irish-British Metallurgy', in J. Waddell and E. Twohig (eds.), *Ireland in the Bronze Age* (Dublin, 1995). To these should be added three papers in M. Ryan (ed.), *The Origins of Metallurgy in Atlantic Europe: Proceedings of the Fifth Atlantic Colloquium* (Dublin, 1979), J. Jackson, 'Metallic Ores in Irish Prehistory: Copper and Tin' (107–25); A. Hartmann, 'Irish and British Gold Types and their West European Counterparts' (215–28); and C. Shell, 'The Early Exploitation of Tin Deposits in South West England' (251–63).

Turning to the archaeology of the different regions: the Atlantic zone of the Iberian Peninsula is treated in several works by R. Harrison, including 'A Reconsideration of the Iberian Background to Beaker Metallurgy', *Palaeohistoria*, 16 (1974), 63–104, *The Bell Beaker Culture of Spain and Portugal* (Harvard, 1977), and 'Ireland and Spain in the Early Bronze Age', *Journal of the Royal Society of Antiquaries of Ireland*, 104 (1974), 52–73.

For Brittany the following will be helpful: S. Cassen and C. Boujot, 'A Pattern of Evolution for the Neolithic Funerary Structures of the West of France', *Antiquity*, 67 (1993), 477–91; A. Sherratt, 'Points of Exchange: The Later Neolithic Monuments of the Morbihan', in A. Gibson and D. Simpson (eds.), *Prehistoric Ritual and Religion* (Gloucester, 1998), 119–38; J. Briard, *Les Depôts bretons et l'âge du Bronze Atlantique* (Rennes, 1965); and the same author's 'Relations Between Brittany and Great Britain during the Bronze Age', in C. Scarre and F. Healey (eds.), *Trade and Exchange in Prehistoric Europe* (Oxford, 1994), 183–90.

Ireland is treated in detail by J. Waddell in *The Prehistoric Archaeology of Ireland* (Galway, 1998) and in the same author's 'The Irish Sea in Prehistory', *Journal of Irish Archaeology*, 6 (1992), 29–40, while the problem of the Beaker period in Ireland is considered by H. Case in 'Irish Beakers in their European Context', in J. Waddell and E. Twohig (eds.), *Ireland in the Bronze Age* (Dublin, 1995), 14–29.

The emergence of elites in the Bronze Age of the Atlantic zone was presented in a classic paper by S. Piggott, 'The Early Bronze Age in Wessex', *Proceedings of the Prehistoric Society*, 4 (1938), 52–106, which though, inevitably, out of date is a seminal account. A more up-to-date discussion of elite burial in Britain, Ireland, Brittany, and the Netherlands is provided in a beautifully illustrated catalogue by P. Clarke, T. Cowie, and A. Foxton, *Symbols of Power* (Edinburgh, 1985). This volume focuses on the wide range of exotic materials that were accessible to the elites through trade networks. Specialist studies of individual materials include: J. Stone and L. Thomas, 'The Use and Distribution of Faience in the Ancient East and Prehistoric Europe', *Proceedings of the Prehistoric Society*, 22 (1956), 37–84; J. Taylor, *Bronze Age Goldwork of the British Isles* (Cambridge, 1980); G. Eogan, *The Accomplished Art: Gold and Gold-working in Britain and Ireland During the Bronze Age* (Oxford, 1994); R. Harrison and A. Gilman, 'Trade in the Second and Third Millennia BC between the Maghreb and Iberia', in V. Markotic (ed.), *Ancient Europe and the Mediterranean* (London, 1977), 91–104; and F. H. Forestier, B. Lasnier, and J. L'Helgouac'h, 'A propos de la "Callaïs" ', *Bulletin de la Sociéte Prehistorique Française*, 70 (1973), 173–80.

Chapter 7. Sailors on the Two Oceans: 1200–200 BC

The general background to European prehistory for this period is summarized in two chapters: K. Wardle, 'The Palace Civilization of Minoan Crete and Mycenaean Greece 2000–1200 BC', and A. Sherratt, 'The Emergence of Elites: Earlier Bronze Age Europe, 2500–1300 BC', in B. Cunliffe (ed.), *Prehistoric Europe* (Oxford, 1998). N. Sandars, *The Sea Peoples* (London, 1978) and A. Harding, *The Mycenaeans and Europe* (London, 1984) offer detailed discussion of the dramatic social and economic changes affecting the Aegean in the second half of the second millennium BC.

Greek colonization is thoroughly covered in J. Boardman, *The Greeks Overseas* (London: revised edn. 1980) and by several important papers in G. Tsetskhladze and F. De Angelis, *The Archaeology of Greek Colonization* (Oxford, 1994). The Phoenicians are given full treatment in D. Harden, *The Phoenicians* (London, 1982) and the elaborately illustrated catalogue and discussion by S. Moscati (ed.), *The Phoenicians* (Milan, 1988). For an up-to-date archaeological treatment of the west Mediterranean see M. Aubet, *The Phoenicians and the West* (Cambridge, 1993).

M. Aubet's book presents in some detail the Phoenician settlements in Iberia. The focal importance of Iberia is further brought out by various papers in B. Cunliffe and S. Keay (eds.), *Social Complexity and the Development of Towns in Iberia* (London, 1995), in particular H. Niemeyer, 'Phoenician Toscanos as a Settlement Model' (67–88), M. Aubet, 'From Trading Post to Town in the Phoenician-Punic World' (47–66), and B. Shefton, 'Greek Imports at the Extremities of the Mediterranean West and East: Reflections on the Case of Iberia in the Fifth Century BC' (127–56). A general overview of the complex systems at work in southern Iberia is given by B. Cunliffe in 'Core-Periphery Relationships: Iberia and the Mediterranean', in P. Bild, T. Engberg-Pedersen, L. Hannestad, J. Zahle, and K.

Randsborg (eds.), *Centre and Periphery in the Hellenistic World* (Aarhus, 1993), 53–85.

The Late Bronze Age trading networks of the Atlantic are the subject of a copious literature, but there is no single overview. Two works, however, are comprehensive, P. Brun, 'Le Bronze Atlantique et ses subdivisions culturelles: essai de definition', in C. Chevillot and A. Coffyn (eds.), *L'Age du Bronze Atlantique* (Beynac, 1991), 11–24, and C. Burgess, 'The East and the West: Mediterranean Influence in the Atlantic World in the Later Bronze Age *c.*1500–700 BC', in the same volume, 25–45. Among the more recent papers of importance are M. Ruiz-Gálvez Priego, 'El occidente de la Peninsula Iberica, Punto de encuentro entre el Mediterraneo y el Atlantico a fines de la Edad del Bronze', *Complutum*, 4 (1993), 41–68; A. Mederos Martín, 'Cambio de rumbo. Interacción comercial entre el Bronce final Atlántico Ibérico y Micénico en el Mediterráneo Central (1425–1050 A.C.)', *Trabajos de Prehistoria*, 54 (1997), 113–34; and the same author's 'La conexión Levantino-Chipriota. Indicios de comercio Atlántico con el Mediterráneo Oriental durante el Bronze final (1150–950 AC)', *Trabajos de Prehistoria*, 53 (1996), 95–115.

The nature of Atlantic society in Iberia is explored in A. Mederos Martín and R. J. Harrison, 'Patronazgo y clientela. Honor, querra y festines en las relaciones sociales de dependencia del Bronce final Atlántico en la Península Ibérica', *Pyrenae*, 27 (1996), 31–52. Items of the feast are discussed in G. Delibes de Castro, J. Fernández Manzano, and J. Celis Sánchez, 'Nuevos "gauchos de carne" Protohistóricos de la Península Ibérica', *Tabona*, 2 (1993), 417–33, and S. Gerloff, 'Bronze Age Class A Cauldrons: Typology, Origins and Chronology', *Journal of the Royal Society of Antiquaries of Ireland*, 116 (1986), 84–115.

J. Briard, in his *Les Depôts bretons et l'âge du Bronze Atlantique* (Rennes, 1965), gives a full account of the Armorican finds in their broader context. Maritime contacts between Britain, Ireland, and the Continent in the Bronze Age are assessed in K. Muckleroy, 'Middle Bronze Age Trade Between Britain and Europe: A Maritime Perspective', *Proceedings of the Prehistoric Society*, 47 (1981), 275–98; M. Almagro-Gorbea, 'Ireland and Spain in the Bronze Age', in J. Waddell and E. Twohig (eds.), *Ireland in the Bronze Age* (Dublin, 1995), 136–48; and G. Eogan, 'Ideas, People and Things: Ireland and the External World During the Late Bronze Age', in the same volume, pp. 128–35.

The vexed question of the Celts is considered in broad outline in B. Cunliffe, *The Ancient Celts* (Oxford, 1997) and for the Atlantic region in more detail by J. Waddell, 'Celts, Celticisation and the Bronze Age', in J. Waddell and E. Twohig (eds.), *Ireland in the Bronze Age* (Dublin, 1995), 158–69, and S. James, *The Atlantic Celts* (London, 1999). P. Sims-Williams, 'Celtomania and Celtoscepticism', *Cambrian Medieval Celtic Studies*, 36 (1998), 1–35, provides wisdom and balance to the debate.

Phoenician exploration of the Atlantic coasts of Iberia and Africa is discussed in: R. Lorris, 'Les Conditions de la navigation sur la côte atlantique de l'Afrique dans l'Antiquité', *Afrique Noire et Monde Méditerranée* (1976), 146–70; M. Aubet, 'El comercio en Occidente: balance y perspectivas', *I Fenici ieoc oggé domani, Richerce Scoperte progetti* (Rome, 1995), 227–43; F. Villard, 'Céramique Grecque du Maroc', *Bull. d'Archéol. Marocaine*, 4 (1960), 2–26; A. Luquet, 'Contribution à l'Atlas Archéologique du Maroc. Le Maroc Punique', *Bull. d'Archéol. Marocaine*, 9 (1975), 238–306; and A. Jodin, *Mogador Comptoir phénicien du Maroc Atlantique* (Rabat, 1966).

The quest for tin in the ancient world has been a favourite topic of study. One of the earliest studies, still very useful, is M. Cary, 'The Greeks and Ancient Trade With the Atlantic', *Journal of Hellenic Studies*, 44 (1924), 166–79. Two other important contributions are C. Hawkes, *Pytheas: Europe and the Greek Explorers* (Oxford, 1977) and R. Penhallurick, 'The Evidence for Prehistoric Mining in Cornwall', in P. Budd and D. Gale (eds.), *Prehistoric Extractive Metallurgy in Cornwall* (Truro, 1997), 23–33.

Chapter 8. Restating Identity: 1200–200 BC

The elite societies of west central Europe, whose floruit lay in the period 550 to 400 BC, were first given emphasis by a seminal paper by S. Frankenstein and M. Rowlands entitled 'The Internal Structure and Regional Context of Early Iron Age Society in South-Western Germany', *Bulletin of the Institute of Archaeology, London*, 15 (1978), 73–112. The theme was taken up and further explored in P. Wells, *Culture Contact and Culture Change* (Cambridge, 1980) and J.-P. Mohen, A.

Duval, and C. Eluère (eds.), *Les Princes Celtes et la Mediterranée* (Paris, 1988). The two best-known of the elite burials have been treated fully in R. Joffroy, *Vix et ses trésors* (Paris, 1979) and J. Biel, *Der Keltenfürst von Hochdorf* (Stuttgart, 1985). The question of the Celtic migrations which came at the end of this period is presented in H. Rankin, *Celts and the Classical World* (London, 1987) and B. Cunliffe, *The Ancient Celts* (Oxford, 1997).

For Iberia the impact of Greek exchange systems is considered in various papers brought together in B. Cunliffe and S. Keay (eds.), *Social Complexity and the Development of Towns in Iberia* (London, 1995), and is discussed in A. Domínguez, 'New Perspectives on the Greek Presence in the Iberian Peninsula', in J. Fossey (ed.), *Proceedings of the First International Congress on the Hellenic Diaspora*. Vol. 1. *From Antiquity to 1453* (Amsterdam, 1991), 109–61, and A. Cabrera, 'Greek Trade in Iberia: The Extent of Interaction', *Oxford Journal of Archaeology*, 17 (1998), 191–206. The Celtiberians have been thoroughly presented in two monographs, A. Lorrio, *Los Celtíberios* (Alicante, 1997) and F. Burillo Mozota, *Los Celtíberios* (Barcelona, 1998).

Long-distance trade and exchange between Continental Europe and the Atlantic zone is discussed in B. Cunliffe, *Greeks, Romans and Barbarians: Spheres of Interaction* (London 1988), esp. Ch. 3, and Y. Roman, *De Narbonne à Bordeaux. Un axe économique au Ier siècle avant J-C* (Lyons, 1983). The influence of La Tène metalwork on Breton pottery has been fully analysed in F. Schwappach, 'Stempelverzierte Keramik von Armorica', *Fundberichte aus Hessen, Beiheft 1* (1969), 213–87. For a background to the development of La Tène art see R. and V. Megaw, *Celtic Art* (London, 1989). Evidence for the elite enclave in the Bourges region is outlined in J. Gran-Aymerich, 'Les Importations etrusques au coeur de la Gaule: Le site princier de Bourges et les nouvelles decouvertes à Lyon et Bragny-sur-Saône', in J. Swaddling, S. Walker, and P. Roberts (eds.), *Italy in Europe: Economic Relations 700 BC–AD 50* (London, 1995). For Hallstatt and other imports to Britain and Ireland see B. Cunliffe, *Iron Age Communities in Britain* (London: 3rd edn. 1991), ch. 16, and J. Waddell, *The Prehistoric Archaeology of Ireland* (Galway, 1998), ch. 8.

The development of settlement in northern Portugal and Galicia is treated in A. Ferreira da Silva, 'Portuguese Castros: The Evolution of the Habitat and the Proto Urbanization Process', in B. Cunliffe and S. Keay (eds.), *Social Complexity and the Development of Towns in Iberia* (London, 1995), 263–90, and in far more detail in the same author's *A Cultura Castreja no noroeste de Portugal* (Paços de Ferreira, 1986), while the evidence for maritime trade is presented in J. Naveiro Lopez, *El Comercio antiguo en el N.W. Peninsular* (Coruña, 1991).

The most convenient summary of the later prehistory of the Armorican peninsula is P.-R. Giot, J. Briard, and L. Pape, *Protohistoire de la Bretagne* (Rennes: 2nd edn. 1995). The remarkable decorated stone stelae are given a full treatment in M.-Y. Daire and A. Villard, 'Les Stèles de l'Age de Fer à décors géométriques et curvilignes. État de la question dans l'Ouest armoricain', *Revue Archéologique de l'Ouest*, 13 (1996), 123–56.

The Iron Age communities of the west of Britain are summarized in B. Cunliffe, *Iron Age Communities in Britain* (London: 3rd edn. 1991). Regional surveys include: N. Johnston and P. Rose, 'Defended Settlement in Cornwall—An Illustrated Discussion', in D. Miles (ed.), *The Romano-British Countryside* (Oxford, 1982), 151–207; I. Armit (ed.), *Beyond the Brochs* (Edinburgh, 1990); K. Edwards and I. Ralston (eds.), *Scotland: Environment and Archaeology: 8000 BC–AD 1000* (Chichester, 1997), ch. 10; J. Ritchie, *Brochs of Scotland* (Princes Risborough, 1988); J. Waddell, *The Prehistoric Archaeology of Ireland* (Galway, 1998), chs. 7 and 8. For two important Irish fieldwork programmes see: C. Cotter, 'Western Stone Fort Project', *Discovery Programme Reports*, 4 (1994), 1–14, and E. Grogan, 'North Munster Programme', in the same volume, pp. 26–72. The question of chevaux-de-frise is discussed in its broader European context in P. Harbison, 'Wooden and Stone Chevaux-de-frise in Central and Western Europe', *Proceedings of the Prehistoric Society*, 37 (1971), 195–225.

Chapter 9. The Impact of Rome: 200 BC–AD 200

General books on the Roman world are many and need no specific introduction. For individual countries the following will be found particularly helpful: J. Alarcão, *Portugal Romano* (Lisbon, 1974); S. Keay, *Roman Spain* (London, 1988); L. Curchin, *Roman Spain: Conquest and Assimilation* (London, 1991); J. Drinkwater, *Roman Gaul* (London, 1983); A. King, *Roman Gaul and Germany* (London, 1990); S. S. Frere, *Britannia* (London: 3rd edn. 1980); P. Salway, *The Oxford Illustrated History of Roman Britain* (Oxford, 1993).

The mineral wealth of western Iberia is discussed in B. Jones, 'The Roman Mines at Río Tintó', *Journal of Roman Studies*, 70 (1980), 146–65; D. Bird, 'The Roman Gold Mines of North-West Spain', *Bonner Jahrbucher*, 172 (1972), 36–64; and B. Jones and D. Bird, 'Roman Gold-Mining of North-West Spain II: The Workings on the Río Duerna', *Journal of Roman Studies*, 62 (1972), 59–74. The process of romanization in south-western Iberia is outlined by J. Edmondson in 'Romanization and Urban Development in Lusitania', in T. Blagg and M. Millett (eds.), *The Early Roman Empire in the West* (Oxford, 1990), 151–78.

The themes of trade and the early romanization of Gaul have generated a considerable literature. B. Cunliffe, *Greeks, Romans and Barbarians: Spheres of Interaction* (London, 1988) provides a general overview. More specific and detailed is C. Goudineau, *Regard sur la Gaule* (Paris, 1998), while the south is treated historically in C. Ebel, *Transalpine Gaul: The Emergence of a Roman Province* (Leiden, 1976). The Roman wine trade is fully discussed in Y. Roman, *De Narbonne à Bordeaux. Un axe économique au Ier siècle avant J-C* (Lyons, 1983), and A. Tchernia, 'Italian Wine in Gaul at the End of the Republic', in P. Garnsey, K. Hopkins, and C. Whittaker (eds.), *Trade and the Ancient Economy* (London, 1983), 87–104. The place of Brittany in the maritime systems has been examined by P. Galliou in *L'Armorique romaine* (Braspars, 1983), esp. ch. 7 dealing with maritime resources. The evidence for maritime trade and exchange between Brittany and Britain is presented in outline in B. Cunliffe, 'Britain, the Veneti and Beyond', *Oxford Journal of Archaeology*, 1 (1982), 39–68, and in more detail by the same author in *Hengistbury Head, Dorset. Volume 1: The Prehistoric and Roman Settlement 3500 BC–AD 500* (Oxford, 1987).

The significance of the British fleet (the *classis Britannica*) is discussed by H. Cleere in 'The Classis Britannica', in V. Maxfield (ed.), *The Saxon Shore: A Handbook* (Exeter, 1989), 18–22. Commercial shipping is the subject of several papers in two conference proceedings: J. du Plat Taylor and H. Cleere (eds.), *Roman Shipping and Trade: Britain and the Rhine Provinces* (London, 1978); and S. McGrail (ed.), *Maritime Celts, Frisians and Saxons* (London, 1990). The maritime relationship between Britain and Ireland in the Roman period is summarized in B. Raftery, *Pagan Celtic Ireland* (London, 1994).

Chapter 10. Migrants and Settlers in the Early Middle Ages: AD 200–800

There are a number of excellent general studies covering the history of this crucial six hundred years. For the earlier part, M. Todd, *The Northern Barbarians* (Oxford: 2nd edn. 1987), E. Thompson, *Romans and Barbarians* (Madison, 1982), and W. Goffort, *Barbarians and Romans, AD 418–584: The Techniques of Accommodation* (Princeton, 1980), all chart the period of crisis which gripped the Roman world and the rapid ethnic and social readjustments that followed from it. J. Wallace-Hadrill, *The Barbarian West 400–1000* (Oxford: revised edn. 1996) remains the classic short study of Europe in the early Middle Ages, while R. Hodges, *Dark Age Economics: The Origins of Towns and Trade AD 600–1000* (London, 1982), as its title suggests, adds an important economic dimension relying heavily on archaeological evidence. K. Randsborg, *The First Millennium AD in Europe and the Mediterranean* (Cambridge, 1991) provides a magisterial overview of modest length with an excellent bibliography.

Turning now more specifically to the Atlantic provinces, the sea began to play an increasingly important role in the latter part of the Roman period. The Channel defences and the fortifications of the 'Saxon Shore' are well summarized in S. Johnson, *The Roman Forts of the Saxon Shore* (London, 1976) and V. Maxfield (ed.), *The Saxon Shore: A Handbook* (Exeter, 1989), which provides an up-to-date assessment of the archaeology of the various coastal installations. The background history of the part which the sea played in the history of Britain in the late third century is outlined in N. Shiel, *The Episode of Carausius and Allectus* (Oxford, 1977), while the fascinating episode of the Gallic empire is fully explored in J. Drinkwater, *The Gallic Empire: Separatism and Continuity in the North-Western Provinces of the Roman Empire AD 260–274* (Stuttgart, 1987). The commercial aspects of later Roman maritime activity are reflected in shipwrecks from London, reported in P. Marsden, *Ships of the Port of London: First to Eleventh Centuries AD* (London, 1994), the wreck from St Peter Port, Guernsey, described in M. Rule and J. Monaghan, *A Gallo-Roman Trading Vessel from Guernsey* (St Peter Port, 1993), and the Sept Îles wreck off the north coast of Brittany, in M. L'Hour, 'Un site sous-marin sur la côte de l'Armorique. L'épave antique de Ploumanac'h', *Revue Archéologique de l'Ouest*, 4 (1987), 113–32.

The folk wanderings which impacted upon the Atlantic territories are well covered in volumes dealing with individual peoples: J. Campbell (ed.), *The Anglo-Saxons* (London, 1982); E. James, *The Franks* (Oxford, 1988), and E. Thompson, *The Goths in Spain* (Oxford, 1969). For the tribes surrounding the Irish Sea, see I. Henderson, *The Picts* (London, 1967); F. Wainwright, 'Picts and Scots', in F. Wainwright (ed.), *The Northern Isles* (London, 1962), 91–116; L. Alcock, *The Neighbours of the Picts: Angles, Britons and Scots at War and at Home* (Rosemarkie, 1993); E. Cowan, 'Myth and Identity in Early Medieval Scotland', *Scottish Historical Review*, 63 (1984), 111–35; M. Dillon and N. Chadwick, *The Celtic Realms* (London, 1967); W. Davies, *Wales in the Early Middle Ages* (Leicester, 1982); H. Mytum, *The Origins of Early Christian Ireland* (London, 1992); D. O'Corráin, *Ireland Before the Normans* (Dublin, 1972). The subject of the early Bretons has generated a considerable literature. Most accessible are N. Chadwick, *Early Brittany* (Cardiff, 1969); L. Fleuriot, *Les Origines de la Bretagne* (Paris, 1982); A. Chédeville and H. Guillotel, *La Bretagne des saints et des rois Ve–Xe siècle* (Rennes, 1984). In P. Galliou and M. Jones, *The Bretons* (Oxford, 1991), the migration period is put into its broader historical conquest. A convenient short introduction to the Breton language is offered by F. Broudic, *Histoire de la langue bretonne* (Rennes, 1999).

The new order which begins to emerge in Europe in the sixth and seventh centuries is referred to in many of the works cited above. To these should be added R. Collins, *Charlemagne* (London, 1998), and W. Watt and P. Cachia, *A History of Islamic Spain* (Edinburgh, 1965).

The Celtic Church and the art created to serve it are conveniently approached through M. and L. de Paor, *Early Christian Ireland* (London, 1958). Some recent debates of a more specialist nature have been brought together in M. Ryan (ed.), *Ireland and Insular Art AD 500–1200* (Dublin, 1987). The masterpieces of Irish early Christian art are brilliantly illustrated in M. Ryan (ed.), *Treasures of Ireland: Irish Art 3000 BC–1500 AD* (Dublin, 1983), accompanied by short discussion chapters. The wanderings of the early monks are thoroughly examined in E. Bowen, *Saints, Seaways and Settlements* (Cardiff, 1977), while the evidence of commerce along the seaways is laid out in J. Wooding, *Communication and Commerce along the Western Sea Lanes AD 400–800* (Oxford, 1996).

Chapter 11. The Coming of the Northmen

The subject of the Vikings has enjoyed a wide popularity and in consequence the literature, both general and detailed, is considerable. Among the best comprehensive accounts are: G. Jones, *A History of The Vikings* (Oxford: 2nd edn. 1984); P. Foote and D. Wilson, *The Viking Achievement* (London: 2nd edn. 1980); J. Graham-Campbell, *The Viking World* (London: 2nd edn. 1989); and P. Sawyer (ed.), *The Oxford Illustrated History of the Vikings* (Oxford, 1997).

The growth of trade in the North Sea region is put into its broad context in G. Duby, *The Early Growth of the European Economy*, trans. H. Clarke (London, 1974). I. Wood, in *The Merovingian Kingdoms 450–757* (London, 1994), considers the earliest medieval trading centres, while the story is taken further in H. Clarke and B. Ambrosiani, *Towns in the Viking Age* (Leicester, 1991). R. Hodges, in *Dark Age Economics* (London, 1982), provides useful summaries of the major trading centres and introduces the archaeology and theory of early medieval exchange systems.

Maritime technology and the art of Viking sailing are well served in a number of books. For Norwegian vessels see A. Brøgger and H. Shetelig, *The Viking Ships: Their Ancestry and Evolution* (Oslo, 1951), and for Danish ships: O. Olsen and O. Crumlin-Pedersen, 'The Skuldelev Ships', *Acta Archaeologica*, 38 (1968), and O. Crumlin-Pedersen, *Viking-Age Ships and Shipbuilding in Hedeby/Haithabu and Schleswig* (Schleswig and Roskilde, 1997).

Viking settlement in Scotland and the Northern and Western Isles is outlined with ample good illustrations in A. Ritchie, *Viking Scotland* (London, 1993). B. Crawford in *Scandinavian Scotland* (Leicester, 1987) gives a more detailed account. The story of the Viking settlement of the northern Atlantic is told in G. J. Marcus, *The Conquest of the North Atlantic* (Woodbridge, 1980). G. Jones in *The Norse Atlantic Saga* (Oxford: 2nd edn. 1986) gives full weight to the Icelandic texts, of which *The Book of Settlements: Landnámabók* is translated by H. Pálsson and P. Edwards (Winnipeg, 1972). Papers from the Eleventh Viking Congress, edited by C. Batey, J. Jesch, and C. Morris as *The Viking Age in Caithness, Orkney and the North Atlantic* (Edinburgh, 1993), reflect much new research.

Viking activity in Ireland is summed up, within the broad compass of early Irish history, in D. O'Corráin, *Ireland Before the Normans* (Dublin, 1972). Other important works include H. Clarke (ed.), *Medieval Dublin: The Making of a Metropolis* (Dublin, 1990); E. Rynne (ed.), *North Munster Studies* (Limerick, 1967); and P. Holm, 'The Slave Trade of Dublin: Ninth to Twelfth Centuries', *Peritia*, 6 (1986), 317–45. For Wales the most convenient account is in W. Davies, *Wales in the Early Middle Ages* (Leicester, 1982). Viking raiding in Brittany is fully chronicled in N. Price, *The Vikings in Brittany* (London, 1989).

Chapter 12. New Centres, New Peripheries: AD 1000–1500

There are several good general discussions of maritime routes and sailing in the medieval period, among which the following contain much that is relevant to this chapter: M. Mollat du Jourdin, *Europe and the Sea* (Oxford, 1993); J. H. Pryor, *Geography, Technology and War* (Cambridge, 1998), and R. Unger, *The Ship in the Medieval Economy 600–1600* (London, 1980). The papers given at an international conference on Atlantic maritime trade were edited by M. Mollat du Jourdin under the title *Les Routes de l'Atlantique: Traveau du neuvième colloque international d'histoire maritime* (Paris, 1969).

The development of maritime commerce between the Mediterranean and the Atlantic is comprehensively treated in F. Fernandez-Armesto, *Before Colombus: Exploration and Colonisation from the Mediterranean to the Atlantic, 1229–1492* (Basingstoke, 1987) and J. Phillips, *The Medieval Expansion of Europe* (Oxford, 1988), and in more specific detail in R. Lopez, 'Majorcans and Genoese on the North Sea Route in the 13th Century', *Revue Belge de Philologie et d'Histoire*, 29 (1951), 1163–79; E. Byrne, *Genoese Shipping in the Twelfth and Thirteenth Centuries* (Cambridge, Mass., 1930); and R. Lopez, 'Market Expansion: The Case of Genoa', *Journal of Economic History*, 24 (1964), 445–64.

Maritime trade along the Atlantic façade has been the subject of a considerable literature, much of it in specialist journals. One collection of papers, introducing many themes, is brought together in E. Carus-Wilson, *Medieval Merchant Venturers* (London, 1954). For Spanish trade, W. Childs, *Anglo-Castilian Trade in the Later Middle Ages* (Manchester, 1978); for Portugal, B. Diffre, *Prelude to Empire: Portugal Overseas Before Henry the Navigator* (Lincoln, Nebr., 1960); and W. Childs, 'Anglo-Portuguese Relations in the Fourteenth Century' in J. L. Gillespie (ed.), *The Age of Richard II* (Stroud, 1997), 27–49; and the same author's 'Anglo-Portuguese Trade in the Fifteenth Century', *Transactions of the Royal Historical Society*, 6th Series, 2 (1992), 195–219. Trade from the Muslim west is well covered in O. Constable's *Trade and Traders in Muslim Spain* (Cambridge, 1994). For Bordeaux, M. James, *Studies in the Medieval Wine Trade* (Oxford, 1971) and J. Bernard, *Navires et gens de mer à Bordeaux vers 1400* (vol. 1) and *vers 1550* (vol. 2) (Paris, 1968); for north-western France, M. Mollat, *Le Commerce maritime normande à la fin du moyen âge* (Paris, 1952) and H. Touchard, *Le Commerce maritime breton à la fin du moyen âge* (Paris, 1967). Ireland is treated in T. O'Neill, *Merchants and Mariners in Medieval Ireland* (Dublin, 1987). Icelandic trade is well covered in: G. Marcus, *The Conquest of the North Atlantic* (Woodbridge, 1980); E. Carus-Wilson, 'The Iceland Venture', repr. in E. Carus-Wilson (ed.), *Medieval Merchant Venturers* (London, 1954), 98–142; and W. Childs, 'England's Icelandic Trade in the Fifteenth Century: The Role of the Port of Hull', *Northern Seas, Yearbook 1995* (Esbjerg, 1995), 11–31.

The role of the Atlantic in the creation of European maritime empires is well covered in P. Butel, *The Atlantic* (London, 1999), J. H. Parry, *The Age of Reconnaissance* (London, 1963), and S. McGrail, 'Columbus' Trans-Atlantic voyages in 1492/3', *Medieval History*, 2 (1992), 76–91.

The importance of salt in the Middle Ages is treated in A. R. Bridbury, *England and the Salt Trade in the Later Middle Ages* (Oxford, 1955), while the context for the pilgrim 'trade' is given in J. Sumption, *Pilgrimage: An Image of Medieval Religion* (London, 1975). For the political context for trade, see J. D. Fudge, *Cargoes, Embargoes and Emissaries* (Toronto, 1995).

Illustration Sources

The author and publishers wish to thank the following for their kind permission to reproduce the illustrations;

P. ii and Chapter openings: The British Library / 568 h.1

1.1 From J.O. Thomson, *History of Ancient Geography* (Cambridge, 1948), fig. 11
1.2 From J.O. Thomson, *History of Ancient Geography* (Cambridge, 1948), fig. 12
1.3 © Musée des beaux-arts, Quimper (France)
1.4 Sotheby's Picture Library
1.6 Royal Geographical Society, London / Bridgeman Art Library
1.7 The British Library / Add Ms 6390 f.8
1.8 AKG London
1.9 J. Martray, *Nous qui sommes d'Atlantique* (Rennes, 1991), 26

2.2 Janet and Colin Bord / Fortean Picture Library
2.3 Bob Evans / Skyscan Photolibrary
2.5 Paisajes Españoles S.A.
2.6 M-Sat Ltd / Science Photo Library
2.7 M-Sat Ltd / Science Photo Library
2.8 Arthus Bertrand / Altitude / Hoa-Qui
2.9 Jacques Briard
2.10 Dúchas, The Heritage Service
2.25 Maurice Gautier
2.28 Georg Gerster / Rapho / Network Photographers
2.31 M-Sat Ltd / Science Photo Library

3.1 Photo: Sean McGrail, Institute of Archaeology, Oxford
3.2 Pepys Library, Magdalene College, Cambridge
3.3 National Museum of Ireland
3.4 After E.V. Wright, *The North Ferriby Boats. A guidebook* (Greenwich, 1976)
3.5 Photo: Institute of Archaeology, Oxford
3.6 Photo: Institute of Archaeology, Oxford
3.7 From P. Marsden, *Ships of the Port of London* (London, 1994), fig. 70
3.8 From P. Marsden, *Ships of the Port of London* (London, 1994), fig. 69
3.9 After S. Jansson, Hjortspringbåd? *Marinar Kæologisk Nyhedsbrev fra Roskilde* 2 (1994)
3.10 From O. Crumlin-Pedersen, 'Skind eller træ? En studie i den nordiske plankebåds konstructive oprindelse' *Sømand, Fisker, Skib og Værft* (Copenhagen, 1970), 213–39
3.5-3.6 Institute of Archaeology, Oxford
3.7-3.8 Museum of London Archaeology Service © MoL
3.10 Vikingeskibsmuseet, Roskilde
3.11 ©National Maritime Museum, London
3.12 John Crook
3.13 Corpus Christi College, Oxford / Bridgeman Art Library
3.14 ©National Maritime Museum, London
3.15 After J.H. Pryor, *Geography, Technology and War* (Cambridge, 1988), fig. 12
3.16 After S. McGrail, *Ancient Boats in North-West Europe* (London, 1998), fig. 14.1
3.17 After S. McGrail, *Ancient Boats in North-West Europe* (London, 1998), fig. 13.1
3.18 Based on C. F. C. Hawkes, *Pytheas: Europe and the Greek Explorers* (Oxford, 1975), fig. 18
3.19 The British Library / Add Ms 27376 f.180v-181
3.20 Based on D. Harden, *The Phoenicians* (Harmondsworth, 1971), fig. 50
3.21 The British Library / Harl Ms 4751 f.69 / The Art Archive
3.22 David Lomax / Robert Harding Picture Library
3.23 Mansell / Time Inc. / Katz Pictures
3.24 ©Patrimonio Nacional / Cantigas de Santa Maria / Institut Amatller d'Art Hispànic
3.25 Photo Images

4.1 After R. G. West, *Pleistocene geology and biology* (London, 1977)
4.2 After L.P. Louwe-Kooijmans, 'The Rhine / Meuse delta: four studies in its prehistoric occupation and Holocene geology' *Analecta Praehistorica Leidensia* 7 (1974), fig. 14
4.3 After T. Darvill, *Prehistoric Britain* (London, 1987), fig. 14

4.4 From B. Cunliffe, *Wessex to AD 1000* (London, 1993), fig. 1.9
4.5 Barry Cunliffe
4.6 National Museum of Denmark
4.7 After S.H. Anderson, 'Tybrind Vig' *Journal of Danish Archaeology* 4 (1985), figs. 14 and 15
4.8 Lars Larsson
4.9 After S.H. Anderson, 'Tybrind Vig' *Journal of Danish Archaeology* 4 (1985), fig. 20
4.10 After P. Mellars, *Excavations on Oronsay* (Edinburgh, 1987), figs. 2.1 and 2.6
4.11 Crown Copyright: Royal Commission on the Ancient and Historical Monuments of Scotland
4.12-4.13 Peter C. Woodman
4.14 From B. Cunliffe, *Wessex to AD 1000* (London, 1993), fig. 1.10
4.15 From B. Cunliffe, *Wessex to AD 1000* (London, 1993), fig. 1.11 with corrections
4.16 After R.J. Schulting, 'Antlers, bone pins and flint blades. Mesolithic cemeteries of Brittany' *Antiquity* 70 (1996), fig. 1
4.17 ©Photo RMN
4.18 After J.E. Morais Arnaud, 'The Mesolithic communities of the Sado Valley, Portugal in their ecological setting' in C. Bonsall, *The Mesolithic in Europe* (Edinburgh, 1989), 615
4.19 Bengt Almgren / Historiska Museet, Lund University
4.20 Musée de Préhistoire, Carnac
4.21 After S.E. Albrethsen and E. Brinch Petersen, 'Excavation of a Mesolithic cemetery at Vedbaek, Denmark' *Acta Archaeologica* 47 (1976), 1–28
4.22 Søllerød Museum, Copenhagen
4.24 After J. Zilhão, 'The spread of agro-pastoral economies across Mediterranean Europe: a view from the far west' *Journal of Mediterranean Archaeology* 6 (1993), figs. 4 and 5
4.26 After J. L'Helgouac'h, *Locmariaquer* (Luçon, 1994), 16
4.27 Maurice Gautier
4.28 After G. Bailloud, C. Boujot, S. Cassen and C.-T. Le Roux, *Carnac* (Paris, 1995), 89
4.29 Hervé Boulé / Éditions Ouest-France
4.30 After P.-R. Giot, *Barnenez, Carn, Guennoc. Vol.* II (Rennes, 1987), figs. B2 and B3
4.31 Cambridge University Collection of Air Photographs: copyright reserved

5.1 National Museum of Denmark
5.2 Musée de Préhistoire, Carnac
5.3-5.4 Musée d'Archéologie du Morbihan, Vannes
5.6 After C.-T. Le Roux, *Gavrinis et les îles du Morbihan* (Paris, 1985), fig. 13
5.7 N. Aujoulat / C.N.P., Ministère de la Culture
5.8 Maurice Gautier
5.10 After G. Daniel, *The prehistoric chamber tombs of France* (London, 1960), figs. 23 and 24
5.11 Dúchas, The Heritage Service
5.12 Information from the Irish Megalithic Survey
5.13 Information from the Irish Megalithic Survey
5.14 After J. Waddell, *The Prehistoric Archaeology of Ireland* (Galway, 1998), fig. 39
5.16 Dúchas, The Heritage Service
5.17 After J. Waddell, *The Prehistoric Archaeology of Ireland* (Galway, 1998), fig. 28
5.18 Dúchas, The Heritage Service
5.19 After J. Waddell, *The Prehistoric Archaeology of Ireland* (Galway, 1998), fig. 30
5.20 Charles Tait / Skyscan Photolibrary
5.22 Crown Copyright: courtesy of Historic Scotland
5.24 After B. Cunliffe, *Wessex to AD 1000* (London, 1993), fig. 3.6
5.25 After B. Cunliffe, *Wessex to AD 1000* (London, 1993), fig. 3.7
5.26 National Monuments Record
5.27 From S. Pigott, *Neolithic Cultures of the British Isles* (Cambridge, 1954), fig. 57
5.29 Deutsches Archäologisches Institut, Madrid (Hermanfrid Schubart KB4-68-14)
5.30–5.33 After E. Shee Twohig, *The Megalithic Art of Western Europe* (Oxford, 1981)
5.34 Dúchas, The Heritage Service
5.35 After E. Shee Twohig, *The Megalithic Art of Western Europe* (Oxford, 1981), figs. 1, 14 and 37
5.36 Adam Woolfitt / Robert Harding Picture Library
5.37 After C.-T. Le Roux, 'Stone Axes of Brittany and the Marches' in T. H. McK. Clough and W.A. Cummins, *Stone Axe Studies* (London, 1979), fig. 3
5.38 Museu Nacional de Arqueologia / Divisão Docu mentação Fotográfica / Instituto Portuguès de Museus;

6.1 Ashmolean Museum, Oxford
6.2 Rijksmuseum van Oudheden, Leiden
6.4 After J.N. Lanting and J.D. Van der Waals, 'Beaker culture relations in the Lower Rhine Basin' *Glockenbechersymposion* (1976), fig. 1
6.7 After W. O'Brien, *Mount Gabriel* (Galway, 1994), fig. 16
6.8 After W. O'Brien, *Mount Gabriel* (Galway, 1994), fig. 25
6.9 William O'Brien
6.10 After R.J. Harrison, *The Bell Beaker cultures of Spain and Portugal* (Cambridge, Massachusetts, 1977), fig. 24
6.11 After R.J. Harrison, *The Bell Beaker cultures of Spain and Portugal* (Cambridge, Massachusettes, 1977), fig. 1 with additions
6.12 ©British Museum
6.13 Fiona Adams
6.14 After G. Eogan, *The Accomplished Art* (Oxford, 1994), figs. 13 and 31
6.15 From P. Harbison, *Pre-Christian Ireland* (London, 1988), fig. 57
6.16 After J. Waddell, *The Prehistory of Ireland* (Galway, 1998), fig. 43
6.17 After Megalithic Survey of Ireland
6.18 Photo: Mick Aston
6.19 After B. Cunliffe, *Wessex to AD 1000* (London, 1993),

fig. 3.16
6.20 After B. Cunliffe, *Wessex to* AD *1000* (London, 1993), fig. 3.17
6.21 After P.-R. Giot, *Brittany* (London, 1960), figs. 36 and 40
6.22 After J. Briard, *Les tumulus d'Armorique* (Paris, 1984)
6.23 ©The Trustees of the National Museums of Scotland 2001, drawing by Marion O'Neil
6.24 ©Photo RMN-Gérard Blot
6.25 From D.V. Clark, T.G. Cowie and A. Foxton, *Symbols of Power* (Edinburgh, 1985), fig. 4.74
6.26 ©The Trustees of the National Museums of Scotland 2001

7.1 From A.H. Layard, *Monuments of Nineveh* I (London, 1848–9), pl. 71
7.2 ©Photo RMN-Hervé Lewandowski
7.4 Paisajes Españoles S.A.
7.5 After M.-C. Fernandez Castro, *Iberia in Prehistory* (London, 1995), fig. 13.2
7.7 Oronoz
7.8 Deutsches Archäologisches Institut, Madrid Peter Witte R 126-93-11)
7.9 From B. Cunliffe, 'Core-Periphery Relationships: Iberia and the Mediterranean' in P. Bilde, T. Engberg-Pedersen, L. Hannestad, J. Zahle and K. Randsborg, *Centre of Periphery in the Hellenistic World* (Aarhus, 1993), 59 (fig. 3)
7.10 From B. Cunliffe, 'Core-Periphery Relationships: Iberia and the Mediterranean' in P. Bilde, T. Engberg-Pedersen, L. Hannestad, J. Zahle and K. Randsborg, *Centre of Periphery in the Hellenistic World* (Aarhus, 1993), 61 (fig. 4)
7.11 Claire Cotter
7.12 After J.R.C. Hamilton, *Excavations at Jarlshof, Shetland* (London, 1956), fig. 14
7.15 Ashmolean Museum, Oxford
7.16 ©British Museum
7.18 Oronoz
7.19 National Museum of Ireland
7.21 After J. Briard, *Les depôts bretons et l'âge du Bronze Atlantique* (Rennes, 1965), fig. 107
7.22 Jacques Briard / Musée d'Archéologie du Morbihan, Vannes
7.23/24 After J. Waddell, *The Prehistoric Archaeology of Ireland* (Galway, 1998), fig. 112
7.24 *left* National Museum of Ireland
7.27 Barry Cunliffe
7.29 Direction du Patrimoine Culturel, Rabat
7.30 M-Sat Ltd / Science Photo Library
7.32 From A. Fox, 'Tin ingots from Bigbury Bay' *Proceedings of the Devon Archaeological Society* 53 (1997), 18

8.2 From B. Cunliffe, *The Ancient Celts* (Oxford, 1997), fig. 53
8.3 From B. Cunliffe, *The Ancient Celts* (Oxford, 1997), fig. 55
8.7 From I. Stead, *The Gauls: Celtic Antiquities from France* (London, n.d.), fig. 4
8.8 Musée des Jacobins-Morlaix
8.10(1) Trustees of the Wisbech & Fenland Museum
8.10(2) Ashmolean Museum, Oxford
8.12 Museu Nacional de Arqueologia / Divisão Documentação Fotográfica / Instituto Portuguès de Museus, photo by José Pessoa
8.14 From B. Cunliffe, *Greeks, Romans and Barbarians* (1988), fig. 24
8.15 ©British Museum
8.18 Barry Cunliffe
8.19 Museu Nacional de Arqueologia / Divisão Documentação Fotográfica / Instituto Portuguès de Museus, photo by José Pessoa
8.21 R.E.M. Wheeler and K.M. Richardson, *Hillforts in Northern France* (London, 1957), fig. 22
8.22 Museu Nacional de Arqueologia / Divisão Documentação Fotográfica / Instituto Portuguès de Museus, photo by José Pessoa
8.24 A.J. Lorrio
8.25 Sociedade Martins Sarmento, Guimarães
8.27 After P.-R. Giot, J. Briard and L. Pape, *Protohistoire de la Bretagne* (Rennes, 1995), 243
8.28 After P.-R. Giot, J. Briard and L. Pape, *Protohistoire de la Bretagne* (Rennes, 1995), 289
8.29 From B. Cunliffe, *The Ancient Celts* (Oxford, 1997), fig. 28
8.31 Steve Hartgroves, Cornwall Archaeological Unit
8.32 Crown Copyright: Royal Commission on the Ancient and Historical Monuments of Wales
8.33 From B. Cunliffe, *Iron Age Communities in Britain* (London, 1991), fig. 13.32
8.34 Crown Copyright: Royal Commission on the Ancient and Historical Monuments of Scotland
8.35 Charles Tait / Skyscan Photolibrary
8.36 Crown copyright: courtesy of Historic Scotland
8.37 From B. Cunliffe, *Iron Age Britain* (London, 1995), fig. 42
8.38 Charles Tait / Skyscan Photolibrary
8.39 Crown Copyright: Royal Commission on the Ancient and Historical Monuments of Scotland
8.40 Slidefile

9.3 Museo Arqueológico Nacional, Madrid
9.4 After D. G. Bird, 'Pliny and the gold mines of north-west Iberia' in T. Blagg, R. Jones and S. Keay (eds.), *Papers in Iberian Archaeology* (Oxford, 1984)
9.5 After D. G. Bird, 'Pliny and the gold mines of north-west Iberia' in T. Blagg, R. Jones and S. Keay (eds.), *Papers in Iberian Archaeology* (Oxford, 1984)
9.6 Photo: D. G. Bird
9.8 Foto Scala, Alverca
9.9 Armando Ferreira da Silva
9.10 Bibliothèque nationale de France
9.11 After J. L. Naveiro Lopez, *El Comercio Antiguo en el N.W. Peninsular* (Coruña, 1991), fig. 35
9.12 Paisajes Españoles S.A.
9.13 From B. Cunliffe, *Greeks, Romans and Barbarians* (London, 1988), fig. 25

9.14 From B. Cunliffe, *Greeks, Romans and Barbarians* (London, 1988), fig. 29
9.15 G. Réveillac/C.N.R.S.
9.16 From B. Cunliffe, *Greeks, Romans and Barbarians* (London, 1988), fig. 34
9.17 From B. Cunliffe, *Greeks, Romans and Barbarians* (London, 1988), fig. 39 with additions
9.20 Maurice Gautier
9.21 From B. Cunliffe, *Greeks, Romans and Barbarians* (London, 1988), fig. 49
9.22 Photo: Bibliothèque Municipale de Boulogne-sur-Mer
9.23 Photo: Barry Cunliffe
9.24 Photo: Patrick Galliou
9.25 Cambridge University Collection of Air Photographs: copyright reserved
9.26 From B. Cunliffe, *Iron Age Britain* (London, 1995), fig. 8.5
9.27 From B. Cunliffe, *Greeks, Romans and Barbarians* (London, 1988), fig. 43
9.28 After J.-Y. Gosselin and C. Seillier, 'Fouilles de Boulogne sur-Mer. Campagnes 1980–1982' *Septentrion* 11 (1981), 19–20
9.30 From R.E.M. Wheeler, 'The Roman Lighthouse at Dover' *Archaeological Journal* 36 (1929), pl. 11
9.31 Museum of London Archaeology Service © MoL
9.33 Skyscan Balloon Photography/English Heritage Photographic Library
9.34 Cambridge University Collection of Air Photographs: copyright reserved
9.37 After D.P.S. Peacock, 'The Rhine and the problem of Gaulish wine in Roman Britain' in J. du Plat Taylor and H. Cleere (eds.), *Roman shipping and trade: Britain and the Rhine provinces* (London, 1978), fig. 44
9.38 Rijksmuseum van Oudheden, Leiden
9.39 From G. C. Boon, 'A Graeco-Roman Anchor-stock from North Wales' *Antiquaries Journal* 57 (1977), fig. 3
9.39 Society of Antiquaries of London

10.2 After E. James, The Franks (Oxford, 1988), figs. 6 and 7
10.4 ©British Museum
10.5 Alet, after L. Langouët, *La Cité d'Alet* (Saint Malo, 1986), 59. Le Yaudet, author
10.6 Photo: Peter Davenport
10.8 ©British Museum
10.9 Photo Source
10.11 Skyscan Balloon Photography/English Heritage Photographic Library
10.13 ©British Museum
10.14/15 After M. Fulford, 'The interpretation of Britain's late Roman trade' in J. du Plat Taylor and H. Cleere (eds.), *Roman shipping and trade: Britain and the Rhine Provinces* (London, 1978), figs. 48 and 49
10.16 J.-C. Fouille, Michel L'Hour/ Drassm, photo Yves Gladu
10.17 After S.J. Keay, *Roman Spain* (London, 1988), 175.
10.20 Huntington Library and Art Gallery, San Marino, California/Bridgeman Art Library
10.23-10.24 Dúchas, The Heritage Service
10.25 After E.G. Bowen, *Saints, Seaways and Settlements in the Celtic Lands* (Cardiff, 1977), fig. 35
10.26 Colour Library Books/Skyscan Photolibrary
10.27 After E.G. Bowen, *Saints, Seaways and Settlements in the Celtic Lands* (Cardiff, 1977), figs. 39, 41 and 45
10.28 From E.G. Bowen, *Britain and the Western Seaways* (London, 1972), fig. 34

11.1 English Heritage Photographic Library
11.3 Rijksdienst voor het Oudheid Kundig Bodemonderzoek, Amersfoort
11.4 National Museum of Denmark
11.5 Antikvarisk-Topografiska Arkivet, Stockholm
11.6 University Museum of National Antiquities, Oslo, photo by Voering
11.8 Ted Spiegel
11.11 ©The Trustees of the National Museums of Scotland 2001
11.12 After A. Ritchie, Viking Scotland (London, 1993), fig. 50
11.13 Crown copyright: courtesy of Historic Scotland, drawing by Alan Braby
11.14 Crown copyright: courtesy of Historic Scotland
11.15 Manx National Heritage
11.17 After F. Mitchel and M. Ryan, *Reading the Irish Landscape* (Dublin, 1997), fig. 152 with additional information
11.18 After P. F. Wallace, *The Viking Buildings of Dublin* (Dublin, 1992)
11.19 National Museum of Ireland
11.20 M-Sat Ltd/Science Photo Library
11.23 Vikingeskibsmuseet, Roskilde
11.24 Giraudon, with special permission from the Ville de Bayeux

12.5 Museo di San Matteo Pisa/Archivio Fotografico Soprintendenza B.A.A.S. di Pisa, Livorno, Lucca e Massa C.
12.6 Galleria delle Carte Geografiche Vaticano/Scala, Florence
12.7 Oronoz
12.8 Maurice Gautier
12.9 Basilica di Sant'Antonio, Padua/Bridgeman Art Library
12.11 V&A Picture Library
12.12 Bibliothèque nationale de France, Ms Fr 2091 f 125
12.13 Oronoz
12.14 Giraudon

13.1 Barry Cunliffe
13.2 Gareth Syvret, Société Jersiaise

Picture Research by Sandra Assersohn

Index